HISTORY OF MY LIFE

GIACOMO CASANOVA

Chevalier de Seingalt

HISTORY OF MY LIFE

FIRST TRANSLATED INTO ENGLISH IN ACCORDANCE
WITH THE ORIGINAL FRENCH MANUSCRIPT

by Willard R. Trask

VOLUMES 9 AND 10

THE JOHNS HOPKINS UNIVERSITY PRESS
Baltimore and London

English translation copyright © 1970 by Harcourt Brace
Jovanovich, Inc.
All rights reserved
Printed in the United States of America on acid-free paper

Originally published as *Histoire de Ma Vie,* Edition intégrale, by
Jacques Casanova de Seingalt, Vénitien, by F. A. Brockhaus,
Wiesbaden, Librairie Plon; Paris, 1960. © F. A. Brockhaus,
Wiesbaden, 1960.

This edition originally published in the United States as a Helen and
Kurt Wolff book by Harcourt Brace Jovanovich, Inc.
Johns Hopkins Paperbacks edition, 1997
9 8 7 6 5 4 3 2

The Johns Hopkins University Press
2715 North Charles Street
Baltimore, Maryland 21218-4363
The Johns Hopkins Press Ltd., London

Library of Congress Catalog Card Number 97-70304

A catalog record for this book is available from the British Library.

ISBN 0-8018-5666-3 (pbk.: Vols. 9 and 10)

HISTORY OF MY LIFE

Volume 9

CONTENTS

Volume 9

LIST OF PLATES

Volume 9

ix

VOLUME 9

I find Rosalie happy. Signora Isolabella. The cook. Biribissi. Irene. Passano in prison. My niece an old friend of Rosalie's.

P O G O M A S, who used the name Passano[1] in Genoa because everyone knew him, introduced me to his wife and his daughter, both of them ugly, dirty, and impudent. I quickly got rid of them in order to eat a hasty dinner with my niece and then to call on the Marchese Grimaldi. I could not wait to find out where Rosalie[2] was living.

A *staffiere* ("confidential servant") of the Senator's told me that His Excellency was in Venice and was not expected back until the end of April. He showed me the way to Paretti's,[3] who had married her six or seven months after I left.

Recognizing me at once, he was obviously delighted to see me, and he left his shop to take me to his wife, who, on seeing me, gave a cry of joy and came to me with open arms. A minute later he left us to return to his business, asking his wife to show me her daughter.

After showing me a six-months-old infant, Rosalie told me that she was happy, that her husband was de-

voted to her in heart and soul, and that, with the help
of the Marchese Grimaldi's patronage, he had plied his
trade to such purpose that he was already working on
his own account.

Rosalie had become a perfect beauty. She was inex-
pressibly grateful to me for having come to see her so
soon after my arrival, and she added in a tone which
allowed no gainsaying that she expected me for dinner
the next day.

"My dear and loving friend, I owe you my good fortune and my peace of mind; let us embrace each other,
but no more; and tomorrow let us beware of speaking
to each other too fondly.[4] But, come to think of it, I have
a surprise for you; wait a moment."

She leaves the room and, two minutes later, comes
back with Veronica.[5] She had engaged her as her chambermaid. Delighted to see her again, and enjoying her
surprise, I embraced her, asking her at once for news of
Annetta;[6] she said she was well and worked at home
with her mother. I told her to send her to me to serve
as maid to my niece for the two or three weeks I should
spend in Genoa. She promises to send her the next day;
but Rosalie bursts into laughter, exclaiming:

"Another niece! But, since she enjoys that privilege, I
hope you will bring her with you tomorrow."

"With pleasure, and the more so because she comes
from Marseilles."

"Marseilles? She might know me, but I don't care.
What is her name?"

Telling her some common name, I say that she is the
daughter of a female cousin of mine in Marseilles; she
does not believe a word of it, but she is happy to see me
still involved in pleasant adventures.

Leaving her, I go to Signora Isolabella's[7] and send in
the Marchese Triulzi's[8] letter. A minute later she comes
to greet me, saying that he had sent her word in advance
and that she was expecting me. She immediately introduced me to the Marchese Agostino Grimaldi della Pie-

tra,[9] her great *cicisbeo*[10] during the prolonged absence of her husband, who was living in Lisbon.

Signora Isolabella's rooms were well appointed; as for herself, at the age of thirty she had a pretty face, a gentle, agreeable character, a small waist, extreme thinness, and a complexion covered with rouge and whitening, but so awkwardly that it was visible at once. It revolted me despite her black eyes, which were superb. A half hour later I take my leave, and I accept an invitation to supper the next day.

Back at my lodging, I am happy to see that my niece has settled very comfortably into a room separated from mine only by a closet in which, I tell her, I will have the maid sleep whom I have engaged for her and whom she will see the following day. She thanks me. I tell her that she will come to dinner with me at a merchant's house as my niece, and she is grateful to me for all the pleasures I provide for her. This girl, whom Croce[11] had infatuated to the point of insanity, was as pretty as an angel, but her well-bred manner and her gentle nature surpassed even her rare charms. I was in love with her, and regret that I had not made her mine the first day gnawed at my soul. If I had taken her at her word, I should have become her lover and, in tranquil possession of her, should perhaps have made her forget Croce completely.

Having scarcely dined, I sat down at table as hungry as my niece, whose appetite was magnificent. We laughed together, finding our supper very bad. I told Clairmont[12] to send up the landlady.

"It is the cook's fault entirely," she said. "He is a cousin of your secretary Passano, who engaged him for you. If he had left it to me I should have given you an excellent cook and at lower wages."

"Have him here for me tomorrow."

"Gladly. But first arrange to get rid of this one. He is quartered on me with his wife and children. It is Passano, who engaged him, who should dismiss him."

"Leave it to me. In the meanwhile engage your cook for me; I will try him day after tomorrow."

I took my niece to her room, I asked her to go to bed without concerning herself about me. I read the gazette. When, after reading it, I went and kissed her and wished her good night, saying that she might spare me the torment of going to bed alone, she made no answer.

The next morning, just as Clairmont was washing my feet, she came into my room to ask me to have coffee with milk made for her because she found chocolate too heating; I at once sent Clairmont to get it, and she knelt down before me to dry me.

"I will not let you do that."

"Why not? It is a token of friendship."

"To give it to anyone but a lover is to degrade yourself."

She lowered her beautiful eyes and sat down beside me. Clairmont came back, dried me, put on my shoes and stockings, and the landlady came up with coffee for her and chocolate for me. She asked her if she wanted to buy a beautiful Pekin silk mantilla[13] in the Genoese style, and I replied that she had only to bring it to her. She went to fetch the milliner; in the meanwhile I gave her twenty Genoese zecchini,[14] telling her to use them for pin money. She accepted them, expressing her gratitude and showing no reluctance when I embraced her. The milliner came up, she made her choice, bargained, and paid.

Passano came to protest to me on the subject of the cook.

"I engaged him by your order," he said, "for the whole of your stay in Genoa at four lire a day with board and lodging."

"Where is my letter?"

"Here: 'Provide me with a good cook, whom I will keep as long as I am in Genoa.' "

"I said 'good,' and he is not good. I am the only competent judge of his goodness."

"You are making a mistake, for he will prove that he is good; he will sue you in court, and you will lose."

"Then you gave him a written agreement?"

"Authorized by you."

"I want to see him at once. Bring him up."

I ordered Clairmont to go for a lawyer. The cook comes up with Passano, and I see the agreement signed by two witnesses and so drawn up that, *stricto jure* ("according to the letter of the law"), I could not but lose in court; I rail, but to no purpose. The cook tells me he is good and that he can find four thousand people in Genoa who will bear written testimony that he is a good cook. The lawyer arrives and tells me the same; he says more: he says I will find no one to say he is bad.

"That may be so," I reply, "but I want him to leave because I want to engage another one; and I will pay him just the same."

"In that case," says the cook, "I will sue you for damaging my reputation."

At that I began alternately laughing and crying, and just then in came Don Agostino Grimaldi.[15] When he heard the story he laughed, shrugged his shoulders, and told me to beware of going to court, for I should lose the case and have to pay the costs as well.

"The person who, if he is not *una bestia* ['an idiot'], has played a rascally trick on you is your secretary, who should have included a clause providing for a trial, as one does with all cooks."

Passano here interrupted him to say that he was neither a rascal nor *una bestia*. The landlady adds that he is his cousin.

At that I pay the lawyer and send him away, and I tell the cook to go downstairs. After that I ask Passano if I owe him any money; he replies that, on the contrary, I had paid him for a month in advance and that he still has ten days in my service.

"Very well, I make you a present of the ten days, and I dismiss you here and now unless your cousin leaves this house today, giving you back the stupid agreement you entered into with him. Now go.''

They all left; whereupon Signor Grimaldi said that I had won my case with Alexander's sword.[16] He asked me to introduce him to the lady he saw there, and I told him she was my niece. He said that Signora Isolabella would be delighted if I would introduce my niece to her, and I excused myself from doing so on the ground that the Marchese Triulzi had not mentioned her in his letter. A moment later he left; and in comes Annetta with her mother. She had become dazzling. The little yellowish spots which she had on her face had disappeared, I thought her teeth had become whiter, she had grown taller, and her bosom, having attained its perfection, was concealed by a gauze fichu. I introduced her to my mistress, whose surprise amused me. I showed her her bed, telling her mother to send her belongings. Having to make my toilet, I told my niece to go to make hers with Annetta, who was delighted to be with me again.

Toward noon, when we were all ready to go out, my landlady came to present my new cook and to give me the agreement which Passano had made with his cousin. This comical victory put me in a mood for enjoyment. I gave my new cook instructions for the dinner I wanted, and I went to Rosalie's in a sedan chair, followed by my niece.

I saw a brilliant company of both sexes, and I observed my niece's surprise when she saw Rosalie and the latter's equal surprise when she saw my niece. Rosalie, embracing her, called her by her name, and she replied with a compliment which she ended by assuring her that the first news she would send her mother would be that she had found her in Genoa, beautiful and happy. As I expected, they went into another room together, and they returned a quarter of an hour later looking very well pleased. But the scene was not yet ended. Paretti comes in, and she introduces my niece to him, saying that she is Mademoiselle xxx. He is delighted; he is in correspondence with her father; he runs out, and a minute later comes back with a letter from her father, which he shows her, and my niece kisses the signature. Seeing her touched to the verge of tears, I cannot hold back mine; I urge Rosalie to tell her husband that there are weighty reasons why he must not inform her father of the news.

The dinner was brilliant, and Rosalie did the honors of it with the greatest ease; but the homage of all the guests was paid to my niece, who, as the daughter of Monsieur xxx, the well-known and wealthy merchant of Marseilles, attracted the attention of a young man whom God had destined to be her husband. How gratified I was to find that I was serving as Heaven's chosen instrument!

As for Rosalie, she astonished me. She seemed really to have been born to be the mistress of a great house. She candidly took the credit for everything I found worthy of praise, even to the beautiful china and the exquisite wines. We rose from table well satisfied and in high spirits.

Tables at cards were proposed; but Rosalie, knowing that I did not like social games, declared that we must play *trente-et-quarante*[17] with everyone joining in. The game filled the time until supper, with no one being able to complain that he had lost too heavily. At midnight we broke up, all of us enchanted with the delightful evening we had spent.

Back at the house, I was no sooner alone with my niece than I asked her how she had come to know Rosalie in Marseilles.

"I made her acquaintance at my house, where she came with her mother to bring the washing. I always liked her. She is two years older than I am. I recognized her at once. She told me that it was you who had made her leave Marseilles, and that she owes her good fortune to you; but she told me nothing in detail. For my part, I told her no more than she must have supposed. I admitted that you are not my uncle, and if she thinks you

are my lover I do not mind. You cannot imagine how
much I enjoyed the evening; you were born to make
people happy.''

''But *La Croix*!'' [18]

''Please do not speak of him.''

She had me on fire. She called Annetta, and I went to
my room. But after putting her mistress in bed, she
came to mine, as I had expected.

''If it is true,'' she said, ''that Madame is your niece,
can I flatter myself that you still love me?''

''Yes, my dear Annetta, I love you; go get undressed,
and then come back to talk with me.''

With that rare girl I spent two charming hours which
momentarily quenched the fire with which I burned for
my niece.

The next morning Passano came to tell me that he
had arranged matters with the cook at a cost of six
zecchini, and I gave them to him, asking him to be more
careful in future.

I went to breakfast at Rosalie's to invite her to dinner
on the next day with her husband and four guests of
her choice, adding that it would be for her to tell me
if a cook I was thinking of engaging was good. After
promising to come, she wanted to know the story of my
amour with Mademoiselle xxx; but when I replied that
I could not tell her the truth, she said that she was not
interested in hearing me make up stories. But she was
delighted when I told her what she had said to me about
her. She asked me if I would mind if she came to my
dinner with the young man who had shown my niece
such great attention at table.

''Who is he? I am curious to know.''

''He is So-and-so. He is the only son of a rich merchant.''

''Bring him. Farewell, my erstwhile love.''

On my way out I asked Paretti to get me a good hire
valet, and he sent me an excellent one that same day.
I found my niece still in bed. I told her that Rosalie

would come to dine with us the next day, and that she could be sure her husband would not write to her father that she was in Genoa. She thanked me, for she was uneasy about it. Having to sup out that evening, I told her that she could go to Rosalie's, unless she would rather sup alone.

"My dear Uncle, your solicitude overwhelms me. I shall go to Rosalie's."

"Are you satisfied with Annetta?"

"By the way, she told me that she slept with you last night and that you were her first lover at the same time that you were her sister Veronica's."

"It is true, but she is an indiscreet chatterbox."

"You must forgive her. She told me that she had consented only after you swore to her that I was your niece; then, too, you must see that she can have confessed the thing to me only out of vanity. She expects it will oblige me to feel a certain respect for her; and she is right. I am bound to respect a girl whom you love."

"I would rather you had the right to be jealous of her. I give you my word that if she does not treat you with due deference, I will turn her out. You may not love me, and I have no right to complain of it; but you are not of a nature to truckle to me."

I was not sorry that my niece had learned that I had Annetta; but I was a trifle piqued by the way she had taken the thing. I thought she felt no love for me, and, what is more, it seemed to me that she was very glad to find that my relation with Annetta freed her from the risk she thought she ran every day when, constantly in my company, she saw me admiring her charms.

We dined alone; and my cook's appetizing dishes made us augur well of him. The valet whom Paretti had promised me arrived; I told my niece that he was hers to command. After an airing in my carriage for a couple of hours I took her to Paretti's and left her there. I went to Signora Isolabella's, where I found a numerous gathering of both men and women of the highest nobility.

The amusement provided until time for the supper was a *biribissi*,[19] to which the women in particular were passionately addicted. The game was forbidden in Genoa; but people were free in their own houses, and the government could say nothing. So the gamesters who owned and operated the game went to the private houses to which they were summoned, and word was sent to the players, who assembled there. That evening, unfortunately for them, the gamesters were at Signora Isolabella's, and so she had a large party. To do as the others were doing, I began playing too. In the room in which we were playing there was a portrait of the Signora dressed as a Harlequiness, and on the *biribissi* board there was a Harlequiness; to pay my court to the mistress of the house, beside whom I was seated, I staked a zecchino on the Harlequiness. The board contained thirty-six figures, the winner was paid thirty-two times his stake. Each player in turn drew a ball from the bag three times in succession. The *biribissi* gamesters numbered three: one tended the bag, another kept the money, the third attended to the board, gathering in the money staked on the various figures as soon as the ball had been drawn. The bank amounted to some two thousand zecchini. The table, a handsome cloth, and four silver candelabra belonged to the gamesters. One could stake as much as one wanted to on a number. I staked a zecchino each time.

Signora Isolabella having been the first to draw, and the bag going round to her right, my turn did not come until last. As fifteen or sixteen people were playing, when my turn arrived I was behind by almost fifty zecchini, for the Harlequiness had never come out. Everyone condoled with me.

But at last my turn arrived, I draw the ball, and it turns out to be the Harlequiness. I am paid thirty-two zecchini. I put them all on the same Harlequiness, it comes out, and they have to pay me a thousand. I leave fifty of them on the figure, and I make my third draw, and the Harlequiness comes out. They give me all the money they have, and, that not being enough, everything is mine—the table, the cloth, the *biribissi* board, and the four silver candelabra. Everyone laughs, the company applaud me, they jeer the crestfallen, bankrupt gamesters, and turn them out. But after the laughter I see that the ladies are inconsolable. The game is over; they are at a loss for something to do. I comfort them by saying that I will bank for the game, and I add that I will not have the odds in my favor: I will pay thirty-six. I was declared charming. I kept them amused until suppertime without either winning or losing. My eloquence finally persuaded Signora Isolabella to accept the whole outfit as a present. The strange turn of events was the subject which kept us amused all through supper. Having remained until all the others were gone, I invited the Signora and the Marchese to dine with me the next day, and they accepted. I had a heavy bag, in which were three hundred [20] zecchini in silver, carried out to my carriage, and I went to Rosalie's to call for my niece, whom I was to take home and who told me that she had spent a delightful evening.

"A very pleasant young man," she said, "whom Rosalie will bring to dine with us tomorrow, said countless flattering things to me, among them that he wants to go to Marseilles to make my father's acquaintance and to pay his court to me. He will have his journey for his pains."

"Why?"

"Because he will not see me. A convent shall be my world. My kind, humane father will forgive me, and I will punish myself."

"That is an idea bred from melancholy, which you should put out of your mind. You are a woman to make the happiness of a husband worthy of you and secure, so far as that is possible, from the vagaries of fortune. The more I study you, the more convinced I am of what I am saying to you."

I observed with pleasure my niece's kind manner to Annetta when she undressed her, and a certain lack of attentiveness in the latter which displeased me. When she came to bed I chided her on the subject, with a gentleness to which she should have replied only by caresses; but not a bit of it, she proceeded to cry. A pretty girl's tears in the arms of a lover ready for amusement put him out of humor.

"Be gay," I said, "or go to your bed."

At these words she broke from my arms and left me to my own devices; I fell asleep in a temper.

The next morning I sternly told her that she had played a scurvy trick on me and that I would dismiss her if she did it again; instead of soothing me, she cried again, and, my patience exhausted, I went to count my money. A half hour later my niece enters and in a soft, feeling voice asks me why I had mortified poor Annetta.

"My dear niece, tell her to behave herself."

At that she smiles, takes a handful of my scudi, and goes. A minute later I see Annetta in high spirits, with her scudi in her apron, come to embrace me and promise she will never cry again in all her life. Such was the nature of my niece, who wanted me to love her and did not want me as a lover. In the code of feminine coquetry, such projects are far from uncommon.

Passano, whom I had not sent for, comes in and congratulates me on my triumph.

"Who told you about it?"

"Everyone at the coffeehouse. It's unheard of, for the *biribissanti*[21] are cheats with nothing to learn. The thing will get you talked about, for everyone says you could not possibly have cleaned them out as you did unless you had come to an understanding with the one who tended the bag."

"My dear fellow, you bore me. Give this coin to your wife and go away."

The gold piece I had given him was worth a hundred Genoese lire.[22] It was a coin which the government had

had struck for internal commerce. There were others worth fifty and twenty-five lire.

I went on counting my gold and silver. Clairmont hands me a note. It was a fond invitation from Irene, who asked me to breakfast with her. My dear Irene in Genoa! After locking up my money I go there in morning dress, I find her well lodged, she tells me that the furniture belongs to her, and her old father, Count Rinaldi, embraces me, shedding tears of joy. He congratulates me.

"Three thousand zecchini," he says, "are something!"

"Yes: practice and luck."

"The amusing thing is that the man who tended the bag is in the pay of the other two *biribissanti*."

"What strikes you as amusing in that?"

"That at no loss to himself he must have been the gainer by half the amount, for except on that condition he would never have made an agreement with you."

"So you believe that?"

"Everybody believes it. The thing can't be otherwise. He's a cheat who has made his fortune by betraying cheats. All the sharpers in Genoa are applauding him and singing your praises."

"As an even greater cheat."

"They don't call you that—far from it. They hail you as a sublime intellect, they congratulate you."

"My thanks to them."

"I heard the story from someone who was present at the delightful encounter. He said that you recognized the ball the second and third time by touch, with the connivance of the man with the bag."

"And you believe that is true."

"I am convinced of it. There's not a gentleman who, in your place, would not have wished he could do the same. But I advise you to take every precaution when you meet the man with the bag to give him his half. You will have spies following you. If you wish, I will see to it for you."

I had self-control enough to remain cool, to make no

answer, to rise, and to push aside Irene, who, as she had done in Milan, tried to keep me from leaving. This slanderous story, which, according to the cheating gamesters' code, did me honor, wounded me to the soul. Passano and Rinaldi had said enough to show me that the thing was on everyone's lips, and I was not surprised that people believed it, but I could not and must not countenance it. I go to the Strada Balbi[23] to tell it to the Marchese Grimaldi and at the same time to return his call. He had gone to sit in court; I am conducted there; I am announced, he comes out, he thanks me for the trouble I have taken, and, after hearing me tell the story which is going the rounds, he replies with a laugh that I should disregard it and not even take the trouble to refute it.

"Then you advise me to admit that I am a scoundrel."

"Only fools will call you that; treat them with the contempt they deserve, unless they say it to your face."

"I should like to know the name of the patrician[24] who is telling the story and who says he was present at the incident."

"He is wrong to tell it; but you would be wrong to try to find out his name. In telling it he does not mean to speak ill of you or to discredit you."

"That is hard to believe. Do you think that if the thing happened as the story says it did, it would be to my honor?"

"Neither to your honor nor to your dishonor. You will be liked for it, people will laugh, and everyone will say that in your place he would have done the same."

"You too."

"Yes. If I had been sure the Harlequiness was in the ball, I would have broken the bank just as you did. I tell you sincerely that I do not know if you won by luck or by skill; but if I had to hand down a decision based on what is more probable, I should say that you knew the ball. Admit that my reasoning is sound."

"I admit it, but granting you a supposition which is

dishonorable to me. Admit, too, that everyone who supposes that I would win by skill insults me.''

''That depends on how one takes it. I admit that they insult you if you feel that you are insulted; but they cannot guess that, and so, having no insulting intention, they do not insult you. In any case, you will not find anyone impudent enough to tell you that you won by skill; but you cannot keep people from thinking so.''

''Very well, let them think it, but let them beware of saying it to me. Good-by, Marchese, until dinnertime.''

I went home angry with Grimaldi, angry with Rinaldi, angry that I had ill-treated Irene, whom I loved, and angry at being angry, for I could have laughed at the whole thing; in the state of moral corruption which prevailed in society, it could not be prejudicial to my honor. My reputation was that of a man of parts, in a sense which, in Genoa more than anywhere else, cast a luster on the name ''rogue,'' which the strait-laced [25] made a term of obloquy. Finally I reflected that, supposing the man with the bag had in fact made an agreement with me beforehand, I should not have scrupled to clean out the *biribissanti* by the means I was believed to have employed, if only to entertain the charming company with the brilliant exploit; but since that was not the case I could not bear having it bruited about as the truth.

I shook myself out of these reflections in order to be in a good humor for the choice company I expected for dinner. I saw my niece appear before me, unadorned with diamonds or a watch or any jewelry at all, her wretched lover having sold everything she possessed; but, well dressed and with her hair done to perfection, she could not have wished to shine more.

Rosalie arrived richly accoutered, then Paretti with his uncle and aunt and two friends, one of whom was the young man who was flattering my niece. Signora Isolabella arrived very late with Signor Grimaldi.

Just before we sat down at table Clairmont announced

a man who wanted to speak with me. I told him to show him in; and it was Signor Grimaldi who said to me that it was the man who tended the bag at the *biribissi*.

"What do you want with me?"

"I have come to ask you to help me a little. I have been dismissed, and I have a family. Everyone thinks that——"

I did not let him finish. I told Clairmont to give him four zecchini, and I sent him away.

We sat down at table, but in comes Clairmont again, this time with a letter for me. I see Passano's handwriting, I put it in my pocket without opening it.

My dinner was very gay, and my cook was given due praise. Signora Isolabella was the dominant figure, but Rosalie and my niece eclipsed her. The young Genoese devoted all his attention to my niece, and I thought she took it in very good part. I wanted to see her fall in love with someone who could rid her of the desperate idea of going to bury herself in a convent. She could not become happy again except by forgetting the wretch who had brought her to the verge of ruin.

Here is Passano's letter:

"I went to the Banchi[26] to change the hundred-lire piece you gave me. It was weighed and, on being found to be ten carats light, was confiscated, and I was ordered to name the person from whom I had received it. You can understand that I could not permit myself to answer the question. I let them take me to prison, and if you do not find a way to get me out I shall be brought to trial. You can also understand that I cannot let myself be hanged. I am—etc."

I hand the letter to Signor Grimaldi. After reading it he took me aside and said it was a very serious matter, which if it got into court could only end at the gallows for whoever had clipped the coin.

"The *biribissanti* will go to the gallows. Let them!"

"Signora Isolabella will be compromised, for *biribissi* is forbidden everywhere. I must speak to the State Inquisitors.[27] Leave it to me. Write Passano to persevere in his silence and tell him you will take care of everything. The law concerning clipped money[28] is severe only in regard to those particular coins, for the government wants them to circulate in Genoa, and to make examples which will teach the clippers to respect them.''

I wrote to Passano accordingly, and I sent for scales. We weighed all the gold pieces I had won at the *biribissi,* and we found that they had been clipped to the extent of two thousand Genoese lire. Signor Grimaldi undertook to cut them up and sell them to a goldsmith.

We found all the tables at cards made up, and Signor Grimaldi proposed that he and I play quinze[29] together. As a two-handed game, it is very tiresome, but I consented. At a limit of four zecchini, I lost five hundred zecchini in four hours.

Toward noon the next day he came to tell me that Passano was out of prison and that the value of his coin had been returned to him. He also gave me twelve or thirteen hundred zecchini which he had received from the goldsmith to whom he had sold the clipped gold pieces. I thanked him for everything and said that I would go to Signora Isolabella's the next day and have my revenge at quinze.

I found him alone with his lady. We were to sup without other company, but we did not sup at all. We sat down to play, and we did not stop until two hours after midnight. I lost three thousand zecchini, of which I paid him a thousand the next day, giving him bills of exchange drawn on myself for the other two thousand. When the bills fell due I was in England and I let them be protested. Five years later he was urged by a traitor to have me arrested in Barcelona; but Signor Grimaldi was a man of honor. He wrote me a letter in which he told me my enemy's name; and he assured me that he would never take any steps to force me to pay. The person who had urged my arrest on him was Passano, who was in Barcelona then, though I did not know it.

I shall tell the story when I come to that time. All those whom I associated with me to use in the tricks I played on Madame d'Urfé betrayed me except a Venetian girl, whom I shall introduce to my dear reader in the following chapter.

Despite these losses I lived well and was not short of money, for, after all, what I had lost had been only the money I had won at the *biribissi*. Rosalie regularly came to dinner with me, and I went to sup at her house every evening with my niece, whose affair of the heart was becoming more serious each day. I told her so, but she would not renounce her intention of entering a convent, and she told me at the beginning of Holy Week that her resolve was now immutable, that day having given her undeniable evidence that she was not pregnant.

She had come to have such a friendship for me, and, since I had been having Annetta, such great confidence in me, that she often appeared in the morning and sat down on my bed when the girl was still in my arms. She laughed to see our fondness, and she seemed to share in our amorous pleasures. It is certain that her presence increased mine. I quenched in Annetta the desires which my niece kindled in me, since I could not quench them with her and in her. Annetta, with her shortsightedness, could not be aware of my frequent preoccupation. My niece knew that her presence gave me pleasure, and I know that what she saw me do could not leave her indifferent. When she thought I was exhausted she would ask Annetta to get up and leave her alone with me because she had business to talk over with me. Annetta would get up and go. Then, left alone with me, she would laugh and have nothing of consequence to say. Sitting beside me in the scantest of attire, she thought that her charms could have no more power over me. She was mistaken, and I took care not to set her right, for fear of losing her confidence. My niece did not know that she was not Annetta and that Annetta was not she. I spared her for my own ends. I felt certain that she would finally grant me the reward which I deserved, at the latest after our departure from Genoa, when we should be thrown together alone in the very free conversation and companionship of travel and in the pleasant idleness which, to replace doing nothing, forces the body and the soul to do everything. One grows tired of talking, of insisting, of reasoning, and even of laughing; one lets oneself go, and one acts because one does not want to know what one is doing. One thinks about it afterward, and one is very glad that it all happened.

But the story of my journey from Genoa to Marseilles was written in the great book of Fate. Not having read it, I could not know what its circumstances were to be. All I knew was that I had to set out, for Madame d'Urfé was waiting for me in Marseilles. The journey was to put in motion a train of events which would decide the destiny of the prettiest of all female creatures: a Venetian girl who did not know me and did not know that I existed to be the instrument of her good fortune. I did not know that I had stopped in Genoa to await her, for I did not know that she was among the number of the living.

Having set my departure for Easter Monday,[30] I still had six days before me. I settled my accounts with the banker to whom Greppi had sent me, and I obtained a letter of credit on Marseilles, though, Madame d'Urfé being in that city, I could not want for money there. I took leave of Signora Isolabella's household, in order to spend the whole week in perfect freedom with no one but Rosalie and her family, often going to her house in the country.

CHAPTER II

*My brother the Abate and his base behavior.
I take away his mistress. Departure from
Genoa. The Prince of Monaco. My niece
conquered. Arrival in Antibes.*

EARLY ON the Tuesday in Holy Week Clairmont
told me that an unknown Abate who refused to give his
name wanted to speak with me. Annetta had gone to
wait on her mistress. I had invited Rosalie, with her entire family and her friends, to dinner that day.

I go out of my room in my nightcap to see who the
Abate might be. I see a figure who falls on my neck and
hugs me. The room was dark. I take him to the window,
and I see the youngest of all my brothers,[1] whom I had
always despised, whom I had not seen for ten years, and
who interested me so little that I did not even ask if he
was alive or dead in the correspondence I maintained
with the Signori Bragadin, Dandolo, and Barbaro.[2]

As soon as his stupid embraces were over I coldly asked
him what chance brought him to Genoa in the pitiable
state in which I saw him, for he was dirty, disgusting,
and in rags; his only advantages were a pretty face, fine
hair, a good complexion, and the age of twenty-nine. He

was born, like Mohammed,[3] three months after my father's death.

"If I am to tell you the whole story of my misfortunes, dear brother, it will be a long one. So let us go into your room and I will relate everything in perfect truthfulness."

"First answer all my questions. How long have you been here?"

"Since last evening."

"Who told you that I am here?"

"Count A. B. in Milan."

"Who told you that the Count knew me?"

"On Signor Bragadin's table in Venice a month ago I read a letter he was writing you, addressed to the Count's house."

"Did you tell him you are my brother?"

"I had to admit it when he said I look like you."

"He told you what is not so: you are a consummate fool."

"He invited me to dinner."

"In those rags. You did me great honor."

"He gave me four zecchini, without which I could never have come here."

"He did a stupid thing. You have become a beggar. Why did you leave Venice, and what do you want of me? I don't know what to do with you."

"Oh, I beg you not to drive me to despair, for really I am capable of killing myself."

"I don't believe a word of it; but why did you leave Venice, where you managed to live on your mass and your sermons?"

"That is the chief point of my story. Let us go in."

"Certainly not. Wait for me here. We will go somewhere and you shall tell me whatever story you please. Take care not to tell my servants that you are my brother, for I am ashamed of it."

I go and quickly put on a *frac*,[4] and I order him to take me to his inn.

"I must tell you that at my inn I am not alone, and that what I have to say to you can be said only in private."

"In whose company are you?"

"I will tell you. Let us go to some coffeehouse."

"But whom are you with? Out with it! Is it a gang of thieves? You sigh?"

"It is a girl."

"A girl? You are a priest."

"Blinded by love, seduced myself, I seduced her. I promised to marry her in Geneva; and I certainly dare not go back to Venice, for I abducted her from her father's house."

"What would you have done in Geneva? You would have been allowed to stay there three days, then you would have been expelled. Let us go to your inn; I want to see this girl you have deceived. You can talk to me privately afterward."

I set out for the inn, the name of which he had told me; he has to follow me; I enter; at that he precedes me and goes up to the fourth floor, where, in a wretched den, I see a very young girl, tall, dark, pretty, appetizing, with a certain haughty pride, who, not in the least embarrassed and making me no salutation, asks me if I am the brother of the liar there who has deceived her. I answer yes.

"Then I call upon your decency and your charity to send me back to Venice, for I will no longer stay with this scoundrel to whom I listened like the idiot I was and who told me all sorts of lies which turned my head. He was to meet you in Milan, where you would give him money to travel by post to Geneva, where he said that priests marry after turning Protestant. He said you expected him, and you were not there. He got hold of some money, I don't know how, and brought me here. Thank God he has found you, for otherwise I would have set off on foot tomorrow, begging for alms. All I have left is the shift on my back. He sold the three others I had

in Bergamo, after selling my trunk and everything in it
in Verona and Bressa. He took my wits away. He made
me believe that the world outside Venice was a paradise;
I wanted to see it, and I left my home; I found that one
is nowhere as well off as in our country. A curse on the
day I first met this impostor! He's a beggarly good-for-
nothing who always talks as if he were preaching. He
wanted to sleep with me as soon as we got to Padua;
but I was not such a fool. I insisted that I would see
this marrying in Geneva first. Here is the written promise he gave me. I make you a present of it; but if you
have a soul capable of kindness, send me to Venice and
so save me from having to go there on foot.''

I listened to this whole tirade standing and in real
astonishment. What gave the tragic scene a touch of
comedy was my brother, who, sitting with his head in his
hands, had to hear out the whole cruel story. But for the
sighs he heaved from time to time I should have thought
he was asleep.

The pathetic adventure strangely touched me. I at
once saw that I must take care of the girl, break off the
ill-assorted match, and send her safely back to her country, which she might not have left but for the confidence
in me which my brother had made her feel. The girl's
typically Venetian nature struck me even more than her
charms; her frankness, her just indignation, her revul-
sion of feeling, her courage, pleased me; she had not
asked me to send her home; but she had convinced me
that I could not honorably abandon her. I could not
doubt the truth of her story, since my brother had preserved the silence of guilt throughout it. The pity he
might arouse in me could not but be accompanied by
scorn.

After too long a silence I promised to send her back
to Venice, escorted by a decent woman, in the coach
which left Genoa every week.

''But you will be in a pitiable situation if you return
home with child.''

"With child? Didn't I tell you he was to marry me in Geneva?"

"Even so——"

"What do you mean? I tell you I never yielded to the least of his desires."

"Remember," my brother said to her in a plaintive voice, "the oath you took that you would be mine forever. You swore it before a crucifix."

As he spoke these words in which he accused the girl of breaking faith, he had risen; but, far from his overawing her, she gave him a backhanded slap with the utmost vigor. I expected a struggle of sorts, which I would not have tried to stop. But not a bit of it: the long-suffering Abate simply turned to the window, raising his eyes to heaven, and burst into tears.

"You are quite a little devil, my beautiful Signorina," I said. "The man whom you are mistreating is unhappy because you made him fall in love with you."

"All I know is that he took my wits away, and that I will not forgive him until I have seen the last of him. That's not the first slap I've given him, I began in Padua."

"You are excommunicated," he said, "for I am a priest."

"I'll give you more of the same."

"No, you will not," I said. "Bundle up your things and come with me."

"Where are you taking her?" said my lovelorn brother.

"To my lodging, and hold your tongue. Just a moment. Here are twenty zecchini, go at once and buy yourself a coat, an overcoat, and some shirts. Do not change your lodging. I will come here to talk with you tomorrow. Give your rags to the poor, and thank God that you found me. Come, Signorina, I will have you taken to my lodging in a sedan chair, for Genoa must not see you in my company, especially since it is known that you arrived here with a priest. I must end this scandalous state of affairs. I will put you in the care of my landlady; take good care not to tell her this ugly story. I will have you dressed suitably at once."

"Let us go. God be praised!"

Turned to stone by the twenty zecchini, he let us leave without uttering a word. I at once instructed my landlady to buy her a dress, shifts, stockings, shoes, and whatever she might need. I was extremely curious to see what the girl would become when her anxieties were relieved. I told Annetta that a girl who had been commended to my care would eat and sleep with her, and, expecting a large and brilliant company, I went to dress. I thought it incumbent on me to tell my niece the whole story, to keep her from judging me unfavorably. She declared that I could not have performed a nobler act, and she became very curious to see the girl, as well as my brother, whom she thought far more to be pitied. I gave her a dress of calencar[5] with a large flower pattern which became her wonderfully well. She aroused my admiration, both for her behavior toward me and for the way in which she treated the young man[6] who was already hopelessly in love with her. She saw him every day, either at my lodging or at Rosalie's. He wrote to her straightforwardly, in the style of a business letter, that since they were well matched in all the essentials of age, station, and fortune, nothing could prevent him from going to Marseilles to ask her father for her hand except some antipathy to his person on her part. When she showed me the letter, asking me for my advice, I congratulated her. I told her that in her place I would not reject his offer, if Signor N. N. was not displeasing to her. She replied that nothing in the young man displeased her, and that Rosalie was of my opinion.

"Then tell him by word of mouth that you will wait for him in Marseilles and that he can be sure of your consent."

"I will tell him so tomorrow."

When I rose from table I went to see Annetta, who was dining in my niece's room with Marcolina;[7] such

was the Venetian girl's name. I very nearly did not
recognize her. But it was not because of her dress, which
was in no way unusual, but because of her face, which
contentment had made a hundred times prettier. Gaiety
had taken the place of anger, which always looks ugly,
and the softness which is born of satisfaction gave her
a countenance in which one saw love. I thought it impossible that the being I saw before me had given my
brother, a consecrated priest, the resounding slap which
I had seen and heard. The two new friends were eating,
laughing at being unable to understand each other.
Marcolina spoke the Venetian dialect, and Annetta, in
revenge, spoke that of Genoa; but the former is charming and every Italian understands it, while the latter is
further from Italian than Swiss is from German. I congratulate Marcolina on her look of happiness.

"I have passed from hell to paradise."

"Indeed, you look like an angel."

"And this morning you called me a devil. But here
beside me is a white angel, such as we have no idea of
in Venice."

"And she is my treasure."

My niece comes in and, seeing me in high spirits with
the two girls, sits down beside me to submit my new
acquisition to a thorough scrutiny. She pronounces her
perfectly pretty, and, after telling her so, gives her a
sweet kiss. Marcolina, always the Venetian, asks her
bluntly who she is.

"I am a niece of the Signore, who is taking me home
to Marseilles."

"Then you would be my niece, too, if I were his sister.
How happy I should be to have such a pretty niece!"

Upon this ensued any number of kisses, which Marcolina received and returned with all the ardor which
Venetian women put into kissing. We left her with
Annetta, and, together with the whole company, went
for a sail about the harbor in a good-sized vessel.

Back at the house about midnight, I asked Annetta,

who was undressing her mistress, where the Venetian
girl was, and, receiving the answer that she had gone to
bed early and was asleep, I took it into my head to go
to see her. She wakes, I sit down beside her, I tell her
that in bed I think her even more beautiful, I make to
embrace her, she holds me off, I do not insist, and we
talk. A quarter of an hour later Annetta comes in, I tell
her to go to bed, and she goes to my room, proud to
show Marcolina that she is my mistress.

I then bring up the subject of my brother, I tell her
of the lively interest she inspired in me the moment I
saw her and of all that I felt inclined to do for her,
whether she wanted to return to Venice or preferred to
go to France with me.

"As your wife?"

"No, for I am married."

"That is a lie, but I don't care. Send me to Venice,
and as soon as possible; I will not be any man's concubine."

At that I became pressing, but using only the gentleness which any woman finds harder to resist than open
force. Laughing the while, Marcolina, when she sees that
I persist although she blocks my every advance, suddenly
gets out of bed clad in a long shift, goes into my niece's
room, and locks the door. At that I went off to bed, but
not at all vexed. Annetta, finding herself made all the
more of, praised Marcolina's decision.

The next morning early I went into my niece's room
to laugh a little over the company which chance had led
me to procure her; and there was reason to laugh.

"Your Venetian girl," she said, "raped me."

Far from defending herself, the other begins giving
her fresh tokens of a continuing fondness, which, being
graciously accepted, enabled me to guess what the two
of them were doing under the covers.

"This," I said to my niece, "is a rude shock to your
uncle's respect for your prejudices."

"Trifling between girls," she replied, "cannot tempt a man who has just come from Annetta's arms."

"But it does tempt me."

So saying, I uncover the two of them. Marcolina cries out, but does not move; my niece feelingly begs me to cover them up again; but what I saw enchanted me too much to let me hurry. Just then Annetta comes in and, obeying her mistress's command, puts the covers back over the bacchantes, thus depriving me of the beautiful vision. Angry with Annetta, I throw her on the bed, and I give the two others a spectacle so interesting that they stop their trifling to watch it with the utmost attention. After the act Annetta swore to me that I had been right thus to avenge myself on their prudery. Rather pleased with the joke, I went to breakfast and, immediately afterward, to the inn to see my brother.

I found him well dressed.

"How is Marcolina?" he asked me sadly.

"Very well. I have put her into decent clothes. She eats and sleeps with my niece's chambermaid, and she is very well satisfied."

"I did not know I had a niece."

"You know it now. I shall send her to Venice in three or four days."

"I hope I may dine with you today."

"No, my dear brother. You are never to show your face in my lodging, for if Marcolina saw you it would distress her. You shall not see her again."

"Oh, I will go to Venice too, even if I should be hanged for it."

"What use is that? She can't bear you."

"She loves me."

"She slaps you."

"Because she loves me. She will become gentle when she sees me decently dressed. You do not know how much I suffer."

"I can imagine it; but I do not allow myself to think

of it, because you are a blasphemer and a fool, a barbarian who deserves no pity; for to satisfy a vile whim you were about to bring a lifetime of misery to a charming girl who was born to be happy. Answer me. What would you have done if I had turned my back on you?"

"I should have gone begging with her."

"She would have beaten you half to death; and she could have gone to the police to rid herself of you."

"But what will you do with me if I let her go back to Venice and do not follow her?"

"I will take you to France and see that you get service under some bishop."

"Service? I was born only to serve God."

"Proud fool! Marcolina was right yesterday when she said that you talk as if you were preaching. Who is your God? What is the service you render him? Ignorant hypocrite! Do you serve him by turning the head of a decent girl, profaning your profession, betraying your religion, which you do not know? Without talents of any kind, you are fool enough to imagine that you can become a Protestant minister when you don't know even the rudiments of theology, when you can't even speak your own language properly. Beware of showing your face in my lodging, for you would force me to have you driven out of Genoa."

"Very well then, take me to Paris! I will go to my brother Francesco,[8] who has a kinder heart than yours."

"Excellent. I will see that you get to Paris. We shall leave in five or six days. Remain at this inn and I will send you word. I shall have my niece, my secretary, and my valet with me, and we will go by sea."

"The sea makes me sick."

"Then you shall vomit."

When I repeated this whole dialogue to Marcolina I saw no sign of interest on her face. She said prettily that she was under no obligation to him except for his having made her acquainted with me. I replied that I forgave him only because he had made me acquainted with her.

"I love you, and if you do not consent to become my mistress it will kill me."

"Never, for I should fall in love with you, and when you left me it would kill me too."

"I will never leave you."

"Very well, take me to France, and there we will begin sleeping together; at the moment you have Annetta, and I am in love with your niece."

The cream of the jest was that my niece had also fallen in love with her, and had told me we must have her eat with us and that from then on she would sleep with no one else. Having acquired the right to witness their sports, I had no objection. At table she told us such amusing stories that they kept us occupied until it was time to go to supper at Rosalie's, where Signor N. N. never failed to be present.

The next day, which was Maundy Thursday, Rosalie came with us to see the processions. I had Rosalie on one arm and Marcolina on the other, both well concealed in their *mezzari*,[9] and Signor N. N. gave his arm to my niece. On the following day, when the same company went to see the processions which in Genoa are called *casacce*,[10] Marcolina pointed out my brother, who kept hovering around us, though always pretending that he did not see us. He was dressed within an inch of his life, and the conceited fool thought that he would make such a good impression on Marcolina that day that she would regret having scorned him; but he must have suffered the torments of the damned, for the Venetian girl, accustomed to manipulating the *zendale*,[11] could use the *mezzaro* even more effectively than a born Genoese woman; he could never be sure that she had seen him. In addition the cruel creature clung so closely to my arm that we appeared to be on the best of terms.

The two girls, become intimate friends, could not bear to have me tell them that their amorous diversions were the only source of their friendship; they promised me

that their toying would cease when we left Genoa, and
that I should begin sleeping between them in the felucca[12]
which would take us to Antibes, in which we were to
spend at least one night, during which we should not undress. I took them at their word, I set our departure for
Thursday,[13] I engaged the felucca, and on Wednesday
I went and told my brother to be on board.

A very cruel moment was that in which I returned my
kind Annetta to her mother's care. Her tears made us
all weep. My niece gave her a dress, and I thirty zecchini,
promising her that I would return to Genoa when I came
back from England; but I never returned there. I informed Passano that he would eat with the Abate whom
he would find on board the felucca. I had it supplied with
food for three days. Signor N. N. promised my niece
that he would be in Marseilles in two weeks, and that
when he arrived their marriage would already be arranged between her father and his. This outcome filled
me with joy, for it assured me that her father would
receive her with open arms. Signor N. N. and Rosalie
and her husband did not leave us until they had to let
us board the felucca.

My felucca, which was of good size, had twelve rowers
and was armed with some small cannon and with twenty-
four muskets, so that we should be able to defend ourselves against pirates. Clairmont had cleverly had my
carriage and my luggage arranged in such a way that
five mattresses were stretched across them at full length,
so that we could have slept and even undressed as if in
a room. We had good pillows and wide covers. A long
tent of serge covered the whole ship, and two lanterns
hung from the two ends of the long beam which held up
the tent. As soon as night fell they were lighted, and
Clairmont brought us supper. Sitting up between my
two young ladies, I served my guests, my niece first, then
Marcolina, then my brother and Passano. Watering the
wine was forbidden, each drank his bottle of excellent
burgundy. After supper, though the wind was very light,

the sail was raised and the rowers rested. I had the lanterns put out, and my two female angels went to sleep, each with her free arm lying across me.

The light of dawn waked me at five o'clock and showed me the two slumbering beauties on either side of me in the same position in which I had seen them when the lanterns were put out. I could not cover either of them with kisses. The one was supposed to be my niece, the other was a girl whom humanity forbade me to treat as my mistress in the presence of a brother who adored her and to whom she had never granted the slightest favor. He was there, overwhelmed by grief and by the sufferings inflicted on him by the sea, which turned his stomach and made him vomit up whatever it contained. There he remained, watching to see if there was any movement under the covers. I felt that I must have pity on him and not risk driving him to despair at a moment when he might easily have thrown himself into the sea and been drowned.

The girls awoke as fresh as roses; and after mutual congratulations on the good sleep we had enjoyed, we stretched and, one after the other, went to the prow to a closet which had been arranged for us and which was necessary to the modesty of my beauties. But I scolded the master of the felucca when I saw that we were only opposite Finale.[14]

"The wind," they all said together, "stopped blowing at Savona."

"We feared we should wake you; but you shall be at Antibes tomorrow."

Cursing the calm, the rowers set to work. Clairmont gave us an excellent broth made from tablets which I always took with me. We dined at noon, and at three o'clock we decided we should like to land at San Remo. The whole crew were grateful to me. We are put ashore there; but I give orders that no one is to leave the felucca. My niece could not keep from laughing openly at my wretched brother, who was constantly taking a mirror from his pocket and giving a sad sigh upon seeing his face, which the sea had robbed of its bloom.

I escorted my two young ladies to the inn, where I ordered coffee. A gentleman comes up to us politely and asks us to do him the honor of going to his house, where we can amuse ourselves playing *biribissi.*

"I thought, Signore, that the game was forbidden in the State of Genoa."

"That is so, but in San Remo we enjoy a number of privileges.[15] It is a fief of the Empire. The *biribissanti* who were in Genoa have been here for several days."

Certain that the sharpers were those whose bank I had broken, I accept the invitation. My niece had fifty louis[16] in her purse; I give Marcolina ten or twelve, and we find ourselves in a drawing room in which there is a large company. Places are found for us; we sit down, and I see the same gamesters whom I had punished at Signora Isolabella's, except for the man who tended the bag. At sight of me they went pale.

"I stake on the Harlequiness," I said to them.

"We have got rid of her."

"How much is in the bank?"

"You see it there. Play is for small stakes here. These two hundred louis are enough. One may stake as little as one pleases, and at most a louis."

"Excellent, but my louis are full weight."

"I believe ours are so too."

"Are you sure of it?"

"No."

"In that case," I said to the master of the house, "we will not play."

"You are right. Bring out the scales."

The owner of the *biribissi* then said that at the end of play he would give four six-franc *écus* for every louis won from him, and no more was needed. In a moment the board was completely covered.

We all staked at a louis. I lost twenty, as did my niece; but Marcolina, who had never seen a *biribissi* and who had never had two zecchini of her own, won a hundred and forty louis. She staked on the picture of an abate, which came out five times in twenty turns. She was given a bag filled with six-franc écus, and we went back to our felucca.

The wind being contrary, we had to be rowed all night, and the sea having become rough, at eight o'clock in the morning I decided to go ashore at Mentone.[17] My niece and Marcolina were unwell. I alone escaped. After locking Marcolina's bag into my trunk, I went ashore with my two girls, telling Passano that he could do likewise with my brother.

We go to the inn. My beauties lie down on a bed. The innkeeper tells me that the Prince of Monaco[18] is in Mentone with his Princess. I decide to call on him. It was thirteen years earlier that I had paid my court to him in Paris. I was the man who, supping with him and his mistress Coralline,[19] kept him from yawning. It was he who had taken me to call on the ugly Duchess of Ruffec;[20] he was not married then, and here he was in his Principality[21] with his wife, by whom he had already had two sons.[22] She was a Marchesa di Brignole, a rich heiress, but even more beautiful and charming than rich; I knew her by reputation; I was curious to see her.

I go there, I am announced, and, after a very long wait, I am shown in. I give him his due by addressing him as Your Highness, which I had never done in Paris, where no one so addressed him. He says that he is pleased to see me again, but with a coldness which belies any pleasure. He hazards a guess that I had stopped because of the bad weather; I say that, if he will permit it, I will stay in his delightful city (which was not delightful) all day; he replies that I am at liberty to do so, and he explains to me that he stays there in preference to Monaco, whose situation both his Princess and he dislike. I ask him to present me, and he orders someone to take me to her.

She was at her harpsichord, accompanying herself in an air; she rises and, no one presenting me, I tell her my name. Nothing is more awkward than a man of my kind announcing himself. The Princess pretends that my name is enough and, to find something to say to me, she tries to remember the commonplaces of the catechism of the nobility under the article "Presentation"; but I do not give her time to be at a loss. I tell her everything in a few words, except that I have two young ladies with me. The Princess was beautiful, affable, and brought up in a way to foster all her talents. She was an only daughter. Her mother,[23] who knew the Prince of Monaco and foresaw that he would make her unhappy, did not want to give her to him; but she had to resign herself to it when she said to her: *"O Monaco, o monaca"* ("Either Monaco, or a nun)."

In comes the Prince, running after one of her maids, who makes off laughing, but the Princess pretends to see nothing and continues the remark she had begun to me. I take my leave, and she wishes me a good journey. I meet the Prince again; he bids me good-by and tells me always to come to see him when I pass that way. I return to the inn, and I order dinner for three.

In the Principality of Monaco there was a French garrison,[24] in return for which the Prince received a pension of a hundred thousand francs. He was right, for the garrison did him honor and gave him a semblance of greatness.

A very smart, dapper young officer,[25] perfumed with ambergris, stops before our open room and, letting effrontery stand for acquaintance, asks us if we will permit him to join his gay humor with ours. I reply coldly that he does us great honor; which is as much as to say neither yes nor no; but a Frenchman who has taken the first step never draws back and is not easily abashed.

After displaying his attractions to my beauties and making several random remarks which he does not give them time to answer, he turns to me and says that, knowing I have spoken with the Prince, he is surprised that he has not invited me to dinner at the palace with these charming ladies. I thought it proper to tell him that I had not informed the Prince of the charming ladies' presence.

No sooner has he heard my answer than he rises eagerly, says that he is no longer surprised, that he will go at once to announce them to His Highness, and so will have the pleasure of dining with us at Court. No sooner has he spoken than he makes for the stairs and is gone.

We all three laugh at the coxcomb's enthusiasm, feeling perfectly certain that we shall dine neither with him nor at the Prince's table.

He comes back a quarter of an hour later in the highest spirits and triumphantly extends an invitation to us from the Prince to dine at the palace. I ask him to thank His Highness and at the same time to beg him to excuse us. I tell him that, the weather having turned fair, I intend to leave at once, after eating a hasty bite. He insists, he protests, but he is finally obliged to leave, crestfallen, to tell the Prince that it is impossible. I thought the thing was over; but not at all.

In another quarter of an hour he comes back looking even more contented; and, completely disregarding me, he tells the ladies that he has described their charms to His Highness with such truth to nature that he had resolved to come to dine with them.

"I have already ordered two more places set," he said, "for I shall have the honor too. You will see him in a quarter of an hour."

"Very well," I said, not hesitating for an instant; "in that case I will go to my felucca to fetch an excellent *pâté* which His Highness will find exquisite. Let us go, ladies."

"You can leave them here, Monsieur. I will keep them company."

"Thank you, but no; they too need some things from the felucca."

"Will you permit me to accompany you?"

"As you please."

I go down, and I ask the innkeeper the price of the dinner.

"Monsieur, everything is paid for. I have just received an order not to tender you a bill."

"That is certainly very handsome of the Prince."

I rejoin the young ladies, and my niece takes my arm, laughing heartily because the French officer was addressing gallantries to Marcolina, who did not understand a word of anything he was saying to her, and he had no way of knowing it for he had not given her time to tell him so.

"We will have a good laugh at table," my niece said to me; "but what are we going to the felucca for?"

"We are going to leave. Be still."

"Leave?"

"At once."

"What a trick to play!"

We go on board the felucca; and the officer, delighted with my fine carriage, falls to examining it. I whisper to the master of the vessel that I want to leave instantly.

"Instantly? The Abate and your secretary have gone ashore, and two of my crew as well."

"That makes no difference. They can come to Antibes by land; it is only ten leagues away; I want to leave, I tell you; make haste."

"Very well."

He pulls up the anchor chain, and the felucca veers off. The astounded officer uncomprehendingly asks me what it means.

"It means that I am going to Antibes; and it gives me great pleasure to take you there."

"That would be a jest indeed! But you are joking."

"I am perfectly serious, and your company is very dear to us."

"What next! Be so good as to put me ashore, for—pardon my impoliteness, ladies—I haven't time to go to Antibes. Some other day!"

"Put the gentleman ashore," I said to the master, "for our company is not to his liking."

"It is not that, on my word of honor, for these ladies are charming, but you must understand that the Prince would have reason to take it ill; for he would believe I had connived with you to play this trick on him, and after all it is not one to be passed over lightly. What will he say? But I can justify myself perfectly. Good-by, ladies, good-by, sir."

Marcolina stood there in complete astonishment, and, understanding nothing of what was going on, she could not laugh at it; but my niece was holding her sides, for nothing was more comical than the way the officer had taken the situation.

Clairmont served us a dinner than which we could have asked for nothing more choice. Everything set us laughing, even the thought of the astonishment of Passano and my stupid brother, which could not but be a scene from comedy, when they arrived at the place and found the felucca gone. I had no doubt that I should see them the next day at Antibes.

At four o'clock we were off Nice, and at six o'clock we landed at Antibes. Clairmont saw to having everything I had brought in the felucca taken to my rooms, waiting until the next day to have my carriage made ready for the road again. We supped in high spirits and with the appetite which one feels on leaving the sea, the very air of which upsets the stomach.

Marcolina, feeling a little tipsy, went to bed and to sleep at once; and my niece would have done likewise, had I not reminded her of her promise, with all the sweetness which love imparts to eloquence. She consented without replying, but with the charming manner which denotes perfect contentment.

Transported with delight to see a readiness so un-

mistakable and one which seemed very much like love,
I got into bed beside her, saying:

"At last the moment of my happiness has come."

"And of mine too."

"Of yours? How can you say that? You have always
refused me."

"Never. I have always loved you, and I bore your indifference in bitterness of heart."

"The first night we spent after we left Milan, you
preferred the pleasure of sleeping alone to that of coming to bed with me."

"Could I do otherwise and not risk making you think
me a girl more a slave to her temperament than to love?
You should have told me that you loved me, and have
convinced me of it by the most ardent attentions. That
would have given me the courage to convince you that
I loved you too, and then you would not have had the
mortification of seeing yourself the only one in love, while
on my side I should not have had that of supposing you
would think you owed only to submissiveness whatever
pleasure you might have received from having me in your
bed. I do not know if you would have loved me less the
next morning; but it is certain that you would not have
esteemed me."

My niece was right, and I acknowledged it; but at the
same time justifying myself, for I had to guard against
her thinking that I could basely demand that she pay
me by her favors for the obligations under which I had
put her. Weighing the question, we saw that, in the
reciprocity of feeling between a woman and a man in
love, it is his part to grant her all the advantages of
consideration and to indulge her in all the ideas which
she may have and which can only humiliate her unless
the man is intelligent enough to interpret them all in
her favor. A woman humiliated can neither love nor forgive the man cruel enough to have debased her soul by
making it entertain the dark idea of humiliation. From
these general truths, however, the soul of a slave, whether

man or woman, must be excepted. Slavery creates mon-sters. So I cannot understand how the Helots[26] can have existed on earth without committing all kinds of crimes.

We spent the sweetest of nights; and she told me in the morning that it was probably only for her own good that we had not begun with that at which we had now arrived, for then she would never have brought herself to accept Signor N. N., though to all appearances he could not but make her happy. I was not a man who would marry.

Marcolina congratulated us in the morning. She swore that she would always sleep alone. She gave us countless caresses.

Passano arrived with my brother as we were about to sit down at table, and my niece having had two more places set, I assented. My brother could not walk.

"I am not used," he said, "to riding horseback, and since my skin is delicate it is not surprising that I am half flayed. But God's will be done. Never in my life have I suffered such pains as I have during this journey, not only in body but even more in mind."

So saying, he gave Marcolina a piteous look, which made us all burst out laughing. My niece, wanting to be amused, said:

"I am sorry for you, dear Uncle."

At the word "Uncle" he blushed, and addressing her as "dear niece," he paid her the stupidest of compli-ments in French, thinking it would surprise us. I told him to be still and to be ashamed of himself, for he had spoken no better than a pig. But the poet Pogomas spoke French no better.

The latter told us that he had no sooner arrived at the place where the felucca should have been and not seen it than he had not known what to think.

"I went," he said, "with the Signor Abate to the inn where I knew you had ordered dinner, to try to find out something; but all I learned was that the innkeeper was expecting you and was also expecting the Prince and an

officer, who were to dine with you. As I was telling him
that he was waiting in vain, since you had left, in comes
the Prince with the officer, very angry, and saying that
he should look for payment from no one but you. The
innkeeper replies that you had tried to pay him before
you left, but that the order he had received from the
Prince himself had kept him from accepting anything.
At this answer the Prince gave him a louis, asking us
who we were. I said that we were in your service, and
that you had not waited for us either. After laughing at
what had happened, the Prince asked me who the two
young ladies in your company were, and I replied that
one of them was your niece and that I did not know the
other; but at that the Signor Abate said that she was
your *cuisine* ['kitchen'] instead of saying *cousine*
['cousin']. You can imagine how the Prince laughed at
his saying *cuisine*. He left, declaring that he would still
find you somewhere and that he would remember the
trick you had played on him. The innkeeper, a worthy
man, felt obliged in conscience to give us a very good
dinner, as he also did to the two sailors, who arrived
later. After dinner we hired two horses, and we slept at
Nice. This morning we came here, sure that we should
find you.''

Marcolina dryly told my dear brother that if he took
it into his head to call her his *cuisine* in Marseilles or
anywhere else, he would have to reckon with her, for she
wanted to be neither his *cuisine* nor his *cousine*. I added
seriously that he should stop trying to speak French, for
the blunders he made disgraced the persons he was with.

When I was preparing to order post horses so that we
could spend the night at Fréjus,[27] a man appears saying
that I owe him ten louis for the stabling of a carriage
which I had left with him almost three years before.[28]
I at once remember that it was when I had carried
Rosalie off from Marseilles. I laugh, for the carriage was
a poor one and not worth even five. I reply that I make
him a present of it. He says he does not want my present,

he wants ten louis. I tell him to take himself off, and I order horses, intending to leave. A quarter of an hour later a fusilier appears and orders me, at my creditor's instigation, to go to speak with the Commandant. I go there, and I see a one-armed individual,[29] who politely tells me to pay the man the ten louis and take my carriage. I reply that since my contract at six francs a month had no terminal date, I do not want to take the carriage.

"And if you never take it?"

"He will be free to leave his claim to his heir."

"Nevertheless, I believe he can legally demand that you either take it or consent to its being sold at auction."

"That may be the case, but I am so magnanimous as to want to spare him the trouble. Not only do I consent to his selling it, I make him a present of it."

"That ends the matter. The carriage is yours," he said to my man.

"I beg your pardon, Commandant, but that does not end it, for I am willing to sell it, but I want the balance."

"You are wrong. As for you, I wish you a good journey; and forgive the ignorance of these people, who want the laws to conform to their ideas."

It was late, and I put off leaving until the next day. Needing a carriage for Passano and my brother, I thought that the one in question might do for them. Passano went to see it, and, having found it in wretched condition, he got it for four louis, and I spent another to put it in condition to reach Marseilles. I was not able to get away until afternoon.

*My arrival in Marseilles. Madame d'Urfé. My
niece is well received by Madame Audibert.
I get rid of my brother and Passano. Regeneration. Departure of Madame d'Urfé. Marcolina's constancy.*

MY NIECE, become my mistress, set me on fire.
My heart bled when I thought that Marseilles was to be
the tomb of my love. All I could do was to go there by
very short stages. From Antibes I went only as far as
Fréjus, in less than three hours; I told Passano to sup
with my brother and to go to bed, ordering a choice
supper, with good wines, for myself and my two girls.
I remained at table with them until midnight; then,
while the hour hand made one revolution, I passed the
time in amorous diversions and in sleep; I did the same
at Le Luc, at Brignoles, and at Aubagne,² where I spent
the sixth delicious night with her, which was the last.

No sooner had we arrived in Marseilles than I took
her to Madame Audibert's,³ having sent my brother and
Passano to the "Thirteen Cantons," ⁴ where they were
to lodge without saying anything to Madame d'Urfé,
who had been staying at the same inn for three weeks,
waiting for me.

It was at Madame Audibert's that my niece had made

the acquaintance of La Croix;[5] she was a woman of wit
and intrigue, who had felt the greatest fondness for
her even from her childhood; and it was by her good
offices that she hoped to obtain her father's forgiveness
and thus return to the bosom of her family. We had
arranged that, leaving her in the carriage with Marcolina, I should go up to see the lady, whom I already
knew, and from whom I should learn where she could
go to lodge while she took all the steps necessary to bring
her plan to a happy issue.

I go upstairs to Madame Audibert, who had seen me
from the window getting out of my carriage and, curious
to know who could be arriving at her house by post, came
to meet me. After I reminded her who I was she consented to go into a room alone with me to learn what I
might want of her. I briefly and truthfully told her the
gist of the whole matter, the misfortune which had forced
Croce to abandon Mademoiselle P. P., my good fortune
in saving her from ruin, my second good fortune in
having introduced her at Genoa to someone who would
present himself in less than two weeks' time to obtain
her hand in marriage from her father, and the pleasure
which I felt in being able to put the charming creature,
whose savior I had been, in her care from that very
moment.

"Where is she?"

"In my carriage, where blinds make her invisible to
passers-by."

"Have her get out, and leave the entire matter to me.
No one shall know that she is in my house. I cannot wait
to embrace her."

I go downstairs; I make her draw her hood down over
her face, and I conduct her to the arms of her sagacious
friend, enjoying the dramatic moment. Embraces, kisses,
tears of joy mingled with tears of repentance, make me
shed them too. Clairmont, to whom I had given instructions, carries up her trunk and everything she had in

the carriage, and I leave, promising that I will go to see her every day.

I get back into my carriage, after telling the postilions where to take me. It was to the house of the worthy old man where I had so happily kept Rosalie.[6] Marcolina was weeping for grief at being parted from her dear friend. I get out at the old man's house; I hastily conclude an arrangement with him by which Marcolina will be lodged, fed, and waited on like a little princess. He tells me that he will put his own niece with her, he assures me that she will never go out and that no one will enter her apartment, which he shows me and which I find charming.

I then go to get her out of the carriage, and I order Clairmont to follow us with her valise.

"Here," I said to her, "is your house. I will come tomorrow to see if you are satisfied, and I will sup with you. Here is your money, changed into gold; you will not need it, but take care of it, for a thousand ducati will give you consideration in Venice. Do not weep, my dear Marcolina, for you possess my heart. Good-by until tomorrow evening."

The old man then gave me the key to his house door, and I went at a fast trot to the "Thirteen Cantons." I was expected, and I was shown to the apartment which Madame d'Urfé had arranged for me to have next to hers. I at once saw Brougnole,[7] who came to bring me her mistress's compliments and to say that she was alone and could not wait to see me.

It would bore my reader to read a detailed account of our interview, for he would find nothing but absurdities in the arguments of the poor woman, who was infatuated with the falsest and most chimerical of doctrines, and, on my side, nothing but falsehoods which had not a shadow or even a semblance of truth. Given over to libertinism, and in love with the life I was leading, I took advantage of the delusions of a woman who,

if she had not been deceived by me, would have wanted
to be deceived by someone else. I gave myself the preference and, at the same time, amusement. The first thing
she asked me was where Querilinte[8] was, and she was surprised when I told her he was there in the inn.

"So it is he who will regenerate me in myself. I am
certain of it. My Genius assures me of it every night. Ask
Paralis[9] if the presents I have prepared for him are
worthy to be given to a leader of the Rosicrucians by
Seramis." [10]

Not knowing what the presents were, and unable to
ask her to let me see them, I replied that we must first
bless them at the planetary hours appropriate to the
ceremonies[11] which we were to perform, and that Querilinte himself could not see them before their consecration.
That being the case, she at once showed me into the
adjoining room, where she took from a desk seven packages which the Rosicrucian was to receive as offerings
to the seven planets. Each package contained seven
pounds of the metal governed by the planet, and seven
precious stones governed by the same planet, each
weighing seven carats: diamond, ruby, emerald, sapphire,
chrysolite, topaz, and opal.

Thoroughly resolved to proceed in such a way that
none of all this should fall into the Genoese's hands, I
said that, as to the method, we must be entirely guided
by Paralis and must begin consecrating the gifts by
putting the packages one at a time in a box made expressly for the purpose. Only one could be consecrated
each day, and we must begin with the Sun. It was a
Friday, we must wait until the next day but one; I had
the box made on the following day, which was Saturday,
with seven compartments. To perform the consecration I
spent three hours a day alone with Madame d'Urfé, so
that the ceremony was not finished until the following
Saturday. During that week I had Passano and my
brother dine with her; completely at a loss to understand her harangues to Passano and myself, my brother

never said a word. Madame d'Urfé, who thought him an imbecile, believed that we intended to put the soul of a sylph in his body, so that he could engender a creature half divine and half human. When she confided this discovery to me she said she would put up with it provided that after the operation he would behave toward her in a way betokening common sense.

I was extremely amused by the spectacle of my brother in despair because Madame d'Urfé took him for an imbecile, and doubly so when he saw fit to say something to her which would convince her that he was a wit. I laughed to see that he would have played the role very badly if I had asked him to play it deliberately; but the buffoon lost nothing by it, for the Marquise, to amuse herself, provided him with the sort of soberly luxurious clothing which would have been affected by an abbé of the most illustrious family in France. The one to whom Madame d'Urfé's dinner was a torment was Passano, who had to answer the lofty questions she asked him and who, not knowing what to say, usually beat about the bush. He yawned, he did not dare to get drunk, he did not adhere to the manners and the politeness which usage decrees at table. Madame d'Urfé said to me that some great misfortune must be threatening the Order, since the great man was so preoccupied.

As soon as I had had the box delivered to Madame and had arranged everything with her to begin the consecration on Sunday, I had the oracle decree that for seven days in succession I must go to the country to sleep, practice perfect abstinence from every mortal woman, and worship the Moon with the proper ceremonies every night at her hour, in the open air, in order to prepare to regenerate her myself in case Querilinte, for reasons purely divine, could not perform the operation in person. In consequence of this command not only was Madame d'Urfé debarred from objecting to my sleeping elsewhere, she was grateful to me for the pains I was taking to ensure the successful outcome of the operation.

On Saturday, then, which was the day after my arrival in Marseilles, I went to Madame Audibert's, where I had the pleasure to see Mademoiselle P. P. delighted with the friendly way in which she had taken her interests to heart. She had spoken to her father; she had told him that his daughter was in her house, and that she hoped for nothing but his forgiveness, so that she could return to the bosom of her family in order to become the wife of a rich young Genoese, who, for the honor of his house, could receive her only from his hands. Her father had replied that he would come on the next day but one to take her to one of his sisters, who lived in a house she owned in Saint-Louis,[12] two short leagues from the city. By staying there perfectly quietly, she could await the arrival of her future husband without giving occasion for any gossip. Mademoiselle P. P. was surprised that her father had not yet heard anything from him. I told her that I would not go to see her at Saint-Louis, but that I would certainly see her again when Signor N. N. arrived, and that I would not leave Marseilles until I had seen her married.

From there I went to Marcolina's, whom I could not wait to clasp in my arms. She received me with heartfelt joy; she said that she would be happy, were it not that she could neither make herself understood nor understand anything that her waiting woman said to her. I saw that it was true, but I saw no remedy for it; I should have had to try to find her a servant who spoke Italian, and it would have been a hard task. She was touched to tears when I conveyed my niece's compliments to her and told her that she would be in her father's arms the following day. She already knew that she was not my niece.

The choice and delicate supper we enjoyed reminded me of Rosalie, whose story delighted Marcolina, who said that I seemed to travel only to bring happiness to unfortunate girls, provided that I found them pretty. Marcolina also charmed me by the appetite with which she ate. The fare one finds in Marseilles is exquisite, except for the poultry, which is of the poorest; but one does without it; we forgave the garlic which is put in all dishes to make them tasty. In bed Marcolina was charming. It had been eight years since I had enjoyed Venetian wantonness in bed, and the girl was a masterpiece. I laughed at my brother, who had been fool enough to fall in love with her. Unable to take her anywhere and wanting her to be amused, I told the landlord to let her go to the theater[13] with his niece every day and to prepare supper for me every evening. The next day I replenished her wardrobe by buying her everything she could want in order to shine like the other women.

The next day she told me that she had infinitely enjoyed the play, though she did not understand a word of it, and on the day after that she surprised me by saying that my brother had taken it upon himself to join her in the box in which she was sitting and had said so many impertinent things to her that if she had been in Venice she would have slapped his face. She thought he had followed her, and she feared she would be harassed.

Back at the inn, I went to his room, where I saw at Passano's bedside a man who was putting away his surgical instruments before leaving.

"What does this mean? Are you ill?"

"I have caught something which will teach me to be more careful in future."

"At sixty years of age, it is too late."

"There is always time."

"You stink of balsam."

"I will not leave my room."

"That will make a bad impression on the Marquise, who thinks you are the greatest of adepts."

"*I don't give a f . . .*[14] *for the Marquise. Stop bothering me.*"

The rascal had never spoken to me in such a tone. I conceal my feelings, and I turn to my brother, who is shaving.

"What did you want with Marcolina at the theater yesterday?"

"I wanted to remind her of her duty and tell her that I was not a man to be her p . . ." [15]

"You insulted her, and me too. You are a wretch and a fool who owes everything to that charming girl, for, without her, I would never even have looked at you, and you dare to go talking your nonsense to her?"

"I have ruined myself with her, I cannot go back to Venice, I cannot live without her, and you are taking her from me. What right have you to her?"

"The right of love, idiot, and the right of the strongest. How is it that, with me, she says she is happy and that she cannot bring herself to leave me?"

"You have dazzled her, and afterward you will treat her as you have treated all the others. In any case, I believe I have the right to speak to her wherever I may find her."

"You shall not speak to her again, I promise you."

Having said which, I take a hackney carriage and go to a lawyer's to inquire if I can have a foreign abbé put in prison for owing me money, though I have not the necessary papers to prove he is in my debt.

"If he is a foreigner, you can give security, have him sequestrated at the inn where he is staying, and make him pay you, unless he proves that he owes you nothing. Does he owe you a large sum?"

"Twelve louis."

"Come with me to the magistrate, where you will deposit twelve louis, and you will have the right to put him under guard at once. Where is he staying?"

"In the same inn as I, and I do not want to have him arrested there. I will have him turned out, I will send him to the 'Sainte-Baume,' [16] which is a disreputable inn, and there I will put him under guard. Meanwhile, here are twelve louis for the security, go get the order, and you will see me at noon.''

''Give me his name and yours.''

After accomplishing this I go back to the ''Thirteen Cantons,'' and I see my brother dressed and about to go out.

''Let us go to Marcolina's,'' I say. ''You and she shall have it out in my presence.''

''With pleasure.''

He gets into the hackney carriage with me, I order the driver to take us to the ''Sainte-Baume,'' and as soon as we are there I tell my brother to wait for me, assuring him that I will come back with Marcolina; but instead I went to see the lawyer, who, having already obtained the order, went at once to take it where it was executed. I then returned to the ''Thirteen Cantons,'' I had all his clothes put in a trunk, and I took them to him at the ''Sainte-Baume,'' where I found him in a room under guard, talking to the astonished innkeeper, who could not understand what was going on. But when he saw a trunk, and when, having taken him aside, I told him my trumped-up story, he left without wanting to hear more. Whereupon, going into my brother's room, I told him that he must prepare to leave Marseilles the next day, and that I would give him money enough to pay for his journey to Paris; but that if he would not go there willingly, I abandoned him, being certain that I knew how to have him expelled from Marseilles.

The pusillanimous fool began crying and said he would go to Paris.

''Then you shall leave tomorrow morning for Lyons; but you must first write me a note stating that you owe twelve louis to the bearer.''

''Why?''

''Because I want you to. On that condition I assure you that I will give you twelve louis tomorrow and will tear up your note.''

''I cannot but do blindly whatever you wish.''

"You can do nothing better."

He wrote the note. I went at once to reserve a place for him in the diligence, and the next morning I went with the lawyer to withdraw the order and recover my twelve louis, which I took to my brother, who left at once with a letter of recommendation to Signor Bono,[17] whom I instructed not to give him any money and to see that he left for Paris in the diligence. I gave him twelve louis, which was more than he needed, and I tore up his note. So it was that I got rid of him. I saw him again in Paris a month later, and, in the proper place, I will recount how he returned to Venice.

But on the previous day, before going to dine alone with Madame d'Urfé, and after taking my brother's trunk to the "Sainte-Baume," I went to talk with Passano, to find out just what was the reason for his ill-humor.

"My ill-humor is due to my certainty that you are about to take possession of twenty or thirty thousand écus in gold and diamonds which the Marquise intended should be mine."

"That is possible. But it is not for you to know whether I will take possession of them or not. What I can tell you is that I shall prevent her from doing anything so foolish as to give you either the gold or the diamonds. If you have any claim to them, go and lay your complaint before the Marquise, I will not stop you."

"So I must put up with having served as the instrument of your impostures without getting any benefit from it? You shall not boast of that. I want a thousand louis."

"You are a wonder."

I go upstairs to the Marquise's apartment. I tell her that dinner is served and that we will dine alone together, since weighty reasons had obliged me to dismiss the Abate.

"He was an idiot. But Querilinte?"

"After dinner Paralis will tell us everything. I have strong suspicions."

"I too. The man seems to me to have changed. Where is he?"

"He is in bed with the foul disease which I dare not name to you."

"That is most extraordinary. It is a work of the dark ones, such as has never happened before, *I believe.*"

"Never, so far as I know; but now let us eat. We shall have a great deal of work to do today after we consecrate the tin." [18]

"So much the better. We must perform a ceremony of expiation to Oromasis, [19] for—horrors!—he was to regenerate me four days hence, and he is in this horrible condition."

"Let us eat, I say."

"I am afraid we shall lose the hour of Jupiter."

"Never fear."

After the ceremony to Jupiter, I put off the one to Oromasis until another day in order to produce a number of cabalistic figures which the Marquise translated into letters. The oracle said that seven Salamanders had transported the real Querilinte to the Milky Way, and that the one who was in bed in the ground-floor room was the black Saint-Germain, [20] whom a Gnomess had put in the terrible condition in which he was in order to make him the executioner of Seramis, who would have died of the same disease before reaching her term. The oracle said that Seramis must leave it entirely to Paralisée Galtinarde [21] (who was I) to get rid of Saint-Germain, and to have no doubt of the successful outcome of the regeneration, since the word [22] was to be sent to me from the Milky Way by Querilinte himself on the seventh day of my devotions to the Moon. The last oracle declared that I was to inoculate Seramis two days after the conclusion of the ceremonies of consecration, after a charming Undine [23] had purified us in a bath in the room in which we then were.

Having thus undertaken to regenerate my good Seramis, I began considering how best to avoid cutting
a poor figure. The Marquise was beautiful, but old. I
might find myself a nullity. At *thirty-eight* years of age,
I was beginning to see that I was often subject to that
disastrous misfortune. The beautiful Undine whom I
would receive from the Moon was Marcolina, who, transformed into a bath attendant, would instantly procure
me the generative power which I should need. I could not
doubt it. The reader will see how I went about having
her descend from the sky.

A note which I received from Madame Audibert made
me go to see her before I went to sup with Marcolina.
She told me joyfully that Monsieur P. P. had received
a letter from Genoa from Signor N. N., who asked him
for his daughter as the wife of his only son, she being
the young lady whose acquaintance he had made at Signor Paretti's, the introduction having been made by the
Chevalier de Seingalt (who was I), who must have taken
her back to Marseilles and restored her to her family.

"Monsieur P. P.," said Madame Audibert, "feels that
he is as greatly indebted to you as a father who loves
his daughter can be to a man who has shown her paternal
kindness. His daughter herself has given him a most
interesting account of you, and he is determined to make
your acquaintance. Tell me when you can sup at my
house. His daughter will not be present."

"I am very glad of it, for Mademoiselle's P. P.'s
fiancé can only esteem his future wife the more when he
learns here that I am her father's friend; but I cannot be
present at the supper; I will come at six o'clock whenever you please and will stay with you until eight, and
the acquaintance will have been made before her fiancé
arrives."

I made the appointment for the next day but one, and
I went to see Marcolina, to whom I told all this news and
gave an account of the way I intended to get rid of my

brother on the morrow, which I have already imparted to my reader.

It was on the next day but one that, as we were going to dinner, the Marquise smilingly gave me a long letter which the scoundrel Passano had written her in very bad French, but which was still understandable. He had filled eight pages to tell her that I was deceiving her, and, to convince her that it was true, he truthfully gave her the whole story of the affair, omitting not the slightest circumstance which could injure me. In addition he told her that I had arrived in Marseilles with two girls whom I was keeping he did not know where, but that it was certainly with them that I went to sleep every night.

Giving the letter back to her, I asked the Marquise if she had had the patience to read it through, and she said that she had not understood a word of it for he wrote in gibberish, and that she did not want to understand it, for he could only have written her lies intended to turn her from her course at a moment when she most needed not to be led astray. Such prudence on her part greatly pleased me, for it was necessary to my plans that she should not suspect the Undine, the sight of whom I should need to set the work of the flesh in motion.

After dining and getting through all the ceremonies and oracles I needed to fortify my poor Marquise in her resolve, I went to a banker to obtain a bill of exchange for a hundred louis on Lyons to the order of Signor Bono, and I sent it to him, instructing him to pay the hundred louis to Passano on the warrant of an advice in my hand which Passano was to present to him in order to receive the hundred louis on the day which he would find specified in the advice. If he presented it after the specified day, he was to refuse payment.

After sending this off, I wrote Bono the letter which Passano was to present to him, in which I said to Bono:

"Pay Signor Passano on sight of this one hundred louis d'or, if it is presented to you this day, April 30,

1763. After this day my order will be null and void."

With this letter in my hand, I went to the room in which the traitor's groin had been pierced by the lancet an hour earlier.

"You are a traitor," I said. "Madame d'Urfé did not read the letter you wrote her, but I read it. Here is the choice I give you, and the only choice, for I am in a hurry. Either decide to let yourself be taken to the hospital at once, for we want no one with your disease here, or decide to leave in an hour to go to Lyons without stopping once, for I give you only sixty hours, which should suffice you to travel forty stages.[24] No sooner have you arrived in Lyons than you will take this letter to Signor Bono, who will at sight of it pay you a hundred louis, which I give you, and after that you can do whatever you please, for you are no longer in my service. I make you a present of the carriage which was taken out of storage in Antibes, and I will now give you twenty-five louis for the expenses of your journey. Choose. But I warn you that if you choose the hospital I will pay you only one month's wages, for I dismiss you from my service here and now."

After thinking a little he said that he would go to Lyons, though at the risk of his life, for he was very ill. I thereupon called Clairmont to pack his trunk, and I informed the innkeeper that the man was leaving, so that he should send for post horses for him at once. After that I gave him the letter addressed to Bono, and twenty-five louis to Clairmont to give to Passano when he saw him in the carriage and ready to leave. After thus disposing of the matter I went to pursue my love affair. I needed to have long conversations with Marcolina, with whom I felt that I was more in love every day. She told me every day that to be completely happy all she lacked was a knowledge of French and the shadow of a hope that I would take her to England with me.

I had never given her any expectation of that, and I became sad again when I saw that I must think of

parting from the girl, who, voluptuous to the marrow,
and no less accommodating, had a natural temperament
which gave her an insatiable appetite for all the pleasures of the bed and of the table, where she ate as much as
I did and drank more. She was delighted that I had got
rid of my brother and Passano, and she begged me to
take her with me to the theater sometimes, where all the
people of fashion approached her kind companion[25] to
learn who she was and berated her because she would
not let her reply. I promised to go with her during the
following week.

"For at the moment," I said, "I am engaged in a
magical operation which keeps me busy all day, and in
which I shall need you. I will have clothes made for you
to disguise you as a boy groom;[26] and so clad you will
present yourself to the Marquise with whom I am staying, at an hour of which I will inform you, and deliver
a note to her. Will you have the courage to do that?"

"Certainly. Will you be there?"

"Yes. She will speak to you, and since you do not
speak French and so cannot answer her, you will pass as
a mute. The note will describe you as such. The same
note will say that you offer to wait on her in the bath,
in my company; she will accept your offer, and at the
hour she appoints you will undress her completely, then
you will do the same, and you will rub her from her toes
to the top of her thighs, and no farther. While you are
doing that in the bath with her, I will strip naked, I will
embrace the Marquise closely, whereupon you will do
nothing but look at us. When I leave her you will wash
her amorous parts with your delicate hands and then dry
them. You will do the same to me, and I will embrace
her closely a second time. At the end of the second time,
after washing her again, you will wash me too and cover
with Florentine kisses[27] the instrument with which I
shall have given her unmistakable signs of my affection.
I will then embrace her for the third time, and this
time your office will be to caress us both until the end

of the skirmish. You will then give us the last ablution
and, after drying us, you will dress her, you will take
what she gives you, and you will return here. You will
see me an hour later.''

''I will do whatever you order me to do, but you must
know how hard it will be for me to do it.''

''No harder than for me, for it will be you whom I shall
want to embrace, and not the old woman you will see.''

''Is she very old?''

''She will soon be seventy.'' [28]

''As old as that? I am sorry for you, my dear Giacometto. And afterward you will come to sup and sleep
with me?''

''Certainly.''

''That's better!''

On the day appointed by Madame Audibert, I saw
my late niece's father, to whom I told everything truthfully, except that I had slept with her. He embraced me
several times, and thanked me again and again for having
done more for her than he could have done himself. He
told me he had received another letter from his correspondent, containing one from his son which was very
modest and respectful.

''He asks for no dowry with her,'' he said, ''but I will
give him forty thousand écus, and we will celebrate the
wedding here, for it is a most honorable marriage.
Everyone in Marseilles knows Signor N. N., and tomorrow I will tell the whole story to my wife, who, in
view of the happy outcome, will grant her daughter
a full pardon.''

I had to promise that I would attend the wedding
party with Madame Audibert, who, knowing that I was
an inveterate gamester, and having high play at her
house, was surprised not to see me there; but I felt that I
was in Marseilles at the time to create, not to destroy.
Everything has its proper season.

I had a waist-length jacket of green velvet made for
Marcolina and breeches of the same material, I gave her

green stockings and morocco leather shoes and gloves of the same color, and a green net in the Spanish fashion, with a long bag behind which held her long black hair. Thus clad she became a figure so worthy of admiration that if she had shown herself in the streets of Marseilles everyone would have followed her, for, aside from all that, the fact that she was a girl was obvious to every eye. Before supper I took her, in girl's clothes, to my inn, to show her where she was to hide in my room after the operation, when the day came for me to perform it.

The ceremonies to the planets being completed on Saturday, I had the oracle declare that Seramis was to be regenerated on Tuesday at the hours of the Sun, of Venus, and of Mercury, which, in the planetary system of magicians, follow one another, as they do in the imaginary system of Ptolemy.[29] They would be the ninth, the tenth, and the eleventh hour of that day, since, being Tuesday, its first hour would belong to Mars. The hours at the beginning of May were each of sixty-five minutes; so the reader, if he knows anything at all about magic, will see that I had to perform the operation on Madame d'Urfé from half past two o'clock to five minutes before six. Early Monday night, at the hour of the Moon, I had taken Madame d'Urfé to the seashore, followed by Clairmont carrying the box, which weighed fifty pounds. Having made sure that we were unobserved, I told Madame d'Urfé that the moment had come, and at the same time I had Clairmont set the box down at our feet, after which I ordered him to wait for us at the carriage. We then addressed a set prayer to Selenis,[30] and we threw the box into the sea, to Madame d'Urfé's great joy, which, however, was no greater than mine, for the box we threw into the water contained fifty pounds of lead. I had the other box in my room, where no one could see it. Back at the "Thirteen Cantons," I left the Marquise there, telling her that I would return to the inn after rendering thanks to the Moon in the same place where I had performed my seven ceremonies.

I went to sup with Marcolina, and while she put on her groom's costume, I wrote with rock alum[31] on white paper in capital letters:

"I am dumb but I am not deaf. I have come out of the Rhone to bathe you. The hour has begun."

"Here is the note," I said to Marcolina, "which you will deliver to the Marquise when you appear in her presence."

I have her go out with me on foot, we enter my inn unseen by anyone, and then my room, where I hide her in a cupboard. I then put on a dressing gown and I enter Madame's room to inform her that Selenis has fixed her regeneration for the next day before three o'clock, and that it must be completed by half past five in order not to risk trespassing on the hour of the Moon, which followed that of Mercury.

"You will arrange, Madame, for the bath to be ready here at the foot of your bed before dinner, and you will make sure that Brougnole shall not enter your room before nightfall.'

"I will tell her to go for a walk; but Selenis had promised us an Undine."

"True; but I have not seen one."

"Ask the oracle."

"As you please."

She herself puts the question, renewing her prayers to the Genius Paralis that the operation should not be deferred even if the Undine does not appear, since she is prepared to bathe alone. The oracle replies that Oromasis's orders are infallible, and that she had been wrong to doubt it. At this reply the Marquise rises and performs a ceremony of expiation. The woman could not move me to pity, for she moved me too strongly to laughter. She embraced me, saying:

"Tomorrow, my dear Galtinarde, you will be my husband and my father. Tell the learned to explain that enigma."

I shut her door, and I go to the cupboard to release

my Undine, who at once undresses and gets into my bed,
where she well understood that she was to spare me. We
slept all night without looking at each other. In the
morning, before calling Clairmont, I had her take breakfast and I instructed her to get back into the cupboard
at the end of the operation, for she must not risk being
seen leaving the inn clad as she was. I repeated all her
instructions, I charged her to be gay and affectionate,
and to remember that she was dumb but not deaf and that
at exactly half past two she must enter and present the
paper to the Marquise, going down on one knee.

Dinner was ordered for twelve o'clock, and as I entered
the Marquise's room I saw the bath at the foot of her bed,
two-thirds filled with water. The Marquise was not there;
but two or three minutes later I see her come out of the
dressing room with a great deal of rouge[32] on her cheeks,
a cap of fine lace, a short blond lace mantle covering her
bosom, which forty years earlier had been of a beauty
unequaled in France, and wearing an old but very rich
dress of cloth of silver and gold. In her ears were two
emerald pendants, and she had on a choker of seven
aquamarines from which hung an emerald which could
not be matched for clarity; the chain which held it was
of some eighteen or twenty very white diamonds of a
carat and a half. On her finger she had the carbuncle
which I knew, which she valued at a million and which
was only paste; but the other stones, which I did not
know she owned, were genuine, as I assured myself later.

Seeing Seramis thus bedecked, I saw that I must flatter
her by my homage; so I went to meet her and made to
kiss her hand on my knees; but she, preventing me, invited me to embrace her. After she had told Brougnole
that she was free until six o'clock, we discussed the subject of our concern until dinner was served.

Clairmont alone was permitted to wait on us at table,
and on that day she would eat nothing but fish. At half
past one I ordered Clairmont to close our apartment to
everyone and to go for a walk until six o'clock if he

wished. Madame began to seem uneasy, and I pretended
to be slightly so too, I looked at my watches, I again calculated the minutes of the planetary hours, and I kept
saying:

"We are still in the hour of Mars, the hour of the Sun
has not yet begun."

At last we hear the clock striking half past two, and
two or three minutes later we see the beautiful Undine
enter, smiling and making her way with measured steps
straight to Seramis, to whom she delivers her paper,
going down on one knee. She sees that I do not rise, and
she remains seated too, but she raises the Genius, accepting her paper, and she is surprised to see it white all
over. I at once hand her a pen; she understands that she
is to consult the oracle. She asks it what the paper is.
I take back the pen, I construct the pyramid for her question, she interprets it, and she finds: *"What is written
under water can be read only under water."*

"I understand it," she says; and she rises, goes to the
bath, dips the opened sheet into it, and reads, in letters
whiter than the paper:

*"I am dumb but I am not deaf. I have come out of the
Rhone to bathe you, the hour of Oromasis has begun."*

"Then bathe me, divine Genius," says Seramis, putting
the paper on the table and sitting down on the bed.

Thereupon Marcolina, following her instructions exactly, takes off her stockings, then her dress, then her shift,
gently puts her feet in the bath, and, in no time at all,
strips bare, steps into the bath up to her knees, while I,
having put myself unaided in the state in which they
both were, beg the Genius to dry Seramis's feet and to
be the divine witness of my union with her, to the glory
of the immortal Horosmadis, King of the Salamanders.[33]

My request is scarcely uttered before the Undine, who
was not deaf, grants it, and I consummate the marriage
with Seramis while admiring the beauties of Marcolina,
which I had never seen so well.

Seramis had been beautiful, but she was as I am today;

without the Undine, the operation would have failed. Yet Seramis, affectionate, amorous, clean, and not in the least repulsive, was not distasteful to me. After the act:

"We must," I said to her, "wait for the hour of Venus."

The Undine purified us where the aspersions of love were to be seen; she[34] embraces the bride, washes her to the top of her thighs, caresses her, is embraced in turn, then she does the same to me. Enchanted by her good fortune and praising the divine creature's charms, Seramis invites me to examine them, I declare that no mortal woman is like her, Seramis becomes tender again, the hour of Venus begins, and, encouraged by the Undine, I undertake the second assault, which would be the most strenuous, for the hour was of fifty-five minutes. I enter the lists, I work for half an hour, groaning and sweating and tiring Seramis without being able to reach the final point and feeling ashamed to cheat her; she wiped from my brow the sweat which dripped from my hair mixed with pomade and powder; the Undine, treating me to the most provocative caresses, preserved what the old body I was obliged to touch was destroying, and nature disclaimed the effectiveness of the means I was employing to reach the finish line. Toward the end of the hour I finally determined to make an end, after imitating all the usual signs which appear at that sweet moment. Emerging from the skirmish the victor, and still threatening, I left the Marquise in no doubt as to my valor. She would have declared Anael[35] unjust; he had indicted me before Venus as a counterfeiter.

Even Marcolina was deceived. The third hour struck, it was time to satisfy Mercury. We spend a quarter of his hour in the bath up to our waists. The Undine enchanted Seramis by the kind of caresses which she gave her, and of which the Regent, the Duke of Orléans,[36] had had no notion; she thought them peculiar to the Geniuses of rivers, so she applauded all the labors which the female Genius performed on her with her fingers. Moved to gratitude, she begged the beautiful creature to bestow her treasures on me, and it was then that Marcolina displayed all the learning of the Venetian school. She instantly became Lesbian, and, seeing me alive in consequence, she urged me to satisfy Mercury; but again I find myself not without thunder but without the power to discharge it. I saw the inexpressible pain which my labors caused the Undine, I saw that Seramis was longing for the end of the skirmish, I could no longer sustain it, I decided to cheat again by an agony accompanied by convulsions which ended in motionlessness, the inevitable consequence of an agitation which Seramis, as she told me afterward, found unexampled.

After pretending to come to myself, I got into the bath, which I left after a brief ablution. I having begun to dress, Marcolina did as much for the Marquise, who watched her with adoring eyes. The Undine dressed at once, and, inspired by her Genius, Seramis took off her necklace and put it around the neck of the beautiful bath attendant, who, after giving her a Florentine kiss, hurried away to resume her place in the cupboard. Seramis asked the oracle if the operation had been perfect. Terrified by the question, I made it reply that the word of the Sun was in her soul, and that at the beginning of February she would give birth to herself with her sex changed, but that she must stay in bed for a hundred and seven hours.

Overjoyed, she declared that the command to rest for a hundred and seven hours was divinely wise. I embraced her, saying that I was going to spend the night outside the city to recover the remainder of the drugs I had left there after the ceremonies I had performed to the Moon, and promising that I would dine with her the next day.

I made infinitely merry with Marcolina until half past seven o'clock, for if I was not to be seen leaving the inn with her I had to wait until dark. I took off the fine wedding coat I had put on and replaced it by a *frac*, and I accompanied her to her lodging in a hackney carriage, taking with me the box with the offerings to the planets which I had so well earned. We were both dying of hunger, but the choice supper we were to have assured us that we should return to life. Marcolina took off her green jacket and put on a dress, after giving me the fine necklace.

"I will sell it, my dear, and give you the money."

"What may it be worth?"

"A thousand zecchini at least. You will go to Venice with five thousand ducati correnti[37] of your own; you will find a husband with whom you will be very well off."

"I give you all the five thousand ducati; and take me with you as your loving mistress; I will love you like my soul, I will never be jealous, I will take care of you as if you were my child."

"We will discuss that, my beautiful Marcolina; but now that we have supped well, let us go to bed, for I have never been so desirous of you as I am at this moment."

"You must be tired."

"Yes, but not exhausted so far as love is concerned, for—thank Heavens!—I was able to distill myself only once."

"I thought it was twice. The good old woman! She is still attractive. Fifty years ago she must have been the greatest beauty in France. When one grows old, one can no longer be pleasing to Love."

"Your way of winding me up was irresistible, but she unwound me even more."

"Do you always need to have a young girl before your eyes when you want to be loving with her?"

"No indeed, for the other times it was not a case of giving her a male child."

"So you have undertaken to make her pregnant. Let me laugh, please. Perhaps she believes she is pregnant, too."

"She certainly believes it, for she is sure that I gave her the seed."

"Oh, what a joke! But why were you foolish enough to promise her three assaults?"

"I thought that, seeing you, I should find it easy, and I was wrong. The flabby skin I was touching was not the skin my eyes saw, and the acme of pleasure would not come. You shall see it is true tonight. Once again: let us go to bed."

"Let us."

By virtue of the comparison I spent a night with Marcolina which equaled those I had spent at Parma with Henriette[38] and at Murano with M. M.[39] I remained in bed for fourteen hours, four of which were consecrated to love. I told Marcolina to dress fittingly and to expect me at the hour for the theater. I could not do her a greater favor.

I found Madame d'Urfé in bed, elegantly attired and with her hair youthfully dressed, and showing a satisfaction which I had never seen in her before. She said she knew that she owed me all her happiness; and she proceeded to argue very rationally from the premise of her delusion.

"Marry me," she said, "and you will be the guardian of my child, who will be your son; by so doing, you will keep me in possession of my entire fortune and have control of what I am to inherit from my brother Monsieur de Pontcarré,[40] who is old and cannot live long. If you do not take care of me next February, when I am to be reborn as a man, who will take care of me? God knows into what hands I shall fall. I shall be declared a bastard, and I shall be forced to lose an income of eighty thousand livres, of which you can keep me in possession. Consider it well, Galtinarde. I already feel within me the soul of a man; I confess it to you, I am in love with the Undine and I want to know if I can sleep with her fourteen or fifteen years hence. If it is the will of Oromasis, he can bring it about. Oh, the charming creature! Have you ever seen a woman so beautiful? What a pity she is dumb. She must have a male water sprite for a lover. But all water sprites are dumb, for in the water it is impossible to speak. I am amazed that she is not deaf. I was surprised that you did not touch her. The softness of her skin is incredible. Her saliva is sweet. Water sprites have a language of gestures, which one can learn. How it would delight me if I could converse with the creature! I beg you to consult the oracle and ask it where I am to lie in; and if you cannot marry me, I think everything I possess should be sold, so that I shall have means when I am reborn; for in my infancy I shall know nothing, and money will be needed to give me an education. By selling everything, it would be possible to invest a large sum which, in trustworthy hands, would suffice to supply all my needs from the interest on it alone."

I replied that the oracle should be our only guide, and that when she became a man and my son I would never allow her to be declared a bastard; and it reassured her. Her reasoning was perfectly sound; but since her argument was based on an absurdity, I could only pity her. If any of my readers is of the opinion that, to act honorably, I should have undeceived her, I am sorry for him; it was impossible; and even if it had been possible I would not have done it, for I should have made her miserable. Her very nature was such that only chimeras could satisfy her.

I put on one of my handsomest coats to take Marcolina to the theater with me for the first time. Chance decreed that the two Rangoni sisters,[41] the daughters of the Roman Consul, took places in the box in which we were. As I had known them since the first time I had been in Marseilles, I introduced Marcolina to them as a niece of mine who spoke only Italian. It was just what was needed to make Marcolina happy, for now she could at last talk with a Frenchwoman in her own Venetian language, which is so full of charm. The younger of the two sisters, far more attractive than the elder, a few years later became Princess Gonzaga Solferino.[42] The Prince who

married her, a man of learning and even of genius,
though poor, was none the less a Gonzaga, being the son
of Leopoldo, also very poor, and a Medini,[43] the sister of
the Medini who died in prison in London in the year
1787. Babet[44] Rangoni, though the poor daughter of a
merchant of Marseilles and Roman Consul, none the less
deserved to acquire the title of Princess, for she had all
the airs and manners of one. She shines under her name
of Rangoni in the list of princes[45] to be found in every
almanac.[46] Her husband, who is extremely vain, is delighted that readers of the almanac should believe that
his wife belongs to the illustrious Modenese family. An
innocuous vanity. The same almanacs call the Medini
who is the Prince's mother a Medici. These little falsehoods, which spring from the pride of the nobility, do
no harm to society. The Prince, whom I saw in Venice
eighteen[47] years ago, was living on a comfortable pension[48] granted him by the Empress Maria Teresa; I hope
that the late Emperor Joseph[49] did not take it from
him, for he deserves it, both by his morals and by his
interest in literature.

At the play Marcolina did nothing but chatter with the
charming younger Rangoni, who tried to persuade me to
bring her to call, but I excused myself. I was considering
how best to send Madame d'Urfé to Lyons, having no
further use for her and finding her presence in Marseilles a burden.

On the third day after her regeneration she gave me
a question for Paralis asking where she was to expect
to die, that is, to lie in, and it was on this occasion that
I made the oracle decree that a rite must be performed
to the water sprites on two rivers at the same hour,
after which the question would be decided; the same
oracle told me to perform three expiations to Saturn
because of the too harsh manner in which I had treated
the false Querilinte, in which rites there was no reason
for Seramis to take part, though she must be present at
the rite to the water sprites.

While I was pretending to think of a place where two rivers were close together, it was she who said that Lyons was watered by the Rhone and the Saône and that nothing would be easier than to do the thing in that city, and I agreed. She having asked the oracle if preparations must be made, I produced the reply that it was only necessary to pour a bottle of sea water into each of the two rivers two weeks before beginning the rite, a series of ceremonies which Seramis could herself perform at the first diurnal hour of the Moon each day.

"In that case," said Seramis, "the bottles must be filled here, for all the other seaports in France are farther from there, and I shall have to set out as soon as I am allowed to leave my bed and then wait for you in Lyons. You see that, since you have to perform expiations to Saturn, you cannot come with me."

I agreed, pretending to feel regret at being obliged to let her leave alone; the next day I bring her two sealed bottles containing salt water from the Mediterranean, I stipulate that she shall empty the bottles into the rivers on the 15th of May (the month in which we then were), promising her that I will be in Lyons before the two weeks are over, and we set her departure for the next day but one, which was the 11th. I wrote down the hours of the Moon for her, and her itinerary so that she would spend the night at Avignon.

After she left I went to stay with Marcolina. On that day I gave her 460 louis in gold, which, with the 140 she had won playing *biribissi*, put her in possession of 600 louis. It was on the day after the Marquise's departure that Signor N. N. arrived in Marseilles with a letter from Rosalie Paretti, which he brought to me the same day. She said that her honor and mine demanded that I present the bearer of her letter to my niece's father. Rosalie was right; but since the girl was not my niece, the thing became awkward. But that did not keep me from telling him, after embracing him warmly, that I would at once present him to Madame Audibert, the intimate friend of his fiancée, who would introduce him, with me, to his future father-in-law, who would later take him to see his daughter, who was two leagues from Marseilles.

Signor N. N. had gone to lodge at the "Thirteen Cantons," where he had at once been told where I was staying; he was delighted to find himself about to attain his dearest wish, and his joy increased when he saw how Madame Audibert received him. She immediately fetched her mantle, got into my carriage with him, and took us to the house of Monsieur N. N.,[50] who, after reading his correspondent's letter, introduced him to his wife, whom he had already informed, saying:

"My dear wife, here is our son-in-law."

I was greatly surprised when, having been previously acquainted with the facts by Madame Audibert, he displayed the tact and presence of mind to introduce me to his wife as his cousin who had made the journey with their daughter. She politely expressed her gratitude, and the awkwardness was over. He at once sent an express messenger to his sister to say that he would dine at her house the next day with his wife, his future son-in-law, Madame Audibert, and a cousin of his whom she did not know. After dispatching the messenger he invited us, and Madame Audibert undertook to convey us in her carriage. She told him that I had with me another niece, of whom his daughter was very fond and whom she would be very glad to see again. He was delighted. Admiring the woman's presence of mind, I was very glad to offer Marcolina this pleasure, and I expressed most sincere thanks to Madame Audibert, who left, saying that she would expect us at her house the next morning at ten o'clock.

I then took Signor N. N. to my lodging, and he came to the theater with Marcolina, who loved to talk and so could not bear to be with French people who spoke only their own language. After the performance Signor N. N. supped with us, and it was at table that I told

Marcolina the good news that she would dine the next day with her dear friend; I thought she would go mad for joy. After Signor N. N. left, we at once went to bed, in order to be ready early the next day. The fiancé did not keep us waiting. At the appointed hour we arrived at Madame Audibert's, who spoke Italian and who, declaring Marcolina a perfect jewel, gave her countless caresses and regretted that I had not made the introduction sooner. At eleven o'clock we arrived in Saint-Louis, where I had the pleasure of witnessing the dramatic scene: Mademoiselle P. P., with a dignity mingled with respect and affection, giving her fiancé the most gracious reception, then thanking me for having been so kind as to introduce him to her father, then passing from seriousness to joy to bestow countless kisses on Marcolina, who was lost in astonishment because her dear friend had not spoken to her at once.

At the dinner everyone was pleased and very gay. I laughed to myself when I was asked why I was sad. They thought I was so because I said nothing; but I was very far from being sad! It was one of the best moments in my life. In those blissful moments my mind was concentrated in the divine tranquility of true contentment, I saw myself the author of the whole delightful comedy, very satisfied to find (on striking the balance) that I did more good than evil in this world, and that, though not born a king, I was able to make people happy. There was not a person at the table who did not owe his particular contentment to me; this reflection gave me a happiness which I could only enjoy in silence.

Mademoiselle P. P. returned to Marseilles with her father, her mother, and her fiancé, who Monsieur P. P. at once insisted must come to stay in his house, and I returned with Madame Audibert, who made me promise to bring Marcolina to supper. It had been settled that the marriage should take place upon the arrival of the answer to a letter which Monsieur P. P. had written to the father of his future son-in-law. We were all invited

to the wedding, and Marcolina was very much flattered
to be included. What a pleasure for me, on our return
from Saint-Louis, to see the young Venetian girl madly
in love! Such is, or should be, the state of every girl who
lives with a man who truly loves her and shows her
attentions; all her gratitude is transformed to love, and
the lover, seeing himself rewarded, becomes all the
fonder.

At supper at Madame Audibert's a very rich young
man, a considerable dealer in wine and his own master,
who had spent a year in Venice and was seated beside
Marcolina, who said countless charming things, showed
that he was not insensible to her attractions. By nature
I was always jealous of all my mistresses, but when I
could foresee their good fortune in a rival who was
coming into being before my eyes, jealousy left me. For
this first time I merely asked Madame Audibert who the
young man was, and I was extremely pleased to learn
that he was of good character and had a hundred thousand écus, together with large wine warehouses in Marseilles and Sète.[51]

The next day at the theater he entered the box in
which we were, and I was delighted to see that Marcolina
received him very graciously. I invited him to sup with
us; he accepted, and was respectful, ardent, and tender.
On his departure I said that I hoped he would do me
the honor some other time; and, left alone with Marcolina, I congratulated her on her conquest, showing her
that she could expect a position in life almost equal to
that which Mademoiselle P. P. had attained; but instead
of finding her grateful, I saw that she was furious.

"If you want to get rid of me," she said, "send me
to Venice; I do not want to marry."

"Calm yourself, my angel—get rid of you? What a
thing to say! What have I ever done to make you think
that you are a burden to me? This handsome, polished,
rich young man loves you, I thought I saw that he is to
your liking; wanting to see you happy and safe from

the whims of Fortune, I point out the prospect of a happy situation for you in the future, and you turn on me? Charming Marcolina, stop crying, you distress me.''

"I am crying because you imagined that I loved him.''

"It was a possibility; I will stop imagining it. Calm yourself and let us go to bed.''

She passed from tears to laughter and caresses in an instant, and we said no more about the wine merchant. The next day at the theater he came to our box, and Marcolina was polite but reserved. I did not dare to invite him to sup with us. At home Marcolina thanked me for not having asked him and said she had been afraid I would do so. It was enough to guide me in the future. The next day Madame Audibert called to bring us an invitation from the wine merchant to sup at his house; I at once turned to Marcolina and asked her if she wished to accept the invitation, and she replied that she was only too happy to be anywhere with Madame Audibert. So she came for us toward nightfall, and she took us to the merchant's, who gave us a supper to which he had invited no one else. We saw a bachelor's house which lacked nothing but a woman fit to do the honors of it and to be its mistress. At the very choice supper the young man divided his attentions between Madame Audibert and Marcolina, who, having made Mademoiselle P. P.'s good manners and easy bearing her own, played her part to perfection. Gay, polite, and discreet, she left me certain that she had set the worthy merchant on fire.

No later than the next day Madame Audibert asked me by a note to come to see her. I went, and, to my considerable surprise, heard her ask me for Marcolina as the wine merchant's wife. I did not think long before replying that I was willing, and that, on sufficient security, I would give her ten thousand écus, but that I could not take the risk of speaking to her on the subject.

"I will send her to you, Madame, and if you can gain her consent I will keep my word; but you must not speak to her about it on my behalf, for it might distress her.''

''I will go for her myself, and she shall dine with me, and you shall come to fetch her in time for the play.''

The next day she came, and Marcolina, whom I had forewarned, went to dine with her. About five o'clock I went to the lady's house, where, finding Marcolina in a charming humor, I did not know what to suppose. They were alone; not having been taken aside by Madame Audibert, I did not want to take her aside, and when it was time for the play we left. On the way Marcolina lavished praise on the lady's excellent character, without saying a word about the affair; but halfway through the play I guessed everything. I saw the young man in the amphitheater,[52] and I did not see him appear in our box, where there were two empty places.

What a pleasure for Marcolina to see me more amorous and fond than ever at supper! It was not until we had gone to bed that, in the sincerity of joy, she repeated to me all that Madame Audibert had said to her.

''I never gave her any answer,'' she said, ''except that I will not marry until you order me to do so. But I am obliged to you for the ten thousand écus which you would be ready to give me. You left the decision to me, and I left it to you. I will go to Venice when you wish it, if you think you cannot take me to England, but I will not marry. It is likely that we shall see no more of the gentleman, who I grant is amiable and whom indeed I could love if I did not have you.''

And in fact we heard no more of him. The day of Mademoiselle P. P.'s wedding arrived; we were invited, and Marcolina appeared at it in my company, without diamonds but otherwise as richly attired as she could wish.

*I leave Marseilles. Henriette in Aix. Irene in
Avignon. Passano's treachery. Madame
d'Urfé's departure for Lyons.*

B U T   F O R my interest in the occasion I should have
found the wedding banquet intolerable. The profusion
of viands, the noisy company, the congratulations, the
interrupted remarks, the insipid jokes, the unrestrained
laughter would have driven me to distraction had it not
been for Madame Audibert, whom I never left. Marcolina
was never far from the bride, who, since she was to return to Genoa a week later, wanted to take her with her,
promising to send her to Venice in trustworthy hands;
but Marcolina would have nothing to do with plans which
would separate her from me. She told me she would go
to Venice when I sent her there of my own free will.
The wedding festivities she was witnessing did not make
her repent in the least of having refused the excellent
match which Madame Audibert had proposed to her. The
bride showed her heartfelt content on her face, I congratulated her on it again and again, she admitted that
she was happy and said that what most gratified her

was that she was sure she would have a true friend at Genoa in Rosalie.[2]

The day after the wedding I made ready to leave. I began by opening the box which contained the offerings to the planets, keeping the diamonds and taking all my money to Roux de Corse,[3] who still had the entire amount which Greppi had placed to my credit; I obtained a letter of credit on Tourton & Baur;[4] for, Madame d'Urfé being in Lyons, I could not lack money there. Three hundred louis which I had in my purse were enough for current expenses. In Marcolina's case, however, I took a different course. I withdrew the six hundred louis she had, I added twenty-five, then I had the whole sum converted into a bill of exchange to her order for 15,000 francs[5] on Lyons, for I still had it in mind to take advantage of a good opportunity to send her home. At the same time I provided her with a separate trunk, into which I had her put all the dresses and underwear I had had made for her. Marcolina had become a beauty and had acquired the manners of good society.

On the eve of our departure we took leave of Madame N. N., supping at her house with her husband and the entire family. She embraced Marcolina fondly, but she showed no less affection for me, the author of all her happiness, despite the presence of her husband, who expressed the greatest friendship for me.

We left the next day, intending to travel all night and not stop until we reached Avignon, but at half past five o'clock, a league beyond the Croix d'Or,[6] the fastening of the pole of my carriage broke, so that we needed a cartwright. We had to resign ourselves to waiting until the nearest one to the place at which we were could come to our aid. Clairmont went to make inquiries at a pretty house on our right at the end of a drive 300 paces long and bordered by trees. I had only one postilion, whom I forbade to leave the four too restive horses. He came back with two menservants from the house which we saw, one of whom brought a message from his master in-

viting me to wait for the cartwright in his house. It
would have been rude of me to refuse such politeness,
which is characteristic of the country and especially of
the nobility. The pole is made fast with ropes, and, leaving Clairmont to guard everything, I go to the house on
foot with Marcolina. The cartwright had been sent for,
and the carriage slowly followed us.

Three ladies accompanied by two gentlemen of rank
come to meet us, one of the latter addresses me, saying
that they cannot be very sorry for the misfortune which
had befallen me since it gave Madame the opportunity
to offer me[7] her house and her services. I turn to the
lady to whom he has pointed and say that I hope I shall
inconvenience her only for a short hour. She curtsies to
me, but I do not see her face. Since the wind of Provence
was blowing very strongly that day, she, like the two
other ladies, had her hood drawn well forward. Marcolina
was bareheaded, and her beautiful hair streamed in the
wind. She replies by curtsies and smiles to the compliments paid to her charms which did not fear the wind;
the gentleman who had first addressed me asks me, offering her his arm, if Madame is my daughter. Marcolina
smiles, and I reply that she is my cousin and that we are
Venetians.

Even the politest Frenchman is so eager to flatter a
pretty woman that he often does not care that the compliment he pays her is at someone else's expense. He
really could not suppose that Marcolina was my daughter, for despite the twenty years between us I did not
look more than ten years the older; so she laughed. We
were about to go in when, a big mastiff in pursuit of a
pretty long-eared spaniel making Madame fear that it
would bite it, she ran to rescue the little dog; and, making a misstep, she fell. We all ran to pick her up; but,
getting up unaided, she said that she had given herself
a sprain and, limping, went up to her apartment with
the same nobleman who had spoken to me. We were no
sooner seated than lemonade was served us, and, seeing

Marcolina at a loss before one of the ladies, who was speaking to her, I offered her excuses, telling the lady the truth. She was beginning to speak broken French, but so badly that I had seen nothing for it but to tell her never to open her mouth. It was better than arousing laughter by foreign expressions. One of the two ladies, the uglier, said to me that she was surprised that the education of young ladies was so neglected in Venice.

"They are not made to learn French!"

"It is a mistake, Madame, but in my country a girl's education includes instruction neither in foreign languages nor in parlor games; that comes when her education is finished."

"Then you are a Venetian too?"

"Yes, Madame."

"One really would not think so."

I bowed in acknowledgment of the unworthy compliment, for, though flattering to me, it was derogatory to my fellow countrymen, but the fact did not escape Marcolina, who gave a little laugh.

"Then Mademoiselle understands French," said the lady who had complimented me, "for she laughs."

"Yes, Madame, she understands everything, and she laughed because she knows that I am just like all other Venetians."

"*Non, Madame, non, Madame,*" said Marcolina, at which there was more laughter.

The Chevalier who had escorted the limping lady to her room returned and said that Madame, having found her ankle swollen, had gone to bed and asked us to go up to her apartment.

She was lying in a big bed in an alcove which was made even darker by curtains of crimson taffeta. She did not have on a hood; but it was impossible to see her well enough to know if she was ugly or beautiful, young or getting on in years. I said that I was in despair at being entirely to blame for her mishap, and she answered in Venetian Italian that it would amount to nothing.

Delighted, for Marcolina's sake, to hear her speak my language, I introduce Marcolina to her, saying that she can pay court to our hostess without speaking French; whereupon Marcolina began talking to her, putting her in high spirits with naïve remarks the amusing side of which it required a thorough knowledge of my country's charming language to appreciate.

"Then Your Ladyship has spent some time in Venice?" I asked.

"Never, but I have often talked with Venetians."

A servant came in to tell me that the cartwright was in the courtyard and that he said it would take him at least four hours to put my carriage in condition to travel. I then asked permission to go down, and I looked at everything. The cartwright lived a quarter of a league away, I was thinking of going there in the carriage itself by fastening the pole to the forecarriage with ropes, when the gentleman who did the honors of the house asked me in the Countess's behalf to sup and spend the night at her house, for, if I went to the cartwright's it would be out of my way, I should not get there until nightfall, and the cartwright, having to work by candlelight, would do everything badly. So persuaded, I told the cartwright to go home and to come back at daybreak with whatever he needed to put me in condition to leave. Clairmont then took everything which was not still tied on the carriage to the apartment I was to occupy. I went to express my gratitude to the Countess, interrupting the laughter which the things Marcolina was saying and the Countess translating aroused from the company. I was not surprised to find that Marcolina had already arrived at the stage of fond caresses with the Countess, who to my regret remained invisible, for I knew her weakness. A table was set for seven, and I hoped I should see her; but not a bit of it, she did not want supper. She did nothing but talk, now to Marcolina, now to me, with a great deal of wit and very correctly. I learned that she was a widow from her dropping the expression "my late husband." I never dared to ask in whose house I was. It was from Clairmont that I learned her name, and then not until I was going to bed; but it made no difference, for I had no knowledge of the family whose name it was.

After supper Marcolina returned to the Countess, sitting down on her bed without so much as "by your leave." Nobody could say a word, for the dialogue between the two new friends was continuous and very animated. When I thought politeness demanded that I should withdraw, I was greatly surprised to hear my supposed cousin tell me that she would sleep with the Countess. The latter's laughter and her "yes, yes" prevented me from telling the madcap that her intention was not far from impertinent. Their mutual embraces showed me that they were of one mind; wishing the Countess good night, I said only that I did not guarantee the sex of the person whom she was admitting to her bed. She answered very distinctly that *the only risk she took lay in which way she would gain.*

Going to bed, I laughed at Marcolina's propensity, which in the same way had won the fond friendship of Mademoiselle P. P. in Genoa. The women of Provence almost all have the same propensity;[8] it makes them only the more charming.

The next morning I rose at daybreak to hasten the cartwright's labors. Coffee was brought to me at my carriage, and when everything was ready I asked if the Countess was visible so that I could go to thank her. Marcolina came out with the Chevalier, who asked me to excuse Madame for not being able to receive me.

"She is," he said with the utmost politeness, "in bed in such dishabille that she dares appear to no one; but she asks you, if ever you come this way again, to honor her house, whether you are alone or in company."

The refusal, though gilded, greatly displeased me; but I concealed my feeling. I could attribute it to nothing but the effrontery of Marcolina, who I saw was in very high spirits, and yet whom I did not want to mortify. After exhausting my stock of compliments, and giving a louis to each of the servants present, I set off.

In rather a bad humor, but able not to show it, I asked Marcolina, after fondly embracing her, how she had spent the night with the Countess whom I had not seen.

"Very well indeed, my friend; we indulged in all the wantonness in which you know two women who love each other indulge when they are in bed together."

"Is she pretty? Is she old?"

"She is young, not more than thirty-three or thirty-four, and I assure you she is quite as beautiful as my darling P. P. I saw all of her this morning, and we kissed each other all over."

"You are a strange one. You cuckolded me with a woman, leaving me to sleep alone. Faithless wretch, you prefer a woman to me."

"It was a passing fancy. But consider that I owed her the kindness, for she was the first to declare her love."

"How?"

"When we were laughing so hard and I embraced her, as you saw, she put her tongue between my lips. You understand that I had to respond in the same fashion. After supper, when I was on her bed, I managed to tickle her you know where, and she did the same to me. After that how could I help anticipating her desire by saying that I wanted to go to bed with her? I made her happy. Look. This proves how pleased she was."

Marcolina shows me a ring set with four stones of the first water of two or three carats each. I am amazed. Such a woman indeed loves pleasure, and deserves to be given it. I bestowed a hundred fond kisses on my beautiful pupil of Sappho,[9] and I forgave her for everything.

"But I cannot understand," I said, "why she did not want me to see her. It seems to me that, to a certain extent, the generous Countess treated me rather like a p. . . ."[10]

"Not at all. On the contrary, I think she felt ashamed to let herself be seen by my lover, for I had to confess to her that such you were."

"Perhaps. That ring, my dear, is worth two hundred louis. How delighted I am to see you happy!"

"Take me to England. My uncle must be there, I will go back to Venice with him."

"You have an uncle in England? Really? It sounds like a fairy tale. You've never mentioned it to me."

"I never mentioned it because I have always been afraid that it would be the very reason why you would not take me there."

"He is a Venetian; what is he doing in England? Are you sure he will give you a good reception? How do you know he is there now, and that he is going back to Venice? What is his name, and how am I to go about finding him in London, where the population is a million?"[11]

"My uncle won't take any finding. His name is Matteo Bosi,[12] and he is valet to Signor Querini,[13] the Venetian Ambassador, who went to congratulate the new King of England[14] with the Procurator Morosini.[15] He is my mother's brother, he left last year, and he told her in my presence that he would be back in Venice in July of this year. So you see we will find him just ready to leave. My uncle Matteo is a kind man, forty years of age, who loves me and who will forgive me for my escapade when he finds that I am rich."

All this was literally true so far as the embassy was concerned; I knew it from Signor Bragadin, and in all the rest that Marcolina had told me I saw the stamp of truth. I find her plan both attractive and well conceived, I give her my word that I will take her to London, delighted thus to have her with me five or six weeks longer. Possessing her, I felt that I was traveling with happiness at my side.

We arrived at Avignon toward the end of the day. We were very hungry, Marcolina had filled me with love; the "Saint-Omer"[16] inn was excellent; I tell Clairmont to take everything we need out of the carriage and to order horses for five o'clock in the morning. Marcolina, who did not like travel at night, shows a pleasure which delights me; but here is what she says to me while we are waiting for supper to be prepared.

"Are we in Avignon?"

"Yes, my dear Marcolina."

"Then, my dear Giacometto, it is at this moment that, as an honest girl, I must perform the task the Countess laid on me this morning before she kissed me for the last time. She made me swear not to speak of it to you until this moment."

"I am very curious. Speak."

"It is a letter from her to you."

"A letter?"

"Will you forgive me for not having delivered it to you until now?"

"Of course, if you promised her you would not. Where is the letter?"

"Wait."

She took a sheaf of papers from her pocket.

"This is my baptismal certificate."

"So I see; you were born in '46."

"This is my certificate of good conduct."

"Keep it."

"This one declares that I was a virgin at the time."

"Excellent. Did a midwife write it for you?"

"It was the Patriarch of Venice."

"Where is the letter?"

"I haven't lost it."

"God forfend! I'll send you back to Aix."

"This is the vow your brother made to marry me as soon as he turned Protestant."

"Give it to me."

"What does 'turned Protestant' mean?"

"I'll tell you later. Where's the letter?"

"Here it is."

"It has no address."

My heart was pounding. I unseal it, and I see the superscription in Italian: "To the most honorable man I have known in this world." I unfold it, and at the bottom of the sheet I see: "Henriette." That was all. She had left the sheet blank. The sight struck me motionless in body and soul. *Io non morii, e non rimasi vivo* ("I did not die, and did not remain alive").[17] Henriette![18] It was her style, her laconism. I remembered her last letter from Pontarlier, which I received in Geneva and which said only: "Farewell." Dear Henriette, whom I had so greatly loved, and whom I felt that I still loved with the same ardor! You saw me, and you did not want me to see you? Perhaps you thought that your charms might have lost the power with which they chained my soul sixteen years ago, and you did not want me to see that in you I had loved only a mortal woman. Ah, cruel Henriette, unjust Henriette! You saw me, and you did not want to know if I still love you. I did not see you, and I could not learn from your beautiful lips if you are happy. It is the only question I would have asked you. I would not have asked you if you still love me, for I know I am unworthy of that, having found it in myself to love other women after loving in you the utmost perfection which Nature has produced. Adorable and generous Henriette! You did not want me to know that you exist until I arrived here, because you feared that I would retrace my steps to have the happiness of seeing you; but I will see you tomorrow. You sent me word that your house would always be open to me. But no. The order which you gave Marcolina shows me that you do not want to see me again now. You may have left this morning, to go God knows where. You are a widow, Henriette. You are rich. Let me imagine that you are happy. Perhaps you only toyed with Marcolina to let me know that you are happy. My dear, my noble, my divine Henriette!

Astonished at my long trance, Marcolina did not dare

In the Harbor of Genoa

Madame d'Urfé

arouse me from it. I did not change my position until the innkeeper came to offer me his compliments and tell me that he had made me a supper such as he knew I liked. I thanked him, and I restored Marcolina to life by fondly embracing her before I sat down at table.

"Do you know," she said, "that you frightened me? You went pale, you spent that quarter of an hour like an idiot. What is it? I knew that the Countess was acquainted with you, but I could not guess that her mere name would have such a tremendous effect on you."

"How did you know that she was acquainted with me?"

"She told me so again and again last night, but she ordered me not to say anything to you until after you had opened her letter."

"What did she say to you?"

"Just what the superscription says. It's odd. The whole letter is nothing but the superscription. Inside there's nothing but her name."

"But that name, my angel, tells everything."

"She told me that if I want to be happy always, I must never leave you. I answered that I was sure of it, but that you wanted to send me home, though you loved only me. I see and I guess that you loved each other dearly. Tell me if it was long ago."

"Sixteen or seventeen years."

"She cannot have been more beautiful."

"Be still."

"And were you lovers long?"

"Four months of perfect and constant joy."

"I shall not be happy as long as that."

"You shall be, my dear Marcolina, with another handsome, honorable man, and of your own age. I am going to England to try to get my daughter away from her mother."

"You have a daughter? The Countess asked me if you were married, and I said no."

"What you said was true. My daughter is not legitimate; she is ten years old. I will show her to you. You will swear she is my daughter."

As we were about to sit down at table, someone came downstairs from the third floor to sup at the common table, where my reader will remember that I had met Madame Stuard.[19] Since our door was open and we were looking at the people who were coming down, we were strangely surprised when we heard a cry and saw the girl who had uttered it come running to us to take my hand and kiss it, calling me her "dear papa." I turn toward the light, and I see Irene,[20] whom I had treated with scant courtesy in Genoa because of the tone her father[21] had taken when he talked to me about the *biribissi* bank I had broken at Signora Isolabella's. I of course draw back my hand and I embrace her. Pretending surprise, the artful creature drops a deep curtsy to Marcolina, who politely returns it and is all ears for the dialogue which was bound to follow such a meeting between the pretty girl and myself, especially when she hears me speak to her in Venetian.

"What brings you here, my beautiful Irene?"

"We have been here two weeks. God, how happy I am to see you! My heart is fluttering. May I sit down, Madame?"

"Yes, yes, sit down," I say, making her drink a little wine, which restores her.

A servant comes up and says she is waited for; she answers sharply that she wants no supper. Marcolina, unexpected as ever, orders the servant to set another place, and shows her satisfaction that her order has not displeased me. The soup being served, I sit down at the table facing the two girls, telling Irene to eat, for we are very hungry. I say that she shall tell us afterward what chance has brought her to Avignon.

Marcolina, seeing that she is eating heartily, says she would have made a mistake not to take supper; the other, pleased to hear herself addressed in Venetian, thanks her

for her interest, and in three or four minutes they have
become good friends enough to embrace each other. I
laugh at Marcolina, who, always the same, fell in love at
sight with all the pretty women she saw. From the brief
dialogues we exchange in the course of eating I learn
that her father and mother are at the common table,
and from her exclaiming from time to time that it is
God's pity for her which has sent me to Avignon, I
gather that she must be in distress. Nevertheless, Irene,
who was as pretty as ever, had assumed an expression of
contentment perfectly in keeping with the gay remarks
Marcolina made to her in her satisfaction at having
learned from her own lips that she had called me "papa"
only because her mother had told her in Milan that she
was my daughter. Marcolina laughed most heartily at the
amusing revelation and looked forward to seeing the
mother, who was supping downstairs and whose lover I
must have been.

We had not yet come to the roast when Count Rinaldi[22]
came in with his wife. I asked them to be seated. Had it
not been for Irene, I should have given the old rascal,
who had tried to lay me under contribution for what I
had won, no very good reception. He scolded Irene for
having had the boldness to enter my apartment without
considering that she must have been unwelcome, in view
of the charming company I was enjoying; but Marcolina
reassured him by saying that Irene could only have given
me pleasure since, as her uncle, I could not but be glad
to see a charming girl in her company.

"I even hope," she added, "that you will allow her to
sleep with me tonight, if the prospect is not unpleasing to
the Signorina."

"Yes, yes," from either side; the new friends embrace,
and I cannot but laugh, though this time the thing did
not please me, for I wanted only Marcolina; but I have
always been able to adapt myself to circumstances.

When the two girls were sure that they would spend
the night together they went wild with joy; I helped on

their delight with good champagne, and I had a large bowl of punch made. Signor Rinaldi and his wife went up to their rooms tipsy; after they left, Irene told us that a Frenchman who had become her lover in Genoa had persuaded her father to go to Nice, where there was high play;[23] that at Nice, having found nothing of what the Frenchman had promised them, she had been obliged to sell some of her belongings to pay the innkeeper, her lover assuring her that he would make it up to her in Aix, where he was certain he would receive a sum of money. At Aix, her lover not having found the people who were to put him in funds again, she had had to give him more of her belongings in order to get them to Avignon, where, so he said, he could not fail to obtain whatever he needed.

"But here," she told me, "he again not finding what he hoped for, and none of us having anything left to sell, my father reproached him so vehemently that the poor young man would have killed himself if I had not prevented it by giving him the lynx-lined cloak you had made for me in Milan, on condition that he would leave. He took it, he pawned it for four louis, he sent me the ticket, assuring me in a very affectionate letter that he was going to Lyons to replenish his purse and would come back to take us to Bordeaux, where we would win great sums. It is twelve days since he left, and we have heard nothing more from him. We haven't a sou, we have nothing left to sell, and the innkeeper threatens to turn us out naked if we do not pay him tomorrow."

"What has your father decided to do?"

"Nothing. He insists that God's Providence will take care of us."

"What does your mother say?"

"She is perfectly calm."

"And you?"

"I undergo continual mortifications, for they say that if I had not fallen in love with the wretch we should still be in Genoa."

"Were you really in love?"

"Alas, yes."

"Then you are unhappy now?"

"Very unhappy; but not because of love, for I've stopped thinking about that, but because of what will happen tomorrow."

"And at the common table no one has fallen in love with you?"

"There are three or four who make advances to me in words; but knowing that we are in need, they do not venture to come to our room."

"Nevertheless you are gay, you haven't the downcast look which distress brings, and I congratulate you."

It was La Stuard's situation all over again.

Marcolina, who was decidedly tipsy, showed that she was very much touched by Irene's story. She embraced her and said that, if I was her father, I ought not to abandon her, and that she should think of nothing but getting a good sleep. They then began to undress, and so did I; but not wanting to skirmish with two, I told them to leave me in peace. Marcolina burst out laughing and replied that I had only to go to bed; which I did, nothing but idle curiosity leading me to watch what Marcolina was doing to the charming Irene, who perhaps found herself engaged in a combat of this nature for the first time in her life.

It was Marcolina who undressed her, at the same time that she undressed herself. When they were both in their shifts Marcolina, always eager for amusement, came to my bed with her arms around Irene and ordered me to embrace her; I told her she was tipsy and that I wanted to sleep; declaring herself insulted, she urged Irene to do as she did, and they forced their way into the bed beside me, where, there not being room enough, Marcolina placed herself on top of Irene, calling her her "wife," while the other played the role very well. I had the strength of mind to remain for more than an hour the spectator of a scene which was always new though I

had witnessed it so many times; but at last, become
ravenous, they both attacked me so violently that I suddenly lost the power to resist, and I spent almost the
whole night abetting the furies of the two bacchantes,
who did not leave me until they saw me become a nullity
and offering no hope of resurrection. We went to sleep,
and I was surprised on waking to see that it was noon.
They were still sleeping, wrapped round each other like
two eels. I sighed when I saw them, thinking of the
true happiness in which the two young creatures were
plunged. I got up without disturbing their sleep, and I
went out to countermand the horses and to tell the innkeeper that I wanted a good dinner at five o'clock and
coffee with milk when I called for it. The innkeeper, who
knew me, and who remembered what I had done for
Stuard, guessed that I would do as much for Count
Rinaldi.

When I returned to my room the two heroines greeted
me with smiles and with the charming proof of confidence
which Nature taught them they should give me, by simul-
taneously displaying, without an atom of jealousy, the
beauties the enjoyment of which they have lavished on
me: an infallible method, according to the constitution
of mankind, of provoking me to give them the good
morning of love. I felt tempted to do so; but the time of
life had set in when I was unconsciously beginning to
hoard my resources. I spent a voluptuous quarter of an
hour on the bed, comparing all their treasures; and unprotestingly letting them call me a miser, I told them to
get up.

"We should have left at five o'clock this morning," I
said to Marcolina, "and it will soon strike one."

"We have enjoyed ourselves," she replied, "and time
spent in enjoyment is never wasted. Are the horses there?
We shall take coffee, I hope?"

They dressed, and while waiting for coffee, I gave
Irene twelve double louis and then four more to get her
cloak out of pawn. Her father and mother came in on

their way from dining to wish us good morning. Irene
did not lose a minute; she proudly gave him the twelve
coins and she told him to love her a little better in future.
He laughed, then he wept, and he left. He came back
half an hour later to tell Irene that he had found an
opportunity to go to Antibes for very little money, but
that they must leave at once, for the driver wanted to
spend the night at Saint-Andiol.[24]

"I am ready."

"No, my angel," I said, "you shall dine with your
dear friend at five o'clock, and the driver will wait. Have
him wait, Signor Rinaldi; my niece will pay him for the
day—won't you, Marcolina?"

"Of course; I shall be very glad to dine here. I foresee
that we shall not leave until tomorrow."

She was right. We dined at five o'clock, we went to bed
at eight, and we indulged in the same sport as the night
before; but at five o'clock in the morning we were all of
us ready. I saw Irene, in her fine cloak, part from Marcolina with tears, and the other do the same. Old Rinaldi
prophesied prodigious good fortune for me in England,
and Irene wept because she was not to me what Marcolina was. We shall meet Irene again ten years hence.

A half hour later we left, and we traveled fifteen stages
without once stopping. We spent the night in Valence,
where we ate poorly; but Marcolina remained very
happy. She did nothing all day but talk to me about
Irene; she said sincerely that if it had been in her power
she would have taken her from her father and brought
her with her. She said she believed she was my daughter,
though her face was not like mine, because of the great
fondness she felt for her.

"How can you expect me to believe she is my daughter,
when I never had anything to do with her mother?"

"She told me the same; she told me that you loved
her for only three days, and that you bought her maidenhead for two hundred zecchini."

"That is true; but I was in love with someone else

then; otherwise I would have bought her from her father for a thousand zecchini."

"You are right. I think, my dear friend, that if I stayed with you, I should never be jealous of your mistresses, provided you let me sleep with them too. I think that is evidence of my good character. Tell me if my reasoning is sound."

"You are good, but you could be just as good without the furious temperament which rules you."

"It is not temperament, for I am not tempted to do it except with the person I love; if it's a woman, I don't care, I enjoy myself just the same."

"Who gave you this inclination?"

"Nature. I began at the age of seven. In ten years I have certainly had more than three or four hundred girl sweethearts."

"And when did you begin doing it with men?"

"When I was eleven years old Father Molin, my confessor, monk of SS. Giovanni e Paolo,[25] wanted to make the acquaintance of the girl with whom I was sleeping at that time; it was during the Carnival. He treated us to a fatherly admonition in the confession box and gave us to hope that he would take us both to the theater if we would resolve to give up our trifling for only a week; we promised; and at the end of the week we went to him and assured him that we had abstained from it. The next day he came, masked, to the house of my sweetheart's aunt, who knew him, and who let us go, thinking there could be no harm in it, for, aside from his being a monk and our confessor, we were too young; my sweetheart was only twelve. After the play he took us to an inn for supper, and after supper he talked to us about our wrongdoing and wanted to see how we were built. He told us that the sin was a great one between girls, whereas between a girl and a man it was of little account, and he asked us if we knew how a man was built; we knew, but we told him we did not. He then said that, if we would promise to keep it a secret, he could satisfy our curiosity; and we promised. Thereupon our confessor showed us his treasure, and in an hour he made us women; and he did it so well that we became the suppliants. Three years later I fell in love with a goldsmith, then your brother made me laugh by falling in love with me and saying that his conscience would not let him ask me for my favors unless he married me. He said it could be done by going to Geneva, and he astonished me by asking me to make the journey with him. Like a fool I decided to do it, and you know the rest. A proof that I never loved him is that I was never curious to know how he was built. He told me at Padua, where I gave him a beating, that I was excommunicated. I had a good laugh.''

We left Valence at five o'clock in the morning, and we reached Lyons at nightfall, going to stay at the ''Parc.'' [26] I at once went to Madame d'Urfé's house on the Place Bellecour;[27] as always, she told me she had been sure I would arrive that day. She wanted to know if she had performed her ceremonies properly, and Paralis, of course, declared that all had been in order, which greatly flattered her; after embracing young D'Aranda, who was with her, I promised to be at her house at ten o'clock the next morning.

We spent it working together to obtain from the oracle all the necessary instructions for her lying-in, for her will, and for finding a way to make sure that, when she was reborn as a man, she would not be reduced to poverty. The oracle decided that she should die in Paris, that she should leave everything to her son, and that her offspring would not be illegitimate, for Paralis promised that as soon as I arrived in London I would send her a gentleman who would marry her. The last oracle was that she must prepare to leave for Paris in three days, together with young D'Aranda, whom I was to restore to his mother's arms in London. His real identity was no longer a secret, for the little rascal had told all. But I had taken care of that in the same way that I had offset

the blabbings of La Corticelli and Passano. I could not
wait to give the little ingrate back to his mother, who
kept writing me saucy letters. I had it in mind to end
her custody of my daughter, who must be ten years old
and who, according to what her mother wrote me, had
become a prodigy of beauty, grace, and talent.

After settling all this I went to the "Parc" to dine
with Marcolina. It was very late, and, since I could not
take her to the theater that day, I went to Signor Bono's
to find out if he had sent my brother to Paris. He said
that he had left the day before, after introducing him
to a certain Passano, my great enemy, whom I should
fear.

"I saw the man," he said, "pale, wasted, unable to
stand; he told me he was going somewhere to die, and
that there was no doubt of it, because you had had him
poisoned; but he is sure, so he says, that he will make
you pay dearly for your crime, and that he will see himself avenged before he dies here in Lyons, where he was
certain that you would arrive. In half an hour, his lips
foaming with rage, he told me the most execrable things
about you. He wants everyone to know that you are the
greatest scoundrel on earth, that you are ruining Madame
d'Urfé by blasphemous lies, that you are a sorcerer, a
counterfeiter, a thief, a spy, a coin clipper, a traitor, a
cardsharper, a slanderer, an issuer of false bills of exchange, a forger of handwriting, and in short the worst
of men, and that he intends to make you known to the
world not by a satire but by a formal accusation in court,
to which he will appeal for just reparation for the wrongs
you have done to his person, his honor, and in fact his
life, for you have killed him by a slow poison. He says
that he is in a position to prove everything he alleges.
My esteem and friendship for you oblige me to inform
you of all that the man said to me, so that you can try
to combat it. This is not a thing to treat lightly, for you
know the power of calumny."

"Where is the traitor?"

"I have no idea."

"How can I find out?"

"If he is purposely hiding so that you cannot discover where he is living, it will be very difficult for you to do so. Nothing is easier than to remain hidden in Lyons, especially when one has money; and Passano has it."

"What can he do against me if he intends to get me into trouble?"

"He can institute criminal proceedings which will break your heart, which will degrade you even if you are the most innocent of men."

"I think I must forestall him."

"That is what you must do, since you do not know where he is; but you cannot avoid publicity."

"You will have no objection, I hope, to testifying in court to all that the slanderous traitor has said to you."

"None whatever."

"Give me the name of a good advocate."

"Here it is; but consider well, for the thing will cause talk."

"Not knowing where the scoundrel has hidden himself, I can take no other course."

If I had known where he was staying, Madame d'Urfé, who was related to Monsieur de Rochebaron,[28] the Commandant of Lyons, would have had him expelled from the city for me.

Smelling a rat, I went to the "Parc," where I drew up a formal complaint. I asked the police court for protection against a traitor who was lying hidden in Lyons and who was threatening my life and my honor; but the next morning Signor Bono, who came to see me very early, advised me against it,

"For," he said, "the police will at once make a search to discover where he is staying, and as soon as your enemy gets wind of it he will attack you in criminal court, after which he will no longer lie hidden. It will be he who will

demand protection against violence on your part. It seems
to me that if you have no important business in Lyons you
might hasten your departure.''

''That is a course which insults me to the soul. I would
die rather than hasten my departure by one hour on the
scoundrel's account. Would that I knew where he has
slunk away ! I would give a hundred louis to find it out.''

''I am delighted that I do not know it, for if I knew
I would tell you, and God knows what you would do. If
you will not hasten your departure, accuse him before
he accuses you, and whenever you see fit I will even
make a written declaration of all that he said to me.''

I went to the advocate whose name Bono had given
me, in order to be guided by his advice. Before telling
him my business I said that it was Signor Bono who had
praised his probity and skill to me. After hearing me
out, the advocate replied that he could be neither my
advocate nor my counsel, for he was already representing my opponent in both capacities.

''But,'' he said, ''do not regret that you have told me
what you intend to do, for everything shall proceed as
if you had not said a word about it to me. Signor Passano's complaint or accusation will not be drawn up until
day after tomorrow, I will not even tell him that he
should act sooner because you might anticipate him, for
it is a circumstance which I have learned only surrep-
titiously and by inadvertence. Do not take it to heart,
Monsieur. You will find other advocates in Lyons as
honest as I am or more so.''

''Would you suggest one to me ?''

''I cannot, but Signor Bono himself can do so.''

''Could you tell me where your client is staying ?''

''His chief concern is to remain hidden, and he is
right. You must understand that I cannot tell you.''

''You are right.''

I put a louis on his table, and he hurried after me to
return it. For once, an honest advocate ! I immediately
thought of setting a spy to follow him; for I wanted

nothing more than to throttle the monster with my own
hands; but where to find a spy? I hurry to see Bono,
who gives me the name of another advocate and advises
me to make haste, for in a criminal case the first to petition always has the advantage. I ask Bono to put me
on the track of a reliable spy who, by following the advocate, will certainly be able to tell me where the scoundrel
is staying; but Bono declines to help me in this way. He
even proves to me that, by having the advocate spied on,
I should be acting dishonorably; and I knew it; but
where is the man whom anger, whether justified or unjustified, does not drive to violence?

I go to see the second advocate, a venerable-looking old
man, whose prudence commands even more respect than
his appearance. After hearing the whole of my business,
he said that he would serve me and would present my
complaint that very day. I told him he must hurry, for
I had learned from the slanderer's own advocate that
the accusation would be presented on the next day but
one.

"That must not be the reason for our hastening, Monsieur, for you cannot abuse the confidence which my
colleague made to you. We must hasten because the nature of the case demands it. *Prior in tempore potior in
jure* ("The earlier in time, the stronger in law"). Prudence demands that the enemy be attacked. Be so kind,
if you please, as to call here at three o'clock this afternoon."

I left him six louis, and he said he would render me
an account of them.

In the afternoon I went to read the complaint, which
I found correct in every particular, and after that I went
to Madame d'Urfé's, where I stayed for four hours constructing pyramids to delight her soul; despite my ill-
humor I could not but laugh at the account she gave me
of her pregnancy, at her certainty of it because of the
symptoms she felt, and at her regret that her having to
die would prevent her from laughing at what the physi-

cians of Paris would say about her bearing a child, which
would be pronounced most extraordinary at her age.

At the "Parc" I found Marcolina very sad.

"You told me we would go to the theater, and I waited
for you. You shouldn't have kept me waiting."

"You are right. Forgive me, dear heart. Urgent business delayed me at Madame d'Urfé's. Be gay."

I needed gaiety, for having to deal with Passano had
upset me. Anger had as much power over me as love. I
slept very badly.

The next morning I went to see my advocate, who told
me that my complaint had already been registered in the
Criminal Magistrate's[29] court.

"We have nothing more to do at present," he said,
"for, not knowing where he is, we cannot serve a sum-
mons on him."

"Cannot I demand that the police ferret him out?"

"You can, but I do not advise you to do so. Let us
wait for him to come to court. The accuser, finding himself accused, will have to think of defending himself and
providing the crimes with which he charges you. If he
does not appear, we will have him sentenced *in absentia*
to all the penalties which are inflicted on slanderers.
Even his counsel will abandon him if he does not appear
as you do."

With my mind somewhat set at rest by the advocate,
I spent the whole day with Madame d'Urfé, who was to
leave the next day; I promised that I would come to her
house in Paris as soon as I had dealt with some matters
which concerned the Order. Her great rule of conduct
was to respect my secrets and never to interfere with
me. Marcolina, who had been bored by being left alone
all day long, breathed again when I told her that I would
now be wholly hers.

The next morning Signor Bono came to my lodging to
ask me to go with him to Passano's advocate, who wanted
to speak to me. The advocate told us that his client was
a madman who really believed that he had been poisoned

and, thus reduced to despair, he was ready for anything.

"He maintains," he told me, "that even if you should have anticipated him, he will have you sentenced to death, for he is ready to go to jail, and he maintains that he will come out of it the victor, since he has witnesses to all his accusations. He shows twenty-five louis d'or which you gave him in Marseilles and all of which are short-weight, and he has two documents from Genoa certifying that you clipped a large number of gold pieces, which a noble Grimaldi had a goldsmith melt so that they should not be found in your possession on the occasion of a search which the government was about to make of your lodging to convict you of your crime. He even has a letter from your brother the Abate testifying against you. He is a madman very sick with the pox, who, if he possibly can, wants to see you die before he does. I take the liberty of advising you to give him money to rid yourself of him. He has told me that he has a family, and that if Signor Bono would give him a thousand louis he would sacrifice all his justified accusations to his needs. He has ordered me to discuss it with Signor Bono. What is your answer?"

"That I will not give him a copper. I will not let him off. He is an infamous slanderer, and I will not stomach what he says about the Genoese coins which Signor Grimaldi took to the goldsmith's. The fact is true, but the wretch aggravates it by slander. I hope to learn today where he is lodging. The foul beast! Why does he hide?"

"I have put off presenting his complaint in order to see if I could prevent the scandal which will follow from it. I shall now go to present it."

"I beg you to do so. In any case, I am much obliged to you."

We left; and Bono was sorry that the thing was bound to make a noise. I went to my advocate's to report the scoundrel's proposal to him. My advocate praised me for not having consented to pay anything to stop the accuser's mouth. He even said that, having Bono as witness,

I could force the advocate not to put off presenting the
complaint, which he must have already drawn up; and
I at once instructed him to take the necessary steps. He
at once sent a clerk to obtain an order from the Criminal
Magistrate directing the advocate to present, within three
days, a criminal complaint against me, which must be in
his hands, on the part of a certain Ascanio Pogomas, alias
Giacomo Passano. I signed.

I was displeased by the three days. He replied that no
other procedure was possible; but that *jacta erat alea*
("the die was cast")[30] and that I must prepare to undergo all the unpleasantness which the case would cause
me even if I came out of it the victor on every point.

Madame d'Urfé having left, I went to the "Parc,"
where, after dining well and employing every means to
raise my spirits, I went out with Marcolina. I took her
to see the fashions at the celebrated milliners' shops; I
bought her everything she could wish for, then I took
her to the theater, where she could not but be pleased
to find the eyes of the entire audience turned to her.
Madame Pernon,[31] sitting beside the box in which we
were, made me introduce her; she embraced her very
fondly after the performance, and from the expression
on both their faces I foresaw that the most intimate
friendship would spring up between them; and it would
have done so if Marcolina had been able to speak French
or Madame Pernon Italian. They were both baffled when
they became aware of their respective ignorance. A
woman who cannot understand her lover and cannot
make herself understood becomes cold. At home Marcolina laughed and confessed to me that when they parted
Madame Pernon had given her a Florentine kiss. It was
the petticoat password.[32] Our supper was enlivened by
the high spirits in which my little presents had put her,
and after it we celebrated our amorous rituals. The next
morning I took Marcolina to see the manufactories,[33]
and I gave her a pretty dress. In the afternoon we were
invited to sup at Madame Pernon's, where Marcolina

could not shine, for no one spoke Italian. Signor Bono, who spoke Italian and who was Madame Pernon's admirer, was not present; we were told that he was ill.

But the next morning early I saw him in my room, looking cheerful but exhausted; he asked me to go out with him in morning dress, he had good news to tell me. He took me to a coffeehouse, and he showed me a letter from the scoundrel in which he told him that he was ready to drop everything, on the advice of his counsel, who had found an accusation against him which he did not want to oppose. "That being the case," the wretch wrote to him, "arrange for Monsieur de Seingalt to give me a hundred louis, and I will leave at once. All will be over."

"I should be a great fool," I said, "to give him more money to escape the law. Let him go if he will and if he can; but I will give him nothing. Tomorrow I will obtain an order for his arrest. I want to see him branded with infamy by the hangman. The slanders he has put upon me are too vile; my honor demands that I force him to prove everything."

Bono replied only that he thought I could consider a clean dropping of the proceedings adequate satisfaction, and that I should prefer it to a formal condemnation which would harm me even in the moment of victory, and he added that the hundred louis were nothing in comparison with what the legal proceedings would cost me. I left him, asking him to excuse me if I could not share his opinion. I went to inform my advocate of the proposal I had rejected, and I told him to take the necessary legal steps to have a warrant for his arrest issued.

The same day I had Madame Pernon to supper, and, Signor Bono being present, Marcolina shone and we were in very high spirits. On the next day but one Bono wrote me that Passano had left Lyons, never to return, and that before leaving he had drawn up a retraction with which I would be thoroughly satisfied when I saw it.

I thought his flight natural; but I also thought it most

unlikely that he would have made a retraction, since he had left of his own free will. So I called on Bono, who astonished me by showing me a retraction as full as possible. He asked me if I was satisfied with it, and I replied that not only was I satisfied, I forgave him too.

"I only think it strange," I said, "that he did not insist on the hundred louis."

"He had the hundred louis,[34] but from me; I was glad to pay them in order not to see publicity given to a piece of baseness which, aside from harming us all, would have given me great pain, for you would have done nothing if I had told you nothing. I would not have said anything to you if you had not told me you are satisfied with the retraction and that you have forgiven him. As for the hundred louis it costs me, I am delighted to have had the opportunity to give you a small token of my friendship. Let us say no more about it, I beg you."

I embraced him affectionately.

I went to dine with Marcolina, and I told her we should leave for Paris in three days.

CHAPTER V

*I meet the Venetian Ambassadors and Marco-
lina's uncle in Lyons. I part from that charming girl and I leave for Paris. Amorous journey with Adèle.*

THE NEXT day I was sitting in the theater behind
Madame Pernon, when I was surprised to see Signor
Querini and the Procurator Morosini enter the box op-
posite to the one in which I was; with them I see Signor
Memmo[1] and Count Stratico,[2] professor in the University
of Padua; they were all people whom I knew and who
were passing through Lyons on their way home from
London.

"Farewell, dear Marcolina," I said to myself. I sit
there impassively, saying nothing to her; she was listening to a remark Signor Bono was making to her; in any
case she knew none of the Venetians. I perceive that
Signor Memmo had noticed me and that he was pointing
me out to the Procurator, who knew me very well; I felt
that I could not avoid going to pay them my respects in
their box.

The Ambassador Morosini received me enthusiastically,
Signor Querini politely enough for a bigot, and Signor
Memmo with emotion, for he remembered that eight years

earlier his mother had been a party to the plot which had
sent me to prison[3] under the Leads. I congratulate the
gentlemen on their brilliant embassy to George III and
on their return to our country, and as a matter of course
I commend myself to their good offices to obtain the
pardon which would permit me to return to it someday.
Seeing me in fine array, Signor Morosini says that I am
luckier than he, for I had to stay away, while nothing
but duty made him go back. He asks me where I have
come from and where I am going; and I say that I have
come from Rome, where the Holy Father had made me
a Cavaliere, and that I am going to London.

"Come to see me," he says, "and I will give you a
little commission."

"Will Your Excellency stay here for some time?"

"Three or four days."

I return to the box in which I was sitting; Marcolina
asks me who the gentlemen I have gone to see are, I
reply, looking at her coldly, that they are the Venetian
Ambassadors on their way back from London. She
changes color, she says nothing more. A moment later
she asks me which of them is Signor Querini, and I point
him out to her.

The play ended, we go down. The Ambassadors were
at the door, waiting for their carriage. Mine happened
to be ahead of theirs in the line.

The Procurator Morosini says to me:

"You have a charming girl there."

Marcolina goes and kisses Signor Querini's hand;
greatly surprised, he thanks her, and asks:

"*Why me?*"

"Because," she answers him in Venetian, "I know
that Your Excellency is Signor Querini."

"What are you doing with Casanova?"

"He is my uncle."

My carriage being there, I excuse myself, I hand
Marcolina into it, and I say:

"To the 'Parc.' "

Marcolina was in despair, for, it having been decided that she should go back to Venice, I must not neglect this opportunity. She supped in tears, while I was far from gay. I said that we had three or four days before us in which to consider how best we might talk with Master Matteo, her uncle; I praised her for having kissed Signor Querini's hand, and I begged her to be gay while we were deciding upon a course, for grief would tear my soul.

We were still at table when I heard in the anteroom the voice of Signor Memmo, a young Venetian, good-natured and highly intelligent. I at once warned Marcolina not to say a word about our affairs and to be gay but dignified. We rise, he makes us resume our places at the table, he drinks with us, and he gives us a full account of the gay supper they had had with the old bigot Signor Querini, whose hand a pretty Venetian girl had kissed. The adventure had delighted them all, and even Signor Querini had been pleased by it.

"May I ask, Signorina, how you come to know Signor Querini?"

"Oh, that is a secret."

"A secret! Ah! How we shall laugh tomorrow! I have come," he said to me, "to invite you in the name of the Ambassador to dine with us tomorrow, together with your charming niece."

"Would you like to go, Marcolina?"

"Con grandissimo piacer. Parlaremo venizian[4] ['With the greatest pleasure. We will talk Venetian']. I simply cannot learn to speak French."

"No more can Signor Querini."

After a sufficiency of most amusing talk, he left, very well pleased, to tell the Ambassadors that they would have me at dinner with Marcolina. She at once came to embrace me, congratulating herself on the fortunate meeting. I told her that she must dress in her best the next day, be charming to everyone at table, and above all pretend not to see her uncle Matteo, who would be sure to wait on his master.

"Leave it to me," I said, "to give the recognition scene all the beauty which can be drawn from it, for I shall bring it about that the person who will take you back to Venice will be Signor Querini himself. Your uncle will look after you at his order."

Delighted with the arrangement, Marcolina promised me all that I asked.

The next morning at nine o'clock I left her at her toilet table and went to see what commission the Procurator Morosini wanted to entrust to me. He gives me a small sealed box which I am to deliver in London to Lady Harrington,[5] together with a letter and a card on which were only these few words: "The Procurator Morosini regrets that he was unable to take a last leave of Mademoiselle Charpillon."[6]

"Where shall I find her?"

"I have no idea. If you find her give her the card; if not, it doesn't matter. You have a dazzling girl with you."

"And I am dazzled by her."

"But how is it that she knows Querini?"

"She saw him by chance in Venice; but she has never spoken to him."

"I can well believe it. We had a good laugh, for Querini attaches great importance to the meeting. But how do you happen to have this Venetian girl with you, who, according to Memmo, doesn't speak French?"

"It is a long story."

"She is not your niece."

"She is more, for she is the mistress of my soul."

"Have her learn French, for in London——"

"I shall not take her to London. She wants to go back to Venice."

"I am sorry for you, if you love her. Will she dine with us today?"

"She is enchanted to have that honor."

Back at the "Parc," I warned her that if, at table or afterward, there was any talk of her going back to Venice, she must say that no one on earth could persuade her to go back unless Signor Querini would take her with him and assume the custody of her property. She was to leave it to me to get her out of any difficulty which might arise from this declaration.

I put on an ash-gray short-napped velvet coat embroidered with silver and gold spangles, a shirt with cuffs of point lace worth fifty louis, and my watches, snuffboxes, rings, and the cross of my order, all of which were set with diamonds and which together were worth at least twenty thousand écus, and with Marcolina, who was as bright as a star, I went at half past one o'clock to the Ambassadors' lodging.

The company consisted entirely of Venetians, and we joined it to bring joy. They were at once delighted to see Marcolina, who made her entrance with all the ease of a French princess. She dropped two solemn curtsies to the two Ambassadors, and a smiling one to the rest of the company. As soon as she found herself seated between two grave Senators, the first thing she said was that she was delighted to see herself the only woman in such a choice company and to see not a single Frenchman. After this sample of her wit, the company knew what tone to take. Amusing remarks were made to her, to which she replied with propriety, she always answered and never questioned, and she gave a charming account of the differences she had observed between French and Venetian manners, which were in many points diametrically opposed.

At table Signor Querini asked her how she had recognized him, and she replied that she had seen him at mass more than fifty times. Signor Morosini, pretending not to know that she wanted to return to Venice, told her that she should study French, which was the language of all countries, for otherwise she would be bored in

London, where Italian was very little spoken. She replied that she hoped I would be so kind as to put her in the company only of people to whom she could talk, as I had done until then, for she foresaw that if she had to learn French by studying it, she would never speak it.

At the end of dinner Signor Querini praised the brilliance of the four stones in her ring and asked where it had been set; she replied that, since it was a present a lady had given her, she did not know. When we left the table the Ambassadors asked me to tell them the story of my escape from the Leads, and I obliged them. My narrative continued for two hours and was never once interrupted. The whole company having noticed that Marcolina shed tears at the place where I was in danger of perishing, she was taken to task at the end of the story. Someone said that, for a niece, she had shown too much concern over my danger, and she replied that, since she had never loved anyone but me, she had no way of knowing what difference there was between one love and another. Thereupon Signor Querini told her that, in human nature, there were five different kinds of love: love of one's neighbor, love of friends, love of family, conjugal love, and love of God; and she listened to his dissertation with the greatest attention. When he came to explaining the love of God the Senator took wing, and then I was more surprised than anyone else in the company to see Marcolina touched to the point of shedding tears, which she quickly dried as if to hide them from the wealthy old man, whom wine had made more of a theologian than usual. Pretending rapture, Marcolina kisses his hand, and the vain enthusiast takes her head and kisses her on the brow, saying:

"*Poveretta* ['Poor little thing']! You are an angel."

We all bit our lips to keep from laughing, and the minx pretended to have lost all her gaiety. I did not really know Marcolina until that day, for she confessed to me at the "Parc" that she had purposely feigned emotion in order to win the old man's heart. When we left them they invited us to dinner on the next day too.

We went to the "Parc," for we both wanted to talk to each other more than to go to the comic opera. I did not have the patience to wait for her to undress before covering her with kisses.

"My dear Marcolina, you wait until the end of our acquaintance to reveal your treasures to me, so that I shall weep all the rest of my life for the mistake I am making in letting you go back to Venice. Today you fettered the hearts of all those who dined with you."

"Then, my friend, I will always do the same; you will make me happy if you will keep me. Did you see my uncle?"

"I think I saw him. Was it not he who always changed your plate?"

"Yes. I recognized him by his ring. Tell me if he looked at me."

"Constantly, and always in astonishment; but I, too, took care not to look at him, for he did nothing but turn his eyes from you to me and from me to you."

"How I wish I knew what he is thinking! You will see something new tomorrow. I am sure he has told Signor Querini that I am his niece and hence cannot be yours. If Signor Querini says so to me tomorrow, I must admit it, must I not?"

"Certainly, but with the greatest dignity, without any truckling, and not giving him any idea that you need him in order to return to Venice. Remember that after all he is not your father and that he has no rights over your freedom. You must also admit that I am not your uncle and that we are bound together only by the fondest friendship. After all, you are shrewd, and I rely on you. Remember to say everything I have told you to say. It must be Querini who takes you to Venice, or nobody. And he must take you as if you were his daughter."

Early the next morning I receive a note from Signor

Querini asking me to call on him as he has something important to say to me. I tell the lackey that I will go at once.

"That's the beginning," says Marcolina. "I am very glad that the thing is taking this turn, for when you come back you can instruct me to act in accordance with what you will have said."

I go to the inn on the Place Bellecour; Signor Querini has me shown in, I see him with the Procurator Morosini; they ask me to be seated, and Signor Querini, after saying that his colleague's presence was no disadvantage, says that he has a confidence to make to me but that, in order to do so, he must ask me to make one to him.

"I have trust enough in Your Excellency's discretion not to keep anything secret from Your Excellency."

"I am obliged to you. That being so, I ask you to tell me sincerely if you know the girl who is with you, for your niece she certainly is not. At least none of us believes that she is."

"She is not my niece; and since I do not know her parents I cannot say that I know her in the sense in which Your Excellency is using the word; but I believe that I know her inmost soul and that I have reason to congratulate myself if I have conceived an affection for her which will end only with my life."

"What you say pleases me. How long has she been with you?"

"About two months."

"Excellent. How did she come into your custody?"

"Permit me not to answer that question, for it concerns her."

"Very well, let us pass over it. Being in love with her, it is impossible that you should not have had the curiosity to ask her who her parents are, who is responsible for her."

"She has told me that she has a father and mother, who are poor but honest people; and, truthfully, I never cared to ask her their names. She has told me only her

Christian name, Marcolina, which perhaps is not hers; but that does not matter to me."

"It is her name."

"It is? Then Your Excellency knows her?"

"Yes. I did not think so yesterday; but I think so now. Two months, and her name is Marcolina; my valet is not mad."

"Your valet?"

"Yes. She is his niece. He learned in London that she ran away from home about the middle of Lent. Marcolina's mother, who is his sister, wrote to tell him so. The prosperous condition in which he saw her yesterday kept him from speaking to her; he even thought he was mistaken; he feared to commit a fault and to be disrespectful to me, seeing that I had her at our table as your niece. But what did she say to you yesterday when you left here, for it is quite possible that she does not know that her uncle Matteo is in my service; but she cannot fail to recognize him. She must have seen him."

"She did not see him, for, being what she is, she would have told me she had done so."

"It is true that he was always behind her. But now let us come to the point of the matter. Tell me, if you are free to tell me, if Marcolina is your wife or if you intend to marry her one day."

"I love her as much as it is possible to love, but I cannot make her my wife; it is a great grief to me, the cause of which only she and I know."

"I respect your reasons, and I do not even ask to know them; but, that being the case, would you object to my interesting myself in her to the point of asking you to let her return to Venice with her uncle?"

"I consider Marcolina fortunate if she has been able to inspire some interest in you, and I am even persuaded that a return to Venice and to the bosom of her family under Your Excellency's protection might efface the stain which she put upon herself by running away. As for letting her go, I certainly cannot oppose it, for I am

not her master. As her lover, I would defend her with
all my power if anyone tried to tear her from my arms
by force; but if she wanted to leave me, I could only
weep and, resigning myself, hope that time would heal
my wound as it has healed so many others.''

"You are very reasonable. Then would you have any
objection to my undertaking this good work? You understand that I should not venture to take any steps without
your consent.''

"I respect the decrees of destiny when they seem to
me to come from a pure source; I adore God, and I yield.
If Your Excellency can persuade Marcolina to leave me,
I will consent to it; but I advise you to go about it
gently; for Marcolina is intelligent, she loves me, and
she knows that she is free; in addition, she counts on me,
and she is not mistaken. Speak to her today, and privately, for my presence might embarrass you both. Wait
until after dinner to speak, for the discussion may take
a long time.''

"My dear Casanova, you are an honest man, and I
swear to you I am delighted to have made your acquaintance.''

"I take my leave, and I assure you that I will say
nothing to Marcolina beforehand.''

Back at the "Parc," I gave Marcolina a full account
of this dialogue, informing her at the same time that I
had promised not to say a word to her about it, but I
told her that she must execute a master stroke to show
Signor Querini that I had not lied when I had told him
she had not seen her uncle.

"You must," I said, "as soon as you see him, show
surprise, speak his name, run to him, and embrace him.
Will you do that? It will make a dramatic tableau, which
at the same time will show everyone what a good heart
you have.''

"Be sure that I will do it very well.''

When she was ready we went to the Ambassadors'
lodging, where, with all their train, we found them wait-

ing only for us. Marcolina, even gayer and more brilliant than on the day before, first paid her respects to Signor Querini and then was gracious to all the others. A quarter of an hour before dinner was served the valet Matteo entered to bring his master, who was seated beside Marcolina, his eyeglasses on a tray. Marcolina, fixing her eyes on the man's face, breaks off an interesting discourse to which she was treating the company, and suddenly says to him:

"My uncle!"

"Yes, my dear niece."

At that she rises, she kisses him, he embraces her fondly, we all show the astonishment which the meeting could not but arouse in us.

"I knew," she said to him, "that you had left Venice to go with your master I don't know where; but I did not know that your master was His Excellency. I am very glad to see you again; you shall take news of me to Venice. You see that I am happy. Where were you yesterday?"

"Here."

"And you did not see me?"

"I did indeed; but your other uncle there——"

"Well, my dear cousin," I said to him, smiling, "let us recognize each other and embrace; Marcolina, I congratulate you."

"What a moment!" said Signor Querini.

The valet left; we resumed our places, but each of us with a different countenance from that of the day before. Marcolina showed the mixture of contentment and regret which remembering its native country arouses in a noble soul. Signor Querini showed admiration and the confidence he felt that he would succeed in his undertaking because he was dealing with a girl who displayed such moderation; in the silence which had fallen Signor Morosini made appropriate comments on the turn which I had given to the little drama. All the others, serious, attentive, curious to know the end of the story, sat with-

out moving or speaking, listening to the extremely interesting monologue which Marcolina was delivering, turning her eyes first to one, then to another. Anyone clever
enough to recognize it would have seen that I was only
dissembling. It was Signor Memmo who courteously tried
to rouse me to the point of saying a few explanatory
words; but in my answers he found only evidence of
contentment.

We sat down at table, and at the second course it was
Signor Morosini who, having learned from me that
Marcolina might consider returning to Venice, ventured
to say to her that, since her heart was free, she could
hope to find in Venice, her native country, a husband
worthy of her.

"As to his being worthy of me, I must be the judge."

"One can also have recourse to discreet persons who
are concerned for the happiness of both parties to a
marriage."

"Pray excuse me. Never. The man whom I marry must
please me; and not after, but before the marriage."

"Who," asked Signor Querini, "taught you that
maxim?"

"My uncle there," she replied, pointing to me; "during the two months I have lived with him he has taught
me, and I believe him, all that we need to know to guide
us in this world."

"I congratulate both the pupil and the master; but,
my dear Marcolina, our guide through this world, which
is morality, is not learned so quickly."

"What His Excellency has just told you," I said to
her, "is true. On the subject of marriage, one must take
the advice of the wise, for all marriages contracted from
inclination prove to be unhappy."

"But please tell me," the Procurator said to her,
"what qualities the man you would choose for a husband
must have."

"I cannot tell you them in detail; but I should suppose
he had them all if he pleased me."

"And if he was a scoundrel?"

"He would not please me. That is why I will never marry a man without knowing him well before I give myself to him."

"And if you are mistaken?"

"I shall weep in secret."

"And poverty?"

"She need have no fear of it, Monsignore," I said, "for Marcolina has fifty écus a month without fail for the rest of her life."

"That casts a different light on the subject," said Signor Querini. "If that is true, my dear child, you enjoy a great privilege, which is being able to live in Venice without needing anyone."

"Yet it seems to me that, if I am to live in Venice, I shall always need the protection of such a nobleman as yourself."

"Well then, my dear child, come to Venice, and I give you my word of honor that I will do whatever lies in my power for you. But how, if I may ask, are you certain of these fifty écus a month? You laugh?"

"I laugh because I am a scatterbrain who does not inquire into her own affairs. If you want to know that, my friend will tell you all about it."

"You were not joking?" the old man asked me.

"Certainly not. Marcolina has a cash capital which will give her a life annuity even higher than the sum I mentioned, but she was very right to say that in Venice she needs Your Excellency's protection, for her capital must be carefully invested. The capital is in my hands, and if Marcolina so wishes, it will be in hers no later than two hours from now."

"That is enough. So, my dear child, you must come to Venice no later than day after tomorrow. There is Matteo, who is beside himself, and who is ready to receive you."

"I love my uncle Matteo and I esteem him; but it is not to him that Your Excellency must entrust me if I decide to come."

"To whom then?"

"To yourself. You have called me by the sweet name of your 'dear child' three times, so take me to Venice as if I were your child, or I will not come; that I tell you. We will leave day after tomorrow for London."

At this declaration, which ravished my soul, the whole company at table looked at one another in silence. It was for Signor Querini to reply, and he had said too much to withdraw. There was silence for half a quarter of an hour. Everyone ate and drank gravely. Matteo changed his niece's plate, trembling. Dessert was being served when Marcolina broke the silence, saying that Divine Providence must be humbly adored, and only after its effects were manifested, for before its consequences it was impossible to judge of good and evil in this world.

"In what connection, my dear child, are you making this reflection," Signor Querini asked her, "and in what connection are you now kissing my hand?"

"I am kissing your hand because for the fourth time you have called me 'my dear child.'"

At that a general laugh restored the table to life; but Signor Querini, not forgetting her reflection on adoring Divine Providence after its consequences, called upon her to explain it.

"I said it," she replied, "because of a thought which came to me in the course of examining myself. I am in good health, I have learned to live, I am seventeen years old, and I have become moderately rich in two months by honest and harmless means. I am happy, for I feel that I am happy. I owe all this to the greatest sin that a decent girl can commit. Must I not humbly bow in thousandfold adoration of Divine Providence?"

"Yes; but, even so, you must repent of the sin you committed."

"It is that which I find difficult, for in order to repent I have to think of it, and when I think of it I cannot repent. On that I must consult some great theologian."

"There is no need. I myself will tell you in the course

Bathtub

After the Play

of our journey how it is done. In repenting, it is not necessary to think of the pleasure the crime you committed gave you.''

Signor Querini, finding himself in the role of an apostle, was falling piously in love with his beautiful proselyte. On leaving the table he disappeared for a quarter of an hour, then, returning, said to Marcolina that if he had a daughter to take back to Venice he would certainly entrust her to no one but Signora Veneranda, his own housekeeper and the woman in whom he had complete confidence.

''I have just spoken to her, and it is all arranged, you will be with her day and night, you will sleep with her, if you choose, and you will eat with us until we reach Venice, where I will myself put you in your mother's hands in the presence of your uncle.''

''Let us go to see Signora Veneranda.''

''Gladly. *Casanova, come with us.*''

We go, and I see a woman of canonical appearance, with whom Marcolina would not fall in love in her fashion, but who seemed sensible and trustworthy. Signor Querini tells her in our presence all that he had just told Marcolina, and the duenna[7] assures him that she will take the best care of her. Marcolina embraces her, she looks pleased, and we return to the company, who are delighted to learn that she is to make the journey.

''I must,'' said Signor Querini, ''see about putting my major-domo in another carriage, for the calash holds only two.''

''Your Excellency need not trouble about that,'' I said, ''for Marcolina has a carriage of her own in which Signora Veneranda will be very comfortable and in which she can put her trunks.''

''You mean,'' she asked me, ''to give me your carriage too?''

I could not answer. I pretended to blow my nose, and I went to the window to dry my tears. Turning round two minutes later, I did not see Marcolina. The Procura-

tor Morosini, touched as I had been, told me that she had
gone to speak to Signora Veneranda. Since everyone
looked sad, and I knew that my own emotion had caused
it, I talked of England, where I was going in the expectation of making my fortune by a project[8] I had in mind
which needed only the approval of the Minister, Lord
Egremont.[9] Signor Morosini said that he would give me
a letter for the Minister and another for Signor Zuccato,[10]
who was the Venetian Resident. Signor Querini thereupon asked him if he would not be compromising himself
with the State Inquisitors by recommending me, and the
Procurator coldly replied that the Inquisitorial Tribunal
had not informed him of the crime I had committed. Signor Querini, a man of extremely narrow mind, shook his
head and did not answer. Marcolina returned, and everyone saw that she had gone away to cry. She came to me
and asked me if I would take her to the "Parc," for
she had to pack her trunk and put a quantity of gew-
gaws she had, and of which she was fond, in boxes. So
we left, having promised to dine there the next day too.
The travelers were to set off on the next day but one.

Back in our room and feeling that nothing could console me, I undressed, ordering Clairmont to have the
carriage gone over and put in condition for a long journey. I flung myself on the bed in a dressing gown, refusing to listen to all the very reasonable things Marcolina was saying to me.

"Consider," she said, "that it is not I who am leaving you but you who are sending me away."

Toward six o'clock Signor Morosini and Signor Querini
entered the courtyard and, before coming upstairs,
stopped to look at my carriage, which the cartwright
was examining. They spoke to Clairmont, then came to
see us. I asked them to excuse me for being in undress.
Signor Querini made me laugh by remarking on the large
number of boxes which Marcolina had to find a way of
getting into the carriage, and he exclaimed admiringly
when he learned that it was the one he had just seen, for

it was very fine. Signor Morosini told Marcolina that if she would sell it to him as soon as she was in Venice he would give her *mille ducati*[11] for it, which was exactly a thousand French écus; it was worth twice as much.

"That," Signor Querini said to her, "will increase your capital."

I then told him that the next day I would bring him a bill of exchange at sight on Venice for five thousand Venetian ducati, which, together with another three thousand which Marcolina could get by selling the valuable jewels she had, and the thousand for the carriage, would give her a capital of nine thousand écus, from which she could obtain a very respectable income. But Marcolina was crying while she laughed and laughing while she cried. My only consolation was knowing that I had made her fortune, as I had done for several others who had lived with me. It seemed to me that I must let her go in order to make room for the others whom heaven had destined for me. We supped gloomily and, despite love, the night we spent was not gay.

The next morning I went to Bono's to obtain a sight draft on Venice, payable to the order of Signor Querini.

It was Marcolina herself who handed it to him at dinnertime, and Signor Querini gave her a receipt in due form. Signor Morosini gave me the letters for England which he had promised me. It was settled that the departure should take place at eleven o'clock the next morning; but we went to their lodging at eight to give Signora Veneranda time to put everything she needed in the carriage. But what a sad night I spent with the girl! She could not understand, and she said it over and over again, how I could be my own executioner; and she was right, for I did not understand it either. In the course of my life I have done countless things I did not want to do, and each time I was driven to it by some occult power which I took it into my head not to resist. I put on boots and spurs, telling Clairmont that I should be back the next day, and when Marcolina was ready I got into the carriage with her and went to the Ambassadors' lodging. After taking her to Signora Veneranda's room I went to talk with Signor Memmo, who treated me to most eloquent commentaries on the heroism I was showing.

After all breakfasting together gloomily enough, for Marcolina's grief, keeping her constantly on the verge of tears, was respected by the entire company, we left, I on the folding seat opposite to the heart which I was tearing from my bosom and to Signora Veneranda, who kept us amused for a long time by her exaggerated comments on the beauty and comfort of the carriage and on her good fortune in riding in it as if she were an Ambassadress, as her master had said to her, for their carriages were nothing in comparison with ours.

We took coffee at Bourgoin[12] while the horses were changed, and the Ambassadors decreed that we should go no farther than Le Pont de Beauvoisin,[13] for Signor Querini did not like to travel at night. We arrived there at nine o'clock and, after supping badly, everyone went to bed in order to be ready to leave the next morning at daybreak. Marcolina went to bed with Signora Veneranda, who not only turned her back to us when she saw me at the bedside, with my head bent over Marcolina's, whose tears mingled with mine, but who, despite her piety, had moved so far over on the bed that there would have been room for me too if I had dared to occupy it. In every woman piety always yields to pity. I spent the night sleeping very badly on the uncomfortable chair which was beside Marcolina's bed. At daybreak I told them to dress, and Signora Veneranda, who had slept as soundly as possible, was greatly surprised when she saw me there and learned that I had stayed there all night.

The horses were harnessed, and a saddle horse which I had ordered to take me to La Tour-du-Pin[14] was ready too. After hastily drinking a cup of coffee we went downstairs, and I took leave of Their Excellencies and the whole company. The last was Marcolina, whom I embraced for the last time and whom I did not see again until eleven years later, when I found her happy. After tearing myself from the door of her carriage, I mounted and stayed there watching her until the moment when the postilion whipped up. Then I left at full gallop, hoping to kill the horse and to perish with it; but death never comes to the wretch who longs for it. I covered eighteen leagues in six hours, and as soon as I saw the ill-fated bed which thirty hours earlier had given me the refuge of love I threw myself on it, not hoping to find in dream what I could no longer possess in reality. However, I slept deeply until eight o'clock and, after ravenously devouring all that Clairmont brought me, I went back to sleep, and in the morning I found myself able to endure life.

Needing distraction, I told Clairmont to inform the innkeeper that I would eat at the public table, and at the same time I told him to find out where there was a decent carriage for sale, for I wanted to leave as soon as possible.

The public table at the Hôtel du Parc was a Land of Cockaigne. The price was thirty sous[15] a head; I could not understand how the innkeeper could make anything on it. The company was good enough; what I liked was its variety. Foreigners came and went, I spoke to no one, and no sooner did someone take my fancy than I did not see him again at the next meal. The third day after Marcolina's departure I was ready to leave. I had bought a carriage of the kind known as a *solitaire,* with three glass windows,[16] two wheels, shafts, springs *à l'Amadis,* and lined with crimson velvet, almost new. I got it for forty louis. I sent two strong trunks to Paris by the diligence, keeping only a portmanteau packed with what I needed, and I was going to leave the next morning in dressing gown and nightcap, determined not to leave my *solitaire* until after fifty-eight stages on the finest road in all Europe. Imagining myself traveling alone, I thought I would be doing homage to my dear Marcolina, whom I could not forget. At table an officer told me that I had obtained the carriage only because the day's notices had made him lose a quarter of an hour. He had already offered thirty-eight louis, and he was on his way to take the owner forty; but my servant had already paid them. On his asking me when I was leaving, I said that I should leave at six o'clock the next morning, expecting to be in Paris in forty-eight hours.

A quarter of an hour later, when I am alone in my room putting my fine jewels and my diamonds away in my jewel case, Clairmont comes in to tell me that the merchant who had been at the table in company with a girl was in the anteroom with her, asking to speak to me. I tell him to send him in, and I shut my jewel case.

"Monsieur, I have come to ask you for a favor which, if you grant it, can cost you only a little inconvenience but which will be of great service to myself and my daughter."

"What can I do for you or for Mademoiselle, since I am leaving tomorrow at six o'clock?"

"I know that, for you said so at table; but it will not keep us from being ready at the hour you have set. I should like to ask you to take my daughter in your chaise; I am, of course, ready to pay for another horse which the post will furnish you, and I will ride on horseback."

"Apparently you have not seen my chaise."

"I beg your pardon, I have seen it. It is a *solitaire*; but the seat is deep, and if you will sit back a little she can very easily find room on the same seat. It is an inconvenience, certainly, but if you could know what a benefit the favor would be to me you would be glad to go to the trouble. All the places in the diligence are taken until next week, and if I am not in Paris in six days I shall lose my living. If I were rich I would hire a chaise and travel post, but that would cost me four hundred francs. The only course which remains to me is to leave by the diligence tomorrow, with my daughter and myself tied to seats on the roof, and you can understand what distress that would cause her. Look, she is crying.''

I look at her attentively, and I see that she is such that, traveling alone with her, I cannot possibly remain within certain bounds. In addition my soul was beset by fears. The torment I had suffered at parting with Marcolina had turned me against not women but love; I had resolved to avoid anything which might lead me to enter into an attachment which could have consequences; my quiet, my peace of mind demanded that I at last adopt this course. ''This girl,'' I said to myself, ''may for my misfortune have so many charms of mind or character that I shall be in danger of falling in love with her if I grant the favor which they ask of me.''

After half a quarter of an hour which I spent in reflection, I answered him, without looking at the young lady, that his situation caused me the greatest distress, but that I did not know what I could do about it, for I foresaw too many difficulties.

''You may suppose, Monsieur, that I could not ride so many posts in succession without stopping; and I assure you that you are mistaken.''

''The horse you are riding may founder. You may be hurt, and if that happens I know myself; I shall have to stop despite you, and I am in a hurry. If you do not consider this reason sufficient, I cannot help it; for in my view it is so.''

''Alas, Monsieur, let us take that risk.''

''There is another risk which I do not wish to tell you. In short, I cannot.''

''Alas, Monsieur,'' said the young lady, in a voice which would melt stone, ''save me from traveling on the roof of the diligence; the very thought makes me shudder; though tied, I shall be afraid, deathly afraid, aside from a sort of indignity which I see in it, perhaps stupidly; but it is not in my power to think otherwise. I implore you to grant me this favor; I will sit at your feet, and I will inconvenience you no more than a dog would do.''

''Enough! You do not know me, Mademoiselle. I am neither cruel nor rude, especially with your sex, and my resistance will make you think the contrary; but that shall not be: I still have too high an opinion of myself to permit you to believe it. The hire of a post chaise is six louis. Here they are. I beg you to accept them, Monsieur. Tomorrow morning I will put off my departure for an hour or two, if necessary, to assume the responsibility for the chaise you will hire, if you are not known, and here are four more louis for another horse, for they will put three to your chaise. Anything over that, you would have spent for two places in the diligence.''

''Monsieur, I reverence your virtue and your generosity lays my soul at your feet; but I do not accept the present you wish to make me. I am not worthy of it. Let us go, Adèle.[17] Excuse us, Monsieur, for having made you waste half an hour.''

''Wait a moment, my dear Father.''

Adèle asked him to wait because her tears were choking her. The scene infuriated me, for the weeping girl, at whom I then looked with more interest, met my eyes with hers and so troubled my soul that I was no longer my own master.

''Calm yourself, my little dear,'' I said to her, ''I yield, for otherwise I could not sleep; but I make one condition,'' I then said to her father. ''You will be willing to ride on the back of my carriage.''

''Gladly, Monsieur; I thought your servant would ride there.''

''No, he goes on horseback. So now everything is arranged. Get to bed, and be ready at six o'clock.''

''Monsieur, I will pay for a horse even so.''

''You will pay for nothing, for it would insult me, and I beg you not to insist, for, just as you told me that you are poor, I tell you that I am rich, so do not feel that you are degrading yourself.''

''Monsieur, I yield, but I will pay for the horse for my daughter.''

''Not even that; you make me laugh. Stop haggling, I beg you, and let us all go to bed. I will set you both down in Paris without its costing you a sou; and after that I will send you about your business. Nothing else is possible. There—Adèle is smiling, and that pleases me.''

''It is the joy my soul feels at being freed from the fear of the diligence roof.''

''I understand that perfectly, and I hope that you will not cry in my chaise, for I loathe gloom. Good-by.''

I went to bed, submitting to the decree of my destiny. I saw that I could not escape the charms of this new beauty; and I forearmed myself to resist any temptation to play the game longer than two days. Adèle was pretty, with blue, very prominent eyes, a complexion of lilies and roses, on the verge of adolescence, and with a bust which promised to develop during the next year. I went to bed thanking the good or evil Genius who was determined that I should not be bored during the short journey.

The next morning at five o'clock Adèle's father came into my room to ask if it made any difference to me if I took the road through the Bourbonnais[18] or through Burgundy.[19]

''Either way, it will make no difference to me, if you have business on one of the two roads.''

''I have, Monsieur. I could collect some money in Nevers.'' [20]

''Then we will go by way of the Bourbonnais.''

A half hour later Adèle, simply but neatly dressed, comes into my room with a look of contentment and wishes me good morning, saying that her father was taking the liberty of putting a small trunk which contained

their clothing behind my chaise; and, seeing me busy
tying up packages, she asks me if she can help me. I answer no, I tell her to be seated, I notice her air of exaggerated timidity and submission; it is not to my liking;
I gently tell her so, and encourage her to take coffee.

When I was about to go down, a man comes to tell me
that the lanterns are not properly fastened to their
springs, that I will certainly lose the candle holders if I
do not order him to mend them, which he will do in less
than an hour. I curse, I call Clairmont, intending to
scold him, but Clairmont says that the lantern maker
himself, inspecting the lanterns without telling him so,
must have loosened them on purpose to make money. It
was the exact truth, I knew the trick, I call him a scoundrel, he answers me too plainly, I kick him in the stomach,
pistol in hand. He goes off swearing, the innkeeper comes
up at the noise, everyone says I am in the right; but
despite that I have to lose an hour, for the moon was not
shining and I had to have the lanterns. Quick, another
lantern maker! He comes, he looks, he laughs, for the
other's trickery was plain to see; and he undertakes to
put in new springs, but it will take him two hours.

"Very well. Be quick about it," I say.

I talk with the innkeeper, asking him if I can have the
other lantern maker sent to prison, even if it will cost me
two louis.

"Two louis? I shall see that it is done at once."

I was fuming with rage, paying no attention to Adèle,
into whom I struck fear. Ten minutes later the Chief of
Police arrives, hears the facts, takes the names of the witnesses, draws up a complaint, and asks me how much my
time is worth an hour. I set an English rate on it,[21] five
louis. The Chief of Police, pocketing the two louis which
I slipped into his hand, writes down the lantern maker's
fine as twenty louis, and leaves, telling me that he will
have him imprisoned at once. I breathe again, I pace up
and down the room, I grow calm, I apologize to Adèle,
who has no idea in what way she has offended me, her

father comes in to tell me that the lantern maker is in prison, that I am right, and that he has testified in writing as an eyewitness with the utmost pleasure.

"Then you saw the scoundrel do it?"

"I beg your pardon. I wasn't there; but it makes no difference, for everyone who saw it, saw it."

At that I threw myself into a chair, weak with laughter. Moreau (such was the name of Adèle's father) then entertained me with his story. He was a widower, he had only Adèle, and he was going to Louviers[22] to work in a manufactory. That was the whole of it; but he had the gift of dragging out a narrative.

An hour later pathos has its turn. Two women in tears, one of them with an infant at her breast, followed by four small children, and all falling to their knees before me, presented a picture the source of which I knew at once. It was the malefactor's mother and wife, come to ask me to show him mercy. The wife spoke first, and irritated me because she said her husband was an honest man and all the witnesses were scoundrels. But the mother calmed me, saying it was possible that he had been guilty of the cheat, but that I ought to forgive it in a man who had to feed all the mouths I saw there and who would stay in prison all his life, for even if he sold everything down to his bed he would never have twenty louis.

"Very well, my good woman, I absolve him so far as I am concerned, and here is my waiver, which I give you in writing. Arrange the rest with the Chief of Police, for I will see neither you nor anyone else again."

Handing her the note, I gave her six francs for the children, and the family left well satisfied. The police clerk came a little later to have me sign my name in their big book, and I had to pay out more money. When the lanterns were mended, I had to pay twelve more francs, and the thing was all over. I got into my *solitaire*, Adèle sat down between my thighs, Moreau got up behind,

Clairmont mounted his horse, and we set off. It was nine
o'clock.

Adèle was awkwardly seated at first; I encouraged her
to sit more easily and she did so; she caused me discomfort only because I saw that she was uncomfortable; she
could rest her back nowhere but on me, and I felt that
I should not urge her to take that liberty, which might
lead to serious consequences. I made her talk of innocent
subjects as far as Bresse,[23] where, while the horses were
being changed, we got out to attend to natural necessities.
Getting back into the carriage, into which Adèle had to
follow me, I held out my hand to help her make the long
stride needed to enter it from the front, for this sort of
carriage has no step. Adèle having to raise her skirt in
front, and directly before my eyes, and then to lift up
her leg a great way, I saw black breeches instead of her
white thighs. The sight displeased me; I said to her father, who was helping her from behind:

"Monsieur Moreau, Adèle has on black breeches."

She blushed, and her father said with a laugh that she
was fortunate to have shown only her breeches.

His answer pleased me; but the thing itself displeased
me, for in France the idea of wearing breeches is an impertinence in a girl, unless she has to ride horseback;
and even then, a girl who is not of the nobility rides without breeches, only taking care to arrange her skirts properly. In Adèle's breeches I thought I saw an insulting
intention, an attempt at defense; a reasonable supposition, but which I thought she should not entertain; the
thought made me angry, and I did not speak to her all
the way to Saint-Symphorien,[24] except now and again to
tell her gently to make herself more comfortable, whereas
all the way to Bresse I had said things to make her laugh.
The young Adèle must have noticed this coolness on my
part, which continued for four hours. At Saint-Symphorien I told Clairmont to ride on ahead, to order me a
good supper for three, and to go to bed and sleep until
dawn the next day. I saw that he was tired; Roanne[25]

was a place which should offer good accommodations. In any case, I was in no hurry.

Halfway through the stage, which is a double one,[26] Adèle said that she must really be inconveniencing me, since I was not as gay as I had been during the first stage; I assured her that it was not so, saying that I was keeping so still only to leave her perfectly undisturbed.

"I am grateful to you, but by doing me the honor to talk to me you will certainly not disturb me. You are not telling me the real reason for your silence."

"If you know what it is, tell it to me yourself."

"Your manner changed as soon as you saw that I had on breeches."

"It is true that their blackness offended me."

"I am sorry; but admit that I could not foresee two things: first, that you would find out I had on breeches, and second that you did not like black."

"You are right; but, chance having shown me the thing, you must also forgive the effect it had on me. The color black gives me gloomy ideas, whereas white would have given me a cheerful one. Do you always wear breeches?"

"Never."

"Then you see that, by wearing them on this occasion, you have done something a little unbecoming."

"Unbecoming?"

"Yes. What would you have said if I had put on skirts this morning? I should have acted unbecomingly. It is the same thing. You laugh?"

"Excuse me, but let me laugh, for I have never heard a more amusing idea. But it is not the same thing, for everyone would have seen you in skirts, while no one could guess that I have on breeches."

I assented to Adèle's analysis, charmed to find that she was intelligent enough to expose my sophism; but I continued not to speak to her.

We supped well enough in Roanne. Adèle's father saw that, but for his daughter, he would neither have supped with me nor made the journey from Lyons to Paris for nothing; he was delighted when I told him that, far from inconveniencing me, she kept me good company. I told him the discussion we had had over breeches and skirts, and, laughing heartily, he said that his daughter was in the wrong, and after supper I edified him by saying that I would sleep in the other room, which had only one bed, leaving him to sleep in the one in which we had supped, where there were two.

When I had taken coffee the next morning Clairmont told me that he would ride ahead and would stop at a place where I could sleep, for, having lost one night, I might as well lose another. This discourse showed me that Clairmont liked to get his night's sleep, and his health was precious to me. I told him to stop at Saint-Pierre-le-Moutier,[27] and to have a good supper prepared for me. In the carriage Adèle thanked me.

"Then you don't like traveling at night?"

"I shouldn't care, if I weren't afraid I should go to sleep and fall on you."

"You would make me happy, my dear Adèle. A girl as pretty as you is a precious burden."

She did not answer. My declaration was made. To be sure that she would be as docile as a lamb, I had to see her come to it of herself. I did not speak to her again until noon, two minutes before arriving at the post station in Varennes.[28]

"My dear Adèle, I am hungry. If I were sure you would eat a fowl with me with an appetite equal to mine, I would dine here."

"Try it, and I will endeavor to do my duty."

So we dined well at Varennes and drank even better. We left tipsy. Moreau confessed that at a gallop he would fall into a ditch, both he and his horse. Adèle, who drank wine two or three times a year, laughed at not being able to stand straight. I comforted her, saying that the fumes of champagne did not last long.

A quarter of an hour later poor Adèle, after resisting

sleep as long as she could, had at last to yield and fell on my chest. She slept soundly for two hours and a half, and I respected her. The only thing I did, and which delighted me, was to make sure that she was no longer wearing breeches, either black or any other color. Her intention was clear; but I wanted to see it fully revealed; to that end I had to hide my discovery from her, at the same time helping her to carry out her plan, whatever it might be. When she woke she thought she had come back from the other world: not only seeing herself in my arms, but finding me in hers, she could not summon words enough to excuse herself. Sheer humanity obliged me to give her a fond kiss to convince her that she had given me pleasure, and that soothed her uneasiness. But in trying to assume a decent position and to arrange her skirts, she uncovered the beginning of her thighs. She quickly covered them again; but my burst of laughter brought one from her, and she had the presence of mind to say that she hoped this time no black had given me gloomy ideas. Certain necessities obliged us to get out at Moulins,[29] where we were instantly assailed by eighteen or twenty women, vendors of knives, scissors, and other knickknacks of all sorts in steel. I made the father and daughter presents of whatever took their fancy; but we laughed heartily at the women, who actually came to blows in their eagerness to sell their wares. We reached Saint-Pierre as night was falling; but in the four hours it took us to travel the nine leagues,[30] Adèle became as familiar with me as if I had been her oldest acquaintance. I held her now on my right thigh, now on my left, so that she could look at me while she spoke; she told me stories, she laughed at those I told her, and if I never gave her a few kisses she thought it was only because I was afraid of displeasing her.

At Saint-Pierre we found an excellent supper, thanks to the efforts of Clairmont, who had arrived there two hours before us and who had already gone to bed. Two large beds which were in the room in which we supped

had been made; I at once told Moreau that he need have
no hesitation over going to bed with Adèle. He replied
that in all the five years since he had become a widower
he had slept with her without ever forgetting that he was
her father; but that on this one night she would sleep
alone, for if he wanted to get his money he would have
to be at Nevers[31] at daybreak and so he must leave at once
and wait for us there.

"If you had told me this beforehand, we should all
have gone to spend the night at Nevers."

"It does not matter. I shall ride the three and a half
stages at a gallop. I entrust my daughter to you. She will
be less near to you than in your chaise."

"Have no doubt of it, Monsieur Moreau. We are both
on our good behavior."

"Do not drink any more, dear Father, for you have to
ride."

After he left I told Adèle to go to bed.

"And if you do not believe I am your good friend, go
to bed fully dressed. I will not be offended, my pretty
little one."

"It would be very wrong of me to give you such a
proof that I distrust you."

She went somewhere, then she came back, closed her
door, and, when she was down to her last petticoat, came
to embrace me. I was writing.

"My beautiful Adèle, my charming sleeper, I am dying
to see you asleep in my arms once more."

"Very well then, come. I will sleep."

"All the time?"

"All the time."

"We shall see. Let us go."

I throw down my pen, and in a minute I take off my
dressing gown, and there is Adèle in my arms, smiling,
full of fire, yielding to me, only begging me a few moments later to spare her. I do whatever she asks; but a
half hour afterward Venus seizes on her with such force
that she grants me everything, only begging me to

preserve her honor, and after the bloodstained sacrifice
I keep my word to her; then we sleep. There is a knock
at the door; it is Clairmont, telling me that five o'clock
has struck. I order coffee. I have not time to give Adèle
a morning greeting; but I promise her that I will make
up for it on the road.

She quickly gets out of bed; she sees the sheets, she
sighs, then she laughs; nevertheless, she rumples up my
bed, then, a little pensive, she takes her coffee, and we
are in the *solitaire*, both amorous, happy, renewing our
ecstasies, and in despair that the journey is not longer.
At Nevers we find the worthy Moreau disconsolate because his debtor cannot give him the two hundred francs
until noon; he does not dare ask me to wait; but I hearten
him by saying that we will dine there if he can have a
good dinner prepared for us. He promises to do so, and
we shut ourselves up in a room to avoid a crowd of
women who wanted to force their wares on us.

He received his money, we dined very well, we left,
and, finding ourselves in Cosne[32] at nightfall, I say that
we will sleep there. Clairmont was waiting for us at
Briare,[33] but that is nothing to me. After a bad supper
Moreau, who had not slept the night before, gives Adèle
the certainty that she can come to bed with me again. The
second night is more delicious than the first. The next
day at Briare we eat the supper which Clairmont had
had prepared for us, and we go to spend the night at
Fontainebleau,[34] where Moreau goes off to sleep in the
small room next to the one in which we had supped and
in which there were two beds. We need only one. It was
there that I had the beautiful Adèle in my arms for the
last time. In the morning I gave her my word that I
would go to see her in Louviers when I came back from
England, but I was unable to keep my promise.

From Fontainebleau to Paris, I took only four hours,
which, occupied by love taking leave, I found passed very
quickly. I stopped on the Pont Saint-Michel[35] at the
shop of a watchmaker, who sold me a watch without my

getting out of my carriage. I gave it to Adèle. I left them at a hostelry on the corner of the Rue aux Ours,[36] and I told Moreau to come for his trunk to the Hôtel de Montmorency, on the Rue de Montmorency,[37] where I intended to put up. I had reasons for not going to stay at Madame d'Urfé's. I dressed quickly, and I went to dine with her.

CHAPTER VI

I drive my brother the Abate from Paris. Ma-
dame du Rumain recovers her voice through
my cabala. A bad joke. La Corticelli. I take
young D'Aranda to London. My arrival in
Calais.

MADAME D'URFÉ received me with a joyful
cry, at once telling young D'Aranda to hand me the
sealed note she had given him that morning. I unseal it,
and I read, after that day's date: "*My Genius told me*
at daybreak this morning that Galtinarde is leaving Fon-
tainebleau and that he will come to dine with me today."

This is a fact. Countless things of the same sort have
happened to me in my lifetime, such as would turn any
other man's head. They amazed me, but, God be praised,
they did not make me lose my power of reasoning. People
cite instances in which they have guessed something before it happened; but they never mention countless other
instances in which they have foretold something which
never came to pass. Six months ago I was fool enough to
bet that a bitch would give birth to five puppies, all
female, the next day, and I won. Everyone was amazed,
except myself.

Of course I expressed my admiration for the prophetic

powers of Madame d'Urfé's Genius, and I rejoiced at the
good health she was enjoying during her pregnancy. Certain that I would arrive, she had sent word to all the
people who were to dine with her that she was ill. We
dined with young D'Aranda, and spent the rest of the
day alone together deciding how best to set about bringing the little fellow to the point of going to London
willingly. The oracle's answers were all obscure, since
I did not myself know what course to take. Madame
d'Urfé's reluctance to tell him to go was so strong that
I could not presume upon her obedience to that extent.
I put off the decision until another day, and I left, assuring her that I would go to dine with her every day until
I set out for London. I went to the Comédie Italienne,[1]
where I saw Madame du Rumain,[2] who was delighted to
see me back in Paris and who begged me to come to call
on her the next day, for she was in the greatest need of
my oracle. But my surprise was great when I saw the
ballet, and La Corticelli among the dancers. I was
tempted to speak to her, not from any feeling of love but
because I was curious to learn her adventures. On my
way out of the theater I saw Balletti,[3] who had retired
from the stage and was living on his pension; he told me
where she lived, the sort of life she was leading, and the
state of her finances. She was in debt, and could not pay
her debts.

"Hasn't she acquired a lover?"

"She had several; but she deceived them all, and she is
in poverty."

I go to sup at my brother's, who was living near the
Porte Saint-Denis,[4] curious to learn how he had received
the Abate.[5] He is delighted to see me again, as is his wife,
and he tells me that I have arrived in time to persuade
our brother the Abate to leave the house of his own free
will, for otherwise he had made up his mind to put him
out.

"Where is he?"

"You will see him in a moment, for we are about to have supper, and eating is his chief employment."

"What has he done to you?"

"There he is, he's coming downstairs. I will tell you all in his presence."

Astonished to see me and to see that I do not look at him, he greets me politely and then asks me what I have against him.

"I consider you a monster. I have the letter which you wrote to Passano. According to your testimony, I am a cheat, a spy, a coin clipper, and a poisoner."

He does not answer and sits down at the table.

My brother speaks to me in his presence as follows:

"When the gentleman came to me, I received him gladly; my wife was delighted to make his acquaintance; I gave him the room above this one, and I told him that my house would be his. After that, to curry favor with us, he said that you are the greatest scoundrel alive on the face of the earth, and to prove it, he told us that, having carried off a girl from Venice to marry her in Geneva, he went to see you in Genoa, he and his lady having not a shirt to their backs and being reduced to begging. It is true, he told us, that you immediately rescued him from poverty by clothing him and thereafter letting him want for nothing; but you traitorously obtained possession of her by putting her in the company of two other girls you had, you took her to Marseilles with you, sleeping with her and with the other girl in his presence, and you finally drove him out of Marseilles, giving him, to be sure, a few louis, but discourteously and simply as charity. He ended his story by telling us that, the crime he had committed in Venice preventing him from returning there, he needed us until he could find a way to support himself by his talents and his priestly profession. As for his talents, he told us that he could teach Italian; but we laughed because he does not speak French and because I was sure he had a very poor knowledge of Italian. So we thought it best to confine our efforts to his being a priest, and the next day my wife spoke to Monsieur de Saincy,[6] the bursar in charge of vacant ecclesiastical benefices, to obtain an introduction for him to the Archbishop of Paris, who, upon receiving a favorable report on his conduct, could employ him in his service, after which he could hope to be given a good benefice. To that end he would have to attend our parish church, and I spoke to the parish priest of Saint-Sauveur,[7] who promised to show him every consideration and at once to appoint an hour for him to say mass, for which he would give him the usual fee of twelve sous. When we informed the Signor Abate here of what we had done for him in four days, he became angry. He told us that he was not a man to put himself to the trouble of saying mass for twelve sous, and that he certainly would not pay court to the Archbishop in the hope of entering his service, for he had no intention of serving. We concealed our feelings. The fact is that in the three or four weeks he has been here he has turned the house topsy-turvy. A manservant of whom I was fond has left because of him, my wife's chambermaid, who took care of her linen, and whom he upbraided for no reason, left yesterday, and our cook, who does not want him in her kitchen, threatens to give notice if we have not authority enough to forbid him to enter it."

"What does he want in the kitchen?"

"To find out the menu for the day; to taste stews; to jabber away at the good woman, telling her what he thought was not good the day before. In short, our brother is an intolerable individual. I am delighted that you have arrived, for I hope that between us we will find a way to send him, tomorrow and no later, to mind his own f...ing business."[8]

"Nothing easier," I replied. "If he wants to stay in Paris, he is free to do so; but you must send his rags to a furnished room tomorrow, and at the same time have him served with a police order forbidding him, as a disturber of your peace, ever to set foot in your house again. If he wants to go away, let him say so, and I undertake to pay for his journey this evening before I leave here.''

''Nothing could be more humane. Well, what do you say?''

''I say,'' replies the Abate, ''that it is the way he drove me out of Marseilles. It is exactly his style. Violence. Despotism.''

''Thank God, you monster, that instead of giving you a beating I give you money. You tried to get me hanged in Lyons.''

''Where is Marcolina?''

''You make me laugh. I have no accounts to render to you. Hurry up. Choose.''

''I will go to Rome.''

''Very well. For a man traveling alone the journey costs only twenty louis; but I will give you twenty-five.''

''Where are they?''

''Just a moment. Paper, pen, and ink!''

''What are you going to write?''

''Bills of exchange on Lyons, Turin, Genoa, Florence, and Rome, and to take you to Lyons tomorrow you will have a paid place in the diligence. You will have five louis in Lyons, another five in Turin, five in Florence, and five in Rome, and here in Paris not a sou from me. Good-by, my sister. I am staying at the Hôtel de Montmorency. Good-by, Cecco.'' [9]

''I will send our excellent brother's trunk to you tomorrow.''

''A very good idea. If I am not there, have it delivered to my manservant. Leave the rest to me.''

''I will send it at eight o'clock.''

The next morning the trunk came, and the Abate too. I had him given a room, and I told the proprietor that I would be responsible for the Abate's board and lodging for three days and no longer. He wanted to talk to me, and I put him off until the next day. I instructed my servant not to let him enter my room, and I went to Madame du Rumain's.

"Everyone is asleep," said the Swiss; "but who are you? for I have an order."

"I am So-and-so."

"Come into my lodge and amuse yourself with my niece. I will be back."

He comes back and he takes me to the chambermaid's room; she gets up cursing.

"What is the matter?"

"You might have come at noon. Madame got home at three o'clock in the morning. It's not nine yet; but she'll be sorry, I'm going to wake her."

I go in, and she thanks me for having had her waked just as I am asking her to excuse me for it.

"Raton, bring us writing materials, and leave us. You are not to come until I call you. I am asleep for everyone on earth."

"I shall go and sleep too."

"Monsieur, how is it that the oracle has deceived us? Monsieur du Rumain is still alive,[10] he was to have died six months ago; it is true that he is not well; but we will ask about that later. The urgent thing now is something else. You know that music is my chief passion and that my voice was celebrated both for its strength and its range. I have lost it, my dear friend; it is three months since I have been able to sing. Monsieur Herrenschwandt[11] has given me every remedy in the pharmacopoeia, and nothing can bring it back to me; I am in despair over it, I am only twenty-nine[12] years old, I am unhappy, it was the only pleasure which made life dear to me. Ask the oracle, I beg you, for a remedy to give me back my voice as soon as possible. How happy I should be if I could sing tomorrow, for instance; I shall have a great number of people here, and everyone would be astonished. If the oracle is willing I am sure it can be done, for there is nothing wrong with my chest. Enough!

that is my question. It is a long one, but so much the better. The answer will be long too, and I like long answers.''

There were times when I liked long questions too, for they gave me time while I was constructing the pyramid to think of what I might answer. What the case required was a remedy for a trifling disorder; but I did not know one, and the honor of the oracle demanded that I give one. I was sure that a healthy regimen would restore her vocal chords to their original state; but it is not the part of an oracle to repeat what any incompetent doctor knows enough to say. So reflecting, I decide to take the course of ordering her to perform a ceremony of worship to the Sun at an hour which would oblige her to follow a regimen which would cure her, without my having to prescribe it for her.

So the oracle told her that she would recover her voice in twenty-one days, if she would begin on the day of the new moon and perform a ceremony to the rising Sun every morning in a room which had at least one window facing the east. To perform this ceremony, a second oracle instructed her, she must have slept for seven hours, and, before going to bed, must bathe in honor of the Moon, keeping her legs in warm water up to the knee. As for the liturgies appropriate to these ceremonies, I told her which psalms she was to read while bathing in order to secure beneficent influences from the Moon, and which ones she was to read before the closed window at the instant when the Sun rose. The oracle's consideration in ordering that the window should be closed greatly pleased the lady, for there might be a wind which would make her catch cold. Lost in admiration of the divinity of this magical remedy, she promised she would punctually carry out all of the oracle's instructions if I would be so good as to bring her the drugs needed for the fumigations.

I promised all that she asked, and to show her my zeal I told her that on the first day I would perform the fumi-

gations myself so that she could learn the method, for the
nature of the two ceremonies demanded that no woman
be present at them. The manner in which she received my
offers showed that she was deeply touched. We had to
begin the next day, which was that of the new moon,
and I went to her house at nine o'clock; for in order to
sleep seven hours before worshiping the rising Sun she
had to go to bed before ten. I was sure that what would
make her recover her voice was the new regimen, and
I was right in my expectation. It was at London that
she gave me the news in a letter which came from her
heart. This lady, whose daughter married Monsieur de
Polignac,[13] loved pleasure, and, frequenting great supper
parties, she could not always enjoy perfect health. She
had lost the beauty of her voice. Having recovered it by
a magical operation, she laughed when she found people
who told her that magic was a chimerical science.

At Madame d'Urfé's I found a letter from Teresa,[14]
young D'Aranda's mother. She wrote me that she would
be obliged to take the step of coming to fetch her son
herself if I did not bring him to her, and that she expected a definite reply at once. I told the boy that his
mother would be at Abbeville in a week and that she
wanted to see him.

"She must be granted the pleasure," I said; "you
shall come with me."

"Gladly; but if you go to London with her, with whom
shall I return to Paris?"

"Alone," said Madame d'Urfé, "preceded by a postilion."

"On horseback. Oh, how I shall enjoy that!"

"But you shall ride only eight or ten stages a day, for
you need not risk your life riding at night."

"I will dress as a courier."

"Yes, I will have a fine jacket made for you, and
chamois breeches, and I will give you a splendid parchment[15] with the arms of France."

"I'll be taken for a courier for the Cabinet, and I will say I am coming from London."

I then pretended to object, saying that a horse might fall and break his neck. By persisting in my opposition I made sure that he would come, for Madame d'Urfé, having suggested the plan in the first place, naturally became the one to whom he must appeal for the favor. I refused to hear a word of it for three days before I granted it to him on condition that he would not travel on horseback but would come with me. Sure that he would return to Paris, he insisted on taking only two or three shirts with him; but sure, on my side, that once I had got him as far as Abbeville he would not escape me, I had his trunk with all his clothes sent to Calais,[16] where we should find it on our arrival. In the meanwhile Madame d'Urfé had a complete courier's outfit made for him and a pair of strong boots which he needed to protect his legs in case of a fall. So it was that this difficult undertaking was made easy by chance.

I spent that afternoon with the banker Tourton & Baur[17] arranging to have my money in London distributed among several bankers, to whom he sent me, as I requested, with strong letters of recommendation. I wanted to make numerous acquaintances.

As I left the Place des Victoires, I thought of La Corticelli,[18] and curiosity took me to call on her. She was living on the Rue de Grenelle Saint-Honoré[19] in a furnished apartment. She was astonished to see me. After a long silence, seeing that I said nothing, she wept, then she said:

"I should not be unhappy if I had never known you."

"You would be just as unhappy, but in some different way, for your misfortunes are the result of your bad conduct. But what are they?"

"Unable to bear being in Turin after you dishonored me——"

"If you go on in that style I shall leave; for I have not

come here to defend myself, but rather to hear the voice of your repentance.''

''And I repent; but it is none the less true——''

''Good-by.''

''Very well, I will tell my story and not say what I think. Sit down. I fled from Turin with Droghi;[20] he was in the corps de ballet, I don't know if you knew him; he used to come to La Pacienza's;[21] he loved me; I let him give me a child. When you arrived in Turin I was pregnant. At my wit's end to decide on a course, for Droghi had no money and did not want to confess our situation to anyone, I gave my lover one of my watches and a ring to sell, and we left. We came here, but we stayed only a week. On the promenade of the Palais-Royal we found Santini,[22] who was going to London with D'Auberval [23] to dance in the opera at the Haymarket;[24] he needed a couple; he gave us a good contract without knowing what we could do, and we left. At London we were not liked, and if we had sued we should have lost, for it was plain to see that I was pregnant, and as for Santini everyone knew that he was a tailor who didn't know how to dance a step. I gave him all my jewels to sell, and so we came back. In the two months we were in London we got twenty guineas[25] into debt, though we lived like beggars, and those barbarians would not even take up a collection for me.

''Santini had a relative in Versailles, a valet at the Court, and when he told him how hard put to it he was to provide for my lying-in at all comfortably, he offered him a lodging; he accepted, and I went to lie in at Versailles, giving birth prematurely to a dead infant after being on the verge of death myself. I came back here, reduced to possessing only one dress. The pantaloon Collalto[26] saw me, became my lover, took care of me, and one day, angry with Santini, who wanted to play the master, he slapped him and turned him out. He was right, for Santini should have shown him respect. Santini went I don't know where, and Collalto got me an engage-

ment at the Comédie Italienne[27] and gave me my freedom. In a short time I had five or six lovers keeping me
one after the other, all of whom left me for trumped-up
reasons, for after all I was not married to them. Collalto
himself left me, angry at finding himself ill with the
same disease which I had. He ought to have forgiven me
and arranged to have me cured; but men are all like
you, merciless. Again I sold everything I had, and I
signed a bill of exchange for four hundred francs which,
having fallen due, and I not being able to pay it, was
protested, and a seizure was executed on my furniture
because it was believed to be mine. The seizure lasted
only twenty-four hours because the landlord, informed of
the fact, was able to assert his rights; but he will have it
taken away in two or three days if I do not pay him his
month in advance, as I have always done. I haven't a
sou, and, to make matters worse, I have been dismissed
from the Comédie Italienne. In a week I will no longer
appear there. I cannot count on another lover, for everyone knows I am ill; I am in the hands of the street-
walkers who prowl on the Rue Saint-Honoré at night.
That is the true picture of the state in which you find
me.''

After this dreadful story she buried her face in a
dirty handkerchief to catch a flood of tears. I was as if
turned to stone, beside myself, and under the mortifying
necessity of recognizing that I was one of the causes of
the horrible abyss in which I saw the wretched girl sunk.
Pity commanded me to do something for her at once.

''What course have you thought of taking?''

''You mock me. I don't know what taking a course
means. To decide on a course one at least has to have
money. I shall be arrested tomorrow. I shall go to prison
and die there. God's will be done. Listen! someone is
coming here. Wait.''

She rises and goes out; I hear her talking; the person
leaves; she comes back, and she tells me that she has

given twenty-four sous to a streetwalker who had brought her a man.

"I told her," she said, "that I have company and that I am engaged for the whole night."

My horror increases; I tell her that I do not think I am capable of relieving her misfortunes either with my purse or with my advice.

"What would you do if you had money?"

"If I had enough of it, I would go and get cured."

"And after that?"

"If I had any left, I would go to Bologna, where I would earn my living by my profession, having perhaps grown wiser."

"But where would you go to be cured, since spies would have you arrested?"

"I have no idea. If Collalto had not abandoned me!"

"Ah, poor Corticelli! You are lost, and permit me to tell you that you are wrong to console yourself by attributing the cause of your misfortunes to others and not to yourself. I would never have abandoned you if you had not acted toward me like the worst of enemies. Dry your tears! I will say no more. I leave, and I promise I will come back tomorrow or the next day and tell you where you shall go to be cured without anyone being able to find you; I will pay whatever it may cost. After you are cured you shall have money enough to go to Bologna; and after that may God bless you! You will not see me again."

At that the poor girl could thank me only by sobbing and holding my hands clasped in hers, which were trembling from the excess of emotion which what I had said to her had aroused in her soul. I stayed there until the outburst was over. At the end of the scene I gave her four louis, and I left in anguish of heart.

Having undertaken to rescue the poor girl from the abyss into which she had fallen, I thought of going to an honest surgeon whom I knew, and who alone could tell me how I could set about putting La Corticelli in an inaccessible place until she was cured. He was my erst-while surgeon Faget,[28] who lived on the Rue de Seine.[29] I take a hackney carriage, I go there, I find him at table with his family; I ask him to finish his supper and then to go to his office with me to hear what I have to say. I tell him the whole story. She is to be cured in six weeks. No one is to know her; she will pay in advance. How much must she pay? She is poor. I am doing a work of charity.

Faget's only answer is to write a note, address it, and hand it to me unsealed, saying:

"The thing is done."

The note ordered the man to whom it was addressed, at the end of the Faubourg Saint-Antoine,[30] to take in the person who would give it to him, and who would pay him a hundred écus, and to dismiss her six weeks later safe and sound. He added that the patient had reasons for not being seen by anyone. Delighted to have finished the business so quickly and so successfully, I go home, I sup, and I go to bed, declining to listen to my brother. I send him word that he can talk to me at eight o'clock. I needed to rest.

At eight o'clock he comes into my room and, stupid as ever, tells me that he had wanted to acquaint me with his plan before I went to bed in order to give me all night to think it over.

"There was no need of that. Do you want to stay in Paris, or go to Rome?"

"Let me have the money for the journey, and I will stay in Paris, giving a written undertaking not to go to see my brother again, or you if you are here. That should suit you just as well."

"You are a fool, for only I can judge what does or does not suit me. Leave my presence at once. I have not time to listen to you. Either Paris without a sou, or twenty-five louis to take you to Rome, parceled out as I see fit."

I call Clairmont and have him turned out of the room.

On my way out I tell the proprietor again that the next
day is the last on which I will pay for the Abate. I was
in a hurry to have done with La Corticelli and her troubles. I went in a hackney carriage to the house in the
Faubourg Saint-Antoine of which Faget's note gave me
the address, in order to see the place where the wretched
girl was to do penance for six weeks. I find an elderly
man with his wife, both of whom seem honest people,
and after giving him Faget's letter to read I tell him
that the girl will come without losing any time, and that
I had come to see everything. At that he shows me a
small room with a bed, a bath, three or four chairs, a
table, a wardrobe, all very clean. He says that she will
eat alone, and that unless her illness is very complicated
he will have her cured at the end of six weeks. He shows
me the doors of seven or eight rooms like the one we are
in, four of which, he tells me, are occupied by sick girls,
all more or less under the same condition of secrecy and
whose names he does not know. I pay him a hundred
écus, he writes the receipt in Faget's name, and I tell
him he is to give the room in which we are to the person
who will come to him with the receipt and the same letter
from Faget. After that I go to the Palais-Royal,[31] where
I happen upon a Venetian named Boncousin,[32] who tells
me that he has come to open a rooming house in Paris,
hoping thereby to make his fortune.

"Relying on what?"

"On two girls whom you know."

"Who are they?"

"I will not tell you. Come to supper with me, and you
shall see them. Here is my address. But you shall pay for
the supper, for I am not rich."

"Very well, I will come the day after tomorrow, for
today and tomorrow I am engaged."

"Will you give me the money now, so that I shall be
sure of it?"

"Gladly; but I did not suppose you had grown so poor.
Here are six francs."

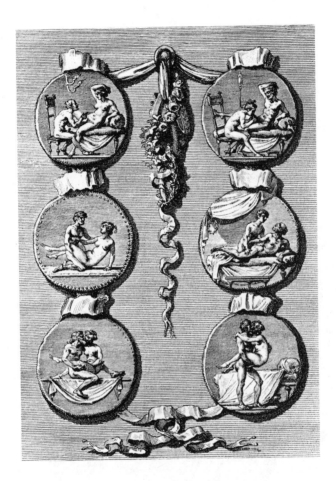

Under Love's Dominion

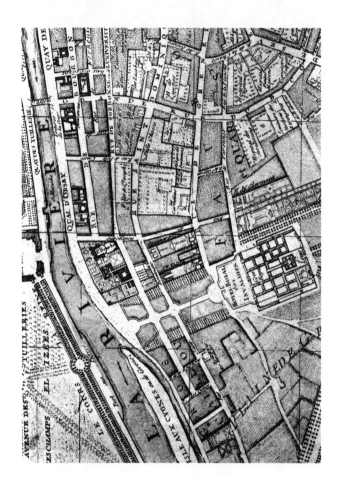

The Rue de Grenelle and Its Environs

"It is very little, if you want to sup well."

"I will pay the rest after the supper. Good-by."

I knew that the man was a scoundrel. He had an inn in Venice. I should not have gone if I had not been curious about the two girls I was supposed to know. I go to dine at Madame d'Urfé's, and immediately after dinner I go to La Corticelli's to comfort her. I find her in bed. She disgusts me by showing me her illness; I tell her what I have done for her and I give her the surgeon's receipt and the letter. I tell her she has only to take a hackney carriage and go there by herself, promising that I will go to see her once before I set off for London and will leave her another hundred écus, which should be enough to take her to Bologna as soon as she is cured. Full of gratitude, she tells me that she will go after dark the next day without saying anything to her maid, whom she will send somewhere so that she can take her shifts and her one remaining dress with her in a bag, and she asks me for two louis more to redeem some clothing which she had in pawn.

Delighted to have rescued La Corticelli from her sad plight, I go to see Madame du Rumain, who had taken leave of all her acquaintances for three weeks. She was a woman of the greatest probity, as polite and polished as possible, but with a manner so oddly affected that it often made me laugh heartily; she talked of the Sun and the Moon as if they were sovereigns whose acquaintance she was about to make. Talking to me one day of the happiness of the saved after death, she said that in heaven the happiness of souls must consist in their loving God "to distraction." I brought her all the drugs and herbs needed to make the perfumes; I told her what psalms to recite; at eight o'clock we ate a light supper together, then she ordered her chambermaid to shut her door and to expect me at ten o'clock, when she was to put me to bed in a room on the third floor which she had had made ready for me, instructing her to let me enter her room at five o'clock in the morning. At half past nine o'clock

I myself put her legs in the bath, the water in which had become warm, I showed her how to prepare the perfumes herself on the following days, I had her recite the psalms, then I dried her legs myself, laughing a little at her expressions of gratitude, and after seeing her to her bed, I went off to bed myself, waited on by her chambermaid, who, young and charming and merry, made me laugh by saying that if I had become her mistress's chambermaid it was only right that she should become mine. I wanted to make free with her; but she ran away, saying that I must save myself in order to be on my mettle with her mistress at five o'clock. She was mistaken.

The next morning at five o'clock I found Madame punctually putting on her shoes and stockings. We went into the adjoining room, from which we could have seen the rising Sun if the Hôtel de Bouillon[33] had not been in the way; but it did not matter. She performed her devotions with the air of a priestess. After that she sat down at her harpsichord, assuring me that she would find it very hard to occupy nine-hour mornings for three weeks in succession, for she did not dine until two. We breakfasted at nine o'clock, and I left her, promising that I would see her again before I set off for London.

I went to the Hôtel de Montmorency to dress, and Clairmont made me laugh by describing my brother's state of alarm because I had not come home to sleep. He was curling my hair when I saw him come in. I rose quickly, asking him, "Paris or Rome?" and he replied, "Rome." At that I told him to wait outside. When I was dressed I had him summoned, and just then my brother the painter came in with his wife to say that they had come to ask me for dinner. I wrote a note to Madame d'Urfé begging her to pardon me if I could not go there; and I told my brother that he had come in time to see the execution of the Abate, who had finally made up his mind to go to Rome however I chose to send him. I sent Clairmont to the office of the Lyons diligence to reserve and pay for a place for him; then in less than half an hour I wrote him four drafts for five louis each—one on Signor Bono in Lyons, another on Signor Zappata in Turin, another on Signor Sassi in Florence, and the last for Belloni in Rome.

"What assurance have I," the fool asked me, "that these gentlemen will pay me the money on sight of these notes?"

"If you are not sure of it, leave them with me, but for good and all. You are always impertinent to your benefactors."

Clairmont came, bringing a ticket for a paid place in the diligence which left at dawn the next day. I gave it to him and I bade him good-by.

"I can dine with you."

"I do not want you. Go and dine with Passano, monster! You sign your name as a witness that I am a coin clipper, and you dare to speak to me? Clairmont, turn him out."

It was unbelievable, but it was true. My sister asked me what I had done with the girl I had carried off.

"I sent her to Venice with ten thousand écus."

"That is all very well, but think of the pain the Abate must have felt when he saw you sleeping with her."

"Fools are made to suffer pain. Did he tell you that she would never let him give her a kiss, and that she beat him?"

"Not at all. He told us she adored him."

After spending three or four hours pleasantly, I took my sister-in-law to the opera,[34] and her husband went home. She complained to me bitterly. In all the six years[35] he had been married to her he had never been able to consummate the marriage.

"I am told," she said, "that I could ask for an annulment, and I cannot because I am mad enough to love him. He is up to his ears in debt, and if I made him give me back my dowry I should ruin him. But, knowing himself, why did he deceive me by marrying me? He is a traitor."

She was right. But my brother said it was not his fault, and that he had hoped that marrying her would put an end to his impotence. After her death he married another woman,[36] who punished him. She reduced him to having to flee from Paris and leave her everything he possessed. I will say more on the subject twenty years hence.[37]

The next morning early my brother the Abate left. I did not see him again until I was in Rome six years later. I will say more on the subject when I come to that time. I spent the day at Madame d'Urfé's, where I finally consented to young Trenti's[38] returning to Paris from Abbeville on horseback, and I set my departure for three days later. I went to the Français[39] to see a new play, which failed.[40] The author wept bitterly; to console him his friends said that only the machinations of the opposition had made it fail; but that did not make up to him for the money the failure would cost him.

Curiosity made me go to the address at which Boncousin had told me he was staying with two girls who knew me. It was on the Rue Montmartre;[41] the house door, the entry, and the floor were indicated; my coachman drove round and round several times, but could never find the house. I get out to look for it on foot, address in hand; a shopkeeper tells me that two foreign girls had arrived at the house next to hers not long since and that they must be living on the fourth floor. I go up, and I ask the woman who opens the door to me for news of two Venetian girls who must have come to lodge with her.

"Lord! I have fifteen, and God damn my soul if I know what country they come from. Come in, and you shall ask them yourself."

This makes me laugh, and I find a flock of wenches making a great racket and coming to me with exclamations as soon as I appear. I beg all the wild creatures to calm themselves, and I do not even think of asking for the Venetian girls for whom I was looking, for it was a

b. . . . . .[42] However, I talk to them all, and except for one, who was English, I find that they are all French. The mistress of the establishment comes to ask me if I want to sup with one of them, I consent, I decline to choose, I put myself in her hands, asking her to give me the one she thought would be most likely to please me.

She gives me one, who immediately takes charge of me, leads me to a room, and a moment later supper is brought and clean sheets are put on the excellent bed. I look at my table companion, and she does not please me. However, I hide the fact, I treat her pleasantly, I eat well, I sit at the table a long time, I send for champagne; having seen me cold to all her cajoleries, she thinks that I want to see her intoxicated; and she is obliging enough to get drunk. By the third bottle she no longer knew what she was saying or what she was doing. She undresses and lies down on the bed as nature made her, she invites me, she comes to me, I let her do what she will, and for the first time in my life I have the pleasure of seeing that she cannot make me become a man. Adèle, Marcolina, my niece P. P., Clementina, and the others were still too present to my memory. The hussy was young, pretty, and well built; but she became nothing when I compared her to the others. At three o'clock in the morning I went home, very well pleased with myself and not at all troubled by the poor idea of my valor with which I must have left the girl.

The next day after dining with Madame d'Urfé I took a hackney carriage to go to see La Corticelli in her retreat without being recognized. I found her sad, but well pleased with her situation and with the gentleness of the surgeon and his wife. I was assured that she would be completely cured. She told me that she had fled from the Rue de Grenelle at nine o'clock, carrying all her clothes with her, and that her maid must be in despair, for she was in debt to her. I gave her twelve louis, and I promised to send her twelve more when she wrote to me from Bologna; and she promised to do so; but the un-

fortunate girl died while she was under treatment.[43] I
learned of it two months later by a letter which Faget
wrote me to London, in which he told me that he did not
know how to send the twelve louis which she had left to
a Signora Laura, whom I must know. I sent the honest
man an address at which he was able to dispatch them to
her.

All those of whom I made use to help me in the magical
tricks which I played on Madame d'Urfé, except Marcolina, betrayed me, and later they all came to bad ends.
The reader will find Passano and Costa in their proper
places.

On the eve of my departure I supped with Madame du
Rumain, who assured me that her voice was already beginning to return; a wise reflection which she made gave
me pleasure. She said that the regimen which ceremonial
observances of this kind obliged her to pursue might contribute to it; I told her she should have no doubt of it.
I was glad to learn that, to set reason on the road to
truth, it was necessary to begin by deceiving it. Darkness
had to precede light. Boncousin, whom I found in the
parterre of the Théâtre Italien, laughed at me when I
complained that the house of which he had given me the
address was nowhere to be found on the Rue Montmartre.
He told me with a laugh that his need for six francs had
driven him to employ the trick to obtain them. I told
him that he should not reveal himself to be a scoundrel
so cheaply.

After taking leave of Madame d'Urfé and assuring her
that I would not fail to keep all my promises, I took the
youth with me in a hackney carriage, together with his
strong boots, which he admired to adoration. I took him
to the Hôtel de Montmorency, whence we set out toward
evening. He had begged me to travel at night, because
he was ashamed to be seen dressed as a courier and not
to be on horseback. On the third day we arrive at Abbeville. I order dinner, he asks me where his mother is, I
reply that we will inquire for her, and I invite him to go

with me to see the cloth manufactory of the Messieurs van Robais.[44]

"But we can find out in a minute whether my mother is here or not."

"Well, if she is not here we will continue our journey, and we shall meet her on the road. We shall certainly meet her before we get to Boulogne."

"Go to see the manufactory, and meanwhile I will sleep."

"As you please."

I go. An hour and a half later I return to the inn, and I do not see the lad. Clairmont was asleep.

"Where is he? I want to dine."

"He rode off at a gallop to fetch the dispatches which you forgot in Paris."

I summon the post master, I tell him that if he does not bring him back to me he can count on being ruined, for he should not have given him a horse except by my order. He calms me and assures me that he will have him overtaken before he reaches Amiens. He gives the order to a postilion, who laughs when he sees that I am uneasy.

"I'd catch him," he says, "even if he left before dawn. He left only an hour and a half ago; he cannot have traveled more than two stages; I travel three in the same time. You will see me with him at six o'clock at the latest."

"You shall have two louis for drink."

I could not eat dinner. I felt ashamed to find myself tricked in this manner by an inexperienced youth. I threw myself on my bed, where I slept until the postilion waked me by bringing in the culprit, who looked like a corpse. Without a word to him, I ordered that he be locked in a room in which there was a good bed, that he be given supper, and that the innkeeper should make himself responsible for him until early the next morning, when I should leave for Boulogne and Calais. I had to let him rest, for he was exhausted. The postilion caught

up with him halfway through the fifth stage, not far
from Amiens. He had been as docile as a lamb. The next
morning I summoned him, and I asked him if he wanted
to come to London with me of his own free will or bound
hand and foot.

"Of my own free will, I give you my word of honor;
but on horseback, and riding ahead of you, for otherwise
I should be dishonored. No one must be able to say that
you set up a hue and cry after me, as if I had robbed
you."

"I accept your word of honor. Order another saddle
horse on my behalf. Come and embrace me."

Perfectly content, he mounted and, keeping ahead of
me all the way, he stopped in Calais at the "Golden
Arm," [45] where he was astonished to find his trunk. I
arrived an hour after him.

CHAPTER VII

My arrival in London. Mrs. Cornelys. I am
presented at Court. I rent a furnished house.
I make many acquaintances. English morality.

I HAD scarcely arrived before I summoned the inn-keeper and had him give me a receipt for my post chaise, which I was leaving with him, countersigning it, and I at once chartered a packet boat[1] so that it should be at my orders whenever I pleased. Only one was disengaged, another was for all passengers who paid six francs a head. I paid six guineas[2] in advance for it, obtaining a receipt, for I had been told that it was at Calais that one began to be in the wrong in all disputes in which one could not produce visible and palpable proof of one's rights. Before the tide falls Clairmont sees to taking all my luggage on board, and I order supper. The innkeeper warns me that louis do not pass current in England, and he changes mine into guineas without taking any profit. I admired his honesty, for the guinea was worth seventeen sous more than the French louis.

Young D'Aranda-Trenti had resigned himself. He stayed with me quietly, proud to have shown me his prowess on horseback. We sit down at table, and I hear the sound of English words at the door of my room. The innkeeper enters and tells me that it is a courier of the Duke of Bedford,[3] the English Ambassador, who was about to arrive on his way back to London, coming from Versailles. The courier was arguing with the master of the packet I had chartered; he told him he had chartered it by letter and that he could not dispose of it; the other replied that he had not received the letter and no one could prove the contrary against him. At that I congratulate myself on having the packet. I go to bed, and early the next morning the innkeeper comes to tell me that the Ambassador had arrived at midnight and that his valet wished to speak to me. I have him shown in and he tells me on behalf of His Lordship, who was in a hurry to get back to London, that if I would relinquish the packet to him I should be at liberty to make the passage to Dover just the same. I then take a pen, and I write my answer in these words:

"My Lord the Duke may dispose of the whole of my packet, except for the space necessary for three people together with my small amount of baggage. I eagerly seize the opportunity to make this small gift to the English Ambassador."

The valet comes back to tell me that the Ambassador thanks me but that he wishes to pay.

"That is impossible, for the fee has been paid."

"He will give you back the six guineas."

"Tell His Lordship that the freedom of the boat is his without paying, but not otherwise; for I do not sell merchandise which I have bought."

A half hour later the Duke himself is announced and enters to tell me graciously that I am in the right, but that he is not wrong to refuse the too great favor which I wish to do him. I agree, with a mortified air, but I do not budge from my position.

"There is," he says, "a middle course. If you will take it, I shall be no less obliged to you. We will each pay half."

"I will take it, My Lord; it is I who shall be obliged to you for the honor you do me. I will not leave until you are ready."

He put three guineas on my chest of drawers without showing them to me, and he left, thanking me. I told the master of the packet to put His Lordship and all his effects on board, and I took no part in the disputes in which he engaged with the Ambassador's officers in order to get his money. It was not my affair.

We crossed the Channel in two hours and a half with the strongest of winds. The next day the search by the customs officers to see if I had any contraband articles struck me as extremely tedious, impertinent, indiscreet, and even indecent; but I had to put up with it and conceal my feelings, for an offended Englishman who has the law on his side is much more impertinent than[4] a Frenchman.

The island called England is a different color from that which one sees on the surface of the Continent. The sea is extraordinary, for being part of the Atlantic Ocean, it is subject to the ebb and flow of the tides;[5] the water of the Thames has a different flavor from that of all the rivers on earth. Horned animals, fish, and everything one eats has a different taste from what we eat, the horses are of a species of their own even in their shape, and men have a character not found elsewhere and common to the whole nation, which make them think themselves superior to all others. This is a supposition common to all nations; each thinks itself the first. They are all right.

I immediately saw the great cleanliness, the substantial fare, the beauty of the countryside and of the great roads; I admired the beauty of the carriages supplied by the post to travelers who have not one of their own; the reasonableness of the posting charges, the ease with which it is possible to pay them, the rapidity of travel, always at a trot, never at a gallop, and the construction of the cities through which I had to pass on my way from Dover to London. Canterbury and Rochester[6] have a large population, though their breadth is nothing in proportion to their length. We arrived in London toward nightfall, eighteen hours after leaving Dover, at the house of Mrs. Cornelys. This was the name assumed by Teresa, daughter of the actor Imer, later wife of Pompeati, the dancer, who had killed himself [7] in Vienna, cutting his belly open with a razor and tearing out his bowels in an instant.

This Signora Pompeati, who in Holland had taken the name of Trenti, had in London taken that of Cornelys, in honor of her lover Cornelius Rigerboos, whom she ruined, of whom I have spoken in my fourth volume.[8] I arrived, then, at the door of her house on Soho Square,[9] opposite that of the Venetian Resident, who lives on the other side of the same square. My arriving at her house was in obedience to the orders she had given me in her last letter. I had written her the day on which I hoped to see her.

I get out, leaving her son in the carriage, thinking that I shall see her at once; but the porter tells me to wait. Two minutes later a manservant brings me a letter in which Mrs. Cornelys tells me to go on to stay at a house to which the servant will show me the way and where she will come to supper with me. I find nothing strange in this. She might have reasons for it. I get in again, and the postilions arrive at the house on the street near the Square to which the servant directs them. A Frenchwoman, named Raucour[10] and excessively fat, and two menservants come to meet us; the stout woman embraces Mr. Cornelys[11] and rejoices at his safe arrival, dropping me a cold curtsy. In less than a quarter of an hour Clairmont, shown the way by La Raucour, puts all my luggage in a room which had a closet through which I could enter the apartment on the front, consisting of three fine rooms, in which the same Raucour had had My Lord Cornelys's trunk put, while he stood there open-mouthed and at a loss to answer when she said to him:

"These two valets are yours, and I am your most humble servant."

I return to my room through the same closet, and though seeing that I am not only badly lodged but lodged as an inferior, I control myself, a rare occurrence, and I do not say a word; I only ask Clairmont where his room is, so that he can go to it and dispose of his trunk, which was there with all of mine. After going, he comes to tell me that the fat lady had shown him his bed in a room in the attic where one of Master Cornelys's two men-servants slept. Clairmont, who knew me, was astonished to hear me answer calmly:

"Very well, take your trunk there."

"Shall I unpack yours?"

"No. Leave that until tomorrow."

Still concealing my feelings, I go back to the room of my master, who was looking exhausted because he had tried to ride a stage on horseback and had never succeeded in making his mount gallop. He was listening to Madame Raucour, who, sitting beside him, was giving him an account of his mother Mrs. Cornelys's splendid position, her extensive enterprises, her immense credit, the magnificent mansion she had had built, the thirty-three servants she kept, two secretaries, six horses, country house, and I know not what.

"How is my sister Sophie?" [12]

"Is her name Sophie? She is called Miss Cornelys. She is a beauty, Sir, a prodigy of intelligence, grace, and talents; she sings, she plays at sight on all instruments, she dances, she speaks three languages and writes them correctly, she has her own governess and her own chambermaid. It is a pity she is too small for her age, for she is eight years old."

She was ten;[13] but since the woman was talking without vouchsafing me a look, I said nothing. My Lord Cornelys, who needed to go to bed, asked her at what time supper was served, and she replied:

"At ten o'clock and no sooner."

For Mrs. Cornelys was busy with her lawyer until then because of a great lawsuit she had against Sir

Frederic Fermer.[14] I thereupon go to my room and, saying nothing, take my hat and cane and set out for a
walk. It was only seven o'clock. Careful not to lose my
bearings, I walk at random, and a quarter of an hour
later I enter a crowded coffeehouse. It was the "Prince
of Orange," [15] notorious for those who frequented it,
who were the dregs of all the scoundrelly Italians who
were in London. I had been told of it in Lyons, and I
had intended never to go there; it was dark, and chance
led me there; nor did I ever set foot in it again. I sit
down by myself, I order a lemonade; and a man sits
down near me to take advantage of the light which was
on my table to read a printed sheet. I see that it is in
Italian. The man was crossing out letters with a pencil
and putting the correction in the margin. "An author,"
I said to myself. I notice that he crosses out a letter in
the word *ancora* and puts an *h* in the margin, to indicate
that he wants it to be printed "anchora." I cannot restrain myself. I tell him that the word *ancora* has been
spelled without an *h* for four centuries.

"I agree, but I am quoting Boccaccio,[16] and one should
be exact in quotations."

"You are right, pray excuse me. You are a man of
letters?"

"In a very small way. I am Martinelli." [17]

"Not in a small way at all. I know you by reputation.
You are related to Calzabigi,[18] and he has talked to me
about you. I have read some of your satires." [19]

"May I ask to whom I am speaking?"

"My name is Seingalt. Have you finished your edition
of the *Decamerone*?" [20]

"I am still at work on it, and always trying to increase
the number of my subscribers." [21]

"If you would like to add me——"

"You do me honor."

He thereupon gives me a ticket, and seeing that it was
only a guinea, I ask him for another, I pay him, and I
rise to leave, saying that I hope to see him again at the

same coffeehouse. I ask him its name, and he tells me, astonished that I do not know it; but he is even more astonished when I tell him that I have just arrived in London for the first time.

"Then you will have difficulty finding your way back to where you are staying, and I will accompany you."

No sooner have we left than he very frankly warns me that the "Prince of Orange," to which chance had led me, is the most disreputable coffeehouse in London.

"But you go to it."

"I can go to it with the safe-conduct of Juvenal's verse: *Cantabit vacuus coram latrone viator* ['The traveler with an empty purse will sing when he meets a robber'].[22] The rogues have no way of getting their teeth into me. I do not speak to them; and they do not speak to me. I have been here for five years, I seek patronage only from Lord Spencer,[23] I occupy myself with literary work,[24] I am single, I earn enough to live in a furnished room and take my dinner at a tavern. I have a dozen shirts and this coat, and I am in good health; *nec ultra deos lacesso*" ("nor do I importune the gods for more").[25]

Such a man, speaking Tuscan with the greatest purity,[26] pleases me. On the way I ask him how I should go about finding a good lodging, and after learning what accommodations I want and how long I intend to stay in London, and what sort of life I want to lead, he advises me to take a whole house for myself, fully furnished and with all the kitchenware and tableware I should need, as well as table linen and bed linen.

"You will be given the inventory," he says, "and as soon as you obtain a surety, you will be lord and master there, domiciled like an Englishman and responsible only to the laws."

I ask him to tell me of such a house; and he at once enters a shop; he speaks to the proprietress, he writes, and then he comes out after copying everything I needed from an *Advertiser*.[27] It was the locations where houses

such as I wanted were to be found. The nearest to where
we were was in a broad street called Pall Mall,[28] and
we went to see it. An old woman who opened the smaller
door to us as soon as he knocked showed us the ground
floor and the three upper floors. Every floor had two
front rooms—each with a closet, which goes without saying in London—and two at the back. In each apartment
there were two beds, one in the room and one in the
closet. Everything was scrupulously clean—porcelain,
mirrors, bellpulls; it was perfection. In a very large cupboard in the room on the ground floor in which the old
woman slept there was all the linen, and in another were
the silver services and services of porcelain and china.
In the kitchen there was an ample supply of pots and
pans, and in the underground apartment, which I did
not expect, there was furniture enough to lodge a whole
family, and a cellar and storerooms to hold everything
necessary for a well-run house. The rent was twenty
guineas a week. I told Martinelli that the house pleased
me and that I wanted to take it at once, so that I could
move into it whenever I pleased.

As soon as he translated my decision to the old woman,
she told him that if I wanted to keep her as housekeeper,[29]
I need not have a surety, it being enough for her if I
would always pay her the week's rent in advance; but
that if I wanted to put someone else in charge of the
house she would need at least two days to go over the
inventory with whomever I should appoint and who, in
that case, would have to give surety. I replied that I
would keep her on condition that she would engage a
maid, whom I would pay and who would take orders
directly from her, but who must speak French or Italian
in addition to English. She promised me that she would
have the maid the next day; I paid her for four weeks in
advance, and she gave me a receipt under the name of
the Chevalier de Seingalt; I never used any other name
in London. Martinelli, delighted to have been of use to
me, left me when, seeing that I was in my street, I

thanked him and wished him good night. I returned to Mrs. Cornelys's, who was still awaited though ten o'clock had just struck. Young Cornelys was asleep on the sofa.

So it was that, despite all those who say that London is a chaos in which a stranger who arrives there needs at least three days to find himself a lodging, I was excellently lodged two hours after I arrived. I was also delighted to have made the acquaintance of Martinelli, of whom I had had a most favorable opinion for six years. He had given me the address of his room, which was above the "Prince of Orange," and that of his printer. Profoundly shocked by the way in which the Cornelys had received me in London, I awaited her impatiently, resolved, however, to put a good face on it.

Three knocks (signifying the mistress of the house) sound at last, and from the window I see her alight from a sedan chair, I hear her coming quickly up the stairs, she enters, she shows that she is glad, and indeed delighted, to see me, but she does not come running to embrace me; she has forgotten how she parted from me at The Hague;[30] she throws herself on her son, she takes him in her arms, she covers him with kisses, which he accepts sleepily and returns coldly, saying:

"My dear Mama, my dear Mama."

I tell her that he is tired and that, for people who need rest, she has kept us waiting too long. Supper is announced, and she does me the honor to take my arm to go in to it in a room which I had not seen. She has the fourth place removed, I ask her for whom it was; and she tells me that it was for her daughter, whom she had left at home because as soon as she had told her that I had arrived with her brother she had asked her if I was in good health.

"And you punished her for that?"

"Certainly, for it seems to me that she should be first interested in her brother's health and in yours only afterward. Do you think I am right?"

"Poor Sophie. I feel sorry for her. Gratitude has more power over her than the ties of blood."

"It is not a matter of feeling, but of accustoming young people to speaking as they should."

She talked a great deal to her son, who never gave her anything but studied answers, always with his eyes cast down, and with respect but with no sign of affection. She told him that she was working to leave him rich after her death, and that she had made me bring him back because he was old enough to help her and to share her work in the house she kept; and at that he asked her what sort of work it was in which she wanted him to share.

"I give," she said, "twelve suppers and balls a year for the nobility and twelve for the citizenry at two guineas a head, and I often have five or six hundred people; the outlay is immense, and, alone as I am, it is impossible that I should not be robbed, for since I cannot be everywhere I have to put my trust in people who perhaps abuse it, but now that you are here, you can oversee everything, my dear son, keep everything under lock and key, write, handle the cash, make payments, take receipts, and go all through the house to see if the ladies and gentlemen are properly served, in short, perform the functions and act the part of master in a house in which you will actually be so as my son."

"Then you believe, my dear Mother, that I shall be able to do all that?"

"Yes, for you will learn."

"It seems to me impossible."

"One of my secretaries will come to live with you in this house, which I have taken for the purpose, and he will instruct you in everything. For a year you will do nothing but learn English and come to my assemblies so that I can introduce you to all the most important people in London; and little by little you will become English; everyone will talk of Mr. Cornelys."

"Cornelys?"

"Yes, that is your name."

"My name? I'll go and write it down so that I shan't forget it."

Thinking that he was joking, she looked at me in some surprise. She told him to go to bed, which he did at once, thanking her. Left alone with me, she said that she thought him badly brought up and too small for his age, and that she saw she must begin, perhaps too late, to have him given a different education.

"What has he learned in six years?"

"He could have learned all the branches of knowledge, for he was in the best boarding school in Paris; but he learned only what he wanted to—playing the flute, riding horseback, fencing, dancing the minuet well, changing his shirt every day, answering politely, making a charming appearance, telling a story prettily, and dressing with elegance. That is all he knows. Since he would never apply himself, he hasn't the shadow of an acquaintance with literature, he cannot write, he cannot figure, he does not care whether he knows or not that England is an island of Europe."

"That makes six lost years. My daughter will laugh at him. But it is I who have brought her up. He will be ashamed when he sees how much learning she has at the tender age of eight; she knows geography, history, languages, music, and she talks with the greatest intelligence. All the ladies are forever snatching her from one another. I keep her in a drawing school all day, she comes home only at nightfall. On Sundays she dines here, and if you will do me the favor of coming to dinner at my house on Sunday, you will see that I have not exaggerated."

It was a Monday. I say nothing; but I find it strange that she does not think me impatient to see her, that she does not tell me to come to supper at her house the next day, that she has not brought her to supper with her. She tells me that I have come to London in time to see

the last assembly of that year,[31] which she was giving for
the nobility, who in two or three weeks would go to spend
the summer in the country.

"I cannot give you a ticket," she said, "for I can give
them only to the nobility; but you can come to it, and,
by keeping near me as a friend of mine, you will see
everything. If I am asked who you are I will say that
you are the person who took care of my son in Paris and
who has come to bring him back to me."

"I am most grateful to you."

We remained at table talking until two o'clock in the
morning; she gave me a full account of her lawsuit
against Sir Frederic Fermer. He claimed that the house
which she had had built,[32] and which cost ten thousand
guineas, belonged to him, for it was he who had given
her the money; but he was in the wrong, according to
the law she cited, for it was she who had paid the workmen and it was to her that they had given the receipts;
hence the house belonged to her; "but the money," said
Fermer, "did not belong to you." She challenged him to
prove it, to produce a single receipt. "It is true," said
the honest woman, "that you more than once gave me a
thousand guineas at a time; but it was generosity on
your part, and nothing strange in a rich Englishman,
since we loved each other, we were living together."

This lawsuit, which in two years she had won four
times, and which did not end because of the legal chi-
canery Fermer employed to challenge her victory, had
cost Mrs. Cornelys a great deal, and at the time we were
talking there was an appeal which would take it to the
Court of Equity,[33] where, *beati possidentes* ("blessed
are they who are in possession"),[34] it would be fourteen
or fifteen years before a decision was handed down. She
told me that the suit dishonored Fermer, and I well
understood that; but I could not understand how she
could suppose it was to her honor; yet that was what
she sincerely believed. Among the different subjects on
which we touched in three hours of conversation she

never asked me if I was comfortably lodged; she did not care to know if I intended to stay in London for some time and what I thought I might do there, and she offered me neither her services nor her credit, for she told me with a laugh that she never had a penny in her purse. She took in more than twenty-four thousand pounds sterling[35] a year; but in these first three years she had spent more than eighty thousand. Even so, she told me, she expected to finish paying all her debts the following winter.

Mrs. Cornelys having shown no curiosity concerning my affairs, I amused myself by telling her nothing about them. She saw no sign of wealth on me; I had only a perfectly plain watch, all my diamonds were in my jewel case. I went off to bed, annoyed but not angry, for at bottom I was very glad to have discovered her bad character. Despite the impatience I felt to see my daughter, I resolved not to see her until Sunday, going to dine at her mother's house, as, for politeness' sake, she had invited me to do.

The next morning at seven o'clock I told Clairmont to put all my belongings into a carriage, and when this was done I went to tell my poor young man, who was still in bed, that I was going to lodge in Pall Mall in the house of which the address was written on the card which I left him.

"What! You are not staying with me?"

"No, for your mother forgot to put me up."

"So she did. I want to go back to Paris."

"Don't do anything so stupid. Consider that now, being in your mother's house, you are in your own, and that in Paris you may no longer find a roof. Good-by. I shall dine with you Sunday at your mother's."

Clairmont arranged all my belongings in my new house in less than an hour. I went out wearing a *frac*,[36] and I took Signor Zuccato,[37] the Venetian Resident, the letter I had from Signor Morosini, the Procurator; he read it, and he said coldly that he was very glad to have

made my acquaintance. I asked him to present me at
Court, and my request set him laughing. I let him laugh,
and I did not set foot in his house again. I went to take
my letter from the same Procurator to Lord Egremont,[38]
who was ill; I left it for him. A few days later he died.
Some time afterward his widow married Count Brühl [39]
Martinskirchen, who is still in London as Minister of the
Elector of Saxony.[40] I went to call on the Count of
Guerchy,[41] the French Ambassador, with a letter from
the Marquis de Chauvelin,[42] who gave him such an
account of me that he invited me to dine with him on
the next day, saying that he would present me at the
Court of St. James's[43] on Sunday after chapel.[44] At the
Ambassador's table the next day I made the acquaintance
of the Chevalier d'Éon,[45] his Secretary of Embassy, who
later caused such a stir all over Europe. The Chevalier
was a woman who, before becoming a diplomat, had been
a captain of dragoons. Despite his considerable knowledge of diplomacy and his masculine manner, I suspected
that he was something less than a man. His drama began
soon afterward, when Monsieur de Guerchy, who was
given a leave of absence, left London. During this week
I presented myself to all my bankers, in whose hands I
had at least a hundred thousand écus. They accepted the
drafts, and in virtue of my letters of recommendation
from Messrs. Tourton & Baur, they offered me their personal services. I went to the Covent Garden[46] and Drury
Lane[47] theaters, unknown to everyone, and to taverns
for dinner, in order to accustom myself gradually to
English ways. Mornings I went to the Exchange,[48] where
I made several acquaintances; it was there that the
broker Bosanquet,[49] whom I had asked to find me a good
servant who, besides English, could speak Italian or
French, brought me a Negro whose honesty he guaranteed. It was Bosanquet, too, who got me an English cook
who could speak French and who moved into my house
at once with his whole family, and it was he who introduced me to several strange confraternities of which I

will speak at the proper time and place. During this same week I also arranged to be initiated into the select bagnios,[50] where a rich man goes to bathe, sup, and sleep with a choice prostitute. It is a magnificent festival, which costs six guineas in all; economy can reduce it to four; but economy spoils pleasure.

On Sunday at eleven o'clock I dressed elegantly, and, wearing my fine rings, my watches, and my order hanging from my neck on a red ribbon, I went to Court, making my way to the last antechamber, where I found the Count of Guerchy. I went in with him, and he presented me to George III,[51] who spoke to me, but in a voice so low that I could reply only by bowing. But the Queen[52] made up for it. I was delighted to see the Venetian Resident among those who were paying their court. As soon as Monsieur de Guerchy spoke my name, I saw that the Resident was surprised, for in his letter the Procurator had called me Casanova. The Queen having at once asked me what province of France I was from, and having learned from my answer that I was a Venetian,[53] looked at the Venetian Resident, who showed by a bow that he had no objection to make. She asked me if I knew the Ambassadors who had left six weeks earlier, and I replied that I had spent three days with them in Lyons, where Signor Morosini had given me letters for Lord Egremont and the Resident. She said that Signor Querini had said many things which made her laugh.

"He told me," she said with a laugh, "that I am a little devil."

"He meant, Madam, that Your Majesty has the wit of an angel."

I should have been glad if she had asked me for what reason[54] it was not Signor Zuccato who was presenting me, for I would have answered in a way which the Resident would not much have enjoyed. After the Court I got into my sedan chair again and was carried to Mrs. Cornelys's house on Soho Square, where I was invited for dinner. A man dressed to appear at Court would not dare to walk through the streets of London; a porter, a loafer, a scapegrace from the dregs of the people would throw mud at him, laugh in his face, push him to make him say something offensive, all in order to have an excuse for engaging him in a fist fight. The democratic spirit prevails in the English people, even far more than it does today in the French; but the power of the constitution holds it in check. In short, the spirit of rebellion is prevalent in every great city, and the great task of wise government is to keep it dormant, for if it wakes it is a torrent which no dam can hold back.

The sedan chair stops at the door of Mrs. Cornelys's house, I tell my Negro, whose name was Jarba,[55] to dismiss my chairmen; I go in, I am conducted upstairs to the second floor, where, after passing through twelve or fourteen rooms, I am shown into that in which Mrs. Cornelys was sitting with two Englishwomen and two Englishmen. She received me with a politeness expressive of the most familiar friendship, and after making me sit down beside her she continued her conversation with her four visitors, speaking English and telling neither them who I was nor me who they were. When her majordomo came to announce that dinner was served, she ordered the children brought down. At sight of Sophie I run to her impulsively to take her in my arms and kiss her; but, following her instructions, she draws back and, dropping me a low curtsy, she pays me a compliment which she has learned by heart, to which I am tactful enough not to reply, for fear of leaving her with nothing to say. Mrs. Cornelys then presents her son to the gentlemen, and tells them that it was I who have brought him back to her after six years during which I had taken charge of his education; she says this in French, and I see with pleasure that everyone present speaks French.

We sit down at table—she between her two children and I, facing her, between the two Englishwomen, one of whom, though no longer young, at once delighted me

with her wit. It was with her that I conversed when I
saw that Mrs. Cornelys spoke to me only casually and
that Sophie, who turned her beautiful eyes from one
member of the company to another, never looked at me;
she quite obviously passed me over; she was carrying out
a command which I thought as absurd as it was rude.
Angry to find that I felt offended, and determined not
to allow myself to show it, I engage the English ladies
and gentlemen in an amusing conversation on the customs I had observed in England, though without the
slightest tinge of criticism, thus setting them laughing
and making them find me an agreeable companion; and
in my turn I never look at Mrs. Cornelys.

The lady next to me, after examining the beauty of
my laces, asks me what is new at Court.

"Everything seemed new to me, Madam, for I never
saw it before today."

"Did you see the King?" Sir Joseph Cornelys[56] asks
me.

"My son," says his mother, "one never asks such questions."

"Why not, my dear Mother?"

"Because the question may be displeasing to the gentleman."

"On the contrary," I said, "it pleased me. For six
years I have been teaching him always to ask. A boy
who never asks anything always remains ignorant."

Mrs. Cornelys sulks and says nothing.

"You still have not told me," the young fellow takes
me up, "if you saw the King or not."

"Yes, my dear boy, His Majesty spoke to me, but I
do not know what he said, whereas the Queen spoke very
clearly."

"Who presented you?"

"The French Ambassador."

"Excellent!" said his mother. "But you must admit
that the last question is too much by far."

"Addressed to someone else, but not to me, who am

his friend. You see that the answer he obliged me to give
does me honor. If I had not wanted it known that I went
to Court I should not have come to dine here dressed as
I am."

"You are right. But since you like to be questioned,
I will also ask you why you had yourself presented by
the French Envoy and not by the Venetian one."

"Because the Venetian Envoy declined to do it; and
he was in the right."

With much other conversation, this brought us to
dessert, and my daughter had not yet said a word.

"My dear daughter," her mother said, "do say something to Monsieur de Seingalt."

"I shouldn't know what to say, my dear Mother. But
ask him to say something to me, and I will answer as
well as I can."

"Very well, my pretty child," I said, "tell me what
you are studying at present."

"Drawing, and if you like I will let you see some of
my work."

"I shall see it with pleasure; but please tell me in
what way you think you have offended me, for you look
guilty."

"I? I have certainly done nothing at which you could
take umbrage."

"You speak to me without looking at me. Are you
ashamed of having beautiful eyes? And now you are
blushing. What crime have you committed?"

"You are embarrassing her," her mother said to me.
"Answer him that you have committed no crime, but
that it is out of respect and modesty that you do not
stare at the people to whom you speak."

She made no answer.

After a short silence the company rose, and the little
girl, after dropping a curtsy, went to fetch her drawings
and came to me.

"Mademoiselle, I will look at nothing unless you will
look at me."

"Come now," her mother said, "look at Monsieur."

"This time," I said to Sophie, "I recognize you. And do you remember having seen me before?"

"Though it was six years ago, I recognized you as soon as you came in."

"How can you have recognized me if you never looked at me? If you knew, my angel, what unforgivably bad manners it is not to look at the person to whom one speaks! Who can have taught you such a bad lesson?"

At that the child looked at her mother, who had gone to the window. When I saw that I had sufficiently avenged myself, and that the English guests had understood everything, I began looking at her drawings and praising everything in detail, congratulating her on her talent and complimenting her mother for giving her so good an education. She was filled with pride by the praise I bestowed now on her daughter, now on herself, and there was an end to lowered eyes. Sophie, seeing that she was free to look at me, constantly availed herself of the unspoken permission; in her physiognomy I saw a beautiful soul, and I silently pitied her for having to live under the domination of her mother, who was a fool. She sat down at the harpsichord, she sang in Italian, after that she accompanied herself on the guitar in some short airs, then her mother[57] wanted her to dance a minuet with her brother, who had learned it in Paris, and who danced very badly because he held himself badly; and his sister, after embracing him, told him so. She danced it at once with me, and her mother, after declaring the minuet superb, told her that she should let me embrace her, which I did, taking her on my lap and giving her all the kisses she deserved, which she returned with all the affection I could wish. Her mother simply laughed, and she embraced her fondly too when, after leaving me, she went to ask her if she was displeased.

She showed me the great room she had had built for balls and for giving supper to four hundred persons all seated at a single horseshoe-shaped table. I was easily persuaded that there was not a bigger room in London. The last assembly was to be given before Parliament closed, five or six days later. She had in her service more than twenty maids and ten or twelve footmen. All these vermin robbed her, she said, but she could not do without them, so it was unavoidable. I left Mrs. Cornelys, admiring her courage and wishing her good fortune.

I had myself carried to St. James's Park[58] to call on Lady Harrington;[59] I had a letter for her,[60] as my reader knows; she lived within the precincts of the Court, for which reason she entertained at her house every Sunday; play was allowed there, for the Park was under the royal jurisdiction. Everywhere else no one dares to play or to give concerts;[61] spies who walk the streets of London listen carefully to hear what sort of noise is being made in the drawing rooms of private houses, and if they suspect there is play or that someone is singing they hide wherever they can and, as soon as they see the door open, they slip in, and they hale to prison all the bad Christians who dare thus fail to respect the most sacred Sabbath, which, however, it is permissible to sanctify by going to taverns to entertain oneself with bottles and the prostitutes with which London swarms.

At Lady Harrington's I go upstairs, I send in my letter, she has me shown in at once, and I find myself among twenty-five or thirty people, men and women, I make my bow to Her Ladyship, who at once tells me that she had seen me with the Queen and that she wished to see me at her house too. For at least three-quarters of an hour I was the only speaker, answering the questions which are invariably the lot of the arriving foreigner. Lady Harrington, still beautiful at the age of forty, famous in London for her influence and for her gallantries, at once introduces me to her husband and her four adolescent daughters, all of them charming: the Ladies Isabella and Amelia Stanhope—I have forgotten the name of the third.[62] She asks me why I have come to London at the time when everyone goes to the country, and I reply that I expect to spend a year there. That leaves her nothing to reproach me with, and she says that so far as it lies in her power she will introduce me to all the pleasures of her country.

"You will see all the nobility," she says, "on Thursday at Soho Square; I can give you a ticket. Here it is. There will be supper and a ball. It costs two guineas."

I give them to her; and she writes on the ticket "Paid, Harrington." I do not tell her that I have just dined with Mrs. Cornelys.

She gets up a game of whist[63] for me, and she asks me if I have letters addressed to other ladies. I tell her that I have a very odd one which I intend to present to the lady the next day. "The letter is the lady's portrait."

"Have you it with you?"

"Yes, My Lady."

"May I see it?"

"Why not? Here it is."

"It is the Duchess of Northumberland.[64] Let us go and give it to her. We will wait until the rubber is scored."

Lord Percy had given me the portrait on the day I had dined with him, saying that it would serve me as a letter of introduction when I presented it to his mother[65] in London.

"Here, Duchess," Lady Harrington said to her, "is a letter of introduction which this gentleman is commanded to deliver to you."

"Ah, yes! He is Monsieur de Seingalt. My son wrote to me; I am delighted to see you. I hope that you will come to my house. I receive company three times a week."

"Then permit me, Your Ladyship, to deliver my precious letter to you in your house."

"Gladly—you are right."

I played whist at very small stakes, and I lost fifteen

guineas, which I paid at once, whereupon Lady Harrington took me aside to give me a lesson worthy to be recorded.

"You lost," she said, "and you paid in gold; I take
it that you have no bank notes with you."

"I beg your pardon, My Lady, I have notes for fifty
and a hundred."

"You should have changed one and paid with it, or
have waited until another day to pay. Here in England
paying in gold is a little unmannerly, though pardon-
able in a foreigner, who cannot know our customs; but
try not to let it happen again. You saw that the lady
smiled."

"Who is she?"

"Lady Coventry,[66] sister of the Duchess of Hamilton."[67]

"Should I apologize to her?"

"Certainly not. She may be well pleased, for she gains
fifteen shillings[68] by it."

I thought it a rather barbed remark. But Lady Coventry was an extremely beautiful brunette. I made the
acquaintance of Lord Hervey,[69] the conqueror of Havana,
an amiable and witty man. He had married Miss Chudleigh,[70] and had had the marriage annulled. This celebrated Chudleigh was maid of honor to the widowed
Princess of Wales;[71] she later became Duchess of Kingston. Her strange adventures are well known. I shall speak
of her at the proper time and place. I went home well
enough pleased with my day. On the next I began eating
at home, and I was well satisfied with my English cook,
who, besides his country's favorite dishes, which he gave
me every day, gave me fowl and very delicate French
ragouts. What pained me a little was that I was alone;
I had neither a pretty mistress nor a friend, and in
London one can invite a gentleman to dine with one at
a tavern, where he pays his share, but not to dinner at
one's own table. People laughed when I said that I ate
at home because at the taverns soup was not served. I

was asked if I was ill. The Englishman is a meat-eater.[72]
He eats scarcely any bread, and he insists that he is
economical because he saves himself the expense of soup
and dessert; which led me to say that an English dinner
has neither beginning nor end. Soup is considered a
great expense, because even the servants will not eat the
beef from which broth has been made. They say it is fit
only to give to dogs. The salt beef which they serve
instead of it is excellent. I tried to get used to their
beer; but I had to give it up after a week. The bitter
taste it left in my mouth was intolerable. The vintner
whom Bosanquet had sent me supplied me with French
wines which were excellent because they were natural;
but I had to pay high prices for them.

On Monday morning Martinelli came to see me. I had
been settled in my house for a week, and I had never
seen him; I asked him to share my soup, and having
learned from him that he had to go to the Museum[73] and
remain there until two o'clock, I went with him to see
the famous collection which does such honor to the English nation. I made the acquaintance of Dr. Maty,[74] of
whom I later had reason to think highly. I will speak of
him when the time comes. At two o'clock we went to
dinner, and Martinelli proved to be an excellent companion, for he instructed me in the customs of the country I was visiting, to which I must conform if I wanted
to live well there. *Dum fueris Romae, Romano vivito
more* ("When in Rome, do as the Romans do").[75]

I told him of my blunder in paying in gold what I
should politely have paid in paper, and after laughing
at it a little, he showed me that it was not only evidence
of the prosperity and wealth of the nation, which gave
its paper the preference over gold, but also a proof of
its blind confidence in its Bank,[76] in which it was convinced that there was all the real value of all the notes
which circulated in the three kingdoms.[77] This preference
for paper over gold was also remarkable because of the
advantage of five pounds in a hundred which the guinea

had over the pound sterling and which the English dis-
regarded. You owe someone a hundred guineas and you
pay him a hundred pounds sterling in paper; he says
nothing, though he is the loser by it, and he thanks you.
By this policy the English nation has doubled its legal
tender. All the wealth it possesses in cash serves it to
carry on external commerce, and it carries on internal
commerce with the tokens which represent the same real
wealth.[78]

After dinner I went with Martinelli to the play at the
Drury Lane Theater. At the beginning of the performance the groundlings in the pit, seeing that they had
been cheated because the promised play was not being
given, raised a row; Garrick,[79] the celebrated actor who
was buried twenty years later[80] in Westminster Abbey,
came forward and tried in vain to talk to the groundlings
and calm them, he was howled down, he had to withdraw,
and the raging mob shouted "Every man for himself!"
and at that I saw the King, the Queen, and everyone else
leave their boxes, make their way out, and abandon the
theater to the rage of the angry populace, which carried
out its purpose amid laughter. In less than an hour everything but the walls was torn down. After this accomplishment the democratic animals all went to get drunk on
spirits at the taverns. In two or three weeks the whole
auditorium was rebuilt, and bills were put up announcing the first performance. When the curtain rose Garrick
appeared to beg the indulgence of the public; but just
as he was beginning his apology a voice from the pit
shouted "On your knees!" and the cry, repeated by a
hundred mouths, forced the Roscius[81] of England to
kneel. There was a burst of applause, and it was all over.
Such is the populace of London, which mocks the King,
the Queen, and all the Princes when they appear in
public; so they very seldom let themselves be seen.

Four or five days after making the acquaintance of
Sir Augustus Hervey, I came upon him in the Green

Garrick, Aickin, and Bransby in Lethe,
a Farce by Garrick

Augustus Hervey Taking Leave of His Family

Park,[82] just as he had finished speaking with someone.

"Who," I asked him, "is that gentleman?"

"He is the brother of Lord Ferrers,[83] who was executed by the common hangman two months ago for killing his valet."

"And you speak to him? Is he not dishonored?"

"Dishonored for that? It would be absurd. Even his brother is not dishonored. He paid with his life for breaking the law, he owes nothing. He is a gentleman who played high. I know of no penalty in our constitution which dishonors. It would be tyrannical. I can calmly break any law, provided that I am ready to submit to the penalty enjoined for breaking it. It is a trifle mad, I admit, but it is my privilege. Dishonor would attach only to a criminal who, to avoid the penalty due for his crime, should have done cowardly or base things unworthy of a gentleman."

"For example?"

"Persuading the King to grant him mercy, asking pardon of the people, any number of things."

"Running away?"

"No, for escaping is a brave act. Observe that, to run away, a brave man needs nothing but his own faculties, whether moral or physical: he fights against death, which he risks by escaping: *Vir fugiens denuo pugnabit* ['The man who runs away will fight again']." [84]

"Then what do you think of highway robbers?"

"They are vermin whom I detest, for they inconvenience society; but at the same time I pity them when I think that their trade keeps the scaffold always before their eyes. You leave London by yourself in a hackney carriage to visit a friend who lives in a village two or three miles away. Halfway there, an agile man jumps on the step of your carriage and demands your purse, holding a pistol to your chest. What do you do then?"

"If I have a pistol I kill him, and if not I give him my purse, calling him a base assassin."

"You would do wrong. If you kill him the law will sentence you to death, for you have not the right to dispose of an Englishman's life; and if you call him a base assassin he will answer that he is not, for he does not attack you from behind, and, by attacking you from the front, he offers you the choice. It is honorable in him, for he could kill you. You can, as you give him the purse he demands, reproach him for living by a vile trade, and he will admit it. He will tell you that he will hold off the gallows as long as he can, but that he knows it is inevitable. He will thank you afterward, and he will advise you never to drive out of London except with an armed servant on horseback, for then a needy robber will not dare to attack you. We English, who know that these vermin exist in our country, travel with two purses, a small one to give to the robbers we may encounter and another with the money we need."

What was I to reply to this discourse? I thought it reasonable. The island called England is a sea in which there are sandbanks, those who navigate it must voyage with due caution. Sir Augustus's lesson pleased me greatly.

Passing from subject to subject, he pitied the fate of the thief who, after stealing seventy thousand pounds sterling on the rise and fall of stocks, and fleeing to France where he thought he was safe, had nevertheless been recently hanged in London.[85]

"A year ago," he said, "the King demanded him from the Duke of Nivernais,[86] the Ambassador of Louis XV, among the conditions of the peace. The Duke, who is witty, answered the Minister[87] that his master would have no objection to ridding France of a thief by restoring him to his country; and in due course he was sent to us, and the nation, delighted to see a compatriot who had dared to cheat it brought to the gallows, was greatly obliged to the acumen of Lord Halifax,[88] who made our neighbors buy peace at the price of a condition so humiliating to them, for they violated the law of nations in respect to the wretch.''

''And so seventy thousand pounds were recovered?''

''Not a penny.''

''How was that?''

''Because what he stole was not found in his possession. Apparently he left the little treasure in the hands of his wife,[89] who lives in great comfort and who, pretty and rich enough, can marry again very advantageously.''

''I am amazed that she has been let alone.''

''What could be done to her? You can understand that she would never have admitted that her late husband had left the money with her. There was not even any thought of making a search to recover the amount. The law against thieves orders them hanged; it says nothing about the stolen property, for it supposes that it has disappeared. Then too, if a distinction were made between thieves who restored what they stole and those who did not restore it, there would have to be two laws and two different penalties, and you see what confusion would follow. In any case it seems to me that two penalties should not be inflicted for the same crime; the penalty of the gallows suffices without adding to it the restitution of the stolen property, if it is not liquid and in a condition to be claimed by the person who owned it before the theft, for afterward the thing stolen no longer belongs to him; it is the thief who has become the owner of it, by violence it is true, but that does not keep him from being really the owner of it, for he can dispose of it. Such being the case, everyone must take great care to keep what is his, for once it has been stolen from him, he sees that restitution is too difficult. I took Havana from Spain, a great theft executed by superior force, and it was given back[90] because I could not put the island of Cuba in my purse, as I did forty million piasters,[91] which were never even mentioned.''

After being treated to several specimens of equally

sublime doctrine, I went with him to the Duchess of
Northumberland's, where I made the acquaintance of
Lady Rochefort,[92] whose husband had just been appointed Ambassador to Spain.[93] The lady was one of
three whose notorious gallantries daily supplied the busy-
bodies of the great city with agreeable stories. The
Duchess told me that she looked for her son to return
every day.

On the day before the assembly at Soho Square Martinelli dined with me, and the subject having come up,
he talked to me of Mrs. Cornelys and of the debts with
which she was burdened, because of which she was reduced to not daring to go out of her house except on
Sundays, on which day debtors could not be arrested.
The enormous expenditures in which she indulged, and
which were not necessary, put her in straits which must
soon reduce her to the last extremity. She owed, he told
me, four times as much as she possessed, even counting
in her house, of which a lawsuit in progress made her
ownership doubtful.

CHAPTER VIII

Mrs. Cornelys's assembly. Adventure at Rane-
lagh House. Disgust with English courtesans.
The Portuguese Pauline.

I GO to Mrs. Cornelys's assembly, giving my ticket
at the door to her secretary, who writes down my name.
I see her, and she congratulates me on having been admitted to the assembly by ticket, saying that she had
been sure she would see me there. Lady Harrington
arrives; she was one of her great patrons; she tells her
that she has a good number of guineas to give to her,
and, seeing me in conversation with her, she adds that
she had imagined we were acquainted but had not ventured to mention it to me.

"Why, My Lady? I consider it an honor that I have
long known Mrs. Cornelys."

"I believe it," she said with a laugh, "and I congratulate you. You must certainly know this charming
girl too."

With that she takes Sophie in her arms, kisses her,
and tells me that if I love myself I ought to love her
too, because she has exactly my countenance. She takes
her by the hand, and she leads her into the crowd, taking

my arm. It was then that I had to listen patiently to
innumerable questions put to Lady Harrington by
women and men who had not yet seen me.

"Is this not Mrs. Cornelys's husband, just arrived?"

"No, no, no," Lady Harrington said to all the busy-
bodies; and I was bored for, to compliment me, everyone said that no child had ever resembled its father as
the little Cornelys resembled me, and I asked her to let
the child go; but she was too much amused to do me
the favor.

"Stay with me," she said, "if you want to meet everyone."

And she sat down, making me sit at her side and keeping the little girl standing in front of her. The mother
comes to pay court to the lady, and, having to answer
the question if I am her husband, she makes up her
mind and says that I am only an old friend and that
everyone has good reason to be surprised at the great
resemblance between her daughter and me. Everyone
laughs and replies that it is not surprising at all; and
Mrs. Cornelys, to change the subject, says that the child
has learned to dance the minuet to perfection.

"We shall see," said Lady Harrington; "send for a
fiddler."

Since we were in a side room and the ball had not yet
begun, a fiddler comes; wishing the child to do herself
honor, I take her out, and the minuet succeeds in earning great applause from the onlookers. The ball began,
and continued until dawn without a break, for people
went to eat in the side rooms in groups at all hours.
I met all the nobility and all the royal family, for they
were all there except the King, the Queen, and the
Princess of Wales. Mrs. Cornelys had taken in more than
twelve hundred guineas, but her expenditure was enormous too, with no attempt to economize and no measures
to prevent theft of every kind. Mrs. Cornelys exhausted
herself presenting her son to everyone, while he stood
like a victim, not knowing what to say and doing nothing

but make low bows, which, delivered to all and sundry, and in England, became the height of awkwardness. I felt sorry for him. In this role of an underling, which he was playing for the first time in his life, he was the most embarrassed youth on earth.

Taken home, I slept all that day, and the next day went to dine at the "Star" Tavern,[1] where I had been told that the prettiest and choicest girls in London were to be found. I had heard this at the reception of a certain Lord Pembroke[2] in Soho Square, who had told me that he went there very often. I enter the tavern, I ask a waiter for a private room. The host, observing that I do not speak English, addresses me in French, sits down with me, orders what I want, and I am so surprised by his polite, grave, and solemn manner that I cannot pluck up courage to tell him that I want to dine with a pretty English girl. I finally tell him in a roundabout way that I do not know if Lord Pembroke has deceived me in saying that I could have the prettiest girls in London there.

"No, Monsieur, he did not deceive you, and if that is what you want you can have as many as you please."

He calls "Waiter,"[3] whereupon a neat young man appears, whom he orders to send a girl for my service, as if he were ordering him to bring me paper and ink. The waiter leaves, and ten minutes later in comes a girl, whose appearance I dislike. I tell the host plainly that she does not please me.

"Give a shilling for the chairmen, and send her away. No one stands on ceremony in London, Monsieur."

I order the shilling given, and I ask for another girl, but a pretty one. The second arrives, worse than the first. I send her away. I also send away the third, the fourth, the fifth, and so on up to the tenth, delighted to see that, far from displeasing the host, my fastidiousness amuses him. I say I want no more girls, I want to dine; but I tell him I am sure the waiter had been making game of me to please the chairmen.

"That may be so, Monsieur; they always do it when they are not told the name and address of the girl who is wanted."

Toward nightfall I go to St. James's Park, I see that it is a day for Ranelagh House;[4] I was curious to see the place, it was far away, I take a carriage, and, alone without a servant, I go there to amuse myself until midnight and to try to make the acquaintance of some pretty girl. The Ranelagh Rotunda pleases me greatly, I eat bread and butter and drink tea, I dance a minuet or two, but make no acquaintances. I see very pretty girls and women, but I dare not make direct advances to any of them. Bored, I decide to leave about midnight, and I go to the door, thinking I shall find my hackney carriage, for I had not paid for it; but it was gone; there I was, cursing in vain; no one could find the carriage I was asking for, and I did not see how I was to get home. A pretty woman who saw the straits I was in and who had been there five or six minutes waiting for her carriage said to me in French that if I lived not far from Whitehall[5] she could take me to my door. I told her where I lived; her carriage arrives; one of her lackeys opens the door, we get in, and she orders her coachman to drive to my house in Pall Mall.

In the carriage, which was very comfortable, I profusely express my gratitude, I tell her my name, I say I am surprised that I had not made her acquaintance at the assembly in Soho. She tells me that she has arrived from Bath[6] that day; I pronounce myself fortunate, I kiss her hands, then her pretty face, then her beautiful bosom, and finding, instead of resistance, only the sweetest yieldingness and the laughter of love, I have no more doubts, and I give her the greatest proof that I find her perfectly to my taste. Making bold to suppose, from the ease with which she had let me have my way, that she had not found me displeasing, I beg her to tell me where I may go to pay my most assiduous court to her during all the time I shall spend in London, and she replies that

we shall meet again. I do not urge her, and in no time
I am back at my house, very well pleased with the adventure. I had spent two weeks without seeing her anywhere, when I found her at last in a house to which Lady
Harrington had told me to go and introduce myself,
giving her name; it was the house of the elderly but
illustrious Lady Betty Germaine.[7] She was not at home,
but she was to return in a few minutes. I see the beauty
who had brought me home from Ranelagh, busy reading
a newspaper; it occurs to me to ask her to introduce me.
So I go to her, she interrupts her reading, hears me out,
and politely replies that she cannot introduce me since
she does not know me.

"I told you my name, Madame. Do you not remember
me?"

"I remember you perfectly; but such escapades are
no ground for claiming acquaintance."

So strange an answer left me dumfounded. She went
on quietly reading her newspaper; Lady Betty Germaine
arrived. For two hours the philosophical beauty amused
herself talking to others, showing not the slightest sign
of being acquainted with me, but answering me politely
when the conversation gave me an opportunity to address
her. She was a noblewoman whose reputation in London
was of the highest.

One morning at Martinelli's, on whom I had never
called before, I asked him who a wench was who kept
kissing her hand to me from a window on the opposite
side of the street; I was surprised when he told me that
she was the dancer Madame Binetti.[8] Less than four
years had passed since, at Stuttgart, she had done me
the great service which my reader may remember; I did
not know that she was in London. I take leave of Martinelli to go to see her all the more eagerly when he tells
me that she is not living with her husband, though he
is to dance with her at the Haymarket Theater.[9]

"I recognized you at once," she said, receiving me.
"I am surprised, my dear doyen, to see you in London."

She called me "doyen" because I was the oldest of all her acquaintances. I said that I had had no idea she was there, and that I could not have seen her dance for I had arrived three days after the opera closed.

"How is it that you are no longer living with your husband?"

"Because he plays, he loses, and he sells everything I own. Then too, a woman of the theater, if she lives with her husband, cannot hope to have a rich lover coming to visit her. Living alone as I do, all my friends can come to see me without fearing anything."

"What should they fear from Binetti? I never thought he was jealous or unduly particular."

"Nor is he. But you must understand that in England there is a law which empowers a husband to have a lover of his wife's arrested if he catches him *in flagrante* with her. He needs only two witnesses. It is enough if he finds him sitting on the bed with her, or in a position which might indicate that he has done something with her which only her husband has a right to do. The law sentences such a lover to pay the husband who claims to have been cuckolded half of what he owns. Several rich Englishmen have been caught in this way, and that is why they do not go to visit married women, especially if they are Italian."

"Then, far from complaining, you should be very glad that he is so accommodating, for, being perfectly free, you can receive whomever you please and grow rich."

"My dear doyen, you do not know the whole of it. As soon as he supposes I have had a present from some man who has come to see me, and of whose visit his spies have informed him, he comes at night in a sedan chair and threatens to turn me out into the street if I do not give him all the money I have. You do not know the base scoundrel."

I gave her my address, asking her to come to dine at my house whenever she pleased, only letting me know the day before. It was another lesson for me on the subject

of going to see women. In England there are very fine
and very good laws, but they are such that they can too
easily be abused. The obligation of jurors to enforce them
to the letter and not otherwise has the result that, since
many of them are not written clearly enough, they are
given an interpretation the very opposite of that which
has usually been placed upon them, and so the judge
finds himself in a quandary. For this reason new laws
and new glosses on the old ones are made in Parliament
every day.

Lord Pembroke, having seen me at the window, came
up to call on me. After being shown over my house and
learning that I had a cook, he congratulated me and said
that there was not a nobleman in London, except those
who always lived there, to whom it would have occurred
to maintain an establishment like mine. He calculated
roughly that, if I wanted to dine and sup with friends,
I would spend three hundred pounds a month. He said
in passing that I ought to keep a pretty girl on the third
or fourth floor, who would cost me very little, and that
since I was a bachelor people who came to know of it
would consider me very sensible.

"Do you keep one in your house, My Lord?"

"No, no, for it is my misfortune that as soon as I have
slept with a woman or a girl I can no longer put up with
her, so I have a new one every day, and without being as
comfortable as you, I spend four times as much as you do.
Observe that I am a bachelor and that I live in London
like a stranger, never eating at home. I am amazed that
you are content to eat alone nearly always, for I know my
fellow countrymen."

"I do not speak English, I like soup, French dishes,
and the best wines; so I cannot put up with your taverns."

He laughed when I told him that at the "Star" Tavern
I had sent away eight or ten girls, and that he had been
the reason for it.

"I did not tell you the names," he said, "of the girls I send for."

"You should have done so."

"But since they did not know you they would not have come, for they are at the disposal neither of the chairmen nor the waiters. Promise me that you will pay them as I do, and I will sign you notes with their names at once. When they see my name you shall have them, I assure you, even here if you wish."

"Here, by all means, I like that much better. Write me the notes at once and set the price, giving the preference to girls who speak French."

"That's a pity, for the prettiest ones speak only English."

However, after thinking for some time, he wrote five or six addresses and signed them with his name. I copied all the girls' names on a separate sheet, setting down the money I was to give them for spending the night or three or four hours with me. It was four guineas or six and, in the case of one of them, twelve.

"Then she's twice as pretty as the others?"

"That's not the reason; it's because she cuckolds a Duke, a peer of Great Britain, who gives her plenty of money but who touches her only once or twice a month."

I asked him if he would someday do me the honor of tasting my cook's fare, and he said he would, but taking potluck.

"And if you do not find me at home?"

"I'll go to a tavern."

Having nothing to do that day, I sent Jarba with one of His Lordship's notes to one of the two girls whom he had rated at four louis,[10] instructing him to tell her that it was for dinner alone with me, and she came. Despite my wanting to find her attractive, she pleased me only enough for a little toying after dinner. When she saw four guineas she left well satisfied. The second girl at four guineas supped with me the next day. She had been very pretty; but I found her gloomy and too meek; I could not bring myself to make her undress. On the third day at Covent Garden I saw an attractive girl, I addressed her in French, and I was delighted to hear her answer; I asked her if she would sup with me, and she asked me what present I would give her.

"I will give you three guineas."

"That will do."

At the end of the play we sup there, I find her charming, I ask her address, and I find that she is one of the three whom His Lordship had rated at six louis. Her name was Kennedy.[11] The other two were sisters; their name was Garrick; they pleased me only briefly. I kept the last, the twelve-guinea one, to crown the feast, and I did not find myself inclined to cuckold the Peer.

The next day I went to see him[12] early, telling him the whole story of the six sultanas whose acquaintance he had procured me.

"I am delighted that Kennedy pleased you, and that she does not know that I gave you her name. I have learned what your taste is. She was the favorite of Berlendis,[13] Secretary to the Venetian Ambassadors. I was able to sleep with her only once."

This Lord Pembroke was young, handsome, rich, and full of wit. He got out of bed, and wanting to take a walk, told his valet to shave him.

"I do not," I said, "see a sign of a beard."

"You will never see one on my face, for I am shaved three times a day."

"How do you manage three?"

"When I change my shirt I wash my hands, and when I wash my hands I wash my face too, and a man's face is washed with a razor."

"At what hours do you perform these three ablutions?"

"When I get up; when I come home to go out to dinner or the opera; and when I go to bed, for the girl who is with me must not find my face unpleasant because of a beard."

I praised his fastidiousness. I noticed that his valet really only drew the razor over his skin, which took less than a minute. I left him, as I had some writing to do. He asked me if I was dining at home, and I said that I was. I thought that he might come; and I guessed right. I instructed my cook to do himself honor, but not to let it appear that it was because I expected anyone.

La Binetti knocked at noon, and, delighted to find me at home, came into my room, saying that she had come to take potluck with me.

"You have done me a great favor, for it bores me always to be alone."

"This time my husband will torture himself and still not guess where I have dined."

The woman still pleased me. She was then thirty-five years of age; but no one would suppose her more than twenty-two or twenty-three. Her whole person had powerful charms, and her fine teeth and splendid lips forced the critical to admit that her mouth was not too large; in addition she had a playfulness which delighted everyone.

At half past one Lord Pembroke enters my room, and he and La Binetti utter simultaneous cries of surprise. I learn from His Lordship that he has been in love with her for six months, that he has written her ardent letters, and that she had always scorned him; and I learn from her that she would never listen to him because he was the most dissolute nobleman in all England, and that it was a pity because he was also the most amiable. The kisses which followed these explanations showed the contentment of the two parties. Praises were bestowed on chance, whose sacred minister I was declared to be, and we sat down at table, where we enjoyed exquisite dishes, both English and French. His Lordship swore that he had nowhere dined as well all that year, and condoled with me for not having company every day. La Binetti was as much of a trencherman and an epicure as His Lordship, and, after sitting at table two hours, we rose in high spirits and with a great desire to make love; but

La Binetti was too well versed in the great game to be weak with the Englishman: countless kisses, but nothing more.

Busying myself over books which I had bought, I let them talk together privately as much as they pleased, and to prevent them from asking me to invite them to dinner together another day, I said that I hoped chance would often grant me such favors. At six o'clock La Binetti had herself carried to the Park,[14] from where she would go home on foot, His Lordship went home to dress, and I went to Vauxhall,[15] where I found Monsieur Malignan, the French officer to whom I had opened my purse at Aix-la-Chapelle.[16] He told me he had something to say to me, and I gave him my address. I found there a man too well known, the Chevalier Goudar[17] by name, who talked to me at some length about gaming and girls; and Malignan introduced to me, as a man of rare parts who could be very useful to me in London, a person some forty years of age, with a Greek countenance, under the name of Mr. Frederick,[18] son of the late Theodore,[19] self-styled King of Corsica, who fourteen years earlier had died destitute in London after coming out of prison, to which he had been confined six or seven years for debt. I should have done better not to go to Vauxhall that day.

To enter the enclosure named Vauxhall one paid only half [20] what one paid at Ranelagh House; but the pleasures to be had there were great. Good food, music, strolls in dark walks where the bacchantes were to be found, and strolls in lantern-hung walks where one saw the most famous beauties in London, from the highest rank to the lowest, side by side.

Amid so many pleasures I was bored because I did not have a dear mistress in my bed and at my table, and I had already been in London for five weeks. My house was the perfect place to keep a mistress in discreetly and comfortably; Lord Pembroke was right: possessing the virtue of constancy, I needed only that to make me happy. But how was I to find in London the girl exactly to my taste

and of a character like that of one of the women I had
so greatly loved? In London I had already seen fifty
girls whom everyone thought pretty, and I had found
not one among them who had completely won me over.
I thought of it continually. A strange idea came to me,
and I acted upon it.

I went to talk to the old woman who was the caretaker
of my house, and, with the maid whom I paid for the purpose acting as my interpreter, I told her that I wanted to
rent the third and fourth floors of my house in order to
have company, and that, though I had the right to do so,
I would make her a present of half a guinea a week. So I
told her to put up a notice at my door in the following
terms, which I wrote out for her on the spot:

*"Third-floor or fourth-floor furnished apartment to be
let cheaply to a young lady alone and her own mistress
who speaks English and French and who will receive no
visitors either by day or by night."*

The old Englishwoman, who had sown her wild oats,
laughed so hard when my maid explained the notice to
her in English that I thought she would die of coughing.

"Why do you laugh so hard, my good woman?"

"I laugh because your notice couldn't be better calculated to make people laugh."

"Then you think no one will come to rent the apartment?"

"On the contrary, I'll have girls coming all day to
see what it means. I'll leave it to Fanny to get rid of
them. Just tell me how much I am to ask per week."

"I will settle the price myself in conversation with
the young lady. Think again, and you'll see that there
won't be so many girls, because I want her to be young,
speaking English and French, and, what is more, respectable, for she is absolutely forbidden to receive visits,
even from her father and mother."

"But there will still be a great crowd gathered at our
door to read the notice."

"So much the better."

The notice was put up the next day and, as the old woman had said, I saw that all the passers-by read it and reread it two or three times, then walked on, smiling. The first two days no one inquired; but on the third day Jarba came to tell me that the strange notice was announced in the *St. James's Chronicle*,[21] in a piece in which the writer made a very witty commentary on it. I told him to bring me a translation of it. The commentator said that the apartment on the second floor of the house with the notice must be occupied by the tenant of the third and fourth floors, who thus sought to procure himself an agreeable companion, sure of being alone in virtue of the condition which was part of the contract. He said that he ran the risk of being the victim of it, for he might find a very pretty girl who, having obtained the apartment cheaply, would use it only to sleep in, or even to go to only once or twice a week, and who might even refuse to receive the landlord if he took it into his head to pay her a visit.

This well-argued commentary pleased me, for it armed me against surprises. That is why the English newspapers are engaging; they chatter about everything that happens in London and they have the art of making trifles interesting.

Lord Pembroke was the first to come and laugh with me over my notice; then Martinelli came to tell me that my notice might be my undoing, for in London there were girls intelligent enough to come on purpose to turn my head.

A full account of all the girls who came for a week or ten days to see the two apartments, and to whom I refused them on various pretexts, is not worth writing. It goes without saying that I found all those whom I dismissed unprepossessing; I saw old women who said they were young, hussies, trollops, saucy wenches, until finally, one day when I was at table, I saw appear before me a girl between twenty-two and twenty-four years of age, tall, simply but neatly dressed, with a noble and serious countenance, beautiful in every way, with black hair and a pale complexion. She enters, making me a very humble curtsy which forces me to rise; she asks me to remain seated and, to oblige me to do so, accepts a chair. I offer her sweetmeats, for she had already impressed me, and she very modestly refuses.

She tells me, not in the French in which she had begun, but in the purest Italian it is possible to speak, and without any foreign accent, that she would like to take a room on the fourth floor and that she hoped I would not refuse her, for she thought she was still young and she would have no difficulty in submitting to the other conditions.

"You are free to use only one room, but the whole apartment will be yours."

"Though your notice says 'cheap' the whole apartment would still be too dear for me, for I cannot spend more than two shillings a week for lodging."

"That is exactly the price I have set for the whole apartment, and four for the third floor; so you see, Signorina, that the whole apartment is yours. The housemaid will take entire care of your room, you can trust her to get you what food you need, and she will have your linen washed. She will also run errands for you, so that you need not go out to attend to trifles."

"Then I will give my maid notice," she said, "and I am not sorry, for she has been robbing me—no more than pennies, but that is still too much for my means; and I will tell your maid what to buy for me every day in the way of food, which she is never to exceed, giving her tenpence a week for her trouble."

"She will be satisfied. I can even say a word in your favor to my cook's wife, who can supply you with dinner and supper for the same money you would spend sending out for your meals."

"I do not think that is possible, for I am ashamed to tell you what I spend."

"If you spend only twopence a day, I would tell her to give you only twopence' worth. I beg you not to be ashamed of having the uprightness to regulate your expenditure by your resources. I advise you to content yourself with the food you can have from my kitchen, where they are always at a loss for what to do with leftovers; and I promise you I will take no part in it. I will only say a word for you to my cook, and I hope you will not object to my taking an interest in you. Wait a moment, and you will see how naturally the whole thing will be attended to.''

I call Clairmont, and I tell him to send up the maid and the cook's wife.

''Tell me,'' I said to the latter, ''at what price you can give dinner and supper in her room to this young lady, who is not rich and who wants only food to keep her alive.''

''I could feed her very cheaply, for you almost always eat alone and you have enough prepared for four.''

''Very good. In that case I hope you will feed her for what she says she wants to spend.''

''I can spend only fivepence a day.''

''And for fivepence a day she will feed you.''

I told the maid to have the notice removed at once and to do everything necessary in the rooms which she chose to occupy on the fourth floor. As soon as they had left, she told me that she would go out only to hear mass on feast days at the chapel of the Bavarian Minister,[22] and once a month to see the person who gave her three guineas to live on. I replied that she was free to go out without accounting for it to anyone. She ended by asking me never to bring anyone to her apartment, to order the portress never under any circumstances to let anyone go up to see her, and even to say that she did not know her if anyone should come inquiring for her. I assured her that the order would be given, and she left, saying that she would come back at once with her trunk. She stopped at the old woman's quarters to pay her for the week and take a receipt. After she left I told all my household to treat the young lady with all possible deference and

courtesy, for what she had confided to me obliged me
to show her perfect respect. I learn that she had come
and gone in a sedan chair, and it surprises me a little.
The old woman sent me word to beware of a trap.

"What trap? I risk nothing if she is respectable, and if
I fall in love with her, so much the better, it is what I
want. I need only a week to know her inside out. What
name did she give you?"

"Here it is: 'Mistress Pauline.'[23] She came here pale,
and she left red as fire."

Very well pleased to have found such a treasure, I feel
content. I did not need a woman to satisfy my temperament, I needed to love and to find great worth in the
object which interested me, on the score of both beauty
and of qualities of soul; and my budding love gained in
strength if I saw that the conquest would cost me effort.
I relegated the possibility of failure to the category of
impossibilities; I knew that there was not a woman in
the world who could resist constant attentions and all the
assiduities of a man who wants to make her fall in love
with him.[24]

I went to the play; and when I returned to the house
the maid told me that the lady had taken a small back
room which was fit only to lodge a servant; but that she
had managed nevertheless by not unpacking her big
trunk, for there were only a small table, four chairs, and
no chest of drawers. She had supped and drunk water,
and she had asked her to tell the cook's wife that soup
and one dish were enough for her; she had replied that
she must take what she was given and that she, the maid,
would eat what was left over. After that she had sat
down to write, and when she had left her she had locked
her door.

"What does she take in the morning?"

"I asked her that, and she said that she ate only a little
bread."

"You shall tell her tomorrow morning that the custom
of this house is that in the morning the cook makes a

present of breakfast to all the people living in it, whether they want coffee or tea or a plate of soup, and tell her that if she refuses the gift it might displease me; but you are not to tell her that I ordered you to tell her so. Here is a crown[25] for you, which I will give you every week so that you will show her every attention. Before I go to bed I will give you a note to carry up to her tomorrow morning, in which I will ask her to leave the servant's room she is occupying and take one in which she will be more comfortable.''

I wrote to her in such terms that she felt obliged to move into a large room; but she remained at the rear of the house. She told me, too, that she had accepted the breakfast of coffee with milk. Wanting to have her dine and sup with me, I was dressing to pay her a visit and to ask her the favor in a way which would make it impossible for her to refuse, when Clairmont announced that young Cornelys wished to speak with me. I received him, laughing and thanking him for the first visit he had paid me during the six weeks we had been in London.

''Mama would never let me come; I can't stand any more. Read this letter, and you will find something which will surprise you. She herself just wrote it in my presence.''

I open it and I find the following:

''Yesterday a bailiff [26] waited until my door was open, entered my house, and arrested me. I had to follow him, and I am in prison in his house; but if I do not furnish security today, he will take me tonight to the real prison of King's Bench.[27] The security is for two hundred guineas,[28] which I owe for a bill of exchange which has fallen due and which I could not pay. Get me out of here at once, my kind friend, for tomorrow I may have the misfortune to see several other creditors, who will have me committed, and if that happens I am lost. Prevent my ruin and that of my innocent family. As a foreigner you cannot stand surety for me; but you have only to say a word to some householder, and you will find him ready. If you have time to stop in where I am, come, and you shall hear that if I had not signed the bill of exchange I could not have given the ball, for all my silver and china were in pawn. My son has the address of the house in which I am held."

Determined to let her go to ruin, I take a pen and I write her in a few words that I am sorry for her, that I have not time to go to see her, and that I should be ashamed to ask my friends to stand surety in the matter of a bill of exchange which had fallen due and the payment of which could not honestly be refused. I seal the letter, I give it to the youth, who wants to leave me the address of the bailiff's house, which I refuse. He goes away gloomily, with a lackey who was waiting at my door for him.

I tell Clairmont to go up to Mistress Pauline's and ask her if I may come to see her. She sends me word that it is for me to say; I go up, and I find her well lodged, with books and writing materials on a table, and on the chest of drawers clothes which indicated neither poverty nor even straitened circumstances. It is she who begins by saying that she is infinitely grateful for the kindness I show her, and I answer her bluntly that it is I who am in need of her.

"What can I do, Signore, to show you my gratitude?"

"You can put yourself to the trouble, Signora, of honoring me with your company at table whenever I have no guests, for, when I am alone, I eat like a wolf and my health suffers from it. If you do not feel inclined to grant me this favor, you will excuse me for having asked it of you, but the arrangements I have made for you in my house will remain in force despite your refusal."

"I shall have the honor, Signore, of eating with you whenever you are alone and you send to tell me so. The only thing that troubles me is that I am not sure if my company can be of use to you or at least entertain you."

"There is no doubt of that, Signora; I am grateful

to you, and I assure you that you will never repent of having shown me this kindness. I even hope that it will be I who will entertain you. You inspired the most lively interest in me yesterday. We shall dine at one o'clock.''

I did not sit down, I did not look at her books, I did not ask her if she had slept well; the only thing I noticed was that when I entered her room I found her pale and that her cheeks were crimson when I left her.

I went for a walk in the Park, in love with her, and firmly resolved to do everything on earth to make her love me, determined that I would owe nothing to mere compliance. My curiosity to know who she might be was extreme; certainly she could only be Italian; but I had promised myself that I would not importune her with the slightest question—a romantic idea, but one which comes into the mind of a man who is thinking of using all possible means to capture the heart of an unknown object in which he is greatly interested.

As soon as I was back at the house Pauline came down without my having sent her word, and this politeness pleased me; so I thanked her heartily for it; since we had half an hour before us I asked her if she had any cause to complain of her health; and she replied that nature had given her so good a constitution that she had never in her life suffered the slightest indisposition, except at sea, where the waves upset her stomach.

''Then you have traveled by sea?''

''Inevitably, for England is an island.''

''You are right, but I could suppose that you are English.''

''That is true.''

On the table in front of the sofa on which we were sitting there was an open chessboard, and, Pauline toying with the pawns, I asked her if she knew the game.

''I play it, and even well, I am told.''

''And I badly. Let us play. My defeats will amuse you.''

We begin, and at the third move Pauline checkmates
me; my king can neither protect himself from her attack nor withdraw. She smiles. We begin again, and she
checkmates me at the fifth move, and with that she enchants me by laughing heartily. I feed my budding love,
observing how perfect her laughter shows her teeth to
be, how much beauty it adds to her face, how capable
her soul, which could feel such gaiety, must be of happiness. I rejoice to think that I will contribute to it with
all my power. We begin the third game, which Pauline
plays inattentively and which we abandon to go to table;
but scarcely have we sat down before Clairmont announces Miss Cornelys and Madame Raucour.

"Tell them I am at dinner and shall not leave the table
for three hours, so they can take themselves off!"

But a minute later little Sophie, forcing her way upstairs, comes running in and goes down on her knees
before me, bursting into tears and unable to speak, for
her sobs stifled her. Touched by this melancholy tableau,
I take her on my knees, I dry her tears, I soothe her by
saying that I know what she wants and that I will do
whatever she asks. At these words Sophie passes from
gloom to contained joy; she embraces me, calling me her
father, her dear father, she makes me weep; I tell her
that I will see to everything after dinner, and that she
will strengthen my resolve if she will dine with me. At
that Sophie goes to embrace Pauline, who was crying too
without knowing why, and we begin dinner. Sophie asks
me to have dinner served to Madame Raucour, whom her
mother had forbidden to enter my presence.

But everything which Sophie said to me during that
dinner, while Pauline, listening in amazement, never
spoke a word, surprised me. Reasoning as if she were
twenty years of age, she did nothing but condemn her
mother's conduct and call herself unfortunate because
her duty obliged her to submit to her authority and obey
her every order blindly.

"Then you do not love her?"

"How should I love her if she keeps me in fear? I am afraid of her."

"Then what made you cry before dinner?"

"The pity I feel for our whole family. Her telling me that only I could touch your heart, that I was her only hope."

"And you were sure that you would persuade me?"

"I hoped to, remembering what you said to me at The Hague. My mother tells me that I was only three years old then, but I know I was five.[29] It was she who ordered me not to look at you when I spoke to you; but you thwarted her. Everyone tells her that you are certainly my father, and at The Hague she told me so herself; but here she tells me I am Monsieur de Montperny's[30] daughter."

"But, my dear Sophie, your mother does herself wrong and she insults you, since she tries to make you pass for illegitimate whereas you are the legitimate daughter of Pompeati, the dancer, who killed himself in Vienna and who, when you were born, was living with her."

"Then if I am this Pompeati's daughter, you are not my father?"

"Of course not, for you cannot be the daughter of two fathers."

"But how is it that I look so much like you?"

"Simply by chance."

Pauline, who was spellbound by our dialogues, said very little to her; but she constantly kissed her. She asked me if the lady was my wife, and when I replied that she was, she called her "dear Mama," which made her laugh heartily. At dessert I gave her four fifty-pound bank notes, saying that she could give them to her mother but that it was to her that I made a present of them.

"With that amount, my dear Sophie, your mother can sleep in her own room tonight."

"Write her that it is to me that you give them, for I should not dare tell her so myself."

"My dear child, I cannot write her that, for it would be to triumph over her in her affliction. Can you understand that?"

"Yes, very well."

"You may tell her that she will be doing me a great favor as often as she sends you to dine or sup with me."

"Oh, write that, please! Dear Mama," she said, looking at Pauline, "ask my papa to write that, and I will dine with you very often."

At that Pauline, laughing unrestrainedly and addressing me as "husband," gravely asked me to write the words on a slip of paper, for they could only show her mother that I loved Sophie, and increase the esteem she ought to feel for her, and I complied. Sophie left with joy in her soul, after covering us with kisses.

"It has been a long time since I laughed so much," Pauline said to me, "and I don't think I ever had a pleasanter dinner in my life. The girl is a rare jewel, and the poor little thing is unhappy. She would not be so if I were her mother."

I then told her who she was, and the reasons I had for showing her mother that I despised her.

"I laugh to think of her telling her that she found you at table with your wife."

"She will not believe it, for she knows too well that marriage is a sacrament which I detest."

"Why?"

"Because it is the tomb of love."

"Not always."

Pauline sighed, lowering her beautiful eyes and changing the subject. Her asking me if I expected to stay long in London, to which I replied that I expected to stay there nine or ten months, justified me, I thought, in asking her the same question, and she replied that she had no idea, for her return to her country depended on a letter.

"May I ask you what your country is?"

"I foresee that I shall have no secrets from you if you

show any interest in them; but please let us allow a few days to pass. I only began to know you today, and in a way which entitles you to my respect.''

''I shall be most flattered if I can win your esteem; but as for respect I am not too fond of it, for it excludes friendship. I aspire to yours, and I warn you that I will try to trap you into according it to me.''

''I think you are too clever at that, and I beg you to spare me. The great friendship which I might conceive for you would make me unhappy when we part, a thing which may happen any day and which I cannot but desire.''

We finished our game, and after it she asked my permission to go up to her room. I should gladly have spent the whole day with her, for I had known very few women with a manner so sweet and gentle. I spent the rest of the day at La Binetti's, who at once asked me for news of Lord Pembroke. She was angry.

''He is a horrible man,'' she said, ''who wants a new woman every day. What do you think of that?''

''I envy him his luck in being able to obtain one.''

''He gets them because women are fools. He caught me because he took me by surprise at your house. Otherwise he would never have had me. You laugh?''

''I laugh because he has had you; you have had him too, so the score is even.''

''It is not even, you don't know what you're talking about.''

At eight o'clock I went home, and Pauline came down at once. The maid was obeying her order by notifying her immediately. ''If Pauline,'' I said to myself, ''has planned to make me fall in love by showing me attentions, we are of the same mind and the thing is done.'' We sat down at table at nine o'clock and stayed there until midnight. I told her amusing stories. When she left she said I made her too forgetful of her misfortunes.

Lord Pembroke came to take breakfast the next morning and to congratulate me on the removal of my notice.

He confessed that he was curious to meet my tenant;
but I said it was impossible because she was of a solitary
disposition and only put up with me because she could
not do otherwise. He did not insist. I told him that
La Binetti loathed him for his inconstancy, and it made
him laugh.

"Shall you dine at home today?"

"No, My Lord."

"I understand."

Martinelli came to amuse me by reading me in Italian
three or four notices like mine which appeared in an
Advertiser published in the City. They were humorous
parodies of mine. One said that there was an empty
apartment suitable for a young and pretty lady who was
leaving her husband because he objected to her having
cuckolded him on the day after their wedding; it named
the house in which the apartment was located, and said
that the fugitive would pay only six shillings a week, but
for that amount she would have board and the master of
the house to sleep with her every night. The other notices
were in the same style and all of them indecent. The
freedom of the press is greatly abused in London. Martinelli politely did not mention my tenant. It was Sunday; I asked him to take me to mass at the Bavarian
Envoy's. I thought I should see Pauline there, but I did
not see her. She took, as she told me later, a place where
she could not be seen. The church was full of people, and
Martinelli pointed out to me a number of lords and ladies
who were Catholics and did not hide the fact.

One of Mrs. Cornelys's lackeys handed me a letter just
as I was entering my house. She said that she could go
out without fear on holy days, and that she wanted to
come to dinner with me. I told him to wait. I at once went
to Pauline's rooms to ask her if she wanted to dine with
Mrs. Cornelys, and she said that she had no objection,
provided that she did not bring any men with her. So I
wrote her to come without any men. She came with

Sophie, who this time did not hesitate to stay in my arms. Mrs. Cornelys, embarrassed by Pauline's presence, took me aside to express her gratitude, which she did with tears, and to impart to me various chimerical ideas which filled her head, all of them calculated to make her rich in a short time. It was Sophie who enlivened our dinner. I could not help telling Mrs. Cornelys that Pauline was a foreign lady to whom I was renting an apartment.

"Then she's not your wife?" Sophie asked me.

"No, I am not so fortunate; I was joking."

"In that case I want to sleep with her."

"When?"

"When Mama will let me."

"We must see," I said, "if the lady wants you."

"She is sure of me," said Pauline, embracing her.

"Very well, Madame, I will leave her with you; I will send La Raucour to fetch her tomorrow morning."

"Tomorrow at three o'clock will be time enough. She shall dine with us."

At that Sophie went to her mother and gave her countless kisses. The woman had no idea of the pleasure it gives one to inspire love.

After Mrs. Cornelys left, I asked Pauline if she would like to go for an excursion with the little girl and myself, somewhere outside London where no one would see us, and she replied that prudence forbade her to go out with anyone at all; so we spent the whole day at home without being bored in the least. Sophie sang Italian, French, and English airs, in which she would have accompanied herself if she had had a harpsichord. She sang English duets with Pauline, which gave me the greatest pleasure. We supped in the same high spirits, and toward midnight I took them up to the fourth floor, telling Sophie that I would come up to breakfast with her if she would wait for me in bed, for I wanted to see if she was as pretty in bed as when she was dressed, and she promised to wait for me. I did not dare ask Pauline to grant me the same favor. So at eight o'clock I found her already up, though in chamber attire.

Sophie, all smiles, hid under the covers when she saw me appear; but as soon as I threw myself down beside her on the bed and began tickling her she put out her little face, which I covered with kisses, and I took advantage of my paternal rights to see exactly how she was built everywhere and to applaud everything she had, immature as it was. She was very small, but ravishingly built. Pauline saw me give her all these caresses without the least thought of evil, but she was wrong. If she had not been there, the charming Sophie would have had in one way or another to quench the fire which her miniature charms had kindled in her papa.

Very well pleased with her, I told her to get up, and we breakfasted very gaily. I spent the whole morning in this way with the two objects who delighted my heart, and after dinner, La Raucour having come to fetch the little girl, I remained with the grown-up Pauline, who was beginning seriously to set me on fire. So far I had not only not embraced her, I had not even taken her by the hand. Sitting beside her after my daughter left, I took one of her hands, pressing my lips to it, and asking her if she was married. She answered yes.

"Have you," I asked, "experienced the love of a mother?"

"No, but I can well imagine it. I have a husband, who has not yet slept with me."

"Is he in London?"

"No, he is very far from here. Let us not speak of him, I beg you."

"Tell me only if, when I lose you, it will be that you may rejoin him."

"Yes. I assure you, that unless you send me away, I will not leave your house except to leave England, and I will not leave this happy island except to go to be happy myself in my country with the husband I have chosen."

"My charming Pauline, I shall remain here unhappy,

for I love you, and I fear that I will displease you if I give you the fondest proofs of it.''

''Alas, I beg you to control yourself, for I am not my own mistress, either to yield to love, or to resist it if you do not spare me.''

''I will obey you, but I shall languish. How can I be so unhappy when I have the good fortune to please you?''

''I have duties, my dear friend, which I cannot neglect without becoming an object of contempt to myself.''

''I should consider myself the most traitorous, the most horrible of men, the most unworthy to be loved by a woman worthy of love, if I could esteem her less for making me happy by yielding to an inclination which I had myself inspired in her.''

''I am glad of that. Nor do I believe you capable of it; but let us calm ourselves, remembering that we may be obliged to part tomorrow. Admit that our parting would be far more painful. If you do not admit it, it shows that your love is not of the same nature as mine.''

''Of what nature, then, is the love which I have had the happiness to inspire in you?''

''It is such that its consummation seems to me only secondary.''

''Then what is primary?''

''Living together in the most perfect harmony.''

''That is a happiness which I possess, and which you possess. We both enjoy it from morning to night. Why can we not also be indulgent to the secondary, which will take only a few minutes of our time, which will bring our loving souls a peace and a quietude which are necessary to us? Admit, too, that this secondary thing supplies the food which keeps the primary in good health.''

''I admit it, but admit, too, that the same food is most often deadly to it.''

''One cannot believe that, my dear friend, when one loves; and I am in that situation. Can you yourself believe that, having me fond and amorous in your arms, you would love me less afterward?''

"No, I do not believe it; and it is precisely for that reason that I fear to make the moment of our parting intolerable."

"I must yield to your powerful reasoning, my charming Pauline. I should like to see with what you nourish your exalted intelligence. I should like to look at your books. Shall we go upstairs? I shall not go out."

"With pleasure, but you will be baffled."

"How?"

"Let us go."

We go up, I approach her books, and I find that they are all in Portuguese, except Milton in English, Ariosto in Italian, and La Bruyère's *Characters*[31] in French.

"All this, my dear Pauline, gives me a high idea of you; but why this preference for Camoëns[32] and all these other Portuguese writers?"

"Because I am Portuguese."

"You Portuguese? I thought you were Italian. At your age you know five languages, for you must also speak Spanish."

"That goes without saying."

"What an education!"

"I am twenty-two years old, but I knew those languages at eighteen."

"Tell me who you are. Tell me everything."

"Everything, and at once, trusting in you without fear, for if you love me you can do me nothing but good."

"And what are all these manuscript notebooks?"

"My story, which I have written here. Let us sit down."

CHAPTER IX[1]

Pauline's story. My happiness. Her departure.

"I AM the only daughter of the unfortunate Count of X-o,[2] whom Carvalho Oeyras[3] caused to be put to death in prison after the attempt on the King's life[4] which was laid to the Jesuits. I do not know whether my father was guilty or not, but I know that the tyrannical Minister did not dare to have him tried or to confiscate his estates, which are mine but which I can never enjoy except by returning to my country.

"My mother had me brought up in a convent under the care of her sister, who was its Abbess and who gave me all kinds of masters—among others an Italian, a native of Leghorn, a learned man, who in six years taught me everything he considered it right to teach me. I found him chary of answering my questions only when they concerned religion; but I comprehended his reserve. I can assure you that his caution, far from displeasing me, made me value him the more highly, for he not only allowed me to think but furnished me with material for thought.

"After my father's death, I was eighteen years old when my grandfather removed me from the convent, despite my having declared that I should like to stay there until an opportunity to marry should present itself. I was tenderly attached to my aunt, who, after my mother's death, did everything in her power to make me less sensible of my loss. My leaving the convent was the moment which decided the destiny of my whole life; if my will did not enter into it, you see that I have nothing to repent of.

"My grandfather sent me to live with the Marquesa of X-o, his sister-in-law, who let me have half of her town house. I was given a governess who was to be in entire charge of me, an assistant governess, a noble maid in waiting, chamberwomen, and pages, who were all in my service but who were nevertheless under the direct orders of my chief governess. But she was a very honorable woman.

"A year after my entrance into society my grandfather paid me a visit to tell me, my governess being present, that Count *Fl*[5] was asking for my hand for his son, who was to arrive from Madrid at about that time.

" 'What answer did you give him, my dear Papa?'

" 'That the marriage could only be welcome to the whole nobility and obtain the fullest approval of the king[6] and the entire royal family.'

" 'Is it certain that I will please my future husband and that he will please me?'

" 'No one has any doubt of it.'

" 'But I doubt it; so we shall see.'

" 'You will make each other's acquaintance before the thing is settled; but nothing to stop it can arise from that.'

" 'I desire that it may be so and I hope it.'

"After he left I told my governess that I would never consent to give myself to a man whose character I did not know beforehand. She made no answer, and when I urged her to tell me if I was right in thinking as I did, she replied that she would never tell me her opinion on that subject. It was as much as to tell it to me outright. I felt sure that my governess thought as I did. No later than the next day I went to visit my aunt the Abbess, who, after hearing my story, said it was to be hoped that the Count would be pleasing to me and I to him; but that even if we disliked each other there was every likelihood that the marriage would take place, for she had reason to believe that the project came from the Princess of Brazil,[7] who looked with favor on Count *Fl.*

"Thus warned, I went home, determined never to give my consent to any marriage in which I should not find everything to my liking.

"Two weeks later the young Count *Fl* arrived, my grandfather presented him to me together with his father at a reception at which several ladies were present. Nothing was said of the marriage; but the newcomer was led into talking at length of foreign countries and the manners of other European nations. I listened to it all most attentively, scarcely ever opening my lips. Having very little experience of the world, I had no standards of comparison by which to judge my would-be future husband; but it seemed to me impossible that the man could aspire to please a woman, and that a day would come on which I should belong to him. He was unabashedly derisive, stupid and bigoted to the point of superstition, ugly and ill built, and nevertheless so conceited that he was not ashamed to give the company a sneering account of the various conquests he had made among ladies in France and Italy.

"I returned home hoping that I had displeased him, and a week of silence confirmed me in my hope; but I was undeceived. It was at my great-aunt's, who had invited me to dinner, that my grandfather, in company with the elder and younger *Fl*, presented the fool to me as my future husband, asking me courteously enough to name the day and hour when I would sign the marriage contract. I replied, none too courteously, that I would

tell him the day and the hour when I had made up my
mind to marry. After coffee I withdrew.

"Some days having gone by since this scene without
my seeing anyone, I was flattering myself that I should
hear no more of the marriage, when my governess sent
me word that Father So-and-so was in my room and
wished to make his bow to me. I went there at once. He
was the Princess of Brazil's confessor, who, after beating
about the bush for some time, told me that Her Royal
Highness congratulated me on my impending marriage
to Count *Fl.* I replied modestly that the matter was not
settled, for I was not yet thinking of marrying. He replied gaily that at my age I was fortunate enough not to
have to think of anything, so I should leave thinking to
those who loved me and in whose charge I had the good
fortune to be, and that, such being the case, my decision
could be made in a moment.

"My replies to his arguments were only smiles; but,
foreseeing the attack to which I should be subjected, I
the next day went with my governess to see my dear aunt
the Abbess, who could not refuse me her advice in my
distress. Her advice could only apply to my subsequent
conduct, for I began by telling her plainly that I would
never consent to the marriage.

"She replied that the Count had been introduced to
her, and that she had really found him intolerable, but
that she feared a way would be found to force me.

"This announcement upset me so much that, not having the strength to reply, I spoke of entirely different
things until the end of my visit. But back at the house I
came to the most unlikely of decisions without consulting
anyone. My governess refusing to have anything to do
with it, I was left with no one around me but idiots.

"I shut myself up in my study, and in a short letter I
communicated my entire situation to my father's executioner, the pitiless Oeyras. I ended it by begging him to
grant me his protection so that I should obtain such a
measure of the King's grace as would save me from all

violence, and from all fear of incurring the disfavor of the Princess of Brazil, in my inalterable resolve not to marry until I chose to do so of my own free will.

"I sent him my letter by a page the next day. Without supposing that the Minister possessed a human heart, I thought I had got to the heart of him. I counted on his pride; I felt certain that, by granting me justice, he would believe he would convince me that he had not been unjust to my father. I was not mistaken.

"On the next day but one a young gentleman came to speak to me on his behalf and, after asking me to hear him privately, told me that I was to reply to all those who urged me to consent to the marriage that I would not consent to it until they should convince me that Her Royal Highness desired it. The Minister asked me to excuse him if, for reasons known to himself, he had not answered me in writing. After speaking these few words the messenger departed, making me a low bow and not waiting for any answer; but you cannot imagine either my surprise at the young man's sudden appearance or the impression he left on my mind.

"What he said to me was more than enough to put me at ease, for the Minister could not have sent me such advice unless he had good reason to assure me that the Princess would no longer concern herself with my marriage; but the thought vanished from my mind the instant the young man left. I followed him with my eyes, completely amazed, and a moment later, amazed by my amazement, I thought I was a fool and I laughed at myself.

"Extraordinary, however, as I thought the impression the young man made on me was, it would have disappeared entirely in a few days, for, having chanced to see him the next week in church, I did not at once recognize him; but later it became powerful. Wherever I went, there I found him, at the theaters, on the promenades, and every time that, coming out of a house at which I had paid a call, I entered my carriage.

"After three or four months, if I happened not to see him in the church to which I had gone I felt uneasy.

"I saw the two Counts *Fl* almost every day at my great-aunt's; but as there was no further question of my marrying, they did not affect me one way or the other. I had forgiven them; but I did not feel happy. The young man, whose name I did not know, appeared before my mind's eye every time I saw my pages, and an indiscreet sigh which escaped me made me blush; I was angry because I guessed the reason for it.

"In this state I entered my chambermaid's room one morning, drawn by the sound of a voice which I did not recognize; I see laces on a table, behind which stood a girl who dropped me a curtsy, and at whom, being at first entirely taken up with the laces, I did not look. When I found no blond lace such as I wanted, the girl said that she would bring me some the next day, and, replying that I should be obliged to her if she would do so, I looked at her. Imagine my surprise when I saw the face of the young man who filled my mind only too often. To doubt it was my only resource. The girl whom I saw there might resemble him; she seemed to me to be taller, and in any case I thought such boldness beyond all likelihood. She left, after gathering up her bundles, without having looked me in the face, which increased my suspicion.

" 'Do you know that girl?' I asked my chambermaid coldly. She replied that she had never seen her before that day. I withdrew.

"Alone and reflecting on the resemblance, I finally ceased to think about it when I came to the conclusion that I was being ridiculous, but I decided to speak to the girl and insist on learning who she was. She might be my young man's sister.

"She did not fail to come back at the same hour with a box full of blond lace, and when I was told of it I did not hesitate to have her shown into my room. Since I spoke to her at once, not without strong emotion, she could not answer without looking at me, after which, convinced that I was not mistaken, I did not have the strength to ask the questions I had ready, for my chambermaid was present. But when, after choosing some pieces of blond lace, I told her to go for the money to pay for them, my astonishment was great when I saw the masquerader drop to his knees before me.

" 'Decide, Senhora,' he said, 'whether I am to live or to die; I am sure that you recognize me.'

" 'Yes, I recognize you, and I can only conclude that you are mad.'

" 'I adore you.'

" 'Rise, for my chambermaid will come back.'

" 'She is in the secret.'

" 'What are you saying!'

"However, he rose, and my maid unabashedly paid him the money. After putting his laces back in the box, he bowed to me and left.

"When he was gone it was only natural that I should talk to my chambermaid, and my duty demanded that I should dismiss her on the spot; but I did not hear that voice of Nature, and so I did not obey the precept which my duty would have dictated to me if I had stopped to consult it.

"Alone in my study, and examining the situation, I saw that it was already too late for me to turn to the police. I ought instantly to have sent word to my governess and had the audacious young man arrested; but my heart had spoken in his favor, and, after that indulgence, punishing my chambermaid would have been absurd. I did nothing; and I tried to believe that she did not know he had told me she was in the secret. I took the course of dissimulation, hoping that I should not see him again and so the whole momentous thing would be as if it had never happened.

"But this hope became nothing less than fear at the end of two weeks which passed without my seeing the young man again in any of the places where chance or his love had brought him into my presence. I felt an

unconquerable curiosity to know at least his name, and
only my chambermaid could tell it to me, for I could
not think of going to inquire of the Count of Oeyras. I
hated her, when, seeing her before me, I imagined that
she might be aware that her crime was known to me, and
that she enjoyed the pain I must suffer from the con-
straint I put upon myself. She might even draw con-
clusions from my silence which would wrong my honor,
and believe that I loved him. Such a suspicion on her
part, which would have outraged me, made me desperate
when I thought that it might exist. As for the foolhardy
young man who had risked incurring my just anger, I
felt that I could only pity him, and, certain that he could
not guess that I loved him, it sufficed me to know that
he must be convinced that I despised him. This certainty
avenged me at the moments when my vanity gained the
upper hand over my love; but it drove me to despair at
other times when, not seeing him again, I thought he
had perhaps resolved to think of me no more and had
already forgotten me. You see that I struggled, and that
as long as the struggle continues, victory always remains
in doubt.

"Any violent state is never permanent, and if nothing
helps it to escape from the oscillation which keeps it in
turmoil, it finally escapes from it by itself to regain
equilibrium.

"Putting on a fichu trimmed with the lace I had
bought from the pretended lace-seller:

" 'What has become,' I said to my sly chambermaid,
'of the girl who sold it to us?'

"Observe that I asked her the question completely
without premeditation. It can only have been my Genius,
whether good or evil, who put it into my mouth.

" 'Apparently fearing,' she replied, 'that Madame
penetrated her disguise, and that her boldness offended
her, she has not dared to reappear.'

" 'Of course I penetrated it; but I am a little surprised, now that I learn that you knew it was a young man.'

" 'I could not fail to know it, since I was acquainted with the person.'

" 'Who is he?'

" 'He is Count *Al*, whom you should have recognized, for you received him four months ago in this very room.'

" 'That is true; and I may even have recognized him; but I should like to know why you lied when I asked you if you knew the girl.'

" 'In order not to embarrass you. I thought you would be displeased to learn that I knew the masquerader.'

" 'It would have been more to my honor if you had supposed the contrary. When you were in your room and I ordered him to leave, saying that he was mad and warning him that you might come back and find him on his knees, he told me that you were in the secret.'

" 'The secret! I considered the thing a joke of no consequence.'

" 'So it is; but on my side I considered it of such consequence that, in order not to dismiss you from my service, I took the course of saying nothing to you, pretending to know nothing.'

" 'I thought the little scene could only make you laugh; and now that I learn that you took it seriously I am really sorry that I can in a way reproach myself with having failed in my duty.'

"This dialogue, in which I saw that my chambermaid was completely justified, set my heart at rest, but did not restore to my mind the peace which it needed. I knew that a certain young Count *Al* was entirely without resources and could hope for nothing but what the Minister's patronage could procure him by giving him employment, and I was not sorry to have learned that this Count *Al* loved me, and the thought that I myself might be the happy instrument of his rise to fortune began to furnish the delightful subject of my daydreams when I was alone. Easily persuading myself that my chamber-maid might be more intelligent than I in considering the young Count's action a prank of no consequence, I con-cluded that I was ridiculous in my excessive scrupulous-ness; but after these rather comforting thoughts another followed which greatly annoyed me, for it was humiliat-ing to me. Count *Al's* resolve not to see me again forced me to attribute to him either a great lack of intelligence or a want of love which I found even more displeasing than his limited ability to reason. If he had been offended by my declaring his behavior that of a madman, he could be neither delicate, nor wise, nor worthy of my fond esteem.

"With my love thus languishing in the cruel uncer-tainty which is often its deathbed, here is what happened to arm it with all the strength needed to make it om-nipotent:

"My chambermaid—without my knowledge, as I learned from her later—wrote to him that he could come to see her disguised in the same way, she being sure that I should not object. He followed her advice, and one fine morning she came into my room laughing and say-ing that the pretended lace-seller was in hers with some trinkets. At this news I laughed too, but forcing myself to do so, for I did not think the thing laughable; but when she asked me if I wanted her to show him in, I assumed a serious manner, asking her if she had gone mad, yet at the same time saying that I would myself go to her room.

"It was that day which saw the momentous negotiation begun. My chambermaid coming and going, we had all the time we needed to open our minds to each other and to make all the declarations we could possibly wish to make. Frankly confessing that I loved him, I sadly made him comprehend that I must forget him, for I could not hope that my relatives would consent to our union. For his part, he told me that his patron the Minister having decided to send him to England as soon as possible, he would certainly die either before he set sail or during the voyage, for without me he could not live, or at least without the hope of one day possessing me. It seemed to me that I could promise him nothing. He asked me if I would permit him to come to see my chambermaid from time to time in the same disguise, whereupon I gave him to understand to what he would expose me and expose himself. He replied that it was enough for him to have nothing to fear on my account, for his visits could never be laid to my door; but I had great reason to fear for him, for disguising himself as he did was a crime. Nevertheless, urging him to be prudent, I assured him that I should always see him with great pleasure.

"Count *Al*, eight inches shorter than I, twenty-two years of age, dressed as a woman, could not be taken for a man by anyone, not even from the tone of his voice or from a certain corpulence. He even has the gestures and manners of our sex, or he easily imitates them. Having very little beard on his chin, when he wants to he takes care that not a trace of it is visible.

"So he continued to visit me two or three times a week for nearly three months, always in my chambermaid's room and always within the bounds of the utmost respect; but even if we had been alone and completely free it would have made no difference; he was too afraid of offending me to attempt anything not consonant with the deference he owed me. But I believe that this restraint on his part as well as on mine was precisely the fuel which the fire of love needed in order to become inextinguishable.

"When we thought of the moment, which could not but come soon, when we should have to part, sadness overwhelmed our minds; but we made no plans, we had no thought of coming to a resolve which would make us happy. Our love itself, bowed down by grief, made us stupid; we flattered ourselves that the cruel moment would never come, or we banished the thought of it; so the moment came, unexpectedly and hence too soon, whether we wanted to arrive at a plan or decide that we would make no plans at all.

"One fine morning my lover, with tears in his eyes, told me the news that the Minister had given him a letter for London addressed to Senhor de Saa,[8] the Portuguese Envoy here, and another, unsealed, addressed to the captain of a frigate[9] which was to arrive from Ferrol,[10] and which, stopping for only a few hours, was to go to England. The Minister ordered the captain to take my lover on board, to treat him with consideration, and to convey him there.

"I instantly conceived the bold plan of going with him, either as his servant or even, without being under the necessity of disguising my sex, as his wife. I saw that my lover was astonished when I imparted my bold plan to him. The excess of his happiness so taxed his faculties that he told me he felt incapable of considering the matter reasonably and that he left me to decide everything. I said that we would discuss it at greater length the next day.

"Seeing the obstacles which I might encounter in leaving my house dressed as a woman, I decided to dress as a man; but since, in the guise of a man, I could play no role but that of my lover's valet, I feared that, in case of need during a sea voyage, I might find myself subjected to fatigues beyond the weakness of my sex. This reflection led me to think of playing the role of master, if the captain did not know Count *Al* personally. But the idea of seeing my lover obliged to perform the duties of my valet being no less distasteful to me, I decided to pass him off as my wife. As soon as we were landed in England we would marry and resume the clothes proper to our true sexes. Our marriage would wipe out the crime of my running away, or of the abduction of which my husband might be accused, and I did not think it within the realm of possibility that the Count of Oeyras would decide to persecute me when I had made the fortune of his protégé. To live until I came into possession of my income, the sale of my diamonds would suffice us. My jewel case was at my disposal.

"My lover either could not or dared not make the least objection the next day when I imparted my extraordinary plan to him. The only insuperable obstacle would have been if the captain of the expected vessel knew him. The risk had to be run. He himself supplied me with the clothes I needed. I was eight inches taller than he.

"I did not see him again until three or four days later, about nightfall. He said that he had received a note from a clerk in the naval office informing him that such-and-such a frigate had arrived from Ferrol and was at anchor in deep water at the mouth of the Tagus[11] so that it should be ready to continue its voyage as soon as the captain, who had left it to carry dispatches to the Prime Minister, had returned on board. The frigate's long-boat[12] was to be at such-and-such a place at midnight, where the captain hoped to find him when he arrived.

"Firm in my resolve as I was, I needed to know no more. He told me the place and the house where he would be waiting for me, and I promised to go there. I shut myself up, pretending to be ill, I put into a small bag what I absolutely needed, together with the jewel case containing all my mother's diamonds, and, dressed as a man, I left my apartment unseen by anyone, and at the end of the hall I went down by a stairway used only by the servants. Even the porter did not see me when I left the house.

"Count *Al*, dressed as a man, fearing that I might lose my way, was waiting for me a hundred paces from my door. He startled me by taking my arm. Together we went to the house where he had left his trunk, which he opened to pack his male attire in it and to take out the women's clothes in which he dressed in less than half an hour. Then, having the man whom he had ordered to carry his trunk and my small bag follow us, he took me to the longboat. We entered it at eleven o'clock. I took from my bag the case containing my small wealth, telling him that I thought it was safer in my pocket.[13] A few minutes after midnight the captain arrived, followed by one of his officers; upon seeing me he said that he had orders from the Minister to show me every consideration, and he was delighted when I introduced my wife, thinking it nothing unusual that the Minister had not informed him that I was taking her on board. In less than an hour we reached the frigate, which was three miles at sea, and anchor was weighed immediately. We were given a very large room, in which there was a wide bed, a folding bed, and a hammock. The captain, after I handed him the letter ordering him to give passage to England to my lover, whom fortunately he had never met, left us. We spent all the rest of the night discussing the great step we had just taken, and when dawn came we were very glad to be out of sight of Lisbon. Needing rest, I threw myself on the folding bed and my lover got into the hammock, without even thinking of undressing. But no sooner had we lain down than the sea began to treat us as it treats all those who are not accustomed to it. During the first twenty-four hours it emptied our stomachs, even trying to bring up what was not in them, and during the next two days we did nothing but sleep and moan; but on the fourth day, tormented by a devouring hunger, we were amazed that we could not satisfy it no matter how much we ate.

"The voyage is a very long one for Europe, since, as you know, it crosses the whole Atlantic,[14] yet we made it in two weeks. My lover having never left his room, the captain never came to pay him a visit; I could attribute it only to politeness, for in our country one can be jealous without fear of being ridiculous. For my part, however, I spent almost all day in the open, amusing myself looking through a spyglass at all the objects which distance did not permit me to distinguish. On the seventh day my heart fluttered when I was told that a vessel which we made out at a moderate distance was a corvette,[15] which, though it had left Lisbon at least a day after we did, would still reach England three days before us.

"We arrived there at dawn, and it was in the port of Plymouth[16] that the frigate dropped anchor.

"The officer whom the captain at once sent ashore to obtain permission to disembark his passengers returned on board toward nightfall, bringing him some packages and letters. After reading one of them more attentively than the rest, he called me aside.

" 'This letter,' he said, 'is from the Count of Oeyras. He orders me, on my life, not to let a young Portuguese lady leave my ship, if she is on board it, unless she is personally known to me. He instructs me to take her back to Lisbon after executing the commissions which will detain me at Cadiz[17] for a few days. On my vessel there are neither unmarried women nor wives, except yours. Prove to me that she is your wife, and I will let you go ashore with her at once; otherwise you must see that I cannot disobey the Minister's order.'

" 'She is my wife, but I have no document to convince you of it.'

" 'That is too bad. She will return to Lisbon with me, respected and well treated, as the Count instructs me; you may be sure of that.'

" 'A wife, sir, cannot be separated from her husband.'

" 'I agree. You are free to return to Lisbon on the corvette; it will be there before her.'

" 'Why can I not return with her?'

" 'Because I am ordered to land you here. Why is your wife not named too in the letter you gave me? If she is not the person whom they want to recover, you can be sure that you will see her again in London.'

" 'Permit me to go and speak with her.'

" 'Certainly, but in my presence.'

"Broken-hearted, I went to tell my lover, addressing him as my wife, by what turn of fate and what cruel order we were condemned to part. He replied, finding the strength to hold back his tears, that we could do nothing but be patient, for we were sure to see each other again in two months at the latest. The captain's presence made it impossible for him to say more. I told him that from London I would at once write to the Abbess, that she was the first person he must see in Lisbon, and that from her he would learn my address. I took good care not to ask him for my jewel case.[18] The captain might have thought it his duty to take custody of it, and the value of the diamonds would have led him to conclude that my pretended wife was a young lady whom I had seduced. We could only surrender to our destiny. Embracing each other, we wept, as the captain did too when he heard me say :

" 'Trust this worthy captain with your honor and mine!'

"The trunk was put into the longboat, and I had to leave my bag behind ; so I found myself with only men's clothes. The customs inspection to which I was subjected showed me all that I possessed : notebooks, letters, books, shirts, two or three coats, a sword, dueling pistols and pocket pistols ; I put the latter in my pockets. I went with my trunk to the inn, where the innkeeper told me at once that if I wanted to leave for London at dawn with two ladies and a clergyman it would cost me only the hire of one horse, and he invited me to sup with these three persons, whose manner showed me that I must not refuse them my company. On their part they found me worthy of theirs. We arrived in this city very early the next day, and got out in the Strand [19] at an inn where, finding myself poorly accommodated, I stayed only for dinner. Afterward I went out to secure a good lodging suitable to the situation in which I found myself. I had a purse containing fifty lisbonines[20] and a ring of about the same value.

"After seeing a number of rooms in different houses I took a fourth-floor one, persuaded by the kind, honest looks of the landlady. Without experience and without recommendations, I could only trust in God and my good intentions, hoping the best from sympathy. The woman pleased me. I at once agreed to ten shillings a week, and I immediately asked her to help me to obtain a perfectly plain girl's wardrobe, no longer daring to go out dressed as I was. No later than the next day my money had bought shifts, dresses, shoes, and all the clothing necessary for a poor girl who wanted neither to dazzle nor to arouse pity nor to follow the path of adventure. Speaking English so well that no one doubted I was an Englishwoman, I knew what demeanor I must maintain to protect myself against all that I had to fear.

"But in less than two weeks I saw that my good landlady's house was not suitable for my purpose, my peace, and my means, for my situation might continue for a long time and, without money, I should have been in the direst misfortune. I determined to leave the house. Since it was for me to say if I would receive visitors, I received none, but I could not prevent the curious from coming to my door all day long, and the more it became known that I received no one, the more of them there were and the more importunate they became. The house in which I was staying was too much frequented. In St. Paul's[21] and near the Exchange as it was, any number of young men came there to eat on the ground floor and the first floor, and they all insisted on trying to cure me of my sadness, though I had no need of it.

"Resolved not to spend more than a guinea a week on the necessaries of life, and having no use for my ring, I decided to sell it, but little by little. An old merchant who lived on the same floor as I, and for whose honesty my landlady vouched, offered me a hundred and fifty guineas for it, and I let him have it on condition that he would pay me the amount at the rate of four guineas a month, and that I could redeem it from him at any time by paying him what he had advanced me. I wanted to keep the cash I had, and which I still have, to return to my country by land when I receive a letter telling me that I can go there with nothing to fear. I do not want to go there by sea. I did not spend much of it for clothing; and I have enough of it left. My ring is worth enough to keep me for three years, and in the year I have already spent here I have received only a third of its value.

"Leaving the house of my kind landlady, who still remains my firm friend, I took a room in a respectable house, once again in the Strand, for the same price, but I was obliged to take a maidservant, for I could never bring myself to eat anywhere but in my room. Having to keep a servant was always a misfortune, for I found none who were not cheats, and you can understand that, wanting to spend only a shilling a day for food, I could not put up with theft. I ate little and, unable to tolerate beer, I drank water. Port wine, excellent in our country, is here expensive and bad. All this abstinence made me lose flesh, I did not know what to do to escape from my wretched situation, when my good angel—if I dare flatter myself it was he—led me to read in an *Advertiser* the strange notice to be seen on your door. After laughing at it, for it was too amusing not to laugh at, I could not resist a wish to go and talk with you. I wanted to see if I could better my condition without increasing my expenditure. Curiosity entered in too, for the *Advertiser* also said that the master of the house was an Italian who apparently did not fear being tricked, and on my side I had no fear of violence, and in that I was mistaken, for there are kinds of violence which it is sweet not to resist. Having been educated by an Italian, I have always felt a great liking for your countrymen."

"Your story, Signora, is one which has interested me very much indeed! You have the intelligence of an angel; and now that I know you are Portuguese I am ready to forgive your countrymen."

"Then you bore us a grudge?"

"I hated you from the time I learned that you allowed

your Vergil to die in poverty[22] two hundred years ago.''

"Camoëns, you mean; but how can you be so fond of him when you do not understand our language?''

"I have read him translated into Latin heroic verse of such beauty that I thought I was reading Vergil.''

"Heavens! What are you saying? This very moment I promise—nay, I make a vow—that I will learn Latin.''

"Excellent—but from me. I will go to live and die in Portugal if you promise me your heart.''

"Why have I not two! Since I have known you I like myself less; I am afraid that I have no constancy.''

"I will be content if you will love me only as if I were your father; but let your father clasp his daughter in his arms sometimes. Please, go on with your story. I still do not know the most essential part of it. What became of your lover? And what did your relatives do when they learned of your flight?''

"On the third day after I arrived in this vast city I wrote a long letter to my aunt the Abbess, in which, in the greatest detail and with perfect truth, I told her all that had happened to me, begging her to protect my fiancé and to support me in my resolve not to return to Lisbon until she could assure me that when I arrived there my marriage would encounter no opposition and that, in possession of my inheritance, I could live openly with my husband. I asked her in the meanwhile to inform me of everything, sending her answers to me, by the name of 'Miss Pauline,' under cover directed to my landlady, whose address I gave her. I sent her my letter by way of Paris and Madrid, for there is no shorter route by land, hence I did not receive her answer until three months later. She informed me that the frigate on which I had left had returned to Lisbon only a week or ten days earlier, and that the captain, having at once sent the Minister word that he had brought back the only woman he had on board, despite the fact that Count *Al* claimed that she was his wife, requested his orders. The Minister, never doubting that the lady was I, ordered the captain, sending him a letter which he was to give the Abbess, to take the lady to her convent and give her into her charge. In the letter the Minister told the Abbess that he was sending her her niece and that he begged her to keep her under safe guard until further order. My aunt was surprised, but she would have been much more so if she had not three or four days earlier received the letter in which I told her my whole story. She thanked the captain, she took her supposed niece into a room in which she locked her up, and she instantly wrote the Count of Oeyras that in accordance with his order she had received into her convent a lady whom His Excellency called her niece, but that since the young lady was neither her niece nor a lady, but a young man dressed as a girl, she could not keep him in her convent. She therefore asked him to send someone to remove him from her custody as soon as possible. After sending the Minister this strange answer, she went to see Count *Al*, who at once fell to his knees before her. My aunt made him rise, telling him that she knew all and showing him my letter. At the same time she told him that, in obedience to her duty, she had just written the Minister that she could not keep a man in her convent, and so he must expect to be taken elsewhere within an hour or two. Thereupon the Count, bursting into tears, begged her good offices in my situation and his own, and gave her my jewel case, which he had kept in his pocket all along and of which the Abbess very gladly took custody. After that she left him, assuring him that she[23] would inform me of everything. She did not see him again, despite the fact that he had to spend part of the night and part of the following day in the room where he was, since the Minister had gone to one of his estates three or four leagues from Lisbon. Not having received her letter until very late, he could not answer her until the next day; but it was an answer which he considered he must deliver in person. The Abbess easily persuaded him of the importance of secrecy in the matter, for violation of the seclusion of her convent entailed the loss of her honor. She gave the proud Minister the letter she had received from me to read, and she told him that my jewel case had been placed in her custody. He replied that she should keep it. He thanked her for the frankness with which she had informed him of everything, and he asked her with a laugh to excuse him if he had sent her a handsome young man to keep her company. After spending a few minutes in thought, he told her that secrecy was of the utmost importance in the matter, and that, such being the case, the masquerader must leave the convent at once and go with him. Since my aunt could not but be of the same opinion, she went for him, took him to the door, showed him to the Minister's carriage, in which he was alone, and made him sit down at his right. She could not tell me what he had done with him, and no one knew anything about it. All Lisbon was curious, for the story was openly told, but with a circumstance which made an essential difference, which she had to let pass, and which must have made the Count of Oeyras laugh. It was, and still is, said in Lisbon that the captain of the frigate delivered me to my aunt by order of the Minister; but that no later than the next day the Minister himself went unaccompanied to remove me from the convent, and that no one knew where he was keeping me. Hence everyone believes that Count *Al* is here in London. Meanwhile it is easy for the Count of Oeyras to remain informed of everything about me, for he knows my name and my address and he has plenty of spies. On the advice of my aunt, I wrote him two months ago that I am ready to return to Lisbon if His Excellency will do me the honor to write me in his own hand that as soon as I arrive in my country Count *Al* will publicly become my husband, with the further condition that no one shall order me to go there, or take me there, even as a friend. Otherwise I declare that I am prepared to spend my whole life in London, where the law guarantees my freedom. I look for the Minister's answer every day.''

This story may seem a romance to those over whom the stamp of truth has no power. Despite the disguised names, a number of highly placed people in Lisbon know who the real actors are; but, being discreet, they will never name them.

So did Pauline and I live, never leaving each other and falling more in love every day precisely because we tried to make our love die of starvation; but it is love which would finally have killed me, for I was growing visibly thinner, I could no longer sleep, and my appetite was failing. Pauline, on the contrary, was putting on flesh and becoming every day more beautiful. I told her that if my sufferings had the virtue of increasing her charms, she ought to keep me from dying, for a dead man has ceased suffering. She convinced me that my decline came not from my love but from the life I was leading, never leaving the house. "If you love me," she said one day, "give me a proof of it. Go out for a ride."

"And afterward?"

"You will find me grateful, and you will eat with appetite and sleep all night."

Quick, a horse, quick, my boots! I kiss her hand, for I had not yet gone further than that, and I set out for Kensington.[24] Finding trotting uncomfortable, I try to make my horse gallop, and he takes the bit in his teeth and, in full career, his four legs slip from under him, and there I am on the pavement directly in front of the Duke of Kingston's[25] house, where Miss Chudleigh at the window recognizes me and sends one of her servants to my rescue. I get up, I want to go to thank her, but I cannot walk on my right foot. I am carried into the drawing room, my boots are pulled off, I am examined, and a valet who is a surgeon announces that it is a sprain with dislocation. He feels the bone, and he declares it pulled out of its socket. He prescribes a week in bed to restore me to health, he puts a great bandage on me, and the charming Miss Chudleigh has me carried home and sends the horse to its owner.

At home, I am put to bed, and a surgeon who lived twenty paces from my house takes off the bandage and laughs at the supposed dislocation. He offers to bet a hundred guineas that it is only a sprain, and he is disappointed.

"For I wish it were a fracture," he says, "so that I could show you who I am."

He was French. I thank him, and I swear to him that I do not need the experiment to be convinced of his skill.

I do not see Pauline. I am told that she has gone out in a sedan chair. I see her come back at last two hours later, very much upset, having learned from the old woman that I had broken a leg.

"Woe to me! I am the cause of it!"

She goes pale, and she falls onto the bed.

"My dear friend, it is nothing. A sprain!"

"The wicked old woman! God be praised! Feel my heart."

"I feel it. Fortunate fall!"

I press my lips to hers, kiss answers kiss,[26] and I bless the sprain. Pauline laughs.

"What are you laughing at?"

"At the rogue Love, who always conquers us."

"Where did you go?"

"I went to redeem my ring, giving the honest man back the forty-eight pounds he had paid me, at the rate of four a month, and I make you a present of it so that you shall have a keepsake to remind you of my friendship. Until I leave, we shall live together as wife and husband, and we will celebrate our nuptials this evening, supping here on your bed, for your sprain and I both forbid you to leave it."

"Ah, my dear Pauline! What news! Permit me to doubt it, I beg you, for being sure of it before it is done would kill me."

"Very well then, doubt it, but only a very little, otherwise your doubt could wrong me. Tired of living with you, loving you and making you unhappy, I made this decision three hours ago, when I saw you mount your horse, and I went to get my ring so that I need not leave your arms again until the fatal letter summoning me to Lisbon arrives. For a week my heart has been in dread of it. No, I want it no more.''

''May the courier who is bringing it be robbed!''

Since she was talking to me standing, I invited her to fall into my arms, but, the door being open, she would not, and to calm me she went to fetch Ariosto, and she insisted on reading me Ricciardetto's adventure with Fiordispina,[27] Princess of Spain, which constitutes the beauty of the twenty-fifth canto of the poem, which I knew by heart. She pretended that she was the Princess and I Ricciardetto, and she delighted in imagining

> *Che il ciel l'abbia concesso*
> *Bradamante cangiata in miglior sesso*

("That heaven had granted her Bradamante, changed into a better sex").[28]

When she came to the stanza which runs

> *Le belle braccia al collo indi mi getta*
> *E dolcemente stringe, e baccia in bocca:*
> *Tu puoi pensar se allora la saetta*
> *Dirizza amor, se in mezzo 'l cor mi tocca*

("Thereupon she throws her lovely arms around my neck and sweetly embraces me and kisses me on the lips; you can imagine if then Love straightens his arrow, if he strikes me in the heart"),[29]

she demanded a gloss on the phrase *baciar in bocca*, and on the love which then stiffened Ricciardetto's arrow. When I gave her the commentary in action, she seemed offended when I surprised her into touching the arrow; but she had to burst out laughing when she came to the two lines:

Io il veggo, io il sento, e a pena vero parmi
Sento in maschio di femmina mutarmi

("I see it, I feel it, and I scarcely think it
true; I feel myself change from a woman to
a man"),[30]

and at two more in the following stanza:

Così le dissi, e feci ch'ella stessa
Trovò con man la veritade espressa

("So I said to her, and I made her
find the truth of it with her own
hand").[31]

She said she was astonished that Rome[32] had not forbidden the poem, in which there were so many "obscenities," but she recanted when I convinced her that only the things which arouse disgust deserve to be called "obscenities." She thought it amusing that Ariosto should have chosen to attribute to a Spanish woman,[33] rather than to one of any other nation, the irregular taste which led her to fall in love with Bradamante. But I thought my turn had come when she read these three lines:

Io senza scale in su la rocca salto
E lo stendardo piantovi di botto
E la nemica mia mi caccio sotto

("Without stairs I mount the rock
and suddenly plant my standard
in it and put my enemy under
me").[34]

I wanted to show her the thing in action then and there, but she said I risked making my sprain worse.

"Then must we wait until I am cured to consummate our marriage?"

"I think so. If I am not mistaken, you cannot avoid making certain movements——"

"You are wrong, my dear; but in any case I will not put it off until tomorrow, you may be sure, even if it costs me a leg. Besides, you will see that there are ways. Are you persuaded? Answer, for your concern makes me uneasy."

"Very well. The wife must obey the husband. I will do whatever you wish."

"When?"

"After supper."

"My dear wife, let us go without supper. We will dine the better tomorrow."

"No. Consider that we must give the servants no reason for suspecting anything."

I assented; but we could not eat, and at ten o'clock we were left to ourselves.

But the charming girl who had had the courage to tell me so clearly that we should become husband and wife after supper did not have the courage to undress in my presence. She could not bring herself to do it; she told me so, laughing at herself.

"But you spent two weeks in the same room with your lover."

"He always stayed in his hammock, with his back to me, when, sitting on my folding bed, I undressed, and it was the same when I dressed in the morning."

"So much virtue is almost beyond belief."

"I think, my friend, that when one has not yet begun it is easier to restrain oneself than to let oneself go. For this first night I will get into bed with you fully dressed."

"Do you want me to dress too?"

"You are cruel. Forgive my weakness."

"But, my angel, do you not see how unworthy of your intelligence this shame is?"

"Let us put out the candles, and in a minute I will come to your arms."

"Quick, let us put them out!"

But despite the drawn curtains a bright moon lit the room enough to let me distinguish the most charming profiles at the favorable distance to which she had with-drawn. The whole maneuver seemed calculated only to make me the more ardent; but Pauline knew that she had no need to use art.

Pauline came to my arms; at first we gathered our forces in a profound silence. Our ardors mingled, and her moans were my assurance that her desires were more intense than those I felt and that her needs were greater than mine. The unavoidable duty of safeguarding her honor made me call a sudden halt and collect in a hand-kerchief the proud tokens of her virtue over which I had just triumphed.

Until that moment love alone had animated me; but after the blood-stained sacrifice I was surprised to find myself filled with respect and gratitude. I strained my powers of expression to convince her that I was sensible of the full extent of my good fortune and that she would always find me ready to expose my life to the plainest risks in order to convince her of my constant affection. After renewing our skirmishes several times, we found ourselves reluctantly unable to conclude the last one, and we fell into a sleep so sound that when we woke we could not believe that we had slept.

Seeing in my arms the greatest of Portuguese beauties, the only descendant of an illustrious family, who had given herself to me and yet who would be mine for only a very short time, I gazed at Pauline, leaning on one elbow and sunk in that sad reflection.

"What are you thinking of, my dear friend?"

"I am trying to convince myself that my happiness is not a dream. If it is real, I want to die before I lose you. I am the fortunate man to whom you have surrendered an inestimable treasure, of which I consider myself un-worthy even though I love you more than myself."

"No, my friend. You are very worthy of it if you can still esteem me, for I have no doubt of your affection."

Moved by the caresses which followed my words, Paul-ine became ardent as soon as she felt that my fire was

renewed, and, letting every beauty which could arouse
my curiosity shine out before my avid eyes, made herself
ready to enjoy my third assault, in the long course of
which I several times saw her in the last extremity of
love. A moment later I ended, showing her those tokens
of my respect of which I had deprived her only in order
to safeguard her honor.

"I swear to you, my friend, that love did not give me
time to think of it. I left it to you, I suppose; but I am
very glad to see that I shall never be tempted to repent
of having surrendered to love's power."

She then got out of bed to dress, laughing because my
presence no longer embarrassed her.

"If the disappearance of shame," she said, "is a result
of acquiring knowledge, tell me why our first parents did
not feel shame until after they had acquired knowledge."

"I have no idea, my angel, but I should like to know
if you put that question to the learned Italian whom you
had as a tutor before you left the convent."

"As a matter of fact, I did."

"What did he answer you?"

"That they were ashamed not of having tasted enjoyment but of having been disobedient. In covering the
parts which had led them astray they thought they re-
pudiated the sin which they had made them commit. But,
whatever people may say, Adam was far more guilty
than Eve." [35]

"How so?"

"Because Adam had received the prohibition from
God himself, while Eve could only have learned of it
from Adam."

"They both received it from God."

"Then you have not read Genesis?"

"You are laughing at me."

"Then you have read it incorrectly, for it says there
clearly that God made Eve after forbidding the thing to
Adam." [36]

"I think it strange that our interpreters do not cite this fact, for it seems to me essential."

"It is because they are rascals, almost all of them enemies of our sex."

"Come now!"

"Let us drop the subject, I beg you; but my tutor was an honest man."

"Was he a Jesuit?"

"Yes, but of the short robe." [37]

"What does that mean?"

"We will discuss it another time."

My dear Pauline was a thinker so attached to her religion that she gave it far more thought than I did. I should never have learned this about her if I had not succeeded in going to bed with her. I have found a great number of women of the same stamp; to enjoy their souls, one must begin by damning them; after that one gains all their confidence, and they have no more secrets from the man who has been fortunate enough to conquer them. For the same reason, that charming sex loves the brave man and loathes the coward, unless sometimes he is a pretty plaything who amuses them but whom at bottom they despise, for if the brave man cudgels him they laugh.

After that heavenly night I decided not to leave my house again so long as Pauline remained in London. My resolve pleased her. I shut my door to everyone, even to the surgeon, for my sprain was disappearing of itself. I had word of it conveyed to the Honorable Miss Chudleigh, who stopped sending a lackey twice a day to inquire after my health.

Pauline having gone up to her room after our amorous battle, she seemed to me an angel incarnate when I saw her again at noon. Her complexion, which a year's abstinence had made too pale, had become tinted with a compound of lilies and roses, and her face had acquired an expression of satisfaction and contentment which my eyes never tired of admiring.

Wanting to have her portrait in miniature, as she wanted to have mine, I wrote Martinelli to send me the most celebrated painter in London for likenesses, and he sent me a Jew,[38] who succeeded perfectly. I later had them set in rings, and it was the only present which Pauline would accept from me, though I should have thought myself all the richer if she had consented to accept everything I owned.

Three weeks passed in this way after our nuptials, every moment of which, always exerting the same influence, made us equally happy. We had become such that we could no longer find the slightest difference between us; it was an unending succession of enjoyments such that we could ask nothing more. Since desires can arise only from needs, we could feel none, for, Nature and Fortune supplying us with everything, there was nothing we could need. Besides, any desire is inseparable from trouble and disquiet, and Pauline and I laughed at the philosophers who would have seen fit to pity us because we had no more desires. It is impossible to have them when one possesses everything, and we possessed everything. It was impossible for us to imagine that we could have been richer or happier, unless we had wished to think of the future; but we did not have time to think of it. This lack of time was the true foundation of our real riches. In a complete satisfaction of our senses, what could have lessened our happiness if we had stopped to examine ourselves strictly? It could have been only our feelings. Our feelings? We should have found our hearts pure.

Every day I found something new and adorable in her admirable character, and she was beginning to flatter herself that the fatal letter which would oblige her to leave would never arrive. She no longer thought of Count *Al* except to make reflections on the physical power of a handsome face, which reason should censure and which chance alone could make effective.

The first day of August was a day of ill omen for her

and for me. For her, who received two letters from Lisbon, and for me because, among others, I received one from Paris giving me the news that Madame d'Urfé was dead.[39] It was Madame du Rumain who wrote me that the doctors declared, on the testimony of her chambermaid Brougnole, that she had poisoned herself by taking too strong a dose of a decoction which she called the "universal medicine." She told me that she had left an insane will, for she bequeathed everything to the first son or daughter she should bear, declaring that she was pregnant. It was I whom she appointed guardian of the infant, which cut me to the quick, for the story must have made all Paris laugh for at least three days. The Countess du Châtelet,[40] her daughter, had laid hands on her rich inheritance in real estate and on her portfolio, in which, to my great surprise, four hundred thousand francs had been found. I was dumfounded; but I contained my grief and my repentance by fixing my attention on the two letters Pauline had received, one from her aunt and the other from the Count of Oeyras, who urged her to return to Lisbon as soon as possible, by sea or land, assuring her that upon her arrival she would be put in possession of all her property and be publicly married to Count *Al.* He sent her a letter of credit at sight for twenty millions. The amount surprised me; however, it came to only about two thousand pounds sterling, for the Portuguese reckon in reis,[41] which is an indivisible coin, like the maravedi[42] in Spain. He advised her to make the journey by sea, and in case she decided to do so, he informed her that Senhor de Saa would arrange for her to embark on a frigate which he named and which should at that time be in some English port. Her aunt the Abbess, whom the Minister had informed, told her the same thing; but Pauline would not hear of the sea or of the Portuguese Envoy Saa, for she did not want to give anyone in Lisbon the slightest justification for saying that she had been forced to return against her will. She was angry that the Minister had sent her the

bill of exchange; for it showed that he thought she was
in need. Nevertheless I convinced her that she ought to
be grateful to him for it, for he did not say that he was
making her a present of it. She would have considered
it an insult. Pauline was rich, and she was high-minded;
the proof is the ring which she had made me accept when
she was practically in poverty, and certainly she did not
count on my purse, though she was sure that I would
never have abandoned her. I always let her believe that
I was very rich.

We spent the whole day sadly, and the night too. It
was not until the next day that she spoke to me as
follows:

"My dear friend, we must part, and what is more we
must make an effort to forget each other, for my honor
demands that in Lisbon I become the wife of a man to
whom everyone cannot but believe that I have already
given myself, and you must feel that as soon as he really
becomes my husband my duty demands that I give him
my undivided heart. I cannot conceive how, otherwise,
I could live happily. But it will not be difficult for me,
once I have seen you for the last time. The first impression, which you have almost blotted out, will regain its
power, and I am sure that I shall love my husband, who
is honest and gentle, as I very well learned during the
few days we lived together.

"After this preamble, my very dear friend, this is
what I must ask of you, and what you must grant me
if only as a favor. You must promise me you will never
come to Lisbon[43] unless I give you permission. I hope
you do not need to have me tell you the reasons which
oblige me to lay this prohibition on you. You must not
risk coming to my country to trouble the peace of my
soul. I could not become criminal without at the same
time becoming unhappy, and you must abhor the idea of
being the cause of it, loving me as you love me, and
knowing me as you know me. Alas, believe me! I imagine
that I have lived with you as your real wife, and as soon

Interior of the Rotunda, Ranelagh

Tender Conversation

as you have left me I shall imagine that I have been widowed and that I am going to Lisbon to contract a second marriage.''

Dissolving in tears and clasping her in my arms, I promised to obey her. She at once replied to the Minister and the Abbess that she would be in Lisbon in October and that she would send them news of her as soon as she was in Spain. Having money enough, she outfitted herself for the journey, she bought a carriage, and she engaged a chambermaid recommended to her by the honest landlady with whom she had lodged at the beginning of her stay in London. In this way she employed the last of the weeks during which she lived with me in London. Claiming it as a return favor, which she could not refuse me, I got her to accept the services of my valet Clairmont, whom I knew to be faithful, as far as Madrid. From Madrid he was, in accordance with my instructions, to rejoin me in London; but his unhappy fate had decreed otherwise for him.

We spent this week in the utmost outward tranquility, and in bitterness of heart and mind. We looked at each other without speaking, we spoke to each other not knowing what we were saying, we forgot to sit down at table to eat, and we went to bed together hoping that love would not let us sleep, but we were mistaken: an involuntary lethargy plunged our grief-burdened senses into the blackness of Styx[44] in the midst of the caresses which sometimes tried to convince us that we were immortal.

Pauline could not refuse either me or herself the pleasure of my accompanying her to Calais.

We left on August 10th; and I was very well satisfied with the appearance of her chambermaid, who had the manner of a governess; and the next day we remained in Dover only long enough for her carriage to be put on board a packet boat, which four hours later landed us at Calais, where Pauline, beginning to try to believe herself,[45] asked me to go to another room to sleep alone.

She left the next morning with four horses, preceded by Clairmont and determined never to travel at night.

The resemblance between this parting at Calais and the one which had lacerated my soul when Henriette had left me at Geneva fifteen years earlier,[46] is striking; striking, too, the similarity in character between those two incomparable women, who differed from each other only in beauty. Perhaps that was what was needed to make me as wildly in love with the second as I had been with the first. Both of them wise, both of them endowed with profound intelligence, it could only be because of the difference in their education that the first was gayer, and had more talents and fewer prejudices. Pauline had the noble pride of her nation, she was inclined to seriousness, and had religion in her heart even more than in her mind. In addition she surpassed Henriette in her fondness for the pleasure of loving and in the ecstasies which follow from it. I was successful with them both because they found me wealthy, otherwise I should have known neither of them. I have forgotten them; but when I recall them I find that Henriette left the stronger impression on me, and the reason is that my soul was more susceptible to impression at the age of twenty-two[47] than at the age of thirty-seven.

I returned to Dover at eight o'clock after a most uncomfortable crossing in a packet boat on which all ten or twelve passengers were seasick. I was only sad.

On arriving in London, I shut myself up in my house, thinking of how I was to go about forgetting Pauline. Jarba put me to bed. He was a reliable, good-hearted young fellow, but when he entered my room the next morning he guilelessly said something which made me shudder, though a minute later I laughed at it. He asked me, on behalf of the old woman who had charge of the house, if I wanted her to put the same notice up at the door.

"What! Devil take it! Does the old witch dare——"

"It's not that. She means no harm."

CHAPTER X

Peculiarities of the English. Castel-Bajac. Count Schwerin. My daughter Sophie in boarding school. My reception at the Thinkers' Club.[1] La Charpillon.

I DID not go out until two days later, but sad, preoccupied, and like a man who had only just arrived. I entered a coffeehouse where twenty people were reading the newspaper. Not understanding English, I sat there quietly watching those who came and went. A merchant who spoke French said to another, who was reading, that So-and-so had killed himself and that he had done well because his affairs were in such disorder that he could only live in poverty.

"You are mistaken, I was present yesterday when his effects were inventoried, for he was in debt to me too, and we all agreed that he had done a stupid thing, for he could have waited another six months before he killed himself, even without putting his affairs in order."

The calculation making me laugh, I went to the Exchange to draw some money. I find Bosanquet, who at once gives me what I ask for; and seeing, on my way out of the room in which I signed the receipt, a man whose countenance aroused my curiosity, I ask him who he is.

"He is a man who is worth a hundred thousand pounds."

"And that other one?"

"He is worth nothing."

"But what I want you to tell me is their names."

"I don't know them. A name means nothing. Knowing a man consists in knowing what amount he commands; for what does his name matter? Ask me for a thousand pounds and give me a receipt for them in my presence under the name of Attila,[2] and that is enough for me. You will repay me not as Seingalt but as Monsieur Attila, and we will laugh."

"But when you sign bills of exchange——"

"That is different, for I have to sign them with the name that the drawer gives me."

I leave him, and I go to the Park; but before entering it I want to change my bank note into coins. I enter the establishment of a fat merchant, a great trencherman whose acquaintance I had made at a tavern, and I ask him to give me guineas for my twenty-pound note, which I threw down on his counter.

"Come back in an hour," he says, "for at the moment I haven't a penny."

"Very well, I will come back on my way out of the Park."

"Take your note; you shall give it to me when I give you the cash."

"It makes no difference. Keep it. I do not doubt your honesty."

"That is madness, my friend, for if you leave me the note I will not give you the cash, if only to teach you a lesson in how to live."

"I do not believe you are capable of so dishonest an act."

"Nor am I; but in the case of something as simple as a bank note, which is no inconvenience to you in your pocket, and left here without your having received the cash, I could more easily persuade myself that I had given you the cash, despite anything you might say to me, than believe you were so stupid as to leave me the note without receiving it."

"You are right."

I go to the Park; I see Martinelli, and I thank him for having sent me his *Decamerone*.[3] He congratulates me on my reappearance in the world, and on the beautiful young lady whose slave I had become, whom Lord Pembroke had seen and found charming.

"What? What? Where did he see her?"

"With you in a carriage and four, at full trot on the road to Rochester,[4] only three or four days ago."

"Very well, I can now tell you that I took her to Calais and that I shall not see her again."

"Shall you rent your apartments again?"

"Never. I was too greatly punished for it, though love treated me well. Come to dine with me whenever you like."

Going toward Buckingham House,[5] I see in the shrubbery to my left a piece of indecency which surprises me. Four or five people at different distances were attending to their needs and showing their behinds to the passers-by.

"It is disgusting," I said to Martinelli; "those pigs should be facing us instead."

"Not at all, for then people would recognize them and would certainly look at them, whereas, showing us their arses as they do, they force us, unless we are especially interested in that part of the body, not to look in that direction."

"Your reasoning is excellent, my friend, but since it is something new for a foreigner, you will excuse me."

"You will have noticed that an Englishman who, walking in the street, needs to make water does not, as we do in our country, go and piss in somebody's doorway or his alley or his courtyard."

"So I have observed. They turn to face the middle of the street and piss there. But people going by in carriages see them, and that is as bad, I think."

"Who tells the people in carriages that they have to look?"

"Very true."

We go to the Green Park, where we come upon Lord Pembroke on horseback; he stops and exclaims when he sees me; I can imagine why, and I tell him that I regained my freedom four days since, and that I felt lonely at my excellent table.

"I am rather curious. I may come today."

He leaves, and, counting on it, I go home to order him a good dinner. Martinelli could not come; but he takes me out of the Park by a gate which I did not know, and he goes far enough with me to put me on the right road.

At the end of a street we see a crowd, at the center of which something curious must have been happening, for everyone was craning his neck to see. Martinelli approaches, stays there a few minutes, then tells me that I shall hear something strange.[6]

"The whole crowd," he said, "is eagerly watching a brave man who will probably die in a quarter of an hour from a blow on the temple he received in a fist fight with another man."

"Is there no remedy?"

"A surgeon who is there maintains that he will not die if he is allowed to bleed him."

"Who can forbid him?"

"That is what is astonishing. The people who forbid him are two men who have bet twenty guineas on his living or dying. One of them said, 'I wager he dies,' the other wagered that he would not die, and the wager was on. There stands the surgeon, wanting to bleed him; the man who wagered he would die will not let him, for if he lives the other will demand his twenty guineas. They refuse to hear of any compromise, so the man may die because of their accursed wager."

"By God, there's an unfortunate man and a pair of pitiless bettors."

"The Englishman has his own ideas on the subject of betting. There is a confraternity or a club called 'The Bettors,' [7] and if you are curious I will get you introduced there."

"Do they speak French?"

"Undoubtedly, for they are men of intelligence and distinction." [8]

"And what do they do?"

"They talk, and when one of them denies something that the other puts forth as a fact, if the other challenges him to bet he must bet, on pain of a fine which goes into the club treasury and which the members divide among them at the end of the month."

"My dear friend, introduce me to this delightful club, which will make me rich, for I shall not hesitate to speak out when I am of a different opinion, and I will not speak at all unless I am sure of what I am saying."

"Be careful, for they are sharp."

"But let us get back to the man who is dying from that blow in a fist fight. What will be done with the man who killed him?"

"His hand will be examined; and if it is found to be 'dangerous,' [9] he will be hanged; if they find his hand is like yours and mine, all that will happen to him is that his hand will be branded."

"I am at a loss; please explain to me. How is a 'dangerous' hand recognized?"

"When it is found to have been branded. Then it is certain that the man has killed another, and when his hand was branded he was warned to be careful not to kill still another, for he would go to the gallows."

"But if the man with the 'dangerous' hand—since there is such a thing—is attacked?"

"He shows his hand; and then everyone is bound to respect him and let him alone."

"And if he is forced?"

"Then he defends himself, and if he kills it means nothing, provided that he has witnesses."

"Fist fighting can easily cause death. I am surprised that it is permitted."

"It is only permitted on a wager. If the two who fight have not thrown a coin or two on the ground before fighting, which is proof positive of a wager, if death results the killer is sentenced to the gallows."

"O laws, O customs!" [10]

It was thus that I learned to know this proud nation. I had a good dinner prepared for the noble Lord, and he did not fail to come to it. Though only the two of us were present, our dinner lasted a long time, for I wanted commentaries on all the fine things I had learned that morning, and especially on the Bettors' Club. The amiable Lord advised me not to join it unless I was prepared to remain perfectly silent for at least a month.

"But if I am asked a question?"

"Evade it."

"Evade it? No doubt I shall do so if I am asked my opinion and I am unable to give it; but in the contrary case, when I am sure, the devil himself won't be able to make me keep still. They are not scoundrels, I hope?"

"Scoundrels? They are all noble, learned, rich, and epicures; but pitiless in accepting and in offering bets."

"But is the treasury well stocked?"

"Very poorly, for rather than pay the fine any one of them would rather lose his stake. Who will introduce you?"

"Martinelli."

"Yes, he will speak to Spencer,[11] who is a member. I have not wanted to join."

"Why?"

"Because I don't like to argue. But you are a strange man."

"What makes you say so?"

"A month shut up with a woman who was in London

for fourteen months and whom no one could ever get to know or even to find out what her country is, and who was known only to you, a foreigner—it's something to nettle us all.''

''How did you know that she was here for fourteen months?''

''Because she first lived in the house of an honest widow, where several people saw her; but she would never let anyone make her acquaintance. Your notice brought her into your hands.''

''Unluckily for me, for I shall never love another woman.''

''Oh, there'll be another in a week. Perhaps tomorrow, if you will come to dine with me in the country. I made the engagement by chance yesterday in Chelsea,[12] where a Frenchwoman who is a beauty asked me to give her dinner. I have sent my orders, and I have informed five or six of my friends who are fond of play.''

''Play for stakes?''

''Of course.''

''Does the charming Frenchwoman like to play?''

''No, but her husband does.''

''What do you call him?''

''It is he who calls himself the Count of Castel-Bajac.''[13]

''A Gascon.''[14]

''Yes.''

''Thin, tall, dark, and marked with smallpox.''

''Just so. I am delighted that you know him. Isn't it true that his wife is a beauty?''

''I have no idea, for it was six years ago that I made his acquaintance, and I did not know that he was married then. I will come, and I am very glad to be of the company. However, I give you one warning: say nothing if he pretends not to know me. He may have good reasons for doing so. I can tell you a story in confidence tomorrow which is not to his credit. I did not know he was a gamester. I will be careful in the company of the bettors, and you, My Lord, be careful in tomorrow's company."

"I will give your Negro my address."

He rode away, and I went to see Mrs. Cornelys, who had written me a week earlier that her daughter was ill, and who complained that she had twice been told that I was not at home when she knew I was there. My only excuse was that I was in love, and she had to allow it; but Sophie's condition alarmed me. She was in bed with continual fever, extremely thin, and looking at me with eyes which told me that she was dying of grief. Her mother was in despair, for she loved her dearly; I thought she would murder me when I told her in the patient's presence that if she died it would be she who had killed her. At that the child said, "No, no," and flung her arms around her mother's neck and soothed her; but before leaving I took her aside and told her that Sophie was dying because she made her too afraid of her and treated her with unbearable tyranny.

"Send her to boarding school for two years," I said, "with nice girls of good family; tell her so this evening, and you will see that tomorrow she will be better."

She replied that a good boarding school, including instruction, cost a hundred guineas a year. I said that, after seeing what school it was, I could pay the master or mistress a year in advance from my own purse. At this offer, the woman, who was really in poverty despite her luxurious style of living, embraced me with tokens of the liveliest gratitude.

"Come with me this instant," she said, "and tell your daughter the news yourself. I want to see her face."

"Gladly."

"My dear Sophie," I said as I entered, "your mother is persuaded that a change of air will restore you to health. If you will go to one of the finest boarding schools in London for a year or two, I will lend her a hundred guineas at once."

"I can only obey my dear mother."

"It is not a matter of obedience. Would you like to go to boarding school? Answer me frankly."

"But would it please my mother?"

"Very much, my dear daughter, if you will go willingly."

"Most willingly."

The child's face became red as fire. I left her, asking her to let me have news of her. I went home to think sadly of Pauline.

The next morning at ten o'clock Jarba asked me if I had forgotten that I was engaged to dine at Lord Pembroke's.

"No, indeed. It is only ten o'clock."

"Very true. But we have twenty miles to travel."

"Twenty miles?"

"Yes, here is the address he left with me. We have to go to Saint Albans." [15]

I think it odd that His Lordship had not told me so; but such are the English. I travel post, which is not difficult in London, for there are post offices everywhere, and I go to his house in Saint Albans in less than three hours. Nothing is finer than the English roads, and nothing more attractive than the English countryside, it lacks only the vine. It is a peculiarity of the very fertile soil of the island that it cannot yield wine. Lord Pembroke's house was not of the largest, but big enough to lodge twenty masters. The lady had not yet arrived; he shows me his gardens, his baths, his gazebos, his underground hothouses for growing fruits out of season; and among other things he showed me a cock, chained in a coop, which really looked ferocious.

"What is that? It's a fine cock, but chained! Why?"

"Because he is ferocious. He loves hens, and he would run away in search of them, and he would kill all the cocks they belong to."

"And why do you condemn him to celibacy?"

"So that he will be in good condition to fight. Look, here is the list of his victories."

He opens a drawer, and he takes out a long sheet of paper on which he had recorded all the fights from which he had emerged the victor after killing his opponent. There were more than thirty of them. He shows me his very bright steel spurs. The cock shook when he saw them, and I could not help bursting into laughter. All on fire, the bird raised his feet to have the spurs put on. After that he shows me his steel helmet.

"But with these advantages he is sure to defeat his opponent."

"Not at all, for when he is fully armed he scorns an unarmed opponent."

"You amaze me, My Lord."

"You will no longer be amazed when you read this."

From a fourth drawer he takes a list showing his entire genealogy. He could prove twenty quarters of nobility, in the male line of course, for if he could have proved them in the female line too, His Lordship would have hung at least the Maltese Cross[16] around his neck. He told me that he had cost him two hundred guineas, but that he would not sell him for a thousand. I asked him if he had offspring; and he replied that he was working at it, but that it was difficult; I do not remember what difficulties he alleged. The English constantly offered my eager curiosity delightful peculiarities.

But up drives a carriage with a woman and two men. I see the scoundrel Castel-Bajac, and a thin man whom Castel-Bajac introduced to His Lordship as Count Schwerin,[17] nephew of the celebrated Field Marshal,[18] killed on what is called the field of honor. An English General Beckw . . . ,[19] who commanded a regiment in the service of the King of Prussia, and who was one of the guests, pays him compliments and says that he had died in his presence; the modest nephew then takes from his pocket the bloodstained ribbon of the Black Eagle[20] which the Marshal was wearing when he received his death wound.

"His Majesty," [21] he informed the company, "permitted me to keep it."

"But your pocket," said an Englishman who was present, "is not the proper place for it."

His Lordship at once took possession of Madame. I examine her, and in comparison with Pauline she seems to me to be nothing. Whiter of complexion because she was blonde, less tall, and without the slightest air of nobility, she does not interest me. When she laughed all her beauty vanished. It is a great misfortune for a pretty woman when laughter makes her ugly—the same laughter which often has the power to make an ugly woman beautiful.

Lord Pembroke, whose place it was to do so, introduced his friends to the lady and the gentlemen, and when he names me, Castel-Bajac, who could have pretended not to know me under the name of Seingalt, expresses his pleasure and embraces me.

We dine in high spirits on English fare, we drink punch, and it is Madame who insists on a little game of faro. His Lordship never plays; so it is General Beckw . . . who offers to make a bank to amuse the company. He puts down a hundred guineas and eight or nine hundred more in bank notes. He politely distributes twenty counters to each punter, saying that each counter is worth half a guinea. Wanting to stake gold against gold, I accept no counters. At the third deal Schwerin was the first who, having lost his twenty counters, asks for twenty more. The banker tells him that he carries no one on his word. The Field Marshal's nephew does not answer and stops playing. At the following deal the same thing happens to Castel-Bajac. Being seated beside me, he asks my permission to take ten guineas from me. I coldly reply that he would bring me bad luck, and I push away his hand. Madame says that her husband had forgotten to bring his portfolio. An hour later the General lays down the cards, and I take my leave, asking

His Lordship and the entire company to dine at my house the next day.

I was back at home by eleven o'clock, without having encountered any highwaymen, as I had expected to do. I had a small purse containing six guineas at their disposition. I had been taught that lesson. I had my cook waked and told him that I should have twelve people to dinner the next day. It was the first fine dinner I was giving. I found a note from Mrs. Cornelys telling me that she would come to dine with me on the following Sunday with "our" daughter, and that we would go to see the boarding school in which she intended to put her.

Lord Pembroke arrived first at my house with the beautiful Frenchwoman, in a carriage which barely seated two. The crowding was favorable for love. The others arrived one or two at a time, and the last were the Gascon and the Prussian.

We sat down at table at two o'clock, and we rose at four, all well pleased with my cook and even more so with my vintner, for despite the souls of forty bottles which we had in our bodies, none of us was drunk.

After coffee the General invited the whole company to sup at his house, and Madame Castel-Bajac asked me to make a bank. Not waiting to be urged, I made one of a thousand guineas, half in gold, half in bank notes. Having neither counters nor slips, I said that I would accept only gold against gold, and that I would stop when I saw fit, without announcing the last deal.

I was delighted to see that the two foreign Counts[22] paid their little debts to the General in bank notes. I changed two of the same notes which they offered me into guineas, and I changed the two notes they had given him for the General. I put these four notes aside under my snuffbox, and play began. Having no croupier, and allowing all the punters to stake, I had to deal very slowly. It was the two Counts who occupied my attention, for they always made mistakes to their own advantage. It annoyed me. Both of them having had the misfortune to lose, and both of them being, luckily for me, out of bank notes, Castel-Bajac took from his pocket a bill of exchange for two hundred pounds and threw it to me, asking me to discount it for him; I reply that I know nothing about bills of exchange. An Englishman looks at it, then hands it back to me, saying that he knows neither the drawer nor the drawee nor the endorser. "I am the endorser," says the Gascon, "and I think that suffices." Everyone laughs, except myself. I politely hand it back to him, saying that he can discount it at the Exchange. He leaves, muttering insults, and Schwerin follows him.

After the departure of the sharpers I continued dealing quietly until very late in the night. When I stopped I was the loser, because of the General, who I saw was having too good luck. Before leaving he took me aside with His Lordship to ask him to see to it that the two swindlers should not come to his house the next night, for if the Gascon had said to him half of what he had dared to say to me he would have had him shown out by the window. His Lordship replied that he could give the message only to his wife. I ask him if the four notes which had come from them, and which I had, might be forged. Seeing that they are brand-new, he replies with a laugh that it is possible.

"What would you do to make sure?"

"I would send them to the Bank[23] to be changed."

"And if the Bank found that they were forged?"

"I would put up with it, or I would have the man who gave them to me arrested."

After giving me the General's address, he left with the lady.

The next day at the Bank I was surprised by the cold indifference with which an unassuming man to whom I had given my four notes, asking him to give me guineas for them, handed them back to me, saying that they were forgeries. He smiled when I asked him to examine them a little more closely. He told me to return them to the person who had given them to me and make him pay me in good money, which I should not find it difficult to do.

I knew very well that it was in my power to have the scoundrels put in prison; but, feeling reluctant to do so, I decide to go to His Lordship's to learn where they were staying. His Lordship was still asleep, one of his footmen takes me to their lodging, and my presence surprises them. I tell them coolly enough that, the four notes they had given me being forgeries, they should at once give me forty guineas. Castel-Bajac replies that he has no money; but that the thing amazed him.

"I can only," he said, "return them to the person who gave them to me, always provided that the notes you have there are the ones we gave you."

At this counterproposal the blood rushes to my head, and I leave them. The same footman, who was waiting for me, takes me to a place where, after being put on oath, I am given a bill [24] which authorizes me to have them arrested. I go to the Alderman,[25] who undertakes to see to it, then I go home very much put out by the shameful business. I found Martinelli, who had come to ask me for dinner. I gave him an account of the matter, not telling him that the scoundrels were to be arrested. The philosopher said that, if he were in my place, he would burn the forged notes. Such heroism may have been mere boasting, but his advice was good. I did not follow it. Thinking to cheer me up, he said that he had agreed with Lord Spencer on a day for my introduction to the Thinkers' Club, and I replied that I no longer wanted to join it. (One often feels resentment toward a wise man who gives one good advice which one has not the courage to follow.)

Toward nightfall I went to the General's, where I found the Countess sitting on Lord Pembroke's lap. We supped gaily; the two wretches did not appear, and no mention was made of them. Getting up from supper, we went into another room, where the table for faro was ready. The General dealt until daybreak, and I went home having lost two or three hundred guineas. I went to bed, and I did not wake until very late.

A man was announced, I had him shown in, and, finding that he spoke only English, I had to summon Jarba to interpret for me. He was the chief constable, who told me that if I would pay for his journey he was sure he could arrest Castel-Bajac at Dover, for which place he had left at noon; he was sure to arrest him before nightfall. I replied, giving him a guinea, that the other would be enough for me, and that he should let the Gascon go to the devil.

The next day being a Sunday, the only day on which the extraordinary Mrs. Cornelys could go about in London, I had her to dinner at my house with my daughter, who, delighted to be on the eve of escaping from her mother's hands, had recovered her health. The boarding school was in Harwich,[26] and we went there after dinner.

The mistress of the establishment was a Catholic noblewoman who, despite her sixty years, still looked fresh and displayed wit and the manners of good society. Having been forewarned by Lady Harrington's recommendation, she gave the young Cornelys the most gracious reception. She had fifteen or sixteen girls at board, the eldest of whom was barely thirteen years of age. I saw them all in the garden, playing innocently together. When Her Ladyship introduced Sophie to them, saying that she was to become their fellow boarder, they all hastened to give her the fondest caresses. Five or six of the young ladies, and one of them more especially, seemed to me angels incarnate, and two or three of them were so ugly that they frightened me. These two extremes are seen in England more than anywhere else. My daughter was shorter than any of the others, but her little face was so pretty that she did not lose courage. She at once made up to all of them, talking with them as if she had known them for a long time. When Her Ladyship invited us to go through the house, they all followed us.

Each girl had a small room next to another which was separated from hers by a half-wall and in which lived a fellow boarder with whom she could talk. They ate four at a table, and six maids took care of them all. They had all kinds of masters, who came to give them lessons in a large room in which I saw harpsichords, harps, guitars, and tables on which there was everything needed for lessons in drawing. Thinking that I was Sophie's father, all the girls talked to me, and I saw that those who could not yet venture to speak French or Italian were mortified. I was in ecstasies. Their short dresses, with an English-style whale-bone corset which left their bosoms entirely bare, put my soul in a stupor.

After going over the whole house, we went with only the headmistress into a room where Mrs. Cornelys gave her the hundred guineas for a year in bank notes and took a receipt. They agreed that the little girl should enter as soon as she came with her bed and her few necessaries. Her mother took care of it all on the following Sunday.

Very early the next day the Alderman's man came to tell me that Count Schwerin was a prisoner in his house, and he gave me a note in which he asked me to come to speak with him. I decided to go when the man told me he had not a penny and that, the charge being one of forged bank notes, he was going to take him to Newgate.[27] I could not quite stomach the idea of letting him go to the gallows. So I went there, and I cannot describe how much I suffered at the sight of his endless tears, his despairing gestures, his admission of his crime, and the basenesses to which he descended to move me to pity. He swore that the notes had been given him by Castel-Bajac, but that he knew from whom he had bought them and that he was ready to tell me the person's name if I would set him free. I said that if he named the person from whom they came he was sure not to be hanged, but that I would keep him in prison nevertheless, sending him fourpence a day until he gave me my money. At that his cries began again, while he swore that he was in utter poverty and showed me his empty pockets. He then offered me, as security, his bloodstained ribbon of the Black Eagle, and I took it into my head that I should like to have it.

So I accepted it, giving him a receipt and undertaking to return it to him when he gave me forty pounds sterling. I wrote out my waiver, I paid the costs of his imprisonment, I burned the forged notes in his presence, and I let him go.

Two days later I saw the self-styled Countess Castel-Bajac appear at my house to tell me that, her husband and her lover having left, she did not know where to turn. She also complained bitterly of Lord Pembroke, who had also abandoned her after she had given him clear tokens of her affection. I said that he would have made a mistake to leave her before that, for he must have considered that she owed him something. She replied that it was true he had given her a good lesson. It finally appeared that, if I wanted to get rid of her, I had to give her what she needed to rejoin her wretched lover in Calais, for she swore to me that she did not want to see Castel-Bajac again, who in any case was not her husband. The reader will see these two persons reappear on the scene three years hence.

About this same time a tragicomic incident did not fail to afford me amusement.

An Italian came to me with a letter from my friend Balletti. He recommended the bearer of the letter to me, Signor Costantini[28] by name, a native of Vicenza, who was in London on business of great importance of which he would inform me. He asked me to be of use to him in any way in my power. Being myself the only judge of the extent of my powers and of my willingness to employ them, I told Signor Costantini that I greatly esteemed the friend who had sent him to me, and that hence he could count upon me.

"Signore," he said, "I arrived in London yesterday

evening, and the long journey having cost me all the money I had, I now command only two guineas, but I know that my wife is here, she is rich, and I can easily find out where she lodges. You know that, as her husband, I can dispose of whatever she possesses.''

''I know nothing about it.''

''Then you do not know the laws of this country?''

''I do not.''

''Too bad; but it is none the less true. I intend to go to her house tomorrow and turn her into the street with the dress she has on and nothing more, for all her furniture, her clothes, her diamonds, in short everything she possesses, is mine. May I ask you to be with me when I stage this fine scene?''

Very much surprised by the situation, and even more so by his proposal, I ask him if he had told my friend Balletti of the matter. He replies that he has confided in no one, and that I am the first person to whom he has spoken of it.

I could not dismiss him as mad, for he had not the slightest appearance of being so, and seeing, furthermore, that the law which he cited very likely existed in England, I answered him briefly that I did not feel inclined to help him in his enterprise, of which in any case I completely disapproved, unless his wife had stolen from him all the things of which he alleged that she was then in possession.

''No, Signore. She stole nothing from me but my honor, and when she left me she possessed nothing but her talent. She came here, and she has made a great fortune. Am I not right to seize it, if only to punish her and avenge myself?''

''That may be so, but since you seem to me a sensible man I ask you what you would think of me if I consented without further ado to be your companion in an enterprise which, despite your arguments, I consider cruel. Add that I might know your wife and might even be her friend.''

"I will tell you her name."

"I beg you to say no more, though I am not acquainted with any Signora Costantini."

"She has changed her name; she calls herself Calori[29] and she sings in the opera at the Haymarket."

"Now I know who she is, but you are wrong to have told me her name."

"It was because I do not doubt your discretion. I am going at once to find out where she lives. That is the chief thing."

He left me, drying his tears, and I pitied him. Nevertheless I was annoyed that he had confided his secret to me. Three or four hours later I went to see La Binetti,[30] who, after telling me that La De Amicis,[31] when she left London, had gone completely mad over the impresario Mattei,[32] who did not love her, told me all the stories I wanted to hear about all the *virtuose*[33] who were then in London. When she came to La Calori, she told me she had had several lovers who had given her a great deal, but that at the moment she had no one but the celebrated violinist Giardini,[34] with whom she was in love. I asked her where she came from and if she was married, and she replied that she was from Vicenza and that she did not believe she was married.

I had almost stopped thinking about this ugly matter when, three days after my conversation with La Binetti, I received a note from King's Bench Prison,[35] which I was surprised to find signed with the name Costantini. The unfortunate man told me that he considered me the only friend he could have in London, and so he hoped that I would have come to see him, at least to give him some good advice.

Thinking it all very strange, and not understanding how it was possible, I take a hackney carriage and I hurry to King's Bench. I find him in despair, with an old English attorney who spoke Italian and whom I knew. Costantini had been arrested on the previous evening on account of several notes to order drawn by his wife, which she had not paid when they fell due. According to these notes his wife appeared to owe the bearers about a thousand guineas. The attorney who was there was the depositary of the notes, which belonged to names which I did not know. There were five of them. He had come to propose some arrangements to the prisoner.

Very much surprised by this infamous trick, which I should not have believed to be such if I had not learned from La Binetti that La Calori, far from being in debt, was rich, I asked the attorney to leave, for I needed to talk with Signor Costantini privately.

"I am arrested," he says, "for debts of my wife's, and I am told that I must pay them because I am her husband."

"It is a trick your wife is playing on you. She found out that you are in London."

"She saw me from her window."

"Why did you put off executing your plan?"

"I would have carried it out this morning; but could I believe that my wife was in debt?"

"Nor is she. These notes are false. They were predated, they were drawn only yesterday. It is a bad business, which may cost her dear."

"But I am in prison."

"Stay there, and count on me. We shall meet again tomorrow."

Indignant at this scurvy trick, and determined to take up the cudgels for the unfortunate man, I go to tell Monsieur Bosanquet the whole story; he replies that tricks of the kind were extremely common in London and that ways of dealing with them had long been known there. He ended by saying that if I took an interest in the prisoner, he would put him in the hands of an advocate who would clear him, and who would make his wife and her lover, who had apparently instigated the thing, repent of trying it. I replied that I was interested in the man, and I asked him to act and even to stand surety for him if that was necessary, being myself ready to vouch for him. I gave him the man's name, and he advised me to take no further steps in the matter.

Five or six days later he came to tell me that Master Costantini had left the prison, and even England, or so the advocate who had undertaken his defence believed.

"How was that?"

"It is perfectly simple. His wife's lover himself, foreseeing the storm, must have persuaded him to accept a sum of money on condition that he would leave, and the poor wretch agreed. So the thing is over; but it is a bit of news which will arouse laughter and which will be read in the papers, and it will even be said that Giardini did very well when he advised Signorina Calori to play this fine part."

I learned later from La Binetti that she had him given two hundred guineas. I was very well pleased, and I wrote Balletti the whole story. Some years later I came upon La Calori in Prague.[36]

A Flemish officer who had served in France and to whose assistance I had come at Aix-la-Chapelle[37] had paid me several visits and had even dined at my house two or three times, and I was sorry that I had not yet, as in duty bound, gone to call on him at his lodging at least once; he made me blush when, running into me in London, he politely reproached me for it. He had his wife and daughter with him. A modicum of curiosity also made me want to go there. It was my evil Genius who took me there, for my good one always kept me from doing so.

When he saw me he fell on my neck, and as soon as he introduced me to his wife, calling me his savior, I had to accept all the compliments which rogues pay to decent people whom they hope to dupe. Five or six minutes later I see an old woman come in with a pretty girl. Monsieur Malignan introduced me, saying that I was the Chevalier de Seingalt of whom he had often spoken to them. The young lady, pretending surprise, said that she had known a Monsieur Casanova who looked very much like me; I replied that that, too, was my name, but that I did not have the happiness to remember her.

"I, too," she said, "had another name then; it was Augspurgher, though now my name is Charpillon;[38] and since you saw me and spoke to me only once, it is easily possible that you have forgotten me, the more so since I was then only thirteen years old. Some time afterward I came to London with my mother[39] and my aunts; we have been here now for four years."

"But where did I have the happiness of speaking with you?"

"In Paris, at the Palais Marchand,[40] you were with a charming lady; you gave me these buckles" (and so saying, she showed them to me on her shoes); "then, encouraged by my aunt, you did me the honor to embrace me."

I then remember her perfectly, and my reader may recollect that at the time I was with the beautiful Baret, the stocking seller.

"Mademoiselle, I remember the occasion very well, and I remember you, but I do not recognize your aunt."

"This lady is her sister, but if you will be good enough to come to tea with us, you shall see her. We are living in Denmark Street,[41] Soho. I will show you that I wrote down the very flattering compliment you paid me."

CHAPTER XI

La Charpillon and the fatal effects of my ac-
quaintance with her.

AT THE name Charpillon I take from my portfolio
the letter which the Procurator Morosini had given me
at Lyons[1] and I hand it to her.

"What do I see! My dear Ambassador! And in all the
three months you have been in London you have never
thought of bringing me his letter?"

"It is true; I should have inquired; but since the
Ambassador showed no particular eagerness, I have neglected this little duty, and I am grateful to the chance
which enables me to perform it."

"Then come to dine with us tomorrow."

"I cannot, for Lord Pembroke told me to expect
him."

"In company, or by himself?"

"By himself."

"I am glad of that. Expect me, too, with my aunt.
Where do you live?"

I give her my address, assuring her that she will do me

both an honor and a favor, and I am surprised to see her laugh.

"Then you are the Italian," she says, "who two months ago posted on the door of his house at this address the strange notice which set everyone laughing?"

"I am he."

"I am told that it cost you dear."

"On the contrary. I owe that notice my happiness."

"It follows that, now that the lady has gone, you must be unhappy. No one knows who she was. Do you really make a secret of it?"

"Certainly; and I would rather die than reveal it."

"Ask my aunt if I didn't want to go to ask you for a room. But my mother would not let me."

"What need have you to find a cheap lodging?"

"None whatever; but I felt a need to laugh and to punish the audacious author of such a notice."

"How would you have punished me?"

"By making you fall in love with me and then treating you so that you suffered the pains of hell. Oh, how I should have laughed!"

"Then you believe it is in your power to make any man you choose fall in love with you, basely planning in advance to become the tyrant of him who has paid your charms the homage which is their due? It is the project of a monster, and it is unfortunate for men that you do not look like one. I shall profit by your frankness to be on my guard."

"In vain. Unless you forgo seeing me."

Since she smiled while maintaining this dialogue, I took it as it was natural to take it; but admiring in her a kind of intelligence which, together with her charms, at once convinced me that she did indeed have the power to make any man love her. It was the first sample of it which she gave me that first day on which I had the misfortune to make her acquaintance.

It was on that fatal day at the beginning of September 1763 that I began to die and that I ceased to live. I was thirty-eight years of age. If the perpendicular line of ascent is equal in length to that of descent, as it should be, on this the first day of November in the year 1797 I think I can count on nearly four years of life,[2] which in accordance with the axiom *motus in fine velocior* ("motion is increased in speed toward the end")[3] will pass very quickly.

La Charpillon, whom all London knew, and who, I believe, is still alive,[4] was a beauty in whom it was difficult to find a defect. Her hair was light chestnut, her eyes blue, her complexion of the purest white, and her stature almost equal to Pauline's, counting in the two inches she would gain when she became twenty, for at that time she was only seventeen. Her bosom was small but perfect, her hands dimpled, slender, a little longer than most, her feet tiny, and her manners assured and well-bred. Her sweet, open countenance bore witness to a soul distinguished by delicacy of feeling and to the nobility of manner which is usually due to birth. It was on these two points that Nature saw fit to lie in her appearance. She ought rather to have told the whole truth there, and lied in all the rest. The girl had deliberately planned to make me unhappy even before she had come to know me; and she told me so.

I left Malignan's house, not like a sensual man who, having a passion for the sex, cannot but feel overjoyed to have met a girl with whom, having recognized her rare beauty, he feels sure that he will easily satisfy all the desires she has inspired in him, but stupefied and surprised that the image of Pauline, which I still had before my eyes, and which, each time I saw a woman who could lay claim to please me, imperiously entered my mind to make me scorn her, did not have the power to render this Charpillon incapable of taking me by surprise. I forgave myself, concluding that what had enchanted me was only novelty and the combination of circumstances, and that disenchantment would soon follow. "I shall cease," I told myself, "to find her marvelous as soon as I have slept with her; nor will that be long in coming."

How could I imagine that she would make difficulties? She had invited herself to dinner with me; she had been the dear friend of the Procurator, whom she had certainly not kept languishing and who must have paid her, for he was neither handsome nor young enough to have made her fall in love with him. Without even flattering myself that I could please her, I knew that I had money, that I was not stingy, and that she would not resist.

Lord Pembroke had become my friend after the charity I had shown Count Schwerin and my restraint in not demanding half of the amount from the General. He had told me that we would arrange a party which would give us a pleasurable day.

When he arrived and saw four places laid he asked me who the two others who would dine with us were, and he was surprised when he learned that they were La Charpillon and her aunt, and that she had invited herself as soon as she had known that it was he who was to dine with me.

"The girl having made me want very much to have her," he said, "I finally found her at Vauxhall one night with her aunt, and I offered her twenty guineas if she would come for a stroll with me in a dark walk. She consented, asking for the money in advance, and I was kind enough to give it to her. She came into the walk; but she immediately dropped my arm, and I did not find her again."

"You should have slapped her face in public."

"I should have brought trouble on myself, and everyone would have laughed at me. She's a fool, whom I now despise. Are you in love with her?"

"I am curious about her, as you were."

"She is a scheming wench who will do everything she can to trap you."

She arrives, and she says the most charming things possible to His Lordship, scarcely looking at me. She laughs; she herself recounts the trick she had played on him at Vauxhall, and she twits him with stupidity for giving her up because of a joke which, on the contrary, should have led him to love her the more.

"Another time," she said, "I will not run away from you."

"That is possible, for I will not pay you in advance."

"Fie! 'Pay' is an ugly word which dishonors you."

His Lordship praised her wit and only laughed at all the impertinent things she said to him in her pique at the indolent lack of attention which he accorded her remarks. After dinner she left us, after making me promise to come to dinner with her on the next day but one.

I spent the whole of the following day with the amiable Lord, who introduced me to the English bagnio,[5] an entertainment which costs a great deal and which I shall not describe, for it is well known to all those who have spent some time in London and have been willing to pay six guineas to enjoy its pleasures. We had two very pretty sisters, whose name was Garrick.

On the appointed day I went to La Charpillon's to dinner, as I had promised to do. She introduces me to her mother, who, though ill and haggard, comes back to my memory at once. In the year 1759 a Genevan named Bolomay[6] had persuaded me to sell her some jewelry for six thousand francs. She had given me two bills of exchange drawn on the same Genevan by herself and her two sisters; her name was Augspurgher. The Genevan who had accepted the bills had gone bankrupt before they fell due, and the three Augspurgher sisters had disappeared a few days later. So I am greatly surprised to find them in England, and still more surprised to be brought to their house by La Charpillon, who, knowing nothing of this underhanded dealing by her mother and her aunts, had not told her that Monsieur de Seingalt was the Casanova to whom they owed six thousand francs.

"Madame, I have the pleasure of recollecting you," were the words I said to her.

"Monsieur, I recollect you too. That scoundrel Bolo-may——"

"Let us not speak of it, Madame; we will leave it for another day. I see that you have been ill."

"Deathly ill, but I am better now. My daughter did not announce you by your name."

"I beg your pardon: it is mine, as was the name I had in Paris, when I made her acquaintance without knowing that she was related to you."

Thereupon the grandmother, who was named Augs-purgher like her daughter, comes in with the two aunts; and a quarter of an hour later three men arrive, one of whom was the Chevalier Goudar, whom I had known in Paris;[7] of the two others, whom I did not know, one was named Rostaing[8] and the other Coumon.[9] They were the three friends of the house, all of them professional sharp-ers, whose office was to bring in dupes and thus provide the means of subsistence which in turn provided theirs. It was to this infamous gang that I saw myself intro-duced, and although I was aware of it at once, I neither fled nor promised myself that I would never set foot in the place again. I thought that I risked nothing if I re-mained on the defensive and nursed no intention but that of entering into a relationship with the daughter; I considered these people merely creatures who had noth-ing in common with my undertaking. At table I fell in with the general atmosphere, I set the tone, I led them on, I was led on, and I became convinced that I would accomplish the whole of my purpose with no difficulty. The only thing which displeased me was a request which La Charpillon made of me after asking me to excuse her for having given me poor fare at her house. She asked me to invite her to supper with the entire company and to appoint the day. I immediately asked her to name it herself, and after consulting the scoundrels, she named it. Four rubbers of whist, at which I constantly lost, brought us to suppertime, and toward midnight I went home, bored and in love with La Charpillon.

Nevertheless I had the strength not to go to see her during the two following days. The third day being the one she had appointed for supper at my house, at nine o'clock I saw her with her aunt.

"I have come," she said, "to breakfast with you and to discuss a piece of business."

"Now, or after we have breakfasted?"

"Afterward, for we must be alone."

In the ensuing private conversation, after informing me of her family's situation at the time, she said that they would cease to be in straits if her aunt, who was in the other room, had a hundred guineas. With that amount she would compound the "balm of life" which would make her fortune. She discoursed on the virtues of the balm, on the large sales of which there could be no doubt in London, and on the profit which I myself would make, since, as was only right, I should have a half share with her in the enterprise; aside from all that, she said that, on receiving the hundred guineas, her mother and her aunts would undertake in writing to repay me the same amount at the end of six months. I replied that I would give her a definite answer after supper.

So saying, and being alone with her, I assume a light-hearted manner, the manner which a polished man assumes, when, in love, he wants to find his way to the favors to which he aspires, and I begin making the appropriate motions on the large sofa on which we were seated; but La Charpillon, with the same lightheartedness, resists my every movement and repeatedly forbids my gently caressing hands to do anything they would; she refuses me hers, she tears herself from my arms, turning her head away when she sees mine within range of giving her a kiss, and finally she gets up and, all smiles, goes to join her aunt in the other room. Forced to smile too, I follow her, and a minute later she leaves, bidding me good-by until that evening.

Left alone and reflecting on this first scene, I find it natural, to be expected, and, above all, in view of her need of the hundred guineas for which she had already asked me, not at all unpromising. I saw very well that I could not hope for her favors unless I gave her the money, and certainly I had no thought of haggling; but she must see too that she should not have it if she took it into her head to play the prude. It was for me to take such measures as would guarantee me against being tricked. Not wanting to dine, I go to walk in the Park, and toward nightfall I am home again.

The company arrives, it is not late, the beautiful child asks me to make a small bank for them, and, after bursting out laughing, which she does not expect, I decline.

"A game of whist, at least," she says.

"Then you are not in a hurry for my answer concerning the matter of which you know?"

"Of course I am. So you have made up your mind."

"Yes, come."

She follows me into the other room, where, after making her sit down on the same sofa, I tell her that I have the hundred guineas and that they are at her disposal.

"You must give them to my aunt, otherwise the gentlemen would think that I had obtained them from you by shameful concessions."

"Very well, I will give them to your aunt; you may count on it."

After these words I made the same approaches to her which I had made that morning, but always to no purpose. I ceased to press her when she said that I would never get anything from her either with money or by force; but that I could hope everything from her friendship when she saw that, being alone with her, I was gentle as a lamb. At that I got up, and she followed me.

Feeling my bile rising, I saw that I could conceal it only by joining in the whist game which had already been arranged. She was in very high spirits, and it annoyed me. Beside me at the table, she exasperated me by a hundred freedoms which would have raised me to the seventh heaven if she had not twice rebuffed me that same day.

After the Seduction

Dancing Lesson at a Boarding School

When the company was leaving she called me aside to say that she would send her aunt to me in the other room if I had really decided to give her the hundred guineas. I replied that it would be necessary to write and that the time was not suitable for it, and when she asked me to fix a time I said, showing her a purse full of gold pieces, that the time would come when she made it come.

Reflecting after she left that the young hussy had undoubtedly laid a deliberate plan to cheat me, I prepared to renounce my pursuit. The failure humiliated me, but I saw a certain courage in accepting it. To distract myself I the next day began going to my daughter's boarding school, taking a basket of sweetmeats with me. I rejoiced Sophie's soul, as well as those of her schoolmates, with whom she shared them all. But the pleasure I felt was greater than theirs. I went there nearly every day. The journey took only an hour and a quarter.[10] I brought them all sorts of trinkets and small articles of attire which delighted them; Her Ladyship was politeness itself to me, and my daughter, who openly called me her dear papa, made me every day more convinced that I had won her heart as I had given her life. In less than three weeks I congratulated myself that I had forgotten La Charpillon and had replaced her by innocent affections, though one of Sophie's schoolmates pleased me a little too much for me to find myself entirely free from amorous desires.

In this state, one morning at eight o'clock I saw before me the coquette's favorite aunt, who said that her niece and the entire family were mortified that I had not put in an appearance since the supper I had given them, and especially herself, to whom her niece had given the hope that I would provide her with the means to compound her "balm of life."

"Yes, Madame, I would have given you a hundred guineas, if your niece had treated me like a friend. She refused me favors which even a Vestal [11] would have granted me, and you know that she is no Vestal."

"Permit me to laugh. She is lighthearted, a bit of a

scatterbrain, she gives herself only when she is sure she
is loved. She told me everything. She loves you, but she
fears that your love is only a passing fancy. She is in bed
with a bad cold, and she thinks she has a slight fever.
Come to see her, and I am sure you will not leave dissatisfied."

At these words all the desire which I had felt to possess
the girl reawoke; and after a good laugh at myself for
it, I asked her at what hour I should go there to be sure
of finding her in bed. She said to go immediately, and
to knock only once. I told her to go and wait for me.

How gratified I was to see that I was about to succeed
in possessing her and that I had made sure I should not
be tricked, for, having put my case to her aunt, and having her on my side, I had no more doubts.

I quickly put on a redingote, and in a quarter of an
hour I am at her door. I knock once, and the aunt comes
tiptoeing to open the door and tell me to come back in
half an hour, for, having to take a bath, she was already
naked in her tub.

"Damn it! one lie after another! The excuse is
trumped up. I don't believe a word of it."

"Truly I am not lying, and if you promise to behave
I will take you to her room on the fourth floor. She can
say what she pleases to me afterward, I'll pay no attention."

"To her room? And she is in the bath? Are you deceiving me?"

"No. Follow me."

She goes up, I follow her. She opens a door, she pushes
me in, then she shuts it, and I see La Charpillon stark
naked in the tub; pretending to think that it is her aunt,
she asks her to bring her towels. She was in the most
seductive position that love could ask; but no sooner has
she seen me than she crouches down and gives a cry.

"Don't cry out, for I am nobody's dupe. Be still."

"Go away."

"No. Let me recover myself."

"Go away, I say."

"Be quiet, and fear no violence."

"My aunt shall pay me for this."

"She is an excellent woman and she will find a true friend in me. I will not touch you, but straighten up."

"What! Straighten up?"

"Take the position you were in when I entered."

"Certainly not, and I beg you to leave."

By dint of trying to double up more effectively, she displayed an even more seductive picture, pretending to trust in gentleness to persuade me to go, after seeing that anger had failed her. But when, though I promised not to touch her, she saw me resolved to quench as well as I could the fire she knew she had kindled in my soul, she turned her back on me, determined that I should neither think that she could take pleasure in seeing me, nor myself get any pleasure from the thought. I knew all this, but needing to recover my sanity, I had to sink to anything to appease my senses, and I was not sorry to see the cheat take effect very quickly. Just then the aunt came in, and I left without saying a word, rather glad to have acquired a feeling of contempt which assured me that feelings of love would have no more power over me.

The aunt overtook me at the door, and, asking me if I was pleased, told me to step into the parlor.

"Yes," I said, "very pleased to have made your acquaintance, and here is your reward."

So saying, I threw her a hundred-pound bank note to make her "balm of life" with, not bothering to wait for the receipt which she offered to give me. I was not brazen enough to give her nothing, whereas the ba..[12] was more than sufficiently so to guess that I should not dare leave her unrewarded.

Back at home, after thoroughly considering what had happened and deciding that I was the victor, I rejoiced; and, recovering all my good humor, I felt certain that I would never again set foot in the house of those women. There were seven of them, counting two maidservants.

Their need to subsist had led them to adopt the course
of rejecting no means to that end, and when in their
councils they concluded that they had to employ men,
they confided in the three I have named, who in their
turn would have had no means of subsistence without
them.

Thinking only of amusing myself, going to the theaters,
to the taverns in the neighborhood of London, and to the
boarding school where my daughter was, I happened to
meet her at Vauxhall with her aunt and Goudar, five or
six days after the scene by the bathtub. I tried to avoid
her, but she at once came up to me, gaily reproaching me
for my bad manners. I answered her harshly; but, pretending not to notice it, she entered an arbor, inviting me
to drink a cup of tea with her. I said that I felt more
inclined to sup, and she replied that in that case it was
she who would accept an invitation from me. I am
willing; I order for four, and to all appearances we are
the best of friends. Her remarks, her gaiety, her charms,
the power of which I had experienced, once again displaying themselves before my weak soul, now all the
weaker from drink, I propose a stroll in the darker walks,
hoping, I add, that she will not treat me as she had
treated His Lordship. She replies sweetly enough, and
with an appearance of sincerity which very nearly deceived me, that she wanted to be mine entirely and in the
light; but that first she must have the satisfaction of
seeing me call on her every day, like a true friend of the
household.

"You shall see me there without fail, but now come
into the walk and give me a little proof of your intentions."

"No! Absolutely not!"

At that I left her, refusing to take her home, and I
went home to bed a little tipsy.

The next morning I heartily congratulated myself on
her not having taken me at my word. The power which
the creature had gained over me was irresistible and I

was convinced that I had no other means of saving myself from becoming her dupe except either not to see her or to continue to see her and renounce enjoying her charms. The second course seeming to me impossible, I decided on the first; but the wench had determined not to let me put it into practice. The way in which she went about accomplishing her purpose must have been the result of her regular discussions with her whole infamous coterie.[13]

At home a few days after the little supper at Vauxhall, I saw before me the Chevalier Goudar, who began by congratulating me on my wise decision to see no more of the Augspurghers.

"For," he said, "if you had continued to go there you would have fallen more and more in love with the girl, and she would have reduced you to beggary."

"Then you must think me a great fool. If I had found her accommodating, she would have found me grateful, but without going beyond my means in the proofs of it I should have given her; and if I had found her cruel I could any day have done what I have done already, and so she would never have reduced me, as you think, to beggary."

"Then you are firmly resolved not to see her again?"

"Yes, firmly."

"Then you are no longer in love with her?"

"I was in love with her, and I have learned how to cure myself of it. In a few days I shall have forgotten her completely. I was no longer thinking of her when the devil contrived that I should meet the four of you in Vauxhall."

"There you are! Be persuaded that the true way to be cured of an unhappy love is not to flee the seductive object, for, when one lives in the same country, it is only too easy to cross her path everywhere."

"What other way is there?"

"Enjoying her. It is possible that La Charpillon does not love you; but you are rich, and she has nothing. You could have had her for a certain sum of money, and you would have been far more pleasantly cured when you had found her unworthy of your constancy, for, after all, you know what she is.''

''I would gladly have taken that course if I had not clearly seen her plan.''

''You would have frustrated it by coming to an agreement with her. You should never have paid in advance! I know the whole story.''

''What can you know?''

''I know that she has cost you a hundred guineas, and that you have not had a single kiss from her. For that amount you could have had her in bed. She herself boasts of having tricked you.''

''She lies. I made her aunt a present of the amount, which she needs, she tells me, to make her fortune.''

''Yes, to compound her 'balm of life'; but admit that, but for her niece, she would never have received it.''

''I admit it; but tell me, please, what leads you to come to say these things to me today, you who are of her coterie?''

''What brings me here, I swear to you, is nothing but friendship for you, and as for your saying that I am of her coterie, I will set you right by telling you the incident which made me acquainted with the girl, and with her mother, her grandmother, and her two aunts.

''Sixteen months ago,'' he went on, ''happening to be at Vauxhall, I saw the Venetian Ambassador, the Procurator Morosini, walking alone. He had just arrived to congratulate the King on his accession to the throne in the name of his Republic. Seeing His Excellency delighting in watching the young London beauties who were strolling here and there, it occurred to me to go to him and say that all those beauties were at his command and that he had only to throw his handkerchief at whichever one of them he was pleased to choose. My remark making him laugh, and continuing to stroll with me while I assured him that I was not joking, he asked me, pointing to a girl, if he could have her too. Not knowing her, I told him to continue his stroll, saying that I would join him presently with the answer. Having no time to lose, and certain, from her manner, that I was not about to make my proposal to a Vestal, I approach the girl and the lady who was with her, and I tell her that the Ambassador is in love with her and that I will bring him to her if she feels inclined to encourage his newborn passion. The aunt says that a nobleman of his rank could only honor her house if he came to it to make her niece's acquaintance. They give me their name and address, and the thing is done. I leave them, and before rejoining the Ambassador I happen upon a great connoisseur whom I ask who a certain Mademoiselle Charpillon, of Denmark Street, Soho, may be.''

''So it was La Charpillon?''

''None other. He tells me that she is a Swiss girl who is not yet a public woman but who to all appearances soon will be, for she is not rich and has a numerous family, all females. I at once overtake the Venetian, and telling him that his business is done, I ask him at what hour on the next day I may introduce him to the beauty, warning him that, since she has a mother and aunts, she will not receive him alone. He has no objection to that; he is even glad that she is not a public woman. He appoints an hour at which I am to go with him, incognito, in a hackney carriage, and I leave him. After informing the girl and her aunt of the hour, and adding that she must pretend not to know who he is, I go home. The next day I introduced him to them, and after spending an hour in perfectly decent conversation with the girl and her aunt without making any proposal, we left. On the way the Ambassador told me that he wanted to have her on the conditions which he would give me at his residence the next day in writing, and not otherwise.

''The conditions were that Mademoiselle should go to live in a small furnished house, which would cost her nothing and in which she was to receive no one. His Excellency would arrange for her to receive fifty guineas a month and would pay for supper whenever he chose to go to sleep with her. He instructed me to find him the house, if the contract, which must be signed by the girl's mother, was agreed to, and to act quickly. In three days I did and settled everything, but demanding a written agreement from the mother that she would give me her daughter for one night after the departure of the Ambassador, who it was known would remain in London only a year."

At this point Goudar took from his pocket the agreement, which I read and reread with as much surprise as pleasure. Then he went on as follows:

"At the end of the year the Ambassador left, and the girl was free. She had Lord Baltimore,[14] Lord Grosvenor,[15] the Portuguese Envoy Saa, and several others, but none of them as his acknowledged mistress. I press the mother to make her give me a night, as she had agreed to do in writing; but she refuses to take me seriously, and the girl, who does not love me, laughs in my face. I cannot have her arrested, for she has not reached the required age; but in a few days I shall obtain a warrant for her mother's arrest, and all London will laugh. Now you know why I constantly go to her house; but you are wrong if you believe that I am involved in the plots which are hatched here. However, I can assure you that they are considering how to get you into their toils again, and that they will succeed if you are not very careful."

"Tell the mother that I have another hundred guineas at her disposal if she can arrange for me to spend a night with her daughter."

"Do you really mean that?"

"I do indeed, but I will not pay the money until the thing is done."

"That is the one sure way not to be taken in. I undertake the commission with pleasure."

I kept the brazen scoundrel to dinner with me. He was

a man who, in the sort of life I was leading in London, could not but be useful to me. He knew everything, and he told me any number of amorous anecdotes which I was very glad to hear. He was, besides, known as the author of several works[16] which, though bad, showed that he had a certain wit. He was then writing his *Chinese Spy*, composing five or six letters a day at the coffeehouses at which he chanced to be. I amused myself by writing a number of them[17] for him, for which he was most grateful to me. The reader will see in what condition I found him some years later in Naples.

No later than the next day I am surprised in my room by La Charpillon herself, who, not gay but serious, tells me that she has not come for breakfast but to demand an explanation from me; at the same time she introduces Miss Lorenzi,[18] I bow to her.

"What explanation do you want, Mademoiselle?"

At these words Miss Lorenzi thinks it proper to leave us alone. She was ugly. It was the first time that I had seen her. I told Jarba to bring her breakfast and to tell the portress that I was at home to no one.

"Is it true, Monsieur, that you sent the Chevalier Goudar to tell my mother that you would give her a hundred guineas for a night with me?"

"It is true. Are a hundred guineas not enough?"

"I will thank you not to jest. It is not a question of bargaining. It is a question of learning if you think you have the right to insult me, and if you think I am one to put up with it."

"If you feel that you have been insulted I admit that I am in the wrong; but I did not expect as much. To whom was I to address myself? For directly to you leads to nothing. You are too fond of deceiving, and you exult only when you break your word."

"I told you that you should never have me either by violence or for money, but only when you have made me fall in love with you by your attentions. Now prove to me that I have failed to keep my word to you. It is you who have failed in your duty to me by your trick of surprising me when I was in the bath, and yesterday by sending to ask my mother to deliver me over to your brutality. Only a scoundrel would undertake that errand for you.''

''Goudar a scoundrel? He is your best friend. You know that he loves you, and that he procured the Ambassador for you only in the hope of having you. The written agreement which is in his possession proves your wrongdoing. You are in debt to him. Pay him, and then call him a scoundrel if you can find yourself innocent by some other ethics than his. Do not cry, Mademoiselle, for I know the source of your tears. It is impure.''

''You do not know it. I tell you I love you; and it is a cruel thing for me to find myself treated in this way by you.''

''If you love me, you have chosen a very poor way to make me believe it.''

''As you have to convince me of your esteem. You began with me as you would have done with a prostitute, and yesterday as if I were an animal without a will of my own, the mere slave of my mother. It seems to me that if you had any consideration you should at least have asked me directly, and not by the mouth of a vile go-between but in writing. I would have[19] answered you in writing, and then there would have been no possibility of deceit.''

''Imagine that I did write to you; what would your answer have been?''

''Observe my frankness. I would have promised to satisfy you, without a word about the hundred guineas, simply on condition that you would pay court to me for only two weeks, coming to my house and never asking the slightest favor of me. We should have laughed, you would have become one of the family, we should have gone to promenades and plays together, and at last, having made me madly in love with you, you would have had me in your arms as you would have deserved to have me, not from compliance but from love. I am astonished that a man like you can be content that a girl whom he loves should give herself to him as an act of compliance. Do you not consider it humiliating, on the one side as well as on the other? I feel ashamed when I think—and I admit it to you—that I have never yet been moved by more than compliance. Alas for me! Yet I feel that I was born to love, and I believed that you were the man whom heaven had sent to England to make me happy. You have done the very opposite. No man has ever seen me cry. You have even made me unhappy at home, for my mother will never have the sum you offered her, even if it were to cost me only one kiss.''

"I am truly sorry to have hurt you; but I see no way of mending it.''

"Come to our house; that will mend it; and keep your money, which I despise. If you love me, come and conquer me like a reasonable lover and not like a brute; I will help you do it, for you must be sure now that I love you.''

This harangue won me over. I gave her my word that I would pay court to her every day and be for her what she wanted me to be; but not for longer than the time she had prescribed. She confirmed her promise, and her brow cleared. She rose, and when I asked her to give me one kiss as a pledge of her good faith, she said with a laugh that I must not begin by violating our conditions. I agreed, and I begged her pardon. She left me in love, and hence full of repentance for all my past conduct toward her. *Amare et sapere vix deo conceditur* ("To love and be wise is scarcely granted to a god").[20]

The adjurations and the arguments to which she treated me, and of which the account I have just given is but a feeble representation, would perhaps have had no power if she had sent them to me in a letter; but delivered *viva voce* they could not but put me in chains. In a letter I should have seen neither her tears nor her captivating features, which all pleaded for her before a judge already corrupted by the God of Love. I began going to see her late in the afternoon of that same day, and in the reception I was given, instead of seeing that they were mocking me in my defeat, I thought I heard applause for my heroism.

> *Quel che l'uom vede Amor gli fa invisibile*
> *E l'invisibil fa veder Amore.*

> ("Love makes what a man sees invisible, and Love makes him see what is invisible.")[21]

I spent the whole of the two weeks without ever taking her hand to kiss it, and I never entered her house without bringing her a costly present, which she made of inestimable value by her enchanting grace and her show of boundless gratitude. In addition, to make the time pass more quickly I arranged some diversion every day, either at one of the theaters or on the outskirts of London. The two weeks must have cost me at least four hundred guineas. The last day finally came.

In the morning I timidly asked her, in her mother's presence, if she intended to spend the night in my house, or at home in her own bed with me. Her mother replied that we would decide that after supper. I agreed, not daring to point out to her that at my house the supper would have been tastier, and hence more costly and more inviting to love.

After supper the mother told me to leave with the company and to come back later. Although laughing to myself at this secrecy, I obeyed; and, returning, here I am at last in the parlor, where I see the mother and the daughter and a bed on the floor. I am free at last of any fear of being duped; but I am surprised that the mother, wishing me good night, asks me if I will pay the hundred guineas in advance.

"For shame!" said her daugher.

And the mother left. We locked the door.

It was the moment when my love was to begin its

escape from slavery. So I go to her with open arms, but, though without harshness, she draws away, asking me to get into bed first while she makes ready to do likewise. I yield to her will, I undress, I get into bed, and, on fire with love, I see her undress, and when she has nothing on but her shift I see her blow out the candles.

Left in darkness, I complain, I say that it is impossible, she replies that she can sleep only in the dark. I think it base, but I control myself. Knowing that modesty could not enter in, I begin to foresee all the resistances whose purpose is to sour the pleasures of love, but I hope to overcome them.

No sooner do I feel that she is in bed than I approach to clasp her in my arms, but I find her worse than dressed. Crouched in her long shift, her arms crossed, and her head buried in her bosom, she let me talk as much as I will and never answers a word. When, tired of talking, I determine to act, she remains motionless in the same position and defies me to do it. I thought her behavior was meant to be a joke; but at last I am convinced that it is nothing of the sort. I see that I am duped, a fool, the most contemptible of men, as I see that the girl is the vilest of whores.

In such a situation love easily becomes rage. I lay hold of her as if she were a bolt of goods, but I can accomplish nothing; it seems to me that her accursed shift is the reason for it, and I succeed in tearing it open behind, from the top to her buttocks; thereupon, my hands becoming claws, I count on the most brutal violence on my part, but all my efforts were vain. I made up my mind to stop when I found my strength exhausted and when, having grasped her neck in one hand, I felt a strong temptation to strangle her.

Cruel night, heartbreaking night, during which I talked to the monster in every possible key: gentleness, anger, reasonableness, remonstration, threats, rage, despair, prayers, tears, vilification, atrocious insults. She resisted me for three whole hours without ever answer-

ing me, and without ever straightening up except once
to prevent me from doing something which would in a
way have avenged me.

At three o'clock in the morning, amazed, stupefied,
feeling my head on fire, I decided to dress in the dark.
I opened the door to the parlor, but finding the street
door locked, I raised a row, and a maidservant came to
open it for me. I walked home, accompanied by a night
watchman[22] whom I went to Soho Square to find. I at
once got into bed, but irritated Nature avenged herself
by refusing me the rest I needed. When it grew light I
took a cup of chocolate, which my stomach refused to
keep down, and an hour later my shivering announced
a fever which did not subside until the next day, leaving
me unable to move my limbs. Ordered to stay in bed and
to diet, I was sure that I should recover my strength in
a few days; but what was balm to my soul was my certainty that I was cured of my insane love, for I felt that
I was free from any thought of revenge. Shame had made
me loathe myself.

The morning on which I had succumbed to the fever,
I had ordered my manservant to shut my door to everyone, to announce no visitors to me, and to put any letters
which might come for me into my desk, for I did not
want to read them until I had recovered my health. It
was on the fourth day that, feeling a little better, I asked
Jarba for my letters. Among those which had come by
post I find one from Pauline, who writes me from Madrid
that Clairmont had saved her life in crossing a river, and
that, not thinking she could find another servant as faithful, she had decided to keep him until she reached Lisbon, whence she would send him back to me by sea. At
the time I thought she had done well; but as it turned
out she caused me to lose Clairmont. I learned four
months later that the ship on which he had taken passage
had been wrecked, and, not seeing him again, I believed,
as I believe today, that he was drowned.

Among the letters which had come by the "penny

post'' [23] I found two from La Charpillon's mother and one from herself. In the first of the two letters which the infamous mother wrote me on the morning after the night I had spent with her daughter, she told me, not knowing that I was ill, that her daughter was in bed with a high fever and covered with bruises from the blows I had given her, which obliged her to sue me in court. In the second letter, written the next day, she said she had learned that I was ill like her daughter and that she was sorry to hear it, her daughter herself having admitted to her that I might have reason to complain of her, but that she would justify herself at our first interview. The letter from La Charpillon was written on the third day. She said she confessed that she had been so much in the wrong that she was surprised I had not strangled her when I had her by the neck, and she swore that she would not have resisted it, for such was her duty in the cruel dilemma in which she had found herself. She said that, feeling certain that I had resolved not to go to her house again, she begged me to receive her at mine once only, since she was eager to inform me of something which would be of interest to me and which she could communicate to me only by word of mouth. In a note which Goudar had written me that morning at my door, he said that he had something to say to me and that he would come back at noon. I at once ordered him admitted.

The extraordinary man began by amazing me with a detailed account of all that had happened to me with La Charpillon during the four hours she had spent in bed with me, even down to the torn shift and the moment when she thought I would strangle her. He said that he had been informed of the entire scene by her mother, to whom the girl had given an exact account of everything. He said that she had not had fever, but that it was true that her whole body was covered with black marks, obvious signs of the blows she had received, and that her mother's great regret was that she had not received the hundred guineas, which I would certainly have paid in advance if her daughter had insisted.

"She would have had them in the morning," I said, "if she had been amenable."

"She had sworn to her mother that she would not be, and do not hope to have her without her mother's consent."

"But why does she not consent?"

"Because she maintains that as soon as you have enjoyed her you will leave her."

"That might be so; but after I had rewarded her adequately, whereas now she is left without being able to hope for anything more."

"Is that your firm resolve?"

"Most firm."

"It is your best course; but I want to show you something which will surprise you. We shall meet again in an hour."

An hour later he comes back, followed by a porter who brought an armchair[24] covered by a piece of cloth up to my room. As soon as we were alone Goudar uncovered the chair and asked me if I would like to buy it. I replied that I should not know what to do with it, besides which it was an unattractive piece of furniture.

"Nevertheless," he said, "the price asked for it is a hundred guineas."

I reply with a laugh that I would not give three for it, and this is what he then said to me:

"The chair you see here has five springs, all of which operate at the same time as soon as a person sits down in it. Their action is very rapid. Two seize the person's two arms and hold them fast; two more, lower down, take hold of his legs, spreading them as far apart as possible, and the fifth raises the back of the seat in such a way that it forces the seated person onto his coccyx."

After telling me this, Goudar sits down, the springs operate, and I see him held by the arms, and otherwise in the same position in which an obstetrician would put a woman whose labor he wanted to make easy.

"Get La Charpillon to sit here," he said, "and your business is done."

After laughing my fill, I tell him I do not want to buy it but that he will do me a favor if he will leave it[25] with me for only a day.

"Not even an hour unless you buy it, and the owner of the contrivance is waiting for me a hundred paces from here."

"Then return it to him and come back for dinner."

He told me what I had to do at the back of the chair to make the springs return to their places and so set him free. He covered it with the cloth again, he summoned the porter, and he left.

The action was infallible, and it was not avarice which kept me from buying the contrivance, for it must have cost its owner far more, but the fear which it inspired in me after I reflected a little. The crime could have cost me my life in the view of English judges, and besides I could not have brought myself deliberately to obtain possession of La Charpillon by force, still less by the action of this formidable contrivance, which would have made her die of fear.

At dinner I told Goudar that, La Charpillon having proposed to pay me a visit, I should have liked to keep the mechanical chair to convince her that I could have had my will of her if I had wanted to. I showed him the letter she had written me, and he advised me to let her pay the visit, if only for curiosity's sake.

Feeling in no hurry to receive the wench with those black marks on her face and bosom, which she would only have paraded to make me blush for my brutal fury, I spent eight or ten days without making up my mind to receive her, Goudar coming every day to inform me of the results of the councils held by the crew of females who were resolved to live only by trickery. He told me that La Charpillon's grandmother was a Bernese woman who had taken the name of Augspurgher without any right to it, being only the mistress of a citizen so named, by whom she had had four daughters; La Charpillon's mother was the youngest of them. This youngest daughter, who was pretty enough, having indulged in conduct not consonant with the wise regulations of the Swiss Government, had been the cause of a decree of exile from the canton for the entire family, which had gone to settle in Franche-Comté,[26] where they had lived for a time on the profits of the "balm of life," the manufacture of which the grandmother directed.

"It was there that La Charpillon was born. Her mother gave her that name, I do not know why, saying that her father was a Count of Boulainvilliers,[27] whose mistress she had been for three months. La Charpillon becoming pretty, her mother concluded that her great good fortune awaited her in Paris, and went there to live; but four years later, seeing that the sale of her balm did not suffice to support her, that La Charpillon, being still too young, did not find a man of substance to keep her, and that the debts she had incurred threatened her with prison, she decided to go to live in London, so advised by Monsieur Rostaing, who had become her lover and who, also burdened with debts, had to flee from France. Five or six months after her arrival in London the mother nearly died from the overdose of mercury she took to cure her of the cruel disease with which Rostaing admits that he infected her.

"Coumon is a Languedocian, an intimate friend of Rostaing's, who serves him, as he does the whole family, by bringing dupes whom he picks up in the coffeehouses of London to their house for games at whist. The profit is always honorably and equally divided into six parts; but what La Charpillon earns from the temporary relations into which she enters in the great nocturnal gatherings in the gardens of London is buried in secrecy; however, I know that her mother supports Rostaing."

Such is the story I learned from Goudar. The man introduced me to the most celebrated courtesans in London, and above all to Kitty Fisher,[28] who was beginning to go out of fashion. In a potshop where we were drinking a bottle of strong beer,[29] which is better than wine, he introduced me to a girl who served there, sixteen years of age, whom I thought a wonder of nature. She was Irish and a Catholic, and her name was Sarah.[30] I wanted to have her, but he would never permit it. He himself was trying to get possession of her, and he told me he was jealous of her. He did in fact get possession of her some time later, and the following year he left England with her. Then he married her. She is the same Sarah Goudar who shone at Naples, Florence, Venice, and elsewhere, always with him, and of whom I will speak four or five years hence. He had hatched the scheme of giving her to Louis XV, putting an end to the domination of Madame Du Barry, but a *lettre de cachet*[31] sent him running. Happy days of the *lettre de cachet,* alas, you are gone forever!

When La Charpillon, after looking in vain for a reply to her last letter, saw two weeks pass without hearing a word about me, she resolved to return to the assault. This must have been the result of an extremely secret council, for Goudar had told me nothing about it.

She was announced as having arrived at my door alone in a sedan chair, a thing so extraordinary that I at once decided to receive her. I saw her before me just as I was taking chocolate; I do not rise, I do not offer her any; but she modestly asks me for some, sitting down beside me and putting out her face for me to kiss, which she had never done before. I turn my head away, but this utterly unexpected refusal does not disconcert her:

"It is," she says, "these still visible marks from the blows you gave me which make my face distasteful to you."

"You lie, I never struck you."

"It makes no difference, your tiger's claws left bruises

all over my body. Look, for you run no risk that what you see will have the power to seduce you. Besides, it is nothing you have not seen before.''

So saying, the scheming wench rises and shows me the whole surface of her body marked here and there with bruises which were still livid despite their age. Coward that I was, why did I not turn my eyes away? Because she was beautiful, and because I loved her charms, and because charms would not deserve their name if they were not more powerful than a man's reason. I pretended to look only at the bruises. Fool that I was! She already knew that I was tasting the poison and even gulping it down; but suddenly she rearranges her clothing and sits down beside me again, sure that I wished the exhibition would continue longer; but I control myself and I say coldly that it had been her own fault if I had hurt her so badly, and that this was so true that I could not even be sure that I had done it.

''I know,'' she said, ''that it is all my fault, for if I had been affectionate, as I ought to have been, I could now show you only the traces of kisses; but repentance blots out crime. I come to ask your forgiveness. May I hope for it?''

''You have it already. I hold nothing against you, and it is I who repent; but I have not yet been able to forgive myself. That is all. Now that you know all, you can leave and cease both to count on me and to trouble my peace in future.''

''It shall be as you wish; I know all, it is true; but it is you who do not know all, and you shall know it, if you will permit me to spend another half hour with you.''

''Since I have nothing to do, you may stay and say what you have to say.''

Despite the haughty role which reason and honor laid it upon me to play, I was greatly touched and, what is far worse, I felt inclined to believe that the girl had come to me again not to deceive me but to persuade me that she loved me, and that she wanted at last to deserve my becoming her fond lover. The speech she made to tell me what I did not know required no more than a quarter of an hour, and she used two, constantly interrupting it by tears and countless digressions. The gist of it was that her mother had made her swear by her soul's salvation that she would spend the night with me as she had spent it, and that she had obeyed her. She offered to be mine as she had been Signor Morosini's, living with me, seeing no more of her mother or any of her relatives, and visiting no one except the people I wanted her to visit, while I was to allow her a certain sum each month, which she would turn over to her mother to keep her from troubling her with actions at law, since she was not old enough to claim independence.

She dined with me, and she made this proposal toward nightfall, when, having seen her listen unprotestingly while I said everything to her that she deserved to hear, I had become calm and resolved to expose myself to temptation once again. A little while before she left I said to her that we could live together as she had proposed, but that I absolutely insisted on sealing the bargain with her mother, and so she should see me at her house the next day. I saw that she was surprised.

It is clear that she would that day have granted me anything I could desire, and that in consequence there would have been no question of resistance in the future and that I should have been safe from any trickery. Then why did I not do what was no less than a duty I owed to myself? Because love, which makes a man a fool, persuaded me that, having that day been the creature's judge, it would have been base in me if I had gone on to become her lover. She must have left with a feeling of contempt and a determination to avenge herself for my coldness. But a man in love cannot see his mistakes until he is no longer in love. Goudar was amazed the next day when I told him of her visit. I asked him to find me a small furnished house for rent by the month in Chelsea, and he undertook to do so. That evening I went to see the scheming wench at her house, but in a sober mood, of the absurdity of which she must have been fully aware. As she was alone with her mother, I hastened to tell the latter my plan: a house in Chelsea, to which her daughter would go to live and in which I should be the master, and fifty guineas a month for her to use as she saw fit.

"I do not care to know," the mother replied, "what sum you will give her a month; but I insist that when she leaves my custody to live elsewhere she shall give me the hundred guineas she should have received from you when you went to bed with her."

I replied that she would give them to her. The girl said that, while the house was being found, she hoped that I would come to see her. I promised I would do so.

No later than the next day Goudar came to tell me that there were a score of houses for rent in Chelsea, and that I should do well to go there with him and have the pleasure of choosing. We went, I chose, and I paid ten guineas in advance for a month, taking a receipt and obtaining acceptance of all the conditions I wanted to stipulate. In the afternoon of the same day I went to seal the bargain with the mother in the daughter's presence, making them both sign the agreement, whereupon I told the daughter to pack her things and come with me. She quickly filled a trunk with her clothes, I had it taken to my new house in a hackney carriage, and a half hour later she appears, ready to leave with me. The mother asks me for the hundred guineas, I give them to her, having no fear of being tricked, for all the girl's possessions were already in my house. We leave, and we arrive in Chelsea, where she declares the house very much to her liking. We take a stroll until nightfall, we talk, we sup in high spirits, then we go to bed, where she grants me some favors sweetly enough, but as soon as I want to proceed to the heart of the matter I am disappointed to encounter difficulties. She alleges reasons of nature, I reply that I do not consider that condition repellent enough to keep me from proving my love to her; but she resists, raising objections which, though groundless, her sweetness and her caresses persuade me to admit, and she puts me to sleep.

On waking in the morning and seeing her sleeping, it occurs to me to convince myself that she had not been lying, and I quickly unlace what prevented me from seeing; she wakes and tries to stop me, but it was too late. I gently reproach her for deceiving me, and she sees me ready to forgive her and my love eager to confirm her pardon; but it is she who refuses to forgive me for having taken her by surprise. She is angry, I try to calm her, and at the same time to force her to yield, she will not, she opposes force to force, and, knowing her tricks, I determine to make an end, but calling her all the names she deserved. She begins to dress, laughing at me so impertinently I am driven to slap her face and give her a kick which knocks her out of the bed; she screams, she stamps her feet, the caretaker comes up, she opens the door to him, she speaks to him in English, with blood streaming from her nose. The man who, as my good luck would have it, spoke Italian, told me that she wanted to leave, and that he advised me not to try to stop her, for she could lodge a very serious complaint, in which case he would have to testify against me. I replied that she could go to the devil if she pleased. She then finished dressing, and after staunching the blood and washing her face, she left in a sedan chair. I spent a long hour there without moving, unable to decide upon anything. I pronounced myself unworthy to live, and I found the girl's behavior incomprehensible and incredible. I finally decided to have the scheming wench's trunk put in a hackney carriage and to go back to my house, where, overwhelmed by melancholy, I went to bed after ordering my door closed to all visitors.

I spent twenty-four hours in reflections, all of which ended by convincing me of my mistakes and making me despise myself. I believe that what follows after a long period of despising oneself is a despair which leads to suicide.

Just as I was going out, Goudar arrived and told me to go back upstairs, for he had something important to say to me. After telling me that La Charpillon was at home,[32] and, having one cheek swollen and black, let no one see her, he advised me to send her her trunk and to give up any claims I might have upon her mother, for she was in the right and determined to ruin me by a calumny which could both ruin me and cost me my life. The reader can easily imagine its nature,[33] and everyone knows how easy it is to make it effectual in London. He said that he had been urged by the mother herself, who did not want to injure me, to act as mediator. After spending the whole day with the man, complaining to the top of my bent like the utter fool I was, I told him to assure the mother that I had no intention of keeping her daughter's trunk, but that I wanted to know if she would have the courage to receive it from me in person.

He undertook to deliver my message, but rightly saying that he felt sorry for me. He said that I was about to walk into their toils again, and that he pitied me; but I did not believe that she would have the courage to receive me, for, according to the agreement she had signed, she would at least have to give me back a hundred guineas; but, contrary to my expectation, Goudar came and reported with a laugh that Madame Augspurgher hoped that I would always continue to be the good friend of her house. I went there at nightfall, I had the trunk put in her parlor, and I spent an hour there without ever opening my mouth, looking at La Charpillon, who was sewing and who now and again pretended to dry her tears, who never raised her eyes to my face, and who two or three times loosened the bandage round her head so that I could see in what a state my slap had put her face.

I continued to go there every evening, always without speaking to her, until I saw that every sign of the damage I had done her was gone. During those five or six days

my repentance for having had the temerity to disfigure
her produced upon my too kindly soul the fatal effect of
leading me to forget all her misdeeds and making me
so much in love with her that, had she but known it,
she could have stripped me of all I had and reduced me
to beggary.

Seeing her prettiness restored, and dying to have her
in my arms once again, sweet and caressing as I had had
her, even though it had been imperfectly, I sent her a
magnificent pier glass made in one piece, and a tea and
coffee service for twelve of Dresden china, writing her
a loving note in which I called myself the basest of men.
She replied that she expected me for supper alone in her
room, when she would give me, as I deserved, the most
unmistakable tokens of her fond gratitude.

Certain that my good fortune now awaited me, I
thought I saw that I should long since have attained it
if I had been clever enough to attack her on the side
of sentiment. In the blind intoxication of enthusiasm, I
decided to put in her hands the two bills of exchange for
six thousand francs which Bolomay had made over to my
order and which gave me the right to send her mother
and her aunts to prison.

Enchanted by the happiness which awaited me and
by the heroic feelings which made me worthy of it, I go
to her house at suppertime, and I am at once very glad
not to see the two sharpers, whom I mortally hated. She
receives me in the parlor, her mother being present, and
I see with pleasure the pier glass over the fireplace and
the Dresden china service set out in order on the mantelpiece. After countless fond expressions, she invites me
to go up to her room, and her mother wishes us a happy
night. We go up, and after a sufficiently appetizing supper, I take the two bills of exchange from my portfolio
and tell her the whole story of them. I end by saying
that I am putting them[34] in her hands to make her certain that, as soon as she has decided to be my mistress
without reservations, I will endorse them to her order,

and to assure her that I am far from thinking of using them to avenge myself for the base treatment I had received from her mother and her aunts. I only stipulate that she shall promise me that they will not leave her hands. She praises my generous act in the highest terms, she promises everything, and she goes and puts them in her jewel case. After that I think I may begin to give her proofs of my passion, and I find her gentle; but as soon as I try to persuade her to crown my flame, she resists, she presses me to her bosom, and she commands her tears to flow. I control myself. I ask her if she will change her mind in bed, she sighs, then she says no. I was not stricken dumb, I was entirely deprived of the power of speech. A quarter of an hour later I rose, and, with an appearance of the greatest calm, I took my cloak, my hat, and my sword.

"What!" she said. "Do you not want to spend the night with me?"

"No."

"Shall we see each other tomorrow?"

"I hope so. Good-by."

I left that accursed house, and I went home to bed.

CHAPTER XII[1]

*Continuation of the preceding chapter, but
far stranger.*

THE NEXT morning at eight o'clock Jarba announces her.

"She has dismissed her chairmen," he says.

"Say that I am asleep and tell her to go away."

But just then she comes in, and Jarba leaves us.

"Be so good," I say quietly, "as to give me back the two bills of exchange which I put in your hands last night."

"I haven't them with me; but why do you want me to give them back?"

At this question, which could only be answered by an explanation in full, I demolished the dike by which the black humor which was poisoning me was confined to the region about my heart. It escaped like a torrent, manifesting itself in invectives and terrible threats. It was an explosion which continued for a long time, and which my nature needed to preserve my life. When, disgracing my reason, my tears began to flow, she seized the opportunity to tell me that she had promised her mother that she would never give herself to anyone in her own house, and that she had now come to mine only to convince me that she loved me and that her desires were equal to those I felt, and indeed she would never leave it, if such was my wish.

The reader who thinks that, at this declaration, all my anger should have vanished, and that I should instantly have made myself sure of her sincerity and the submission inseparable from it, is mistaken. He does not know that the passage from irritated love to black anger is short and swift, while the passage from anger to love is long, slow, and difficult. The distance is the same; but when anger is seconded by indignation, a man becomes absolutely incapable of any fond feeling. To brute hatred indignation adds noble scorn, which, sprung from reason, strengthens him and makes him invincible. Its duration depends on his temperament. It does not yield until it no longer exists. My temperament was such that, in me, simple anger lasted only a moment: *irasci celerem tamen ut placabilis essem* ("I become angry quickly, even as I am quickly appeased"),[2] but when indignation has entered in, my proud reason has always made me inflexible until forgetfulness supervened to restore me to my original state.

When La Charpillon on that occasion offered herself completely to my desires, she knew, she was certain, that my anger or my pride would keep me from taking her at her word. This sort of knowledge, reader, is the daughter of philosophy in you and in me; but in a coquette it is the daughter of nature.

The young monster left me toward nightfall, to all appearances mortified, downcast, and disconsolate, saying only these few words:

"I hope you will come back to me as soon as you have come back to yourself."

She spent eight hours with me, during which she interrupted me only five or six times to deny suppositions on my part which were true but which it was vital to her not to let pass. I never troubled to have dinner brought, but it was so that I should not have to eat with her.

After she left I found myself in a condition in which my only need was to rest; but I took a bowl of broth, then I slept fairly well. On waking I found that I was calm, and, recollecting the previous day, I thought that La Charpillon had repented of her wrongdoing, of which I thought I had seen her convinced when she left. It seemed to me that I had become indifferent to her and to everything to do with her. Such was the state to which the God of Love brought me in London

Nel mezzo del cammin di nostra vita

("In the mid way of our life")³

at the age of thirty-eight. It was the end of the first act of my life. The second closed on my departure from Venice in 1783. The third will apparently close here,⁴ where I am amusing myself writing these memoirs. The comedy will then have ended, and it will have had its three acts. If it is hissed, I hope that I shall not hear anyone tell me so; but I have not yet informed my reader of the last scene of this first act, and it is, I believe, the most interesting.

> *Chi ha messo il piè sull'amorosa pania*
> *Cerchi rittrarlo, e non v'inveschi l'ale,*
> *Che non è in somma amor se non insania*
> *A giudizio de' savj universale.*

> ("Let him who has set his foot on the birdlime of love try to draw it back, and not entangle his wings in it, for love is nothing but madness, according to the universal judgment of the wise.")⁵

I went to walk in the Green Park, where I saw Goudar coming to meet me. I needed the scoundrel. He said that he had come from La Charpillon's, where he had found everyone in high spirits, and that though he had several times brought the conversation around to me he had never succeeded in getting a word out of them. I told him that I despised her, together with her whole family, and he praised me. He came to dine with me, then we went to the Walsh[6] woman's, where the celebrated Kitty Fisher came to wait for the Duke of xx, who was to take her to a ball. She had on over a hundred thousand crowns' worth of diamonds. Goudar told me I could seize the opportunity to have her for ten guineas, but I did not want to do so. She was charming, but she spoke only English. Accustomed to loving only with all my senses, I could not indulge in love without including my sense of hearing. She left. La Walsh told us that it was at her house that she swallowed a hundred-pound bank note on a slice of buttered bread which Sir Richard Atkins,[7] brother of the beautiful Mrs. Pitt,[8] gave her. Thus did the Phryne[9] make a present to the Bank of London.[10] I spent an hour with Miss Kennedy, who had lived with the Venetian Secretary of Embassy Berlendis.[11] She became drunk and indulged in all sorts of wantonness; but the image of La Charpillon, which was always with me, left me no appetite for possessing the charming Irish-woman. I returned to my house, melancholy and discontented. It seemed to me that I ought to renounce La Charpillon for ever; but, in consideration of my own honor, I should not leave her with the victory or with reason to boast that she had got the two bills of exchange from me for nothing. I resolved to make her give them back to me, either willingly or by force. I had to find a way to do it; and here is what made me believe that I had found it.

Monsieur Malignan, at whose lodging I had made the infernal creature's acquaintance, came to invite me to dinner there. Since he had dined at my house more than once with his wife and daughter, I could not refuse him, the more so since he asked me to send him two dishes prepared by my excellent cook. However, I did not agree to go until I had asked him who the persons were whom he had invited. He named them, and, not knowing them,

I promised I would go. It was on the next day but one. I found there two young ladies from Liège, one of whom very soon interested me; it was she who introduced her husband, whom Malignan had not introduced to me, and another young man who I thought was paying court to the other lady, who she said was her cousin. The company being to my liking, I was hoping to spend a pleasant day, when, just after we all sat down at table, in comes La Charpillon, who gaily says to Madame Malignan that she would not have come to ask her for dinner if she had known she had so many guests. She was warmly received, and was given the place at my left; at my right was the lady from Liège whom I had already found very agreeable.

I saw that I was caught. If La Charpillon had arrived before dinner was served, I should have found some excuse to leave; but it was too late for that. The course I adopted all through the dinner was to disregard the intruder completely and to devote all my attention to the lady from Liège. After we rose from the table Malignan gave me his word of honor that he had not invited her, and I pretended to believe him.

The two ladies and gentlemen were to embark for Ostend three or four days later, and, speaking of their departure, the agreeable lady said that she was sorry to leave England without having seen Richmond.[12] I at once asked her to grant me the favor and the honor of showing it to her no later than the next day, and, not waiting for her to answer me, I invited her husband, her cousin, and, one after the other, the entire company, except La Charpillon, at whom I did not even look. The excursion was applauded and the invitation accepted.

"Two carriages seating four," I added, "will be ready tomorrow morning at eight o'clock, and there will be exactly eight of us."

"And I will make the ninth," said La Charpillon, fixing her eyes on my face with unexampled effrontery, "and I hope, Monsieur, that you will not turn me away."

"Certainly not, it would be impolite. I will precede you all on horseback."

"No, no! I will hold Mademoiselle Émilie on my lap."

She was Malignan's daughter. A quarter of an hour later I leave the drawing room to attend to something and, coming back, I encounter the brazen hussy, who says that I have insulted her most outrageously, and that I owe her amends or she will avenge herself.

"Begin," I said, "by giving me back my bills of exchange, and we will discuss the matter afterward."

"You shall have them tomorrow."

About ten o'clock I leave the company, after promising that I will not go on horseback and that the two carriages will be at Malignan's house, where we will all breakfast. I made all the arrangements accordingly.

The next morning after breakfast Malignan, his wife, his daughter, and the two gentlemen got into one carriage, and I had to get into the other with the two beautiful ladies and La Charpillon, who appeared to have become the married lady's intimate friend. The arrangement could not but put me in a bad humor. We arrived at Richmond in an hour and a quarter, and after ordering a good dinner we went to see the apartments, then the gardens, the weather being superb. It was autumn.

The informality of our stroll affording her the opportunity, La Charpillon comes up to me and says that she wants to give me back my bills of exchange at her house. At that I reproach her with her constant course of deceit, her base character, and her infamous behavior, I call her a who . . .,[13] I name the men with whom she has been, I swear to her that I hate her, and that it is she who must fear my vengeance; but she was well versed in her trade, she let me talk, holding my arm and smiling, but asking me to speak softly, for I might be heard. I was heard, and I was glad of it.

At noon we went to dinner, and La Charpillon, sitting beside me, indulged in innumerable wanton words and

Playing Whist

Under the Spell of the Coquette

gestures, all intended to make everyone believe that she was in love with me, and not caring if anyone thought she was hurt by the scorn which I showed for all her advances. She really made me angry, for no one could help concluding that I was a fool and that she was openly mocking me. I suffered a great deal at that dinner.

After dinner we returned to the garden, and La Charpillon, stubbornly determined to triumph, clings to my arm, and, knowing all the sites, after a few turns she takes me to the maze.[14] It was here that she wanted to put her powers to the test. She pulls me onto the grass with her, and launches a full-scale amorous attack, with expressions of passion and the fondest love. By displaying the most interesting part of her charms to my sight, she finally succeeded in seducing me; but I still do not know if it was love or a strong desire for revenge which determined me to surrender. However that may be, everything made me sure that she was to be mine, that she could not wait to prove it to me, and that she certainly had no idea of putting any obstacle in my way.

With this thought in mind, I become gentle and tender, I recant, I ask her a thousand pardons, I swear that I will no longer demand that she give me the bills of exchange, and that all that I possess is hers, and after these preliminaries, signed and confirmed by fiery kisses, I think I see that she herself invites me to gather the laurel of victory, but just at the very moment when I am certain that I shall possess her, she curvets and throws me out of the saddle.

"What now! What insane behavior!"

"Enough of this, my dear friend. I promise to spend the night at your house, in your arms."

She was still in them as she spoke the words; but my soul, my blood, the tumult of my heart left me unable to do anything but satisfy myself. Holding her clasped in my left arm with all the strength which the extreme of fury gave me, I take from my pocket a knife with a pointed blade, I unsheathe it with my teeth, and I put the point of it to her throat, which was bare except for a thin collar. I threaten to kill her if she moves.

"Do whatever you will. I ask you for nothing but my life; but after you have satisfied yourself I will not leave this place. I shall have to be taken to the carriage by force, and nothing shall stop me from telling the reason for it."

She did not need to threaten me, for I had recovered my reason the moment after the one which had decided me to cut her throat. I rose without answering her by a single word, and after picking up my knife, my hat, and my walking stick, I set out to find my way back from the bowling green[15] where I had been within a hair's-breadth of my ruin.

Can anyone believe that she followed me, that she took my arm, as if nothing had happened? It is impossible that a seventeen-year-old girl can be what she was without having gone through a hundred skirmishes of the same sort. Once the feeling of shame is overcome, she grows used to it, and she glories in it. When we rejoined the company I was asked if I had felt ill; but no one noticed the least change in her.

We returned to London, where, saying that I felt indisposed, I thanked the company and went home.

This episode made the strongest impression on my mind. I could not sleep. I knew beyond doubt that if I did not resolve to avoid every chance of seeing the girl I was absolutely lost. Her countenance cast a spell which I could not resist. So I decided not to see her again; but at the same time, ashamed of the weakness I had shown in entrusting the two bills of exchange to her and in letting myself be tricked every time she had promised to return them to me, I wrote her mother a note in which I advised her to force her daughter to send them back to me, or to prepare for proceedings on my part which would make her suffer.

After sending her the note I went out to distract myself, and after dining at a tavern I went to see my daughter at her boarding school, then I returned home, where Jarba handed me a sealed letter which had come by the "penny post." I open it, and I see that it is signed Augspurgher. It was the answer from La Charpillon's mother. Here is what it contained: "I am very much surprised that you should address yourself to me to obtain the two bills of exchange for six thousand French livres which you say you deposited with her. She has just told me that she will return them to you in person when you have grown wiser and have learned to respect her."

Reading this impertinent letter sent the blood to my head so violently that I forgot my morning's resolution. I put pistols in my pocket and I make my way to Denmark Street, Soho, intending to cane the wench into giving me back my letters. I had taken the pistols only to keep the upper hand of the two sharpers who supped there every night. I arrive in a fury, but I walk past the door, for I see the hairdresser waiting to be admitted. This hairdresser was a handsome young man who went every Saturday after supper to put up her hair in curl papers. Going to the nearest street corner, I stop, reflecting that I should do better to wait until the hairdresser was gone. Taking my stand just around the corner, a half hour later I see Rostaing and Coumon come out of the house, and I am very glad of it. It meant that supper was over. I hear eleven o'clock cried, and I am surprised that the hairdresser is staying so late. Three quarters of an hour later I see a maidservant come out with a candle in her hand, looking for something which must have fallen out of the window. I enter without compunction, I open the door to the parlor, which was two steps from the street door, and I see, in the words of Shakespeare, the "beast with the two backs" [16] stretched out on the sofa: La Charpillon and the hairdresser. On my appearance the wench gives a cry, her fancy man breaks away from her; but my stick begins descending on him without mercy or reprieve, and without leaving him time to rearrange his clothing. La Charpillon was trembling between the wall and the end of the sofa, not daring, by leaving there, to face the rain of blows from my stick, which might descend on her. The uproar brings the maids, then the aunts, then the paralytic mother; the hairdresser flees, and the three furies let fly at me with insults and imprecations which I find so unjustified that my righteous wrath descends on the furniture. The first objects I broke to pieces were the handsome pier glass and the china service I had given them. Their words angering me more and more, I smashed chairs to bits by hitting them against the floor; then, picking up my cane, I announced that I would break their heads open if they did not stop shouting. Quiet then fell.

Having thrown myself down on the sofa, for I was exhausted, I order the mother to give me my bills of exchange; but just then in comes the night watch.[17] To this night watch, which consists of a single man who walks about his district all night carrying a lantern and a long stick, is entrusted the safety and the peace of the whole vast city. There is one such everywhere. No one dares not to respect him. Putting three or four crowns into his hand, I told him to go away. He left, I shut the door, and, returning to the sofa, I again demanded my bills of exchange from Madame Augspurgher.

"I haven't them, ask my daughter for them."

"Send for her."

The two maids say that, when I began breaking up the chairs, she had fled by the street door, and that they did not know where she might have gone. At this news, the mother and the aunts are in tears:

"My daughter alone at midnight in the streets of London!"

"My niece is lost, where has she gone?"

"Accursed be the hour when you came to England to make us all wretched!"

Thinking of the terrified girl running through the streets at that hour, I tremble.

"Go," I say coldly to the two maids, "and look for her in the neighbors' houses, you will certainly find her. Come back and bring me news that she is safe, and you shall each have a guinea."

They went out, and one of the aunts followed to tell them where they might find her.

But when they saw that I was taking a part in the search for the girl, that I was alarmed by the danger in her running away, then it was that their complaints, their reproaches began again with all the more vigor. I remained there without a word, not only seeming to tell them that they were right, but on the way to being convinced myself that all the fault was mine. I waited impatiently for the maids to return. They finally arrive an hour after midnight. Breathless, and showing every sign of despair, they say they have searched everywhere, she is nowhere to be found. I give them two guineas nevertheless, and I remain there motionless and in terror, reflecting on what a dreadful part the horrible fear which my fury must have inspired in her might play in the disappearance of the unfortunate girl. How weak and stupid is a man in love!

Extremely affected by the disastrous turn of events, I do not hide my sincere repentance from the old cheats. I implore them to have her sought for everywhere as soon as the next day dawns, and to let me know instantly, so that I can hasten to beg her forgiveness on my knees and never see her again as long as I live. In addition I promise to pay for all the furniture I have broken, and to leave my bills of exchange in their hands, signing a receipt with my name. Having thus, to the eternal shame of my reason, made honorable amends to those whose souls laughed at honor, I left, promising two guineas to the maid who should bring me the news that the unfortunate girl had been found.

At the door I found the watch, who was waiting to see

me home. Two o'clock had struck. I flung myself on my bed, where six hours of sleep, though broken by hideous phantasms and agonizing dreams, probably saved me from losing my reason.

At eight o'clock in the morning I hear a knocking, I run to the window, and I see one of my enemies' maids; with my heart pounding I shout that she is to be shown up, and I breathe again when I learn that Miss Charpillon had just come home by sedan chair, but in a pitiable condition. She had at once gone to bed.

"I came at once to tell you the news, not for the two guineas, but because I pity you."

The word "pity" takes me in at once; I give her the two guineas, I make her sit down near me, and I ask her to tell me all the details of her return. I feel certain that the maid is honest, that she has my interests at heart, and that if need be she will serve me faithfully. I am very far from suspecting that she may have an understanding with the mother. But how could I be so excessively stupid? It was because I needed to be so.

She began by telling me that her young mistress loved me and that she only played a part in deceiving me because her mother insisted on it.

"I know that, but where did she spend the night?"

"She took refuge with a shopwoman beyond Soho Square, where she spent the whole night, sitting uncomfortably in the shop. She has just gone to bed with a high fever. I am afraid it will have consequences, for she is in her critical days."

"That is not true, for with my own eyes I saw the hairdresser——"

"Oh, that makes no difference. He is not so particular."

"She is in love with him."

"I do not think so, though she often spends hours with him."

"And you tell me she loves me?"

"Oh, that has nothing to do with it."

"Tell her that I will go to spend the day at her bedside, and bring me her answer."

"I will send the other maid."

"No. She does not speak French."

She left, and, not having seen her reappear, at three o'clock in the afternoon I resolve to go myself to see how she is. Scarcely have I knocked once before her aunt comes to speak to me at the door and asks me not to come in, swearing that if I come in I will either kill or be killed. Her two friends were there, furiously angry with me, and the poor girl was delirious from a burning fever. She did nothing but cry out, "There is my murderer, there is Seingalt. He wants to kill me. Save me."

"In God's name, go away."

I go home, in despair and certain that I have been told the simple truth. Sunk in melancholy, I spend the whole day without eating, for I cannot swallow, and the whole night unable to sleep, with violent chills. I drank strong spirits, hoping to make myself drowsy. All was in vain; I vomited bile, I felt very weak, and the next morning at nine o'clock I went to La Charpillon's door, which was opened only a crack, as on the day before. The same shameless aunt came to say, absolutely forbidding me to enter, that the poor girl had had two relapses, that she was in convulsions and delirious, that she still constantly thought she saw me in the room, and that Dr. So-and-so said that if her condition grew worse during the next twenty-four hours she would die.

"She was having her menses," she said, "and the fright stopped them. It is terrible."

"Accursed hairdresser!"

"Youthful weakness! You should have pretended not to see anything."

"G . d d . . n it!¹⁸ What are you saying? You Swiss filth! You think that is possible? Take this."

I left, giving her a ten-pound note. Coming out of the street, I meet Goudar; I tell him, I beg him, to go to see how La Charpillon is, and to come to spend the whole day with me if he can. My expression terrifies him, he goes; and an hour later he came to tell me that the whole household was in despair, for the girl's life was in danger.

"Did you see her?"

"No. They told me that she kept throwing herself out of the bed stark naked, and that no one could see her."

"Do you believe it?"

"A maid who has always told me the truth assured me that she had gone mad because her period had stopped. In addition she has a continual fever and convulsions. I believe it all, for it is the usual consequence of a great fright in a girl who is in her critical period. She said you are the cause of it."

I then told him the whole story, describing the inability to control myself which came over me when I saw the hairdresser. Goudar could only say that he was sorry for me; but hearing that I had not been able either to eat or to sleep for forty-eight hours, he wisely told me that such grief could cost me my life or my reason. I knew it, and I saw no remedy for it. He spent the day with me, and he was useful to me; I could not eat, but I drank a great deal; unable to sleep, I spent the night pacing back and forth in my room, talking to myself like a madman.

I kept sending my Negro all day to find out how she was; and he always brought me back ill-omened answers. On the third day I go to her door myself at seven o'clock in the morning. After I have been kept waiting in the street for a quarter of an hour the door is opened part way, and I see the weeping mother, who, not letting me in, tells me that her daughter is on her deathbed. Just then a thin, pale, tall old man comes out, saying to her in Swiss German that there is nothing to do but to trust in God and obey his will. I ask her if he is the physician; she replies that the time for a physician has passed, that he is a minister of the Gospel, and that there is another upstairs.

"She can no longer speak; in an hour at the most she will be no more."

At that moment I feel as it were an icy hand clutching my heart. I let her burst into tears, and I leave saying that it is true that I was the ultimate cause of her daughter's death, but that she was the first cause of it. My trembling legs take me home, resolved to give myself the death which I thought the surest. In accordance with this terrible determination, at which I arrive with perfect coolness, I order my door shut to everyone. Then I go to my room, I put my watches, rings, snuffboxes, purse, and portfolio in my strongbox, which I put in my desk. I then write a short letter to the Venetian Resident, in which I tell him that after my death all my possessions are the property of Signor Bragadin.[19] I seal my letter, I lock it up in the same desk with the strongbox in which I had all my money, my diamonds, and my jewels, and I put the key in my pocket, in which I keep only two or three guineas in silver. I also put in my pocket my good pistols, and I go out, firmly intending to drown myself in the Thames at the Tower of London.[20] In accordance with this resolve, formed and fostered not by anger or love but in the cold light of reason, I go to a shop to buy as many lead balls as my pockets could hold and the weight of which I could manage to carry as far as the Tower, to which I intended to go on foot. I set out for it, and, reflecting on what I am about to do, I conclude that I could take no wiser course, for, if I remained alive, I should be in hell every time the image of La Charpillon arose in my memory. I even congratulate myself on its costing me no effort whatever to adopt this course; in addition I rejoice that I am just enough to punish myself, having found myself guilty of the unforgivable crime of cutting short the life of a charming object which Nature had created for love.

I walked slowly because of the immense weight I was carrying in my pockets, which assured me that I should die at the bottom of the river before my body could reappear by rising to the surface. Halfway across Westminster Bridge,[21] I come upon Sir Wellbore Agar,[22] a rich and amiable young Englishman who enjoyed life by catering to his passions. I had made his acquaintance at Lord Pembroke's in Saint Albans, then he had dined at my house, then at General Beckwith's, and we had always spent our time together very gaily, conversing on topics dear to the young. I see him, and I try to pretend that I do not see him, but he comes and catches me by the lapels.

"Where are you bound? Come with me, unless you are going to get someone out of prison, and we will have a good laugh."

"I cannot. Let me go."

"What is the matter with you, my dear friend? I do not recognize you."

"Nothing is the matter."

"Nothing is the matter? You don't see your expression. You are on your way, I swear, to do something disastrous. It's plain from your face. There's no use denying it."

"I tell you there's nothing the matter. Good-by. I will go with you some other day."

"Come now, my friend! You have a black look. I won't leave you. I will go with you."

He looks at one side of my breeches, and he catches a glimpse of a pistol, he looks at the other, he sees the mate to it, he takes my hand, he says he is sure I am going to fight, and that, as my friend, he insists upon looking on, assuring me that he will not try to interrupt the meeting. I assure him with a smile that I am not going to fight, and, without thinking what it would lead to, I find myself saying that I was only going for a walk.

"Excellent," says he. "In that case I hope my company will be agreeable to you, as yours is precious to me. We'll dine at the 'Cannon.' [23] I will go now to send someone to tell the girl who was to dine with me alone to bring along a young Frenchwoman who—Goddamme!—[24] is charming. We will make two couples.''

''My dear friend, pray excuse me, I am sad, I need to go somewhere by myself to get over it.''

''You shall go tomorrow, if you still need to, but I assure you that three hours from now you will be gay. If not, I will keep you company in your gloom. Where do you intend to dine across the river?''

''Nowhere, for I am not hungry. I've eaten nothing for more than three days. I can only drink.''

''You amaze me. Now I see the whole thing. It's a cholera morbus which can make you lose your mind, as one of my brothers did, who died of it.''

The young man, so insistent, arguing so justly, seems to me not lightly to be dismissed. ''I could,'' I said to myself, ''carry out my plan after we part. The most I risk is living five or six hours longer;

Credete a chi n'ha fatto esperimento

('Believe him who has had the experience'),[25]

says Ariosto.''

The reader can believe me when I say that all those who have killed themselves because of a great grief have only anticipated the madness which would have overcome their reason if they had not become their own executioners, and that hence all those who have gone mad could have escaped that misfortune only by killing themselves. I did not come to my resolve until I should have lost my reason if I had waited only one day more. Here is the corollary. A man should never kill himself, for it is possible that the cause of his grief will cease before madness sets in. This means that those whose souls are strong enough never to despair of anything are fortunate. My soul was not strong, I had lost all hope, and I was going to kill myself like a man of wisdom. I owe my salvation only to chance.

When Agar hears that I was going to the other side of

the bridge only to amuse myself, he says that I may just
as well turn back, and I let him persuade me; but a half
hour later, unable to walk any longer because of the lead
in my pockets, I ask him to take me to some place where
I can wait for him, for I am completely exhausted. I
gave him my word that I would wait for him at the
"Cannon," and I went there. When I was safely in the
tavern, I emptied my pockets of the too heavy packets,
putting them in a closet.

While waiting for the pleasant young man, I reflected
that he might prove to be the cause which would annul
my suicide. He had already prevented it, for he had delayed it. "That being so," I reasoned to myself, not like
a man who hoped but like a man who foresaw, "it is
possible that Agar, Esquire,[26] is the being to whom I
shall be indebted for my life." It remained for me to
determine whether he was doing me good or evil. The
conclusion to which, in accordance with my philosophy,
I came again was that, in respect to absolute and decisive acts, we are our own masters only up to a certain
point. I considered that in a certain sense it was by force
that I found myself sitting there in the tavern waiting
for the young Englishman to return, for it is certain
that, taking only moral force into consideration, I had
had to yield to force.

A quarter of an hour after he returned, the two young
light-o'-loves, one of whom was French, came, bringing
gaiety written on their charming faces. They were made
for joy; they lacked nothing of all that could kindle desires in the coldest of men. I was fully aware of their
merits, but since I did not give them the reception to
which they were accustomed when men found them
pleasing, they began to think me an invalid.[27] Though
I was at death's door, I felt an assertion of my self-
esteem which forced me to play a role resembling that
of the man I ought to be. I gave lifeless and cheerless
kisses, and I asked Agar to tell the English girl that if
I were not half dead I should find her charming. They

condoled with me. A man who has neither eaten nor slept
for three days is certainly insensible to the seductions of
Venus. Words would not have persuaded them if Agar
had not told them my name. I had a reputation, and I
saw that they were filled with respect. All three of them
put their hopes in the influence of Bacchus. I was more
than sure that they were mistaken.

The dinner being in the English style, that is, without
soup, I was absolutely unable to swallow either a bit of
roast beef [28] or a little pudding.[29] I ate nothing but some
oysters, drinking some rather good Graves and enjoying
Agar's skill in keeping them both occupied. At the
height of the gaiety he suggested that the English girl
dance the hornpipe[30] naked, and she consented, provided
that we could find some blind musicians[31] and that we
would all undress too. I said to Agar that I would do
whatever he wanted, but that I could neither dance, for
I could not stand on my legs, nor become such as the
charms of our two heroines ought to make me. I was
excused on condition that if the spectacle brought me to
life I would follow their example, and the two girls
swore that it would not escape them. The blindmen were
found, they came; and we locked ourselves in.

While the blindmen, who had sat down, tuned their
instruments, the two beauties and the athlete, who was
twenty-five years of age, put themselves in the state of
nature, and the performance began. It was one of those
moments in which I learned many truths in this world.
In that one I saw that the pleasures of love are the effect,
and not the cause, of gaiety. The three bodies were
magnificent, the dancing, the posturings, the gestures
seductive; but no emotion told me that I was sensible to
them. The male dancer maintained his conquering appearance even as he danced; I was astonished that I had
never made the experiment on myself. After the dance
he paid them both homage, going from one to the other,
and he did not stop until he saw that Nature, in need of
rest, declared him incapable. The Frenchwoman came

to see if I showed any sign of life, and, finding me powerless, said that it was all over with me.

The girls dressed, and I asked Agar to give the French woman four guineas for me and to pay for everything, for I had only some small change. Could I have guessed that morning that, instead of going to drown myself, I should make one at so charming a party? My indebtedness to the Englishman made me put off my suicide until the next day. When the girls were gone, I wanted to leave Agar, but he would not let me. He insisted that I looked better than I had in the morning, that the oysters which I had eaten and had kept down showed that I was in need of distraction, and in short that I could be well the next day and eat dinner if I went with him to spend the night at Ranelagh House.[32] He persuaded me to go there. I left the waiter at the "Cannon" my six packets, telling him that I would come back for them the next morning at nine o'clock, and I got into a hackney carriage with Agar to obey the Stoic maxim which had been inculcated into me in my happy youth: *Sequere Deum* ("Follow the God").[33]

We enter the fine rotunda, which was full of people, with our hats pulled down over our eyes. We had our arms around each other's shoulders. I stop for a moment to wait until a woman who was dancing a minuet in front of me with marked grace, and only whose back I saw, should turn to repeat the same steps in the opposite direction. What made me want to see her face was that she had on a dress and a hat exactly like a dress and a hat which I had given to La Charpillon; in addition, she was of the same stature; but this last observation did not concern me, for at that moment La Charpillon must be dead or at least on her deathbed. The dancer, then, starts off in the other direction; I look at her, and I see La Charpillon herself. Agar told me afterward that at that moment he thought I would fall down in an epileptic fit: the arm I had around his shoulders shook and contracted spasmodically.

I overcome my surprise and my spasm by a salutary doubt. There may be only a resemblance. The young woman, her attention fixed on her partner, had not noticed me; I remain where I am, waiting for her to come back in my direction, when I should see her only a step away and face to face; but just then she raises her arms to make her curtsy at the end of the minuet, and I go up to her as if I wanted to take her for the next dance. She looks at me, and she at once turns and walks away. I say nothing, and certain of the fact, I feel that I must go to sit down. A cold sweat instantly bathed my whole body. Agar, convinced that I am on the verge of a fit, advises me to take a cup of tea, to which I reply by asking him to leave me alone and to go and amuse himself.

The revolution which, in less than an hour, had taken place in my entire being made me fearful of its consequences, for I was shaking from head to foot and a violent palpitation of the heart made me doubt if I could stand even if I dared to rise. How the strange paroxysm would end terrified me, I could not but think that it would kill me.

My fear was not groundless. Having proved unable to bring me to my death, it gave me a new life. What a prodigious change! Feeling that I had grown calm, I fixed my eyes with pleasure on the rays of light which made me ashamed; but my feeling of shame assured me that I was cured. What contentment! Having been immersed in error, I could not recognize it until after I had emerged from it. In the dark one sees nothing. I was so amazed at my new state that, not seeing Agar reappear, I began to believe that I should not see him again. "That young man," I said to myself, "is my Genius, who assumed his appearance to restore me to my senses."

It is certain that I should have been confirmed in this insane idea if I had not seen him reappear an hour after he left me. Chance might have decreed that Agar should find some girl who would have persuaded him to leave Ranelagh House with her. I should have gone back to London alone, but certain that I had not been saved by Agar. Should I have recovered my senses if I had not seen him until some days later? I do not know. Men easily go mad. There has always been a seed of superstition in my soul, of which I am certainly not proud.

Agar finally comes back, in high spirits but very uneasy about my condition. He is astonished to see me glowing with health and surprised to hear me making amusing comments on the objects which took my fancy in the beautiful rotunda.

"My friend," he said, "you are laughing, you are no longer sad."

"No. I am hungry, and I need to ask a great favor of you, if you have not some important business tomorrow which will prevent your granting it."

"I am free until day after tomorrow, and entirely at your service."

"Here is what I have in mind. I owe you my life— my life, I tell you. But, for your gift to be complete, I need to have you spend tonight and all day tomorrow with me."

"I am yours to command."

"Then walk about, and come back for me whenever you are ready."

"Let us go at once, if you like."

"Let us go."

On the way I tell him nothing. When we enter my house I find nothing new except a note from Goudar, which I put in my pocket. It was an hour after midnight. We are served supper, and Agar is surprised to see me eat with ravenous appetite. He laughs and congratulates me. After supping well, he goes to bed and I do likewise. I sleep very soundly until noon; I go to breakfast in his room, and I tell him every detail of the whole horrible story, which would have ended with my death if I had not happened to meet him halfway across

Westminster Bridge, and if he had not read my terrible resolve in my distracted countenance. At the end of the story I take his hand, I open my desk, I make him read my will, and, retrieving my purse, I give him the five or six guineas I owe him. After that I unseal Goudar's note, which contained only these few words:

"I am sure that the girl in question, far from being on her deathbed, has gone to Ranelagh with Lord Grosvenor."

Agar, young but very sensible, is thunderstruck. Convinced that he had saved my life, he congratulates himself, and we embrace. The character of La Charpillon and her mother's perfidy seem to him beyond belief, and as for the bills of exchange whose loss I regretted because, having them, I could have taken some slight revenge by sending her mother and her aunts to prison, he said that it was still in my power to have them arrested and force them to restore them to me, and the more so since I had kept the letter from the mother acknowledging the debt and admitting that I had only consigned them to her daughter on deposit.

I at once resolved to have them arrested, but I did not tell him so. After spending the whole day in high spirits with me, he left to sup with his mistress. I swore him eternal friendship, and I owed it to him. The reader will see hereafter the punishment the kind young man had to undergo for having served me so well.

Full of vigor the next morning, gay as a man who has just won a great victory, I go to the attorney who had served me in my case against Count Schwerin,[34] and he, after hearing the facts, told me that I was justified and that my right to have the scheming woman arrested was unquestionable. So I went to Holborn,[35] where I made a statement on oath, and I received the order to have the mother and the two aunts arrested. The man who had arrested Schwerin was willing to serve me again in the arrest of the women; but he did not know them, and he had to know them. He was sure he could obtain entrance to their house and take them by surprise; but he also had to be sure that the women he arrested were the ones named in the warrant.

"There might," he said, "be other women with them."

His objection was justified; so, having no one who could do the thing, for Goudar would never have undertaken it, I resolved that I would myself show the man into the house at an hour when I could be sure that the malefactors would all be together in the parlor.

I told him to be waiting in Denmark Street at eight o'clock, with a hackney coach at his orders, and to enter as soon as the door was opened for him. I assured him that I would enter at the same time, and that I would turn them over to him myself; and the thing was done accordingly in every particular. He entered the parlor with one of his constables, followed by me. I at once pointed out the mother and the two aunts to him, then I hurried away, for La Charpillon, dressed in mourning, standing with her back to the fireplace, though I only glanced at her, terrified me. I believed, and I felt, that I was cured; but the wound having only just healed over, I do not know what would have happened if at that moment she had had the presence of mind to throw herself on my neck and beg me to spare her mother and her aunts. As soon as I saw them all touched by the powerful rod,[36] I left, relishing the pleasure of vengeance, and almost certain that they would find no one to go bail for them; their pi..s,[37] who were there, were petrified.

The pleasure of revenge is great, and those who procure it are happy when they taste it; but they were not happy when they sought it. The happy man is the impassive man,[38] who, not knowing what it is to hate, never thinks of avenging himself. The animosity with which I had the three women arrested, and the terror in which I left their house as soon as I saw the girl, prove that I was not yet free. To be so completely, I had to forget her.

The next morning Goudar came to me in high spirits, showing every sign of great contentment. He said that what I had had the courage to do proved either that I was cured of my passion or that I was more in love than ever. He had just come from La Charpillon's, where he had found only the grandmother, in despair and consulting an advocate.

He said that he had arrived at their house just as I was leaving it, and that he had stayed there until they had had to resign themselves to being taken to the house of the man who was executing my warrant. They had refused to go; they had insisted that he should wait until morning, when they were certain to find sureties, and their two bravoes had drawn their swords to prevent the man from using force; but the brave officer of the police had disarmed them and carried away their swords together with the three prisoners. The girl had wanted to go too, to keep them company; but she had left them in order to take every possible step to keep them from going to prison. Meanwhile the bailiff had them under guard at his house.

Goudar ended by saying that, as their friend, he would pay them a visit, and that if I were willing to enter into some arrangement he would be glad to act as mediator. I thanked him, and I said that the only way by which the women could get out of prison was to give me my money.

Two weeks[39] passed without my hearing anything more of the matter. No protests on their part, and no proposals for an arrangement. La Charpillon went to dine with them every day, and it was she who paid for their keep. It must have cost her a great deal, for they occupied two rooms and their cruel host did not allow them to send out for meals. If they had not agreed to it, he would have taken them to King's Bench.[40] Goudar said that La Charpillon had told her mother and her aunts that she would never bring herself to come to me to ask for their freedom, even if she were sure that merely speaking

to me would reduce me to doing whatever she wanted.
In her eyes I was the most loathsome of monsters. I went
to see my daughter nearly every day, and I had completely recovered my good spirits.

During these two weeks I had looked everywhere for
Agar in vain, and at last I was pleasantly surprised to
see him enter my room one morning with a friendly and
smiling countenance.

"Where on earth have you been hiding?" I asked him.
"I have looked everywhere for you and not found you."

"It is Love, my dear friend, who has kept me in his
impenetrable prison. I have come to bring you money."

"On whose behalf?"

"On the part of the Augspurgher ladies. Give me a
receipt and the necessary declaration, for I am to go
myself to restore them to the arms of the unhappy
Charpillon, who has done nothing but weep for two
weeks."

"I know her tears; but I wonder that she should have
chosen as her protector the man who freed me from her
chains. Does she know that I owe you my life?"

"All she knew was that we were at Ranelagh together
on that evening you saw her dance when you thought
she was dead; but she heard the whole story from me
after she had made my acquaintance."

"I take it that she came to you to persuade you to
speak to me in her favor."

"Not a bit of it. She came to tell me that you are a
monster of ingratitude, for she loved you and she gave
you unmistakable proofs of her affection; but now she
loathes you."

"God be praised! But it is strange that she should
have made you fall in love with her in order to obtain
her revenge on me. My dear friend, she is fooling you,
for it is you whom she is punishing."

"In any case it is a sweet punishment."

"I want you to be happy, but take care of yourself!"

Agar counted me out two hundred and fifty guineas, and I canceled my bills of exchange and renounced all my claims in writing. He went away satisfied. After this, did I not have reason to believe that the whole matter was ended? But I was sadly mistaken.

About that time the Hereditary Prince of Brunswick,[41] now the reigning Duke, married Princess Augusta, the King's sister. The Common Council,[42] having resolved to make him an English citizen and to give him the accompanying prerogatives, the Goldsmiths' Company[43] enrolled him among its members, having the Lord Mayor[44] and the Aldermen[45] give him the diploma in a gold box. The Prince, who was the first gentleman of our world, added this new luster to his nobility, which dated back fourteen centuries.

On this occasion Lady Harrington arranged that Mrs. Cornelys should make two hundred guineas. She lent her house in Soho Square to a cook who gave a ball and supper for a thousand persons[46] at three guineas a head. The groom, the bride, and the entire royal family, except the King and Queen, were present. For my three guineas I, too, was among the guests, but standing with six hundred others, the long tables in the great hall having accommodated only four hundred. I saw Lady Grafton[47] seated beside the Duke of Cumberland,[48] and astonishing all the other ladies by wearing her hair without powder and combed straight down in front so that it covered half of her forehead. They all exclaimed at it. They said that she was out of her mind, insane, absurd, and deserved to be booed, for she was making herself ugly; but in less than six months dressing the hair à la Grafton became general; it crossed the water and spread all over Europe, where it still persists, having, however, most unjustly, lost its name. It is the only fashion which can boast an antiquity of thirty-four years, though it was howled down on its first appearance. As in the case of spectacles in general, first receptions are to be distrusted. They are often wrong. A great many excellent plays, both French and English, failed at their first performances.

At this supper, for which the man who had produced it had received three thousand guineas, there was all

> *Che puote cor pensar può chieder bocca*
> ("That the heart could imagine and the
> mouth desire")[49]

in the way of both food and drink; but, since I did not dance and was not in love with any of the beauties who decorated the festival, I left at one o'clock in the morning. It was a Sunday, that sacred day on which in London no one fears prison except criminals. Nevertheless, this is what befell me.

Splendidly dressed, I was going home in a carriage, my Negro Jarba being up behind with another manservant whom I had recently engaged. The carriage has scarcely entered my street when I hear someone call my name:

"Good evening, Seingalt."

I put out my head and I reply:

"Good evening."

I instantly see men armed with pistols, two at the right, two at the left, and two others who had stopped the carriage; I hear them call out:

"By order of the King!"

My servants ask them what they want, and one of them replies that they mean to take me to Newgate Prison, for Sunday is no protection to criminals. I ask what crime I have committed; I am told that I shall learn that in prison. My Negro says that I have the right to know it before I go there; they answer that the judge is asleep; and he retorts that I will wait until he gets up, and the passers-by, who had stopped at the disturbance, cry out that I am in the right. The head constable gives in and takes me to his quarters in the City.[50] I found myself in a large room on the ground floor, in which there were nothing but some benches and large tables. My servants, after dismissing the carriage, came to keep me company, whereupon the six constables, declaring it their duty not to leave me, had me told that I must have food and drink brought for them. I ordered Jarba to satisfy them and to be mild and polite. I had to prepare to spend five hours there. The hour of the hearing was seven o'clock.

Having committed no crime, I could be there only as the result of a calumny, and knowing that justice in London was equitable, I was perfectly at ease, resolved to put up peaceably with a misfortune which could only be of short duration. If I had obeyed the old maxim, which I knew well, never to answer an unknown voice which addresses one at night, I should have avoided this misfortune, but the error was committed, so I could only be patient. I amused myself with humorous reflections on my swift passage from the most brilliant assembly in London to the infamous company in which I found myself, richly dressed as I was.

Dawn came at last, and the proprietor of the pothouse[51] where I was came downstairs to see who the criminal who had spent the night under his roof might be. His anger at his henchmen, who had not waked him to give me a room, made me laugh again, for he saw himself the loser by at least a guinea, which he would have made me pay for his courtesy. Someone finally announced that the magistrate[52] was sitting and that it was time to bring me into his presence. A sedan chair was called to carry me, for, dressed as I was, the mob would have thrown me into the gutter if I had gone on foot.

I enter a large room, where I find myself among fifty or sixty persons who at once fix their eyes on the barbarian who dares to show himself clad in such offensive finery.

At the far end of the room I see, seated in a raised armchair, the person who was apparently to inform me of what crime I was accused. He was the "sergens-fil," whom I prefer to call the "Criminal Court Magistrate." The accusations were read to him, he was addressed, he replied; and he hurriedly dictated the sentences, for the poor man was blind. He had a black bandage two inches wide which went around his head and covered his eyes. Since he could not see, it made no difference to him if they were covered. Someone beside me encouraged me, saying that he was a just judge, a man of intelligence, kind-hearted, and the author of several celebrated novels. In short, the man was Mr. Fielding.[53]

When my turn came the secretary who was beside him whispered it to him and, the complaint apparently naming me "Casanova, Italian," he called me by that name, telling me in perfect Italian to come forward for he had something to say to me. At that I made my way through the crowd and, arrived at the bar, I said:

"Eccomi, Signore" ("Here I am, My Lord").

All of the following dialogue between the honest magistrate and myself was conducted in Italian, and I wrote it down word for word the same day. I am happy to give my reader the following faithful and literal translation of it.

"Signor di Casanova, Venetian, you are sentenced to the prisons of His Majesty the King of Great Britain for the rest of your natural life."

"I am curious, Sir, to know for what crime I am sentenced. Will you be so good as to inform me of it?"

"Your curiosity is justified, Signor Venetian. In our country the courts do not consider that they have the right to sentence a person without informing him of his crime. You are accused, and the accusation is supported by two witnesses, of having attempted to scar a girl's face. It is she who calls upon the law to safeguard her against this outrage, and the law must safeguard her against it by sentencing you to prison. So prepare to go there."

"Sir, it is a calumny. It is possible, however, that, examining her own conduct, she may fear I might think of committing that crime. I can swear to you that I have never thought of such a base act.''

''She has two witnesses.''

''They are false ones. Who is this girl?''

''She is Miss Charpillon.''

''I know her, and I have never given her anything but tokens of affection.''

''Then it is not true that you intend to disfigure her?''

''It is false.''

''In that case I congratulate you. You shall dine in your own house; but you must furnish two sureties. Two householders must vouch to us that you will never commit this crime.''

''Who will dare to vouch that I will never commit it?''

''Two honest Englishmen whose esteem you have earned and who know that you are not a rogue. Send for them, and if they arrive before I go to dinner you shall be set free at once.''

I go out at once, and the constables take me back to the place in which I had been. I give my servants in writing all the names of householders I can remember, charging them to tell them the reason which obliged me to inconvenience them. I urge them to make haste, and they leave. They were to come back before noon; but they did not come back, so the magistrate went to dinner. However, I comforted myself with the knowledge that he would sit after dinner too. But suddenly I hear most unpleasant news.

The chief constable, accompanied by an interpreter, comes to tell me that he is there to take me to Newgate.[54] This is the prison in London to which only the lowest and most miserable criminals are sent. I tell him through the interpreter that I am waiting for sureties, and that he can take me to prison at nightfall if they do not come. He refuses to do so. He says that as soon as my sureties arrived I would be fetched from the prison, so it should make no difference to me. The interpreter whispers to me that the man was certainly paid by the other side to do me the injury of putting me in prison, and hence that it was in my power to remain where I was by giving him money. I ask how much, and after speaking with him privately he comes to tell me that ten guineas would persuade him to keep me where I am until nightfall. I at once had him reply that I was curious to see Newgate Prison. So a hackney coach was sent for, and I was taken there.

Upon my entrance into that inferno, a crowd of wretches, some of whom were to be hanged within the week, applauded my arrival, at the same time jeering at my fine array. Seeing that I do not speak to them, they become angry and begin treating me to insults. The jailer[55] quiets them, assuring them that I do not speak English, and he takes me to a room, informing me of what it will cost me and of the prison rules, as if he were sure I was to stay there a long time.

But a half hour later in comes the same man who wanted to make ten guineas by keeping me in his house and who tells me that my sureties are waiting for me before the magistrate and that my carriage is at the door. I thank God, I go downstairs, and once more I am before the man with the bandaged eyes. I see there Mr. Pagus,[56] my tailor, and Maisonneuve,[57] my vintner, who greet me and congratulate themselves on being able to do me this small service. Not far from me I see La Charpillon with Rostaing, an attorney, and Goudar. My sureties go to give their names to a clerk, who questions them and who then goes to speak to the magistrate, who approves them and informs them of the amount for which they are to stand surety for me. They sign, and the magistrate immediately tells me to sign for twice the amount for which my sureties had signed, and at the same time affably tells me that I am free. I go to the clerk's table to sign, asking him how much the security comes to, and he replies that it comes to forty guineas, my sureties having vouched for twenty each. I sign, saying to Goudar that Miss Charpillon's beauty would perhaps have been rated at ten thousand if the magistrate had seen her. I ask the names of the two who had served as her witnesses, and I am shown the names of Rostaing and Bottarelli.[58] I cast a disdainful look at Rostaing, who was there, pale as a corpse; a feeling of pity keeps me from looking at La Charpillon. I asked the clerk if I had to pay the costs, and he answered no, which gave rise to a dispute between him and the attorney employed by the beauty, who stood there in the utmost mortification because she could not leave until the costs of my arrest were paid. During this time I saw three or four other Englishmen arrive, who had come to stand surety for me. They all begged me to forgive the English laws, which were too often hard upon foreigners. I finally got home, eager to go to bed after spending a day which was one of the most tiresome of my whole life.

CHAPTER XIII

Bottarelli. Letter from Pauline, in care of Senhor de Saa. The avenging parrot. Pocchini. The Venetian Guerra. I meet Sara again: my plan to marry her and follow her to Switzerland. The Hanoverian mother and daughters.

THE FIRST act of my comedy having ended in this fashion, the second began the next day. As I get out of bed, I hear a noise at my door, I go to the window to see what it is, and I see Pocchini,[1] the infamous scoundrel who had robbed me at Stuttgart and whom my reader may remember. He was trying to enter without waiting to be announced, and just then he saw me. I told him that I could not receive him, and I closed the window.

A quarter of an hour later in comes Goudar with a copy of an English newspaper called the *St. James's Chronicle*, in which there was a brief account of my adventure, beginning with my arrest as I left Soho Square and ending with my return to my house a free man by virtue of security amounting in all to eighty pounds sterling. My name and La Charpillon's were disguised; but Rostaing's and Bottarelli's were given in full,[2] the writer of the account praising them. I asked Goudar to take me at once to see Bottarelli, whose acquaintance I wanted to make. Martinelli, who arrived at the same time, insisted on going with me too.

On the fourth floor of a dilapidated house we enter a room where we see the picture of poverty, composed of a woman, four children, and a man writing at a table. The man was Bottarelli. He rises, I ask him if he knows me, he answers no, whereupon I tell him that I am the Casanova whom his testimony had sent to Newgate the day before.

"Signore, I am sorry for it; but look at my family. I was in need of two guineas; I will serve you for nothing when you wish it."

"Are you not afraid you will be hanged?"

"No, Signore, for a false witness is not sentenced to the gallows. The law provides that we shall be deported; but nothing is harder in London than to convict a witness of having testified falsely."

"I am told that you are a poet."

"Yes, Signore. I have lengthened the *Didone*[3] and shortened the *Demetrio*." [4]

I left the scoundrel after giving his wife a guinea from pure charity. She gave me a copy of a book by her husband entitled *The Secret of the Freemasons Exposed*.[5] He was a monk in Pisa, his native city, which he had left with her, a nun. He had married her in London.

About this time Senhor de Saa himself—which greatly surprised me—brought me a letter from my dear Pauline which confirmed the unhappy fate of my faithful Clairmont.[6] She had already become the wife of Count *Al.* What surprised me even more was that he swore to me that he had known who she was from the moment she arrived in London. Trying to make it appear that they know more than they really know is the weakness of nearly all diplomats. Yet Senhor de Saa was a perfect gentleman. La Charpillon had treated him almost as she had treated me.

But now for an event which cannot but interest every reader with a sense of humor.

Strolling about the city one morning, I came to a place called the "Parrot Market."[7] Seeing a pretty one in a brand-new cage, I asked what language it spoke, and I was told that, being very young, it spoke none. I gave the ten guineas which were asked for it and I sent it home. Resolved to teach it a few interesting words, I decided to put it near my bed and constantly say to it in French, "Miss Charpillon is more of a whore than her mother." I began the thing as a joke, and certainly with no malicious intention. In less than two weeks the obedient parrot learned the few words so well that it repeated them from morning to night, with the addition that, after uttering them, it gave a great burst of laughter, a thing which I had not meant to teach it.

It was Goudar who said to me one day that if I sent my parrot to the Exchange I could certainly get it sold for fifty guineas. I at once adopted his happy idea, not in a spirit of avarice but in order to have the pleasure of calling the scheming creature who had treated me so ill a wh . . . ,[8] and at the same time to be safe from the law, which is extremely severe in that respect.

So I entrusted the business to Jarba, my parrot being an appropriate piece of merchandise for an Indian.

For the first two or three days my parrot, which spoke French, did not have a large audience; but as soon as someone who knew the heroine noticed the praise which the indiscreet bird bestowed on her, the circle grew bigger, and people began bargaining for the right to own the cage. Fifty guineas appeared to be too much. My Negro wanted me to sell the whole thing more cheaply; but I would never consent to it. I had fallen in love with my avenger.

How I laughed when, at the end of seven or eight days, Goudar told me what effect my talking parrot, offered for sale on the London Exchange, had had upon La Charpillon's family. Since the person who was selling it was my Negro, no one had any doubt that it belonged to me and that I had taught it to speak. He said that the girl not only was not offended by the thing but that she thought it very amusing and laughed at it all day. The ones who were in despair were her aunts and her mother, who had consulted several advocates on the subject, all of whom had replied that there were no laws to punish a calumny the author of which was a parrot, but that they could make the joke cost me very dear if they could prove that the parrot was my pupil. For this reason Goudar warned me that I must be careful not to boast that the bird had gone to school to me, for two witnesses could ruin me.

The ease with which false witnesses can be found in London is really scandalous. One day I saw a notice put up in a window and bearing in capital letters the one word "witness." It meant that the person who lived in the apartment was a professional witness.

An article in the *St. James's Chronicle* said that the ladies who considered themselves insulted by the parrot must be very poor and entirely friendless, for if they had bought the parrot as soon as they learned of its existence the story would scarcely have become known. It said that the thing could only be a revenge, and, without naming me, it said that the author of it deserved to be an Englishman. Happening to encounter Agar, I asked him why he did not buy the parrot. He replied, laughing at first but then becoming serious, that the parrot amused everyone who knew the persons concerned, and he refused to say more. Jarba at last found a buyer, and he brought me fifty guineas. Goudar told me that it was Lord Grosvenor.[9] That nobleman loved La Charpillon, but as an occasional diversion and no more. This jest concluded my acquaintance with the coquette, whom I later often encountered in London at promenades and theaters without even remembering what had happened to me on her account, so indifferent had I become to her.

As I entered St. James's Park one day from the direction of Buckingham House, two girls who were drinking milk in a ground-floor room called to me. Not knowing them, I was going on, when a young officer in English uniform came running after me to say that the young ladies were Italian, that they knew me, and that they had something to say to me. I went there at once, thanking him.

I was surprised, when I entered the room, to see Pocchini, wearing a uniform, and to hear him gaily say that he had the honor of presenting his daughters to me. I replied coolly that I remembered my snuffbox and my watches, which two other daughters of his had stolen from me in Stuttgart. He said I was lying. At that I throw the rest of the milk in a glass in his face and I leave. I was without a sword. The English officer follows me and says that I shall not leave without granting satisfaction to his friend, whom I had insulted.

"Tell him to come out and go with you to the Green Park, and I promise to give him a caning in your presence, unless you want to fight in his place; but in that case give me time to fetch my sword. Do you know this man, whom you call your friend?"

"No, but he is an officer, and it is I who took him to drink milk with his daughters and who brought you into our room."

"Very well, I will fight to the death to give you the satisfaction you demand; but I warn you that your friend is a thief and the pi..[10] for his daughters. Be off, I will wait for you."

After a quarter of an hour all four of them come out, the girls go to take a walk, and the Englishman and Pocchini follow me. Seeing people still about, I enter Hyde Park[11] and I stop.

Pocchini begins by addressing me; but I interrupt him, raising my cane and telling him that I will beat him with it if he does not draw his sword; he replies that he will never draw it against a man without a sword, and at that I give him a light blow. The coward cries out and calls me a bully, and the Englishman, after laughing loudly, asks me to excuse him, takes my arm, and we

The Thames at the Tower of London

English Armchair
Upholstered in Tapestry

retrace our steps, leaving the cursing coward to make off in another direction.

On the way I give him a detailed account of the fellow's dealings, and he admits that he is a scoundrel; but he says that unfortunately he is in love with one of his daughters. Arriving at St. James's Park, we see the two girls, and I laugh when I see Goudar between them. I ask him how he happens to know them, and he replies that their father the Captain, who had sold him some jewels, had introduced them to him. They laugh, and they ask me where I left him. I say that I gave him a caning; and they reply that I have done well. The Englishman, amazed at the infamous character of the wenches, begs my pardon, embraces me, and swears as he takes his leave that I shall not see him with them again.

A notion of Goudar's, with which I had the weakness to fall in, led me to dine with them at a tavern near Charing Cross.[12] The scoundrel got them drunk and, in the frankness of their intoxication, made them say more than enough to get their pretended father hanged. He did not live with them, but he visited them at night to make them give him whatever money they had earned. He often brought them men, and he had taught them to steal and to make the theft appear to be a joke when it was discovered. They gave him the stolen goods, and they did not know what he did with them.

At that I laughed to see Goudar, who had told me in the Park that he had made Captain Pocchini's acquaintance by buying jewels from him.

After this bad dinner I went home, leaving it to Goudar to see them to their lodging. He came the next morning to tell me that when they arrived there they were arrested and taken to prison; and that he had just come from the house in which the Captain lived, where the landlord had told him that he had not come home since the day before. The honest Goudar told me he would be sorry if he did not see the wretched man again,

for he owed him ten guineas for a watch which the girls
might have stolen but which was worth twenty.

Three or four days later he told me that Pocchini had
left London with an English maidservant whom he had
engaged, having gone to choose her in a place which he
named to me, where there were always three or four
hundred such, ready to enter the service of the first
comer. The proprietor of the place vouched for their
fidelity. Goudar had learned from the proprietor that the
maid whom Pocchini had chosen was very pretty, and
that he had left with her at once, going to the Thames
to embark. Goudar declared it an excellent speculation.
He regretted that the gold watch was still in his hands,
for he was always afraid he would meet the man from
whom the virtuous girls had stolen it. I never heard what
became of them, but we shall meet Pocchini again a few
years hence.

I went almost every day either to see my daughter at
her boarding school or to spend a few hours with Dr.
Maty[13] at the British Museum. One day I found with
him an Anglican clergyman whom I asked how many
different sects of Christians there were in England. Here
is his answer, which I added to my memoirs that very
evening:

"No one can be sure, for almost every Sunday a new
one springs up and another perishes. A man, whether in
good faith or to make his fortune, chooses one holy day
or another to take his stand in some public place and
speak, and immediately a few idle and curious passers-by
gather around him. He expounds some passage in the
Bible which, in his opinion, makes a difference in dogma.
His interpretation pleases some of the idlers, who applaud him and invite him to come the following Sunday
to a tavern, where they promise him a select company
of listeners. He goes, he expounds his doctrine more
forcefully, he is talked about, he maintains theses, his
disciples increase in number, they give themselves some
specious name, and there is the sect in its infancy, with

the Government knowing nothing about it and indeed unable to learn anything about it until it manages to exert some political influence. I believe this is the way in which all the different sects of our religion began.''

About this time Signor Steffano Guerra,[14] a Venetian patrician who was traveling by leave of the State Inquisitors, an eccentric of the first water, who after his travels returned to his country more ignorant than when he had left it, lost a suit against an English painter whom he had commissioned to paint a miniature portrait of one of the most beautiful ladies in London. Guerra had undertaken in writing to pay the English painter twenty-five guineas for the lady's portrait. When the painter finished his work he took it to him, and Guerra, declaring it a poor likeness, told him to keep it for himself and refused to pay him the money which he had agreed to pay. The Englishman, according to the custom of the country—for that is always the first step there— had the Venetian arrested, who at once gave bail and took the case before the appropriate judge. He was sentenced to pay. He appealed, he lost again, and finally he was obliged to pay. Guerra said that he had ordered a portrait, and that a picture which was not a likeness could not be called a portrait, and that therefore he could not be sentenced to pay. The painter said that it was a portrait because he had made it after the lady's face. The judge in his decision said that since Guerra had made the painter work, and he had to live by his work, he must pay him unless he could prove that the painter had not used all his talent to make the portrait a likeness. All England pronounced it a very just decision, and so did I. But Signor Guerra pronounced it unjust. The portrait and the suit cost him a hundred guineas.

Malignan's daughter died during these days of the smallpox at the same time that her father, at Bath, received a slap from a Lord who liked to play piquet and did not like it when those who played against him took it into their heads to improve upon fortune. I gave him money to bury his daughter and to leave the island. He died when he arrived in Liège, and his wife sent me word of it, assuring me that if he had lived he would have paid his debts.

Shortly after I arrived in London I learned that M. F.[15] was there as Chargé d'Affaires for the Canton of Bern.[16] I called at his lodging, and he did not receive me; nor did he return my call. I thought that, having got wind of certain familiarities in which I had indulged at Bern with the charming Sara, his younger daughter,[17] he did not want to put me in a position to renew them in London. Then, too, the man was a little mad. So I gave the matter no further thought, and I had entirely forgotten his discourtesy; but here is what happened to me six months later at a performance by the English comic opera troupe at Marylebone.[18] The entrance fee for the performances, at which one had to sit at a small table, was only a shilling, but one had to eat and drink, or at least drink a pot of beer.

I go, then, to the small theater, and by pure chance I sit down beside a girl without at once looking at her face; but two or three minutes later I see an enchanting countenance which I think is not new to me; but I attribute it to beauty itself, which can never appear new to a man in whose soul its divine lineaments are engraved. I see her in profile, then in half profile, and I feel certain that I am seeing her for the first time. However, I saw her smile when I looked at her, and it seemed that the persistence with which I stared at her must be the reason for it. One of her gloves drops at my feet, I pick it up and give it to her, and she thanks me in French, letting me see black eyes which pierce my soul.

"Then Madame is not English?" I say in a most submissive voice.

"Monsieur, I am Swiss, and you know me."

At this answer, which could not be fuller, I draw back my head, I look to her right, and I see Madame M. F. and, next to her, a girl,[19] and then Monsieur M. F. I rise to pay my respects to the lady, whom I esteemed, and I bow to her husband, who answers me only by a very cold inclination of the head. I ask her what her husband can have against me to account for such behavior, and she whispers to me that Passano[20] had written him dreadful things about me.

But what pleasure I then took in justifying myself to his daughter, who in three years had become such that I could not recognize her! She knew it, and her blush convinced me that she remembered all that had taken place between us in my housekeeper's[21] presence; but I was eager to know if she would admit it or if she would not think it her duty to disavow what she had every right to lay entirely to her own innocence. If Sara had conceived this plan I should have scorned her, for, with the intelligence I knew her to possess, she could not possibly have wanted to use it to overcome her temperament.

Having found some excuse to rise, she struck me by her presence. She was only in bud when I knew her in Bern; I now saw her in a maturity which was all the more seductive because it had only just flowered.

"Charming Sara," I said, "you have so dazzled me that I must ask you two questions necessary to the peace of my soul. Tell me if you remember our triflings at Bern."

"Yes."

"Tell me quickly if you are offended by my remembering them at this moment with extreme pleasure."

"No."

Who is the man in love who would have been willing to risk wounding her delicacy by asking her the third question? Sure that Sara would make me happy, and even flattering myself that she could not wait to do so, I surrendered to all the ardor of my desires, and I determined to convince her that I deserved her heart.

Since the man who served refreshments to people who ordered them was hovering near our table, I asked Madame M. F. to do me the favor of letting me offer them

some green oysters.[22] She accepted after the usual demurrals, and after that I do not stop at oysters but during
the hour and a half our supper lasted I had him bring
everything that was proposed to me, surprised that I was
offered a leveret, a most uncommon dish in London except
on the tables of noblemen, who, having hunting preserves,
are very jealous of them. Quantities of champagne,
spirits, larks, pipits, truffles, and sweetmeats—I was not
surprised when the waiter, showing me the bill, said that
I must pay ten guineas; but I was amused by the zeal
of M. F., who took it upon himself to protest the amount.
I quietly asked him to lower his tone, I paid, and I rewarded the waiter with half a guinea. The honest Swiss,
pale and serious an hour earlier, had become red-faced
and affable. Sara looked at him and pressed my hand. I
was exultant.

On our way down the short stairway after the performance, he asked me if I would name a time[23] at which
he could come to pay his respects to me. For answer, I
embraced him. His servant told him there were no hackney carriages and so they must wait. It was raining in
torrents. A little surprised that he should have gone there
with his whole family without having a carriage of his
own, I urge him to use mine, which had a folding seat,
and I send for a sedan chair for myself. He cannot refuse
my carriage, but on condition that he will be the one
to go in the sedan chair. I had to give in, and, taking the
folding seat, I saw Madame M. F. and her two daughters
home. On the way the lady expressed herself in the most
obliging terms, putting the blame, though without rancor,
on her husband for the discourtesy which had been shown
me. When I replied that I would avenge myself by waiting on her assiduously in future, she pierced my heart
by telling me that they were on the eve of their departure.

"We were to leave day after tomorrow," she said,
"and our apartment must be vacated tomorrow, for the
people who have rented it will come to occupy it the
next day. Some business which my husband must finish

obliges him to stay in London for another seven or eight days, so tomorrow we have two tasks on our hands: first to find ourselves a lodging, and next to move."

"Then you have not yet found a place to stay?"

"My husband says he is sure to find one tomorrow morning."

"Furnished, I suppose, for since you are about to leave you must have sold your furniture."

"It has all been sold, and we must have it transported to the purchaser at our own expense."

Hearing that M. F. had already found a lodging for himself, I thought that if I offered to lodge them, Madame F. might put me down as one of those who offer what they are sure will be refused, so I said nothing, very much displeased with my evil Genius,[24] who was making me lose the charming Sara just when I had found her again. My hope having lessened, my love grew weaker.

Arrived at the door of Madame's house, we get out, and the very politeness which obliges her to invite me to come upstairs shows me that she is only urging it upon me for form's sake. She lodged on the third floor and her daughters on the fourth. Everything being topsy-turvy, she asks me to go up with her daughters, since she had to speak with the landlady. There being no fire, Sara remains alone with me, her sister having gone to the next room to light one. Happy moment, which was, if that is possible, less than a moment! What charms! What an exchange of joy in two ecstasies which, on a bed already unmade, instantly became one! We had time neither to say a word to each other, nor to savor the nectar which Venus gave us, nor to reflect upon the precious gift bestowed on us by Love, Nature, and Fortune. Someone comes up the stairs, it is Monsieur M. F., it is over.

If the man had had eyes he would certainly not have recognized me. My whole face must have showed a perturbation of the most extraordinary kind. It must have been composed of a joy stifled at its birth, of the pallor

of a fear which had just escaped being surprised, and
of an infinite mingling of such shades of expression as
are depicted on a countenance animated by feelings of
fondness, gratitude, constancy, triumph, and exultation,
all of them in tumult.

After making mincemeat of all the compliments which
are always boring but at that moment were intolerable,
I left, looking, I must suppose, distracted. I arrived at
my house in such a state of enthusiasm that I determined
to leave England with Sara, having no doubt that my
company would be agreeable to the whole family. In the
course of the night I made all my plans for the journey;
and, greatly regretting that I had not managed to persuade Madame M. F. to accept an apartment in my house
for the few days she was to remain in London, I rose at
daybreak to oblige her to accept it even if her husband
should have found another.

So I go there; and at the door, I come upon M. F., who
tells me that he is going to rent two rooms for a week,
since he has to vacate the apartment he is occupying
on that very day. I reply that his wife had informed me
of all the circumstances, that I myself had rooms enough
to lodge him, and that I insisted that he give me the
preference. I ask him to go upstairs with me; he says
that the whole family is in bed; but we go up, and his
wife exhausts herself in excuses. It is her husband who
tells her that I want to rent him an apartment. He makes
me laugh; I tell him that I do not want it to cost him
a single copper, and that the pleasure he would give me
would sufficiently pay me. After many polite demurrals,
hearing me swear that he will not inconvenience me, he
accepts. We agree that he shall come toward nightfall,
and I return home to order my two apartments made
ready, leaving it to M. F. to deal with having all his
furniture conveyed to the person who had bought it. My
satisfaction was extreme.

An hour later two young ladies are announced. I go

down myself to see what they want and to tell them to leave, since I am busy; and I am surprised to see Sara and her sister. No sooner have they come upstairs and sat down than she tells me with great dignity that the principal tenant of the house in which they were living would not let them take out the furniture until he had received the forty guineas which her father owed him, despite the fact that a merchant in the City had assured him that he would pay the amount within the week.

"Here," she said, "is a note of Papa's, payable to the bearer at the place specified. Could you do my papa this small favor?"

I take the note, which was in English, and I give her a fifty-pound bank note, telling her that she can bring me ten pounds' change that evening. She thanks me unaffectedly; she leaves, and I see her to my door, charmed, delighted with the confidence she had shown in me by asking me for this small service. M. F.'s need for forty guineas does not lead me to suppose him in serious straits; and I am extremely glad to have been of some use to him and to have convinced him that he had been mistaken in treating me as of no account.

I dine sparingly in order to sup the better with the Swiss angel, the new object of my worship. After dinner I write letters to make the time pass more quickly; and toward nightfall M. F.'s valet arrives at my house with three large trunks, night bags, and boxes. He leaves, telling me that his master will very soon be there with the whole family; but six o'clock comes, and seven, and eight, and nine, and I am surprised to see no one. Not understanding the reason for it, I decide to go myself to see what is causing the delay.

I go upstairs, and the sight I see astounds me: M. F., his wife, and his daughters, who, as soon as they see me, dry their tears. I also see two shady-looking men. I guess at once what it must be, and assuming an air of gaiety, I say to M. F.:

"I would wager that some avaricious creditor has had you arrested for some debt which you cannot pay at once."

"That is so; but I am sure I shall be able to pay it in five or six days, and that is why I put off leaving until a week from tomorrow."

"Then you were arrested after you sent me your trunks?"

"A quarter of an hour later."

"And what have you been doing for these four hours?"

"I have sent to find sureties."

"And why did you not send for me?"

"I am obliged to you, but you are a foreigner; only householders[25] can serve as sureties."

"Even so you should have sent to let me know, for I have had an excellent supper prepared for you, and I am dying of hunger."

What increased the lugubriousness of the scene and made my playful tone a little too saucy was the room, in which there were only three chairs and a candle whose long wick gave a smoky light. It occurred to me that his debt might exceed my means, which made me hesitate to ask him what amount was in question.

Sara being the only one in the family who spoke English, I ask her if she has asked the man who brought the warrant how much he needed to set them free. She replies that he was asking only a security of a hundred and fifty pounds, or the same sum in ready money, because of a bill of exchange drawn by her father. She makes him repeat the information, and the man displays the bill.

"And when your father has paid," I ask Sara, "shall we go to supper?"

The question draws a smile from her, I give the amount to the man, who hands me the bill, and I put it in my portfolio, saying to M. F. that he shall pay it to me before he leaves England.

After this scene I embraced M. F., who for once was crying for joy, then Madame, then her daughters, and

I saw the four of them to my house on foot, raising all their spirits except Madame's, who could not overcome her melancholy.

After supping well and enjoying the pleasure of seeing M. F. tipsy, I admired the charming Sara, who, proffering countless excuses for having forgotten it, handed me a ten-pound bank note, the change from the fifty I had given her that morning.

My pleasure was no less perfect when I saw that they were delighted with the apartments which I had had made ready for them. Wishing them a good night's sleep, I said that I would board them until they left, and that if my company was agreeable to them I would take them to Switzerland myself.

On waking in the morning I cast a summary glance at my physical and moral state, and I find that I am happy; I examine my feelings, and I perceive them to be so well justified that I do not complain of not being in control of them. A heroic sensibility whose pure spring is in my soul makes me lenient toward a sensuality of which I had too often been the victim in my past life. I loved Sara, and I felt so certain of possessing her heart entirely that I put desires out of my mind. Desires arise from needs, they are troublesome, they are inseparable from doubt, they torture the mind. Sara was mine, and she had given herself to me when no possibility of interest could have made the source of her passion suspect.

I go up to see her father, whom I find unpacking his trunks, and, seeing his wife downcast, I ask her if she is feeling well. She replies that her health is perfect but that, being afraid of the sea, she could not be cheerful on the eve of taking a sea voyage. M. F. asks me to excuse him for his not being able to breakfast with us; he must go to finish some business. The young ladies come down, and we breakfast. I ask Madame why she has not opened all her trunks. She replies with a smile that one would be quite enough to contain the possessions of the whole family, and that she is going to sell everything they do not need. Seeing some handsome coats, a great deal of fine linen, and other things of value, I say it is really a pity; she answers calmly that the things are all very well in their way, but that the satisfaction of paying debts is still better. I earnestly say that she should sell nothing; that, since I have decided to go to Switzerland with her, I will pay her debts myself; and that she can repay me at her convenience. She is astonished, and she says she had not believed that I was speaking seriously.

"Perfectly seriously," I reply, "and here is the object of my hopes."

So saying, I take Sara's hand, and I press my lips to it. She blushes and, looking at her mother, makes no reply.

Thereupon Madame M. F. treated me to a very long discourse in which I saw candor and wisdom in their fairest light. She gave me a frank and detailed account of the situation of the family, and of her husband's inadequate means. She excused him for having contracted debts in London in order to live there above the reach of poverty; but she modestly condemned him for having insisted on bringing his whole family with him. He could have lived there alone, limiting himself to one servant; but with the family the two thousand crowns a year which the Bernese Government gave him had simply not gone far enough. She told me that her old father[26] had had influence enough to persuade the Government to pay his debts, but that to make up for it the Government had decided not to continue sending a Chargé d'Affaires[27] to London. A banker, she said, would be entrusted with receiving the interest on the capital sums which the Republic possessed in England. She said she believed that Sara was happy to have pleased me, but that she was not sure her husband would consent to the marriage.

At the word "marriage," which had not entered my mind before, I saw Sara blush, and the idea pleased me; but I foresaw difficulties.

On returning to my house M. F. said to his wife that two secondhand dealers would come in the afternoon; but, thereupon telling him my plan to accompany him to Switzerland, I easily convinced him that he should keep all his possessions, doing no more than to become my debtor for two hundred guineas, on which he would pay me interest until he was in a position to return them to me. Delighted by my proposal, he insisted on drawing up the contract in proper form that day, and the next day we confirmed it in the office of Monsieur Vanneck,[28] who signed it as witness. At the same time I gave him back his bill of exchange and his note for forty guineas, giving him ten more to make the amount an even two hundred.

We did not speak of marriage, his wife having told me that she would mention my proposal to him in private.

It was on the third day that he came down to my room alone to discuss the matter with me. He told me that his wife had informed him of my intentions, which were an honor to him, but that he absolutely could not give me Sara, for he had promised her to Monsieur de W.[29] before he left Bern, and that family interests prevented him from going back on his word, the more so since his father[30] would never, so long as he lived, give his consent to a union which difference of religion could not but make unhappy. All in all, this exposition did not displease me. I said that the circumstances might change with the passing of time, and in the meanwhile it would satisfy me if he would grant me his friendship without stint and would leave it entirely to me to arrange for the journey we were to make. He swore, embracing me, that he set the greatest store by my friendship, that he would take no part in the arrangements for our journey, and that he was delighted, as was his wife, that his young daughter had won my heart.

After this frank explanation, I gave Sara, in the presence of her father and mother, all the indications of my affection which I could give her without infringing on decency and on the respect which I owed them. Sara visibly breathed only love.

It was on the fifth day that I went up to her room, and that my love became ardent, for I found her still in bed and alone. After the first time I had not again been in a situation of freedom with her. I throw myself on her neck, covering her face with kisses, and I see her tender but cold. My fire increases, I hope to quench it, and she resists, gently but strongly enough to raise a barrier to my desires. I ask her with all the sweetness of love why she opposes my ecstasy. She begs me to ask no more of her than she was granting.

"Then you no longer love me."

"Oh, my dear friend, I adore you."

"Then why this refusal after you have given me entire possession of yourself?"

"It is the one thing that contents me. You made me happy. I saw you as much in love as I, and that should be enough for us."

"It is impossible, my dear Sara, that your change of attitude does not have a reason. If you love me, renouncing yourself must be painful to you."

"It is, my dear friend, but I must bear it. The reason which determined me to fight against my passion does not spring from weakness but from what I owe myself. I have contracted obligations toward you which I cannot pay you with my person except by degrading myself in my own eyes. When I gave myself to you, when you gave yourself to me, we owed each other nothing. My soul, being now in slavery, shrinks from giving what, when it was free and in love, it gave to love. It rejoiced in itself."

"Oh, my dear Sara! What strange metaphysics, inimical to me and even more to yourself! It leads your mind to invent sophisms which deceive you. Have some consideration for my delicacy, and be reassured. No, my angel, you owe me nothing."

"Admit that you would have done nothing for my father if you did not love me."

"I will not admit it, my dear friend. My esteem for your mother could easily have led me to do the same thing. Consider, after all, that, lending him a small amount, it is possible that I did him that slight service without thinking of you."

"It is possible, but I cannot help believing the contrary. No, I cannot bring myself to pay the debts of my mind at the expense of my heart."

"On the contrary, sensibility should make your heart all the more ardent."

"It could not be more so."

"I am indeed unfortunate! Can what I have done to lay me open to punishment? Do you not understand, my divine Sara, that you are punishing me?"

"Alas! spare me that cruel reproach, I beg you, and let nothing diminish your affection. Let us go on loving each other."

This dialogue is only the hundredth part of what kept us engaged until dinnertime. Madame M. F. came in, and, seeing me sitting at the foot of her daughter's bed, she laughed and asked me why I did not let her get up.

I answered her with serene tranquility that a most interesting subject had made two hours pass only too quickly.

Going to my room to dress, and reflecting on the change in the enchanting girl, I decide that her resolve could be only momentary. I even attributed it to an extraordinary increase in her passion. I felt certain that the fit could be only of the briefest duration. I needed to believe it, for otherwise I did not feel that I had the strength to play up to a whim which, after all, smacked of novel-reading.

So we dined in very high spirits, and in everything we said Sara and I presented her mother and father with a picture of perfect friendship beyond any possibility of change. I took them to the Italian opera which was being given at Covent Garden, then we returned to my house, where, after a good supper, we went to bed in the most perfect peace of mind.

I spent the whole of the next morning in the City, settling my accounts with the bankers who still had money of mine, and I had them all give me bills on Geneva, for my departure was settled, and I took a fond farewell of the honest Bosanquet.[31] I could stay in London only five or six more days. In the afternoon I hired a carriage for Madame M. F., who had to pay some farewell visits, and I paid one of the same to my daughter's boarding school, where she, shedding tears, begged me to take care of her; then I decided to call on her mother, for Sophie had made me promise to do her that favor.

At supper that evening we talked of our journey, which was to be entirely arranged by me, and M. F. agreed with me that, instead of going by way of Ostend, we should do better to take ship for Dunkirk.[32] M. F. had only a few small pieces of business to finish. He had paid all his debts, and he told me that he would arrive in Bern with some fifty guineas still in his purse after paying two-thirds of the cost of the journey.

I had to agree to his doing so, but I was determined never to show him the accounts. I hoped that in Bern I should succeed in obtaining Sara's hand as soon as I made sure of her consent, for I had not yet talked to her about it.

It was on the next day, after breakfasting with the whole family, and Sara's father having gone out on business, that I took Sara's hand in her mother's presence and I asked her in tones of the most perfect love if I could be sure she would grant me her heart if, when we were in Bern, I could succeed in obtaining her father's consent, her mother having assured me that I should certainly have hers. Scarcely has the subject been raised before Madame M. F. rises, saying in the most amiable way that since our discussion might well take a long time she would leave us until noon, and, so saying, she took her elder daughter with her and went to pay calls.

Sara, immediately returning to the subject, said that she could not understand how I could have any doubt of her consent, after the proofs of her affection which she had given me, and after the unmistakable tokens of it which I had received. With her face the picture of candor, love, and gratitude, she said that if she became my wife she was sure that she would never cease to be happy, that she would never have any will but mine, and that when she followed me nothing in her native country could make her regret it.

My softened soul cannot resist the energy and the sweetness of these words. I clasp the amorous Sara in my arms, and I see her sharing my transports; but she implores me to restrain them when she sees me on the verge of giving her that proof of them which every fond lover feels that he must share with the object of his adoration. Clasping me in her arms, she implores me not to demand of her what she is not willing to give me until she should be mine by the bond of marriage.

"What! you have the heart to drive me to despair? Consider that your resistance may cost me my life. Good God! Is it possible that you should love me and that at the same time this fatal resolve should not be abhorrent to your love? Yet you want me to be sure that you love me."

"Yes, my loving friend, be sure of it."

"Alas, that certainty cannot suffice me if you divorce it from a proof which ever accompanies it."

Seeing my tears flow, Sara was touched to the point of feeling a faintness which obliged her to throw herself on the bed, which was only two steps away. Her pallor frightened me. I made her smell some drops[33] which I had in a flask, at the same time rubbing her temples, and she opened her eyes, offered me her lips, and seemed to be contented by a kiss which assured her that my soul had grown calm.

In this situation the mere thought of taking advantage of her condition to satisfy my desires would have horrified me if it had entered my mind. Not being in a deep enough faint not to have seen my restraint, she recovered her faculties, which were perhaps restored to her by the ardor of the kisses which I printed on her lips, her eyes, her arms, and her beautiful hands. Sitting up again, she said that I had now given her further proof of my tender affection.

"What! can you imagine that I could have been base enough to take advantage of your faintness to procure an enjoyment which you would not have shared?"

"Certainly not; yet I would not have resisted, but perhaps I should have ceased to love you."

"Good God! Can I believe my ears? Divine creature! You hold me spellbound. I am lost."

After saying this, I sat down at her bedside, and I gave myself over to the most melancholy reflections, which Sara never once interrupted. Finally her mother came back and asked her why she was lying down. She replied that she had felt unwell.

Her father, too, came back soon afterward, and we dined, but in very low spirits. What had happened to me, and what I had learned directly from the lips of a girl whose heart was as pure as her passion was strong, had plunged me into the deepest dejection. After this last scene, I had nothing left to hope for; and knowing my temperament, I knew that I must think about myself. It had been only six weeks since God had helped me to throw off the chains in which La Charpillon had bound my will even though I had known all the baseness of her character; and I now saw myself in danger of becoming the victim of an angel whose virtues my reason could not but admire. It was impossible for me to be governed by them, and, not even certain that she would become my wife, I foresaw my destruction. She would have been the cause of it; and I should not have had the poor consolation of having the right to complain of it.

Such were my reflections after her fainting fit, and they could not act in me until after they had ripened.

In the City there was a sale of choice merchandise which was to be parceled out by means of a lottery; Sara had read the announcement of it in some newspaper. I invited her and her mother to go to the City with me to take chances in the lottery.

It was a sort of fair in — Square, at which the women who owned them disposed of a number of fine articles at their proper price, but by means of a lottery. An article, for example, which was worth ten guineas was drawn for when ten tickets at a guinea each had been sold; the person who had drawn the lucky ticket when his turn came won it.

We found the place full of people of the greatest distinction, among them the Countess of Harrington and her daughters Lady Stanhope and Lady Amelia. The mother had a strange case on her hands at the time. She was having officers of the law make an investigation at her house to find the thief [34] who had stolen six thousand pounds sterling from her husband, whereas all London had no doubt that she herself had made away with the money.

Madame M. F. declined to take part in the lottery, but she did not think she should deny my request to her daughters to take tickets on my behalf. So I gave them a few guineas, and they were lucky. That is to say that, for ten or twelve guineas which they lost, they took home merchandise worth sixty. After the usual demurrals they allowed me to make them a present of it all. There were a length of fine linen, two Indian dresses, and a ruby necklace which, it having fallen to Sara, her father undertook to sell before they went back to Switzerland, where sumptuary laws [35] were in force.

In love with Sara, and sure that she would no longer grant me more than trifling favors, I did not put off speaking my mind. After supper, before we rose from the table I informed the amiable family that, not being certain that Sara could become my wife, I had decided to put off my visit to Bern until some other time. Her father said that it was a wise decision, and that I could maintain a correspondence with his daughter. She seemed to assent, but I saw that she showed no eagerness to comply.

I spent a cruel night. It was the first time in my life that I found that I was loved and yet unhappy because of the strangest of whims. Weighing the reasons which she alleged, and finding them groundless, I ended by concluding that my caresses had offended her.

In the course of the three last days I several times found myself alone with her, but never let myself indulge in transports, thereby earning sweet tokens of her gratitude in the form of childish caresses. I finally learned that if enforced abstinence usually exacerbates love, it can also have the opposite effect. In the long run Sara would have reduced me to indifference, for I should never have found her unworthy of my friendship. A different character, a Charpillon who deceived me and made me furious, in short a coquette who keeps hope forever alive and whom one never obtains, at last arouses scorn and often hatred.

They all set off, taking ship on the Thames for Ostend.[36] I went with them as far as the estuary, then returned by water. I gave Sara a letter for Madame W. This Madame W. was the learned Hedwig,[37] of Geneva, whom Sara did not know. Two years later[38] Sara became the wife of another Monsieur W., and she was happy.

Nowadays when I ask for news of my old acquaintances from people coming from their countries, or natives of them, I listen to them attentively; but the interest they arouse in me is less strong than the interest I take in some fragment of history, some incident five or six centuries old and unknown to all the learned. For our contemporaries, and even for the companions of our early follies, we feel a kind of contempt which may very well spring from the contempt which at certain moments we feel for ourselves. Four years ago I wrote a letter to Madame G.[39] in Hamburg. My letter began as follows:

"After a silence of twenty-nine years." She did not even answer me. When my reader learns who Madame G. is he will laugh. Two years ago I had set out for Hamburg; but my guardian Demon made me return to Dux.[40]

At the opera in Covent Garden Goudar came to me to ask me if I wanted to go to La Sartori's[41] concert, at which I should see a brand-new English girl to whom La Sartori herself was giving singing lessons. She spoke Italian. She was a jewel. I must, he said, make haste, for the first nobleman who saw her would make off with her on the instant.

Having just lost Sara, I was not anxious to make a new acquaintance, but I had to see the girl. I went there; I was bored, and that pleased me. However, she was pretty. A Livonian who called himself Baron Henau,[42] young and with an interesting face, appeared to be smitten by the charming pupil of the *virtuosa* Sartori. After supper she offered us tickets at a guinea for a new concert, and I took two, giving one of them to Goudar. The Livonian Baron took fifty and paid her for them on the spot. I at once saw that he wanted to capture her by storm, and his attitude pleased me. I thought he was wealthy. I let him take me in. He made himself agreeable to me, and we became friends. The reader will soon see the consequences of this fatal friendship.

To forget Sara, I needed another Sara. She was the pretty Irish girl[43] who brought us our bottle of strong beer when we went to the pothouse where she served; but Goudar was jealous of her.

Walking with him in the Park, I go on ahead to let him talk with two girls whose faces, so far as I could see them under their hats, struck me as pretty. This is what he said to me after he let them go.

"A Hanoverian lady,[44] a widow and the mother of five daughters, came here two months ago, bringing all of them with her. She lives in a house on Leicester Fields Square.[45] She is appealing to the Court for reparation for the damage done her by a detachment of the army then commanded by the Duke of Cumberland.[46] The mother being ill, or so it is said, keeps to her bed and lets no one see her. She sends her two elder daughters to solicit the recompense for which she asks. They are the two girls you just saw. But they can accomplish nothing. I have even been told that the Ministers no longer give them a hearing. They are all of them pretty. The youngest is fourteen years of age and the eldest twenty-two. They speak German, French, and English; they politely receive everyone who goes to call on them, though all of them always remain in the room. They accept money if it is offered them, but they do not ask for it. I went there three or four days ago from curiosity, and they received me quite well; but since I did not give them anything I dare not go back there by myself. If you are curious, let us go there.''

''How can I help being curious after hearing your account of them? Let us go at once; but if the one I find attractive does not grant me some favors I will not give them the usual guinea.''

''You will not give it, for they do not even allow one to take them by the hand.''

''Are they Charpillons?''

''Very likely. But you will see no men there.''

We go up to a second floor, and in a large drawing room I see three pretty girls and a sinister-looking man. I pay them the usual compliments, which, though they acknowledge them by curtsying, do not lighten their air of gloom. Goudar goes to the man and speaks to him, and the man replies. Goudar shrugs his shoulders and tells me that we have come at a bad moment.

''The man,'' he says, ''is a bailiff, who insists that he will take the mother to prison unless she pays the landlord twenty guineas she owes him, and they haven't a copper among them. When he has taken her to prison the landlord will turn all the girls out into the street. They will then go to stay in the prison with the mother, and their lodging will cost them nothing.''

"That is not so. They can eat there if they pay for it, but they could not stay there, for only the prisoners are given lodging in prisons."

I ask one of the girls where their sisters are.

"They have gone," she answers, "to look for money, for sureties will not do; the landlord insists on ready money at once."

"What do you owe twenty guineas for?"

"For the rent of the apartment and some meals; and we have nothing to sell."

"A sad situation. And what does your mother say?"

"She is ill in bed; at the moment she is crying. She is absolutely incapable of leaving her bed; and they want her to go to prison. The landlord has just given her the comfort of saying that he will have her carried there."

"What barbarity! But I think you pretty, and I am rich. I could be of some good to you if you were good to me."

"I do not know what good you are talking about."

"Your mama can tell you. Go and talk with her."

"Sir, you do not know me. We are decent girls and, what is more, girls of good birth."

After uttering these words, the little beauty turned away to cry. The two others, who were as pretty as she, stood there not saying a word. Goudar said to me in Italian that unless we consoled the poor creatures in due form we were cutting a very poor figure there, and we went down the stairs.

VOLUME 9 · NOTES

1. *Pogomas . . . Passano:* Giacomo Passano, of Genoa (died ca. 1772), actor, writer, and adventurer. His pen name, Ascanio Pogomas, is an anagram from Giacomo Passano (cf. Vol. 7, Chap. VII, n. 6). For C.'s previous dealings with him, see Vol. 7, Chap. VII, and Vol. 8, Chaps. IV, V, VI, and X.

2. *Rosalie:* A young woman from Marseilles with whom C. had had a liaison and who married a Genoese merchant ca. 1761 (cf. Vol. 7, Chaps. IV and V).

3. *Paretti:* Probably invented name of the Genoese merchant whom Rosalie married. In Vol. 7, Chap. V, C. abbreviates it to "P-i"; here he gives it in full for the first time.

4. *Speaking to each other too fondly:* The text has, "de nous tutoyer" ("of addressing each other as *tu*").

5. *Veronica:* Veronica Alizeri (born 1734). Cf. especially Vol. 7, Chaps. V and VI.

6. *Annetta:* Maria Anna Alizeri (born after 1734), Veronica's younger sister; cf. Vol. 7, Chap. VI.

7. *Isolabella:* Name of a rich Genoese mercantile family (cf. Vol. 8, Chap. X).

8. *Triulzi:* Marchese Carlo Triulzi, also Trivulzi (ca. 1719-1789), abate, antiquarian, and art collector (cf. Vol. 8, especially Chap. VII).

9. *Grimaldi della Pietra:* Giovanni Agostino Grimaldi, Marchese della Pietra (1734-1784), Genoese patrician and holder of a fief in the Kingdom of Naples.

10. *Cicisbeo:* Italian word of unknown derivation, designating the recognized gallant of a married woman. Grimaldi married Isabella Morelli, of Florence, ca. 1760.

11. *Croce:* Antonio Croce, otherwise Della Croce, De la Croix, Marchese di Santa Croce, also known as Castelfranco and Crosin (died after 1796), Italian adventurer (cf. especially Vol. 8, Chap. X).

12. *Clairmont:* Also Clairmon, Clermont (died 1763), C.'s valet (cf. Vol. 8, Chap. VI).

13. *Mantilla:* After being adopted in France, the Spanish mantilla became fashionable in Genoa in the 18th century.

14. *Genoese zecchini:* The Genoese zecchino was a gold coin worth 13 lire, 10 soldi. It was minted from 1718 to 1827.

15. *Don Agostino Grimaldi:* See note 9 to this chapter.

16. *Alexander's sword:* Reference to the story of Alexander the Great cutting the Gordian knot which he had been unable to untie.

17. *Trente-et-quarante:* Card game using six full packs (312 cards in all); its rules are extremely complicated. Any number of persons may play against a single banker.

18. *La Croix:* C., speaking French to his "niece," uses the French form of Croce's name (cf. note 11 to this chapter).

19. *Biribissi:* A favorite gambling game, especially in Genoa, played with a board with figures and numbered compartments and with correspondingly numbered balls drawn from a bag. The figures often represented human beings or animals; on the board C. here describes, the figures were characters from the *commedia dell'arte*.

20. *Three hundred:* As appears from what precedes and what follows, this is a slip of C.'s for three *thousand*. And he here calls the coins silver, while later he calls them gold.

21. *Biribissanti:* The organizers of a *biribissi*.

22. *A hundred Genoese lire:* A gold coin worth 100 lire, the genovino d'oro, was minted in Genoa from 1758.

23. *Strada Balbi:* Now the Via Balbi and one of the finest streets in Genoa, with old palaces of the nobility.

24. *Patrician:* The informer could only be a patrician, for none but members of the Genoese nobility were invited to such evening occasions.

25. *The strait-laced:* Text, "les jansénistes," used generically in the 18th century to designate persons of rigid morals, from the name of the founder of a reform movement influential in France in the 17th century (cf. Vol. 4, Chap. VI, n. 9).

26. *Banchi:* Probably an abbreviation for the most important bank in Genoa at the time, the Società delle compere e dei banchi di San Giorgio; but it is also possible that Passano went to the Exchange, the Loggia di Banchi.

27. *State Inquisitors:* From 1625 Genoa had a State Inquisition, modeled after that of Venice, made up of six patricians presided over by a Senator. They had far less power than the Venetian State Inquisitors.
28. *Law concerning clipped money:* It was promulgated on April 13, 1763.
29. *Quinze:* Card game for from two to six persons, played with two packs of 52 cards.
30. *Easter Monday:* In 1763 Easter Monday fell on April 3. Among C.'s papers there is a document showing that he transferred several pieces of jewelry as pledges to the Marchese Grimaldi on April 15, 1763. Hence he cannot have left Genoa before the latter date.

CHAPTER II

1. *Youngest of . . . my brothers:* Gaetano Alvisio (or Luigi) Casanova (1734-1783), ordained a subdeacon in 1755; in prison by order of the Venetian Council of Ten from 1767 to 1769; from 1771 preacher in Rome.
2. *Bragadin, Dandolo, . . . Barbaro:* One of the several passages in C.'s memoirs which show that he maintained a correspondence with the three Venetian patricians whose friendship he had won as a cabalist in 1746. (See especially Vol. 2, Chaps. VII and VIII.)
3. *Mohammed:* According to the old Islamic biographies of Mohammed, he was born after the death of his father Abdallah.
4. *Frac:* In the 18th century in France, a colored coat with full skirt and a high collar; the word now designates a different kind of garment.
5. *Calencar:* A colored fabric from India. The original, to specify its color, adds "couleur de cane." French *cane* means "duck" (as opposed to drake). If the reading is not a misreading, the color would seem to be indeterminable.
6. *The young man:* See Chap. I of this volume.
7. *Marcolina:* Obviously a fictitious name.
8. *My brother Francesco:* Francesco Casanova (1727-1802), in the 18th century a well-known battle and landscape painter; worked in Paris from 1758, made a member of the Académie Royale de Peinture in 1763.

9. *Mezzari:* The *mezzaro* was a sort of hood of oriental material, worn by Genoese women.

10. *Casacce:* Religious processions on Maundy Thursday and Good Friday, attended by the entire city.

11. *Zendale:* A kerchief of black silk, big enough for two ends of it to be crossed over the breast and knotted behind, worn by Venetian women.

12. *Felucca:* A lateen-rigged vessel, commonly three-masted, used chiefly in the Mediterranean, and propelled either by sails or by oars.

13. *Thursday:* C. cannot have left Genoa until after April 15, 1763 (cf. note 30 to Chap. I of this volume).

14. *Finale:* On the Italian Riviera, some 40 miles west of Genoa.

15. *San Remo . . . privileges:* Originally a fief of the Holy Roman Empire, from 1361 a so-called "città convenzionata" of the Republic of Genoa. As such, its constitution gave it considerable autonomy. After conflicts in the 18th century the Republic withdrew the city's privileges.

16. *Louis:* French gold coin worth 24 francs.

17. *Mentone:* Town on the Riviera, now marking the boundary between France and Italy; in C.'s day it belonged to the Principality of Monaco.

18. *Prince of Monaco:* Charles Maurice Grimaldi, Count of Valentinois and Prince of Monaco (1727-1790).

19. *Corallina:* Cf. Vol. 3, Chap. IX.

20. *Ruffec:* Catherine Charlotte Thérèse, Duchess of Ruffec (1707-1755), mother-in-law of the Prince of Monaco (cf. Vol. 3, Chap. IX, and note 22 to this chapter).

21. *His Principality:* The Principality of Monaco, independent until 1731 and from then until 1793 under French protection, in C.'s time included not only Monaco but also Roquebrune and Mentone, both of which became French possessions in 1861. From 1814 to 1911 the Principality was under the protection of the Kingdom of Sardinia; since 1911 it has had the status of an independent State.

22. *Wife . . . two sons:* The Prince of Monaco had married Maria Caterina, Marchesa di Brignole-Sale (1739-1813), in 1757. Their two sons were Honoré IV (1758-1819) and Joseph Marie Jérôme Honoré (1763-1816), later called Prince Joseph of Monaco. The marriage was annulled in

1770. C. appears to combine events from different periods in his account.

23. *Her mother:* Anna Balbi, Genoese noblewoman; she was married to Gian Francesco Maria, Marchese di Brignole-Sale (died 1769), who was Doge of Genoa from 1746 to 1748.

24. *French garrison:* France kept a garrison in Monaco to guard her border against Italy.

25. *Young officer:* Probably the commander of the garrison; in 1763 he was a certain Alexandre Millo.

26. *Helots:* The lowest social class in ancient Sparta, probably the descendants of the original population conquered by the Dorians. They were serfs and had no civic rights.

27. *Fréjus:* On the French Riviera, some 50 miles west of Monaco on the road to Toulon and Marseilles.

28. *Carriage . . . three years before:* See Vol. 7, Chap. IV. In Oct. 1760 C. had agreed to pay 6 francs per month for the stabling of his carriage. The time is now April 1763, hence some 30 months later, which would make C. owe some 180 francs. Ten louis = 240 francs.

29. *One-armed individual:* Baron Prosper Marie de Lesrat; he had lost one arm in battle in 1744.

CHAPTER III

1. *Chapter III:* A marginal note at the beginning of this chapter reads: "1762-1763." However, the time is April 1763. C. left two versions of this chapter, both of which are contained in the ms. The version printed in the Brockhaus-Plon edition is the one which gives the more detailed account of Madame d'Urfé's "regeneration." The other version, as represented by Schütz in the first German edition, is shorter, but, in addition to the matter contained in the longer version, it reports a visit by Madame d'Urfé to Aix-en-Provence, during which she calls upon the good offices of her old friend the Duke of Villars, Governor of Provence, to rid her of Passano, which causes C. some anxiety.

2. *Le Luc . . . Brignoles . . . Aubagne:* Post stations on the old post road from Antibes to Marseilles, which turned inland from the coast at Fréjus.

3. *Madame Audibert:* Died after 1772; she maintained a gaming room in Marseilles (cf. Vol. 7, Chap. IV).

4. *"Thirteen Cantons":* The Auberge des XIII Cantons was a Swiss hostelry on the Cours Belzunce; it was considered the best establishment of its kind in Marseilles. It survived into the 19th century. C. had stayed in it during his first visit to Marseilles (cf. Vol. 7, Chaps. III ff.).

5. *La Croix:* See note 11 to Chap. I. C. here first wrote "Crosin," then struck it out and substituted "La Croix."

6. *Rosalie:* See Vol. 7, Chap. IV.

7. *Brougnole:* Chambermaid to Madame d'Urfé. For C.'s various spellings of the name, see Vol. 8, Chap. III, n. 7.

8. *Querilinte:* Name invented by C. for an imaginary Rosicrucian adept, after whose release from prison Madame d'Urfé's "rebirth" was to take place. C. intended to pass Passano off as Querilinte (cf. Vol. 8, Chap. I).

9. *Paralis:* Name of the spirit to whom C. ostensibly addressed his cabalistic questions and to whom he attributed the answers to them. The name first appears in C.'s memoirs in connection with his cabalistic sessions with his three patrician friends in Venice (cf. Vol. 2, Chap. VIII, n. 18).

10. *Seramis:* C.'s cabalistic name for Madame d'Urfé, first used here and probably modeled after that of the legendary Babylonian queen Semiramis.

11. *Ceremonies:* In common with occult doctrine in general, the ceremonies are based on the Ptolemaic system, according to which the earth, as the center of the universe, was circled by 7 planets: Sun, Moon, Mercury, Venus, Mars, Jupiter, and Saturn; each planet was given its corresponding metal and precious stone. Medieval occultism greatly increased the number of such correspondences.

12. *Saint-Louis:* Then a separate village, now one of the northern suburbs of Marseilles, with extensive harbor works.

13. *The theater:* Then the Théâtre Vacon in the street of the same name; it existed from 1738 to 1789, in which year it was demolished to make room for a fish market. It was replaced by the Grand Théâtre, on the Rue Beauvau, which still stands.

14. *F . . .:* C. writes "f . . ." (for *foute*).

15. *P . . .:* C. writes "maq . . . . ." (for *maquereau*).

16. *"Sainte-Baume":* A second-rate inn which existed at the

time on the Rue de l'Arbre, a street north of the Canebière and parallel to it.

17. *Bono:* Giuseppe Bono (died 1780); established himself in Marseilles as a silk merchant and banker in 1756. C. has already mentioned him in Vol. 8, Chap. IV.

18. *Tin:* Tin was the metal of the planet Jupiter.

19. *Oromasis:* C.'s version of the name of a legendary Rosicrucian adept (cf. Vol. 8, Chap. I, n. 10).

20. *Saint-Germain:* See Vol. 8, Chap. I.

21. *Paralisée Galtinarde:* C. does not explain why he here gives himself this new cabalistic or Rosicrucian name; the first element of it is obviously derived from Paralis (for which see note 9 to this chapter); with some letters left over, the two elements together form an anagram for "de Seingalt."

22. *Word:* Semen. C. has previously used the term in this sense in both occult and mundane contexts; see Vol. 5, Chap. V, n. 58, and Vol. 8, Chap. IV, n. 34.

23. *Undine:* A female water spirit, one of the elemental geniuses of water according to occult doctrine (cf. Vol. 2, Chap. VII, n. 22).

24. *Stages:* A stage corresponded to a journey of two hours.

25. *Companion:* I.e., her landlord's niece.

26. *Boy groom:* C. writes "en Jacquet," from English "jockey" (originally a diminutive of Jack or Jock), used in the French of the time to designate a boy in livery who served as a postilion or rode behind his master's carriage.

27. *Florentine kisses:* The *bacio alla fiorentina* is defined by the commentators as a kiss in which the giver pinches the receiver's cheeks between thumb and third finger; but the definition scarcely applies in the present context.

28. *Seventy:* Madame d'Urfé was only 58 years old in 1763.

29. *System of Ptolemy:* See note 11 to this chapter. Though preserved in astrology, the Ptolemaic system had long been supplanted in astronomy.

30. *Selenis:* C.'s name for the genius of the moon (cf. Vol. 8, Chap. III, n. 18).

31. *Rock alum:* Alum from the rock was considered the purest. Used as a writing fluid, it produced colorless characters, which became visible after the application of water.

32. *Rouge:* In France, the use of rouge was restricted to women of the nobility; however, actresses and prostitutes usurped the privilege.

33. *Horosmadis:* Possibly another version of the name "Oromasis" (see note 19 to this chapter), but here applied to the King of the Salamanders. According to occult doctrine, salamanders were elemental spirits who presided over fire (cf. Vol. 2, Chap. VII, n. 22).

34. *She:* The text has "il" ("he"), which must be either a slip or a misprint for "elle."

35. *Anael:* The Angel Anael, in cabalism the messenger of Venus (cf. Vol. 8, Chap. I, n. 11).

36. *Orléans:* Philip, Duke of Orléans, was Regent of France from 1715 to 1723 during the minority of Louis XV; Madame d'Urfé was the Duke's mistress in her younger days.

37. *Ducati correnti:* The ducato corrente of Venice, money of account (6 lire, 4 soldi).

38. *Henriette:* See Vol. 3, Chaps. I-V.

39. *M. M.:* C. first wrote "Marie-Mathilde," then crossed it out and substituted "M. M." For his relation with her, see Vol. 4, Chaps. I-IX.

40. *Pontcarré:* Geoffroy Macé Camus, Seigneur de Pontcarré, brother of Madame d'Urfé, Councilor of State from 1753.

41. *The two Rangoni sisters:* Nothing is known of the elder; for the younger, see the following note. C. here says that he had met them during his first stay in Marseilles, but in his account of it (Vol. 7, Chaps. III-IV) he does not mention them.

42. *Princess Gonzaga Solferino:* Elisabetta Rangoni (died 1832) was married at some date after 1763 to Luigi Gonzaga, Prince of Castiglione delle Stiviere, Marchese of Medole and Solferino (1745-1819), son of Leopoldo Gonzaga, Prince of Solferino and Venetian patrician (died 1760).

43. *A Medini:* Elisabetta's mother, née Elena, Countess Medini, was married to Prince Leopoldo Gonzaga in 1744. Her brother, Count Tommaso Medini (1725-1788?), man of letters and adventurer, became a friend of C.'s and later his enemy (cf. Vols. 11 and 12).

44. *Babet:* French diminutive of Elisabeth.

45. *Rangoni . . . princes:* A noble family named Rangoni is

documented in Modena from 1149. But the Roman Consul of the same name was obviously not descended from it.

46. *Almanac:* A yearbook listing the titled families of Europe. A surviving example is the *Almanach de Gotha*.

47. *Eighteen:* Text, "dix-huit," substituted for "douze," which had been substituted for an original "deux." C. left Venice for the last time in 1783. The substitutions go to show that he revised his memoirs at intervals over a considerable period of years.

48. *Comfortable pension:* Prince Gonzaga was granted a yearly pension of 10,000 gulden in 1772 in return for ceding his rights to the Principality of Castiglione, in the Duchy of Mantua, to Austria.

49. *The late Emperor Joseph:* Joseph II (1741-1790), son of Francis I and Maria Teresa, Emperor from 1765. C.'s referring to him as no longer living shows that he wrote, or at least revised, this part of his memoirs after 1790.

50. *N. N.:* A slip of C.'s for P. P., the initials under which he conceals the name of his "niece's" father.

51. *Sète:* Town some 20 miles southwest of Montpellier, and still an important port for the shipment of wine.

52. See Vol. 3, Chap. VIII, n. 46.

CHAPTER IV

1. *Chapter IV:* In the ms. this chapter is preceded by a marginal note: *Antecedentibus sublatis*, indicating the suppression of an unstated number of pages. However, there is no break in the narrative. Cf. note 1 to Chap. III.

2. *Rosalie:* C. first wrote a name which he afterward crossed out so heavily that it can no longer be read. The name cannot in any case have been Paretti; perhaps he first wrote Rosalie's maiden name, or the real name of her husband.

3. *Roux de Corse:* Georges Roux de Corse, Marquis de Brue, was a well-known merchant, shipowner, and banker in Marseilles.

4. *Tourton & Baur:* Parisian banking house founded in 1755; its offices were on the Place des Victoires.

5. *15,000 francs:* A louis being worth 24 francs.

6. *Croix d'Or:* Old name of a crossroads north of Marseilles on the way to Aix-en-Provence.

7. *It gave Madame the opportunity to offer me:* C. first phrased this so that the invitation came from the gentleman who was speaking, then changed it to the present form. According to Charles Samaran, *J. Casanova* (1914), the house to which C. refers must be the château of Luynes (a few miles south of Aix); it belonged to the Margalet family. So Henriette's real name may have been Margalet.

8. *Have the same propensity:* This assertion of C.'s is unsubstantiated elsewhere.

9. *Pupil of Sappho:* The Greek poetess Sappho (ca. 600 B.C.) lived on the island of Lesbos and gathered girls about her, as her pupils and as votaries of Aphrodite and the Muses in its capital, Mitylene. The community was later misunderstood, so that Sappho came to be regarded as the most celebrated representative of Lesbian love.

10. *P . . .:* C. writes "maq. . . . . ." (for *maquereau*, "pimp").

11. *A million:* In 1760 the population of London was 676,000; by the end of the century, however, it had reached nearly a million. C.'s figure, then, is approximately that of the date at which he was writing.

12. *Bosi:* No Matteo Bosi being known as a servant of Querini's, the name appears to be an invention of C.'s.

13. *Querini:* Tommaso Querini (1706 - after 1763), Venetian patrician and Procuratore di San Marco. However, Venice did not have an ambassador in London, but merely a resident, who, from 1761 to 1764, was Giovanni Girolamo Zuccato. The reference here is to an embassy extraordinary to congratulate King George III on his accession. The members of the embassy reached London on June 8, 1762, and did not leave it until June 3, 1763. C.'s encounter with these Venetian envoys (described in the next chapter) cannot have taken place in Lyons, since they did not reach that city on their return journey until July 11, whereas extant letters of C.'s show that he was already in England by the middle of June. The meeting may have taken place in Paris at the beginning of June; or, more probably, C. met, not the two envoys themselves, but some members of their suite who

were sent back to Venice before them and were in Lyons
early in June.

14. *King of England:* George III (1738-1820), of the House
of Hanover; he ascended the throne in 1760.

15. *Morosini:* Francesco Lorenzo Morosini (1714-1793), Venetian patrician and diplomat, Procuratore di San Marco in
1755, Venetian Ambassador in Paris 1748-1751.

16. *"Saint-Omer":* The Hôtel de Saint-Omer, in Avignon, still
exists on the Rue du Limas. Casanova had already stayed
there in 1760 (cf. Vol. 7, Chap. III).

17. Piero Chiari no doubt rightly ignores the suggestion of the
German commentators that this is altered from Ariosto,
Orlando furioso, XV, 47: *Che colui morto, ed io rimanga
vivo.*

18. *Henriette:* See Vol. 3, Chaps. I-V.

19. *Madame Stuard:* See Vol. 7, Chap. III. Her real name was
Marie Anne Constance Louise des Grafs.

20. *Irene:* Irene Rinaldi. See Vol. 8, Chap. VII; she was probably Irene Balzali (died after 1790), Italian actress.

21. *Her father:* See the following note.

22. *Count Rinaldi:* Probably the assumed name of an adventurer and professional gambler who died before 1774; see
Vol. 2, Chap. VIII, and Vol. 8, Chap. VII.

23. *High play:* The French Consul in Nice, Jullien, maintained
a well-known gambling room in his house, himself acting as
banker.

24. *Saint-Andiol:* Some 12 miles southeast of Avignon on the
road to Aix-en-Provence and Marseilles.

25. *SS. Giovanni e Paolo:* The Church of SS. Giovanni e Paolo
(in Venetian, S. Zanipolo) is one of the finest architectural
monuments in Venice; it was built in Gothic style by the
Dominicans from 1246 to 1430.

26. *The "Parc":* The Hôtel du Parc was then considered the
best inn in Lyons; it was in the former Place des Carmes
(now Rue d'Algérie), in the northern part of the old city;
it survived into the 19th century.

27. *Madame d'Urfé . . . Bellecour:* Madame d'Urfé owned a
house on the Place Bellecour, which was laid out in 1713 and
is still the center of Lyons.

28. *Rochebaron:* François de La Rochefoucauld, Marquis de

Rochebaron (1677-1766), Lieutenant-General and Commandant of Lyons.

29. *Criminal Magistrate:* Text, "lieutenant criminel." ("Criminal Lieutenant" in Vol. 5, Chap. X, p. 235 and n. 45, should
be corrected accordingly.)

30. Attributed by Suetonius (*Lives of the Caesars,* "Divus
Julius," 32) to Julius Caesar when he crossed the Rubicon
and thus began the civil war. It became a proverbial expression in the sense, "There is now no turning back."

31. *Madame Pernon:* Wife of a manufacturer in Lyons (cf.
Vol. 8, Chap. IV).

32. *Petticoat password:* Text: "le mot du jupon"; the word
of recognition among Lesbians.

33. *Manufactories:* No doubt the world-famous silk factories
of Lyons.

34. *He had the hundred louis:* C. here appears to refer to
events which took place from June to September of 1763.
Documents preserved at Dux show that Passano was still
in Lyons (or had returned there) in Sept. 1763, at which
time he received an order for 1000 francs drawn on the
banker Bono by C. Perhaps he received more than one such
order.

CHAPTER V

1. *Memmo:* No doubt one of the three Memmo brothers, Venetian patricians, whom C. had long known; most probably
Andrea Memmo (1729-1793), a Senator and the Venetian
Envoy first in Rome and from 1777 in Constantinople; his
name does not appear among those of the official members
of the embassy to London, but it is possible that he accompanied it in a private capacity.

2. *Stratico:* Count Simone Stratico (1730-1824), Professor of
Medicine, Mathematics, and Physics at the University of
Padua from 1755, and at the same time in the employ of
the Venetian Government; he was an official member of the
embassy to London.

3. *His mother . . . prison:* Lucia Memmo, née Pisani, married
to the Venetian patrician Pietro Memmo in 1719. She seems
to have been instrumental in sending C. to prison in 1755,

for she accused him to the State Inquisitors of converting her sons to atheism. (Cf. Vol. 4, Chaps. XI and XIII.)

4. *Con . . . venizian:* The words are in the Venetian dialect.

5. *Lady Harrington:* Caroline Stanhope, Countess of Harrington, née Fitzroy (died 1784), married in 1746 to William Stanhope, Viscount Petersham, who became the second Earl Harrington in 1756.

6. *Mademoiselle Charpillon:* Marie Anne Geneviève Augspurgher, known as "La Charpillon" (ca. 1746 - after 1777); she spent her childhood in Paris as Mademoiselle de Boulainvilliers (cf. Vol. 5, Chap. XI), then became a courtesan in London (cf. especially Chaps. XI and XII of this volume).

7. *Duenna:* C. writes *"duegna,"* for Spanish *dueña.*

8. *A project:* C. was probably thinking of a lottery such as he had instituted in Paris in 1757 with the Calzabigi brothers. In 1763 there were already two lotteries in England, both of them under attack from the Opposition in Parliament. C. doubtless thought he could propose a scheme which would be advantageous to the Treasury.

9. *Egremont:* Charles Wyndham (1710-1763), from 1751 Earl Egremont, English Secretary of State. Since he died on Aug. 21, 1763, C. could not lay his plans before him.

10. *Zuccato:* Giovanni Girolamo Zuccato, Secretary of the Venetian Senate, from 1761 to 1764 Venetian Resident in London.

11. *Mille ducati:* Italian, "a thousand ducats." The Venetian ducato was originally a gold coin minted from 1284 to 1540, when it was replaced by the zecchino. In the 17th century a new ducato was minted, with a value of 14 lire.

12. *Bourgoin:* Some 25 miles southeast of Lyons, on the old road to the Mont Cenis and Turin.

13. *Le Pont de Beauvoisin:* On the same road, some 20 miles east of Bourgoin.

14. *La Tour-du-Pin:* Between Bourgoin and Le Pont de Beauvoisin. However, the sequel shows that C. did not break his journey there but covered the whole distance to Lyons (some 45 miles) on horseback without a stop.

15. *Sous:* The French sou was a silver coin worth 1/20th of a franc. There were 30-sou pieces, also of silver.

16. *Solitaire . . . glass windows: Solitaire* is obviously a designation for a carriage seating one person. The use of glass

windows in carriages is documented from 1631 (in Spain).
Springs were introduced during the reign of Louis XIV;
springs *à l'Amadis* have not been identified.

17. *Adèle:* Nothing is known of Adèle Moreau and her father
except what C. himself recounts. The names are probably
fictitious.

18. *The Bourbonnais:* Former French province, corresponding
to the old Duchy of Bourbon, situated north of the Massif
Central; its capital was Moulins.

19. *Burgundy:* Former French province northeast of the Bourbonnais; capital, Dijon.

20. *Nevers:* Town in the upper valley of the Loire, some 30
miles north of Moulins and some 14 miles north of Saint-
Pierre-le-Moutier.

21. *I set an English rate on it:* Text: "Je le taxe à l'anglaise.
. . ." The wealth and extravagance of Englishmen was proverbial on the Continent in the 18th century. As the sequel
shows, the "rate" was five louis per hour.

22. *Louviers:* In the valley of the Seine, some 20 miles south
of Rouen.

23. *Bresse:* C. here writes "La Bresse," but later on "Bresse."
In either case he is in error. La Bresse was the name of a
county belonging to the Duchy of Burgundy and lying northeast of Lyons; its capital was Bourg-en-Bresse. The first
post station on the road which C. took from Lyons to Roanne
was L'Arbresle (some 15 miles northwest of Lyons).

24. *Saint-Symphorien:* Saint-Symphorien-de-Lay, a village on
the road from Lyons to Roanne, some 12 miles southeast of
Roanne.

25. *Roanne:* City in the upper valley of the Loire. C.'s stopping
there for the night made his day's journey just under 55
miles.

26. *Double one:* A normal stage was reckoned at about two
hours.

27. *Saint-Pierre-le-Moutier:* In the valley of the Allier, some
19 miles north of Moulins. This makes the day's journey just
over 71 miles.

28. *Varennes:* Varennes-sur-Allier, in the valley of the Allier,
some 20 miles south of Moulins.

29. *Moulins:* Capital of the Bourbonnais.

30. *Nine leagues:* The league as a measure of distance varied

in different times and countries. The distance between Moulins and Saint-Pierre-le-Moutier is about 19 miles.

31. *Nevers:* See note 20 to this chapter.

32. *Cosne:* In the valley of the Loire, about 32 miles north of Nevers.

33. *Briare:* On the road to Paris, about 16 miles north of Cosne.

34. *Fontainebleau:* Famous for its château, about 37 miles south of Paris. From Cosne to Fontainebleau is some 78 miles.

35. *The Pont Saint-Michel:* Bridge in Paris, connecting the Île de la Cité with the Latin Quarter. First built of wood in 1378, it was replaced by a stone bridge in 1618. As was the practice in Paris and other cities, the Pont Saint-Michel had houses and shops on either side; they were not removed until 1769.

36. *Rue aux Ours:* Street in the present 3rd Arrondissement.

37. *Rue de Montmorency:* First officially so named in 1768, it is also in the 3rd Arrondissement not far from the Rue aux Ours. At the time there were two hostelries by this name in Paris, the better known of which was on the Rue Mazarine; C. chose the less pretentious one, on the Rue de Montmorency.

CHAPTER VI

1. *Comédie Italienne:* The Comédie Italienne performed at the time in a house on the Rue Mauconseil (1st Arrondissement), next to the Church of Saint-Eustache.

2. *Madame du Rumain:* Constance Simone Flore Gabrielle, née Rouault de Gamaches (1725-1781), married in 1746 to Charles Yves Levicomte, Comte du Rumain; her second husband, whom she married in 1771, was Jean Jacques Gilbert, Marquis de Fraigne. For C.'s previous relations with her see Vols. 5 and 8.

3. *Balletti:* Antonio Stefano Balletti (1724-1789), Italian actor and dancer, friend of C.'s (see especially Vols. 2 and 3); he appeared at the Comédie Italienne in Paris from 1742 to 1769. He did not actually retire until the latter date; but an accident long kept him from performing.

4. *Brother's . . . Porte Saint-Denis:* In 1762 Francesco Casa-

nova lived on the Carré de la Porte Saint-Denis (on the border between the 4th and 10th Arrondissements); he married on June 26th of that year and then lived with his wife on the Rue des Amandiers Popincourt in the so-called Faubourg Saint-Antoine, outside the city walls (near the present Place de la Bastille).

5. *The Abate:* C.'s and Francesco C.'s younger brother Gaetano Alvisio Casanova (1734-1783). Cf. Chaps. II and III of this volume.

6. *Saincy:* Louis Pierre Sébastien Marchal de Saincy was "économe général du clergé" from 1750 to 1762.

7. *Saint-Sauveur:* The Church of Saint-Sauveur stood where the Rue Saint-Sauveur crosses the Rue Saint-Denis (2nd Arrondissement); it was demolished in 1793.

8. *Mind . . . business:* C. writes "de l'envoyer . . . se faire f. . . . ." (for *foutre*).

9. *Cecco:* Italian diminutive for Francesco.

10. *Monsieur du Rumain . . . alive:* Madame du Rumain's first husband (see note 2 to this chapter) did not die until 1770.

11. *Herrenschwandt:* Anton Gabriel Herrenschwandt (died 1785), of Swiss extraction, from 1755 physician in ordinary to the Duke of Orléans and the Swiss Guard Regiment in Paris. C. here writes (more or less phonetically) "Hereschouand."

12. *Twenty-nine:* Madame du Rumain, born in 1725, was already 38 years of age in 1763.

13. *Daughter . . . Polignac:* Constance Gabrielle Bonne du Rumain (1747-1783) was married in 1767 to Marie Louis Alexandre, Marquis de Polignac (died 1768).

14. *Teresa:* Teresa Imer (1723-1797), Italian singer, married to Angelo Pompeati in 1745; under the name of Trenti, she directed a theater in the Austrian Netherlands from 1756 to 1758 and from 1760 lived in London as "Mrs. Cornelys."

15. *Parchment:* Text, "placard," an official document on parchment, which was not folded but rolled.

16. *Calais:* In the 18th century Calais was already the port most used for the crossing to England, since the distance to Dover on the opposite side of the Channel was the shortest (about 22 miles).

17. *Tourton & Baur:* See note 4 to Chap. IV of this volume.

18. *La Corticelli:* Maria Anna Corticelli (1747-1767 or 1773), Italian dancer. For C.'s previous relations with her see Vol. 7, especially Chaps. VII and VIII, and Vol. 8, especially Chaps. III and V. It would seem that here, as elsewhere, C. confuses events of his stays in Paris in 1763 and 1767, and that this interview with La Corticelli did not take place until 1767. Cf. note 27 to this chapter.

19. *Rue de Grenelle Saint-Honoré:* The present Rue de Grenelle (7th Arrondissement) in the former Faubourg Saint-Germain is still the site of a number of mansions from the 18th century (now housing ministries and embassies). The addition "Saint-Honoré" suggests that in C.'s time there was a Rue de Grenelle in the Faubourg Saint-Honoré or near the Rue Saint-Honoré (1st Arrondissement). The fact that, according to his account, C. seems to have walked to La Corticelli's lodging from the office of Tourton & Baur on the Place des Victoires (2nd Arrondissement) supports this suggestion.

20. *Droghi:* Nothing more is known of him.

21. *La Pacienza:* See Vol. 8, Chap. V.

22. *Santini:* Nothing is known of a dancer named Santini who had been a tailor.

23. *D'Auberval:* Jean Bercher (1742-1806) used the names D'Auberval and Dauberval; he made his debut as a dancer in Turin in 1759, settled in Paris in 1761, where by 1770 he had won high esteem in his profession.

24. *The Haymarket:* The "King's Theatre in the Haymarket," London, was built in 1705; from 1708 it principally housed Italian opera.

25. *Guineas:* The guinea was a gold coin worth 21 shillings, minted from 1662 to 1813 and made of gold from the Guinea Coast of Africa, whence the name; it is now only money of account.

26. *Collalto:* Antonio Collalto-Matteucci (ca. 1717-1777), famous Italian actor of the period, from 1759 succeeded Carlo Veronese in the role of Pantalone at the Comédie Italienne in Paris.

27. *An engagement at the Comédie Italienne:* Documents show that La Corticelli (Maria Anna Corticelli) appeared in Turin in October 1763, danced in Venice in 1764, and first came to Paris in 1765, where she was a member of the corps de

ballet at the Comédie Italienne until 1767. Another dancer of the same name appeared at the same time in Paris, perhaps Rosa Corticelli, sister of Maria Anna. C. confuses events which occurred during his stays in Paris in 1763 and 1767.

28. *Faget:* Jean Faget (ca. 1700 to 1762), celebrated Parisian physician (cf. Vol. 5, Chap. X).

29. *Rue de Seine:* In C.'s time there were two streets of this name, one in the parish of Saint-Germain, the other in the parish of Saint-Victor, by which names they were distinguished. The present Rue de Seine is in the Faubourg Saint-Germain (6th Arrondissement).

30. *Faubourg Saint-Antoine:* It was situated beyond the present Place de la Bastille.

31. *Palais-Royal:* The reference is to the garden in the inner court of the Palais-Royal, then a favorite promenade and meeting place.

32. *Boncousin:* Either Silvestro or Lodovico Boncousin (also Beaucousin), proprietor of a hostelry in Venice (cf. Vol. 2, Chap. VIII).

33. *Hôtel de Bouillon:* The Hôtel de Bouillon, built as a private house by Mansart in the 17th century, is now No. 17, Quai Malaquais, and since 1892 has belonged to the École Nationale Supérieure des Beaux-Arts.

34. *The opera:* In the 18th century performances of opera were given in the theater of the Palais-Royal until 1763, when the auditorium was destroyed by fire. From 1764 to 1770 they were given in the Tuileries Palace.

35. *Six years:* Unmistakable evidence that C. confused events of his stays in Paris in 1763 and 1767. Francesco Casanova did not marry until June 1762.

36. *He married another woman:* Francesco Casanova's first wife, Marie Jeanne Jolivet, died before 1775; in that year he married Jeanne Catherine Delachaux (1748-1818).

37. *Twenty years hence:* One of several indications that C. originally planned to continue his memoirs beyond the year 1774.

38. *Trenti's:* C. here calls Teresa Imer's son by one of the names she used (cf. note 14 to this chapter). Giuseppe Pompeati had himself assumed the name of Count d'Aranda (cf. Vol. 5, Chap. X).

39. *The Français:* Unofficial name of the theater in which the Comédie Française performed.

40. *A new play . . . failed:* Probably *La Manie des arts ou la matinée à la mode,* by Marc Antoine Jacques Rochon de Chabannes (1730-1800); it had its first performance at the Comédie Française on June 1, 1763.

41. *Rue Montmartre:* The Rue Montmartre, in the 2nd Arrondissement, runs from the Church of Saint-Eustache to the Boulevard Montmartre.

42. *B . . . . . . :* C. writes "b. . . . ." (for *bordel*).

43. *Died . . . treatment:* Maria Anna Corticelli probably died in the Hôtel-Dieu (public hospital) in Paris in 1767, though it is possible that she did not die until 1773. C. again appears to confuse events of his stays in Paris in 1763 and 1767.

44. *Van Robais:* In the 17th century the Hollander Josse van Robais founded a manufactory for fine fabrics in Abbeville under the patronage of the Finance Minister, Colbert; in the 18th century it became one of the most celebrated establishments of the kind in France. Abbeville is still a center of the textile industry. C. writes "de Varobes."

45. *The "Golden Arm":* No inn of this name is known to have existed in Calais in the 18th century. But see Vol. 10, Chap. III, n. 24.

CHAPTER VII

1. *Packet boat:* Properly, a vessel carrying passengers and mail. C., who writes "paq-bot," perhaps uses the term incorrectly.

2. *Guineas:* See note 25 to the preceding chapter.

3. *Bedford:* John Russell, Duke of Bedford (1710-1771), from 1744 First Lord of the Admiralty, from 1748 Secretary of State; from 1762 to 1763 he was in France as Envoy Extraordinary negotiating the Peace of Fontainebleau. Contemporary documents show that he arrived in Dover on the evening of June 11, 1763. If C. really traveled with him, this establishes the date of C.'s arrival in England.

4. *More impertinent than:* C. writes "plus impertinent du," an Italianism.

5. *Ebb and flow of the tides:* C. had previously known only the Mediterranean, in which the tides are little perceptible.

6. *Canterbury . . . Rochester:* Towns on the road from Dover to London.

7. *Had killed himself:* Angelo Francesco Pompeati did not commit suicide until 1768. Cf. Vol. 5, Chap. VI, n. 56.

8. *My fourth volume:* C. uses his own numeration, which is neither preserved nor indicated in the Brockhaus-Plon edition. For the events referred to, see Vol. 5, Chap. VII, and especially Vol. 6, Chap. I.

9. *Her house on Soho Square:* Teresa Imer (see note 14 to the preceding chapter), now Mrs. Cornelys, had rented Carlisle House, on the east side of Soho Square, from the noble family of Howard in 1760; here she gave her suppers and balls for the nobility and for well-to-do commoners. The house of the Venetian Resident, Zuccato, was on the same square.

10. *Raucour:* She has not been identified.

11. *Mr. Cornelys:* Young Giuseppe Pompeati, known in Paris as Count d'Aranda, in London becomes Mr. (or Sir Joseph) Cornelys.

12. *Sophie:* Illegitimate daughter of Teresa Imer-Pompeati by C. (or, according to her mother, by the Marquis de Montperny). She was born between Dec. 1753 and March 1, 1754.

13. *She was ten:* According to C.'s account (cf. Vol. 3, Chap. XIII, and Vol. 5, Chap. VI), Sophie was born in Dec. 1753. If this is true, at the time of which he is writing she was 9 years old.

14. *Fermer:* Probably George Fermor, Earl Pomfret (1724-1785), who married Anna Maria Drayton in 1764. Giuseppe Pompeati was later tutor to his son. There is no record of a Sir Frederic Fermer or Fermor.

15. *The "Prince of Orange":* Located opposite the Haymarket Theater, this coffeehouse was a favorite resort of the artists who appeared there in opera.

16. *Boccaccio:* The first edition of Boccaccio's *Decamerone* (1353) uses both the earlier spelling, *anchora*, and the later, *ancora*. Martinelli's edition uses only the spelling *ancora*.

17. *Martinelli:* Vincenzo Martinelli (1702-1785), Italian writer, went to London in 1748 and did not return to Italy until 1772.

18. *Calzabigi:* Ranieri Calzabigi (or da'Calzabigi) (1714-1795),

with his brother Giovanni Antonio and C., organized the Military School Lottery in Paris in 1757 (see especially Vol. 5, Chap. II).

19. *Your satires:* Probably Martinelli's *Lettere familiari e critiche* (London, 1758) or his *Istoria critica della vita civile* (London, 1752).

20. *Your edition of the Decamerone: Decamerone di Giovanni Boccaccio cognominata Principe Galeotto, Diligentemente corretto, ed accresciuto della Vita dell'Autore, ed altre Osservazioni Istoriche e Critiche, Da Vincenzio* [sic] *Martinelli.* Though it bears the date 1762 on its title page, it was probably not published until 1763 or 1764.

21. *Subscribers:* In the 18th century books were often published "by subscription," which in practice meant that they were not printed until a number of subscriptions sufficient to cover the cost had been obtained. C.'s translation of the *Iliad* and his *Icosameron* were published by subscription.

22. Juvenal, *Satires, 10, 22:* C. has already quoted it in Vol. 8, Chap. IX, but with the variant *cantat.*

23. *Spencer:* John, Baron Spencer of Althorp and Viscount Spencer, from 1765 1st Earl (1734-1783), owner of the celebrated "Althorp Library," patron of Martinelli.

24. *Literary work:* Among other works, Martinelli composed the first history of England to be written in Italian (*Istoria d'Inghilterra*, 3 vols., London, 1770-1773) and a history of the government of England and the English colonies (*Storia del Governo d'Inghilterra e delle sue colonie in India e nell'America settentrionale,* London, 1776), in which he prophesied the revolt of the English colonies in North America. He may well have been working on these books at the time he first met C.

25. Altered from Horace, *Odes,* 2, 18, 11-12, where the text has "nihil" instead of "nec."

26. *Speaking Tuscan with the greatest purity:* The language of Tuscany and especially of Florence was considered the purest Italian.

27. *Advertiser:* By the middle of the 18th century London already had 53 newspapers. The one with the largest circulation was the *Public Advertiser.* There was also a *Daily Advertiser.*

28. *Pall Mall:* A fashionable street in the 18th century, and still so today. C. writes "Pale-male."

29. *Housekeeper:* C. writes "Ausekeper."

30. *The Hague:* Finding Teresa Imer-Pompeati on the verge of destitution in Holland late in 1758, C. had taken her son Giuseppe to Paris with him. They had parted not at The Hague but at Rotterdam. (See Vol. 5, Chap. VI and especially Chap. VII.)

31. *The last assembly of that year:* Contemporary sources show that Mrs. Cornelys's last assembly had already taken place on May 19th; it was followed by a ball for her exclusive benefit on May 26th. So C. must be confusing the first ball of the winter of 1763 (Dec. 2nd) with the last ball of the spring of the same year. He first wrote "which she gave that spring," then substituted "of that year" (doubtless in the sense of "that season").

32. *House . . . built:* Since Carlisle House already existed, "built" is a misstatement; Teresa's expenditures on it can have been only for alterations and embellishments.

33. *Court of Equity:* One of the two chambers of the Exchequer Court, which decided cases involving the Crown and cases in civil law.

34. Legal phrase, of uncertain origin, alluding to the privilege by which a person in possession is not required to prove that he is rightfully so.

35. *Pounds sterling:* Money of account until 1816, but in the 18th century already the basis for the denominations in which bank notes were issued. 1 pound $= 20$ shillings of 12 pence each.

36. *Frac:* See note 4 to Chap. II of this volume.

37. *Zuccato:* See note 10 to Chap. V of this volume.

38. *Egremont:* See note 9 to Chap. V of this volume.

39. *Brühl:* Hans Moritz, Count Brühl, Lord of (Herr auf) Martinskirchen (1736-1809), Saxon and Polish Ambassador in St. Petersburg, in Paris, and, from 1764 to 1795, in London; from 1765 member of the Royal Society; in 1767 he married Alicia, née Carpenter (died 1794), widow of Earl Egremont. C. writes "de Brühl Messekicken."

40. *The Elector of Saxony:* Friedrich August III, Elector from 1763; in 1806 he became the first King of Saxony (until 1827).

41. *Guerchy:* Claude Louis François Régnier, Comte de Guerchy (1715-1767), French Ambassador in London from 1763 to 1767. Since he did not arrive there until Oct. 17, 1763, and presented his credentials on Oct. 21st, C. cannot have called on him until the latter date.

42. *Chauvelin:* François Claude, Marquis de Chauvelin (1716-1773), French officer and statesman. C.'s friendship with him dates from their meetings in Turin, where Chauvelin was the French Ambassador from 1754 to 1765. At this point in the ms. C. crossed out a surprising phrase: "qui en vertu de ma naturalisation m'annonçait pour Français" ("who in virtue of my naturalization announced me as French"). Since in the sequel C. crossed out a similar formula (cf. note 53 to this chapter), it may safely be assumed that he really became a French citizen. Presumably, after the events of the French Revolution, he ceased to attribute any value to his French citizenship; this would account for these suppressions. C. had already referred (Vol. 5, p. 174, of the present translation) to the possibility of his becoming a French citizen and being granted a patent of nobility. It is possible that his naturalization was accompanied by the grant of the title of Chevalier de Seingalt, in which case the name would not be a mere invention of C.'s. It is striking that all of his French friends, including those who belonged to the high nobility, always addressed him as de Seingalt in their letters, and with no overtones of mockery or condescension.

43. *Court of St. James's:* That is, of St. James's Palace, which was built under Henry VIII from 1532 to 1533 and remained the royal residence until 1809, in which year it was largely destroyed by fire. "The Court of St. James's" is still the official designation of the British Court.

44. *Sunday after chapel:* At the period presentations at Court were made every Sunday after service in the Chapel Royal.

45. *D'Éon:* Charles Geneviève Louis Auguste André Timothée, Chevalier d'Éon de Beaumont (1728-1810), French diplomat, from 1755 secret agent for Louis XV, in 1762 secretary to the Duke of Nivernais during the latter's term as Envoy Extraordinary to conclude the peace negotiations in London, then secretary to the Count of Guerchy, with whom he immediately fell out. He was the author of a great many political and historical works (13 vols., Amsterdam, 1775).

From 1777 to 1785 he lived in Paris as a woman, an imposture which excited intense curiosity at the time and to which C. refers. See also Vol. 10, Chap. I.

46. *Covent Garden . . . theater:* The most celebrated theater in London at the time; built toward the end of the 17th century, it was destroyed by fire in 1808. The present Covent Garden Theater, also known as the Royal Opera House, was built in 1858.

47. *Drury Lane Theater:* Built in 1663 and destroyed by fire in 1672, it was rebuilt in 1674 by Wren in the street of that name. From 1705 it housed acting companies only, opera being given at the King's Theater. It was several times gutted by the London populace (cf. note 79 this chapter); in 1809 it was destroyed by fire. The present building dates from 1812.

48. *The Exchange:* The Royal Exchange, in the City of London. The original building, destroyed in the Great Fire of 1666, was replaced in 1670. Among other offices it contained those of the Lord Mayor of London and those of the Royal Exchange Insurance Office, one of whose directors was Samuel Bosanquet (see the following note).

49. *Bosanquet:* Samuel Bosanquet, probably of French Protestant origin; from 1755 a director of the Royal Exchange Insurance Office.

50. *Bagnios:* A brothel of a special kind, sufficiently described in the text (C. writes "Begno").

51. *George III:* From 1760 King of England; the third English monarch of the House of Hanover (1738-1820).

52. *The Queen:* Sophie Charlotte, Princess of Mecklenburg-Strelitz (died 1818), from 1761 consort of George III.

53. *I was a Venetian:* At this point in the original ms. C. crossed out: "n'était français que pour m'être naturalisé" ("was French only because I had been naturalized"). Cf. note 42 to this chapter.

54. *For what reason:* C. here crossed out: "je m'étais fait français" ("I had become French").

55. *Jarba:* Iarbas, King of Mauritania, unsuccessful suitor of Dido (Vergil, *Aeneid*, IV, 36, 196, 326), figures as Jarba in several dramatizations of the Aeneas-Dido story, among them Metastasio's *Didone abbandonata*.

56. *Sir Joseph Cornelys:* C. ironically uses young Pompeati's new name.

57. *Her mother:* Text, "elle," the grammatical antecedent of which is Sophie, but which seems rather to designate her mother.

58. *St. James's Park:* Adjacent to the royal palace and subject only to the royal jurisdiction.

59. *Lady Harrington:* See note 5 to Chap. V of this volume.

60. *A letter for her:* Given to C. by Morosini in Lyons (see Chap. V of this volume).

61. *No one dares to play or to give concerts:* There were extremely strict laws against breaking the Sabbath.

62. *The third: Sic,* but C. has just said that he met four of them. They were: Caroline (1747-1767), Isabella (1748-1819; C. writes "Belle"); Amelia (1749-1780; C. writes "Émilie"), and Henrietta (1750-1781); they all bore the title Lady Stanhope.

63. *Whist:* The favorite card game in England at the period, played by four players with 52 cards.

64. *Duchess of Northumberland:* Elizabeth, Countess Percy (ca. 1716-1776); she did not become Duchess of Northumberland until 1766.

65. *Lord Percy . . . presented it to his mother:* See Vol. 8, Chap. VI.

66. *Lady Coventry:* Lady Mary Coventry, née Gunning (1732-1760), sister of Elizabeth (1733-1790), who became Duchess of Hamilton in 1752 and Lady Campbell in 1759.

67. *Duchess of Hamilton:* See the preceding note. But since Lady Mary Coventry died in 1760, the person referred to must be either the Duchess of Hamilton herself or Lord Coventry's second wife, Barbara, daughter of Lord St. John. However, their marriage did not take place until Sept. 1764.

68. *Gains fifteen shillings:* C. had paid in gold pieces (guineas), each of which was worth 21 shillings; if he had paid in bank notes, he would have paid in pounds, each of which was worth 20 shillings. The difference came to 15 shillings.

69. *Hervey:* The Honorable (not "Sir," as C. later writes) Augustus John Hervey (1724-1779) did not become Earl of Bristol until 1775; hence in 1763 he was not yet a Lord. He distinguished himself as an Admiral in naval engagements in the West Indies.

70. *Miss Chudleigh:* Elizabeth Chudleigh (ca. 1720-1788), married secretly in 1744 to Augustus John Hervey, whom she left after their wedding night; the marriage was annulled in 1769. In the same year she was married to Evelyn Pierrepont, Duke of Kingston-upon-Hull. The legality of the marriage was contested, and she was sentenced for bigamy but fled to the Continent.

71. *Princess of Wales:* Augusta, Princess of Saxe-Gotha (1719-1772), married in 1736 to Frederick Louis, Prince of Wales, who died in 1751; mother of George III of England.

72. *Meat-eater:* C. uses (or coins?) the term "criophage," from the Greek word κριοφάγος, "devourer of rams." "Ram-eater" being inapplicable in reference to English diet, one is left with the more specific possibility "mutton-eater," and the less specific one "meat-eater."

73. *The Museum:* The British Museum. Founded in 1753, in C.'s day it was still housed in Montague House, Bloomsbury.

74. *Maty:* Matthew Maty (1718-1776), first a practicing physician, later Librarian of the British Museum and Secretary of the Royal Society.

75. Proverbial expression, of uncertain origin, but already established in the Middle Ages.

76. *Its Bank:* The Bank of England, founded in 1694.

77. *The three kingdoms:* England, Scotland, and Ireland.

78. *Real wealth:* In the ms. there follows a section about a page in length, which, though C. canceled it, is still legible enough to show that he went on to treat various financial and economic problems of the time.

79. *Garrick:* David Garrick (1717-1779), famous English actor; part owner and manager of the Drury Lane Theater. The gutting of a theater by the disappointed or offended audience was a not uncommon occurrence at the period. The most notable examples, the so-called Drury Lane Riots, took place on Jan. 25 and Feb. 24, 1763.

80. *Twenty years later:* Garrick was buried in the so-called Poets' Corner of Westminster Abbey in 1779.

81. *Roscius:* Quintus Roscius Gallus (126-62 B.C.), celebrated Roman actor.

82. *The Green Park:* Between St. James's Park and Hyde Park. C. writes "Grim-parc."

83. *Lord Ferrers:* Laurence Shirley, Earl Ferrers (C. writes "Ferex"), born 1720, was hanged at Tyburn on May 5, 1760, for the murder of his major-domo Johnson. The brother to whom C. refers is presumably Washington Shirley, who inherited the earldom after 1760.

84. C. used this proverb as the epigraph to his *Histoire de ma fuite* (1788), ascribing it to Horace; but it does not occur in Horace's works. It appears on the title page of a work by Petronio Zecchini, whom C. attacked in his *Lana caprina* (1772).

85. *Thief . . . hanged in London:* John Rice, an exchange broker, who was hanged at Tyburn for forgery on May 4, 1763.

86. *Nivernais:* Louis Jules Henri Barbon Mancini-Mazarini, Duke of Nivernais (1716-1798), French diplomat, in Rome from 1749 to 1752, in Berlin and London from 1762 to 1763. He was a member of the French Academy.

87. *The Minister:* I.e., Lord Halifax (see the following note).

88. *Halifax:* George Montagu Dunk, Earl of Halifax (1716-1771), English Secretary of State from 1762.

89. *His wife:* The fact is, however, that Mrs. Rice was arrested; 4700 pounds sterling in bank notes were found in her corset.

90. *Havana . . . was given back:* During the Seven Years' War England took a number of places in the West Indies, among them Havana in 1762. After securing a booty of 30 million gulden, she returned the city to Spain on July 6, 1763.

91. *Piasters:* Another name for the peso, a Spanish silver coin which circulated in all the Spanish colonies from the 16th to the 19th century. The text at this point has: "comme j'ai mis, or division, quarante millions . . ." where "division" might suggest that the 40 million was Hervey's *share* of the booty but where the phrase makes no sense as it stands.

92. *Lady Rochefort:* Probably Lady Lucy Rochford, née Young (1723-1773), married in 1740 to William Henry Nassau de Zulestein, Earl of Rochford, English diplomat.

93. *Husband . . . Ambassador to Spain:* The 4th Earl of Rochford (see note 92) was English Ambassador in Madrid from 1763 to 1766.

CHAPTER VIII

1. *"Star" Tavern:* C. first wrote "Staren-taverne dans le Pique-Dille" (for Piccadilly), then crossed out the last three words. There were several "Star" Taverns in London at the time.

2. *Pembroke:* Henry Herbert, Earl of Pembroke (1734-1794); he was married to Lady Elizabeth Spencer, daughter of the Duke of Marlborough, in 1756, though C. later makes him say that he is a bachelor. It is possible that he maintained a bachelor establishment in London. He was a notorious libertine.

3. *Waiter:* C. writes *"Weter."*

4. *Ranelagh House:* A then celebrated pleasure resort in Chelsea, with extensive gardens. Its principal feature was the Ranelagh Rotunda, built by Sir Thomas Robinson and opened to the public in 1742. In the center of the pavilion, which had a diameter of 150 feet, an orchestra played for dancing. Supper was served in the 50 boxes which lined its circular wall. The Rotunda was demolished in 1805. C. presumably saw an advertisement of the place displayed in St. James's Park.

5. *Whitehall:* Originally the name of a palace which became a royal residence under Henry VIII. All of it except the "banqueting house," which still stands, was destroyed by fire in 1698. C. writes "Wite-ale."

6. *Bath:* Well-known English watering place, with medicinal springs, already famous in Roman times.

7. *Lady Betty Germaine:* Lady Elizabeth Germaine (died 1769), daughter of Lord Berkeley, married to Sir John Germaine, of Drayton.

8. *Madame Binetti:* Anna Binetti, née Ramon (died 1784), Italian singer, married in 1751 to the French dancer and theater director Georges Binet. In 1760 she had helped C. escape from the Duke of Württemberg's officers in Stuttgart (cf. Vol. 6, Chap. III).

9. *Haymarket Theater:* In addition to the Kings Theater in the Haymarket there was the Little Theater, in which not only comedies and pantomimes were given but also performances by dancers and acrobats. C. writes "Hai-marcket."

10. *Louis:* C.'s alternation between guineas and louis is natural, since both coins had very nearly the same gold content.

11. *Kennedy:* Probably the well-known courtesan Polly Kennedy. She lived on Great Russell Street and was for a time the mistress of Lord Bolingbroke.

12. *Him:* I.e., Lord Pembroke.

13. *Berlendis:* Giovanni Berlendis, Venetian Secretary of Embassy in London from 1762 to 1763, Venetian Resident in Turin from 1768.

14. *The Park:* St. James's Park.

15. *Vauxhall:* The oldest and most celebrated pleasure resort in London. It existed as Spring Garden from 1661, and was reopened in its later form, as Vauxhall Gardens, in 1732. It was open from nine o'clock in the evening to four in the morning; it had a pavilion, a semicircular arcade, and an orchestra. It ceased to exist in 1859. The present Vauxhall Park is not on the same site.

16. *Malignan . . . Aix-la-Chapelle:* See Vol. 8, Chap. III.

17. *Goudar:* Ange Goudar (1720 - ca. 1791), adventurer and journalist, published *L'Espion chinois ou l'envoyé secret de la Cour de Pékin pour examiner l'état présent de l'Europe* ("The Chinese Spy, or the secret envoy from the Court of Peking to examine the present state of Europe") (1764, and many subsequent editions). See note 16 to Chap. XI of this volume.

18. *Mr. Frederick:* More often known in C.'s day as Colonel Frederick; probably a Polish adventurer named Wigliariski who adopted the name Neuhoff in 1758 and claimed to be the son of Baron von Neuhoff (see the following note).

19. *Theodore:* Theodor Stephan, Baron von Neuhoff (ca. 1690-1756), became a page to the Duke of Orléans at Versailles in 1709, was later in the service of Bavaria; deeply in debt, he tried to better his fortunes in Spain, where about 1717 he married Lady Sarsfield (died 1720 or 1724), one of the Queen's Ladies-in-Waiting. With the support of the Bey of Tunis, he led an expedition to Corsica in 1736 and was proclaimed King of Corsica as Theodore I. He died in poverty in London in 1756.

20. *Only half:* According to contemporary sources the entrance fee at Vauxhall Gardens was 1 shilling, at Ranelagh House a half crown (2½ shillings).

21. *St. James's Chronicle:* Founded in 1761 and published thrice weekly. J. Rives Childs has found the announcement

in the *Gazetteer and London Daily Advertiser* for July 5, 1763.

22. *Chapel of the Bavarian Minister:* Catholics were not granted freedom of worship in England until 1829; in C.'s time only 0.8% of the population were avowed Catholics. Mass was celebrated only in the chapels of the Ambassadors of Catholic countries. The Bavarian Minister in London was then Baron (later Count) Joseph Franz Xaver von Haslang; the embassy chapel was on Warwick Street, Golden Square.

23. *Pauline:* Of this Pauline, only daughter of a Portuguese Count, nothing is known except what C. relates of her or makes her relate.

24. *Fall in love with him:* C. here added, then canceled, a passage of which only the first few words can still be read ("This was true, but I generalized the rule too much; and I was cruelly"), which may have been intended to be an anticipatory reference to his disappointment in La Charpillon.

25. *Crown:* Silver coin minted from 1551; value, 5 shillings.

26. *Bailiff:* C. here writes "belai" and later "bili," "bilai," in accordance with the former pronunciation.

27. *King's Bench:* Prison for debtors and persons sentenced by the Court of King's Bench. It was built in 1758, later became a military prison, and was demolished in 1880.

28. *Guineas:* Here, and in a number of later instances, C. writes "pièces" instead of his more usual "guinées." (The other instances will not be noted.)

29. *Three years old then . . . five:* Sophie must have been born between Dec. 1753 and March 1754. It would follow that at the time of C.'s stay in Holland (from Oct. 1758 to early in 1759) she was in fact five years old. In the ms. C. first wrote "two" and "four," then corrected them to "three" and "five." (Cf. Vol. 5, Chap. VII.)

30. *Montperny:* Théodore Camille, Marquis de Montperny (died 1753), was major-domo to the Margravine of Bayreuth from 1746; he died in Paris in 1753. He may have been the father of Teresa Pompeati's second daughter (who was born on Feb. 14, 1753, and seems to have died young), for her sponsors in baptism were the Margrave Friedrich von Ansbach-Bayreuth and his sister.

31. *La Bruyère's* Characters: *Les caractères de Théophraste,*

traduits du grec, avec les caractères ou moeurs de ce siècle
(1688).

32. *Camoëns:* Luiz Vaz de Camões (ca. 1524-1580), famous
Portuguese poet, author of the epic poem *Os Lusíadas* ("The
Lusiads").

CHAPTER IX

1. *Chapter IX:* The regular handwriting and the unusually
small number of corrections in the ms. of this chapter suggest that it represents a careful revision of an earlier version.
C.'s story of Countess Pauline X-o has been regarded by
many Casanovists, especially in Portugal, as pure invention,
since no documents to substantiate it have yet been found
in either Portuguese or English archives. However, a number
of details, pointed out in the following notes, seem to testify
to the essential truth of the story.

2. *X-o:* This abbreviation, and the name Pauline, are certainly
pseudonyms. At the conclusion of Pauline's narrative, C.
himself says that the real names are disguised. Since the
Prime Minister Pombal's many reforms had made him im-
placable enemies among the nobility and the Jesuits, the
measures he took after the attempted assassination of the
King (see note 4 to this chapter) were especially severe;
even today the total number of those imprisoned after being
tried for high treason, at least 30 of whom belonged to the
highest nobility, is not known.

3. *Carvalho Oeyras:* Sebastião José de Carvalho e Mello, Count
of Oeyras (1699-1782), known in history as the Marquis of
Pombal (a title which, however, he did not receive until
1770), one of the most important statesmen of the era of
enlightened absolutism. Portuguese Envoy first in London
(from 1738), then in Vienna (from 1745), he was made
Minister for Foreign Affairs by King Joseph Emanuel I in
1750 and Prime Minister in 1756.

4. *Attempt on the King's life:* The attempted assassination
of Joseph Emanuel I of Portugal (1715-1777, King from
1750) took place on the night of Sept. 3-4, 1758; he was
wounded by a bullet. A number of noblemen, among them
Don José Aveiro, were arrested and executed; the Jesuits,
accused of being the instigators of the plot, were banished

from Portugal in 1759. Since the trials for high treason were conducted in secret, it is likely that some of those who were condemned were innocent.

5. *Count Fl:* Like the other characters in the story, he cannot be identified.

6. *Approval of the King:* In accordance with a law of Jan. 29, 1739, marriages by members of the nobility had to be approved by the King. Since C. was probably not especially well versed in Portuguese law, his mentioning this detail tends to substantiate his narrative.

7. *The Princess of Brazil:* The heir presumptive to a King of Portugal had the title Prince (or Princes) of Brazil. Here the reference is to Joseph Emanuel's eldest daughter, Maria Francisca Isabella, who married the Infant Pedro Clemente, the King's brother, in 1760, and ascended the throne on the death of her father in 1777.

8. *Saa:* The Portuguese Envoy in London from 1756 to 1770 was Martinho Mello e Castro, Count of Galvas. Count de Saa was only his representative during his absence from London as a delegate to the peace conference at Fontainebleau.

9. *Frigate:* In the 17th century, a three-masted ship-rigged war vessel; but in the 18th century the term was also applied to three-masted merchant vessels of the same rig.

10. *Ferrol:* Either the Spanish port in the northwestern province of La Coruña (now El Ferrol del Caudillo), or the Portuguese port Pharol de Santa Maria, at the mouth of the Tagus, some 18 miles west of Lisbon.

11. *The Tagus:* Spanish Tajo, Portuguese Tejo, the longest river on the Iberian Peninsula; it rises some 120 miles east of Madrid, flows past Toledo, and finally crosses Portugal. Lisbon is situated on the estuary by which it enters the Atlantic.

12. *Longboat:* Launch capable of being sailed or rowed and carried by a large vessel to afford communication between the mother ship at anchor and the shore.

13. *My pocket:* See note 18, below.

14. *Crosses the whole Atlantic:* An exaggeration, since a voyage from Portugal to England has to cross only the Bay of Biscay.

15. *Corvette:* A fast war vessel ranking in the old navies next below a frigate.

16. *Plymouth:* Port city in southwestern England, some 200 miles from London. Since it appears from Pauline's subsequent narrative that she made the journey to London in one day, C. probably confused Plymouth with Portsmouth, which is only some 75 miles from London.

17. *Cadiz:* Seaport, and capital of the province of the same name, in southwestern Spain.

18. *Not to ask him for my jewel case:* This contradicts Pauline's earlier assertion that she put the jewel case in her own pocket. Alternatively, the *ma* ("my") of the earlier account may be a slip (or a typographical error? Laforgue read *sa*) for *sa* ("his").

19. *The Strand:* Still one of the principal streets in London, running from the City to the present Trafalgar Square. In the 18th century many noble families had residences on it.

20. *Lisbonines:* Portuguese, *lisbonina*; another designation for the *dobra*, Portuguese gold coin minted from 1722 and worth 4 escudos or 4000 reis.

21. *St. Paul's:* The district around St. Paul's Cathedral.

22. *Your Vergil . . . die in poverty:* During his last years the poet Camoëns (cf. note 32 to the previous chapter) lived on the alms which a slave begged for him at night; he died of the plague in 1579.

23. *She:* Text, "il"; but obviously a slip (or an editor's misreading?) for "elle."

24. *Kensington:* Now part of London, near Hyde Park, but in C.'s day a village with a royal residence, Kensington Palace, which still exists.

25. *Kingston:* Evelyn Pierrepont, Duke of Kingston (1711-1773), lived for some years with his mistress Elizabeth Chudleigh in Kingston House, a mansion facing the Princes Gate entrance to Hyde Park. He did not marry her until 1769.

26. *Kiss answers kiss:* Text, "le double baiser sont"; perhaps, rather, a metaphor from gaming with dice: "out comes double-kiss."

27. *Ricciardetto . . . Fiordispina:* In the 25th canto of his *Orlando furioso* Ariosto tells how Ricciardetto won the love

of Fiordispina, who had fallen in love with his sister Bradamante disguised as a knight.

28. Ariosto, *Orlando furioso*, XXV, 42.

29. *Ibid.*, 54. "Dirizza," in the last line of the quoted passage,
can mean both "straighten" and "direct, aim." C. takes it
in the former sense.

30. *Ibid.*, 64.

31. *Ibid.*, 65.

32. *Rome:* The reference is to the Papal Curia as censor of
books.

33. *A Spanish woman:* Ariosto makes Fiordispina a Princess
of Spain.

34. Ariosto, *Orlando furioso*, XXV, 68.

35. *Adam . . . more guilty than Eve:* C. has the "beautiful
theologian" Hedwig make exactly the same point in Vol. 8,
Chap. IV.

36. *God made Eve . . . after . . . Adam:* See Genesis 2:16 ff.

37. *Jesuit . . . of the short robe:* The Jesuit order accepted
lay affiliates whose high position could make them useful to
it; they were not obliged to wear the dress of the order.

38. *A Jew:* Probably the then well-known miniature painter
Jeremiah Meyer (1735-1789).

39. *Madame d'Urfé was dead:* Madame d'Urfé did not die
until 1775; she left a perfectly rational will in favor of her
grandson Achille du Châtelet. C. knew that she was alive,
for a letter from his friend Bono, dated Nov. 10, 1763, and
found at Dux, told him that she was then staying on her
estate in the country. No Casanovist has yet suggested any
plausible reason for C.'s making this obvious misstatement.

40. *The Countess du Châtelet:* Adelaïde Marie Thérèse, Marquise (not Comtesse) du Châtelet-Fresnières, née d'Urfé
(1717 - after 1776), Madame d'Urfé's daughter, whom she
disinherited.

41. *Reis:* Plural of real, a Portuguese coin originally of silver,
then of copper, later only money of account. In 1763 1000
reis were worth 5 shillings 7 pence; so Pauline received about
5250 pounds sterling.

42. *Maravedi:* Spanish coin, originally of gold, then successively
of silver, of an inferior alloy, and of copper, with a steadily
diminishing value.

43. *"You will never come to Lisbon":* It would seem that, despite Pauline's prohibition, C. did visit Portugal, either before or after his stay in Spain (1767-1768); however, he gives no account of such a visit in his memoirs, though he several times writes of intending to go to Lisbon (e.g., Vol. 10, Chap. II).

44. *Styx:* In Greek mythology, the principal river of the underworld.

45. *To believe herself:* Text: "commençant à vouloir se croire," which seems to require a complement, probably, in view of the end of her last speech to C., "veuve." Read: "beginning to try to believe that she was a widow."

46. *Fifteen years earlier:* C. and Henriette parted at the end of 1749 or the beginning of 1750 (cf. Vol. 3, Chap. V).

47. *Twenty-two:* C. was 25 when he met Henriette.

CHAPTER X

1. *The Thinkers' Club:* Later in this chapter C. refers indifferently to a Thinkers' Club and a Bettors' Club. Neither of them has been identified.

2. *Attila:* King of the Huns (5th century).

3. *Decamerone:* For Martinelli's new edition of this work, see notes 16, 17, and 20 to Chap. VII of this volume.

4. *Rochester:* City on the Thames estuary on the old road from Dover to London.

5. *Buckingham House:* Originally built by John Sheffield, Duke of Buckingham, it was bought in 1762 by King George III, who made it his residence and in 1775 ceded it by parliamentary decree to his consort Queen Charlotte, after which it was known as "The Queen's House." After extensive alterations it became the new royal residence, as Buckingham Palace, in 1837. C. writes "Bukingan aus."

6. *Something strange:* According to the English Casanovist Bleackley, the same incident is recounted in a letter of Horace Walpole's to Sir Horace Mann written in 1750. It is possible that Martinelli told C. the story, and that the latter gave it a place in his memoirs as his own experience.

7. *"The Bettors":* Cf. note 1 to this chapter.

8. *Undoubtedly . . . distinction:* The text has "Sans doute il

y a des gens" etc., literally, "No doubt there are men of intelligence and distinction in it."

9. *"Dangerous":* As C. explains a few lines farther on, a man-slayer's hand was branded.

10. *"O laws, O customs":* In C.'s day instantly recognizable as a parody of Cicero's famous "O Tempora, O Mores" (*Catiline* I, 1, 2).

11. *Spencer:* See note 23 to Chap. VII of this volume.

12. *Chelsea:* Now a part of London; in the 18th century still a village on the Thames outside of the city.

13. *Castel-Bajac:* Louis, Marquis (not Count) de Castel-Bajac. See Vol. 5, Chap. X.

14. *A Gascon:* A native of Gascony, a district of southern France between the Garonne and the Pyrenees. Gascons were notorious for boasting.

15. *Saint Albans:* A small city with a celebrated cathedral, some 25 miles northwest of the center of London.

16. *Maltese Cross:* Symbol of the order of the Knights of Malta. Only persons who could prove 16 quarters of nobility were admitted to it.

17. *Schwerin:* Heinrich Bogislav Detlef Friedrich, Count von Schwerin (after 1738 - ca. 1800), lost great sums at play, became an adventurer, and was arrested in Hamburg in 1767 at the instigation of his family; after he was freed (1786) he lived on his estate of Schwerinsburg.

18. *Field Marshal:* Kurt Christoph, Count von Schwerin (1684-1757), uncle of Heinrich Bogislav (see the preceding note); officer in the Prussian service, adviser to Frederick the Great during the First Silesian War; he was killed at the battle of Prague while serving as Field Marshal General.

19. *Beckw . . . :* John Beckwith (died 1787), English Brigadier-General during the Seven Years' War. There seems to have been no reason why C. should not have given his name in full here, as he does in Vol. 10.

20. *The Black Eagle:* Founded by Frederick I on the occasion of his coronation in 1701, it was considered the leading Prussian order; in the 18th century its membership was limited to 30; the limitation was removed in the 19th century. The order was abolished in 1918.

21. *His Majesty:* Here Frederick the Great.

22. *The two foreign Counts:* Castel-Bajac and Schwerin.

23. *The Bank:* Text, "la banque," presumably meaning the Bank of England.

24. *Bill:* C. writes "bil," perhaps for "bill of particulars."

25. *Alderman:* In the 18th century London had 25 aldermen, one for each district of the city.

26. *Harwich:* Important Channel port. But its being some 70 miles from London, whereas C. later says that the journey there took only an hour and a quarter, makes it impossible that it was the site of the school. Bleackley has shown that there was a well-known Catholic girls' boarding school in Hammersmith, then a village on the outskirts of London. But its headmistress was a nun, which does not agree with C.'s account.

27. *Newgate:* The oldest prison in London, dating from the 12th century; thieves, murderers, and forgers were confined to it. The building was demolished in 1902.

28. *Costantini:* Probably an invented name. According to C. he was the husband of the Italian singer Angela Calori (see the following note).

29. *Calori:* Angela Calori (1732 - ca. 1790), Italian singer. She was the Teresa whom C. so greatly loved and whom he first knew as Bellino, whom he later calls Teresa Lanti, and to whom he also refers as married to a Roman named Cirillo Palesi ca. 1760 (cf. especially Vol. 2, Chaps. I and II, and Vol. 7, Chaps. VII and VIII). That all these names designate the same person is revealed only by a passage in Vol. 10, Chap. IX, which C. canceled but which can still be read. See note 36 to that chapter.

30. *La Binetti:* See note 8 to Chap. VIII of this volume.

31. *De Amicis:* Anna Lucia de Amicis (ca. 1740-1816), famous Italian singer of the period, whose great triumphs were achieved in *opera seria.*

32. *Mattei:* An opera impresario named Mattei is documented in St. Petersburg in 1770; the reference here may be to the same person.

33. *Virtuose:* Italian: leading female theatrical performers, whether actresses, singers, or dancers; also, women of virtue. Here, as in Vol. 7, Chap. VIII, C. may be playing on the double meaning of the word.

34. *Giardini:* Felice di Giardini (1716-1796), celebrated Italian violinist of the period.

35. *King's Bench Prison:* See note 27 to Chap. VIII of this
    volume.
36. *La Calori . . . Prague:* See Vol. 10, Chap. IX.
37. *A Flemish officer . . . Aix-la-Chapelle:* His name was
    Malignan. For C.'s earlier encounters with him see Vol. 8,
    Chap. III, and Chap. VIII of this volume.
38. *Charpillon:* Marie Anne Geneviève Augspurgher (Aus-
    purgher), known as La Charpillon (ca. 1746 - after 1777),
    celebrated courtesan in London.
39. *My mother:* Rose Elisabeth Augspurgher (ca. 1720 - after
    1764), native of Bern, from which she was banished for her
    dissolute life; she settled in Paris for a time, then in London.
40. *Palais Marchand:* Alternative name for the old Palais de
    Justice, in which there were many shops. It was in one of
    these that C. had first met La Charpillon (then known as
    Mademoiselle de Boulainvilliers) and had bought her a pair
    of shoe buckles. (In Vol. 5, pp. 253-254, of the present
    translation, where the episode is recounted, "earrings" should
    be corrected to "buckles" in each instance. The error, re-
    vealed by the present context, was due to the fact that C.
    often abbreviates "boucles d'oreille" [earrings] to "boucles.")
41. *Denmark Street:* This street, in the Parish of St. Giles in
    the Fields, still exists. The name Decharpillon has been
    found in the tax lists of the parish for 1763 and 1764.

CHAPTER XI

1. *Letter . . . Morosini . . . Lyons:* See Chap. V of this
   volume.
2. *I can count on nearly four years of life:* C. was wrong in his
   reckoning for he died only seven months later, on June 4,
   1798.
3. Galileo Galilei, *De Motu*, Chap. 19.
4. *Is still alive:* Nothing is known of La Charpillon after 1777.
   From 1773 to 1777 she was the mistress of the English politician John Wilkes (1727-1797) in London.
5. *Introduced . . . bagnio:* C. seems to have forgotten that he
   had already found his own way to a bagnio. See Chap. VII
   of this volume and *ibid.*, n. 50.
6. *Bolomay:* David Bolomay, watchmaker, originally of Lau-
   sanne. C. says nothing of this incident in his account of his

stay in Geneva; in any case, he was not there in 1759 but in 1760.

7. *Goudar . . . Paris:* C. fails to mention that he had already encountered Goudar again in London (see Chap. VIII of this volume, and *ibid.*, n. 17).

8. *Rostaing:* Antoine Louis Alphonse Marie, Count Rostaing (died after 1793); according to Paris police records, he was a young man in 1753. Though he was a professional gambler, his title seems to have been genuine.

9. *Coumon:* Nothing is known of this person except that he came from the southern French province of Languedoc.

10. *Journey . . . an hour and a quarter:* See note 26 to the preceding chapter.

11. *Vestal:* In Roman antiquity, one of the six virgin priestesses devoted to the goddess Vesta under a vow of perpetual chastity. Used as a type of virginity.

12. *Ba . . :* C. writes "maq . . ." (for *maquerelle,* "bawd").

13. *Coterie:* C. writes "avec toute son infâme" (omitting the necessary noun). This chapter shows an unusually large number of such slips, perhaps due to haste in copying (see the following notes 19, 25, 32, and 34).

14. *Baltimore:* Frederick Calvert, Earl Baltimore (1731-1771).

15. *Grosvenor:* Richard, Earl Grosvenor (1731-1802).

16. *Author of several works:* In addition to his *Chinese Spy* (see note 17 to Chap. VIII of this volume) Goudar wrote not only other satirical pieces but also works on economic and political subjects. The *Chinese Spy* was a series of letters from an imaginary Chinese visitor to Europe, in imitation of Montesquieu's celebrated *Lettres persanes* ("Persian Letters").

17. *Amused myself by writing a number of them:* There is no way of determining which, if any, of the letters of the *Chinese Spy* were contributed by C.

18. *Lorenzi:* Nothing is known of this person, whose name would indicate that she was Italian. The "Miss" is C.'s.

19. *Would have:* C. writes: "Je vous aussi repondu," where "aussi" is a slip for "aurais" or "aurais" is omitted.

20. Ascribed to Publilius Syrus (1st century A.D.). C. has quoted it earlier—oddly enough, just before his first meeting with La Charpillon (then Mademoiselle de Boulainvilliers); see Vol. 5, Chap. XI, and *ibid.*, n. 22.

21. Ariosto, *Orlando furioso,* I, 56.

22. *Night watchman:* C. here writes "crieur d'heures," but later "Wach." Since there was no street lighting in London in C.'s time, late walkers often engaged the service of a link-boy, or of a night watchman with his lantern. C. describes the organization and the functions of the "night watch" in the following chapter.

23. *Penny post:* A postal service established in 1683 and confined to London. There were six offices in various parts of the city at which letters could be deposited. The charge was one penny. Londoners were very proud of the service, which was the only one of its kind in Europe.

24. *An armchair:* Not an invention of C.'s, for chairs of the kind are described in various English and French works treating of the period.

25. *It:* C. writes "les" instead of "le."

26. *Franche-Comté:* District of France west of the Swiss Jura, formerly the independent County of Burgundy.

27. *Boulainvilliers:* Anne Gabriel Henri Bernard de Rieux Boulainvilliers, Marquis de Saint-Soire (1724-1798), well-known libertine.

28. *Kitty Fisher:* Catherine Mary Fisher (1740-1767), well-known English courtesan, mistress of Augustus John Hervey, Earl Bristol, in 1759; she later married a Mr. Norris. C. writes "Keti-ficher."

29. *Strong beer:* C. writes *"Strombir."*

30. *Sarah:* Nothing is known of her origins except that she was Irish. She married Goudar some time after March 1764, followed him to Naples in 1767, became the mistress of King Fernando IV of Naples and later of Count Buturlin; Goudar left her, and she died in Paris ca. 1800.

31. *Lettre de cachet:* Originally, a sealed letter, especially one emanating from the sovereign; in the period before the French Revolution, often used to convey arbitrary orders for imprisonment.

32. *At home:* C. writes "chez," without the necessary "elle."

33. *Calumny . . . imagine its nature:* Probably C. was to be accused of pederasty, which in England was then punishable by death.

34. *Them:* C. writes "le" (for "les").

CHAPTER XII

1. *Chapter XII:* At the beginning of this chapter in C.'s ms. is the marginal notation *"duobus omissis"* ("two [pages] omitted"). As before, the reference would seem to be to an earlier version, for there is no break in the narrative.

2. Horace, *Epistles,* I, 20, 25; already quoted by C. in Vols. 1 and 2.

3. Dante, *Commedia,* "Inferno," I, 1.

4. *Here:* At Dux in Bohemia, where C., serving as librarian to Count Waldstein, began to write his memoirs about the year 1790 and where he died on June 4, 1798.

5. Ariosto, *Orlando furioso,* XXIV, 1 (where the text has "Chi mette il piè . . .").

6. *Walsh:* Proprietress of a well-patronized bordello in Cleveland Row and generally known in her day as "Mother Walsh" (also Walch, Welch). There was also a "Mother Wells," who is documented in 1753 at Enfield Wash, 10 miles from London, and who is known to have moved to London about 1760; she may be the same person.

7. *Atkins:* Sir Richard Atkins, Bart. (ca. 1728-1756); his mistress was not Kitty Fisher but Fanny Murray. The gesture of eating a bank note on a slice of bread and butter was attributed to several well-known courtesans and actresses.

8. *Mrs. Pitt:* Penelope Pitt, neé Atkins (ca. 1725-1795), married the English diplomat George Pitt (later Baronet Rivers; 1722-1803) in 1746.

9. *Phryne:* Celebrated Greek hetaira of the Periclean period (4th century B.C.), here used generically for courtesan.

10. *Bank of London:* No doubt for "Bank of England."

11. *Berlendis:* See note 13 to Chap. VIII of this volume.

12. *Richmond:* Then a village on the Thames, west of London, now part of Greater London. There was a royal summer residence there, Richmond Lodge, with a fine garden.

13. *Wh . . . :* C. Writes *"p. . . . ."* (for *putain*).

14. *Maze:* In Richmond Park there was a small Gothic building called "Merlin's Cave," around which Queen Caroline had a maze planted.

15. *Bowling green:* C. writes "boulingrin," perhaps meaning simply "lawn."

16. *"Beast with two backs":* Othello, Act I, scene 1, line 118.

17. *Night watch:* Cf. note 22 to the preceding chapter.

18. *G . d d . . n it:* C. writes "Sacr . . ." (for one of a number of blasphemous expressions).

19. *Bragadin:* Matteo Giovanni Bragadin (1689-1767), Venetian patrician and Senator, C.'s faithful friend and patron (see especially Vol. 2, Chap. VIII).

20. *Tower of London:* The only remaining portion of the old fortifications of London; the oldest part of it, the White Tower, was built by William the Conqueror in 1078. From the 16th century to 1820 it served as the State Prison.

21. *Westminster Bridge:* The second bridge over the Thames, built in 1750 (reconstructed 1856-1862); it crosses the river near the Houses of Parliament. C.'s route is puzzling, for he did not need to cross the Thames to go to the Tower of London from his house in Pall Mall, since they were both on the same side of the river.

22. *Agar:* Sir Wellbore Ellis Agar (1735-1805), son of the Member of Parliament Henry Agar. C., who had trouble with the titles of English baronets and knights, here calls him "le Chevalier Egard." Cf. note 26 to this chapter.

23. *The "Cannon":* The well-known Cannon Coffee House in Cockspur Street, at the southwest corner of the present Trafalgar Square. It was named after its proprietor, Patrick Cannon.

24. *Goddamme:* C. writes *"Dieudamne."*

25. Ariosto, *Orlando furioso,* XXIII, 112; already quoted by C. in Vol. 1, Chap. X.

26. *Agar, Esquire:* C. here writes "Esqʳ Egard."

27. *An invalid:* Text, "un cacochyme"; i.e., one suffering from cacochymia, a vitiated state of the body fluids, especially the blood.

28. *Roast beef:* C. writes "Rochebif."

29. *Pudding:* C. writes "boudin," a normal French word meaning "sausage." However, it seems probable that it represents his attempt to transcribe English "pudding," which is more likely than sausage to have formed part of an English dinner at the time.

30. *Hornpipe:* C. writes "Rompaipe."

31. *Blind musicians:* C. writes "aveugles," which means "blind-men," but the context shows that the need was for blind musicians.

32. *Ranelagh House:* See note 4 to Chap. VIII of this volume.

33. Stoic maxim, which Cicero (*De finibus*, III, 22) attributes to one of the Seven Sages. It was a favorite maxim of C.'s, who seems first to have been impressed by it when it was interpreted for him by his early patron the Venetian patrician Alvise Gasparo Malipiero (cf. Vol. 1, Chap. VI).

34. *Attorney . . . Schwerin:* The attorney was a Mr. White-head. For C.'s dealings with Count Schwerin, see Chap. X of this volume.

35. *Holborn:* District of London, now one of its metropolitan boroughs; most of the courts were situated there. C. writes "Haiborn."

36. *The powerful rod:* The London constables carried no arms but only a rod some three feet long tipped with the royal crown. Anyone whom they touched with it was bound to follow them without resisting; in case of resistance, it was the duty of any citizen present to help the constables do their duty.

37. *Pi . . s:* C. writes "maq . . . . . ." (for *maqueraux*).

38. *The impassive man:* C. writes "l'ataraxe," i.e., "the man in possession of ataraxia," from Greek ἀταραξία, "without disturbance."

39. *Two weeks:* In his *Mémoire justificatif*, found at Dux, C. writes that the amount in question was 4000 francs and that the Augspurghers were released on bail after two days in custody.

40. *King's Bench:* See note 27 to Chap. VIII of this volume.

41. *Brunswick:* Karl Wilhelm Ferdinand (1735-1806), Hered-itary Prince of Brunswick, married Augusta, Princess of Saxe-Gotha (1737-1813), daughter of the Prince of Wales (Frederick Louis, 1707-1751), in 1764; he became the Duke of Brunswick-Wolfenbüttel in 1780.

42. *Common Council:* Established in the 13th century as the municipal council of the City of London, it was, and still is, made up of the Lord Mayor, the Aldermen, and (at present) 206 councilors elected from the wards.

43. *Goldsmiths' Company:* Properly, The Wardens and Com-monalty of the Mystery of Goldsmiths of the City of London;

it was one of the twelve great guilds, ranking fifth in importance. Established in the 12th century, in 1756 it had 198 members, who met in their magnificent Hall in Foster Lane, built about 1407 and surviving until 1829. (The present Goldsmiths' Hall dates from 1835.) The Prince was presented with a gold box containing a document conferring the freedom of the City on him, but not by the Goldsmiths' Company.

44. *Lord Mayor:* Title of the Mayor of London from the 13th century, made official in 1545. He was elected from among the Aldermen.

45. *Aldermen:* Text: "échevins." Strictly speaking, the presentation was made by the "Court of Common Council."

46. *A thousand persons:* The newspapers of the time put the number at 250.

47. *Lady Grafton:* Lady Anne Grafton, née Liddell (1736-1804), married in 1756 to Augustus Henry Fitzroy, Earl Euston and Duke of Grafton. The marriage ended in divorce in 1769; her second husband, whom she married in the same year, was John Fitzpatrick, Earl of Upper Ossory. She was a friend of the celebrated writer Horace Walpole.

48. *Cumberland:* William Augustus, Duke of Cumberland (1721-1765), was the third son of King George II.

49. Ariosto, *Orlando furioso,* IV, 32.

50. *To his quarters in the City:* The commentators suggest that C.'s "chez lui" (translated "to his quarters") refers to a "watchhouse" (guardhouse); if this is correct, it must have had a pothouse on the ground floor, for C. later speaks of it as "the pothouse where I was" ("[le] cabaret ou j'étais") and of the chief constable as the proprietor ("Maître") of it. "The City" was and still is the term applied to the oldest part of London, on the left bank of the Thames.

51. *Pothouse:* See the preceding note.

52. *Magistrate:* C. writes "Sergens-fils" (and later "sergensfil" and "Sergentsfil"). What English judicial title he intended to represent is unclear. The magistrate who heard the case was the Justice of the Peace for Westminster and Middlesex; he sat in the famous Bow Street Police Office and Magistrate's Court, near Covent Garden. Unfortunately, the records of the court for the period were destroyed at the beginning of this century.

53. *Fielding:* C. confuses the writer Henry Fielding (1707-1754), who was also a judge in the Westminster and Middlesex district until 1751, with his successor, his half-brother Sir John Fielding (1721-1780). He was blind in consequence of an accident he suffered at the age of 19 while serving in the army.

54. *Newgate:* See note 27 to Chap. X of this volume.

55. *The jailer:* The jailer of Newgate Prison from 1754 to 1792 was a Richard Akerman.

56. *Pagus:* John Pagus, tailor, of Church Street, St. Ann's.

57. *Maisonneuve:* C. was arraigned on Nov. 27, 1763; his sureties were John Pagus (see the preceding note) and Lewis Chateauneu of Marylebone Lane. For Chateauneu C. substitutes a name of similar meaning (Maisonneuve). Chateauneu was C.'s vintner.

58. *Bottarelli:* Giovanni Gualberto Bottarelli, of Siena, writer, librettist, and adventurer; he lived from 1741 in Berlin and from ca. 1755 in London. As the author of an anti-Masonic book (*L'Ordre des francs-maçons trahi et le secret des Mopses dévoilé,* 1745), he was perhaps an enemy of C.'s, since the latter was a Freemason.

CHAPTER XIII

1. *Pocchini:* Antonio Pocchini (1705-1783), Venetian adventurer, of patrician birth; he was arrested in 1741 and banished to the island of Cerigo (Cythera). It was there that C. met him for the first time (cf. Vol. 2, Chap. IV). He appeared in Padua in 1746, and later in many European cities, almost always in the company of girls whom he passed off as his daughters but to whom his relation was really that of fancy man and pimp. (Cf. especially Vol. 6, Chap. I.)

2. *My name . . . given in full:* No such account has been found in any of the London newspapers of the time.

3. *Didone: Didone abbandonata* (Dido Forsaken), tragedy by Metastasio (1724), was set to music by a number of composers in the 18th century. The first performance of it (music by Domenico Sarri) was given in Naples in 1724.

4. *Demetrio:* Heroic drama by Metastasio; first performance (music by Caldara), Vienna, 1731. Nothing is known of

Bottarelli's versions of these two works; but he specialized in "arrangements" of operas.

5. *The Secret . . . Exposed:* See note 58 to the preceding chapter.

6. *Fate . . . Clairmont:* The English Casanovist Bleackley has found that the packet boat *Hanover,* en route from Lisbon to England, sank off Falmouth on Dec. 2, 1763. Sixty of her passengers drowned and only two or three were saved.

7. *"Parrot Market":* No doubt Parrot Yard, in East Smithfield in the eastern part of London.

8. *Wh ...:* C. writes "p ....." (for *putain*), though he has written the word in full a few lines earlier.

9. *Grosvenor:* See note 15 to Chap. XI of this volume.

10. *Pi ..:* C. writes "maq ....." (for *maquereau*).

11. *Hyde Park:* St. James's Park, the Green Park, and Hyde Park are contiguous.

12. *Charing Cross:* In the 18th century the name of a section of London as well as that of a large square occupying much the same site as the present Trafalgar Square. C. writes "Chirincras."

13. *Maty:* See note 74 to Chap. VII of this volume.

14. *Guerra:* Steffano Guerra (born 1708), Venetian patrician.

15. *M. F.:* Louis de Muralt-Favre, member of the Bernese Council of Two Hundred, appointed Financial Commissioner in London in 1762; errors having been discovered in his accounts, he was recalled in 1763. For C.'s earlier relations with him and his family see Vol. 6, Chap. VIII.

16. *Chargé d'Affaires for the Canton of Bern:* In 1720 Bern had created the post of Financial Commissioner in London; the Commissioner's duty was to collect the interest on the large amounts of capital which Switzerland had begun to invest in England from 1709, after the War of the Spanish Succession.

17. *Sara . . . younger daughter:* See Vol. 6, Chap. VIII. C. exchanges the names of Muralt-Favre's two daughters. The elder, Marguerite, was about 16 years old in 1763, the younger, Sara, was only 13.

18. *Marylebone:* Name of a district of London. From 1740 to ca. 1777 it was the site of Marylebone Gardens, a pleasure resort with a hall for concerts and theatrical performances.

19. *A girl:* The rest of the story supports the contention that

C. paid his addresses not to Sara but to the elder daughter, Marguerite.

20. *Passano:* Giacomo Passano, alias Pogomas. See Chaps. I-III of this volume, and for C.'s still earlier dealings with him, the references in note 1 to Chap. I.

21. *My housekeeper:* Madame Dubois. See Vol. 6, Chaps. VI ff.

22. *Green oysters:* The flat oysters from the mouth of the Charente; so called from the greenish color of their shells.

23. *A time:* The Brockhaus-Plon edition gives: "si je le mettais en temps pour," which is either an (unnoted) slip of C.'s or a typographical error for "si je le mettais un temps pour."

24. *Genius:* C. writes "de mon mauvais qui," omitting the necessary noun, which must have been "démon," "génie," or the like. Some other small slips in this chapter, having been sufficiently exemplified in the notes to the preceding chapter, are here passed over in silence.

25. *Householders:* C. writes *"Auskepers."*

26. *Her old father:* No doubt her stepfather, Montolieu, who was a member of the Genevan Council of Two Hundred.

27. *Not to continue sending a Chargé d'Affaires:* After recalling Muralt-Favre in 1763 the Republic of Bern abolished the position of Financial Commissioner in London and entrusted the collection of interest to the London banking house of Vanneck.

28. *Vanneck:* Sir Joshua Vanneck (died 1777), banker in London, later appointed banker there to the Canton of Bern.

29. *Monsieur de W.:* Friedrich von Wattenwyl (Frédéric de Vatteville); he married one of Muralt-Favre's daughters (it is not clear which one) but not until 1785.

30. *His father:* Samuel de Muralt (1680-1764), member of the Bernese Council.

31. *Bosanquet:* See note 49 to Chap. VII of this volume.

32. *Instead of . . . Ostend . . . Dunkirk:* Perhaps out of consideration for Madame Muralt, who dreaded the sea, since the route by way of Dunkirk involved a shorter Channel crossing.

33. *Drops:* C. writes "gouttes de soie," for which Laforgue suggested "gouttes de Savoie"; in any case, the meaning must be some kind of smelling salts.

34. *Find the thief:* The theft of 3000 pounds sterling (not 6000, as C. writes) took place on Dec. 3, 1763, while Lord and

Lady Harrington were at the opera; some months later the Harringtons' porter, a certain John Wesket, was found guilty of the crime and was hanged. However, Lady Harrington had been suspected.

35. *Sumptuary laws:* See Vol. 6, Chap. VIII, n. 9.

36. *Taking ship . . . for Ostend:* Either the plan to make the journey by way of Dunkirk (see note 32 to this chapter) was abandoned or C. made an error here.

37. *Hedwig:* C.'s name for Anne Marie May (born 1731), who later married Gabriel von Wattenwyl (de Vatteville) (1734-1792). For C.'s acquaintance with her, see Vol. 6, Chap. IX, and especially Vol. 8, Chap. IV.

38. *Two years later:* See note 29 to this chapter.

39. *Madame G.:* Doris Greve, née Droopen, married a Hamburg merchant on May 1, 1764. C. first met her in Berlin in the summer of 1764 (cf. Vol. 10, Chap. III).

40. *I had set out for Hamburg . . . return to Dux:* C. did go to Berlin from Dux in 1795, intending to go on to Hamburg; instead he returned to Dux.

41. *La Sartori:* There were at least four Italian female singers of this name in the 18th century. The concert to which C. refers took place on March 18, 1764, in the King's Theater in the Haymarket (not, as C. writes, in the Covent Garden Theater).

42. *Henau:* As appears later (cf. Vol. 10), he was not a Baron but the son of a Livonian merchant.

43. *Irish girl:* See note 30 to Chap. XI of this volume.

44. *A Hanoverian lady:* C. later says that she was from Stöcken, then an estate near Hanover, now a suburb of the city. The municipal archives of Hanover do not record the names of the owners of the estate in 1763 and 1764, when C. first met the family in London. In 1789 Stöcken belonged to Chamberlain von Schwicheldt (Count of the Empire from 1790). His father, August Wilhelm von Schwicheldt (1708-1766), Hanoverian Minister and diplomat, married Marianne Hippolyte, née von Fabrice, in 1741. They had five children: three daughters, Bertha Augusta (born 1744), Luise Charlotte Sophie (born 1749), Amalie Oelgarde (born 1755), and two sons. It is perfectly possible that C., attempting, as usual, to preserve the anonymity of his sweethearts, made all five children daughters. The Von Schwicheldts were not

created Counts until 1790; but C. can very well have heard of it and applied the title retrospectively. August Wilhelm von Schwicheldt did not die until 1766, but he appears to have entered on his last illness in 1764; this would account for his entrusting his business in London to his wife. It is also possible that Frau von Schwicheldt described herself to C. as already a widow. In any case, the coincidences between the *five* recorded Von Schwicheldt children and the *five* daughters C. attributes to the Hanoverian lady, together with the appearance of the unusual names *Hippolyte* and *Augusta* in both accounts, is perhaps indicative if not conclusive.

45. *Leicester Fields Square:* Now Leicester Square. C. writes "la place d'Esterfil."

46. *Reparation . . . Duke of Cumberland:* The Duke of Cumberland (see note 48 to the preceding chapter) was Commander-in-Chief of the British Army. It is possible that British troops did damage in the Electorate of Hanover during the Seven Years' War. At any rate, early in 1764 a commission was set up in London to investigate demands for reparations from Hanover. Unfortunately the records of the commission have not been preserved.

HISTORY OF MY LIFE

Volume 10

CONTENTS

Volume 10

LIST OF PLATES

Volume 10

VOLUME 10

CHAPTER I[1]

The Hanoverian mother and daughters.

JUST AS we reach the street door we meet the two sisters on their return, looking more calm than sad. I see two beauties who astonish me; but what surprises me even more is one of them dropping me a curtsy and saying:

"Are you not the Chevalier de Seingalt, Monsieur?"

"Yes, Mademoiselle, and very much distressed by your misfortune."

"Would you do me the honor to go upstairs again?"

"I cannot; I have urgent business."

"I ask you for only a quarter of an hour."

I cannot refuse. The girls were the two elder daughters. The one who had asked me to go up spent the quarter of an hour giving me an account of her family's misfortune in Hanover, their journey to the Court of St. James's to obtain reparation, their fruitless efforts, the necessity they had been under to go into debt in order to live, the illness which prevented their mother from acting in person, the barbarity of the landlord, who, refusing to wait any longer, was going to send their mother to prison and turn them out into the street, and the further and even more cruel barbarity of all their acquaintances, from whom they had just asked help and who had refused it.

"We have, Monsieur, nothing to sell, nothing; and today we have only two shillings to buy bread to live on."

"Who are those who, knowing you, have the heart to abandon you in such distress?"

"So-and-so, So-and-so, So-and-so, Lord Baltimore,[2] the Marchese Caraccioli,[3] the Neapolitan Ambassador, Lord Pembroke."[4]

"It is unbelievable, for I know that the three last are high-minded, rich, and generous. There must be some good and weighty reason, for you are all beautiful; and to these gentlemen beauty is a letter of credit at sight."

"Yes, Monsieur, there is a reason. These high-minded and rich noblemen abandon and despise us. Our situation does not inspire pity in them because, they say, we are fanatics. We refuse to grant them favors which are contrary to our duty."

"That is to say, they find you attractive, and they maintain that you should be willing to quench the desires which you kindle in them, and they refuse you their money because, feeling no pity for them, you will not grant them the slightest favor. Is that it?"

"Exactly."

"In that case they are right."

"They are right?"

"Certainly. I think as they do. We abandon you to your duty. Ours is to keep our money to foster the passions which, at the same time that they war on us, give us happy moments. We care neither to be considered virtuous nor to pay beauties who seduce us by their charms, only to make us languish afterward. I will go so far as to tell you that your misfortune at this juncture is that all of you are pretty; you would easily find twenty guineas if you were ugly; I would give them to you myself, for then I should not lay myself open to two cutting reproaches. No one would say that I had performed this act of benevolence because I was a slave to my inclination for gallantry, nor could anyone say that I had helped you in the hope of obtaining what, according to your doctrine, I shall never obtain."

It was the only way to talk to the girl, who was gifted with charms and a dazzling eloquence. I saw that she was taken aback. I asked her how it happened that she knew me, and she replied that she had seen me at Richmond [5] with La Charpillon.[6] I thereupon told her that La Charpillon had cost me two thousand guineas, and that she had never granted me a kiss; but that it would not happen to me again. Her mother then called to her, she went to see what she wanted, and she came out a moment later to say that she begged me to come in, for she had something to discuss with me.

I go in, and I see a woman forty-five years of age, sitting up in bed and not looking as if she were ill. Keen eyes, an intelligent countenance, and a crafty air warned me to be on my guard; it comes to me that she looks rather like La Charpillon's mother.

"What can I do to serve you, Madame?"

"Monsieur, I heard all that you said to my daughters. You did not speak to them like a father, you will admit."

"Madame, I am a professed libertine, and if I had daughters I am sure they would not need the services of a preacher. I told your daughters what is my opinion, and what must be your opinion too if you are wise. I can feel only admiration for girls who insist on parading their virtue; I shall never be their friend. If your daughters want to be virtuous, well and good; but let them not go about tempting men. I take my leave, and I assure you I shall not see them again."

"One moment, Monsieur! My husband was Count So-and-so.[7] They also deserve respect for their birth."

"In that case what greater respect can I show them than not to see them again?"

"Does not our situation arouse your pity?"

"Very greatly, but I fight against what it inspires in me, because they are pretty."

"What a reason!"

"A very strong one. I should be said to have been duped by my feeling. If they were ugly, I would give you twenty guineas on the spot, and I should be admired; but since they are pretty, if you want twenty guineas you shall have them tomorrow morning; but I must have one of your daughters tonight."

"What language to a woman of my station! No one has ever said such a thing to me."

"Forgive my frankness, and permit me to leave your presence, asking you to excuse me. Good-by, Countess."

"We are today reduced to eating nothing but bread."

"If that is the case, I will dine with them and I will pay for dinner for them all."

"You are too strange. They will be gloomy, for I am about to be taken to prison. You will be bored. Instead, give them what you would spend."

"No, Madame. For my money I want at least to enjoy with my eyes and my ears. I will have your arrest put off until tomorrow. By tomorrow, Providence may have intervened."

"The landlord refuses to wait."

"Leave that to me."

I then tell Goudar[8] to ask the landlord what he will take to send the bailiff away for only twenty-four hours. Goudar goes, and comes back to tell me that the landlord will dismiss the bailiff if I will give him a guinea and find him a surety who will pay him the twenty guineas if Madame absconds during the twenty-four hours.

My vintner[9] lived in the house next door; I tell Goudar to wait for me; I run there, and I persuade him to talk with the landlord and give him the written security he demands, together with a guinea, which I give him. After that I go upstairs again, and I give the girls the good news that they have time to enjoy themselves until the next day. A quarter of an hour later, as soon as the bailiff was gone, I explain to Goudar the agreement to which I had come with the mother, and I ask him to arrange for a dinner for eight to be brought in. Goudar goes, and having already obtained the entrée to Madame's room, I enter it, bringing with me all her daughters, who were amazed at the way in which I had completely upset all the rules and regulations of the household.

"Here, Madame," I say, "is all I have been able to do for you. Your daughters are charming, they were all born for love, they all interest me equally, I have procured you a respite of twenty-four hours for nothing, I shall dine and sup with them without asking for a kiss, and if tomorrow you have not changed your way of thinking I will withdraw the twenty-guinea security which I have had put up, and I will trouble you no longer."

"What do you mean by 'changing my way of thinking'?"

"Sending a virtue of which I am the sworn enemy to the devil."

"My daughters will never prostitute themselves, either to you or to any other man."

"And I will sing their praises all over London as models of virtue, and I will go and spend my money with girls as wanton as I am. La Charpillon shall have been the last to trick me."

"You took a terrible revenge. I laughed heartily at your parrot. You are a vicious man."

"Extremely vicious. Believe me, you have made a very undesirable acquaintance today."

Goudar returned after attending to everything, and we took leave of Madame, who thought it unbecoming to show herself to Goudar too. I was the only man, according to her, to whom she had done that honor in London. Our English dinner was good enough; but the pleasure I felt was extreme when I saw the five Countesses eating

with ravenous appetites. My vintner next door sent me
six bottles of Pontacq,[10] which, enchanted by such a land
of Cockaigne, they emptied like heroines; but the poor
creatures, unaccustomed to wine, all became tipsy. Their
mother had devoured everything I sent her and drunk a
bottle of an old wine which she preferred to Pontacq.
Despite their tipsiness I kept my word, and neither
Goudar nor I took any liberties with them. We supped
in equally high spirits, and no less abundantly, and
after a big bowl of punch I left them, in love with them
all and at a loss to foresee if I should have the strength
to acquit myself as well the next day.

"It all depends," said Goudar, as he saw me home,
"upon not giving them a penny before the climax. You
began by playing the part of a rake; if you do not keep
it up you are done for."

I saw that he spoke as a past master, and I determined
to convince him that I knew as much about it as he did.

Impatient the next day to learn the result of the council which the invalid mother must have held with the
five daughters, I went to their lodging at ten o'clock.
The two elder sisters were not there; they had gone out
at eight o'clock to call on all the people whose hearts
they hoped to touch and whom they had not had time
to visit on the previous day. The three younger girls
came running to me, like little water spaniels making
much of their master when he comes home; but not only
do they turn away their pretty faces when they see me
put mine forward to kiss them, they refuse me their
hands too. I tell them they are in the wrong, and I knock
at their mother's room; she asks me to come in and
thanks me for the charming day I had given them.

"I have come to see if I am to withdraw my security."

"It is for you to say, but I do not believe you capable
of it."

"There you are mistaken, Countess. You know the
human heart, but you have not studied the mind, or you
imagine that everyone's mind is less intelligent than

yours. I inform you that all your daughters put me in ecstasies yesterday; but, should it kill me, I will give you no token of friendship until you have abandoned your infamous system of ethics."

"Infamous?"

"Yes, infamous; I said enough to you on the subject yesterday. Good-by, Madame."

She did not want to let me go, but, neither listening to her nor looking at the young enchantresses, I made my way down the stairs, and I went to see Maisonneuve, my vintner, to tell him to withdraw the security. Then with the heart of a tiger, I went to call on Lord Pembroke, whom I had not seen for three weeks. As soon as I mentioned the Hanoverians to him he burst out laughing, and he said that there was nothing for it but to force the b . . . . . s to become proper wh . . . s.[11]

"They came here yesterday to tell me the state they are in, and, far from helping them, I laughed at them. They had nothing to eat, and I did not even allow my hand to give them a guinea; they got a dozen out of me on three occasions by making me hope, and then they disappointed me. They are all cast in the same mold as La Charpillon."

I told him what I had done and what I hoped to do at the cost of twenty guineas—but paid afterward. For the eldest, and then as much again for each of the four others.

"I had the same idea, but I do not believe you will get your way, for Baltimore offered two hundred guineas for all of them, and the bargain fell through because they demanded the money in advance. They called on him yesterday, and he gave them nothing. They disappointed him five or six times. We'll see what they will do when their mother is in prison. You'll see that we shall get them cheaply."

I go home to dine, Goudar arrives, he had just been at their house, the bailiff was there, he had told them that he would wait only until four o'clock; the two

elder sisters had vainly spent four hours going everywhere in search of people who would be charitable. They
had sent a dress to the pawnbroker[12] to get money for
something to eat. I thought it inconceivable.

I expected to see them at my house, and I guessed
rightly; we were at dessert when they appeared before
us. The eldest sister used all her eloquence to persuade
me to keep my security in force another day; but she
finds me inflexible unless she will fall in with a plan
which I will explain to her in my bedroom. She comes,
leaving her sister with Goudar; whereupon, making her
sit down beside me, I put twenty guineas in front of
her as the price of her favors. She scorns them. I find
her refusal galling; I consider myself insulted; I use
force, supposing that her resistance will be slight; I am
mistaken; she threatens to scream, and at that I calm
myself, but I ask her to go; and she leaves with her
sister.

I go to the theater with Goudar, and afterward I go to
my vintner Maisonneuve, to learn what has happened.
He tells me that the bailiff had had the mother carried
to his house, that the youngest daughter had insisted on
following her, and that he had no idea where the four
others were.

I go home, very much distressed. I felt that I had
treated them too harshly; but I saw all four of them
before me just as I was going to supper. The eldest, who
was always the spokesman, told me that their mother
was in prison and that they would all spend the night
in the street if I refused them a room, even one without
a bed.

"You shall have," I said, "rooms and beds; and I
will have a fire lit for you; but I want to see you eat. Sit
down."

They sat down, everything to be found in the kitchen
was brought, and they ate, but gloomily and drinking
only water. Annoyed by this behavior, I told the eldest
that she could go to bed on the third floor with her

sisters; but that she must leave at seven o'clock in the morning and not come to my door again. They went upstairs.

The eldest sister came into my room an hour later, just as I was going to bed, saying that she must speak with me privately. I ordered Jarba[13] to leave.

"What will you do for us," she said, "if I spend the night with you?"

"I will give you twenty guineas, and I will lodge and board you all so long as you remain amenable."

She began to undress, without a word in answer, and she came into my arms after vainly asking me to put out the candles. I found nothing but submission. She let me do what I would, and that was all; she did not honor me with a single kiss. The celebration lasted no more than a quarter of an hour. My only resource was to imagine that I had Sara[14] in my arms. In amorous intercourse illusion is a necessity.[15] Her cowardly stupidity made me so angry that I got up, I gave her a twenty-pound note, and I told her to dress and go to her room.

"Tomorrow morning," I said, "you shall all leave, for I am not pleased with you. Instead of giving yourself to love, you have prostituted yourself. Shame on you!"

She dressed, and she left without answering me, and I went to bed very ill pleased.

The next morning at seven I saw before me the second sister, whose name was Victoire.[16] She had waked me. I asked her very coldly what she wanted. She replied that she hoped to make me pity them enough to keep them in my house a few more days, and to count on her gratitude.

"You must forgive my sister," she said, "who has already told me everything. She could not give you tokens of love because she is in love with an Italian who is in prison for debt."

"I suppose you are in love with some man too."

"No. I love no one."

"Then you could love me?"

So saying, I embrace her, and I find her gentle and loving. I tell her that she has won the day, and she replies that her name is Victoire. Victoire gave me two delicious hours, which more than made up to me for the bad quarter of an hour I had spent with her sister.

After the performance I told her that I was wholly hers and that she had only to have her mother carried to my house as soon as she was set free, and I saw that she was astonished when I gave her twenty guineas; she did not expect it, so she showed her gratitude as lovingly as possible. I was the happiest of men; I ordered dinner and supper for eight every day, and I had my door closed to everyone, except to Goudar. Spending money like water, I was heading for ruin, and I thought of going to replenish my purse in Lisbon.

Toward noon the mother arrived in a sedan chair and at once went to bed. I went to see her, and I listened without surprise to all the praises she bestowed on my virtues. She wanted to make me believe that she was certain the forty guineas I had given her daughters were not in compensation for their favors. I left her to enjoy her hypocrisy.

I took them to the performance at Covent Garden,[17] where the castrato Tenducci[18] surprised me by introducing his wife to me; I thought he was joking, but it was true. He had married her and, having already had two children, he laughed at those who said that, being a castrato, he could not have any. He said that a third testicular gland, which had been left him, was enough to prove his virility, and that his children could not but be legitimate since he recognized them as such.

Back at the house, I supped deliciously with all the girls, and Victoire came to bed with me, delighted to have conquered me. She said that her sister's lover, who was a Neapolitan and who claimed to be the Marchese della Pettina,[19] would marry her as soon as he was freed from prison, that he was expecting money, and that her mother was delighted that her daughter was to become a Marchesa.

"How much does he owe?"

"Twenty guineas."

"And the Neapolitan Envoy lets him stay in prison for that trifling amount?"

"He refuses to receive him, because he left Naples without his King's[20] permission."

"Tell your sister that if the Neapolitan Envoy will tell me that he has a right to the name he uses, I will have him out of prison tomorrow."

I went to invite my daughter to dinner together with one of her schoolmates of whom I was very fond, leaving her six guineas to buy herself a fur-lined coat. She said she would send them to her mother, and she asked me to invite her to dinner too. I told her to do it herself. Back in London, I went to see the Marchese Caraccioli. He was a most agreeable man, whose acquaintance I had made in Turin.[21] I found with him the celebrated Chevalier d'Éon,[22] and I did not need to take him aside to ask him for information about the young man in prison.

"He is," he replied, "what he says he is, but I will not receive him or give him money until he arranges for the Marchese Tanucci[23] to write me that he has permission to travel. At that time I will get him out of prison."

I asked him no more questions, and I amused myself for an hour listening to the Chevalier d'Éon tell him his situation. He had abandoned his post at the Embassy because of ten thousand francs which the Ministry of Foreign Affairs in Versailles had refused to pay him and which were his by right. He had put himself under the protection of the laws of England, and, after obtaining two thousand advance subscriptions at a guinea, he had in the press a large quarto volume[24] in which he made public all the letters he had received from the Ministry in the past five or six years. About this same time an English banker deposited twenty thousand pounds sterling in the Bank of London, offering to wager[25] them that the Chevalier d'Éon was a woman. A company took up the wager; but neither of the two parties could be declared the winner unless Monsieur d'Éon would allow himself to be examined in the presence of witnesses. He had been offered ten thousand guineas, but he had laughed at the bettors. He always said that an examination of the sort would dishonor him, whether he was a man or a woman. Caraccioli said that it could dishonor him only if he were a woman; but I maintained the contrary. At the end of a year the wager was declared void; but three years later[26] he received a pardon from the King, and he appeared in Paris dressed as a woman and wearing the Cross of St. Louis.[27] Louis XV had always known the secret; but Cardinal Fleury[28] had taught him that monarchs should be impenetrable; and the King remained so all his life.

Back at home I gave the lovesick Hanoverian twenty guineas, telling her to have her Marchese come to dinner with me, for I wanted to make his acquaintance. I thought she would die with delight.

It was just then that Augusta, who was the third of the sisters,[29] in collusion with Victoire and apparently with her mother as well, made up her mind to earn twenty guineas. She did not find it difficult. She was the one whom Lord Pembroke had wanted to have. The thing was arranged at once, and Victoire, to my great satisfaction, yielded her place to her.

The five girls were like five excellent dishes which an epicure is determined to taste. My good appetite made me think that the last was always the best. So Augusta remained my mistress.

On the following Sunday I found myself entertaining a large number of guests. Mrs. Cornelys, who did not fear to be arrested on Sundays, was there with her son, and Sophie was embraced in turn by all the Hanoverians, who devoured her with kisses. I gave a hundred to Miss Nancy Stein,[30] her schoolmate, who was thirteen years old and who set me on fire. They were attributed to fatherly love. Miss Nancy, whom I thought something divine, was the daughter of a rich merchant. I told her that I wanted to make her father's acquaintance, and she replied that I should see him at three o'clock. I at once gave orders that he should be admitted.

The person who, in this brilliant company, cut a very sorry figure was the poor Marchese della Pettina; he was not at his ease in it. He was a tall, thin young man, not ill built; but he was revoltingly ugly and as stupid as possible; he thanked me for what I had done for him, saying that, by seizing the opportunity to be of service to him, I had done a good stroke of business, for he was sure that the day would come when he would do a hundred times as much for me. Yet the Hanoverian was in love with him.

My daughter took me to my room to show me her fine fur-lined coat, and her mother followed her to congratulate me on the splendid seraglio I had acquired, saying that she had often thought of providing herself with a male one, but that she had foreseen that there would be insuperable difficulties. I can well believe it. The bit . . .[31]

At table we were very gay. I was between my daughter and Nancy Stein. I felt happy. Mr. Stein arrived while we were still eating oysters. He repeatedly embraced his daughter, with all the affection of the English; it is peculiar to that nation. "I could eat you up," the Englishman said as he kissed his daughter; and he spoke the truth. A kiss is nothing but the expression of a desire to eat the object one kisses.

Mr. Stein had dined, but he nevertheless ate four dishes of twenty-five escalloped oysters, which my cook prepared to perfection; and he did great honor to the oeil-de-perdrix[32] still champagne. We spent three hours at table, and we spent the rest of the day on the fourth floor, around a harpsichord on which Sophie accompanied the airs which her mother sang. Her son played brilliantly on his transverse flute. Mr. Stein vowed to me that he had never in his life enjoyed a greater pleasure,

the more so because, the day being Sunday, it was a
forbidden pleasure. I took the risk and I was lucky. At
seven o'clock the Englishman presented my daughter
with a pretty ring and took leave of me, taking her back
to the school with his daughter. The Marchese della
Pettina told me that he did not know where to look for
a room; I replied that he could find one anywhere, and I
gave his fiancée a guinea, telling her to give it to him
and to ask him not to come to my house again until I
invited him.

When everyone had left, I took all the girls to her
room to see their mother, who was in good health, eating,
drinking, and sleeping well. She did not read, still less
write; but she was not bored, when she went to prison
she insisted on being carried, she was always in bed, and
her only happiness was to do nothing. However, she told
me that she was always thinking about her daughters,
who were happy only because of the laws she laid down
for them. I could scarcely keep from laughing. Having
Augusta on my lap, I asked the mother for permission
to give her a kiss, whereupon she preaches a sermon
justifying the kiss of paternal affection.

The next morning I saw the Marchese Caraccioli passing my window; he asked me if he might come up, and
I begged him to do me the honor. I sent for the eldest
sister, telling him that she was to marry Signor Pettina
as soon as his money arrived. Here is what he said to
her:

*"He is a Marchese, he is poor, he will never receive a
soldo, and when he goes back to Naples he will be locked
up by order of the King, and when he comes out his
creditors will have him sent to prison in the Vicaria."* [33]

This salutary advice had no effect.

After the Envoy left, I was to go for a ride on horseback. Augusta comes to tell me that, if I like, her sister
Hippolyte[34] will go with me.

"She rides like an equerry; last year at Pyrmont[35]
she made a brilliant impression."

"That's amusing. Tell her to come down."

She begs me to grant her the favor and assures me that she will do me honor.

"I am willing, but you have no men's clothes to dress in."

"That is true."

"Then we will ride tomorrow."

I spent the whole day having everything she needed made for her, and I fell in love with her when Pagus,[36] my tailor, had to measure her for breeches. Everything was to be ready for the next day. The horseback ride kept us amused all during supper. Hippolyte, in the greatest delight, came to my room to put her sister Augusta to bed. I began by pretending to trifle; but Augusta herself made the trifling become serious; she advised her sister to spend the night with us, and she followed her advice, so certain of my consent that she did not even ask me for it. In the morning I gave her twenty guineas, more than satisfied with the night I had spent.

Pagus came with fawn-colored velvet breeches and a matching vest, which became her perfectly. Hippolyte was surprisingly beautiful. We mounted, followed by Jarba; we dined at Richmond, and we did not come home until evening. But at table I noticed that Gabrielle,[37] who was the youngest of the sisters, was looking sad. Asked the reason for her sadness, she answers that she can ride just as well as Hippolyte. I comfort her by saying that I will give her the pleasure on the next day but one, and she could not be happier. Hippolyte swears to me that she has nothing but courage, and that she has never ridden; but the other assures me that she will ride as well as her sister. I promise to take them both, and they are satisfied.

The charming Gabrielle, aged fifteen, saw me to my room, and her kind sisters left me alone with her. She began by telling me that she had never had a lover, and she unresistingly let me convince myself that it was true.

Of all the five sisters, Gabrielle was the one who would have made me constant, if I had been capable of constancy; she was the only one who made me regret her mother's departure when she decided to leave a few days later. In the morning I added a ring to the twenty guineas which went without saying, and we spent the day having a habit made for her so that she could ride the next day with her sister; but she chose green.

Gabrielle, docilely following her sister's instructions, rode as if she had gone to riding school for two years. We went at a walk until we were outside the city, then at full gallop to Barnes,[38] where we stopped for an hour to have breakfast. We covered the ten miles in twenty-five minutes. The rays which shone from the faces of the two girls in the intoxication of their delight were fiery; I adored them and adored myself. But just as we were mounting again Lord Pembroke arrives and stops. He was on his way to Saint Albans.[39] He admires the two girls, who are sitting on their capering horses, he does not recognize them, he asks me if he may pay his addresses to them. I reply that he may. He approaches them, and he recognizes them. After a brief conversation I see that he is astonished; he congratulates me; he asks me if I am in love with Augusta; I lie, saying that I love only Gabrielle; he asks me if he may come to my house, and I assure him that it will give me great pleasure. He promises to come as soon as possible, and we leave him.

We give our horses their heads, and we return to London. Gabrielle, completely exhausted, at once went to bed. I left her asleep after giving her lively tokens of my constant love. I ordered supper served.

Gabrielle slept until the next morning, and when she waked to find herself in my arms she began philosophizing.

"How easy it is," she said, "to make oneself happy in this world when one is rich! And how hard it is to be powerless to do so when one sees happiness around one and knows that one cannot attain it because one has no money! Yesterday I was the happiest girl on earth. Why cannot I be so every day!''

I philosophized too, but gloomily; I saw myself near the end of my resources, and I thought of Lisbon. If I had been rich the Hanoverians would have kept me in their chains to the end of my life. It seemed to me that I loved them not as a lover but as a father, and the thought that I slept with them was no impediment to my feeling, since I have never been able to understand how a father could tenderly love his charming daughter without having slept with her at least once. My inability to entertain such a conception has always convinced me, and convinces me still more forcibly today, that my mind and my material part are one and the same substance. Gabrielle, speaking with her eyes, told me that she loved me, and I was sure that she was not deceiving me. Can one conceive that she would not have had that feeling if she had had what is called virtue? That is another idea which I find incomprehensible.

The next day the Englishman Pembroke came to our house, and our dinner with the noble Lord was very gay. Augusta bewitched him. He made her proposals the only effect of which was to set her laughing, for he always stipulated that he would not pay until after he had received her favors, a condition which she would never accept. Nevertheless, when he left he gave her a ten-pound note, which she accepted with great dignity. The next morning he wrote her a letter to which I will return in a moment. A half hour after His Lordship left, my girls' mother sent for me. Here is what she said to me in private, after a most feeling prologue on the subject of the unfailing kindnesses with which I blessed her whole family.

''Convinced as I am,'' she said, ''that you love my daughters like the fondest of fathers, I want them to become your real daughters. I offer you my hand and my heart; be my husband,[40] and you shall be their father, their master, and mine. What is your answer?''

I should have burst out laughing if I had not been overwhelmed by astonishment, indignation, and scorn. What effrontery! Sure that her proposal would disgust me, in making it to me she had no other object than to convince me that she believed my affection for her daughters was innocent. She knew the contrary; but by doing as she did she intended to justify herself; she insulted me, but that was nothing to her. Not to attack her openly, I replied that her proposal did me great honor, but that it was of such consequence that I must ask her for time before I gave her my answer.

In my room I found the sweetheart of the wretched Marchese, who told me that her happiness depended on a certificate from the Neapolitan Envoy stating that her lover was really the Marchese della Pettina. He needed only the certificate to obtain two hundred guineas at once. It was what he needed to return to Naples with her immediately, where she was sure that he would marry her. He would, she said, have no difficulty in obtaining the King's pardon. She appealed to me, only I could obtain her this favor from the Neapolitan Envoy. I promised I would go to see the Marchese Caraccioli for the purpose that very day.

I went there, and the intelligent Marchese made no difficulty about attesting that the person who used the name, and who had recently come out of prison, was what he claimed to be, so far as the name was concerned. I saw her beside herself with joy when, coming home, I handed her the certificate.

*Augusta becomes Lord Pembroke's mistress
by a contract drawn up in due form. The
King of Corsica's son. Monsieur du Clau, or
the Jesuit Lavalette. Departure of the Hano-
verians. My balance sheet. Baron Henau. The
Englishwoman and the keepsake she leaves me.
Daturi. My flight from London. The Count of
Saint-Germain. Wesel.*

WHEN WE rose from table my maid handed Augusta
a letter, which she could not give me to read, for it was
written in English; but she explained it to me, in her
sisters' presence. His Lordship[2] offered her fifty guineas
a month, guaranteed for three years, lodging at Saint
Albans, table and servants, if she would accept him as
her lover, to say nothing of what she could expect from
his gratitude if she found herself able to love him.

I told her that I could give her no advice in the matter,
and she went upstairs to her mother, who refused to come
to a decision without consulting me, for, as she put it,
I was the wisest and most virtuous of men. The upshot
of the consultation was that, as soon as His Lordship
had furnished a merchant well known on the Exchange
as guarantor of the contract, her daughter should accept,
for her conduct would be such that she could be sure
His Lordship would end by marrying her.[3] Nothing else,
the mother declared, was possible. Otherwise she would
never have consented to it, for her daughters, being

Countesses, were not the sort of girls to be anyone's mistress. So Augusta wrote accordingly, and in three days His Lordship concluded the business, coming to dine at my house with the merchant who signed the contract, at the foot of which I also, in all honor, signed as witness and as a friend of the mother, into whose presence I escorted the merchant, who saw her sign away her daughter, and acted as the witness. She declined to see His Lordship; she embraced her daughter, with whom she made a secret agreement whose purport I never learned. But the same day on which Augusta left my house was made memorable by another singular event.

The day after the one on which I gave the certificate to the Marchese della Pettina's fiancée, I took my dear Gabrielle horseback riding with Hippolyte. On returning home I found at the door the man who went by the name of Mr. Frederick[4] and who was said to be the son of the King of Corsica, Theodore, Baron von Neuhoff,[5] who, as everybody knew, had died in London. Mr. Frederick said that he wished to speak with me privately, and I let him come up. When we were alone he said that he knew I was acquainted with the Marchese della Pettina, and since he was about to get a bill of exchange for two hundred guineas discounted for him, he needed to know if he was well enough off in his own country to make it certain that he would honor the bill when it fell due.

"I must know this," he said, "for the persons who will discount the note want me to endorse it."

"I know him; but I will tell you nothing of his resources, for I first made his acquaintance here, and it is from the Envoy of the King of Naples that I know beyond doubt that he is what he claims to be."

"If the persons to whom I have broached the matter do not take it up, would you discount it? You should have it cheap."

"I am not in business. I am not interested in profits of this sort. Good-by, Mr. Frederick."

The next morning Goudar came to tell me that Monsieur du Clau[6] wanted to speak with me.

"Who is he?"

"He is the celebrated Jesuit Lavallette whose bankruptcy ruined the Society of Jesus in France. He retired here, and he must command a great deal of money; I advise you to hear what he has to say. I met him in a reputable house, and, knowing that I am acquainted with you, he addressed himself to me. What can you risk by listening to him?"

"Very well. You may take me to see him."

He leaves, he arranges the hour, and after dinner we go to call on the man, whose face I am very much interested in seeing; he begs my pardon, and after Goudar leaves he shows me a bill of exchange of the Marchese della Pettina's, who is asking him to discount it; he had told him that he could inquire of me concerning his resources, for his rank was known to everyone in London. I give Father Lavallette du Clau the same answer I had given the son of the late King of Corsica. I leave him, angry with the fool of a Pettina, who was causing me all this trouble. I see that he is intriguing, and I decide to have the Hanoverian tell him to put an end to it.

I did not find an opportunity that day. The next day I went horseback riding with my girls. At dinner I had Lord Pembroke, who had obtained Augusta. I waited until evening to speak to her elder sister, who had gone out and did not come back. At nine o'clock I receive a letter from her, containing one in German to her mother. She told me in a few words that, certain she could not obtain her mother's consent, she had gone away with her lover, who had raised money enough to return to his country, where he would marry her. She thanked me for all I had done for her, and she begged me to give the enclosure to her mother, to comfort her, and to make her listen to reason, assuring her that she had not gone off with an adventurer but with a man of a rank equal to her own. I show my three girls their eldest sister's letter, and I tell them to go up with me to their mother's room. Victoire said that we should wait until the next day, for the terrible news would prevent her from sleeping. We supped gloomily.

I saw the girl ruined, and I reproached myself with being the cause of it, for if I had not got him out of prison he could have done nothing. The Marchese Caraccioli had been right to tell me that I had done a stupid good deed. I consoled myself a little in the arms of my dear Gabrielle.

How I suffered the next morning when I had to calm the despair into which the mother fell when she read the German letter! She wept, she talked wildly, she blamed me because I had got him out of prison and then had let him see her daughter in my house. One should never point out their errors to people in distress, for after giving their sorrow full vent, they admit them all, and they feel under an obligation to the person who has let them talk on uncontradicted.

After this incident I spent two very happy weeks with Gabrielle, whom Hippolyte and Victoire regarded as my wife. Riding horseback nearly every day, Gabrielle had become as skillful as her sister; she made me happy, and I made her so in every way, and especially in the constancy which led me always to treat her sisters simply as good friends, without ever letting the memory that I had slept with them encourage me to take liberties which would have offended her. I had had dresses made for them, I had supplied them with linen, I lodged them well and fed them well; and, enjoying all the pleasures to be enjoyed in London, they adored me like a little god who made them happy; they pretended, and tried to believe, that it would never end.

On my side I was approaching the exhaustion of all my material and moral resources. I had no more money, I had sold all my diamonds and all my other precious stones; I had nothing left but snuffboxes, watches, cases

of various sorts, and sundry trifles of which I was fond
and which I did not have the heart to sell, for I should
not have received a fifth of what they had cost me. It
had been a month since I had paid either my cook or
my vintner; but I saw no reason to be any more perturbed than they were; entirely occupied by my love for
Gabrielle, I thought of nothing but keeping her affection
by countless attentions. Upon this happy state of indolence, Victoire intruded one morning to tell me sadly
that her mother had decided to go back to Hanover. She
no longer hoped for anything at Court, she had nothing
more to do in London. She said that she wanted to take
her bones to her native country and that she must lose
no time, for, despite her good appetite, she felt nearer
to death every day.

"And when does she intend to carry out this splendid
plan?"

"In three or four days."

"And without a word to me, as if she were leaving an
inn?"

"No, on the contrary, she told me that she wants to
talk with you privately."

I go upstairs, and she complains that I never come to
see her, ending by saying that, since I had scorned the
hand she had offered me, she no longed wanted to lay
herself open to criticism or even to calumny. She thanked
me for all that I had done for her daughters, adding that
she was leaving before she lost the three who remained
to her. In any case, she said that I was at liberty to go
with her, and to stay as long as I pleased in a country
house she owned near the capital. I could answer her
only that she was a free agent, and that my situation
did not permit me to marry.

On the same day Victoire sent to tell her attorney
that her mother wanted to speak with him; he came, he
carried out all her instructions, and three days later
everything had been arranged for her to leave on the
packet for Ostend. It was when I rose that morning that

I learned from Victoire that they were to be on board at four o'clock; nevertheless, Hippolyte and Gabrielle insisted on going riding, as we had decided we should do the day before. The girls enjoyed it; but I was inconsolable, as I usually was when I had to part from the object of my love. Back at the house I went to bed, I refused to dine, and I did not see the three sisters until after they had packed all their things. When I told Gabrielle that her leaving me made me miserable, she could think of no answer but that I was at liberty to go with her. When it was time for them to leave, I got up, not wanting to see their mother in my room; I saw her in hers, lying on the sofa, two men being ready to carry her to my carriage, which was at the door. My servants had attended to having all her possessions taken on board the boat. After seeing that I should not give her anything for the journey, she told me, in an outburst of sincerity, that she had in her purse a hundred and fifty guineas which I had given to her daughters, all three of whom were there in tears.

When my servants came back to tell me that they were gone, I ordered my door shut to everyone. I spent three days in gloom, making up my accounts. In the month I had passed with the Hanoverians I had spent all the money I had received from my jewels, and I was more than four hundred pounds sterling in debt to my vintner and all the other merchants who supplied my daily table. Determined to go to Lisbon[7] by sea, I sold the cross of my order, six or seven gold boxes, after removing the portraits[8] they contained, all my watches except one, and two trunks full of clothes. After paying everyone, I found myself with eighty guineas at my disposal. I left my fine house, and I went to lodge at Mrs. Mercier's,[9] a hundred paces from Soho Square, for a guinea a week, keeping only my Negro servant, whom I had every reason to believe faithful. Having taken these steps, I wrote Signor Bragadin[10] to send me two hundred zecchini[11] at once by a sight bill; I did not need to take more from the money I must have in Venice, from which I had taken nothing for five years.

In this situation, and firmly resolved as I was to leave London not only not a copper in debt but without borrowing even a guinea from anyone, I quietly awaited the bill of exchange from Venice in order to say good-by to everyone and to set sail for Portugal to see what Fortune might have in store for me there. Two weeks after the Hanoverians left, toward the end of February 1764, I go, led by my Evil Genius, to the "Cannon" tavern[12] to dine, as I always did, in a room alone. The table had been laid for me, when I see Baron Henau[13] come in, napkin in hand, to tell me that, if I wished, I could have my dinner sent into the room next door, where he was alone with his mistress.

"I am grateful to you, for a man alone becomes bored."

I see the young Englishwoman with whom I had dined at La Sartori's,[14] and to whom the Baron had been so generous. She spoke Italian, she was talented and charming; I am delighted to find myself in her company, and we dine gaily. After two weeks of abstinence it is not surprising that the pretty English girl aroused desires which I nevertheless concealed, for her lover, who set the tone, treated her with respect. I could do no more than say that I thought the Baron the most fortunate of men. Toward the end of dinner, noticing three dice on the mantelpiece, she quickly goes to get them and says:

"Let us play for a guinea, which we will spend on oysters and champagne."

We do so, it falls to the Baron to pay, he rings, the waiter comes, and he obeys. As we are eating the oysters she says:

"Let us play for which of us will pay for dinner."

We play, and it falls to her. Sorry to see myself getting off scot-free, I invite the Baron to stake two guineas against me, hoping that I shall lose them; but not a bit of it, luck is against him; he loses, I offer him his revenge, he loses, I tell him I will stay with him up to a hundred guineas, he thanks me, and he plays on, hoping to recoup, and in half an hour he owes me a hundred guineas. He asks me to go on, I reply most politely that luck is against him and he might be cleaned out, and that I should be sorry to profit by it. At this refusal he curses Fortune and the indulgence I seemed to be showing him; he rises, he takes his walking stick and he leaves, saying that he will pay me when he returns.

Left alone with the pretty English girl, I am surprised to hear her say that she was sure I had been playing on half shares with her.

"If you guessed that such was my intention, you must also have guessed that I find you charming."

"I observed that too."

"And do you regret it?"

"On the contrary, provided that my first guess was right."

"I promise you fifty guineas as soon as he pays me."

"Yes, but he must know nothing about it."

"And he shall not."

No sooner was this agreement reached than I give her proof of the reality of my inclination, very well pleased by her acquiescence and heartily welcoming this glimmer of good fortune at a time when gloom alone seemed to be my portion. Our business was hastily concluded, for our door was not locked. I had time to ask her only her address and at what hour she was at home, and especially if I must be very careful in her lover's presence, to which she answered only that he did not give her enough to expect her to be his alone. I put her address in my pocket, promising that I would go to spend the following night with her.

The Baron comes back just when we have concluded our arrangements. He tells me that he has gone to a merchant to discount the bill of exchange which he throws on the table before me, and that he had refused to accept it, despite the fact that it was at sight on one of the leading houses in Cadiz and drawn to his order by a reputable house in Lisbon. He shows me his endorsement, I look at the amount of the note, I see millions, and I am at a loss to understand it; he laughs and tells me that the millions were maravedis,[15] which, paid in pounds sterling, came to about five hundred pounds. I said that if the signature of the drawers was known, it was surprising that the merchant had refused to discount it for him.

"Why don't you go to your banker's?"

"I know none. I came here with a thousand lisbonines[16] in my pocket, which I have spent. I did not think of obtaining letters of credit. I cannot pay you unless this note is discounted. If you know anyone at the Exchange, you could do me the favor."

"If the signature is known, I will get it done for you tomorrow morning."

"In that case I will make it over to your order at once."

He signs his name on it. I promise to return his note to him or to give him his money at noon the next day; he gives me his address, he invites me to dine with him, and we part.

Early the next morning I go to Vanneck, who declines to discount the bill; I find Bosanquet, who tells me that Mr. Lee[17] needed it and would accept it at once; I go there, he tells me that my note is better than bank notes; he calculates, he shows me his figures, and he gives me five hundred and twenty pounds and some shillings, after first, of course, having me endorse it. I at once go to the Baron's, I show him the figures, and I give him his money in good bank notes. He thanks me, he gives me two fifty-pound bank notes, then we dine, we talk of his beautiful mistress, I ask him if he is very much in love with her, he says he is not because she has other lovers. He even says that if she pleases me I need only speak out.

"For ten guineas you can sup with her."

I think the Baron's frankness very commendable, I

nevertheless have no intention of going back on my word to the beauty. I went to her house, and as soon as she learned that I had brought her the fifty guineas she ordered an elegant supper, then she gave me so pleasant a night in her arms that it banished all my gloom. When, on leaving, I gave her the fifty guineas, she told me that she would give me supper whenever I wished for six. Pleased with her honesty, I promised to visit her often.

The next day I received by the penny post[18] a short letter in bad Italian from a man who signed himself "your godson Daturi."[19] He was in prison for debt, and he appealed to my charity to give him a few shillings for food. I had nothing to do; the word "godson" aroused my curiosity, I take a hackney carriage, and I go to the prison to see this unknown "godson" Daturi. I see a handsome youth twenty years of age, who takes his baptismal certificate from his pocket; I see his name, and mine as his father's gossip, his mother's name, the parish in Venice in which he was born, and I remember nothing. He undertakes to recall it all to me if I will hear him out, for his mother has talked to him about me countless times, telling him how she had known me and giving him hope that he would come upon me somewhere in Europe. Hearing his story I remembered everything, and even more than he could hope, for there were things which his mother had not told him. The young man whom I had held at the font as the son of Daturi, who was an actor, was perhaps my own son. He had gone to London with some acrobats to play the *pagliaccio*,[20] he had quarreled with the troupe, he had been dismissed, he had gone into debt to the amount of ten pounds, and he had been put in prison. After his story, without telling him anything about the circumstances of his birth, I had him released and I told him to come to my lodging every morning for two shillings to live on.

A week after this work of charity I found myself with a bad case of a foul disease which I had already had three times[21] and of which I had been cured by dint of mercury and my excellent condition. In the course of the week I had spent three nights with Baron Henau's fatal Englishwoman, whom I should never have met if Goudar had not taken me to La Sartori's. This disease, which it is not permissible to name in decent society, overtook me at a very poor time, that is to say, at a very unfortunate juncture, for it can never come at a good time. I was on the eve of taking a sea voyage across the entire Atlantic Ocean,[22] and, though Venus was born in that element,[23] the air of her birthplace is extremely bad for those who are suffering from her noxious influences. I consider my situation, and I resolve to take the great cure[24] immediately in London. In six weeks, I was certain, I could recover my health and arrive in Portugal fit to meet any demands on my person.

I go out, and I do not, as I had more than once done at the beginning of my pilgrimage through this world, go like a fool to reproach the Englishwoman who had infected me; instead I go to a learned surgeon to strike my bargain with him and to shut myself up in his house. To this end I pack my trunks, as if I were about to take ship to leave England, except that I send my Negro with all my fine linen to my laundress, who lived six miles from London and had the finest customers in the city.

On the very morning when I was all ready to leave Mrs. Mercier's house to stay at the surgeon's, I am handed a letter brought by messenger. I open it and see that it is signed Lee; he writes me what I copy from the original letter, which I have before my eyes:

"The bill of exchange which you gave me is forged, send me at once the 520 pounds I gave you, and if the person who cheated you does not return them to you, have him arrested. I beg you not to force me to have you arrested tomorrow. Lose no time, for your life is at stake."

I was alone, and very glad to be alone so that I could throw myself on my bed and let my body relieve itself

of a terrifying cold sweat, and have time to calm myself
after a fit of shivering which took me from head to foot.
I saw the gallows before me, inescapably, for no merchant would give me five hundred and twenty guineas
on the spot, and the trial which would end by my being
sentenced to be hanged would not be put off for a month.
If I had a month before me, I should certainly have had
five hundred and twenty guineas from Venice; but things
of this sort are not easily arranged in London. Burning
with the fever which had followed my shivering fit, I
take pistols, which are ready loaded, I tell my Negro to
wait for me, and I say the same to Daturi, who was on
the stairs waiting for me, expecting to receive the two
shillings which I gave him every day.

I go to Baron Henau's, intending to blow out his
brains if he does not at once give me the money, or to
keep him in my sight until I had had him arrested. I
arrive at his house, I go upstairs, and the landlady tells
me that he had left for Lisbon four days earlier.

The Baron was a Livonian, who was hanged at Lisbon
four months later. I learned it at Riga two months after
his misfortune overtook him. I mention it now for fear
I shall forget it when my reader is at Riga with me at
the beginning of October of this year.

As soon as I learned that he had gone, I saw that I
must at once decide on a course. I had only ten or twelve
guineas; it was not enough. I go to the Venetian Jew
Treves,[25] to whom I had been recommended by the
Venetian banker Count Algarotti[26] and whose services
I had never employed. I consider neither Bosanquet nor
Vanneck nor Salvador,[27] because they might already
know of my situation. I go to Treves, who had nothing
to do with those important bankers, and I at once ask
him to discount a bill of exchange which I immediately
draw on Count Algarotti in the paltry amount of a
hundred Venetian zecchini, and I write the advice to
Signor Algarotti, telling him to apply for reimbursement
to his relative Signor Dandolo,[28] who had recommended

me to him. The Jew at once discounts the bill in cash.

Lee had given me twenty-four hours, and the worthy Englishman was incapable of going back on his word to me; but nature did not allow me to trust in it. I did not want to lose my linen or three broadcloth coats with linings of a different color which were at my tailor's. I take Jarba to my room, and I ask him if he would rather I should give him twenty guineas on the spot and dismiss him, or if he would prefer to remain in my service, undertaking to leave London in a week to join me in the place from which I should write him that I had stopped to wait for him.

"Sir, I do not want a copper, I wish to remain in your service, I will join you wherever you let me know that you are. When shall you leave?"

"In an hour; but it can cost me my life if you tell anyone."

"Why do you not take me with you?"

"Because I want you to bring me my linen, which is at the laundress's. I intend to give you now approximately what money you will need to join me."

"I do not want anything. You shall pay me what I have spent when you see me in your presence. Wait."

He goes to his little room; he comes back at once, and he shows me sixty guineas which he had and offers them to me, saying that he had credit enough to get another fifty. I refuse, but his act makes me sure of him. So I tell him that in four or five days Mrs. Mercier will give him the letter telling him where he is to come, and I instruct him to buy a small trunk to pack my linen and my laces in.

After that I go to my tailor, who had the broadcloth in lengths for the coats he was to make me and the gold braid for one of them. I let him know that I want to get rid of it all, and he buys it from me himself for thirty guineas, which he pays me on the spot. After that I go to La Mercier's, I pay her a week's lodging for my Negro, I put my luggage on a carriage, and I go with

Daturi to sleep at Rochester.[29] I could not go farther. The young man saved me. I was in convulsions and delirious. I ordered post horses to take me to Sitting-bourne;[30] and he would have none of it. He astonished me. He went for a doctor, who had me bled instantly, and six hours later he pronounced me fit to leave. The next morning I was at Dover, where I stopped only half an hour because the tide, the captain of the packet boat told me, would not let me stay longer. He did not know that it was just what I wanted. I paid the usual six guineas for the crossing, which took six hours because there was very little wind. From Dover I wrote my Negro to come to join me at Calais, and Mrs. Mercier wrote me that she had given him my letter; but my Negro did not come. My reader will learn two years hence where I found him. I stopped at Calais, and I at once went to bed in the "Golden Arm," [31] where I had left my post chaise. The best doctor in Calais at once came to take care of me. My burning fever, complicated by the venereal poison which was circulating in my veins, put me in a state which made the doctor despair of my life. On the third day I was at death's door. A fourth bleeding exhausted all my strength and kept me in a lethargy of twenty-four hours' duration, which, followed by a salutary crisis, restored me to life; but it was only after a strict course of diet and treatment that I was in a condition to leave two weeks after I arrived.

Weak, distressed that I had had to leave London at the cost of considerable loss to Mr. Lee, that I had had to run away, that I had found my Negro unfaithful, that I must abandon my plan of going to Portugal, that I had no idea where to go, that my health was so undermined that it was doubtful if I should recover it, that I looked frightful, had lost flesh, that my skin was yellow and all covered with pustules impregnated with celtic humors,[32] which I had to think about dispersing, I got into my post chaise with my godson Daturi, who, sitting behind, acted as my servant and performed that office very well. I had written to Venice to send me at Brussels the bill of exchange for a hundred pounds sterling which I was to have received in London, to which I did not dare to write. I changed horses at Gravelines[33] and went on to spend the night at the "Conciergerie" [34] in Dunkirk.

The first person I saw upon leaving my chaise was the merchant S., the husband of the Teresa[35] whom my reader may remember, the niece of Tiretta's[36] mistress, whom I had loved nearly seven years earlier. He recognizes me, he is amazed to find me so changed; I tell him that I am recovering from a severe illness, I ask him for news of his wife, he says that she is in good health and that he hopes I will come to dine with him the next day. I reply that I must leave at daybreak, but he will not listen to reason; he insists on my seeing his wife and their three young children; and since I had made up my mind to leave the next morning he said he would come back with his wife and his whole family. How could I refuse? I replied that he should sup with me.

The reader may remember how I loved this Teresa, whom I had resolved to marry. I remembered it only to feel the more unhappy, knowing how distasteful she would find the creature I had become.

She came a quarter of an hour later with her husband and her three sons, the eldest of whom was six years of age. After the usual compliments, and the unpleasant truth, which bored me, concerning the poor state of my health, she sent the two younger boys home, keeping only the eldest to sup with me, for she had good reason to believe that he would be of interest to me.[37] The boy was charming, and since he looked very much like his mother her husband never doubted that he was the boy's father in law and in nature. I laughed to myself at finding children of mine all over Europe. At table she gave me news of Tiretta. He had entered the service of the Dutch East India Company,[38] and he had taken part in a revolt in Batavia,[39] where his complicity had been discovered and he might well have been hanged if he had not, as I did in London, had the good luck to escape by flight. It is not very difficult in this world, when one lives the life of adventure, to get oneself hanged for trifles if one has not one's wits about one and is not very careful.

The next day I went by way of Ypres to Tournai,[40] where, having seen two grooms exercising horses, I asked to whom they belonged.

"To the Count of Saint-Germain,[41] the adept, who has been here for a month and who never goes out. He is going to make the fortune of our province by establishing manufactories. Everyone who passes through the city wants to see him, but he remains in seclusion."

Such an answer makes me want to see him. No sooner have I arrived at the inn than I write him a note in which I inform him of my wish and ask him to name a time. Here is his answer, which I still have and which I only translate into French.[42]

"My occupations make it necessary for me to receive no one; but you are an exception. Come at the time which is most convenient for you; you will be shown to my room. There will be no need for you to speak either my name or yours. I do not offer you half of my dinner, for my food is suitable for no one, least of all for you if you still have your old appetite."

I went there at nine o'clock. He had a beard an inch long, and more than twenty distilling flasks containing liquids, some of which were in digestion on sand at its natural temperature. He told me that he was working on colors to amuse himself, and that he was establishing a manufactory of hats to please Count Cobenzl,[43] Plenipotentiary of the Empress Maria Theresa in Brussels. He said that he had given him only twenty-five thousand florins, which would not be enough, but that he would make up the difference. We spoke of Madame d'Urfé, and he told me that she had poisoned herself [44] by taking too strong a dose of the universal medicine.

"Her will shows," he said, "that she thought she was pregnant, and she could have been so if she had consulted me. The operation could not be easier, but it is impossible to be sure if the offspring will be male or female.''

When he learned what my disease was, he begged me to remain in Tournai only three days and to do as he told me. He assured me that I should leave with all my pustules discharged. After that he would give me fifteen pills which, taken one at a time, would completely cure me in fifteen days. I thanked him for everything, and accepted nothing. After that he showed me his archeus,[45] which he called Atoeter.[46] It was a white liquid in a small phial like several others which were there. They were sealed with wax. On his telling me that it was the universal spirit of nature, and that the proof of it was that the spirit would instantly leave the flask if the smallest hole were made in the wax with a pin, I asked him to perform the experiment for me. He thereupon gave me a phial and a pin, telling me to do it myself. I pierced the wax, and I instantly saw the phial empty.

"It is magnificent, but what use is it?''

"I cannot tell you.''

Ambitious, as usual, not to let me go without having astonished me, he asked me if I had any coins, and I took those I had from my pocket and put them on the table. He then rose, telling me nothing of what he was going to do. He took a burning coal, which he put on a metal plate, then he asked me for a twelve-sou piece[47] which I had there before me, he put a small black grain on it, and he put the coin on the coal, then he blew on the coal with a blowpipe, and in less than two minutes I saw with my own eyes that my coin turned red. He then told me to wait until it cooled, which took place in a minute. After that he told me, with a laugh, to pick up my coin and take it with me, for it was mine. I saw at once that it was gold, but, though I was sure he had removed mine by sleight-of-hand and substituted the gold one, which he could very easily have silvered, I did not want to reproach him with it. After praising him, I told him that, another time, in order to be sure of astonishing the most clear-sighted of men, he should tell him before-hand what transmutation he was about to perform, for then a thinking man would have looked carefully at his silver piece before he put it on the burning coal. He replied that those who could doubt his knowledge were not worthy to speak to him. Such talk was characteristic of him. This was the last time I saw that celebrated and learned impostor, who died in Schleswig six or seven years ago.[48] The twelve-sou piece was pure gold. Two months later in Berlin I gave it to Earl Marischal Keith,[49] who showed an interest in it.

I left Tournai the next day at four o'clock in the morning, and I stopped in Brussels to await the answer to the letter I had written to Signor Bragadin in Venice asking him to have the amount of the bill of exchange I was to have received in London paid to me there. I received his letter five days after I arrived, with a bill of exchange for two hundred Dutch ducats[50] on Madame Nettine.[51] I was thinking of staying there to take the great cure, when Daturi came to tell me that he had just learned from a ropedancer that his father, his mother, and his whole family were in Brunswick, where, if I would go there, he assured me that I should find whatever attendance I could want and that I should be made to feel perfectly at home. He persuaded me at once. I knew the Hereditary Prince, who now reigns;[52] in addition I was curious to see Daturi's mother after twenty-one years.[53] So I left for Brussels immediately, but at Roermond[54] I felt so ill that I began to think I could not continue my journey. Passing through Liège, I went to see Madame Malignan,[55] finding her a widow and in poverty. Thirty-six hours in bed made me believe I could bear up, and I left in my post chaise, which kept me in despair because the post horses were not accustomed to shafts; I resolved to get rid of it at Wesel. No sooner had I arrived at the inn than I went to bed, and I told

Daturi to discuss exchanging it for a four-wheeled carriage.

The next morning I was very much surprised to see General Beckwith[56] in my room. After the usual questions and condolences on the state of my health, the General said that he would himself buy my chaise and would give me a carriage in which I could travel comfortably all through Germany, and the thing was done then and there; but when the worthy Englishman heard my account of the condition I was in, he persuaded me to take the cure at Wesel, where there was a young physician, a graduate of the school at Leiden,[57] who was very cautious and very skillful. Nothing is easier than to change the mind of a sick and melancholy man, who has no plan, who is in search of fortune, and who, with *Sequere Deum*[58] as his maxim, does not know where it may await him. General Beckwith, who was in garrison with his regiment at Wesel, immediately sent for Dr. Peipers,[59] and insisted on being present at my whole confession and even at my examination. I do not want to disgust my reader by describing the wretched state I was in. The young doctor, who was gentleness itself, told me to lodge at his house, where his mother and his sisters would give me all the attendance I could want, and where he assured me that I should be cured in six weeks if I would obey all his instructions. The General encouraged me to make up my mind to it, and I felt inclined to do so, for I wanted to be able to amuse myself in Brunswick, and not go there only to arrive paralyzed in every limb. So I assented, despite my son, who hoped for the honor of getting me cured in his house. Dr. Peipers would not hear of any fixed agreement. He said that when I left I should give him what I pleased, and that he would certainly be well satisfied with it. He left to have his room made ready for me, for he had only one, saying that I could go there an hour later. I had all my baggage taken there, and I arrived at his house in a sedan chair, holding a handkerchief before my face, ashamed to show myself to the mother and sister of the worthy doctor, who was there in company with several girls at whom I did not dare to look.

As soon as I was in my room Daturi undressed me and I went to bed.

My cure. Daturi beaten by soldiers. Departure for Brunswick. Redegonda. Brunswick. The Hereditary Prince. The Jew. My stay in Wolfenbüttel. Library. Berlin. Calzabigi and the lottery in Berlin. Mademoiselle Belanger.

AT SUPPERTIME the doctor came to my room with his mother and one of his sisters, both of whom assured me that they would accord me every attention. Their good character was depicted on their faces.

As soon as they withdrew he informed me of the system he would follow to restore me to health. A sudorific decoction and mercurial pills were to free me from the poison which was carrying me to the grave. I must adhere to a strict diet and refrain from all mental exertion. I assured him that he would find me obedient to all his directions. He promised to read the newspaper to me himself twice a week, and he at once gave me the news that Madame de Pompadour was dead.[1]

So I am condemned to a rest which, according to him, was necessary to the success of his treatment, but which, on the other hand, was murderous, for I felt that the boredom would kill me. The doctor himself feared it, and he advised me to let his sister come and do needlework in my room with two or three girls who were her dear

friends. My bed being in an alcove with curtains, they
would not inconvenience me. I asked him to procure me
the diversion, and his sister was delighted to be able to
do me the favor, for the room I occupied was the only
one in the house with windows on the front. But this
foresight on my doctor's part was fatal to Daturi.

Having been educated in nothing but his profession,
the youth could only be bored to spend the entire day
with me; so when he saw that, having excellent company,
I could do without him, he ceased to think of anything
but amusing himself all day, roaming about now in one
part of the city, now in another. On the third day of
our stay in Wesel he was brought home at nightfall badly
beaten. He had gone to amuse himself in a guardhouse
with some soldiers who had picked a quarrel with him,
and who had ended by giving him a masterly thrashing.
He was in a pitiable state. Covered with blood and with
three teeth[2] missing, he wept as he told me of his misfortune, begging me to avenge him. I sent my doctor with
the story to General Beckwith, who came to tell me that
he did not know what he could do about it and that the
only service he could render me was to send him to the
hospital to be cured. Having no broken bones, he recovered his health in a week, and I sent him to Brunswick
with a passport from General Salenmon.[3] The three teeth
he had lost in the affray saved him from the risk of being
made a soldier, as he might have been if he had had
them all.[4] He set out on foot, and I promised I would
go to see him as soon as I was well enough to leave.

He was a handsome, well-built youth. He could scarcely
write, and he had been taught nothing but ropedancing
and the art of pyrotechnics.[5] He was courageous, and he
had pretensions to honesty. He was a little too fond of
wine, and he had no more than the usual inclination for
the fair sex. I have known a number of men who owed
their success to women, despite their indifference to the
sex.

At the end of a month I was in good health and able

to leave, though I had become very thin. The idea of myself which I left in Dr. Peipers's house is not like me so
far as my character is concerned. He thought me the
most patient of men, and his sister and her pretty friends
the most modest. All my virtues came from my illness.
To judge a man, one must examine his conduct when he
is healthy and free; ill or in prison, he is not the same.

I presented Fräulein Peipers with a dress, and I gave
the doctor twenty louis. On the day before my departure
I received a letter from Madame du Rumain,[6] who, having learned from my friend Balletti[7] that I was in need
of money, sent me a draft for six hundred florins on the
Bank of Amsterdam. She wrote me that I was to repay
her the amount at my convenience; but she died before
I could fulfill the obligation.[8]

Having decided to go to Brunswick, I could not resist
the temptation to go to Hanover. When I remembered
Gabrielle,[9] I still loved her. I was not thinking of stopping there, for I was no longer rich, and my convalescent
state prescribed that I should husband my returning
health. I wanted only to surprise her, paying her a short
visit at her estate, on which she had told me that she was
living near Stöcken.[10] Curiosity also entered in.

So I had decided to leave at daybreak, all alone in the
carriage which the English General had given me in exchange for my two-wheeled one; but it was not to be.

A note from the General, in which he asks me to come
to supper with him, where I will find guests from my
own country, obliges me to accept the invitation. If we
remain at table until late in the night, I am prepared
to leave still later. So I go to General Beckwith's, after
promising my doctor that I will abstain from any excess.

What a surprise when, entering the room, I see the
Parmesan Redegonda,[11] with her swine of a mother! She
did not at once recognize me; but her daughter instantly
named me, saying that I had grown very thin. I told her
that she had grown more beautiful, and it was true.
Eighteen months added to her age could only have in-

creased her charms. I told her that I had just got over
a serious illness, and that I was leaving for Brunswick
at dawn.

"And so are we," she replied, looking at her mother.

The General was delighted to see that we knew each
other, and adds that we could go there together, and I
reply with a smile that it would be difficult, unless the
Signorina's mother had adopted new principles. She
replies that she is the same as ever.

The company wants to go on playing. The General was
dealing at a small faro bank. There were two or three
other ladies and some officers, and the stakes were very
small. He offers me a *livret*,[12] and I decline, saying that
I never play when I am traveling.

At the end of the deal the General says to me that he
knows why I am not playing, and he takes some English
bank notes from his portfolio.

"These are the same notes," he says, "which you gave
me in payment in London six months ago.[13] Take your
revenge. They come to four hundred pounds sterling."

"I have no wish," I say, "to lose as much as that. I
will lose only fifty guineas, in paper too, to amuse you."

So saying, I take from my purse, in which I had two
hundred ducats in gold, the bill of exchange which the
Countess du Rumain had sent me.

He goes on dealing, and at the third deal I find I am
ahead by fifty guineas, which he pays me in English
paper as soon as I said that I had had enough. Just then
supper is announced, and we go to sit down at table.

Redegonda, who had learned French very well, amused
the whole company. She was to enter the service of the
Duke of Brunswick,[14] as second musical *virtuosa*, by
contract with Nicolini,[15] and she had just come from
Brussels. She complained of having undertaken to make
the journey by post coaches, in which she was very uncomfortable, and so much so that she was sure she would
arrive in Brunswick very ill.

"Here is the Chevalier de Seingalt," says the General

to her, "who is all alone and whose carriage is excellent. Go with him."

Redegonda smiles, Redegonda's mother asks me how many seats my carriage has, and the General answers for me that it seats two. The mother then says that the thing is impossible, for she did not let her daughter travel alone with anyone. At this reply everyone burst into laughter, including Redegonda, who, after laughing, said that her mother was always afraid that someone would murder her.

The conversation then turned to other subjects, and we remained at table in high spirits until one o'clock. Redegonda, without much urging, sat down at the harpsichord and sang an air which pleased the entire company.

When I made to leave, the General invited me to breakfast, saying that the post coach did not leave until noon and that I owed the courtesy to my beautiful compatriot, and she joined in, reproaching me with certain occurrences at Florence and Turin,[16] where she had nothing to reproach me with; but I yielded, though I went off to bed, being in need of sleep.

The next morning at nine o'clock I take leave of the doctor and his whole family and I go to the General's on foot for breakfast, having left orders that, as soon as the horses were harnessed, my carriage was to be ready at his door, for I was determined to leave after breakfast without fail. A half hour later Redegonda arrives with her mother, and I am surprised to see her with her brother,[17] who had served me as temporary valet while I was in Florence.

After the breakfast, which was very gay, my carriage being there ready, I make my bow to the General and the whole company, all of whom had left the room to see me set off. Redegonda, asking me if my carriage is comfortable, gets in, and I simply get in after her, without having the slightest plan in mind; but my surprise was not small when, no sooner had I got in than I saw the postilion start off at a fast trot. I was on the verge of calling to him to stop, but, seeing Redegonda laughing at the top of her lungs, I let him go on, ready, however, to order him to stop as soon as Redegonda, having laughed her fill, should tell me that it was enough. But not a bit of it. We had already gone half a league before she began to speak.

"I've been laughing so hard," she said, "to think what interpretation my mother will put on this godsend of a joke, for I meant to get into your carriage only for a moment; then I laughed at the postilion, who certainly could not have been carrying me off by your order."

"Certainly not."

"But my mother will think the contrary. Isn't it amusing?"

"Most amusing; but I am very glad it has happened. My dear Redegonda, I will take you to Brunswick, and you will be better off here than in the post coach."

"Oh, that would be carrying the joke too far. We'll stop at the first post station, and wait there for the coach."

"You may do so if you like; but not I! I shall certainly not oblige you to that extent."

"What! You would have the heart to leave me at the post station all alone?"

"Never, my charming Redegonda. You know I have always loved you. I am ready to take you to Brunswick, I say again."

"If you love me you will wait and restore me to the arms of my mother, who must be in despair."

"My dear heart, do not expect that."

The young madcap began laughing again, and while she laughed I formed and perfected the charming plan of taking her with me to Brunswick.

We arrived at the station; there were no horses; I won the postilion over, and after some light refreshments we arrive at the next post station about nightfall, having found the road bad. I order horses, and I let Redegonda say what she will. I knew that the coach would arrive there before midnight, and that the mother would regain possession of her daughter. It was a disappointment which I would not stomach. I went on all night, and I stopped at Lippstadt, where, despite the unusual hour, I ordered a meal. Redegonda needed sleep as much as I did; but she had to resign herself when I quietly told her that we should sleep at Minden. At that I saw her smile, for she well knew what she had to expect. We stopped there, and we spent five hours in the same bed. She only resisted a little for form's sake. If she had had an honest mother when I made her acquaintance at La Palesi's[18] in Florence, I should never have become involved with La Corticelli,[19] who brought me all kinds of trouble. After my too short stay in Minden I stopped that evening in Hanover, where, at an excellent inn, we supped choicely. I found there the same waiter who had been at the inn in Zurich when I waited at table on the ladies from Soleure.[20] Miss Chudleigh had dined there with the Duke of Kingston,[21] then she had left for Berlin. He had made them an iced *salbottière*[22] with ten lemons, of which they had eaten only a little; we took advantage of it, then we retired to a bed made up in the French manner.

What woke us the next morning was the noise of the post coach arriving. Whereupon Redegonda starts protesting that she will not have her mother finding her in bed, and I start summoning the waiter to tell him not to bring to our room a woman who, on leaving the coach, would demand to be brought there; but it was too late. Just as I am opening the door, in comes the mother with her son, and finds us both in our shifts. I tell her son to wait outside, and I close my door. The mother begins scolding and complaining that we have deceived her, and she threatens me if I will not give her back her daughter. Her daughter, telling her the story in detail, convinces her that only chance had made her leave with me. Her mother finally consents to believe her.

"But," she says to her daughter, "you cannot deny, you wanton, that you slept with him."

She replies with a laugh that that was another matter, and that nobody does any harm asleep. She goes and kisses her, and she calms her by telling her that she will get dressed and will make the journey to Brunswick with her in the coach.

Peace having thus been made, I dressed, I ordered horses, and, after giving them breakfast, I went on to Brunswick, where I arrived three hours before them. Redegonda made me lose my desire to pay a visit to Gabrielle, who must have been with her mother and her two sisters on the estate[23] of which she had told me the name.

I went to lodge at a good inn,[24] and I at once sent Daturi word that I had arrived. I saw him appear before me elegantly dressed and impatient to introduce me to the magnificent Signor Nicolini, who was the theatrical impresario-general for the city and the Court. This man, who was thoroughly versed in his trade and who enjoyed the good will of the generous Prince his master, to whom his daughter Anna[25] was mistress, lived in luxury. He insisted on putting me up, but I managed to excuse myself. However, I accepted his invitation to his table, which was worthy of my consideration not only for his excellent cook but also for the charm of the company, which was far more likely to give pleasure than one made up of persons of quality, where gaiety freezes in the chill of etiquette. Nicolini's was made up of people of talent. Votaries, male and female, of music and the dance offered my mind the most satisfying of pictures. I was convalescing, and I was no longer rich. Otherwise I should not have ended my stay in Brunswick so soon. No later than the next day Redegonda came there to dinner. Everyone knew, though I do not know how, that it was with me she had traveled from Wesel to Hanover.

On the next day but one the Crown Prince of Prussia[26] arrived from Potsdam to see his future wife,[27] daughter

At a Sickbed

At the Mirror

of the reigning Duke. He married her in the following year, and everyone knows that the marriage turned out badly[28] because of a passing fancy of the charming Princess's, which cost the man who had dared to seduce her, or who had let himself be seduced, his head. In the latter case she did a grave wrong in accusing him.

There were magnificent entertainments at Court, and the Hereditary Prince,[29] now the reigning Duke, was gracious to me. I had made his acquaintance in Soho Square at the great picnic supper on the day after he received the freedom of the City of London.[30]

It was twenty-two years since I had loved Daturi's mother. Remembering her beauty, I was curious to see her again. Age had damaged her so cruelly that I was sorry I had made her receive me. I saw that she was ashamed of her ugliness; but her ugliness enabled me not to blush for my former inconstancy. The transition from beauty to ugliness in the face of a woman whose features are of a decided cast is too easy.

On a great plain some distance from the city the Hereditary Prince reviewed six thousand infantrymen in the service of Brunswick. I went; it rained in torrents all day, and the spectators, both foreigners and the native nobility, and chiefly ladies, were very numerous; among others I saw the Honorable Miss Chudleigh, who asked me when I had left London. That celebrated lady was wearing a muslin dress with nothing under it but a shift, and the heavy rain had so soaked it that she looked worse than naked. She seemed to enjoy it. The other ladies sheltered from the downpour under tents. The rain was not allowed to impede the maneuvers of troops who did not fear fire.

Having nothing to do in Brunswick, I was thinking of leaving for Berlin to spend the rest of the summer more agreeably. I needed a greatcoat, I buy the cloth from a Jew who offers to discount foreign bills of exchange for me, if I have any. Nothing could be simpler. I had the draft for fifty louis on the Bank of Amsterdam which

Madame du Rumain had sent me; I take it from my portfolio, and I offer it to the Israelite. After reading it carefully, he says he will come back in half an hour to discount it for me in Dutch ducats. He comes back with the money. The bill was to my order, Seingalt, and I endorse it by signing that name, and he goes away, satisfied with the two per cent he has made, the usual profit on all bills of exchange drawn on the Bank of Amsterdam. No later than the next morning I see in my room the same Jew, who tells me to return his money and take back my bill, or to give him security until the return of the post by which he would learn if my bill of exchange was accepted as good by the banker on whom it was drawn.

Astonished by the fellow's insolent behavior, and certain that my bill was good, I tell him that he is mad, that I am sure of my bill, and that I will give him no security. He replies that he means to have either the money or security, in default of which he will have me arrested, for I was known. At these words the blood rushes to my head, I take my walking stick and, after administering five or six blows, I turn him out, I shut my door, and I dress to go to dine at Nicolini's. I tell no one what has happened.

Determined to leave in two or three days, the morning after this incident I go for a walk outside the city, and I encounter the Hereditary Prince alone on horseback, followed by a groom at a hundred paces. I bow to him, I see him stop, I approach.

"So you are about to leave?" the charming Prince asks me affably. "I learned of it this morning from a Jew who came to tell me that you had given him a caning because he demanded security from you for a bill of exchange which he discounted for you, and which he was given reason to believe was forged."

"I do not remember, Monseigneur, what I may have done in a first impulse of well-justified anger against a scoundrel who dared to threaten that he would prevent my leaving, saying that I was known; but I know that my honor forbids me to withdraw my bill and to give security, and that nothing but arbitrary authority could prevent me from leaving."

"That is true, for it would be an injustice; but the Jew is afraid he will lose the hundred ducats, he says that he would not have given them to you if you had not mentioned my name."

"He lies."

"He says that you signed with a name which is not yours."

"He lies again."

"In short, he is a Jew who has had a beating, or so he claims, and who is afraid of being duped. He is a creature who moves me to pity, and whom I want to prevent from looking for some way to keep you here until he learns that the bill you made over to his order has been honored in Amsterdam. I will myself have the bill taken up from him this very morning, for I have no doubt of its genuineness. Thus you are free to leave whenever you choose. Good-by, Monsieur de Seingalt; I wish you a very good journey."

After this compliment the Prince left, not waiting for any answer I might give him. I might have told him that, by himself having the bill taken up from the Jew, he made it possible for him to say that His Highness had done me that favor, and that the whole city would believe it, to the injury of my honor.

Princes endowed with a pure heart and a magnanimous soul often lack the attention to detail necessary to spare the delicacy of the person to whom they wish to give an obvious token of their esteem. The Prince's action toward me was a little too much due to his generous character. He could not have treated me differently if he had supposed me a scoundrel and yet had wished to convince me that he forgave me, by taking upon himself all the bad consequences of my dishonesty. "And perhaps that is what he thinks," I said to myself a moment after he left. "Why is he interfering? Why does he not pretend to know nothing of this ugly business? Is it the Jew whom he pities, or is it I? If it is I, I must teach him a lesson, though without humiliating the hero."

Such are my reflections on my way to my lodging at the conclusion of our dialogue. I consider his wishing me a good journey very much out of place at that particular time. Such a piece of politeness, coming from a Prince whom I could not but regard as sovereign, actually became an order to leave.

I therefore resolved neither to remain in Brunswick, for by remaining there I could have given occasion for a verdict in the Jew's favor, nor to leave, for I could have given the Prince reason to think that by leaving I was profiting by the kindness he had shown me in making me a present of the fifty louis which I should have returned to the Jew if I had been guilty.

In accordance with this reasoning, arrived at by prudence, rarefied by honor, and worthy to have been hatched by a sounder head than mine, I order horses, I pack my trunk, I dine, I pay the innkeeper, and without troubling to take leave of anyone I go to Wolfenbüttel, intending to stay there for a week and sure that I shall not be bored, for it is there that the third-finest library in Europe[31] exists. I had long wanted very much to examine it at my leisure.

The learned librarian, all the more polite because his politeness was as devoid of ceremony as it was of affectation, told me on my first visit that he would not only put a man at my disposition in the library to fetch me all the books I asked for, but that he would bring them to my room, not excepting the manuscripts which are the chief treasure of that celebrated library. I spent a week without ever leaving it except to go to my room, and without ever leaving my room except to go to it. I did not see the librarian again until the last day, to thank him an hour before I left. I lived in the most perfect peace, never thinking of the past or of the future, my work preventing me from knowing that the present existed. I see today that to be a true sage in this world I should have needed only a concatenation of very small circumstances, for virtue always had more charms for me than vice. In short, I was never wicked, when I was so, except in the exuberance of my heart. From Wolfen-büttel I carried away a great number of views on the *Iliad* and the *Odyssey* which one finds in no scholiast and of which the great Pope[32] had no knowledge. Some of them are to be found in my translation of the *Iliad*,[33] the rest are here[34] and will remain lost. I will burn nothing, not even these memoirs, though I often think of it. I foresee that I shall never find the right time to do it.

I returned to Brunswick and to the same inn, and I at once sent word of my arrival to my godson Daturi. How glad I was when I became convinced that no one in Brunswick knew that I had spent that week only five leagues away! He told me that people said that before I left I had taken the bill of exchange back from the Jew, and that nothing more was said about it. Yet I was sure that the reply must have come from Amsterdam, and that the Hereditary Prince must have known all the time that I was in Wolfenbüttel. My godson invited me to dinner at Nicolini's. It went without saying, for I had not taken leave of him, and I wanted to set off the next day. And now for what happened to me at dinner, and which had to stand me in stead of full satisfaction.

We had come to the roast when a valet of the Hereditary Prince entered with the stupid Jew whose insolence I had punished in an access of anger.

"I am ordered, Monsieur," he said, "to beg your pardon for having suspected your bill of exchange on the Bank of Amsterdam of being a forgery. I have been punished by losing the two per cent which I should have gained by keeping it for myself."

I replied that I wished that that had been the only punishment he had received.

The impresario Nicolini did not fail to plume him-

self on the satisfaction which His Most Serene Highness
had had me accorded at his table, and I was willing to
flatter his vanity. Toward nightfall I asked him if he had
any commissions for me in Berlin, and I took my leave;
but now for what made me put off my departure for
another day.

At my inn I found a note from Redegonda, who, after
complaining that I had never once called on her during
my stay in Brunswick, asked me to come to breakfast
with her in a small house outside the city, directions for
reaching which she gave me. She told me that I should
find her not with her mother but with a young lady who
was an old acquaintance of mine, whom I should be very
glad to see again. She asked me to come without fail at
the hour she named.

I loved Redegonda, and I had neglected her in Brunswick, not so much on account of her mother as because
I was not in a position to make her some handsome present. So I thought I should not fail to appear at her
breakfast, curiosity also making me want to see the girl
whom she called an old acquaintance of mine.

So I went to the house at the appointed hour, and I
found her, beautiful and charming, in a parlor on the
ground floor, with a young *virtuosa* whom I had known
when she was a child, the same year that I had been imprisoned under the Leads. I pretended to be glad to see
her again; but, giving my principal attention to Redegonda, I did my utmost in the way of polite excuses and
then of polite compliments on the pretty little house in
which I saw her. She said that she had rented it for six
months, but that she never slept there.

After coffee we were about to go for a stroll in the
garden, when we saw the Prince come in politely asking
Redegonda, with a very gracious smile, to excuse him
for the chance which had led him to interrupt her conversation.

At that I understood everything, and I understood why
the beauty had urged me in her note to keep the appoint-

ment without fail. In ten or twelve days Redegonda had made a conquest of the charming Prince, who was always disposed to gallantry but who during the first year of his marriage to a sister of the King of England [35] felt it incumbent on him to pursue his amours incognito. We spent an hour strolling, talking of London and Berlin and never saying a word about the bill of exchange or the Jew. I saw him delighted by my praise of the library at Wolfenbüttel, and laughing heartily when I said to him that but for the nourishment of good books the bad food I had eaten there would have killed me.

After paying Redegonda a very gracious compliment, he mounted his horse a hundred paces from the house. Left alone with my fellow countrywoman, far from urging her to grant me favors, I advised her to cherish the personage who had just left us; but she would never admit to anything.

I went back to my inn for the rest of the day, and I left the next morning at dawn.

At Magdeburg an officer to whom I gave a letter from General Beckwith showed me all the most secret parts of the fortress[36] and kept me for three days in company with girls and gamesters. I took good care of my health and I replenished my purse, contenting myself with honesty.

I went straight to Berlin, not caring to stop at Potsdam, since the King was not there. The sandy roads made me spend three days traveling eighteen short German leagues.

I went to lodge at once at the "City of Paris." [37] In this inn I found everything I could wish, both for my comfort and my straitened means. The mistress of the inn, whose name was Rufin and who was French, being thoroughly well versed in her trade, had given her establishment a most favorable reputation. A half hour after my arrival she came to my room to ask me if I was satisfied with it and to settle terms with me for everything. She had a common table, and she made those who

wished to eat in their rooms pay double. I said that I
did not want to eat at the common table, and that, eating
in my room, I did not want to pay more, leaving it to
her to diminish the portions, and she agreed to it on condition that I should sup with her at a small table, which
would cost me nothing and at which the only company
would be her friends. To repay her, as in duty bound,
for her politeness, I accepted her condition with expressions of friendship. Being tired from the journey, I did
not begin supping with her until the next day. She had
a husband who did the cooking and never came to the
table, and a son who did not come to it either. The people
with whom I supped were an old gentleman, very sensible, and very agreeable company, who lodged in a room
next to mine and who was Baron Treyden,[38] whose sister
was married to the Duke of Kurland, Jean Ernest Birhen
or Biron.[39] This amiable man became my friend, and
remained so during all of the two months I spent in
Berlin. A merchant from Hamburg, named Greve,[40] with
his wife whom he had just married and whom he had
brought to Berlin to see the wonders of the Court of a
warrior King. The woman was as amiable as her husband.
I paid assiduous but perfectly honorable court to her.
A very cheerful man, whose name was Noël,[41] who was
the sole and greatly cherished cook of the King of Prussia.
He came to supper with his wife only seldom, for he
seldom had the time for it. Noël had only a scullery boy,
and the King of Prussia never had another cook. I met
his father in Angoulême, famous for his good pâtés. Noël,
Minister[42] of the French Directory[43] at The Hague, is, I
am told, the son of the cook, whom in any case I found
to be most amiable. But for Noël's skill, the famous
atheistic physician La Mettrie[44] would not have died
of the indigestion to which he fell a victim at Lord
Tyrconnel's,[45] for the excellent pâté which cost him his
life had been made by Noël. La Mettrie very often supped
with La Rufin during his lifetime, and I was very sorry
not to have made his acquaintance. He was learned, and

excessively gay. He died laughing, though there is no death more painful, it is said, than death from indigestion. Voltaire told me that he did not believe there had ever been on earth a more determined atheist or one who better supported his position, and I was convinced of it when I read his works. It was the King of Prussia himself who, in the presence of the Academy,[46] delivered his funeral oration, in which he said that it was no wonder that La Mettrie admitted only matter, for all the mind [47] which could exist was in his possession.

It is only to a King who takes it into his head to become an orator that a witticism can be permitted in the gravity of a funeral oration. However, the King of Prussia was never an atheist; but it makes no difference, for belief in a God never influenced either his morals or his acts. It is claimed that an atheist, who, preoccupied with his philosophy, thinks of God, is better than a theist who never thinks of him.

The first call I made in Berlin was on Calzabigi,[48] younger brother of the Calzabigi with whom I had joined at Paris in 1757 to establish the lottery which was first called the Military School Lottery and then, after the death of Pâris-Duverney,[49] the Royal Lottery.

This Calzabigi, whom I found in Berlin, had left both Paris and his wife, who was still known as La Générale Lamothe,[50] to establish the same lottery in Brussels, where, having wanted to live in luxury, he went bankrupt in 1762, despite all that Count Cobenzl [51] had done for him. Forced to leave, he arrived at Berlin in some style and presented himself to the King of Prussia. A rather good speaker, he persuaded the King to establish the lottery in his domains, conferring the directorship on him and giving him the fine title of Councilor of State.[52] He promised His Majesty a revenue of at least two hundred thousand crowns,[53] asking for only ten per cent on the receipts for himself, and the operating expenses.

It was all granted him. The lottery had been established for two years, it was doing well, and fortunately had

never suffered an unlucky drawing; but the King, who
knew that the unlucky drawing could come, and who
could not help fearing it, signified to Calzabigi that he
no longer wanted the lottery to continue on his responsibility. He turned it over to him, contenting himself with
a hundred thousand crowns; this was what the Italian
opera cost him.[54]

I arrived at Calzabigi's precisely on the day when the
King had sent him notice of this disagreeable decision.

After talking to me of our former dealings and of our
vicissitudes, he told me of this unexpected occurrence.
He said that the current drawing would still be on the
King's responsibility, but that he must have notices put
up informing the public that, beginning with the next
drawing, His Majesty would take no part. He needed
a capital of two million crowns, or he foresaw the end
of the lottery, for there would be no one to risk his
money in it if he were not sure he would be paid if he
won. He offered me ten thousand crowns a year if I could
persuade the King to let the lottery continue on his responsibility; and reminding me of the time seven years
earlier, when, arriving in Paris, I had been able to convince the whole Council of the Military School that the
lottery was certain to make a profit, he urged me to
undertake the same thing.

"The augury spoke clearly," he said, "and there is no
superstition in believing that it is the Good Genius of
the lottery which brought you to Berlin precisely yesterday."

I laugh at his illusion, and I feel sorry for him. I
demonstrate to him the impossibility of convincing a
mind which says, "I am afraid and I don't want to be
afraid any longer." He invites me to stay for dinner,
and he introduces Madame Calzabigi to me. I am surprised on two counts: the first is that I thought La
Générale Lamothe was still alive, the second, that in
Madame Calzabigi I recognize Mademoiselle Belanger.[55]
I pay her the usual compliments, I ask her for news of

her mother, she sighs and begs me not to speak to her of her family, for she could recollect only misfortunes.

I had known Madame Belanger in Paris, the widow of an exchange broker, who had only this rather pretty daughter and who I thought was well off. Seeing her married, and apparently complaining of her lot, I understand nothing, and I do not feel much curiosity; but after making me give my opinion on his excellent cook, my good friend also wanted my opinion on his horses and his elegant carriage. He asked me to escort his dear wife on a drive in the park and to stay for supper, for it was his best meal. He had a great deal of work to do, the next day but one being the day of the drawing.

We were scarcely in the carriage before I asked her by what fortunate combination of circumstances she had become my friend's wife.

"His wife," she replied, "is still alive, so I have not the misfortune to be his wife; but everyone in Berlin believes that I am. When my mother died three years ago, I was left with nothing, for she lived on an annuity. Having no relatives rich enough for me to call upon them for help, and not wanting help from someone who would have given it to me only at the price of my honor, I lived for two years on the money I obtained from the sale of all my poor mother's furniture and belongings, going to lodge with a kind woman who did tambour work and who made her living by it. I paid her so much a month, and I learned. I never went out except to go to mass, and I was dying of melancholy. The more my money diminished, the more I trusted in divine Providence; but having finally come to the point where I had not a sou, I appealed to Signor Brea,[56] of Genoa, whom I believed incapable of deceiving me. I asked him to find me a good situation as a chambermaid, thinking it not too much to suppose that I had all the talents necessary for that employment. He promised to bear it in mind, and five or six days later he offered me the following employment and indeed persuaded me to accept it.

"He read me a letter from Signor Calzabigi, whom I had never met, in which he commissioned him to send him to Berlin a decent girl, of good birth, well brought up and reasonably pretty, for he intended to keep her with him in the position of his wife and to marry her on the death of his real wife, who, being old, could not live long. Since the girl for whom he asked him could not be supposed to be rich, he instructed him to give her fifty louis to outfit herself, and another fifty for her journey from Paris to Berlin with a maid. Signor Brea was legally empowered to undertake on Signor Calzabigi's behalf that when the young lady arrived in Berlin she would at once be received by him as his wife and presented as such to all the persons who should frequent his house. He would keep a chambermaid of her choice for her, she should have a carriage and horses, and he would supply her with a wardrobe appropriate to her position, giving her so much a month for pin money, as was usual. He undertook to give her her freedom at the end of a year if his company or Berlin should prove displeasing to her, and in that case to give her a hundred louis, leaving her all that he had given her or had had made for her use. But if the young lady consented to remain with him, waiting for the time when he would marry her, he would settle ten thousand écus on her by a deed of gift, which she would bring him as her dowry when she became his wife, and if he should die before then she would have the right to pay herself ten thousand écus from all his possessions.

"With all these excellent conditions," she went on, "Signor Brea persuaded me to leave my native country and come here to dishonor myself, for it is true that everyone pays me the honors due to a wife, but it is beyond likelihood that people should not know that I am not so. I arrived here six months ago; and for six months I have been wretched."

"Wretched? Has he not fulfilled the conditions stipulated between you and Signor Brea?"

"He has fulfilled them all; but his poor health does not permit him to hope that he will outlive his wife, and since the ten thousand écus which he made over to me by deed of gift cannot become my dowry if he dies, I shall have nothing, for he is riddled with debt, and his many creditors will pay themselves from his household goods instead of me. Add that I cannot bear him, precisely because he loves me too much. You can understand my meaning. He is killing himself little by little, and he makes me wretched."

"In any case you can return to Paris six months hence, or do whatever you please as soon as you are set free. You will receive a hundred louis, and you will be well outfitted."

"Then I should enter upon the last stage of my dishonor in Paris instead of entering upon it here. In short, I am unhappy, and the good Brea is the cause of it; but I cannot hold it against him, for he did not know that his friend here has nothing but debts. Now that the King is about to withdraw his guarantee, we foresee the end of the lottery, and Calzabigi's bankruptcy follows inevitably."

Since nothing was exaggerated in Mademoiselle Belanger's narrative, I had to agree that she was to be pitied. I advised her to try to sell the deed of gift for ten thousand écus which Calzabigi had executed for her. He could not have an objection to her doing so. She replied that she had thought of it; but that to accomplish it she needed a friend, for she foresaw that she could not sell it except at a great loss. I promised her I would think about it.

At supper we were four. The fourth was a young man who had been employed in the *castelletto*[57] of the lottery in Paris, and who had followed Calzabigi first to Brussels, then to Berlin, to share his fortunes. He seemed to be in love with La Belanger, but I did not think she had granted him her favors. He was in charge of the *castelletto*, and he was General Secretary of the lottery. At dessert Calzabigi asked me to give my opinion on a proposal which he had written and which he wanted to publish to obtain a capital of two million, which he needed in order to maintain his credit. At that the lady withdrew to go to bed.

This woman, who could not be more than twenty-five or twenty-six years of age, Nature had made to please. She had no sparkling wit, but she had that knowledge of the usages of society which in a woman counts for more than wit. Her confidence in me inspired me to no more than friendly feelings, and I was glad of it.

Calzabigi's proposal was brief and clear. He invited all those whose wealth was generally known not to put a sum in cash in the treasury of the lottery but to set down their names for some amount which there was no doubt of their ability to cover. If the lottery should lose in a drawing, the subscribers would have to meet the loss, each paying his pro rata share; when there was a profit from any drawing, they would divide it in accordance with the same scale. I promised to give him my thoughts in writing the next day. The capital had to amount to three million crowns. I left him until dinnertime the next day.

Here is the form, entirely different from his, which I gave to his proposal. 1. A capital of only one million should be enough for him. 2. The million was to be divided into a hundred shares at ten thousand crowns each. 3. Each shareholder must give his name to a designated notary, who must answer for the shareholder's solvency. 4. The dividend was to be paid three days after each drawing. 5. In case of loss the shareholder must reestablish his share, again before a notary. 6. A cashier, chosen by four-fifths of the shareholders, should supervise the cashier of the lottery, who would remain the depositary of the receipts in cash. 7. Winning tickets should be paid the day after the drawing. 8. On the day before the drawing, the cashier of the lottery should give the shareholders' cashier an accounting of the receipts and lock the cashbox with three keys, one to remain in his hands, the second in those of the other, and the third in those of the Director-General of the lottery. 9. The only ventures the receivers of the lottery would accept should be on the simple drawing, the ambo, and the terno, and the quaterna[58] would be abolished as making the lottery risk too great a loss. 10. Neither on the terno, the ambo, nor the drawing would it be permitted to stake more than a crown or less than four groats, and no ventures would be accepted after twenty-four hours before the drawing. 11. One-tenth of the receipts should belong to Signor Calzabigi, Director-General of the lottery, but all the operating costs should devolve upon him. 12. He should have the right to own two shares without having the notary answer for his solvency.

When Calzabigi read my proposal I saw from his expression that he did not like it; but I predicted to him that he would find shareholders only on these conditions or on conditions even more unwelcome.

He had reduced the lottery to a sort of *biribissi*;[59] his luxurious style of living gave offense; it was known that he was getting more and more into debt, and the King could not help fearing some piece of roguery one day or another, though he had a comptroller on the watch who could count.

The last drawing under the King's sanction took place, and the numbers which came out of the wheel of fortune amused the whole city. The lottery lost twenty thousand crowns over and above all the receipts, and the King of Prussia at once sent them to his Privy Councilor Calzabigi. It was said that, when the news of the loss was brought to him, he burst out laughing, saying that he expected it and congratulating himself on the blow being light in comparison with what it might have been.

I thought it my duty to go to supper with the Director to comfort him. I found him in consternation. He made the painful but well-founded reflection that this unfortunate drawing would render it more difficult to find wealthy men inclined to furnish the capital for the lottery. It was the first time the lottery had lost, and the thing had happened at the worst possible time.

However, he did not lose courage, and he began the next day to take steps, informing the public, by a printed announcement, that the receiving offices of the lottery would remain closed until new capital had been obtained to provide security for all those who would continue to risk their money.

CHAPTER IV

*Lord Keith. Appointment with the King of
Prussia in the garden of Sans Souci. My con-
versation with the monarch. La Denis. The
Pomeranian cadets. Lambert. I go to Mitau.
My excellent reception at the Court and my
administrative tour.*

IT WAS on the fifth day after my arrival in Berlin
that I presented myself to the Earl Marischal, who after
the death of his brother was called Keith.[1] I had last
seen him in London, on his way from Scotland, where he
had been repossessed of his properties, which had been
confiscated when he had followed King James. The King
of Prussia had had influence enough to obtain this grace
for him. He was then living in Berlin, resting on his
laurels, enjoying his retirement, always in the King's
favor, and taking no more part in anything at the age
of eighty years.

Simple in his manner, as he had always been, he told
me that he was glad to see me again, immediately asking
me if I was passing through Berlin or if I intended to
remain there for some time. My vicissitudes being known
to him in part, I said that I should be glad to settle there
if the King, giving me some employment suitable to my
small talents, would graciously take me into his service.
But when I asked him for his countenance in the matter,

he said that his speaking to the King about me beforehand would do me more harm than good. Priding himself
on knowing men better than anyone else, he liked to judge
them for himself, and it very often happened that he
found desert where no one else had suspected it, and vice
versa. He advised me to write him that I aspired to the
honor of speaking with him.

"When you speak with him," His Lordship said, "you
may tell him in passing that you know me, and then I
think he will ask me about you, and I know that what
I shall reply will not harm you."

"I, unknown as I am, write to a King with whom I
have no connection! It would not enter my mind to do
such a thing."

"Do you not wish to speak with him? That is the
connection. There should be nothing in your letter but
the declaration of your wish."

"Will he answer me?"

"Have no doubt of it. He answers everyone. He will
write you where and at what hour he will be pleased to
see you. Do it. His Majesty is now at Sans Souci.[2] I am
curious to learn what sort of conversation you will have
with a monarch who, as you see, acts in a manner which
proves that he has no fear of being taken in."

I did not delay for a single day. I wrote to him in the
simplest style, though most respectfully. I asked him
when and where I might present myself to His Majesty,
and I subscribed myself "Venetian," dating my letter
from the inn where I was staying. On the next day but
one I received a letter written by a secretary, but signed
"Fédéric."[3] He wrote me that the King had received my
letter and had ordered him to inform me that His
Majesty would be in the garden of Sans Souci at four
o'clock.

I go there at three, dressed in black. I enter the courtyard of the palace by a small door, and I see no one, not
a sentinel, not a porter, not a footman. Everything was

in the deepest silence. I go up a short flight of stairs, I open a door, and I find myself in a picture gallery.[4] The man in charge of it offers me his services, but I thank him and decline, saying that I am waiting for the King, who had written me that he would be in the garden.

"He is," he said, "at his chamber concert, at which he is playing the flute, as he does every day immediately after his dinner. Did he give you an hour?"

"Yes, four o'clock. Perhaps he has forgotten."

"The King never forgets. He will come down at four o'clock, and you had better go to wait for him in the garden."

I go there, and soon afterward I see him, followed by his reader Catt[5] and a pretty spaniel. Scarcely has he seen me before he approaches, and, taking off his old hat with a mocking look, he names me by my name and asks me in a terrifying voice what I want with him. Surprised by this reception, I am at a loss; I look at him, and I say nothing.

"What is this? Speak. Are you not the man who wrote to me?"

"Yes, Sire; but I no longer remember anything. I thought that the King's majesty would not dazzle me. It shall not happen another time. The Lord Marischal should have warned me."

"So he knows you? Let us walk. What did you want to talk to me about? What do you think of this garden?"

At the same time that he asks me what I want to say to him, he tells me to talk to him about his garden. To anyone else I should have replied that I had no knowledge of gardens; but to a King, who supposed that I was a connoisseur, I should have appeared to be giving the lie. So, at the risk of giving him a specimen of my bad taste, I replied that I thought it magnificent.

"But," he said, "the gardens of Versailles are far finer."

"No doubt, Sire, if only because of the fountains."

"True; but if there are no fountains here it is not my fault. I have spent three hundred thousand crowns in vain to bring water here for them." [6]

"Three hundred thousand crowns? If Your Majesty spent them all at once, the fountains should be here."

"Aha! I see you are a hydraulician."

Was I to tell him that he was mistaken? I was afraid of offending him. I bent my head. Which is to say neither yes nor no. But the King did not care—thank God—to converse with me on that science, of which I knew not even the first principles. Without pausing for so much as a moment he asked me what the forces of the Republic of Venice were at sea in time of war.

"Twenty rated ships, Sire, and a great number of galleys."

"And for land forces?"

"Seventy thousand men, Sire, all subjects of the Republic, taking only one man per village."

"That is not true. You seem to want to make me laugh by talking such nonsense to me. But you are certainly a financier. Tell me what you think about taxes."

It was the first conversation I had had with a King. Observing his style, his outbursts, his sudden shifts, I thought I was called upon to play a scene of Italian improvised comedy, where, if the actor is at a loss, the groundlings hiss him. So I answered the proud King, assuming the financier's arrogance and adjusting my expression to match, that I could talk to him about the theory of taxation.

"That is what I want, for the practice does not concern you."

"Considered as to their effects, there are three kinds of taxes, one of which is ruinous, the second necessary, unfortunately, and the third always excellent."

"I like that. Go on."

"The ruinous impost is the royal tax, the necessary one is the military, the excellent one is the popular."

"What does all that mean?"

I had to take my time, for I was making it up.

"The royal tax, Sire, is the one which the monarch imposes on his subjects to fill his coffers."

"And it is always ruinous, you say."

"Without doubt, Sire, for it destroys circulation, the soul of commerce and the support of the State."

"But you consider the military tax necessary."

"But unfortunately so, for war is certainly a misfortune."

"Perhaps. And the popular?"

"Always excellent, for the King takes it from his subjects with one hand and with the other pours it into their bosom in very useful institutions and in measures calculated to increase their happiness."

"You doubtless know Calzabigi?"

"I ought to know him, Sire. Seven years ago we established the Genoese lottery in Paris."

"And in what category do you put that tax, for you will grant me that it is one?"

"Yes, Sire. It is a tax of the excellent kind when the King assigns the profit from it to the support of some useful institution."

"But the King may lose by it."

"One time in ten."

"Is that the result of certain calculation?"

"As certain, Sire, as all political calculations."

"They are often erroneous."

"I beg Your Majesty's pardon. They are never so when God is neutral."

"It is possible that I think as you do on the subject of moral calculation, but I do not like your Genoese lottery. I consider it a swindle, and I should not want it even if I had material proof that I should never lose by it."

"Your Majesty thinks like a wise man, for the ignorant people could not risk their money in it unless they were carried away by a fallacious confidence."

After this dialogue, which, all in all, does only honor to the intelligence of that illustrious monarch, he vacillated; but he did not find me at a loss. He enters a peristyle[7] enclosed by a double colonnade, and he stops before me, looks me up and down, then, after thinking a moment:

"You are," he says, "a very fine figure of a man."

"Is it possible, Sire, that after a long, rigorously scientific dissertation Your Majesty can see in me the least of the qualities which are the glory of your grenadiers?"

After a kindly smile, he said that since Lord Marischal Keith knew me he would speak to him about me, then he saluted me, taking off his hat, as he never failed to do, no matter to whom, with the greatest generosity.

Three or four days later the Earl Marischal gave me the good news that I had won the King's favor, and that His Majesty had told him that he would think about giving me some employment. Extremely curious to see at what he would employ me, and nothing urging me to go elsewhere, I decided to wait. When I did not sup at Calzabigi's the company of Baron Treyden at my hostess's table afforded me great pleasure, and, the weather being extremely fine, walking in the park made the whole day pass agreeably for me.

Calzabigi very soon obtained permission from the King to operate the lottery on the responsibility of anyone he chose, paying him six thousand crowns in advance at each drawing; and he at once reopened his receiving offices, after brazenly informing the public that the lottery would operate on his responsibility. His lack of credit did not prevent the public from staking, and in such numbers that the receipts gave him a profit of nearly a hundred thousand crowns, with which he paid a good share of his debts; and he took back the obligation for ten thousand écus which he had executed for his mistress, giving her the amount in cash. The Jew Ephraim[8] took the ten thousand écus, guaranteeing her the capital and paying her interest at six per cent.

After this lucky drawing Calzabigi had no difficulty in finding guarantors for a million divided into a thousand shares, and the lottery continued for two or three years without calamities; even so, Calzabigi went bankrupt and returned to Italy to die. His mistress married and returned to Paris.

During this time the Duchess of Brunswick,[9] the King's sister, came to pay him a visit with her daughter, whom the Crown Prince married the next year.[10] On this occasion the King came to Berlin and had an Italian opera performed for her at the small theater in Charlottenburg.[11] On that day I saw the King of Prussia dressed as a courtier, wearing a coat of lustrine with gold braid on all the seams and black stockings. His appearance was most comical. He entered the theater with his hat under his arm and escorting his sister, leading her by the hand and drawing the looks of all the spectators, for only the very old could remember seeing him appear in public except in a uniform and boots.

But at the performance what surprised me was to see the celebrated Denis[12] dance. I did not know that she was in the King's service, and, strong in the warrant of a very old acquaintance with her, I at once decided to pay her a visit in Berlin the next day.

When I was twelve years old my mother, having to leave for Saxony, had me come to Venice for a few days with my kind Doctor Gozzi.[13] Having gone to the theater, what seemed to me very surprising was a girl eight years old who, at the end of the play, danced a minuet with enchanting grace. The girl, whose father was the actor who played the part of Pantalone,[14] so charmed me that I afterward entered the box in which she was undressing to pay her my respects. I was dressed as an abate, and I saw her greatly surprised when her father told her to stand up so that I could embrace her. She did so most graciously, and I was most awkward. But I was so filled with happiness that I could not help taking from a woman who was selling jewelry there a small ring which the little girl had thought pretty but too expensive, and making her a present of it. She then came and embraced me again, with her face full of gratitude. I paid the woman the zecchino which was the price of the ring, and I went back to my Doctor, who was waiting for me in a box. My heart was in a pitiful state, for the zecchino I had given for the ring belonged to my master the Doctor, and although I felt that I was desperately in love with Pantalone's pretty daughter, I felt even more strongly that what I had done could not have been more foolish, not only because I had spent money which was not mine but because I had spent it like a dupe to obtain only a kiss.

Obliged the next day to account to the Doctor for his zecchino, and not knowing where to borrow it, I spent a most uneasy night; but the next day it all came out, and it was my mother herself who gave my master the zecchino; but I still laugh today when I think of how ashamed it made me feel. The same woman who had sold me the ring at the theater came to our house when we were dining. Showing pieces of jewelry which were declared too expensive, she praised me, saying that I had not thought the price of the ring I had given the Pantaloncina[15] too high. No more was needed to bring an accusation down on me. I thought I should end it all by asking to be forgiven and saying that it was love which had made me commit the crime, assuring my mother that this was the first and last it would make me commit. At the word "love" everyone did nothing but laugh, and I was so cruelly made fun of that I firmly resolved that it should be the last love of my life; but thinking of Giovannina, I sighed; she was so named because she was my mother's godchild.[16]

After giving me the zecchino, she asked me if I wanted her to invite her to supper; but my grandmother objected, and I was grateful to her for it. It was on the next day that I went back to Padua with my master, where Bettina[17] easily made me forget the Pantaloncina.

After this incident I never saw her again until that evening in Charlottenburg. Twenty-seven years had passed. She must have been thirty-five years of age. Had I not learned her name, I should not have recognized her, for at the age of eight her features could not be formed. I could not wait to see her alone in her room and to learn if she remembered the incident, for I did not think it possible that she could recognize me. I asked if her husband Denis was with her, and I was told that the King had banished him[18] because he ill-treated her.

So the next day I am driven to her house, I send in my name, and she receives me politely, saying, however, that she did not believe she had ever had the pleasure of seeing me anywhere before.

It was then that I gradually awakened the greatest interest in her by talking to her of her family, her childhood, and the grace by which she enchanted Venice when she danced the minuet; she interrupted me to say that she was then only six years old, and I replied that she could not have been more, as I was only ten when I fell in love with her.

"I could never tell you so," I said, "but I have never forgotten a kiss you gave me at your father's order in return for a little present I made you."

"Say no more. You gave me a ring. You were dressed as an abate. I have never forgotten you either. Is it possible that it is you?"

"It is I."

"I am delighted beyond measure. But since I do not recognize you, it is impossible that you should recollect me."

"Certainly, for if I had not been told your name I should not have thought of you."

"In twenty years, my dear friend, the face takes on a different form."

"Say rather that at the age of six one's features are not yet molded."

"You can be a good witness that I am only twenty-six years old, despite the evil tongues which make me ten more."

"Let them talk. You are in the flower of your years and made for love; and I consider myself the happiest of men now that I have been able to tell you that you are the first to have inspired amorous feelings in my soul."

After this exchange, we quickly became affectionate; but experience had taught us both to stop where we were and to leave anything else until later.

La Denis, still young, beautiful, and fresh, reduced her age by ten years; she knew that I knew it, nevertheless she wanted me to accept it, and she would have hated me if, like an idiot, I had chosen to demonstrate a truth to her which she knew as well as I did. She did not care about what I was bound to think, she left that to me. It is even possible that she considered I should be grateful to her for giving me a warrant, by her very plausible lie, to rid myself of ten years as she was doing, and she declared herself ready to bear witness for me if the occasion arose. Diminishing their ages is a sort of duty for women of the theater, principally because they know that, despite all their talent, the public turns against them when it becomes known that they are old.

Considering the fine sincerity with which she had let me see her weakness a very good omen, I had no doubt that she would be kind enough to accept my fond addresses and not make me languish long. She showed me over her whole house, and seeing her lodged with the greatest elegance in every respect, I asked her if she had a particular friend, and she replied with a smile that everyone in Berlin believed that she had, but that everyone was wrong about the principal characteristic of the friend she had, for his relation to her was more that of a father than of a lover.

"Yet you deserve a real lover, and I think it impossible that you can do without one."

"I assure you that I do not give it a thought. I am subject to convulsions, which are the bane of my life.

I wanted to go to the baths at Teplitz,[19] where I am assured that I should be cured of them, and the King refused me permission; but I shall have it next year."

She saw that I was ardent, and thinking that I saw her pleased by my restraint, I asked her if she would take it amiss if I visited her frequently. She replied with a laugh that, if I did not mind, she would say she was my niece or my cousin. At that I said to her, without laughter, that it could be true, and that she was perhaps my sister. The arguments for this probability leading us to speak of the fondness which her father had always felt for my mother, we proceeded to caresses which, between relatives, have never been suspect. I took my leave when I felt that I was about to carry them too far. Showing me to the stairs, she asked me if I would dine with her on the next day. I accepted.

Returning to my inn on fire, I reflected on the concatenation of events, and at the end of my reflections I thought that I paid my debt to Eternal Providence by admitting to myself that I was born fortunate.

When I arrived at La Denis's the next day, all the people she had invited to dinner were already there. The first who fell on my neck to embrace me was a young dancer named Aubry,[20] whom I had known in Paris as a member of the *corps de ballet* at the Opéra, then at Venice as leading serious dancer and famous for having become the lover of a most illustrious lady and at the same time the paramour of her husband, who otherwise would not have forgiven his wife for setting up as his rival. Aubry played against the two of them, and he had so shown his mettle that he slept between the husband and the wife. At the beginning of Lent the State Inquisitors sent him to Trieste. Ten years later I find him at La Denis's, where he introduces his wife to me, also a dancer, and known as La Santina,[21] whom he had married in Petersburg, whence they were on their way to spend the winter in Paris. After Aubry's compliments I

see approaching me a fat man who says that we were
friends twenty-five years before, but that we were so
young that we could not recognize each other.

"We knew each other in Padua," he said, "at Doctor
Gozzi's, and I am Giuseppe dall'Oglio." [22]

"I remember. You were engaged for the service of
the Empress of Russia[23] as a very accomplished violoncellist."

"Exactly so. I am now on my way back to my country,
not to leave it again; and this is my wife, whom I introduce to you. She was born in Petersburg, and she is the
only daughter of the famous violin teacher Madonis.[24]
In a week I shall be in Dresden, where I look forward
with particular pleasure to embracing Signora Casanova,
your mother.[25]

I was delighted to find myself in this choice company,
but I saw that recollections twenty-five years old were
displeasing to my charming Madame Denis. I turned
the conversation to the events in Petersburg which had
raised the great Catherine to the throne, and Dall'Oglio
told us that, having taken some part in the conspiracy,[26]
he had prudently decided to ask permission to resign his
post; but that he had become rich enough to be able to
spend all the rest of his life in his native country without
needing anyone.

La Denis then told us that only ten or twelve days
earlier she had been made acquainted with a Piedmontese
named Odart,[27] who had also left Petersburg after having directed the entire conspiracy. The reigning Empress
had ordered him to leave, making him a present of a
hundred thousand rubles.[28]

He had bought an estate in Piedmont, thinking that
he should live a long life there in peace and prosperity,
for he was only forty-five years old; but he chose the
wrong place. Two or three years later a thunderbolt
entered his room and killed him in an instant. If the
blow fell on him from an all-powerful and invisible
hand, it was not that of the Guardian Genius of the

Russian Empire seeking to avenge the death of the Emperor Peter III, for if that unhappy monarch had lived and reigned he would have been the cause of countless misfortunes.

Catherine, his wife, recompensing them generously, sent away all the foreigners who helped her to rid herself of a husband [29] who was her enemy, and the enemy of her son[30] and of the whole Russian nation; and she showed her gratitude to all the Russians who had helped her to ascend the throne. She sent on their travels all the noblemen who had reasons not to like the revolution.

It was Dall'Oglio and his pretty wife who made me think of going to Russia if the King of Prussia did not give me such employment as I wanted. They assured me that I should make my fortune there, and they gave me excellent letters.

After they left Berlin I became La Denis's lover. Our intimacy began one evening after supper when she was seized by a fit of convulsions which lasted all night. I spent it at her bedside, and the next morning I received the recompense rightly due to constancy. Our amorous relation continued until I left Berlin. Six years later I renewed it in Florence, and I will speak of it when I come to that time.

A few days after Dall'Oglio left, she was kind enough to take me to Potsdam to show me everything worth seeing there. No one could find anything to object to in our intimacy, for she had already told the world in general that I was her uncle, and I always called her my dear niece. Her protector the General [31] had no doubt that she was such, or pretended not to doubt it.

At Potsdam we saw the King parading his First Battalion, every soldier of which had a gold watch in the fob of his breeches. It was thus that the King rewarded the courage with which they had subjugated him as Caesar subjugated Nicomedes[32] in Bithynia. No secret was made of it.

The room in which we slept at the inn where we put

up faced a corridor through which the King passed
when he left the palace. The window blinds being closed,
our hostess told us the reason for it. She said that La
Reggiana,[33] a very pretty dancer, stayed in the same
room in which we were, and that the King having seen
her stark naked as he went by one morning had immediately ordered her windows shut; that had been four
years earlier, but they had never been opened again.
He was afraid of her charms. His Majesty, after his
amour with La Barberina,[34] became entirely negative.
Later we saw in the room in which the King slept portraits of La Barberina, of La Cochois,[35] sister of the
actress whom the Marquis d'Argens[36] married, of the
Empress Maria Theresa before her marriage, with whom
his desire to be Emperor had made him fall in love.

After admiring the beauty and elegance of the apartments in the palace, it was surprising to see how he himself was lodged. We saw a small bed behind a screen in
one corner of the room. No dressing gown and no slippers; the valet who was there showed us a nightcap
which the King put on when he had a cold; usually he
kept on his hat, which must have been awkward. In the
same room I saw a table in front of a sofa, on which
were writing materials and some half-burned notebooks;[37]
he told us that it was the history of the last war, and
that the accident which had set fire to the notebooks had
so annoyed His Majesty that he had abandoned the work.
But he must have taken it up again later, for after his
death it was published,[38] and it was little esteemed.

Five or six weeks after my brief conversation with the
famous monarch, the Earl Marischal told me that the
King offered me a post as tutor to a new corps of noble
Pomeranian cadets[39] which he had just established. Their
number being set at fifteen, he wanted to give them five
tutors; thus each tutor would have three of them, and
would have a salary of six hundred crowns and board
with his pupils. The fortunate tutor thus needed the six
hundred crowns only for clothing. His only duty would

be to accompany them everywhere, and to Court too on
gala occasions, wearing a gold-laced coat. I must make
up my mind as quickly as possible, for four were already
appointed, and the King did not like to wait. I asked
His Lordship where the academy was, so that I could go
to see the place, and I promised him a reply no later
than the next day but one.

I needed a self-possession which was not in my nature
to keep from laughing at this absurd proposal from a
man in other respects so intelligent. But my surprise was
still greater when I saw the quarters of these fifteen
gentlemen from prosperous Pomerania. I saw three or
four drawing rooms almost without furniture, a number
of rooms in which there was nothing but a wretched bed,
a table, and two wooden chairs, and the young cadets,
all twelve or thirteen years of age, ill combed, ill dressed
in uniforms, and all with the countenances of peasants.
I saw them cheek by jowl with their tutors, whom I took
to be their valets, and who looked at me closely, not
daring to imagine that I was the colleague whom they
expected. Just as I was thinking of leaving, one of the
tutors puts his head out a window and says:

"The King is arriving on horseback."

His Majesty comes upstairs with his friend Q. Icilius[40]
and goes to inspect everything. He sees me, and he says
not a word to me. I had the glittering cross of my order
on a ribbon around my neck[41] and an elegant taffeta
coat. I was dumfounded when I saw the great Frederick
in a sort of fury looking at a chamber pot which was near
a cadet's bed and which displayed to the curious eye the
tartarous sediment which must have made it stink.

"Whose bed is this?" said the King.

"Mine," replied a cadet.

"Very good, but it is not you I am angry with. Where
is your tutor?"

The fortunate tutor thereupon presented himself, and
the monarch, addressing him as "clodhopper," gave him
a thorough dressing down. The only consideration he

showed him was to tell him he had a servant at his orders, and that it was his duty to see that the place was kept clean.

After watching this cruel scene, I slipped away, and I went to the Earl Marischal's, impatient to thank him for the brilliant lot which Heaven was offering me through his agency. He could not but laugh when I told him the whole thing in detail, and say that I was right to scorn such a post; but he said at the same time that I must go to thank the King before I left Berlin. However, he undertook to tell His Majesty that I had found the post unsuitable. I told His Lordship that I was thinking of going to Russia; and I began in earnest making my arrangements for the journey. Baron Treyden encouraged me in the enterprise, promising to recommend me to his sister the Duchess of Kurland, and I at once wrote to Signor Bragadin to get me an introduction to a banker in Petersburg who would pay me the monthly sum I needed to live there in comfort.

Propriety demanded that I go there with a servant, Fortune presented me with one when I was at a loss to find him. A youth from Lorraine came to La Rufin's carrying all his possessions under his arm. He told her that his name was Lambert,[42] that he had just arrived in Berlin, and that he wanted to lodge at her inn.

"Certainly, Monsieur, but you must pay me from day to day."

"Madame, I haven't a copper; but I shall have money from home when I write them where I am."

"Monsieur, I cannot put you up."

Seeing him leaving with a mortified air, I told him that I would pay for him for that day, and I asked him what he had in his bag.

"Two shirts," he replied, "and a score of books on mathematics."

I took him to my room, and finding him fairly well educated, I asked him what chance had brought him to the condition he was in.

Visitors to a Sick Gentleman

*Library of the Duke of Brunswick
in Wolfenbüttel*

"At Strassburg," he said, "a cadet from such-and-such a regiment slapped my face in a coffeehouse. The next day I went to him in his room and I killed him on the spot. I at once went back to the room in which I was lodging, I put my books and some shirts in this bag, and I left the city with only two louis and a passport in my pocket. Always traveling on foot, my money lasted me until this morning. Tomorrow I shall write to Lunéville, where my mother is, and I am sure that she will send me money. I intend to ask for a post in the Engineers Corps here, for I think I know enough to make myself useful, and if worst comes to worst I will turn soldier."

I told him that I would have him given a servant's room and money for food until he received the help he expected from his mother. He kissed my hand.

I did not think him an impostor, for he stammered; nevertheless, I at once wrote to Baron von Schaumburg[43] in Strassburg to find out if what he had told me was true.

The next day I talked with an officer of the Engineers Corps, who told me that he had so many well-educated young men in the regiment that no more were taken unless they were content to serve as common soldiers. I thought it a pity that the youth should have to resign himself to this step. I began spending hours with him, compass and ruler in hand, and, finding him well taught, I thought of taking him to Petersburg with me, and I told him so. He replied that I would be his good angel, and that he would serve me during the journey in any capacity I wished. He spoke French badly, but since he came from Lorraine I was not surprised; what did surprise me was that not only did he not know even the rudiments of Latin, but, writing a letter at my dictation, he misspelled every word. Seeing me laugh, he showed no shame. He said that he had gone to school only to learn geometry and mathematics, being very glad that the boring subject of grammar had nothing to do with the sciences. But, skilled in analysis though he was, the fellow was extremely ignorant in all the other branches of knowledge. He knew nothing of society, and in his manners and his bearing he was in no way different from a real peasant.

Ten or twelve days later Baron von Schaumburg wrote me from Strassburg that no one knew Lambert and that there had not been a cadet in his regiment, the name of which I gave him, who had been killed or wounded. When I showed him the letter to reproach him with his lie, he said that, wanting to enter the military service, he had thought he must prove that he was brave, and that I must excuse him, as I must for his telling me that his mother would send him money. He expected money from no one, and he assured me that he would serve me faithfully and that he would never lie. I laughed, and I told him that we should leave in five or six days.

I went to Potsdam with Baron Bodissoni,[44] of Venice, who wanted to sell the King a painting by Andrea del Sarto,[45] intending to let the King see me too, as the Earl Marischal had advised me to do.

I saw him at the parade, on foot. No sooner did he see me than he came to me and asked me when I expected to leave for Petersburg.

"In five or six days, Sire, if Your Majesty gives me permission."

"A good journey to you. But what do you hope for in that country?"

"What I hoped for here, Sire—to please its ruler."

"Have you a recommendation to the Empress?"

"No, Sire, I have only one to a banker."

"That is really worth much more. If you come this way on your return, I shall be glad to have you tell me news of that country. Good-by."

Such are the two conversations I had with that great King, whom I did not see again. After taking leave of all my acquaintances, and receiving from Baron Treyden a letter to Baron Keyserling,[46] Grand Chancellor at Mitau, which enclosed one to Her Highness the Duchess,

I spent the last evening with my sweet Denis, who bought my post chaise. I left with two hundred ducats in my pocket, which would have sufficed me for the rest of my journey, if I had not lost half of them at Danzig at a party with young merchants. This little misfortune prevented me from spending several days at Königsberg, where I had a letter of recommendation to Field Marshal Lehwald,[47] who was its Commandant. I stayed there only one day, to have the honor of dining with the amiable old man, who gave me a letter to General Voeikov[48] at Riga.

Having money enough to arrive in Mitau like a nobleman, I engaged a four-seated carriage and six horses, and in three days I arrived at Memel, with Lambert, who slept through the whole journey. At the inn I found a Florentine *virtuosa* named Bregonzi,[49] who treated me to countless caresses, saying that I had loved her when I was still a boy and an abate. She told me circumstances which showed me that the thing was decidedly possible, but I could never remember her face. I saw her again six years later in Florence when I saw La Denis, who was lodging in her house.

About noon on the day after I left Memel a man who was all by himself in the open country, and whom I at once saw was a Jew, came to tell me that I was on a strip of territory belonging to Poland and that I must pay a certain duty on any merchandise I might have; I tell him that I have no merchandise, and he replies that he must search me. I tell him he is mad, and I order my coachman to drive on. The Jew goes to the horses' reins, the coachman does not dare get rid of the scoundrel with his whip, I get out with my cane and my pistol in hand, and after receiving a few blows he leaves me, but during the affray my traveling companion did not even trouble to get out of the carriage. He told me that he did not want the Jew to be able to say that we were two against one.

I arrived in Mitau[50] two days after this encounter, and I went to lodge opposite the palace.[51] There were only three ducats left in my purse.

The next morning at nine o'clock I called on Baron Keyserling, who had scarcely read Baron Treyden's letter before he introduced me to the Baroness his wife and left me with her to take Her Highness the Duchess her brother's letter.

Madame Keyserling had me served a cup of chocolate by a Polish maid whose beauty was dazzling. She stood before me, saucer in hand, with her eyes cast down, as if she wanted to leave me free to examine her rare beauty. At that time I was overtaken by a whim which I could not resist. I adroitly take from my pocket my three solitary ducats, and, putting my cup back on the saucer, I put the three ducats there with it, and I talk to the Baroness in reply to the questions she had asked me about Berlin.

A half hour later the Chancellor came back to tell me that the Duchess could not receive me at once, but that she invited me to supper followed by a ball. I at once excuse myself from attending the ball, saying, as was the fact, that I had only summer attire and a black coat. It was the beginning of October, and the weather was cold. The Chancellor went back to Court, and I went back to my inn.

A half hour later a chamberlain came to bring me Her Highness's compliments and to say that the ball would be masked, and so I could go to it in a domino. One could be got from the Jews.

"The ball," he said, "was to have been in evening dress; but Court messengers were sent to tell all the nobility that it would be masked because a foreigner who was passing through Mitau had sent his trunks on ahead."

I replied that I was sorry to have been the cause of the change; but he assured me that, on the contrary, a masked ball was freer and more to the taste of the Duchy. After telling me the hour he left.

Prussian money not passing current in Russia, a Jew came to ask me if I had any Friedrichsthaler,[52] offering to exchange them for ducats without any loss to me. I replied that I had only ducats, and he said that he knew it and even that I gave them very cheaply. As I did not understand what he meant, he said that he would give me two hundred ducats if I would have him repaid them in rubles at Petersburg. A little surprised to find him so easygoing, I said that I would take only a hundred, and he paid them over to me on the spot. I gave him an assignment on the banker Demetrio Papanelopulo,[53] for whom Dall'Oglio had given me a letter. He thanked me, and he left, saying that he would send me some dominoes. Lambert followed him to order some stockings from him. He told me a moment later that he had told the innkeeper that I threw ducats out the window, having given three to one of Baroness Keyserling's chambermaids.

So it is that nothing in the world is easy or difficult except as the result of how one goes about it, and also according to the whims of Fortune. I should not have found a copper in Mitau had it not been for my piece of bravado with the three ducats. It was a wonder, which the girl must have at once made known, and the Jew, to profit by the exchange, at once came running to offer ducats to the magnificent nobleman who thought so little of them.

I had myself carried to Court at the appointed hour, where Baron Keyserling at once presented me to the Duchess, and she to the Duke, who was the celebrated Biron,[54] or Birhen, who had been the favorite of the Empress Anna Ivanovna and the Regent of Russia after her death, then was sentenced to live in Siberia for twenty years. He was six feet tall, and one saw that he had been handsome; but age makes beauty disappear. On the next day but one I had a long conversation with him.

A quarter of an hour after my arrival the ball began with a polonaise. Since I was a foreigner, the Duchess thought it her part to grant me the honor of dancing with her. I did not know the dance; but it is so easy that everyone knows it without having had to learn it. It is simply a procession composed of a number of couples, the first of which has the privilege of directing the turns to right or left. Despite the uniformity of the steps and gestures, the dance helps the couples to display their grace. It is the most majestic and the simplest of all dances in which all the persons present at a ball can show themselves.

After the polonaise there were minuets, and a lady who was rather old than young asked me if I knew how to dance the "Amiable Conqueror." [55] I said that I did, not at all surprised by the lady's wish, for she might well have shone in it in her youth. It had not been danced since the days of the Regency.[56] The younger women thought it wonderful.

After an elaborate contradance, through which I escorted Mademoiselle de Manteuffel,[57] the prettiest of the Duchess's four ladies in waiting,[58] she sent me word that supper had been served. So I went to offer her my arm, and I found myself seated beside her at a table laid for twelve, at which I was the only man. The other eleven were all old dowagers. I was surprised that in the small city of Mitau there were so many matrons of that age among the nobility. The Duchess did me the honor constantly to address me, and at the end of the supper she offered me a glass of what I thought was Tokay; but it was only old English beer. I praised it. We went back to the ballroom.

The same young chamberlain who had invited me to the ball introduced me to all the noble ladies of the city; but I did not have time to pay court to any of them.

The next day I dined at Baron Keyserling's, and I turned Lambert over to a Jew to be properly dressed.

The following day I was invited to dine at Court with the Duke, where I saw only men. The old prince kept me talking. The conversation toward the end of dinner having turned to the resources of the country, which consist only in mines and in semimetals, I made bold to say that such resources, being dependent upon exploitation, became precarious, and to justify my assertion I talked on the subject as if I had known it perfectly both in theory and in practice. An old chamberlain who had charge of all the mines in Kurland and Zemgale,[59] after letting me say all that enthusiasm brought to my mind, himself discoursed on the subject to make some objections but at the same time to approve all the plausible things I had found to say concerning the considerations of economy on which the whole utility of the exploitation depended.

If I had known when I began speaking as an expert that I was being heard by a true expert, I should certainly have said far less, for I was extremely ignorant on the subject; but I should have lost by it, for I should not have made the impression I did. It was the Duke himself who was pleased to think that I knew a great deal.

After dinner he took me to his study, where he asked me to give him two weeks if I was not in a great hurry to reach Petersburg. On my declaring myself at his orders, he said that the same chamberlain who had spoken to me would take me to see all the establishments he had in his duchies, where I would be so good as to write down all my observations on the economy with which they were conducted. I at once consented, and it was arranged that I should leave the next day. The Duke, very much pleased by my readiness to satisfy his wish, at once sent for the chamberlain, who promised to be at the door of my inn at dawn with a carriage and six.

No sooner had I got home than I packed, and I ordered Lambert to be ready to leave with me with his case of mathematical instruments, and when I told him what was afoot he assured me that, though he was not acquainted with the science in question, he would be glad to put all his knowledge at my disposal.

We left at the hour appointed, three in the carriage, with a manservant up behind and two others preceding us on horseback, armed with saber and musket. Every two or three hours we came to some place where we changed horses; and we refreshed ourselves by eating something and drinking good wine from the Rhine or from France, of which we had an abundant supply in the carriage.

In our tour, which continued for two weeks, we stopped at five places where there were establishments for workers in copper mines or iron mines. In order to write something everywhere, I did not need to be an expert, but only to reason soundly, principally on the economical conduct of the operation, which was what the Duke had principally urged upon me. In one place I corrected what I found useless, and in another I prescribed an increase in the working force in order to increase the revenue. At one of the principal mines, where thirty workmen were employed, I prescribed a channel leading from a small river which, though very short, because of its incline should, on the opening of a sluice gate, turn three wheels which would enable the director of the mine to dispense with twenty men; and under my guidance Lambert produced a perfect plan of the installation, measured the altitudes, drew the sluice gate and the wheels, and himself set out the markers indicating the elevations of the terrain along the channel on either side to its termination. By means of other channels I drained whole valleys in order to recover greater quantities of the sulphurs and vitriols with which the terrains which we examined were impregnated.

I returned to Mitau delighted not to have practiced any imposture but to have reasoned and discovered in myself a talent I had not known that I possessed. I spent the whole of the next day putting my observations in final form, and having the drawings which I annexed to them copied on a larger scale.

The day after that I went to present the Duke with all my observations, for which he showed himself extremely grateful, and at the same time I took my leave of him, thanking him for the honor he had done me. He said that he would have me driven to Riga in one of his carriages, and that he would give me a letter for Prince Charles,[60] his son, who was in garrison there. The wise old man, ripe in experience, asked me if I would rather have a jewel or its value in money. I replied that from such a prince as he I preferred to receive money, though the honor of kissing his hand was enough for me. At that he gave me a note ordering his cashier to pay me at sight four hundred albertsthaler.[61] I received them in Dutch ducats, struck at the mint in Mitau. The albertsthaler is worth half a ducat. I went to kiss Her Highness the Duchess's hand, and I dined for the second time with Baron Keyserling.

The next morning the young chamberlain whom I knew brought me the Duke's letter to his son and wished me a good journey, saying that the Court carriage which was to take me to Riga was at the door of the inn. I left well satisfied, with the stammering Lambert, and, after changing horses halfway through the journey, I was at Riga at noon, where I at once sent the Duke's letter to his son, Major-General in the Russian service, Chamberlain, and Chevalier of Alexander Nevski.[62]

CHAPTER V[1]

My stay in Riga. Campioni. Sainte-Hélène.
D'Aragon. Arrival of the Empress. Departure
from Riga and my arrival in Petersburg. I go
everywhere. I buy Zaïre.

PRINCE CHARLES DE BIRON, youngest
son of the reigning Duke, Major-General in the Russian
service, Chevalier of Alexander Nevsky, informed in advance by his father, received me very well. Thirty-six
years of age, with a pleasant though not handsome face,
polite without stiffness, speaking French well, he told me
in a few words all that I could expect from him if I
thought of staying in Riga for some time. His table, his
friends, his pleasures, his advice, and his purse were what
he offered me; no lodging, for his own was cramped; but
he at once found me fairly comfortable quarters; he
called on me at once, and he made me come to dinner
with him at once, just as I was. The first person who
struck me was Campioni,[2] the dancer, of whom, my
reader may remember, I have spoken two or three times
in these memoirs. Campioni was a man above his profession. He was made for good society, polished, obliging,
a libertine, without prejudices, fond of women, of good
food, of high play, prudent, discreet, and living with

equanimity both when Fortune favored him and when she turned against him. We were both delighted to find each other there. Another guest was a Baron de Sainte-Hélène,[3] of Savoy, with his young wife, who, though not ugly, was insignificant. The Baron, portly and fat, was a gamester, a trencherman, a heavy drinker, who possessed the art of getting into debt and persuading his creditors to wait. It was his only talent, for in all other respects he was extremely stupid. Another guest was an Adjutant of the Prince's, who was his familiar spirit. A young lady twenty years of age, pretty, tall, and thin, dined at his side; she was his mistress.[4] Very pale, melancholy, abstracted, eating almost nothing because, she maintained, everything was bad; in addition, she said she was ill. Her face was the very picture of discontent. The Prince from time to time tried to induce her to laugh, to cheer up, to drink some wine; she refused everything with disdain and even with resentment; whereupon the Prince made fun of her and laughingly told her that she was being ridiculous. Nevertheless we spent an hour and a half at table gaily enough. After dinner the Prince had business, and, after telling me that, in default of anything better, his table should be mine morning and evening, he left me in the care of Campioni.

This old friend, my fellow countryman, saw me to my lodging and, before showing me Riga, took me to his house to make me acquainted with his wife and his whole family. I did not know that he had married again. I found his supposed wife to be a very agreeable Englishwoman, thin, and full of wit; but she did not interest me as much as his daughter, who was only eleven years old, but who was as intelligent as if she had been eighteen; in addition, she was pretty, she danced well, and she accompanied herself on the mandolin in little airs. This unripe girl, a little too affectionate, at once conquered me, her father congratulated her, but her mother mortified her by calling her a pissabed—a deadly insult for a girl of precocious intelligence.

In the course of our walk Campioni brought me up to date on everything, beginning with himself.

"I have been living with this woman for ten years," he said. "Betty, whom you think charming, is not my daughter; the others are. I left Petersburg two years ago, and I live well here from a dancing school which I keep, at which I have pupils of both sexes who do me honor. I gamble at the Prince's, where I sometimes win and sometimes lose, without ever having been able to win enough to pay a creditor who persecutes me because of a bill of exchange I issued in Petersburg. He can put me in prison, and I expect it every day. The bill is for five hundred rubles. He will not accept payments on account. I am waiting for the big freeze, and then I will find a way to escape by myself, and I will go to Poland, from where I will send my wife money enough to live on. The Baron de Sainte-Hélène will escape too, for he holds out against his creditors only by his eloquence. The Prince, whom we go to see every day, is very useful to us, for at his house we can play; but if some calamity befell us from which we could be saved by money alone, he could not help us, for, riddled with debts as he is, he has no money, and the daily expense he has to meet is too large in comparison with his revenue. He plays, and he always loses. His mistress costs him a great deal, and she makes him wretched with her ill-humor, for she demands that he keep his word to her. He promised to marry her after two years, and on that condition she let him give her two children. She will have nothing to do with him now, for she fears he will give her a third. So she is a constant annoyance to him, and you will never see her anything but very peevish, as you saw her today. He found her a lieutenant who would be ready to marry her, but she wants at least a major."

The next day at dinner the Prince had as guests the Commanding General, Voeikov,[5] for whom I had a letter from Marshal Lehwald,[6] Baroness Korff,[7] of Mitau, Madame Evtinov,[8] and a beautiful young lady who was to marry the Baron Budberg[9] whom I had known at Florence, Turin, Augsburg, and Strassburg, and whom I may have forgotten to mention. All these acquaintances made me spend three weeks very agreeably, during which I was particularly delighted by General Voeikov, who had been in Venice fifty years earlier, when the Russians were called Muscovites and the creator of Petersburg[10] was still alive. He made me laugh by his praise of the Venetians of those days, whom he supposed to be the same at the time he was talking to me.

It was from the English merchant Collins[11] that I had the news that the self-styled Baron Henau,[12] who had given me the forged bill of exchange in London, had been hanged in Portugal. He was a Livonian, the son of a poor shopkeeper and employed as a clerk in his business.

At that time a Russian, who had been in Poland on a mission from his Court, having to return to Petersburg, had the misfortune to stop at Riga, where he lost twenty thousand rubles on his word at faro at the Prince of Kurland's. The dealer was Campioni. The Russian signed bills of exchange in payment for the amount; but as soon as he was in Petersburg he went to the Tribunal of Commerce[13] to protest his own bills, declaring them null and void, in consequence of which not only were the winners defrauded of the large sum on which they were counting, but play was forbidden under strict penalties even in the houses of general staff officers. The Russian who committed this base act was the same man who betrayed Elizabeth Petrovna's[14] confidence, when she was making war on the King of Prussia, by informing her nephew Peter, proclaimed successor to the throne, of all the orders which she sent to her generals. Peter in turn passed all the information on to the King of Prussia, whom he worshiped.[15] On Elizabeth's death Peter III made him Chief Judge of the Tribunal of Commerce, announcing with the most shameless lack of discretion of what nature his obligations to him were. The faithless

Minister did not consider that it dishonored him. Campioni was the dealer, but it was the Prince who had made the bank; I had a ten per cent interest in it, which was to be paid to me when the Russian honored the first of his bills of exchange; but when I said to the Prince at table that I did not believe the Russian would pay, and that I would gladly sell my share for a hundred rubles, the Prince took me at my word and paid me; so I was the only one to profit from the game.

At this same time[16] the Empress Catherine II, wanting to see the states of which she had become the ruler, and also to let herself be seen, passed through Riga on her way to Warsaw, where she had gained the preponderant influence by putting her old acquaintance Stanislaus Poniatowski[17] on the throne. It was at Riga that I saw that great princess for the first time. I witnessed the affability and the smiling sweetness with which she received the Livonian nobility in a great room, and the kisses on the lips which she gave to all the noble young ladies who came to kiss her hand. Those who surrounded her were the Orlovs[18] and the three or four others who had been at the head of the conspiracy. To amuse her faithful servants she told them most graciously that she would make them a small faro bank of ten thousand rubles. The sum, in gold, was immediately brought, together with cards. Catherine sat down, took a pack, pretended to shuffle, held it out for anyone to cut, and she had the pleasure of seeing her bank broken on the first deal. It could not be otherwise unless the punters were fools, for, the pack not having been shuffled, one knew what would be the winning card as soon as one had seen the card before it. She left the next morning for Mitau, where she was received under triumphal arches of wood, either because stone was too scarce or because there had not been time to build them so solidly.

But the next day at noon there was general consternation when it became known that a revolution was even then breaking out in Petersburg. There had been an

armed attack on the fortress of Schlüsselburg,[19] in which
he was held, in an attempt to free the unfortunate Ivan
Ivanovich,[20] who had been proclaimed Emperor in his
cradle and whom Elizabeth Petrovna had dethroned. Two
officers who were garrisoned in the fortress and to whom
the illustrious prisoner was entrusted killed the innocent
Emperor to prevent his being carried off, and captured
the bold man[21] who had ventured the great stroke by
which, if he had succeeded, he was sure to have risen
to the highest fortune. The death of the innocent Emperor had created such a sensation in every part of the
city that the prudent Panin,[22] fearing an uprising, at
once sent courier after courier to inform Catherine that
her presence was necessary in the capital. For this reason
she left Mitau twenty-four hours after she arrived there,
and, instead of going to Warsaw, she returned at full
gallop to Petersburg, where she found submission and
tranquility. Policy decreed that she should reward the
murderers of the unfortunate Emperor, and she sentenced to the executioner's ax the man who in his ambition for greatness had tried to bring about her downfall.

Everything that has been said about her having an
understanding with the murderers is pure calumny. Her
soul was strong, but not evil. When I saw her at Riga
she was thirty-five years of age and had reigned for two
years. Though she was not beautiful, whoever examined
her had reason to be pleased, finding her tall, well built,
gentle, easy of access, and above all never perturbed.

At this same time a friend of the Baron de Sainte-
Hélène arrived from Petersburg on his way to Warsaw.
He was the Neapolitan Marchese Dragon, who called
himself D'Aragon,[23] a great gamester, a fine figure of a
man, and with the courage to risk his life, sword in hand,
whenever anyone worth the trouble picked a quarrel with
him. He was leaving Russia because the Orlovs had persuaded the Empress to prohibit games of chance. It was
thought strange that the Orlovs should have had gaming
prohibited, for they lived by nothing else before they

took that other, more dangerous road to fortune; yet there is nothing strange in it. The Orlovs knew that gamesters who have to live by play are necessarily cheats; they were therefore right to obtain the prohibition of an occupation in which one could survive only by trickery. They would not have done it if they had not attained to opulence. On the whole, they were good-hearted. Alexis[24] had acquired the scar on his face in a pothouse. The man who had given it to him with a knife was one from whom the bearer of the scar had won money. As soon as Alexis found himself rich, the first person whose fortune he made was the man who had scarred him.

This Neapolitan Dragon, whose first accomplishment was to win at cards, and whose second was to handle his sword well, having left Copenhagen in the year 1759 with the Baron de Sainte-Hélène, went to Petersburg by way of Stockholm and of Viborg in Ingria.[25] It was still the reign of Elizabeth; nevertheless Peter, Duke of Holstein,[26] designated to be her successor, cut a great figure. Dragon took it into his head to go to the fencing school where that prince often went to amuse himself practicing with the foils. Dragon, with his Neapolitan swordplay, defeated everyone. The Grand Duke Peter took umbrage at the Neapolitan Marchese Dragon who had come to Petersburg to defeat the Russians at fencing. So one morning he took a foil, he defied him to come on, and he beat him hollow for two full hours, at the end of which he left congratulating himself on having been victorious over the Neapolitan who had defeated all the best Russian swordsmen, thus having shown that he was better than all the others.

After the prince was gone Dragon bluntly said that he had let himself be beaten for fear of offending him. This boast, as might be expected, was immediately carried to the Grand Duke, who flew into a rage and swore that he would force him to do whatever he knew how to do, and at the same time he sent a command to the foreigner to be at the fencing school the next day.

Dragon d'Aragon having gone there, the prince, as soon as he saw him, reproached him for what he had said. D'Aragon denied nothing, he said that he had feared to fail in the respect he owed him; but the prince replied that he would have him banished from Petersburg if he did not beat him as he had boasted he could do.

"In that case," replied the Neapolitan, "Your Highness shall be obeyed; you shall not touch me, and I hope that instead of being angry you will grant me your protection."

They spent the whole morning fighting in every possible fashion, and the Grand Duke was never able to touch D'Aragon. The prince at last threw down his foil, made him his fencing master, and gave him a commission as Major in his regiment of Holstein Guards. Soon afterward he asked him for permission to hold a bank at faro at his Court, and three or four years later he found himself in possession of a hundred thousand rubles, which he was taking with him to the Court of the new King Stanislaus, where all games were permitted. When he arrived in Riga Sainte-Hélène presented him to Prince Charles, who asked him to show his mettle the next morning, foil in hand, against himself and two or three of his friends. I was one of them. He beat us all. His diabolical skill having angered me, for I knew that I was excellent, I found myself saying to him that I should not be afraid of him with bare swords. He at once calmed me by saying that with bare swords his style of fighting would be entirely different. The Marchese left the next day and at Warsaw he found sharpers[27] so proficient that, not wasting their time fencing with him, in less than half a year they won all his money.

A week before I left Riga, where I stayed for two months, Campioni departed incognito, helped to escape by the excellent Prince Charles; and three or four days later the Baron de Sainte-Hélène likewise made off from his creditors without taking leave of them. He wrote a note to the Englishman Collins, to whom he owed a thousand crowns, that, as a man of honor, he was leaving his debts where he had made them. I shall speak of these three persons in the course of the next two years. Campioni left me his Schlafwagen,[28] which obliged me to travel to Petersburg with six horses. I left his daughter Betty with great regret, and I maintained a correspondence with her mother during all the time I was in Petersburg. I left Riga on December 15th, in atrociously cold weather, but I did not feel it. Traveling day and night, shut up in my Schlafwagen, which I never left, I arrived there in sixty hours. This speed was due to the fact that at Riga I had paid in advance for all the stages, so that I received a post passport from the Governor of Livonia, who was a Marshal Braun.[29] The journey is about equal to the one from Lyons to Paris, for the French league is about equal to four versts[30] and a quarter. On the coachman's seat I had a French man-servant, who offered me his services as far as Petersburg gratis, asking only for permission to ride in front of my carriage. He served me very well, poorly clad though he was, bearing up under three nights and two days of very severe cold and nevertheless remaining in good health. I did not see him again in Petersburg until three months after my arrival, when, covered with gold braid, he sat beside me at the table of Count Chernichev,[31] as *uchitel* [32] to a young Count who was sitting beside him. I shall have occasion to speak of the office of *uchitel* in Russia. The word means "tutor."

Young Lambert, lying beside me in my Schlafwagen, did nothing but eat, drink, and sleep, without ever saying a word to me, for he could only talk in his stutter about mathematical problems, in which I was not interested at every hour of the day. Never the least attempt at a joke or at an amusing or critical observation on what we saw; he was boring and stupid; which gave him the privilege of never being bored. At Riga, where I presented him to no one because he was not presentable, all he did was to go to a fencing school, where, having picked up an acquaintance with some idlers, he went to a pot-house to get drunk on beer with them; I did not know how he got the small amount of money he needed for it.

During all the short journey from Riga to Petersburg I stopped only a half hour at Narva,[33] where it was neces-sary to show a passport which I did not have. I told the Governor that, being Venetian and traveling only for my pleasure, I had never thought I should need a pass-port, my Republic not being at war with any power and there being no Russian envoy in Venice.[34]

"If Your Excellency nevertheless finds difficulties," I said, "I will go back where I came from; but I will complain to Marshal Braun, who gave me a post pass-port, knowing that I had obtained a passport from no power."

The Governor thought for a little, then he gave me a sort of passport, which I still have, with which I entered Petersburg not only without being asked if I had any other but without my luggage being searched. From Caporya[35] to Petersburg there is nowhere to eat or sleep except in a private house which does not belong to the post. It is a desert in which not even Russian is spoken. It is Ingria, where the people speak a special language[36] which has nothing in common with other languages. The peasants of the province amuse themselves stealing what little they can from travelers who lose sight of their carriages for a moment.

I arrived in Petersburg just when the first rays of the sun were gilding the horizon. As we were exactly at the winter solstice, and I saw the sun appear, at the end of a vast plain, at precisely twenty-four minutes after nine o'clock, I can assure my reader that the longest night in that latitude lasts eighteen hours and three quarters.

I went to lodge in a wide, handsome street called the Millionnaya.[37] At a very reasonable rent I was given two rooms in which I saw not a piece of furniture; but two beds, four chairs, and two small tables were brought at once. I saw immensely big stoves; I thought it would take a great quantity of wood to heat them, but the fact proved to be exactly the contrary; only in Russia is the art of building stoves known, as the art of making cisterns or wells is known only in Venice. When it was summer I examined the inside of a big rectangular stove twelve feet high and six feet wide which was in the corner of a large room; inside it I saw, from the grate where the wood was burned to the top of it, where the pipe began by which the smoke first escaped, to escape afterward through the chimney—I saw, I say, channels[38] all of which led upward in serpentine bends. These stoves keep the room which they heat warm for twenty-four hours by means of the hole at the top, which is at the end of the large pipe and which a servant closes, by pulling a cord, as soon as he is sure that all the smoke from the wood is gone. As soon as he sees, through the small window at the bottom of the stove, that all the wood has become embers, he shuts in the heat above and below. Very rarely is a stove heated twice a day, except in the houses of great noblemen, where the servants are forbidden to shut the stoves at the top. The reason for this prohibition is very wise. It is as follows:

If it happens that a master, arriving tired from hunting or a journey and needing to go to bed, orders his servant to heat the stove, and if the servant, either by inadvertence or from haste, shuts the stove before all the smoke is gone, the sleeping man does not wake again. He commits his soul to his creator in three or four hours, moaning and not opening his eyes. Whoever first enters the room in the morning finds the air heavy, stifling, he sees the man dead, he opens the window at the bottom of the stove, a cloud of smoke bursts out of it, he opens the door and the windows, but the man does not revive, he looks in vain for the servant, who has run away, but who is found with astonishing ease and who is hanged without mercy, though he swears that he did not do it on purpose. An excellent policy, for were it not for this wise law, any servant could poison his master with impunity.

After coming to terms both for heat and for food, and finding everything cheap (which is no longer the case, everything there being now as dear as in London),[39] I bought a chest of drawers, and a large table at which I could write and to put my books and papers on.

The language which I found known to everyone in Petersburg, except the common people, was German, which I understood with difficulty but in which I expressed myself about as I do today. Immediately after dinner my landlord told me that there was a masked ball at Court, gratis, for five thousand people. The ball went on for sixty hours. It was a Saturday. The landlord gives me a ticket, which was necessary and which the masker had only to show at the entrance to the Imperial Palace.[40] I decide to go to it; I had the domino which I had bought in Mitau. I send for a mask, and chairmen carry me to the Court, where I see a great number of people dancing in several rooms in which there were orchestras. I walk through the rooms, and I see buffets at which all those who were hungry or thirsty were eating and drinking. Everywhere I see joy, freedom, and the great profusion of candles which lighted all the places to which I went. As I should expect, I find it all magnificent, superb, and worthy of admiration. Three or four hours passed very quickly. I hear a masker saying to another near to him:

"There's the Empress, I am sure; she thinks no one can recognize her; but you will see Grigori Grigorievich Orlov[41] *in a moment; he has orders to follow her at a distance; he is wearing a domino not worth ten kopecks,*[42] *like the one you see on her."*

I follow him, and I am convinced of it, for I hear more than a hundred maskers say the same thing as she passes, all of them, however, pretending not to recognize her. Those who did not know her bumped against her in making their way through the crowd, and I imagined the pleasure she must take in the assurance it gave her that she was not recognized. I often saw her sit down among people who were conversing in Russian, and who were perhaps talking of her. In so doing she exposed herself to unpleasantness, but she had the rare satisfaction of hearing some truths, which she could never flatter herself that she heard spoken by those who were paying court to her without masks. At a distance from her I saw the masker who had been given the name of Orlov, though he never lost sight of her; but in his case everyone recognized him because of his great stature and the way he always kept his head bent forward.

I enter a room in which I see a contradance in the form of a quadrille, and I am pleased to find it being danced perfectly in the French manner; but what takes my attention from it is a man who enters the room alone disguised in the Venetian manner, bautta,[43] black cloak, white mask, cocked hat as in Venice. I feel sure that he is a Venetian, for a foreigner never succeeds in dressing exactly as we do. He comes by chance to watch the contradance beside me. It occurs to me to accost him in French; I say that I had seen many men in Europe disguised in the Venetian manner, but never one so successfully as he, to the point that one would take him for a Venetian.

"I am Venetian."

"Like myself."

"I am not joking."

"Nor am I."

"Then let us speak Venetian."

"Speak, I will answer you."

He then speaks to me, and I see from the word *Sabato,* which means Saturday, that he is not Venetian.

"You are," I say, "a Venetian, but not from the capital, for you would have said *Sabo.*"

"I admit it; and from your language I judge that you may be from the capital. I thought the only Venetian in Petersburg was Bernardi."[44]

"You see that it is possible to be mistaken."

"I am Count Volpati,[45] of Treviso."

"Give me your address and I will call on you and tell you who I am, for I cannot tell you here." [46]

"There it is."

I leave him, and two or three hours later what attracts me is a girl in a domino, who was surrounded by several maskers and who was speaking Parisian in falsetto in the style of the balls at the Opéra.[47] I do not recognize her by her voice, but from her language I am sure that she is someone I know, for there were the same catchwords, the same exclamations, which I had made fashionable in Paris wherever I went at all frequently: "Oh, how agreeable!" "The dear man!" A number of these phrases, which I had originated, arouse my curiosity. I stay there, not addressing her, having the patience to wait until she unmasks to steal a look at her face; and at the end of an hour I am able to do it. She has to blow her nose; whereupon, to my great surprise, I see La Baret,[48] the stocking seller at the corner of the Rue Saint-Honoré, whose wedding party at the Hôtel d'Elbeuf [49] I had attended seven years earlier. What had brought her to Petersburg? My old love reawakens, I approach her, and I say in falsetto that I am her friend from the Hôtel d'Elbeuf.

It stops her short, she does not know what to say to me. I whisper into her ear "Gilbert," "Baret," truths which could be known only to her and to a lover; she begins to become curious, she talks only to me; I talk to her of the Rue des Prouvaires,[50] she sees that I know everything about her, she rises, she leaves the company she was with and comes to walk with me, begging me to tell her who I am when I assure her that I had been her fortunate lover. She begins by asking me to tell no one what I knew about her, she says that she left Paris with Monsieur de Langlade,[51] Councilor of the Parlement of Rouen, that she had left him later for a comic opera impresario[52] who had brought her to Petersburg as an actress, that she called herself Langlade, and that she was being kept by Count Rzewuski,[53] the Polish Ambassador.

"But who are you?"

Certain, by then, that she could not refuse me amorous visits, I showed her my face. Mad with joy as soon as she recognized me, she said that it was her good angel who had brought me to Petersburg, for Rzewuski having to return to Poland, it was only on a man like myself that she could count to enable her to leave Russia, where she could no longer bear to be and where she had to practice a profession for which she felt she was not born, for she could neither act nor sing. She gave me her address and an hour, and I let her pursue her way about the ball, extremely delighted to have made this discovery.

I went to a buffet, where I ate and drank very well, then I returned to the crowd, where I saw La Langlade talking with Volpati. He had seen her with me and he had gone to pump her to find out who I was; but, preserving the secrecy which I had enjoined on her, she had told him I was her husband, and she called to me by that name, saying that the masker refused to believe it was true. The young madcap's confidence was of the sort that is made at a ball. After several hours I was ready to go back to my inn; I took a sedan chair, and I went to bed, intending not to rise until it was time to go to mass. The Catholic church was served by Recollect monks,[54] who wore long beards. After sleeping deeply, I am surprised, when I open my eyes, to see that it is not yet light. I turn over on the other side, I go back to sleep, but I wake again a quarter of an hour later, and I feel sorry for myself because I can only sleep in short naps. When day appears I rise, thinking that I had spent a very bad night; I call, I dress, I send for a hairdresser, and I tell the servant to hurry, for, it being Sunday, I want to go to mass; he replies that it is Monday, that I had spent twenty-seven hours in my bed; I understand, I laugh, and I persuade myself that it is true, for I felt I was dying of hunger. That is the only day which I can say

I really lost[55] in my life. I had myself carried to the
house of Demetrio Papanelopulo, who was the Greek
banker with whom I had a credit of a hundred rubles a
month. I found myself very well received, on Signor
dall'Oglio's[56] recommendation; he invited me to come to
dine with him every day, and he at once paid me the
month which was already due, showing me that he had
honored the draft I had executed in Mitau. He found me
a manservant, for whom he vouched, and a carriage by
the month for eighteen rubles, which came to a little
more than six zecchini. The cheapness of it astonished
me; but it is no longer so today. He insisted that I dine
there that day, and it was at his table that I made the
acquaintance of young Bernardi, the son of the one who
had been poisoned because of suspicions the story of
which it is not for me to tell.[57] The young man was in
Petersburg trying to obtain payment of the sums for
which his late father was the creditor for diamonds which
he had sold to the Empress Elizabeth. He was lodging at
Papanelopulo's, and he ate his meals there, paying him
board. Count Volpati came after dinner and told of the
encounter he had had at the ball with an unknown man
who must be Venetian and who had promised to call on
him. Since he knew me only by name, he supposed it
could only be I as soon as the banker introduced me to
him, and I did not deny it.

The Count was about to leave; he was already in the
Gazette, as was the custom in Russia, where no one was
given a passport until two weeks after the public was
informed that he was about to leave.[58] For this reason
the merchants very easily give credit to foreigners, and
foreigners think twice before they contract debts, for
they can hope for no grace. Bernardi could not wait to
be rid of Count Volpati, who was the lover of a dancer
named La Fusi,[59] with whom he could not hope to accomplish anything until after his departure. This Fusi,
after Volpati left, managed things so well with the
young, inexperienced man in love that she got him to

marry her, which did him the greatest harm in the eyes
of the Empress, who had him paid and would not listen
to those who solicited some post for him. Two years after
I left he died, and I do not know what became of his
widow.

The next day I took a letter to the then Colonel Pyotr
Ivanovich Melissino,[60] now a General in the Artillery.
The letter was from Signora dall'Oglio, whose lover he
had been. He received me very well, he presented me to
his extremely agreeable wife, and he invited me to supper
once and for all. His house was managed in the French
style; there was gaming, and afterward everyone supped
informally. There I met his elder brother,[61] who was
Procurator of the Synod [62] and who was married to a
Princess Dolgoruki; the game played was faro; the company was made up of people who could be relied on
neither to go about complaining of their losses nor boasting of their winnings; thus it was certain that the Government would not find out that the law against gaming
was being broken. The person who kept the bank was a
Baron Lefort, the son of the celebrated one.[63] The one
I saw there was then in disgrace because of a lottery he
had set up in Moscow at the coronation of the Empress,
and for which she herself had provided the funds to
amuse her Court. The lottery having gone bankrupt because of a lack of management, calumny had laid the
disaster to the Baron by raising the suspicion that he was
the guilty party. I played for small stakes, and I won a
few rubles. Supping beside him, I improved the acquaintance, and, seeing him at his own house later, he informed
me of his vicissitudes. Speaking of gaming, I praised the
noble indifference with which Prince xxx had lost a
thousand rubles to him. He laughed, and he told me that
the exalted gamester whose noble disinterest I had admired did not pay.

"But honor?"

"Honor is not lost here on that account. There is a tacit
understanding that a person who loses on his word pays

if he wants to, and if he does not want to that is his privilege. The person who won from him would make himself ridiculous by demanding payment."

"It is a system which entitles the banker to refuse to carry anyone on his word."

"Nor does the gamester take offense at it. He leaves, or he puts pledges on the table. There are young scions of the highest nobility who have learned to cheat and who boast of it; a Matiushkin[64] defies all the foreign sharpers to win from him. He has just obtained leave to travel for three years. He says he is sure he will come back to Russia very rich."

At Melissino's I made the acquaintance of a young officer of the Guards named Zinoviov,[65] a relative of the Orlovs, who introduced me to the English Envoy Macartney,[66] a handsome young man of great intelligence, who had the weakness to fall in love with Mademoiselle Shitrov,[67] one of the Empress's ladies in waiting, and the boldness to get her with child. The Empress considered this English freedom an impertinence, forgave[68] the young lady, who danced very well at the Imperial Theater, and had the Envoy recalled. I met the brother of the lady in waiting, already an officer,[69] a handsome youth of great promise. At the exalted spectacle of a performance at the Court itself, at which I saw Mademoiselle Shitrov dance, I also saw Mademoiselle Sievers dance; she is now Princess N. N.,[70] whom I saw four years ago at Dresden with her daughter, who was very well brought up and clever at drawing. Mademoiselle Sievers enchanted me. I fell in love with her without ever being able to tell her so, for I was never introduced to her. She danced to perfection. The castrato Putini[71] enjoyed her good graces, which he certainly deserved both by his talent and his intelligence. He even lodged at Count Sievers's. It was the castrato Putini who brought to Petersburg the Venetian chapelmaster Galuppi,[72] called Buranello, who arrived there the next year, when I was leaving.

Demetrio Papanelopulo introduced me to the Cabinet
Minister Olsuviev,[73] heavy and fat, full of wit, and the
only man of learning I knew in Petersburg, for he had
not become learned by reading Voltaire but by having
gone to Uppsala to study[74] in his youth. That rare man,
who loved women, wine, and choice viands, invited me
to dine at Locatelli's[75] at Ekaterinhof,[76] an imperial residence which the Empress had given to the old theatrical
impresario for his lifetime. He was astonished when he
saw me; but I was even more so to see that he had become a caterer, for that was what he did at Ekaterinhof,
where, for a ruble a head, without wine, he gave excellent
meals to all who went there. Monsieur Olsuviev introduced me to another Secretary of the Cabinet, Teplov,[77]
who was fond of handsome youths, and whose virtue was
that he had strangled Peter III, who had kept the arsenic
from killing him by drinking lemonade. The person who
introduced me to the third Secretary of the Cabinet,
Yelagin,[78] who had spent twenty years in Siberia, was
the dancer Mécour,[79] his mistress, to whom I had brought
a letter from La Santina,[80] whose acquaintance I had
made when she passed through Berlin. A letter from
Dall'Oglio which I took to Luini,[81] a castrato musician
very skilled in his art, handsome and extremely agreeable, gained me a most cordial reception in his house,
where the table was exquisite. La Colonna,[82] who was first
singer, was his mistress. They lived together to torment
each other. I did not see them in agreement even one
day. It was at his house that I made the acquaintance
of another castrato, well versed in his art and agreeable,
whose name was Millico[83] and who, constantly going to
the house of the Master of the Imperial Hunt, Naryshkin,[84] mentioned me to him so often that the amiable
nobleman, who had some smattering of letters, wanted
to make my acquaintance. He was the husband of the
celebrated Maria Pavlovna.[85] It was at the Master of the
Hunt's magnificent table that I made the acquaintance of
the *kaloyer*[86] Platon,[87] now Archbishop of Novgorod,

then preacher to the Empress. This Russian monk understood Greek, spoke Latin and French, he was intelligent,
he was handsome; it was natural that he should make
his fortune in a country where the nobility have never
condescended to intrigue for ecclesiastical dignities.

I took a letter from Dall'Oglio to Princess Dashkov,[88]
who lived three versts from Petersburg, exiled from the
Court when, after helping the Empress to mount the
throne, she expected to share it with her. Catherine hum-
bled her ambition. I found her dressed in mourning
because of the death of the Prince her husband, who had
died in Warsaw. It was she who spoke of me to Monsieur
Panin[89] and who three days later wrote me a note in
which she said that I could go to see him whenever I
wished. I thought it admirable behavior on the Empress's
part: she had disgraced Princess Dashkov, but she did
not prevent her chief Minister from paying court to her
every evening. I heard from people worthy of credence
that Count Panin was not Princess Dashkov's lover but
her father. The Princess is today the President of the
Academy of Sciences. Its learned members would blush
to have a woman at their head if they had not found her
a Minerva. What is still wanting in Russia is the spectacle
of some celebrated woman commanding its armies.

A thing which I saw[90] with Melissino, and which struck
me, was the ceremony of the blessing of the waters on
the Day of the Epiphany, performed on the Neva covered with five feet of ice. The children are baptized by
immersion, being plunged into the river through a hole
made in the ice. On that particular day, it happened that
the pope who was doing the immersing let the child he
was putting into the water slip from his hands.

"*Drugoi*," he said.

That is, "Give me another one"; but what I found
wonderful was the joy of the father and mother of the
drowned child, who certainly could only have gone to
Paradise, having died at that fortunate moment.

I took the letter from the Florentine Signora Bre-

gonzi,[91] who had given me supper in Memel, to the friend
whom she had assured me I could persuade to be useful
to me. The friend was a Venetian named Signora Roccolino;[92] she had left Venice to sing on the stage in Petersburg, knowing no music and never before having practiced the profession. The Empress, after laughing at her
for her folly, sent her word that there was no position
for her; but what did Signora Vincenza (for so she was
called) do then? She struck up an intimate friendship
with a Frenchwoman, the wife of one Proté,[93] a French
merchant who lodged at the Master of the Hunt's. This
woman, who was in possession of that nobleman's heart,
was at the same time the confidant of his wife Maria
Pavlovna, who, not loving her husband, was delighted
that the Frenchwoman freed her from the obligation of
submitting to her matrimonial duties if he took it into
his head to demand them of her. But La Proté was the
most beautiful woman in Petersburg. In the flower of her
age, to all the graces of gallantry she joined the most
refined taste in dress. No woman could adorn herself as
she did; extremely gay in company, she united all voices
in her favor; when La Proté was mentioned in Petersburg
everyone was jealous of the Master of the Hunt's good
fortune in possessing her. Such was the woman whose
confidant Signora Vincenza had become. She invited to
her house the men who were in love with her and who
were worthy of consideration, and La Proté never failed
to go there. Signora Vincenza did not scruple to accept
the presents which gratitude procured her from one direction or another.

As soon as I saw Signora Vincenza I recognized her;
but, at least twenty years having passed since what had
happened between us had taken place, she showed no
surprise that I had forgotten it, and she took care not
to remind me of it. Her brother, whose name was
Montellato, was the man who, one night when I was
leaving the Ridotto,[94] came to murder me in the Piazza
San Marco, and it was in her house that a plot had been

hatched which would have cost me my life if I had not jumped out the window into the street. She gave me exactly the reception which one gives to a dear fellow countryman, an old friend whom one encounters far from home; she told me her misfortunes in detail, and at the same time she boasted of her courage. She needed no one, she said, and she lived gaily with the most agreeable women in Petersburg.

"I am amazed," she said, "that, dining at the Master of the Hunt Naryshkin's as often as you do, you have not met the beautiful Madame Proté, she is the Master of the Hunt's heart and soul; come and take coffee with me tomorrow, and you will see a prodigy."

I go there, and I find her above praise. Being no longer rich, I use my wit to make an impression on her; I ask her what her name is, she says that it is Proté, I reply that she thereby declares herself to be *"pro me"*; I explain the pun[95] to her; I jest, I tell her stories, I let her know that she has set my soul on fire, I do not despair of coming to be happy in time, and the acquaintance is made. From then on I never went to the Master of the Hunt's without going to her room before and after dinner.

About this time, the Polish Ambassador having returned to Warsaw, I had to break off my liaison with La Langlade, who accepted an advantageous proposal which Count Bryus[96] made her. I then ceased to go to her house. That charming woman died six months later of smallpox. I longed to make progress with La Proté. To that end, I gave a dinner at Locatelli's in Ekaterinhof, to which I invited Luini with La Colonna, a Guards officer named Zinoviov,[97] La Proté, and Signora Vincenza with a violinist who was her lover. The gaiety of the dinner having set the guests on fire, after coffee each cavalier tried to disappear with his lady, profiting by which I began to take possession of the beauty, without, however, coming to the heart of the matter because of an interruption. We all went out to see what Luini, who had gone hunting, would bag in the park; he had brought his guns and his dogs for the purpose. Having left the imperial residence a hundred paces behind with Zinoviov, I point out to him a peasant girl whose beauty was surprising; he sees her, he agrees, we walk toward her, and she runs away to a hut, which she enters; we enter it too, we see her father, her mother, and the whole family, and she herself in a corner of the room, like a rabbit afraid that the dogs it saw would devour it.

Zinoviov—who, parenthetically, is the man who spent twenty years in Madrid as the Empress's envoy—talks to the father in Russian for a long time; I see that the subject is the girl, for her father calls her and I see her come forward obediently and submissively and stand before the two of them. A quarter of an hour later he leaves, and I follow him, after giving the fellow a ruble. Zinoviov tells me that he had asked the father if he would give her into service, and that the father had replied that he would be willing, that he must get a hundred rubles because she still had her maidenhead.

"You see," he said, "that there is nothing to be done."

"What do you mean? Suppose I were willing to give the hundred rubles?"

"Then you would have her in your service, and you would have the right to go to bed with her."

"And if she did not want it?"

"Oh, that never happens. You would have the right to beat her."

"Then suppose that she is willing. I ask you if, after enjoying her and finding her to my liking, I could go on keeping her."

"You become her master, I tell you, and you can even have her arrested if she runs away, unless she gives you back the hundred rubles you paid for her."

"And if I keep her with me, how much a month must I give her?"

"Not a copper. Only food and drink, and letting her

King Frederick II of Prussia

The Dancer Madame Denis

go to the bath every Saturday so that she can go to church on Sunday.''

''And when I leave Petersburg can I make her go with me?''

''Not unless you obtain permission and give security. Though she has become your slave, she is still first of all the slave of the Empress.''

''Excellent. Arrange it for me. I will give the hundred rubles, and I will take her with me, and I assure you I will not treat her as a slave; but I put myself in your hands, for I should not want to be cheated.''

''I will strike the bargain myself, and I assure you that I shall not be cheated. Do you want me to do it at once?''

''No, tomorrow; for I do not want the company to know of it. Tomorrow morning I will come to your house at nine o'clock.''

We all returned to Petersburg together in a phaeton, and the next morning at the appointed hour I was at Zinoviov's, who was delighted to do me this small favor. On our way he said that if I liked, in a few days he would get me together a seraglio of as many girls as I could want. I gave him the hundred rubles.

We arrive at the peasant's hut, the girl being there. Zinoviov explains the matter to him, the peasant thanks St. Nicholas[98] for the good fortune he has sent him, he talks to his daughter, I see her looking at me, and I understand that she says yes. Zinoviov then tells me that I must assure myself that she is a virgin, since in signing the agreement I must state that I had bought her for my service as such. My upbringing made me reluctant to insult her by examining her; but Zinoviov encouraged me, saying that I would be doing her a favor by enabling myself to testify to the fact to her parents. At that I sat down and, taking her between my thighs, I explored her with my hand and found that she was intact; but to tell the truth I would not have called her a liar even if I had found her maidenhead gone. Zinoviov counted out the hundred rubles to the father, who gave them to his daughter, whereupon she put them in her mother's hands, and my manservant and the coachman came in to sign as witnesses to what they did not know. The girl, whom I at once gave the name Zaïre,[99] got into the carriage and drove to Petersburg with us dressed as she was in coarse cloth and without a shift. After thanking Zinoviov I stayed at home for four days, never leaving her until I saw her dressed in the French style, simply but neatly. My martyrdom was not knowing Russian; but it was she who, in less than three months, learned Italian—very badly, but well enough to tell me whatever she wanted to. She began to love me, then to be jealous; once she came very near to killing me, as my reader will see in the next chapter.

CHAPTER VI

Crèvecoeur. Baumbach. Journey to Moscow.
Continuation of my adventures in Petersburg.

ON THE same day that I took Zaïre home with me
I dismissed Lambert. He got drunk every day, I no
longer knew what to do with him. There was no opening
for him except as a common soldier. I obtained a passport for him, and I gave him what money he needed to
return to Berlin. Seven years later in Görz[1] I learned
that he had entered the Austrian service.

Zaïre, having become so pretty by the month of May
that, wanting to go to Moscow, I did not dare to leave
her in Petersburg, I took her with me, dispensing with a
manservant. The pleasure I took in hearing her talk to
me in Venetian was inconceivable.[2] On Saturdays I went
to the Russian baths[3] to bathe with her in company with
thirty or forty other people, both men and women and
all stark naked, who, looking at no one, supposed that no
one looked at them. This lack of modesty had its source
in innocence of intention. I was amazed that no one
looked at Zaïre, who seemed to me the original of the
statue of Psyche which I had seen in the Villa Borghese.[4]

Her breasts were not yet developed, she was in her thirteenth year; nowhere did she show the indubitable imprint of puberty. Snow white as she was, her black hair made her whiteness even more brilliant. But for her accursed jealousy, which was a daily burden to me, and the blind faith she had in what the cards which she consulted every day told her, I should never have left her.

A young Frenchman with a handsome face, whose name was Crèvecoeur[5] and who showed that he had had an upbringing worthy of his birth, arrived in Petersburg with a Parisian girl whom he called La Rivière,[6] young and not ugly, but who had no talent, and no education except that which is acquired by all girls in Paris who offer their charms for sale. The young man came to bring me a letter from Prince Charles of Kurland, who said no more to me than that if I could be of use to the couple he would take it as a favor. He brought me the letter, accompanied by his fair lady, at nine o'clock in the morning, just as I was breakfasting with Zaïre.

"It is for you to tell me," I said, "in what way I can be of use to you."

"By admitting us to your company, by introducing us to your acquaintances."

"As for my company, I am a foreigner, it amounts to very little. I will go to see you, you shall come to me when you like, and I shall find it a pleasure; but I never eat at home. As for my acquaintances, you must see that, as a foreigner, I should go beyond what is permissible if I presented you and Madame. Is she your wife? I shall be asked who you are and what has brought you to Petersburg. What am I to say? I am surprised that Prince Charles did not send you to others."

"I am a gentleman from Lorraine. I came here to amuse myself; Mademoiselle Rivière there is my mistress."

"I cannot imagine to whom I can introduce you on those grounds, and in any case I think that you can see the customs of the country and amuse yourselves without needing anyone. The theaters, the promenades, even the pleasures of the Court are open to all. I imagine that you are not short of money.''

''On the contrary, I have no money, and I expect none from anyone.''

''And I have none left either; and you astonish me. How can you have been so foolish as to come here without money?''

''It is she who says that we need none except from day to day. She made me leave Paris without a copper, and until now she seems to be right. We have managed to live everywhere.''

''Then it is she who has the purse.''

''My purse,'' she said, ''is in the pockets of my friends.''

''I understand, and I see that you must find friends in all the inhabited globe; if I had a purse, for friendship of that kind I would open it to you too. But I am not rich.''

Baumbach,[7] of Hamburg, whom I had known in England, from which he had fled because of debts, had come to Petersburg, where he had had the good fortune to enter the military service; son of a rich merchant, he had a house, servants, and a carriage, he liked prostitutes, good food, and play, he got into debt in all directions. He was ugly, lively, and filled with the spirit of libertinism. He arrives at my lodging just in time to interrupt the conversation I had begun with the strange young woman whose purse on her travels was in her friends' pockets. I introduce Monsieur and Madame, telling him everything except the matter of the purse. Baumbach, in ecstasies over the encounter, makes advances to La Rivière, who receives them in the manner of her trade, and in a quarter of an hour I laugh to see that she was right. Baumbach invites them to dine at his house the next day, and begs them to go with him that very day to Krasni-Kabak,[8] where he will give them an informal dinner; he asks me to be one of the party, and I accept. Zaïre asks me what is afoot, for she does not understand French, and I tell her. She says that since it is to be a party at Krasni-Kabak, she wants to go there too, and I say that she may, for it was pure jealousy and I feared the consequences, which consisted in ill-humor, tears, and fits of despair, which had more than once driven me to beat her; it was the best way to convince her that I loved her. After the beating she became affectionate little by little, and peace was made with the rites of love.

Baumbach, very well pleased, went to attend to some business, promising to return at eleven o'clock, and while Zaïre got dressed, La Rivière treated me to a discourse intended to convince me that so far as knowledge of the world went I was the most ignorant of men. What astonished me was that her lover was not at all ashamed of the role he played. The only excuse he could offer me was that he was in love with the wench; but I could not accept it.

Our party was gay. Baumbach talked only to the adventuress, Zaïre sat on my lap the greater part of the time, Crèvecoeur ate, laughed in season and out of season, and went for a walk; the beauty challenged Baumbach to play quinze[9] for twenty-five rubles, which he lost very gallantly and which he paid her, obtaining nothing in exchange but a kiss. Zaïre, very glad to have been on an excursion during which she feared I would be unfaithful to her, said a thousand amusing things to me about the Frenchwoman's lover, who was not jealous of her. She could not understand how she could bear having him so sure of her.

"But I am sure of you, and yet you love me."

"That is because I have never given you reason to think me a wh. . . ."[10]

The next day I went to Baumbach's alone, being sure that I should find there some young Russian officers, who would have annoyed me too much by flirting with Zaïre in their language. At Baumbach's I found the traveling couple, and the two Lunin brothers,[11] then Lieutenants, now Generals. The younger of the two brothers was blond and pretty as a girl; he had been loved by the Secretary of the Cabinet Teplov,[12] and, like an intelligent youth, he not only defied prejudice, he deliberately set about winning the affection and esteem of all men of position, in whose company he was always to be found, by his caresses. Having supposed the Hamburger Baumbach to have the same inclination which he had found Monsieur Teplov to possess, and not being mistaken, he would have thought it insulting to me not to make me of their company. With this idea in mind he took a place beside me at table, and he lavished such pretty attentions on me during dinner that I really thought he was a girl in men's clothing.

After dinner, when I was sitting before the fire between him and the traveling Frenchwoman, I declared my suspicion to him, but Lunin, jealous of the superiority of his sex, immediately displayed his, and, curious to know if I would remain indifferent to his beauty, he laid hold on me, and thinking himself convinced that he had pleased me, put himself in a position to make himself and me happy. And it would have happened if La Rivière, angry that a youth should infringe on her rights in her presence, had not taken him by the waist and forced him to put off his exploit to a more suitable time.

The struggle made me laugh; but not having been indifferent to it I saw no reason to pretend that I was. I told the wench that she had no right to interfere in our business, which Lunin took to be a declaration in his favor on my part. Lunin displayed all his treasures, even those of his white bosom, and defied the wench to do as much, which she refused, calling us b . . . . . . ; we replied by calling her a wh . . . ,[13] and she left us. The young Russian and I gave each other tokens of the fondest friendship, and we swore that it should be eternal.

The elder Lunin, Crèvecoeur, and Baumbach, who had

gone for a walk, came back at nightfall with two or three friends who easily consoled the Frenchwoman for the poor entertainment we had given her.

Baumbach made a bank at faro, which continued until eleven o'clock, when he had no more money, and we supped. After supper the great orgy began. La Rivière held her own against Baumbach, the elder Lunin, and his friends the two young officers. Crèvecoeur had gone to bed. I and my new friend alone appeared to keep our heads, calmly watching the encounters which quickly succeeded one another, each different from the last, and of which poor Crèvecoeur's mistress always bore the brunt. Offended that she interested us only as spectators, she from time to time vented her spleen against us in the most cruel sarcasms; but we laughed at them. Our attitude was like that of two virtuous old men who look with tolerance on the extravagances of unbridled youth. We parted an hour before dawn.

I arrive at my lodging, I enter my room, and by the purest chance I avoid a bottle which Zaïre has thrown at my head and which would have killed me if it had struck me on the temple. It grazed my face. I see her throw herself down in a fury and beat her head on the floor; I run to her, I seize her, I ask her what is the matter with her, and, convinced that she has gone mad, I think of calling for help. She calms her frenzy, but bursting into tears and calling me "murderer" and "traitor." To convict me of my crime she points to a square of twenty-five cards, in which she makes me read in symbols the whole of the debauch which had kept me out all night. She shows me the wench, the bed, the encounters, and even my sins against nature. I saw nothing; but she imagined that she saw everything.

After letting her say everything necessary to relieve her furious jealousy, I threw her accursed abracadabra into the fire, and, looking at her with eyes in which she could see both my anger and the pity I felt for her, and telling her in so many words that she had very nearly killed me, I declare that we must part for ever on the morrow. I say it was true that I had spent the night at Baumbach's, where there was a wench, but I naturally deny all the excesses she accused me of. After that, needing sleep, I undress, I get into bed, and I go to sleep, despite everything that, lying down beside me, she did to win her pardon and assure me of her repentance.

After five or six hours I am awake, and, seeing her sleeping, I dress, thinking how best to get rid of a girl who, one day or another, might very well kill me in her jealous rages. But how could I carry out my intention when I saw her on her knees before me, despairing and repentant, begging me to forgive her, to take pity on her, and assuring me that in future I should find her as gentle as a lamb? The upshot of it was that, taking her in my arms, I gave her unmistakable tokens of the return of my affection, on condition, which she swore to fulfill, that she would not consult the cards again as long as she lived with me. I had decided to go to Moscow three days after this occurrence, and I filled her with joy by assuring her that I would take her with me. Three things in particular had made the girl love me. The first was that I often took her to Ekaterinhof to see her family, where I always left a ruble; the second was that I had her eat with me when I invited people to dinner; the third was that I had beaten her two or three times when she had tried to keep me from going out.

Strange necessity for a master in Russia: when the occasion arises, he has to beat his servant! Words have no effect; nothing but stirrup leathers produce one. The servant, whose soul is only that of a slave, reflects after the beating, and says: "My master has not dismissed me, he would not have beaten me if he did not love me, so I ought to be attached to him."

Papanelopulo[14] had laughed at me when, at the beginning of my stay in Petersburg, I said to him that, being fond of my Cossack, who spoke French, I wanted to attach him to me by kindness, chastising him only with words when he drank himself senseless on spirits.

"If you do not beat him," he said, "the day will come when he will beat you."

And it happened. One day when I found him so much the worse for drink that he could not wait on me I thought it best to scold him in harsh words, threatening him only by raising my walking stick. As soon as he saw it in the air, he ran at me and seized it; and if I had not instantly knocked him down he would certainly have beaten me. I dismissed him then and there. There is no better servant in the world than the Russian, tireless at work, sleeping on the threshold of the room in which his master sleeps so that he can run to him as soon as he calls, always submissive, bandying no words with him even when he is clearly in the wrong, and incapable of stealing from him; but he becomes a monster or an imbecile when he has drunk a glass of spirits, and it is the vice of all the common people. A coachman exposed to the severest cold, often all night long, at the door of a house where he is keeping watch over his horses, knows no other way of maintaining his resistance than to drink brandy. If he drinks two glasses of it he may fall asleep on the snow, where he sometimes does not wake again. He dies frozen. The misfortune of losing an ear, the whole nose except the bone, a piece of cheek, a lip, frequently occurs if one is not careful. A Russian saw that I was about to lose an ear one day when I arrived at Peterhof [15] in a sleigh, the cold being very dry. He at once rubbed me with a handful of snow until the whole cartilage which I was going to lose came back to life. Asked how he had known that I was in danger, he said that is easy to know, for the part attacked by the cold turns extremely white. What surprised me, and what I still find incredible today, is that the lost part sometimes comes back. Prince Charles of Kurland assured me that he lost his nose one day in Siberia, yet he got it back again the following summer. Several muzhiks[16] assured me of the same phenomenon.

During this time the Empress had a commodious wooden amphitheater built, as large as the whole square in front of her palace, which was built by the Florentine architect Rastrelli.[17] The amphitheater, intended to accommodate a hundred thousand spectators, was the work of the architect Rinaldi,[18] who had been in Petersburg for fifty years and who never wanted to return to his native Rome. In the interior of this edifice Catherine intended to give a tournament for all the valiant cavaliers of her Empire. There were to be four quadrilles, in each of which a hundred warriors, richly clad in the costume of the nation they represented, were to contend, jousting against each other on horseback, for prizes of great value. The whole Empire had been informed of the magnificent festival, which was to be given at the sovereign's expense; and the Princes, Counts, and Barons began to arrive from the most distant cities with their fine horses. Prince Charles of Kurland had written me that he would arrive too. It had been decided that the day on which the festival would take place would be the first day of fair weather; and nothing was more sensible, for a whole fair day without rain or wind or threatening clouds is a very rare phenomenon in Petersburg. In Italy we count on good weather; in Russia they count on bad. I laugh when Russians traveling in Europe talk of their fine climate. It is a fact that during the whole of the year 1765 there was not one fine day in Russia; the irrefutable proof of which is that it was impossible to hold the tournament.[19] The wooden structure of the amphitheater was covered over, and it was held the next year. The horsemen spent the winter in Petersburg; those who did not have money enough to stay went home. One of the latter was Prince Charles of Kurland.

Everything being arranged for my journey to Moscow, I got into my Schlafwagen with Zaïre, with a manservant who spoke Russian and German up behind. For eighty rubles an *izvozchik*[20] contracted to take me to Moscow in six days and seven nights with six horses. It was cheap, and, not taking the post, I could not expect to travel faster, for the journey was seventy-two Russian stages, which made five hundred Italian miles[21] more or less. It seemed to me impossible, but that was his business.

We left when the cannon shot from the citadel told us that day was done; it was toward the end of May, when one no longer sees any night in Petersburg. But for the cannon shot which announces that the sun had sunk below the horizon, none would know it. One can read a letter at midnight there, the moon does not make night lighter. People say it is beautiful, but it annoyed me. This continual day lasts for eight weeks. During that time no one lights candles. It is different in Moscow. Four and a half degrees of latitude less than at Petersburg make a candle always necessary at midnight.

We reached Novgorod in forty-eight hours, where the *izvozchik* allowed us five hours' rest. It was there that I saw something which surprised me. Invited to drink a glass, the coachman looked very gloomy, he told Zaïre that one of his horses would not eat, and he was in despair, for he was sure that, not having eaten, it could not go on. We all go out with him, we enter the stable, and we see the horse listless, motionless, with no appetite. Its master began haranguing it in the gentlest of tones, giving it looks of affection and esteem calculated to inspire the animal with sentiments which would persuade it to eat. After thus haranguing it, he kissed the horse, took its head in his hands and put it in the manger; but it was useless. The man then began to weep, but in such a way that I was dying to laugh, for I saw that he hoped to soften the horse's heart by his tears. After weeping his fill, he again kisses the beast and again puts its head in the manger; but again to no purpose. At that the Russian, in a towering rage at such obstinacy in his beast, swears vengeance. He leads it out of the stable, ties the poor creature to a post, takes a big stick, and beats it with

all his strength for a good quarter of an hour. When he
can go on no longer, he takes it back to the stable, puts its
head in the trough, whereupon the horse eats with ravenous appetite, and the *izvozchik* laughs, jumps up and
down, and cuts a thousand happy capers. My astonishment was extreme. I thought that such a thing could
happen only in Russia, where the stick has such virtue
that it performs miracles. But I have thought that it
would not have happened with a donkey, which stands
up under a beating much more stubbornly than a horse.
I am told that today blows are not as much in fashion in
Russia as they were at that time. The Russians, unfortunately, are beginning to become French.[22] A Russian
officer told me that, from the time of Peter I, who, when
he was displeased, rained blows from his stick on his
Generals, the Lieutenant had to receive his Captain's
blows with submission, the Captain the Major's, the
Major the Lieutenant-Colonel's, the latter the Colonel's,
who in turn had to receive them from the Brigadier-
General. All this has changed today. I learned this at
Riga from General Voeikov,[23] who had been brought up
by the great Peter and who was born before the birth of
Petersburg.[24]

I think I have said nothing about that city, which is
today so celebrated and whose existence I still consider
precarious, when I think of it today. It required a genius
like that of that great man, who amused himself by
giving the lie to Nature, to think of building a city
which was to become the capital of his whole immense
Empire in a place where the terrain cannot be less favorable to the labors of those who doggedly try to make
it fit to hold up the palaces which are every day built
there of stone, at enormous expense. I am told that the
city has reached maturity today, to the glory of the great
Catherine; but in the year 1765 I saw it still in its infancy. Everything seemed to me ruins built on purpose.
The streets were paved in the certainty that they would
have to be repaved six months later. I saw a city which

a man in a hurry must have had built in haste; and in fact the Czar gave birth to it in nine months. But the nine months were its time of coming to birth; the child had perhaps been conceived long before. Contemplating Petersburg, I reflected on the proverb: *Canis faestinans caecos edit catulos* ("A bitch in a hurry bears blind pups") ;[25] but a moment later, admiring the great design, I said, with utmost respect: *Diu parturit leaena sed leonem* ("The lioness is long in giving birth, but she bears a lion").[26] A century from now I prophesy a magnificent Petersburg, but raised at least twelve feet, and then the great palaces will not fall into ruin for lack of piling. The barbarous architecture brought there by the French architects and fit only to build houses for marionettes will be proscribed; and Monsieur Betskoi,[27] a man of intelligence be it said, will no longer exist to give the preference over Rastrelli and Rinaldi to a Delamotte,[28] a Parisian who astonished Petersburg by constructing a four-story house the wonderful thing about which, according to him, was that no one could either see or guess where the staircases were.[29]

We arrived in Moscow as our man had promised us we should do. It was not possible to arrive there more quickly, traveling always with the same horses; but by post one goes there rapidly.

"The Empress Elizabeth," a man who was there said to me, "made the journey in fifty-two hours."

"I can well believe it," said a Russian of the old school, "she issued an ukase in which she prescribed the time, and she would have got there still faster if the time she prescribed had been shorter."

It is a fact that in my day it was not permitted to doubt the infallibility of an ukase; whoever ventured to doubt that an ukase, which means "decree," could be carried out was considered guilty of lèse-majesté. In Petersburg I was crossing a wooden bridge with Melissino, Papanelopulo, and three or four others, when, one of them hearing me criticize the meanness of the bridge, said that it would be built of stone by the day of a certain public function on which the Empress was to cross it.[30] Since it was only three weeks to the day, I said it was impossible; a Russian, looking at me askance, said that it was not to be doubted, for there had been an ukase; I was going to reply, but Papanelopulo pressed my hand and made me a sign to say nothing. In the end the bridge was not built, but that did not put me in the right, for, ten days before the day, the Empress issued a second ukase in which she decreed that it was her good pleasure that the bridge should not be built until the following year.

The Czars of Russia have always used, and still use, the language of despotism in everything. One morning I saw the Empress dressed in men's clothing to go riding. Her Grand Equerry, Prince Repnin,[31] was holding the bridle of the horse she was to mount, when the horse suddenly gave the Grand Equerry such a kick that it broke his ankle. The Empress, with a look of astonishment, ordered the disappearance of the horse and announced that death would be the punishment of anyone who dared in future to bring the offending animal before her eyes. The title which is still given today to all Court posts is a military title, which shows the nature of the government. The Empress's head coachman has the rank of colonel, as does her head cook; the castrato Luini had the rank of Lieutenant-Colonel, and the painter Torelli[32] had only the rank of captain, since he had only eight hundred rubles a year. The sentinels who stand with crossed muskets at the inner doors of the Empress's apartments ask the person who wants to enter what his rank is, to learn if they are to uncross their muskets to let him go in; the word is *Kakoi rang?* ("What rank?") When I was asked this question for the first time, and the meaning was explained to me, I was at a loss; but the officer who was there asked me how much I had a year, and when I answered him that I had three thousand rubles he at once gave me the rank of general, and I was allowed to pass. It was in this room that a moment later

I saw the Empress stop at the door and take off her gloves
to give the two sentinels her beautiful hands to kiss. It
was by this sort of informal behavior that she kept the
affection of this body of guards, which was commanded
by Grigori Grigorievich Orlov, and on which the safety
of her person depended in case of a revolution.

Here is what I saw the first time that I followed her
to her chapel where she was going to hear mass. The
protopapas, or bishop,[33] received her at the door to offer
her the lustral water, and she kissed his ring at the same
time that the prelate, decorated with a beard two feet
long, bent his head to kiss the hand of his sovereign, who
was at once his mistress in things temporal and his patriarch. During the whole mass she showed no sign of
devotion; hypocrisy was unworthy of her, with a smiling
glance she dignified now one now another of the congrega-
tion, from time to time speaking to her favorite, to whom
she had nothing to say; but she wanted to glorify him by
showing all who were present that it was he whom she
distinguished and set above all others.

One day as she left the opera house, where Metastasio's
Olimpiade[34] had been performed, I heard her say these
exact words:

"The music of this opera has given everyone the greatest pleasure, and so I am delighted with it; but I was
bored listening to it. Music is a beautiful thing, but I do
not see how one can love it passionately, unless one has
nothing important to do and to think about. I am having
Buranello[35] brought here now; I am curious to see if he
will be able to make music become something to interest
me."

This is the style in which she always spoke. I will report in the proper place what she said to me on my
return from Moscow. We lodged at a good inn, where
I was given two rooms and where my carriage was put
in a stable. After dinner I engaged a two-seated carriage,
and I took a hire valet who spoke French. My carriage
was for four horses, for the city of Moscow is made up

of four cities,[36] and one has to drive great distances through unpaved or badly paved streets if one has many visits to make. I had five or six letters, and I wanted to leave them all; sure that I should not get out of the carriage, I took with me my dear Zaïre, who, a girl of thirteen, was curious about everything. I do not remember what feast the Greek Church was celebrating that day, but I still remember the deafening ringing of bells which I heard in every street, for I saw churches everywhere. Wheat was being sown then for the harvest in September, and we were laughed at for sowing it eight months earlier than they did, whereas not only is it unnecessary but it can only make the harvest smaller. I do not know who is right, but it is possible that we are all right.

I took to their addresses all the letters I had received in Petersburg from the Master of the Hunt, from Prince Repnin, from my banker Papanelopulo, and from Melissino's brother. The next morning I received visits from all the persons to whom I had been sent. They all invited me to dinner with my dear girl. I accepted the dinner of the first to come, who was Monsieur Demidov,[37] and I promised all the others that I would go to them in turn on the following days. Zaïre, instructed in the role she was to play, was enchanted to show me that she deserved the distinction I was conferring on her. Pretty as a little angel, wherever I took her she was the delight of the company, who did not care to inquire if she was my daughter, my mistress, or my servant. In this respect, as in many others, the Russians are an admirable people. Those who have not seen Moscow cannot say that they have seen Russia, and those who have known Russians only in Petersburg do not know the Russians, for at Court they are all different from what they are by nature. In Petersburg they can all be considered foreigners. The citizens of Moscow, and especially the rich ones, pity all those whom rank, interest, or ambition has ''expatriated''; for their fatherland is Moscow, and they consider

Petersburg nothing but the cause of their ruin. I do not know if this is true, but I say what they say.

At the end of a week I had seen everything: manufactories, churches, old monuments, natural-history collections, libraries, which did not interest me, the famous bell,[38] and I observed that their bells are not hung so that they swing, like ours, but immovably. They are rung by a rope fastened to the end of the clapper. I found the women prettier in Moscow than in Petersburg. They are gentle by nature and very accessible, it is enough to offer to kiss their hands to obtain the favor of a kiss on the lips. As for the fare, I found it profuse and without delicacy. Their table is always open to all their friends; and a friend brings five or six people to dinner without notice, sometimes even arriving when dinner is ended. It is unheard of for a Russian to say: *"We have dined, you have come too late."* They have not the baseness of soul required to utter those words. It is for the cook to see to it, and dinner begins over again; the master or the mistress makes much of the *gosti*.[39] They have a delicious drink[40] the name of which I have forgotten, but better than the sherbet[41] one drinks in Constantinople in the houses of all the great nobles. They do not give their servants, who are very numerous, water to drink, but a concoction which is not unpleasant to the taste, which is healthy and nutritious, and so cheap that with a ruble they make a large cask of it. I observed the great devotion they all have for St. Nicholas.[42] They pray to God only through the intercession of this saint, whose image must stand in a corner of the room in which the master of the house receives visitors. The person who enters bows first to the image, then to the master; if the image by some chance is not there, the Russian, after looking all over the room for it, is nonplused, does not know what to say, and loses his head. The Russian is in general the most superstitious of all Christians. His language is Illyrian,[43] but his liturgy is entirely Greek; the common people do not understand a word of it, and the clergy, themselves ignorant, are delighted to keep them in ignorance. I was never able to make a *kaloyer* who spoke Latin understand that the only reason why we Romans, when we sign ourselves with the cross, move our hand from the left shoulder to the right, while the Greeks move theirs from right to left, is that we say *spiritus sancti* while they say, in Greek, *agios pneuma*.

"If you said *pneuma agios,*" I said to him, "you would sign yourselves as we do, or we would do it as you do if we said *sancti spiritus.*"

He replied that the adjective had to be before the substantive, because one could not utter the name of God without preceding it by an honorific epithet. Of this caliber are almost all the differences which separate the two sects, to say nothing of a great number of lies, which I found among them as among us.

We returned to Petersburg in the same way in which we had come from it; but Zaïre would have wished me never to leave Moscow. Being with me at every hour of the day and the night, she had become so much in love that I was distressed when I thought of the moment when I should have to leave her. The day after my arrival I took her to Ekaterinhof, where she showed her father all the little presents I had given her, telling him in great detail all the honors she had received as my daughter, which made the good man laugh heartily.

The first piece of news which I heard at Court was of an ukase ordering the building of a temple, to be dedicated to God, in the Morskaya,[44] opposite the apartment in which I was living. It was Rinaldi whom the Empress had chosen to be the architect of it. Philosopher[45] that he was, he had told her that he must know what emblem he was to put above the portal of the temple, and she replied that he was to use no emblem, simply writing Gᴏᴅ in large letters there, in whatever language he chose.

"I will put a triangle."

"No triangle. Gᴏᴅ, and that is all."

Another piece of news was the flight of Baumbach,

who had been caught at Mitau, where he believed he was
safe; but Monsieur de Simolin[46] had arrested him. The
poor fool was in custody and his case was serious, for it
was a matter of desertion. However, he was spared the
full penalty and sent to garrison in Kamchatka.[47] Crèvecoeur and his mistress had left with some money, and a
Florentine adventurer named Bilioti[48] had fled, taking
eighteen thousand rubles from Papanelopulo; but a certain Bori, Papanelopulo's familiar spirit, had caught him
in Mitau too, and had brought him back to Petersburg,
where he was in prison. During these days Prince Charles
of Kurland arrived, and he sent me word of it at once.
I went to call on him at the house in which he was
staying, which belonged to Monsieur Demidov, who, own-
ing iron mines, had taken it into his head to have the
house built entirely of iron. Outside walls, stairway,
doors, flooring, partitions, ceiling—everything was of
iron, except the furniture. He did not fear fire. The
Prince had brought with him his mistress, ill-humored
as ever, whom he could no longer put up with because
she was really intolerable, and he was to be pitied, for he
could only get rid of her by giving her a husband, and
a husband such as she demanded was not to be found. I
paid her a visit, but she bored me so much with her complaints of the Prince that I did not go back again. When
the Prince came to see me and saw my Zaïre, and reflected
how little my happiness, and hers, cost me, he learned
how every sensible man who needs to love should keep a
concubine; but man's stupid hankering after luxury
spoils everything and turns every sweet to bitterness for
him.

I was thought happy, I liked to appear so, and I was
not happy. From the time of my imprisonment under
the Leads I had become subject to internal hemorrhoids
which troubled me three or four times a year, but at
Petersburg it became serious. An intolerable pain in
the rectum, which returned every day, made me melancholy and wretched. The octogenarian physician Sino-

paeus,[49] whom I told of it, gave me the unhappy news that I had an incomplete fistula, of the sort called blind, a sinus which had formed in my rectum. There was no remedy but the cruel lancet. According to him I must make up my mind to undergo the operation at once. The first thing was to find out the height of the sinus, and to that end he came to my lodging on the day after I had confided in him, with a good surgeon who examined my intestine by introducing a lint probe covered with oil into my anus; drawing it out, he learned its height and extent by observing the place on the probe where the little stain from the running humor of the fistulous cavity had remained. The little cavity of my sinus, the surgeon told me, was two inches away from the sphincter; the base of the sinus might be very big; my pain came from the fact that the acrid lymph which filled the sinus was corroding the flesh to open a way of escape, which would make my fistula complete and the operation easier. After this opening which nature would bring about, he said, I should be relieved of the pain but be much more inconvenienced by the continual flow of pus which I should have in the region. He advised me to be patient and to wait for this beneficial effect of nature. He said, thinking that it would comfort me, that complete fistula in the anus was a very common complaint throughout the province in which the excellent water of the Neva was drunk, for it had the faculty of purifying the body by forcing out the noxious humors. For this reason everyone in Russia who suffers from hemorrhoids is congratulated. My incomplete fistula, by obliging me to live in accordance with a regimen, was perhaps good for my health.

The Colonel of Artillery Melissino invited me to a review three versts from Petersburg, where the Commanding General, Alexis Orlov, was to give dinner to the principal guests at a table set for eighty. The party were to see a drill with the cannon which was supposed to fire twenty times a minute. I went with the Prince of Kurland, and I admired the exact fulfillment of the expectation. The field cannon, served by six artillerymen and loaded by them twenty times in one minute, fired as many shots while advancing toward the enemy. I saw it, holding a watch with a second-hand. In three seconds, the cannon was swabbed out at the first, loaded at the second, and fired at the third.

At the big table I found myself beside the French Secretary of Embassy,[50] who, wanting to drink in the Russian fashion and thinking that Hungarian wine was as light as champagne, drank it to such purpose that when he rose from table he could not stand. Count Orlov set things to rights by making him go on drinking until he vomited, and then he was carried off asleep.

In the high spirits which reigned at the dinner I enjoyed some samples of the country's wit. *Fecundi calices quem non fecere disertum* ("Who has not been made eloquent by many cups?").[51] Since I did not understand Russian, Monsieur Zinoviov, who was seated beside me, explained all the witticisms of the guests which were followed by applause. They were delivered, glass in hand, as a toast to someone, who must reply in the same strain.

Melissino rose, holding a large goblet filled with Hungarian wine. Everyone fell silent to hear what he would say. He toasted his General, Orlov, who was opposite him at the other end of the table. Here is what he said:

"*May you die on the day you find yourself rich.*"

The applause was general. He was praising Monsieur Orlov's great generosity. He might have been criticized, but in lively company one does not consider so curiously. I thought Orlov's reply more sensible and more noble, though no less Tartarian,[52] for it, too, had to do with death. Rising in his turn, holding a big goblet,

"*May you never die,*" he said, "*except by my hands.*"

Still louder clapping.

The wit of the Russians is forceful and striking. They care nothing for subtlety or elegance of expression; they go to the point roughshod.

At this same time Voltaire had sent the Empress his

Philosophy of History,[53] written for her and dedicated to her in a dedication six lines long. A month later a whole edition of the same work, three thousand volumes in all, arrived by water and disappeared entirely in a week. All the Russians who could read French had the book in their pockets. The leaders of the Voltaireans were two very intelligent noblemen, a Stroganov[54] and a Shuvalov.[55] I saw some verses by the former as fine as those of his idol, and twenty years later a superb dithyramb[56] by the latter; but the subject of it was the death of Voltaire, which seemed to me very strange, for a poem of that genre was never used for a sad subject. In those days Russians with pretensions to literature, whether they were noblemen or the more lettered among the military, knew, read, and praised only Voltaire, and, after reading all that Voltaire had published, believed that they were as learned as their idol; I told them that they should read the books from which Voltaire had taken his learning, and they would perhaps come to know more than he. "Beware," a wise man said to me in Rome, "of arguing with a man who has read only one book." [57] Such were the Russians in those days; but I have been told, and I believe it, that they are profound today. In Dresden I knew Prince Beloselski,[58] who, after being Ambassador in Turin, returned to Russia. The Prince was determined to geometrize the human intelligence; he analyzed metaphysics; his little book classified the soul and reason; the more I read it, the more highly I admire it. It is a pity that an atheist can put it to wrong use.

But here is a sally of Count Panin's, tutor to Paul Petrovich,[59] heir presumptive to the Empire, who was so submissive to him that, at the opera, he did not dare to applaud an air sung by Luini until he had given him permission.

When the courier bringing the news of the sudden death of Francis I,[60] the Roman Emperor, arrived, the Empress was at Krasnoe-Selo,[61] the Count-Minister was in the palace at Petersburg with his august pupil, who was then eleven years of age. The courier came at noon to deliver the dispatch to the Minister, who stood facing those who were present at his audience, of whom I was one. Paul Petrovich was at his right. He unseals the dispatch, he reads it in a low voice, then he says, addressing no one in particular:

"Here is important news. The Roman Emperor has died suddenly. Full Court mourning, which Your Highness," he said to the Prince, looking at him, "will wear three months longer than the Empress."

"But why am I to wear it longer?"

"Because, as Duke of Holstein, Your Highness has a seat in the Diet of the Empire, a privilege," he added, turning to the bystanders, "which Peter I so greatly desired and was never able to obtain."

I observed the attention with which the Grand Duke listened to his mentor, and how well he managed to hide the joy he felt. This method of instruction pleased me greatly. Give ideas to the young mind, and leave it to disentangle them. I praised it to Prince Lobkowitz,[62] who was there, and who carried my reflections even further. Prince Lobkowitz made everyone like him; he was preferred to his predecessor Esterházy,[63] and that is saying a great deal, for Esterházy had won all hearts. Prince Lobkowitz, with his high spirits and his affability, was the life of every occasion which he attended. He was paying court to the Countess Bryus,[64] who was the reigning beauty, and no one believed that he was unsuccessful.

At that time a great infantry review[65] was held twelve or fourteen versts from Petersburg; the Empress was there, with all the ladies of the Court and the principal courtiers; two or three villages near the place had houses, but so few that it was very difficult to obtain lodgings in them; even so, I wanted to attend it, partly to satisfy Zaïre, who was ambitious to show herself in my company. The festivities were to go on for three days, there were to be fireworks made by Melissino, a mine was to blow up a fort, and there were to be a number of military maneuvers on a great plain, which should furnish a most interesting spectacle. I went there in my Schlafwagen with Zaïre, having no doubt that I should obtain the lodging, whether good or bad, which I needed. It was at the time of the solstice, and there was no night.

We arrive at eight o'clock in the morning at the place where, on this first day, the maneuvers went on until noon, and afterward we stop in front of a tavern, where we have food brought to us in the carriage, for the place was so full that we could not have found room. After dinner my coachman goes everywhere to look for some sort of lodging, but none is to be found. What of it?—not wanting to go back to Petersburg, I decide to lodge in my carriage. That was what I did for all the three days, and what was declared excellent by all those who had spent a great deal and who had been very poorly lodged. Melissino told me that the Empress had declared my expedient very sensible. My house, of course, was movable, and I placed myself at the points which were always the safest and the most convenient in respect to the place where the maneuvers were to be held on that particular day. In addition my carriage was expressly made to afford perfect comfort on a mattress, for it was a sleeper. I was the only person who had such a carriage at the review; visits were paid me, and Zaïre shone in doing the honors of the house in Russian, which I was very sorry I did not understand. Rousseau, the great J. J. Rousseau, ventured to declare the Russian language a dialect of Greek.[66] So stupid a mistake does not seem to be consonant with a genius so rare, yet he fell into it.

During the three days I often conversed with Count Tott,[67] the brother of the one who then held a post in Constantinople, who was known as Baron de Tott. We had first known each other in Paris, then in The Hague, where I had the good fortune to be useful to him. He was then away from France in order to avoid difficulties into which he would have run with his fellow officers at the Battle of Minden.[68] He had come to Petersburg with

Madame Soltikov,[69] whose acquaintance he had made in Paris and with whom he had fallen in love. He lodged in her house, he went to Court, where he was well regarded by everyone. He was very gay, his mind was well furnished, and he was also a handsome young man.[70] Two or three years later he was ordered by the Empress to leave Petersburg, when the war against the Turks was brought on by the troubles in Poland.[71] It was claimed that he was maintaining a correspondence with his brother, who was then working at the Dardanelles to prevent the passage of the Russian fleet commanded by Alexis Orlov. I do not know what became of him after he left Russia.

He greatly obliged me in Petersburg by lending me five hundred rubles which I have never had an opportunity to return to him, but I am not dead yet.

During these days Monsieur Maruzzi,[72] a Greek man of business who had been a merchant in Venice and who had given up business in order to become a free man, arrived in Petersburg, was presented at Court, and, having a pleasant countenance, was introduced to all the great houses. The Empress distinguished him because she was considering making him her Chargé d'Affaires in Venice. He paid court to Countess Bryus; but his rivals did not fear him; rich though he was, he was afraid to spend, and in Russia avarice is a sin which women do not forgive.

During this time I made journeys to Tsarskoye-Selo, Peterhof, Oranienbaum, and Kronstadt;[73] one should see everything when one goes anywhere and wants to say one has seen everything. I wrote on several subjects in an attempt to enter the civil service, and I presented my productions, which were seen by the Empress; but my efforts were useless. In Russia only men who are expressly sent for are regarded. Those who go there by their own choice are not esteemed. Perhaps this is right.

CHAPTER VII

I see the Czarina. My conversations with that great sovereign. La Valville. I leave Zaïre. My departure from Petersburg and my arrival in Warsaw. The Princes Adam Czartoryski and Sulkowski. The King of Poland, Stanislaus Poniatowski, called Stanislaus Augustus I. Theatrical intrigues. Branicki.

I WAS thinking of leaving at the beginning of the autumn, and both Monsieur Panin and Monsieur Olsuviev kept telling me that I ought not to go until I could say that I had spoken to the Empress. I replied that I regretted it too, but that, having found no one who would present me, I could only complain everywhere of my bad luck.

It was finally Monsieur Panin who told me to take a walk early in the Summer Garden,[1] where she went very often and where, meeting me by chance, it was likely that she would speak to me. I gave him to understand that I should like to meet Her Imperial Majesty on a day when he was with her. He named the day, and I went there.

Strolling by myself, I looked at the statues bordering the walk, which were of inferior stone and very badly executed, but which became comic by reason of the names engraved on them. A weeping statue offered the reader the name of Democritus, a laughing one was Heraclitus, an old man with a long beard was named Sappho, and an old woman with shrunken breasts was Avicenna.[2] They were all in the same style. Just then I see, halfway down the walk, the sovereign advancing, preceded by Count Grigori Orlov and followed by two ladies. Count Panin was at her left, and she was speaking to him. I stand aside to let her pass, and as soon as she is within range she asks me, with a smile, if the beauty of the statues had greatly interested me; I reply, following her, that I thought they had been put there to impose on fools or to arouse laughter in people who had some acquaintance with History.

"All I know," she replied, "is that my worthy aunt,[3] who in any case was not one to trouble about investigating trifles of the sort, was imposed on; but I hope that you have not found everything you have seen in our country as absurd as these statues."

I should have offended against both truth and good manners if, to this frankness on the part of a lady of her caliber, I had not shown her that in Russia what was laughable was nothing in comparison with what was admirable; and thereupon I entertained her for more than an hour on everything of every sort which I had found remarkable in Petersburg.

The course of my remarks having led me to mention the King of Prussia, I pronounced a eulogy on him, but at the same time respectfully taking the monarch to task for his habit of never letting the person who was answering a question he had put to him finish his answer. She then gave a gracious smile, and she asked me for an account of the conversations I had had with him, and I told her everything. She was kind enough to say that she had never seen me at the *courtag*.[4] This *courtag* was a concert of instrumental and vocal music, which she gave in her palace every Sunday after dinner and to which everyone could go. She walked up and down at it, and she spoke to those to whom she wished to accord that honor. I said that I had been to it only once, it being my misfortune that I was not fond of music. She then said, smiling and looking at Monsieur Panin, that she knew someone else who had the same misfortune. She meant herself. She stopped listening to me to speak to Monsieur Betskoi, who was approaching, and, Monsieur Panin having left her, I also left the garden, delighted with the honor I had been accorded.

Of medium stature, but well built and with a majestic bearing, the sovereign had the art of making herself loved by all those who she believed were curious to know her. Though not beautiful, she was sure to please by her sweetness, her affability, and her intelligence, of which she made very good use to appear to have no pretensions. If she really had none, her modesty must have been heroic, for she had every right to have them.

Some days later Monsieur Panin told me that the Empress had twice asked him for news of me, and that he was sure I had pleased her. He advised me to watch for opportunities to meet her, and he assured me that, having already had a taste of my quality, she would signify to me that I should approach her whenever she saw me anywhere, and that if I wanted employment, she might think of me.

Though I did not myself know for what employment I might be fitted in a country which, furthermore, I did not like, I was nevertheless very glad to know that it might be easy for me to obtain some sort of access to her Court. With this idea in mind, I went to the garden every morning. Here is a full account of the second conversation I had with her. Seeing me from a distance, she sent me word by a young officer to approach her.

As there was talk everywhere of the tournament which the bad weather had prevented from being held, she asked me, for the sake of asking me something, if a show of the sort could be given in Venice, and I answered by discoursing at some length on the sort of shows which could not be given there, and on those which were given there[5] and which could not be given anywhere else, which

amused her; and in this connection I said that the climate
of my native country was more fortunate than that of
Russia, for fair days were common there, while in Petersburg they were very rare, despite the fact that foreigners
found the year there younger than anywhere else.

"That is true," she said, "for in your country it is
eleven days older."

"Would it not be," I went on, "an act worthy of
Your Majesty to adopt the Gregorian calendar? [6] All the
Protestants conformed to it, and England did so too,
fourteen years ago, excising the last eleven days of February, and she has already gained several millions by
it. In this general agreement Europe is astonished that
the old style remains in force here, where the sovereign
is the visible head of her Church, and where there is an
Academy of Sciences. It is thought, Madame, that the
immortal Peter, who ordered that the year should begin
on the first of January,[7] would also have ordered the
abolition of the old style, if he had not thought he should
conform to England, which was then the moving spirit
of all the commerce of your vast Empire."

"You know," she said, affably and slyly, "that the
great Peter was not a learned man."

"I believe, Madame, that he was a great deal more.
The monarch was a true and sublime genius. What served
him instead of learning was a delicate tact which led him
to judge rightly of all that he saw and thought could
increase the happiness of his subjects. It was the same
genius which always kept him from making a misstep,
and which gave him the strength and the courage to root
out abuses."

The Empress was about to answer me, when she saw
two ladies to whom she sent word to approach.

"I will answer you with pleasure on another occasion," she said, and turned to the ladies.

The "other occasion" arrived a week or ten days later,
when I thought that she no longer wished to speak to
me, for she had seen me and had not sent to summon me.

She began by telling me that what I wanted her to do for the glory of Russia was already done.

"All the letters," she said, "which we write to foreign countries, and all the public acts which may be of interest to History, we countersign with the two dates, one under the other, and everyone knows that date which is in advance by eleven days is the modern one."

"But," I ventured to object, "at the end of this century the extra days will become twelve."

"Not at all, for that has also been done. The last year of this century, which, in accordance with the Gregorian reform, will not be bissextile[8] among you, will not be so among us either. Thus no real difference remains between us. Is it not true that this reduction suffices as soon as it stops the progress of the error? It is even fortunate that the error is one of eleven days, for that being the number which is added every year to the epact,[9] we can say that your epact is ours, with only the difference of a year. We even have it together during the last eleven days of the tropical year.[10] As for the celebration of Easter, we must leave it to take care of itself. You have the equinox set at the twenty-first of March, we have it at the tenth, and the same objections which the astronomers make to you, they make to us; sometimes it is you who are right, sometimes it is we, for after all the equinox often arrives one, two, or three days later or earlier; and as soon as we are sure of the equinox, the law of the March moon[11] becomes of no account. You see that you are often not in agreement even with the Jews, whose embolism[12] is said to be perfect. To conclude, this difference in the celebration of Easter does not disturb public order or the due maintenance of it, or cause any change in the important laws pertaining to government."

"What Your Majesty has just said is very wise and fills me with admiration; but Christmas——"

"It is only there that Rome is in the right, for you were going, I think, to tell me that we do not celebrate it during the days of the solstice, when it should be cele-

brated. We are aware of it. Permit me to say to you that
it is a carping observation. I prefer letting this slight
error remain to causing all my subjects great pain by
removing from the calendar eleven days which would
take away their birthdays or their name days from two
or three million souls, and even from them all, for it
would be said that with unheard-of despotism I had deprived everyone of eleven days of life. People would not
complain aloud, for that is not the way here, but they
would whisper to one another that I am an atheist and
that I am clearly attacking the infallibility of the Council of Nicaea.[13] This laughably simple-minded criticism
would not make me laugh. I have much more agreeable
things to laugh at.''

She had the pleasure of seeing me surprised and of
leaving me in my surprise. I felt certain that she had
studied the subject on purpose to dazzle me, or that she
had conferred with some astronomer after I had mentioned the reform to her in our last conversation. Monsieur Olsuviev told me some days later that it was quite
possible that the Empress had read some little treatise
on the subject which said everything about it that she
had said to me and even more, and that it was also possible that she was perfectly well versed in the subject.

With great modesty of manner, she expressed her
opinion precisely, and her mind seemed as imperturbable
as her humor, whose even tenor was shown by her smiling
countenance. Since she had made a habit of it, it could
not cost her much effort; but that takes nothing from
the merit of the thing, for to do it one must have a
strength above the ordinary impulses of human nature.
The Empress's bearing, the very opposite of that of the
King of Prussia, showed me a genius far greater than
the latter's. The kindly exterior by which she offered
encouragement assured her of profiting, whereas the
other, with his brusqueness, was in danger of being the
loser by it. Catherine, with her undemanding manner,
could demand more and obtain it. When one examines

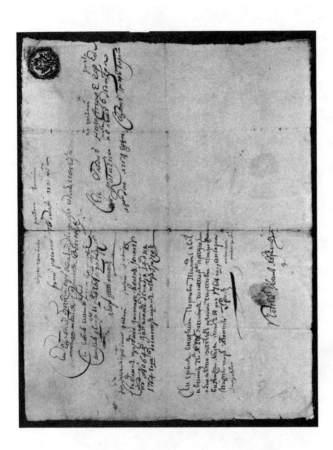

*Customs Authorization for Casanova's Journey
from Riga to St. Petersburg*

Russian Women's Bath

the life of the King of Prussia one admires his courage, but one sees at the same time that, but for the aid of Fortune, he would have been defeated, and when we examine that of the Empress of Russia we do not find that she counted much on the help of the blind goddess. She accomplished things which, before she mounted the throne, appeared great enterprises to all Europe; it seems that she wanted to convince all Europe that she found them small.

In one of those modern journals in which the journalist abandons his proper function to draw the reader's attention to himself, making bold to reveal his thoughts without a care for the reader whom they may offend, I read that Catherine II died happy,[14] as she had lived. She died, as everyone knows, a sudden death. Now this journalist, calling such a death happy, informs us, without telling us, that it is such a death which he would wish for himself. That is all very well—every man to his taste; and we can wish it to him since that is what he wants. But if, for such a death to be happy, it is necessary to suppose that the person whom it suddenly strikes wished for it, who told him that Catherine desired it? If he supposes the desire in her because of the profound intelligence which everyone attributed to her, we might ask him by what right he decides that a profound intelligence must regard a sudden death as the happiest of all deaths. Is it because he so regards it himself? But if he is not a fool, he ought to fear he may be wrong; and if he is in fact wrong, he is proved a fool. So the journalist is convicted of being a fool whether he is wrong or not wrong. To know which he is, we should have to question the late Empress today.

"Are you well satisfied, Madame, to have died a sudden death?"

"What nonsense! You could only put such a question to a woman in despair or to a woman who, because of her poor constitution, had to fear a painful death after a long and cruel illness. I was happy, and I was in very good health. No greater misfortune could befall me, for it is perhaps the only one which, not being a fool, I had no reason ever to expect. The misfortune prevented me from finishing a hundred things, which I should very easily have finished if God had granted me the least little illness the slightest symptom of which could have made me foresee the possibility of my death; and I can assure you that, to prepare myself for it, I should not have needed to have my doctor predict it to me. But not a bit of it. It was an order from Heaven which obliged me to set out on the greatest of journeys, without leaving me time to pack my things, when I was not ready. Am I to be called happy in having succumbed to this death because I did not have the grief of seeing it arrive? Those who suppose that I should not have had the strength to resign myself peacefully to a law of nature common to all mortals must have seen in me a cowardice with which, to tell the truth, I do not believe I ever in my life gave anyone reason to suspect that I was tainted. In short, I can swear to you today, naked spirit as you see me, that I should confess myself satisfied and happy if the too severe decree of Heaven had granted me only twenty-four hours of good sense before my last moment. I should not complain of its injustice."

"What, Madame! You accuse God of injustice?"

"How could I do otherwise, since I am damned? Do you believe it possible that a damned soul, even if on earth it had been the guiltiest of the living, can consider just a decree which condemns it to be unhappy for all eternity?"

"Indeed I consider it impossible, for recognizing the justice of your sentence would to a certain extent console you."

"That is very well argued, and a damned soul must be inconsolable for ever."

"Nevertheless, there are philosophers who, because of your sudden death, pronounce you happy."

"Fools, you should say, for everything I have said

to you shows that my sudden death proves me unfortunate, even were I happy today."

"A powerful argument. May I make bold to ask you, Madame, if you admit the possibility of an unhappy death followed by eternal happiness, or of a happy death followed by carnal punishment?"

"Neither is among possibilities. Eternal happiness is a continuation of the contentment of the soul at the moment when it departs from matter, as eternal damnation must be that of a spirit which departs from it feeling torn by remorse or vain regrets. But enough, for the torment to which I am condemned does not permit me to say more to you."

"Tell me, I beg you, what that torment is."

"Boredom. Farewell."

After this long poetic digression the reader will be grateful to find me returning to my subject.

Monsieur Panin having told me that the Empress would leave for Krasnoe-Selo in two or three days, I let myself be seen, foreseeing that it would be for the last time. So I went to the garden; but, rain beginning to fall, I was about to leave, when she sent for me to come to a room on the ground floor in which she was walking with Grigori Grigorievich and another lady.

"I forgot," she said, with an air of dignity tempered by the most polite condescension, "to ask you if you think the correction of the calendar is without error."

"The correction itself confesses it, Madame, but the error is so small that it cannot produce a perceptible change in the length of the solar year until nine or ten thousand years hence."

"I have come to the same conclusion, and, that being the case, it seems to me that Pope Gregory should not have admitted the error. The legislator must never show either weakness or a concern with trifles. I was tempted to laugh, a few days ago, when I saw that, if the correction had not done away with the radical error by suppressing the bissextile year at the end of the century, the world would have had one year more in the course of fifty thousand years, during which time the equinox would have moved a hundred and thirty times, always backward, through all the days of the year; and Christmas would have been celebrated in summer ten or twelve thousand times. The Supreme Pontiff of the Latin Church found an easy acceptance for his wise reform which he would not have met with in my Church, scrupulously attached as it is to its ancient usages."

"Yet I believe that Your Majesty would have found your Church obedient."

"I have no doubt of it; but what a grief for my clergy to see themselves forced to deny their due to a hundred saints whose festivals fall on one of the eleven excised days! You have only one each day,[15] but we have ten or twelve. I will tell you further that all the ancient States are attached to their ancient laws; they say that if they have survived they cannot but be good. I have been told that your Republic begins the year on the first of March,[16] and I think that this custom, far from denoting barbarism, is an honorable monument celebrating her long life. In addition, I think that one is less wrong to begin the year on the first of March than on the first of January. But does it not cause some confusion?"

"None, Madame. The two letters M. V.[17] which we add to the date during the months of January and February make any mistake impossible."

"Venice is also distinguished by her arms, which obey no rule of heraldry, since the representation itself cannot, properly speaking, be called an escutcheon. She is also distinguished by the amusing figure she makes of her patron the Evangelist, and by the five Latin words she addresses to him, in which, I am told, there is a grammatical error.[18] An error to be respected because of its antiquity. But is it true that you do not divide the twenty-four hours of the day into twice twelve?"

"Yes, Madame: and we begin counting them at the beginning of the night." [19]

"What will not habit do! It seems easier to you. Whereas I should find it very difficult."

"Your Majesty, looking at a watch, would know how many hours of the day were still left, and, to find it out, would not need to hear the cannon shot from the citadel which informs the public that the sun has passed to the other hemisphere."

"That is true; but for your one advantage of knowing the hour at which the day ends, we have two. We know that at twelve o'clock in the day it is always noon, and always midnight at twelve o'clock at night."

She spoke to me of the customs of the Venetians, of their love for games of chance, and in that connection she asked me if the Genoese lottery was established there.

"I was urged," she said, "to permit it in my domains, and I should have consented; but on condition that the amount risked should never be less than a ruble, in order to keep the poor from playing, who, incapable of reckoning, think it is easy to get a *terno*."

In reply to this observation, which was based on profound wisdom, I made her a very low bow. This was the last conversation I had with that great lady, who was able to reign for thirty-five years without ever making a crucial mistake and without ever departing from moderation.

Not long before I left, I gave an entertainment at Ekaterinhof for all my friends, with a fine display of fireworks which cost me nothing. It was a present from my friend Melissino; but my supper at a table for thirty was exquisite and my ball brilliant. Despite the slimness of my purse, I thought it incumbent on me to give my good friends this token of my gratitude for all the kindnesses they had shown me.

Since I left with the actress Valville,[20] it is here that I must tell my reader how I made her acquaintance.

I went all alone to the French theater, and I took a seat in a third-tier box beside a very pretty lady who was there all alone and whom I did not know. I speak to her, now to criticize, now to praise the work of an actress or actor, and she always replies with an intelligence as seductive as her charms. Enchanted by her, toward the end of the play I make bold to ask her if she is Russian.

"I am a Parisian," she replied, "and an actress by profession. My stage name is Valville, and if you do not know me I am not surprised, for I arrived here only a month ago, and I have acted only once, in the role of the soubrette in *Les Folies amoureuses*." [21]

"Why only once?"

"Because I did not have the good fortune to please the sovereign. But since I am engaged for a year she ordered that I be paid the hundred rubles which are due me every month, and at the end of the year I shall be given a passport, my journey will be paid for, and I will leave."

"I am sure that the Empress thinks she is doing you a favor by paying you when you do not have to work."

"She must certainly think so, for she is not an actress. She does not know that, by not acting, I lose more than she gives me, for I am forgetting my profession, which I have not yet learned completely."

"You should let her know that."

"I wish she would grant me an audience."

"That is not necessary. You certainly have a lover."

"No one."

"It is unbelievable."

No later than the next morning I send her a note in the following terms:

"I wish, Madame, to enter upon a liaison with you. You have inspired in me desires which trouble me and which I challenge you to satisfy. I ask you to invite me to supper, wanting to know in advance how much it will cost me. Having to leave for Warsaw next month, I offer you a place in my sleeping carriage, which will cost you only the inconvenience of letting me lie beside you. I know how to obtain a passport for you. The bearer has orders to wait for an answer, which I hope to read in terms as clear as those of this note."

Here is her answer, which I received two hours later:

"Having, Monsieur, the great art of breaking off any liaison with the greatest ease when I find it ill assorted, I have no difficulty in consenting to enter into one. In regard to the desires I have inspired in you, I am sorry that they trouble you, for they flatter me, and I could bring myself to satisfy them only in order to make them stronger. As for the supper which you ask of me, you will find it ready this evening, and we will bargain afterward for what follows it. The place which you offer me beside you in your sleeping carriage will be precious to me if, in addition to my passport, you have influence enough to get my journey to Paris paid for me. I hope that you will not find my terms less clear than yours. Good-by, Monsieur, until this evening."

I found La Valville all alone and very pleasantly lodged; I approached her, and she received me as if we were old friends. Proceeding at once to what interested her more than anything else, she said she would consider herself fortunate to leave with me, but that she doubted if I could get the necessary permission. I repeated that I was sure of it if she would present such a petition to the Empress as I would write for her, and she promised to present it, giving me ink and paper to write it at once. Here it is, in a few lines:

"Madame, I beg Your Imperial Highness to consider that, remaining here for a year doing nothing, I should lose my art all the more easily since I have not yet learned it completely. Hence your generosity becomes more harmful than useful to me; it would fill me with gratitude if Your Imperial Highness would carry it so far as to give me permission to leave."

"What?" she said. "No more than that?"

"Not one word more."

"You say nothing about the passport or the money for the journey, and I am not rich."

"Present this petition, and either I am the greatest fool on earth or you will have not only the money for your journey but all your salary for a year."

"That would be too much."

"It is certain. You do not know the Empress, and I know her. You must have it copied, and present it in person."

"I will copy it myself. My hand is very legible. I really feel as if I had composed it myself, for it is exactly in my style. I believe you are more of an actor than I am, and I want to begin studying under you this very evening. Let us have supper."

After a light and sufficiently choice supper, which La Valville seasoned with countless amusing Parisian expressions which I knew well enough, she made no difficulty about granting me the rest. I went downstairs only for a moment to dismiss my carriage and tell my coachman what to say to Zaïre, whom I had already told that I might go to Kronstadt and spend the night there. He was a Ukrainian, of whose loyalty I had more than once had proof; but I saw at once that, if I became La Valville's lover, I could no longer keep her with me.

In this actress I found the same character and the same qualities which one finds in all French girls who, having charms and some sort of education, consider that merit enough to entitle them to belong to only one man; they want to be kept, and the title of mistress is far more flattering to them than that of wife.

During the intermissions she told me some of her adventures, which made me guess her whole story, which was not long. The actor Clairval,[22] who had gone to Paris to recruit a troupe of players[23] for the Court at Petersburg, having met her by chance and found her intelligent, had convinced her that she was a born actress, even though she had never had any notion of it. The idea had dazzled her, and she had signed the agreement and received one from the recruiter without even troubling to look at his credentials. She had left Paris with him and with six others, actors and actresses, among whom she was the only one who had never in her life appeared on the stage.

"I thought," she said, "that just as among us a girl enters the Opéra in the chorus or the ballet without ever having learned to sing or dance, one joined a company of actors in the same way. How could I have thought anything else when an actor like Clairval told me that I was born to shine on the stage and proved it to me by taking me with him? Before giving me a written engagement he insisted only on hearing me read and making me learn two or three scenes from different plays, which he had me act in my room with him, who, as you know, plays valets to admiration; and certainly he did not mean to deceive me. He deceived himself. Well, two weeks after we arrived here I made my debut, and I got what they call a 'slap in the face,' about which I really don't care, for I don't feel it."

"Perhaps you were afraid."

"Afraid! Just the contrary. Clairval told me that if I had been able to show a little fear the Empress, who is kindness itself, would have thought it her duty to encourage me."

I left her in the morning after seeing my petition written out in her hand and excellently copied. She assured me that she would present it herself the following morning, and I accepted her invitation to a second supper for the day when I should have parted from Zaïre, whose story I told her. She praised my discretion.

French girls who have sacrificed themselves to Venus, if they have intelligence and some education, are all of the same stamp as La Valville; they have neither passion nor temperament, and so they do not love. They are accommodating, and their project is always one and the same. Able to break off a liaison at will, they enter into one with the same facility and always in a smiling humor. This is not from stupidity, but from a deliberate system. If it is not the best one, it is at least the most convenient.

Back at my lodging, I found Zaïre apparently calm, but sad; this displeased me more than anger, for I loved her; but I had to make an end and prepare to suffer all the grief which her tears would cause me. Knowing that I must leave and that, not being Russian, I could not take her with me, she was concerned about what was to become of her. She would belong to the man to whom I should give her passport, and she was very curious to know who he would be. I spent the whole day and the night with her, giving her tokens of my affection and of the grief I felt at being obliged to part from her.

The architect Rinaldi, a man of sense, who was seventy years of age[24] and who had been in Russia for forty, was in love with her; he had told me several times that I should be doing him the greatest favor if I would leave her to him on my departure, offering to give me twice what she had cost me, and I always answered him that I would never leave Zaïre to anyone with whom she would not have wanted to be of her own free will, since I intended to make her a present of the amount I should be paid by the person who acquired her. This did not please Rinaldi, for he did not venture to suppose that he pleased her; yet he hoped.

He came to me on the morning which I had decided should see the end of the business, and, speaking Russian very well, he explained to the girl all that he felt for her. She replied in Italian that, since she could belong only to the person to whom I should leave her passport, it was to me that he should address himself, and that in any case she had no inclination in the matter, neither disliking nor feeling a fondness for anyone. Unable to get a more affirmative answer from her, the worthy man left after dining with us, hoping little, but still asking for my good offices.

After he was gone I asked her to tell me sincerely if she would hold it against me if I left her to that worthy man, who would certainly treat her as if she were his own daughter.

Just as she was about to answer, I was handed a note from La Valville, in which she asked me to come to her at once, to hear some news which would please me. I immediately ordered horses put to my carriage.

"Very well," said Zaïre in a perfectly calm voice, "go about your business, and when you come back I will give you a definite answer."

I found La Valville very happy. She had waited for the Empress on her way from the chapel to her apartment, and, asked by her what she was doing there, she had given her the petition. She had read it as she walked on, and with a sweet smile had told her to wait. Three or four minutes later, having written on it, she had had the petition returned to her, addressed to the Secretary of the Cabinet Yelagin.[25] Inside it she had written four lines in Russian, which Monsieur Yelagin had himself translated for her, she having at once gone to him with the petition. The Empress ordered him to deliver to the actress Valville a passport, her salary for a year, and a hundred Dutch ducats for her journey. She was certain to receive it all in two weeks, because she could not receive the passport from the police until two weeks after an announcement of her departure was published.

The grateful Valville showed me how much my friend she was, and we settled the time of our departure. I had mine announced in the city *Gazette* three or four days later. Having promised Zaïre that I would come home, and being curious what her answer would be, I left her, assuring her that I would live with her as soon as I had put the girl I had to leave in Petersburg in good hands.

After supping with me in a very good humor, Zaïre asked me if, when he took her, Signor Rinaldi would pay me back the hundred rubles I had given her father; I answered that he would.

"But now," she said, "it seems to me I am worth much more, since you are leaving me all that you have given me and since I can make myself understood in Italian."

"I see that, my little dear; but I don't want it said that I made a profit on you, and the more so because I have already decided to make you a present of the hundred rubles I shall receive upon giving him your passport."

"Since you want to make me such a fine present, why do you not rather put me back in my father's hands with my passport? Don't you see that that would be still more generous? If Signor Rinaldi loves me, you have only to tell him to come to see me at my father's house. He speaks Russian too, they will agree on a price, and I will not object. Shall you be sorry if he does not get me so cheaply?"

"Certainly not, my dear child; on the contrary, I shall be very glad to have been of use to your family, for after all Signor Rinaldi is rich."

"That will do, and you will always be dear to my memory. Let us go to bed. You shall take me to Ekaterinhof no later than tomorrow morning. Let us go to bed."

That is the whole story of my parting from the girl who was the cause of my leading a more or less regular life in Petersburg. Zinoviov told me that, if I had furnished security, I could have left with her, and that he would himself have done me the favor. I declined, thinking of the consequences. I loved her, and it would have been I who became her slave; but it may be that I should not have reflected so sagely if at the same time I had not fallen in love with La Valville.

Zaïre spent the morning getting her things together, now laughing, now crying, and she saw my tears each time she left her trunk to come and kiss me.

When I left her at her father's, giving him her passport, I saw her whole family on their knees before me, addressing me in terms which are due only to the divinity. But Zaïre looked very much out of place in the hovel, for what they called a bed was only a big straw mattress on which the whole family slept together.

When I told Signor Rinaldi what had happened he

took it in good part. He said that he hoped to have her, and that, if he had the girl's consent, he would easily agree on the price with her father; and he began going to see her the next day; but he did not get her until after I left; he was generous to her, and she stayed with him until he died.

After this sad parting La Valville became my only mistress, and in three or four weeks I was ready to leave with her. I took into my service an Armenian merchant who lent me a hundred ducats and who cooked well in the oriental fashion. I got a letter of recommendation from the Polish Resident[26] to Prince Augustus Sulkowski,[27] and another from an Anglican clergyman[28] to Prince Adam Czartoryski;[29] and having put a good mattress and bed covers in my sleeping carriage, I lay down in it with La Valville, who found this way of traveling as agreeable as it was comical, for we were actually in bed.

We stopped at Caporya[30] the next day to dine, having a plentiful supply of food and good wines in my carriage. Two days later we met the famous chapelmaster Galuppi, surnamed Buranello, who was going to Petersburg with two friends and a *virtuosa*. He did not know me, and he was greatly surprised to find at the inn where he stopped a good Venetian dinner and a man like myself who received him with a compliment in our mother tongue. He embraced me again and again when I told him my name.

The rain having spoiled the roads, it took us a week to get to Riga, where I did not find Prince Charles of Kurland. We took four more days to get to Königsberg, where La Valville, who was expected in Berlin, had to leave me. I let her have my Armenian, to whom she gladly paid the hundred ducats I owed him. Two years later I found her in Paris, and I will speak of her in the proper place. We parted very gaily, and none of the sad reflections which usually accompany partings such as ours came to trouble our good humor. We had been lovers only because we had attached no importance to love; but we

felt the most sincere friendship for each other. It was at
Klein-Roop, a place not far from Riga, where we stopped
and spent the night, that she offered me her diamonds
and all the money she had. We lodged at Countess
Löwenwolde's,[31] to whom I had brought a letter from
a Princess Dolgoruki.[32] The Countess had in her service,
as governess of her children, the pretty Englishwoman,
Campioni's wife, whom I had met in Riga the year before.[33] She told me that her husband was in Warsaw and
lodging at Villiers'.[34] She gave me a letter in which she
begged him to think of her. I promised her I would have
money sent to her, and I kept my word. I found little
Betty as charming as ever, but still ill-treated by her
cruel mother, who seemed to be jealous of her.

At Königsberg I sold my sleeping carriage, and, being
now alone, I engaged a place in a four-seated carriage
and went to Warsaw. My three companions were Poles
who spoke only German; so I was thoroughly bored during all the six days it took me to make the unpleasant
journey. I went to lodge at Villiers', where I was sure I
should find my old friend Campioni.

I found him doing well, and well lodged. He kept a
dancing school, and a considerable number of pupils,
male and female, brought him enough to live on comfortably. He was delighted to have news of Fanny and
the children, and he sent her money; but he did not
think of having her come to Warsaw, which was what
she wanted. He assured me that she was not his wife. He
told me that the famous Marquis d'Aragon[35] had left
Warsaw after losing all the money he had won in Russia
to sharpers sharper than himself; but the person who
had made a great fortune was Tomatis,[36] who was the
manager of the *opera buffa* and of a Milanese dancer
named Catai[37] who, by her charms far more than her
talent, was the delight of the city and the Court; but
Tomatis controlled her completely. Games of chance being permitted, he named to me the gamesters who had
set up shop there. One was a Veronese woman named

Giropoldi, who lived with a Lorrainese officer named Bachelier,[38] who kept the bank at faro. A dancer who had been the mistress of the famous Afflisio in Vienna brought in the customers. La Giropoldi passed her off as a virgin ; however, she was the woman by whom Afflisio had had a daughter whom he had educated at the Conservatorio dei Mendicanti[39] in Venice and who was with him in Bologna when he was arrested by order of the Archduke Leopold, Grand Duke of Tuscany, who sent him to end his days in the galleys. Another sharper who had set up shop with a Saxon woman was Major Saby,[40] of whom I have spoken during my second stay in Amsterdam. Baron Sainte-Hélène[41] was there too; but his principal talent consisted in getting into debt and persuading his creditors to wait; he was staying in the same inn with his wife, a pretty and honest woman, who would have nothing to do with his business. He told me of several other adventurers, and I was very glad to be informed at once of all these people, whose company I must avoid for my own advantage.

The next day I engaged a hire lackey and a carriage by the month, a necessity in Warsaw, where it was impossible to walk. It was toward the end of the month of October 1765.

My first step was to take the letter from the Anglican clergyman to Prince Adam Czartoryski, General of Podolia. He was sitting at a large table covered with notebooks and surrounded by forty or fifty people, in a huge library which he had made his bedroom. Yet he was married to an extremely pretty Countess Fleming,[42] whom he had not yet got with child, because, she being too thin, he did not love her.

After reading the letter, which was four pages long, he said to me most politely in choice French that he had the highest regard for the person who had sent me to him and that, being very busy, he asked me to come to supper with him, "if I had nothing better to do."

I return to my carriage and am driven to the door of

Prince Sulkowski, who had then been appointed Ambassador to Louis XV. The Prince was the eldest of four brothers, and had a profound intelligence and any number of projects, all admirable, but all in the style of those of the Abbé de Saint-Pierre.[43] Being on the verge of leaving to go to the Cadet Corps, he read the letter, then he told me that he had a great deal to say to me. He added that "if I had nothing better to do" he would take it as a favor if I would come to dine with him alone at four o'clock. I replied that I would do myself that honor.

From there I went to a merchant named Kempinski, who, on Papanelopulo's instructions, was to pay me fifty ducats a month. My lackey having told me that there was a rehearsal of a new opera at the theater, to which anyone might go, I went to it, and I spent three hours there known to no one and knowing no one. I found the actresses and the dancers pretty, but most of all La Catai, who appeared as prima ballerina and did not know how to make a step but was generally applauded, especially by Prince Repnin,[44] the Russian Ambassador, whose word was law.

Prince Sulkowski kept me at table for four mortal hours, pumping me about everything except what I could know. His specialty was policy and commerce, and, finding me at a loss, he shone. He took a liking to me, I believe, precisely because he never saw me in anything but admiration.

About nine o'clock, "having nothing better to do"— the phrase which I found on the lips of all the great Polish noblemen—I called on Prince Adam, who, after announcing my name, made me acquainted with all his guests by theirs. They were Monseigneur Krasicky,[45] Prince-Bishop of Warmia; the Grand Notary to the Crown Rzewuski,[46] whom I had seen in Petersburg as the lover of the unfortunate Langlade, who soon after died of smallpox; the Palatine of Vilna, Oginski,[47] and General Ronikier,[48] and two others whose names I have forgotten; the last person he named to me was his wife, whom I found very charming. A quarter of an hour later I see a fine-looking nobleman enter, and everyone rises. Prince Adam names me, and at once says to me very coldly:

"It is the King."

This way of confronting a stranger with a King is certainly not one to take away his courage or to dazzle him with majesty, but it is still a surprise, and its too great simplicity is unnerving. At once dismissing the idea that it might be a trick, I advanced two paces, and, when I was about to kneel, His Majesty put out his hand for me to kiss with an air of the greatest affability. Just as he was going to ask me the usual questions, Prince Adam gave him the long letter from the Anglican clergyman, who was very well known to him. After reading it the charming sovereign, still standing, began asking me questions, all of them concerning the Empress and the principal personages of her Court, to which I replied with details which he showed interested him greatly. A quarter of an hour later supper was announced, and the King, still listening to me, led me to the table and made me sit at his right. The table was round. Everyone ate except the King, who presumably had no appetite, and I, who would have had none even if I had not dined at Prince Sulkowski's, so gratified was I by the honor of keeping the whole company listening to me alone.

After rising from table the King commented on everything I had said, with a grace and in a style than which nothing could have been more winning. When he withdrew he said to me that he would always see me at his Court with very great pleasure. When I was about to leave, Prince Adam said that if I wanted him to present me to his father I had only to come to his house about eleven o'clock the next day.

The King of Poland was of medium stature, but very well built. His face was not handsome, but intelligent and interesting. His eyesight was poor, and when he was not speaking one might have thought him melancholy; but when he spoke his eloquence shone, and when the subject on which he was speaking allowed it he inspired gaiety in all those who heard him by the keenness of his wit.

Well enough satisfied with this beginning, I returned to my inn, where I found Campioni with an agreeable company of girls and gamesters, who had not yet finished supper. After staying there an hour, more from curiosity than from enjoyment, I retired.

The next morning at the appointed hour I made the acquaintance of that rare man, the magnificent Palatine of Russia.[49] He had on a dressing gown and was surrounded by gentlemen all in the national costume, all booted, all with mustaches, their heads bare and shaven. He stood among them, talking now to one, now to another, affably but seriously. As soon as his son, who had mentioned me to him beforehand, spoke my name the Palatine unbent, giving me a reception in which I saw neither pride nor familiarity. Though not what is called a fine figure of a man, he had a handsome countenance and great dignity, and was well spoken. He neither intimidated nor encouraged; this enabled him to know as he was the man with whom he wished to become acquainted. After hearing that in Russia I had done nothing but amuse myself and become acquainted with the Court, he concluded that I had come to Poland only for the same purpose, and he said that he would make it possible for me to meet everyone. He said that, being a bachelor and alone, he would be pleased if I would eat at his table morning and night every day when I did not have some other engagement.

Withdrawing behind a screen, he had himself dressed, then, after showing himself in the uniform of his regiment, which was in the French style, and wearing a blond wig with a pigtail and long side whiskers in the manner of the late lamented King Augustus III,[50] he made a bow which included everyone, and he retired to the inner apartments, which were the lodging of the

Palatiness his wife, who had not yet wholly recovered from an illness to which she would have succumbed but for the ministrations of the physician Reumann, who was a pupil of the great Boerhaave. The lady was a Dönhoff,[51] an extinct family, as the last heir of which she had brought the Palatine an immense dowry. It was when he married her that he resigned the Cross of Malta. He had won his wife by a duel with pistols on horseback, in which, after receiving the lady's promise that she would grant him her heart, he had the good fortune to kill his rival. From this marriage he had only Prince Adam and a Princess, today a widow, named Lubomirska,[52] and at that time Straznikowa from the name of the office her husband held in the royal army.

It was the Prince Palatine of Russia and his brother,[53] who was Grand Chancellor of Lithuania, who were the first fomenters of the troubles in Poland, which was then only just born. Discontented with the little esteem in which they were held at Court, where the King had no will but the pleasure of his favorite, Count Brühl,[54] the Prime Minister, the two brothers assumed the leadership of the conspiracy, which sought nothing less than to dethrone the King and put on the throne, under the protection of Russia, a young man, their nephew, who, having gone to Petersburg in the suite of an Ambassador,[55] had succeeded in gaining the good graces of the Grand Duchess, who soon afterward became Empress and who died in this year 1797.[56] The young man was Stanislaus Poniatowski, the son of Constance Czartoryska, their sister, and of the famous Poniatowski,[57] the friend of Charles XII.[58] Fortune decreed that he did not need a conspiracy to mount a throne[59] of which *dignus fuisset si non regnasset* ("he would have been worthy if he had not reigned").[60]

The King who was to be dethroned died, and then the conspirators acted openly; and I will not repeat to my reader the events which put Stanislaus on the throne, which on my arrival in Warsaw he had occupied for nearly two years. I found Warsaw brilliant. Preparations were then being made to hold the Diet,[61] and everyone was eager to see what it would reveal in regard to Catherine II's pretensions in recompense for all that she had done to make it possible for Poland to give herself a Piast King.[62]

At dinnertime I found at the Russian Palatine's three tables laid for thirty or forty each. I was told that this was a daily occurrence. The luxury of the Court was nothing compared to that which shone at the Prince Palatine's. Prince Adam told me that I was to take a place every day at the table at which his father sat. On that day he presented me to the pretty Princess his sister,[63] and to a number of Palatines and Starosts,[64] having later gone to make my bow to whom, in less than two weeks I became known in all the great houses and hence was invited to all the great banquets and balls which were given almost every day in one house or another.

Not having money enough to frequent the gamesters, or to obtain a tender acquaintance with some girl of the French or the Italian theater, I took a fancy to the library of Monseigneur Zaluski,[65] the Bishop of Kiowia, and especially to himself. I spent almost every morning there, and it was from him that I received authentic documents concerning all the intrigues and secret plots whose purpose was to overthrow the entire old system of Poland, of which that prelate was one of the principal supporters. But his constancy was unavailing. The prelate was one of those whom agents of the Russian despotism carried off under the eyes of the King, too weak to dare to resist, and sent to Siberia.[66] This happened some months after my departure.

Thus the life I led was very regular. I spent the afternoons at the Russian Prince Palatine's to make up his table at *tressetti*,[67] an Italian game for which he had a great liking and which I played well enough for the

Prince never to be so well pleased as when he could have me as his partner.

But despite my good behavior and my economy, three months after I arrived I was in debt, and I had no resources. Fifty sequins[68] a month which I received from Venice did not suffice me. Carriages, lodging, two servants, and the necessity of being always well dressed kept me in straits, and I did not want to confide in anyone. I was right. A man in need who asks help from a rich man loses his esteem if he obtains it, and wins his scorn if he refuses it.

But here is how Fortune sent me two hundred ducats. Madame Schmidt,[69] whom the King had his reasons for lodging in the palace, sent me word to sup with her, adding that the King would be there. At the supper I saw with pleasure the charming Bishop Krasicky, the Abate Ghigiotti,[70] and two or three others, who were amateurs of Italian literature. The King, whom I never saw in a bad humor in company, and who, besides, was very well read and knew all the classics as no King ever knew them, brought up some anecdotes of ancient Roman writers, citing manuscript scholiasts who left me with nothing to say and whom His Majesty was perhaps inventing. Everyone talked; I was the only one who, being in a bad humor and not having dined, ate like an ogre, replying only in monosyllables when politeness demanded it. The conversation having turned to Horace, and each of the company quoting one or two of his maxims and giving his opinion on the profound philosophy of the great poet of reason, it was the Abate Ghigiotti who forced me to speak, saying that unless I was of his opinion I ought not to remain silent.

"If you take my silence," I said, "as confirmation of the preference you accord to that thought of Horace's over several others, I will take the liberty of saying that I know others which give nobler expression to a courtier's policy, for *nec cum venari volet poemata panges* ("if he wants to go hunting, do not compose verses''),[71] which pleases you so much, is after all only a satire, and not at all a delicate one.''

"It is difficult to combine delicacy with satire.''

"Not for Horace, who even pleased Augustus by doing it, which is to the credit of the monarch who, by the protection he accorded to the learned, made his name immortal and inspired crowned sovereigns to emulate him by taking his name and even disguising it.''

The King of Poland, who on his accession to the throne had taken the name Augustus, became serious and could not refrain from interrupting me.

"Who, pray,'' he asked me, "are the crowned sovereigns who took the name of Augustus in disguise?''

"The first King of Sweden,[72] who called himself Gustavus; it is a perfect anagram of Augustus.''

"Most amusing. It is an anecdote worth relating. Where did you find it?''

"In a manuscript of a professor at Uppsala which I saw at Wolfenbüttel.''

The King, who at the beginning of supper had also cited a manuscript, thereupon began laughing heartily. But after laughing his fill he returned to the subject, asking me in what well-known maxims of Horace's— leaving manuscripts aside—I found marked evidence of a delicacy which made his satire agreeable.

"I could quote several, Sire, but here is one, by way of example, which seems to me very beautiful and, above all, modest. *Coram rege,* he says, *sua de paupertate tacentes plus quam poscentes ferent.*[73]

"That is true,'' said the King, and Madame Schmidt asked the Bishop to translate the passage.

" 'In the King's presence,' '' he replied, " 'those who do not speak of their need will obtain more than those who speak of it.' ''

The lady said that the maxim did not seem to her satirical. After having spoken so much, it was for me to be silent. And the King himself turned the conversation to Ariosto, saying that he wished we might read him together. I replied, making him a bow, with Horace: *Tempora queram* ("I hope the time may come").[74]

It was on the next day, as he came away from mass, that the generous and too unfortunate Stanislaus Augustus, giving me his hand to kiss, put into mine a carelessly made packet, telling me to thank Horace and to say nothing about it to anyone. In it I found two hundred gold ducats, and I paid my debts. From that day on I went almost every morning to the so-called "wardrobe,"[75] where the King, while his hair was being dressed, spoke freely to those who went there only to amuse him. But he never thought of reading Ariosto. He understood Italian, but not enough to speak it, still less to appreciate the great poet. When I think of this prince and of the great qualities I found him to possess, it seems to me impossible that he committed so many errors as a king. Outliving his country[76] is perhaps the least of them. Not finding a friend who would kill him, I venture to say that he should have killed himself; but he did not need to seek his executioner in a friend, for, had he imitated Kosciuszko,[77] a single Russian would have sufficed to send him to immortality.

Warsaw became very brilliant during the Carnival. Foreigners came there from every corner of Europe for no other reason than to see the fortunate mortal who had become a king despite the fact that no one could have guessed that he would become one when he was in the cradle. After seeing him and speaking with him everyone admitted that he gave the lie to those who called Fortune blind and foolish. But his eagerness to show himself was extreme. I saw him become uneasy when he knew there were some strangers in Warsaw whom he had not yet seen. No one needed to be presented to him, for the Court was open to all, and when he saw people he did not know he was the first to speak to them.

Here is something which happened to me toward the end of January, and which it seems to me I should re-

cord, however the reader may judge of my way of thinking. It was a dream, and I have already confessed somewhere that I have never been able to keep from being a
trifle superstitious.

I dreamed that, dining in good company, one of the
guests threw a bottle in my face which covered it with
blood, and that having instantly run my sword through
the body of the aggressor I got into a carriage to leave.
That is all; but here is what reminded me of the dream
that same day.

Prince Charles of Kurland, who had arrived in Warsaw during this time, invited me to go to dinner with
him at Count Poninski's,[78] then Major-Domo to the
Crown, the man who later occasioned much talk, was
created a Prince, and then was proscribed and cruelly
slandered. He kept a good house in Warsaw, and he had
a very agreeable family. I had never called on him, because he was in favor neither with the King nor with his
relatives.

Halfway through the dinner a bottle of champagne
burst without anyone touching it, and a splinter, striking
my forehead, cut a vein, from which the blood, spurting
rapidly, quickly flowed over my face, my coat, and the
table. I get up with all the others; quick, a bandage; the
cloth is changed, and everyone sits down to finish dinner.
That is all.

I am dumfounded, not by the incident, but because
I recollect the dream, which, but for the little mishap, I
should never have remembered. Someone else would perhaps have told the company the whole dream, but I have
always been too afraid of being taken for a visionary or
a fool. I did not even pay much attention to it myself,
for my dream differed from what had happened in its
most important circumstances. Two more of them were
verified a few months later.

La Binetti, whom I had left in London, arrived in
Warsaw with her husband and the dancer Pic.[79] They
had come from Vienna, and they were on their way to

Petersburg. She brought a letter of recommendation to the King's brother,[80] the Prince and General in the Austrian service, who was then in Warsaw. I learned all this at supper at the Prince Palatine's on the day she arrived, from the mouth of the King himself, who said that he wanted to persuade them to stay in Warsaw so that he could see them dance, for which he would pay them a thousand ducats.

Impatient to see her and to be the first to give her this good news, I went to see her at Villiers' inn[81] very early the next morning. Very much surprised to find me in Warsaw, and still more so by the news I gave her that Fortune was sending her a thousand ducats, she called Pic, who seemed to doubt it; but a half hour later Prince Poniatowski himself came to inform her of His Majesty's wish, and she granted it. In three days Pic arranged a ballet, and the costumes, the scenery, the orchestra, the supporting dancers were all supplied by the diligent Tomatis, who had unlimited powers and who spared nothing to please his generous master. The couple were so well liked that they were engaged for a year and given carte blanche; but this was taken in very bad part by La Catai, for not only did La Binetti eclipse her but she took away her admirers. For this reason Tomatis saw to it that La Binetti was subjected to several annoying occurrences on the stage, which made the two leading dancers relentless enemies. Within ten or twelve days La Binetti had a house furnished with the utmost elegance, plain plate, silver-gilt dishes, a cellar with exquisite wines, an excellent cook, and a crowd of admirers, among others the Stolnik Moczynski[82] and the Podstoli to the Crown Branicki,[83] the King's friend, who lodged in an apartment next to his.

The audience at the theater was divided into two parties, for La Catai, though her talent was nothing in comparison with that of the new arrival, felt under no obligation to yield the precedence to her. She danced in the first ballet, and La Binetti in the second, and those who applauded the former were mute upon the appearance of the latter, and the party of the latter made not a sound when the former danced. My obligations to La Binetti were very strong and of very long standing; but my duty was even stronger toward La Catai, who had on her side the whole Czartoryski family, all their relatives by marriage, and all who were dependent on them; among others, Prince Lubomirski,[84] Straznik to the Crown, who honored me with his approbation on every occasion, and who was her principal admirer. Now it is obvious that I could not desert to La Binetti without earning the scorn of all those to whom it was incumbent on me to show the greatest deference.

La Binetti reproached me bitterly, and it was in vain that I explained my reasons to her. She insisted that I stop going to the theater, telling me, without condescending to explain herself further, that she was preparing to be revenged on Tomatis in a way which would make him repent of all the rudeness he continued to show her. She called me the oldest of all her acquaintances, besides which I still loved her and I cared nothing for La Catai, who, though prettier than La Binetti, was subject to epileptic fits.

Here is the cruel way in which she made poor Tomatis feel the first effect of her hatred.

Xavier[85] Branicki, Podstoli to the Crown, Chevalier of the White Eagle,[86] Colonel of a regiment of Uhlans, still young, with a handsome face, who had served six years in France, and the King's friend, who had just come from Berlin, where he had treated with the great Frederick as envoy from the new King of Poland, was La Binetti's principal lover. It is to him that she must have confided her grievances, and it is he whom she must have charged to avenge her on a man who, as director of the theater, let slip no opportunity to make things unpleasant for her. Branicki, on his side, must have promised her he would avenge her, and, if the opportunity were long in coming, to create it. This is the course of events in all affairs of the kind, and no other conjectures are more probable. But the way the Pole went about it is unique and most extraordinary.

On February 20th Monsieur Branicki went to the opera and, contrary to his custom, after the second ballet he went to the stage box in which La Catai was undressing to make his bow to her. Tomatis was the only person with her, and he remained there. He thought, as she did, that, having broken with La Binetti, he had come to assure her of a conquest to which she was indifferent; nevertheless, she was very polite to a nobleman whose homage was not to be scorned except at great risk.

When La Catai was ready to go home, the opera being already over, the gallant Podstoli offered her his arm to escort her to her carriage, which was at the door, and Tomatis followed her. As it happened, I was at the door too, waiting for my carriage; snow was falling in great flakes. La Catai arrives, the door of the vis-à-vis[87] is opened, she gets in, and Monsieur Branicki gets in too, and Tomatis is left there motionless and astounded. The nobleman tells him to get into his carriage and follow him; Tomatis replies that he will ride in no carriage but his own, and he asks him to be good enough to get out. The Podstoli shouts to the coachman to drive on, Tomatis orders him to stay where he is, and the coachman obeys his master. Thereupon the Podstoli, obliged to get out, orders his hussar to slap the offender's face, an order which was carried out to the letter and so rapidly that poor Tomatis was not given time to remember that he had a sword which he could at least have plunged into the body of the brute who had thus insulted him. He got into his vis-à-vis and he went home, where, apparently with no choice but to stomach the slap, he could not eat supper. I had been invited there; but after witnessing this more than scandalous incident I did not have the heart to go. I went home, sad and thoughtful, afraid that I had myself received at least some small part of the infamous slap. I wondered whether the insult could have been planned with La Binetti, and, examining the succession of events, it seemed to me impossible, for neither La Binetti nor Branicki could have foreseen Tomatis' display of bad manners.

CHAPTER VIII

My duel with Branicki. Journey to Leopol and return to Warsaw. I receive the King's order to leave. My departure with the unknown young woman.

REFLECTING AT home on this sorry event, I decided that, in entering Tomatis' vis-à-vis, Branicki had not gone beyond what the laws of gallantry permitted. He had acted without ceremony; he would have done the same thing if Tomatis had been his intimate friend; he could foresee an Italian jealousy, but he could not foresee that Tomatis would oppose him in any such way as he did; had he foreseen it, he would not have laid himself open to the insult unless he was determined to kill the man who dared to put it upon him. As soon as he received it, nature urged him to seek vengeance, and he chose the vengeance which came into his mind: a slap! It was too much, but it was less than if he had killed him. People would have said that he had murdered him, even though Tomatis had a sword too, for Branicki's servants would not have given him time to unsheathe it.

Nevertheless, I concluded that Tomatis should have killed the servant, even at the risk of losing his own life on the spot. It demanded less courage of him than the courage which enabled him to force the Podstoli to the Crown to get out of his carriage. It seemed to me that Tomatis had made a great mistake in not foreseeing that Branicki would resent the insult violently, and hence in not immediately putting himself on guard when Branicki received it. The whole blame, in my opinion, fell upon La Catai, who should never have let the Podstoli hand her into the carriage.

The next morning the thing was the news of the day in good society everywhere. Tomatis remained indoors for a week, vainly begging the King and all his patrons for vengeance, and obtaining it nowhere. The King himself did not know what kind of satisfaction he could procure for the foreigner, for Branicki maintained that he had returned insult for insult. Tomatis told me in confidence that he would surely have found a way to avenge himself, if it would not have cost him too dear. He had spent forty thousand sequins on the two spectacles,[1] which he would infallibly have lost if, by taking vengeance, he had made it necessary for him to leave the Kingdom. The only thing which consoled him was that the regard shown him by the great families whose favor he enjoyed was redoubled, and that the King himself, at the theater, at the tables at which they were together, on the promenades, and everywhere, spoke to him and was extremely gracious to him.

La Binetti alone relished the occurrence and triumphed. When I went to see her she rallied me by condoling with me on the misfortune which had befallen my friend, as she called him; she bored me, but I could neither be certain that Branicki had acted only at her instigation, nor guess that she bore a grudge against me too; but even if I had known it I should not have taken her seriously, for the Podstoli could do me neither good nor harm. I never saw him, I had never spoken to him, he could have no hold on me. I did not even see him at the palace, for he was never there at the hours when I went there; and he never came to the Prince Palatine's, not even in the suite of the King when he came there for supper. Monsieur Branicki was a nobleman whom the whole nation detested, for he was completely Russian,[2] a great supporter of the dissidents,[3] and the enemy of all those who would not bow under the yoke which Russia wanted to lay on the ancient constitution. The King loved him because of their old friendship, for he was under personal obligations to him, and for political reasons.[4] The monarch had to straddle the ditch, for he had as much to fear from Russia, if he declared himself opposed to the settlement which had been agreed upon, as he had to fear from his country, if he had acted openly in accordance with it.

The life I was leading was exemplary, no love affairs, no gaming; I worked for the King, hoping to become his secretary, I paid my court to the Princess Palatine, who liked my company, and I played *tressetti* with the Palatine against any two others whom chance brought. On the fourth of March, on the eve of the feast of St. Casimir,[5] which was the name of the King's elder brother,[6] the Prince and Grand Chamberlain, there was a great dinner at Court, and I went to it. After dinner the King asked me if I was going to the theater that day. A comedy in Polish was to be given for the first time. This novelty interested everyone, but it was a matter of indifference to me, for I did not understand a word of Polish; I told the King so.

"Never mind that; come to it. Come in my box."

At these words I bowed, and I obeyed. I was standing behind his chair. After the second act there was a ballet in which the Piedmontese dancer La Casacci[7] so pleased the King with her dancing that he clapped his hands— an extraordinary favor. I knew her only by sight; I had never spoken to her; she was not without talent; her great admirer was Count Poninski, who, every time I went to dine with him, reproached me for going to call on other dancers and never going to La Casacci's, where one was very well received. After the ballet it came into my head to leave the King's box and go by way of the stage to La Casacci's little box and congratulate her on the justice the King had done to her talents. I pass La Binetti's box, which was open, and I stop for a moment; Count Branicki, who was said to be her lover, enters, and, making a bow, I leave, and I enter La Casacci's box; surprised to see me in her presence for the first time, she reproaches me pleasantly; I pay her compliments, I promise I will call on her, and I embrace her. During the embrace Count Branicki enters; it had been only a minute since I had left him in La Binetti's box; it was clear that he had followed me; but why? To pick a quarrel; he had a grudge against me. He was with Bisinski,[8] Lieutenant-Colonel of his regiment. Upon his appearing, I rise, both out of politeness and to leave; but he stops me by addressing me in these words:

"I entered here, Monsieur, at a bad moment for you; it seems that you love this lady."

"Certainly, Monseigneur, does not Your Excellency consider her worthy of love?"

"Perfectly so; and what is more I will tell you that I love her, and that I am not of a humor to put up with rivals."

"Very well! Now that I know it, I will no longer love her."

"Then you yield to me?"

"On the instant. Everyone must yield to such a nobleman as you."

"Very well; but a man who yields takes to his legs."[9]

"That is a trifle strong."

As I utter the words I go out, looking at him and showing him the hilt of my sword, three or four officers who were there being witnesses to the whole incident. I had not yet taken four steps outside the box when I hear myself honored with the title of "Venetian coward"; I turn, saying to him that, outside the theater, a Venetian coward could kill a Polish bravo, and I go down the great stairs which gave on to the street. I wait there a quarter of an hour, hoping to see him come out and to make him unsheathe his sword, not being, like Tomatis, restrained by the fear of losing forty thousand sequins; but not seeing him, and perishing from the cold, I call my servants, I have my carriage brought up, and I am driven to the Prince Palatine's, where the King himself had told me he was to sup.

Alone in my carriage, my first impulse having subsided a little, I congratulate myself on having resisted his violence, not having drawn my sword in La Casacci's box, and I even feel very glad that the bully had not come down, for he had Bisinski with him armed with a saber, who would have murdered me. The Poles, though generally polite enough nowadays, still keep a good deal of their old nature; they are still Sarmatians or Dacians[10] at table, in war, in the fury of what they call friendship. They refuse to understand that, a man alone being a match for another man, it is not permissible to go in a gang to cut the throat of someone who is alone and whose quarrel is with only one man. I clearly saw that Branicki had followed me, urged on by La Binetti and resolved to treat me as he had treated Tomatis. I had not received a slap, but it was almost the same thing; three officers had been witnesses that he had sent me about my business, and I recognized that I was dishonored. The power to bear that stigma not being in my nature, I felt certain that I should decide on a course, but I did not know which one. I needed full satisfaction, and I considered how best to obtain it, but by some moderate means which would leave me with a foot in both camps. I got out at the house of the King's uncle, Prince Czartoryski, Palatine of Russia, determined to tell the King the whole story and leave it to His Majesty to force Branicki to beg my pardon.

As soon as the Palatine sees me he gently reproaches me for having kept him waiting a little too long, and we sit down to play our usual game of *tressetti*. I was his partner.[11] At the second game which we lose, he reproaches me with my mistakes, he asks me where my mind is.

"Four leagues from here, Monseigneur."

"When one plays *tressetti*," he replied, "with a gentleman who plays for the pleasure of playing, one is not allowed to have one's mind four leagues away."

So saying, the Prince throws his cards on the table, rises, and goes walking about the room. I remain at the table, nonplused, then I go to the fireplace. It could not be long before the King would be there. A half hour later the Chamberlain Pernigotti[12] arrives and tells the Prince that the King could not come. This announcement rends my soul; but I conceal my feelings. Supper is ordered; it is served, I take my usual place at the Palatine's left; we were eighteen or twenty at the table. The Palatine showed that he was displeased with me. I did not eat. Halfway through supper in comes Prince Kaspar Lubomirski,[13] Lieutenant-General in the Russian service, and sits down at the other end of the table, facing me. As soon as he sees me he condoles with me in a loud voice on what had happened to me.

"I am sorry for you," he says. "Branicki was drunk; and from a drunken man a gentleman cannot receive an insult."

"What happened, what happened?"

Such was the reply of the whole table. I say nothing. Lubomirski is questioned, he answers that since I am saying nothing it is for him to say nothing too. The Palatine then stops scowling and asks me amicably what had happened between me and Branicki.

"I will tell you everything in detail after supper, Monseigneur, in a corner of this room."

The conversation turned upon indifferent matters until the end of the meal, and when the company rose, the Palatine, whom I followed, went to the small door by which he was accustomed to retire. In five or six minutes I tell him the whole story. He sighs. He condoles with me, and he says I was justified in having my mind four leagues away when I was playing.

"I ask Your Highness to advise me."

"I never give advice in affairs of this kind, for they demand that one do a great deal or do nothing."

After this dictum, which proceeded from wisdom itself, he enters his apartment. I thereupon go for my fur, I get into my carriage, I go home, I go to bed, and my naturally good constitution makes me enjoy a sleep of six hours. Sitting up at five o'clock in the morning, I consider what course I am to take. "A great deal or nothing." I immediately reject the "nothing." So I must make a choice among the "great deal." I find only one: to kill Branicki or force him to kill me, if he will honor me with a duel, and in case, not wanting to fight, he cheats me out of a duel, to murder him, taking my measures carefully and even risking losing my head on the scaffold afterward. In this determination, and having to begin by proposing a duel four leagues from Warsaw, since the Starosty[14] extended four leagues in every direction and duels were forbidden within it on pain of death, I write him the following note, which I now copy from the original, which I still have.

"March 5, 1776, at 5 o'clock in the morning.

"Monseigneur, yesterday evening at the theater Your Excellency wantonly insulted me, having neither a right nor a reason to behave to me in that fashion. That being so, I conclude that you hate me, Monseigneur, and that hence you would be glad to remove me from the number of the living. I can and I will satisfy Your Excellency. Be so good, then, Monseigneur, as to call for me in your carriage, and to take me where my defeat cannot make you guilty under the laws of Poland, and where I may enjoy the same advantage if God so far helps me that I kill Your Excellency. I should not, Monseigneur, make this proposal to you were it not for the idea I have formed of your generosity. I have the honor to be,

"Monseigneur, Your Excellency's very humble and very obedient servant Casanova." [15]

I send my lackey to take this letter to him an hour before dawn at his apartment in the palace, next to the King's. I tell my servant to deliver it into no hand but his, and, if he was asleep, to wait until he woke to obtain a reply. I waited for it only half an hour. Here is a copy of it:

"Monsieur,

"I accept your proposal; but you will have the goodness to tell me at what hour I shall see you. I am, Monsieur, entirely your very humble and very obedient servant, Branicki, Podstoli C. P." [16]

Delighted with my good fortune, I instantly reply that I will be at his apartment the next day at six o'clock in the morning, to go with him to settle our quarrel in a safe place. He replies, asking me to name the arms and the place, adding that the whole affair must be ended in the course of the day. I thereupon send him the length of my sword, which was thirty-two inches, saying that the place depended upon him, provided it was outside the Starosty. He replies at once by this note, which was the last:

"Pray come to see me at once, Monsieur, and you will do me a favor. In consequence I send you my carriage. I have the honor to be, etc."

I reply by only four lines to tell him that, having a great deal to do, I had to spend the whole day at home, and that, having decided that I would not go to him unless I was sure that we should go to fight at once, he must excuse me if I sent him back his carriage.

An hour later the nobleman himself arrives at my lodging, he enters my room, leaving his suite outside and sending away two or three people who were there to speak with me. After shutting and bolting the door, he

sat down on my bed, in which I was finding it more
convenient to write. Not understanding what this meant,
I take up two pocket pistols which I had on my night
table.

"I have not come here to kill you, but to tell you that
when I accept a proposal to fight I never put it off until
the next day. So we shall fight today or never."

"I cannot do it today. It is Wednesday, the day of the
post; I must finish something which I must send to the
King."

"You shall send it after we have fought. You will not
be left dead, believe me, and in any case, if you succumb,
the King will forgive you. A man who is dead is beyond
the reach of any reproach."

"I have a will to make, too."

"Now it's a will! So you fear you will die. Fear it no
longer. You will make your will fifty years from now."

"But what objection can Your Excellency have to
putting off our duel until tomorrow?"

"I do not want to be cheated. We shall both of us be
put under arrest today by order of the King."

"It is impossible, unless you inform him."

"I? You make me laugh. I know that trick. You shall
not have challenged me in vain. I want to give you satisfaction; but today or never."

"Very well. This duel is too dear to my heart for me
to give you an excuse for not fighting it. Come to fetch
me after dinner; for I need all my strength."

"With pleasure. For my part, I prefer to sup well
afterward. But by the way, what is this about the length
of your sword? I want to fight with pistols. I do not
draw swords with unknown people."

"What do you mean, 'unknown'? I can give you
twenty witnesses in Warsaw that I am no fencing master.
I will not fight with pistols, and you cannot oblige me
to do so, for you gave me the choice of weapons, and I
have read your letter."

"Well, strictly speaking you are right, for I know that

I gave you the choice; but you are too much of a gentleman not to fight with pistols if I assure you that you will be greatly obliging me. It is the least favor you can do me. I will tell you further that one risks less with pistols, for one usually misses one's shot, and I assure you that if I miss you we shall fight with swords as much as you please. Will you grant me this pleasure?"

"I like your way of putting it, for I find it witty. I feel inclined to grant you this barbarous pleasure, and, at the cost of some effort, I am even able to share in it. So," I went on, "I accept the new arrangement for our duel, upon these precise conditions. You will come with two pistols, which you will have loaded in my presence, and I shall be allowed to choose mine. But if we miss each other, we shall fight with swords until the first blood, and no longer, if that is what you want, for I feel ready to go on until death. You will come to fetch me at three o'clock, and we shall go where we are safe from the laws."

"Excellent. You are a man one can like. Permit me to embrace you. Give me your word of honor that you will say nothing to anyone, for we should be arrested."

"How can you think I would take that risk, when I would travel leagues on foot to deserve the honor you are kind enough to do me?"

"So much the better. Then it is all settled. Good-by until three o'clock."

This dialogue is authentic, and has been known to everyone for the past thirty-two[17] years. As soon as the insolent bravo left me I put into a sealed envelope all the papers which belonged to the King, and I sent a servant to fetch the dancer Campioni, in whom I had perfect confidence.

"Here is a packet," I said to him, "which you will return to me this evening if I am alive, and which you will take to the King if I am dead. You can guess what is afoot, but remember that if you speak I am dishonored, and that I further declare to you that you will not have a more bitter enemy in the world."

"I understand perfectly. If I were to disclose the affair to those who would certainly put a stop to it, it would be said that it was at your instigation. I want you to come out of it with honor. The only advice I make bold to give you is not to spare your opponent, even if he were the emperor of the world. Your respect could cost you your life."

"I know that from experience."

I ordered a tasty dinner, and I sent to the Court for some excellent Burgundy wine; Campioni dined with me. The two young Counts Mniszek,[18] with their Swiss tutor Bertrand,[19] came to pay me a visit while I was at table, and were witnesses to my good appetite and my unusual gaiety. At a quarter before three o'clock I asked everyone to leave me alone, and I went to the window to be ready to go down as soon as the Podstoli arrived at my door.

I saw him at a distance in a berlin[20] with six horses, preceded by two grooms on horseback who were leading two saddle horses, by two hussars, and by two aides-de-camp. Four menservants were up behind his carriage. He stops at my door, I quickly go down from my fourth floor, and I see that he is accompanied by a Lieutenant-General and by a chasseur, and, with one foot on the step of the carriage, I turn to my servants and I order them not to follow me and to stay in the house and wait for my orders. The Podstoli says to me that I may need them; I reply that if I had as many as he has I would bring them, but that, having only this wretched pair, I prefer to put myself in his hands unattended, sure that he will provide me with attendance if I need it. He replies by giving me his hand as a pledge that he will take care of me before himself. I sit down, and the carriage drives on. He had given the order in advance, for no one said a word. It would have been absurd if I had asked where we were going. These are moments when a man must watch over himself. The Podstoli saying nothing, I thought it my part to ask him some inconsequential questions.

"Do you expect, Monseigneur, to spend the spring and summer in Warsaw?"

"I expected so yesterday; but you may keep me from doing it."

"I hope that I shall not interfere with any of your plans."

"Have you ever served as a soldier?"

"Yes; but may I inquire why Your Excellency asks me the question, because——"

"For no reason, no reason at all. I asked it simply to say something."

At the end of a half-hour's drive the carriage stops at the entrance to a beautiful garden.[21] We get out, and, followed by all the Podstoli's suite, we go to a green arbor which was not green on the fifth of March, at one end of which there was a small stone table. The chasseur puts on the table two pistols a foot and a half long, takes from his pocket a bag of powder, then a pair of scales. He unscrews the pistols, weighs the powder and the balls, then loads them, screws them to the mark, and crosses them. Branicki, unperturbed, invites me to choose. The Lieutenant-General asks him in a loud voice if it is a duel.

"Yes."

"You cannot fight here; you are within the Starosty."

"That does not matter."

"It matters a great deal, I cannot be a witness; I am on guard at the castle, you have taken me by surprise."

"Enough. I will be responsible for everything; I owe this gentleman a satisfaction."

"Monsieur Casanova, you cannot fight here."

"Then why have I been brought here? I defend myself anywhere, even in a church."

"Lay your account of the matter before the King, and I assure you he will take your side."

"I will do so gladly, General, if His Excellency will only say to me in your presence that he is sorry for what happened between us yesterday."

At my proposal Branicki gives me a black look and says in an angry voice that he has come there with me to fight, not to parley. I then say to the General that he can bear witness that, so far as it lay in my power, I wanted to avoid the duel. He withdraws, with his head in his hands. Branicki urges me to choose. I throw off my fur, and I take up the first pistol which comes to hand. Branicki, taking the other, says that he guarantees on his honor that the pistol I am holding is perfect. I reply that I shall test it on his head. At this terrible reply he turns pale, he throws his sword to one of his pages and shows me his bared chest. However unwillingly, I see that I must do the same, for my sword was my only weapon after the pistol. I show him my chest too, and I fall back five or six paces, the Podstoli does likewise. We could not fall back farther. Seeing him determined, as I was, with the mouth of his pistol toward the ground, I take off my hat with my left hand, asking him to do me the honor of firing at me first, and I put my hat on. Instead of firing at once, the Podstoli lost two or three seconds drawing himself up and hiding his head behind the butt of his pistol; but the situation did not demand that I wait upon his every convenience. I fired at him at the same instant that he fired at me, and there was no doubt of it, for all the people in the nearby houses said that they heard only one report. When I saw him fall, I quickly put in my pocket my left hand, which I felt was wounded, and, throwing down my pistol, I ran to him; but what was not my surprise when I saw three naked sabers raised against me in the hands of three noble assassins, who would instantly have made mincemeat of me where I had dropped to my knees beside him, if the Podstoli had not turned them to stone by shouting in a voice of thunder:

"Villains, respect this gentleman."

At that they withdrew, and I went to help him get up, putting my right hand under his arm while the General helped him on the other side. In this fashion we took him to an inn which was a hundred paces from the garden. The Podstoli walked very much bent over, and stealing curious glances at me, for he could not understand where the blood came from which he saw streaming over my breeches and my white stockings.

No sooner have we entered the inn than the Podstoli throws himself into a big armchair, he stretches out, his clothes are unbuttoned, his shirt is raised as far as his stomach, and he sees that he is wounded to the death. My ball had entered his abdomen at the seventh true rib on the right and had gone out under the last false rib on the left. The two holes were ten inches apart. The sight was alarming: it seemed that the intestines had been pierced and that he was a dead man. The Podstoli looks at me and says:

"You have killed me, and now get away, for you will lose your head on the scaffold: you are in the Starosty, I am a high officer of the Crown, and here is the ribbon of the White Eagle. Get away at once, and if you have no money take my purse. Here it is."

The full purse drops, I put it back in his pocket, thanking him and saying that I have no need of it, for if I was guilty of killing I would instantly lay my head on the steps of the throne. I said that I hoped his wound would not be mortal, and that I was in despair over what he had forced me to do. I kiss his forehead, I leave the inn, and I see neither carriage nor horses nor servants. They had all gone to fetch a doctor, a surgeon, priests, relatives, friends. I find myself alone and without a sword in a countryside covered with snow, wounded, and not knowing the way back to Warsaw. In the distance I see a sleigh with two horses, I shout, the peasant stops, I show him a ducat, and I say:

"Varsaw." [22]

He understands me, he raises a mat, I lie down in the

sleigh, and to keep me from being splashed he covers me with the mat. He drives at a fast canter. Half of a quarter of an hour later I meet Bisinski, Branicki's faithful friend, on horseback, riding at full gallop, with his bare saber in his hand. If he had paid any attention to the sleigh he would have seen my head, and he would certainly have cut me in two like a reed. I arrive in Warsaw, I have the peasant drive me to Prince Adam's palace to ask him for sanctuary, and I find no one. I decide to take refuge in the Recollect[23] monastery, which was a hundred paces away. I dismiss my sleigh.

I go to the door of the monastery, I ring, the porter, a pitiless monk, opens the door, sees me covered with blood, supposes that I have come to save myself from the law, tries to shut his door, but I do not give him time. A kick in the belly knocks him down, legs in the air, and I go in. He shouts for help, some monks arrive, I tell them that I want sanctuary, and I threaten them if they refuse to grant it. One of them speaks, and I am led to a room which looks like a dungeon. I submit, sure that they will change their minds in a quarter of an hour. I ask for a man to go to summon my servants, who come at once, I send for a surgeon and Campioni. But before they arrive, in comes the Palatine of Podlasie,[24] who had never spoken to me but who, having fought a duel in his youth, seized the opportunity to tell me the details of it as soon as he heard the honorable details of mine. A moment later I saw the Palatine of Kalisz[25] come in, with Prince Jablonowski,[26] Prince Sanguszko,[27] the Palatine of Vilna, Oginski, all of whom at once began reviling the monks who had lodged me like a galley slave. They excused themselves by saying that I had got in by maltreating the porter; which made the princes laugh, but not me, for I was suffering a great deal from my wound. They at once gave me two fine rooms.

Branicki's ball had entered my hand through the metacarpus under the index finger, and, after breaking my first phalanx, had lodged there; its force had been weakened by the metal button on my waistcoat and by my abdomen, which it had slightly wounded near the navel. The ball had to be extracted from my hand, which was causing me great discomfort. A surgeon and adventurer named Gendron, who was the first to be found, came to extract it by making a cut on the opposite side, which made my wound twice as long. While he performed this painful operation on me, I told the princes the whole story, having no difficulty in concealing the agony which the unskillful surgeon caused me when he put in the pincers to take hold of the ball. Such is the power of vanity over the human mind.

After the surgeon Gendron left, the Prince Palatine's arrived and took charge of me, undertaking to get rid of the other, whom he called a vagabond. At the same moment in came Prince Lubomirski, the husband of the daughter of the Prince Palatine of Russia, who astonished us all by telling us everything that had happened immediately after my duel. As soon as Bisinski, having arrived at Wola, saw his friend's dreadful wound, and did not see me, he set off like a madman, swearing that he would kill me wherever he found me. He went to Tomatis' house, finding him in company with his mistress, Prince Lubomirski, and Count Moczynski. He asked Tomatis where I was, and as soon as he heard Tomatis reply that he knew nothing about it, he fired a pistol at his head. Upon this murderous act, Moczynski took him around the waist to throw him out the window, but Bisinski got free of him by three strokes of his saber, one of which slashed his face and knocked out three of his teeth.

"After that," Prince Lubomirski went on, "he took me by the collar, holding a pistol to my throat and threatening to kill me if I did not take him out to his horse in the courtyard so that he could leave without fear of Tomatis' servants. Which I instantly did. Moczynski went home, where he will have to remain for a long time under the care of a surgeon, and I went home to observe all the confusion into which the city has been thrown because of your duel. It is rumored that Branicki is dead, and his Uhlans are looking for you on horseback, galloping everywhere to avenge their Colonel by butchering you. A good thing for you that you are here! The Grand Marshal [28] has surrounded the monastery with two hundred dragoons, on the pretext of making sure you do not escape; but really to prevent that frenzied mob from forcing their way into the monastery to butcher you here. Branicki is in great danger, the surgeons say, if the ball pierced his intestines, and they are sure of his life if they were not touched. They will know which is the case tomorrow. He is lodging at the Grand Chamberlain's,[29] not having dared to go to his apartment at Court. However, the King went to see him at once. The General who was present at the duel says that what saved your life was your threat to Branicki that you would wound him in the head. Having tried to protect his head, he put himself in an awkward position, and he missed you. But for that, he would have pierced your heart, for he fires at the sharp edge of a knife and cuts the bullet in two. The other piece of good fortune you had was your not being seen by Bisinski, who could not suppose that you were under the mat in the sleigh.''

''The great good fortune I had, Monseigneur, was that I did not kill Branicki, for I should have been butchered on the spot if he had not said three words which stopped his friends, who already had their sabers raised over me. I am sorry for what has happened to Your Highness and to the kind Count Moczynski. If Tomatis was not killed by Bisinski's shot, it shows that his pistol was empty.''

''I think so too.''

Just then an officer of his household brings me a note from the Palatine of Russia. ''See,'' he writes me, ''what the King has just sent me, and sleep in peace.'' Here is what I read in the note the King wrote to him, which I have kept. ''Branicki, my dear Uncle, is in a very bad way, and my surgeons are with him to give him all the help of their art; but I have not forgotten Casanova. You can assure him of his pardon, even if Branicki should die.''

I printed a respectful kiss on the note, and I showed it to the noble company, who expressed their admiration for a man truly worthy of his crown. I needed to be left alone, and they left me. After they went, my friend Campioni gave me back my packet and shed tender tears over the event which did me immortal honor. He had stayed in a corner, where he had heard everything.

The next day visitors came in crowds, together with purses filled with gold from all the magnates who were opposed to Branicki's faction. The household officer who presented me with the purse on behalf of the nobleman or the lady who sent it to me said that, being a foreigner, I might be in need of money, and that on that assumption his master or mistress took the liberty of sending me some. I expressed my thanks and refused the purse. I sent back at least four thousand ducats, and I prided myself on it. Campioni declared my heroism absurd, and he was right. I repented of it afterward. The only present I accepted was the dinner for four persons which Prince Adam Czartoryski sent me every day; but I did not eat. *Vulnerati fame crucientur* (''The wounded must be made to suffer the pangs of hunger'') [30] was the favorite maxim of my surgeon, who was no genius. The wound in my abdomen was already suppurating, but on the fourth day my badly swollen arm and the blackening of my wound, which threatened gangrene, made the surgeons decide, after conferring together, that my hand must be amputated. I learned this strange news early in the morning when I read the *Court Gazette*, which was printed at night after the King had signed the manuscript. I laughed heartily at it. I laughed in the faces of all those who came that morning to condole with me, and just as I was making fun of Count Clary,[31] who was trying to persuade me to let them perform the operation, in came not the surgeon but the surgeons.

"Why three of you, gentlemen?"

"Because," said the one who regularly attended me, "before proceeding to amputation I wanted to have the consent of these learned men. We shall now see what state you are in."

He removes the bandage, he draws out the drain, he examines the wound, its color, then the livid swelling, they speak together in Polish, then the three of them together tell me in Latin that they will cut off my hand at nightfall. They are all in high spirits, they tell me I have nothing to fear, and that it will make me sure of recovering. I reply that I am the lord and master of my hand, and that I will never allow them to perform this absurd amputation.

"There is gangrene present, and tomorrow it will rise into the arm, and then we shall have to cut off the arm."

"Very well then, you will cut off my arm; but in the meanwhile, to judge by what I know about gangrene, I saw none in me."

"You do not know more about it than we do."

"Go away."

Two hours later begin the tiresome visits of all those whom the surgeons had told about my obstinacy. The Prince Palatine himself writes me that the King was astonished at my want of courage. It was then that I[32] wrote the King that I did not know what to do with my arm without my hand and, that being the case, I would let my arm be cut off when the gangrene became visible.[33]

My letter was read by everyone at Court. Prince Lubomirski came to tell me that I had been wrong to make so light of those who were concerned for me, for after all it was impossible that the three best surgeons in Warsaw should be deceived in so simple a matter.

"Monseigneur, they are not deceived, but they think they can deceive me."

"To what purpose?"

"To flatter Count Branicki, who is very ill, and who perhaps needs this comfort in order to recover."

"You will permit me not to believe anything so unlikely."

"But what will you say when I am proved to be right?"

"If that happens I will admire you, and you will be praised for your firmness; but it must happen first."

"We shall see this evening if the gangrene has attacked my arm, and tomorrow morning I will have my arm cut off. I give Your Highness my word for it."

In the evening the surgeons who come are not three but four; they unwrap my arm, which was twice its natural size, I see that it is livid to the elbow; but when the drain is taken out of the wound I see that the edges of it are red and I see pus; I say nothing. Prince Sulkowski and the Abbé Gourel,[34] of the Prince Palatine's household, were present. The four surgeons decide that, the arm being infected, they are no longer in time to amputate the hand, and so the arm will have to be cut off at the latest the next morning. Tired of arguing, I tell them to come with the necessary instruments, and that I will submit to the operation. They go off very well pleased, to take the news to Court, to Branicki's, to the Prince Palatine's; but the next morning I ordered my servant not to let them enter my room; and the thing was over. I kept my hand.[35]

On Easter Sunday I went to mass with my arm in a sling, though I did not wholly recover the use of it until eighteen months later. My cure took only twenty-five days. Those who condemned me found themselves obliged to praise me. My firmness did me immortal honor, and the surgeons had to admit that they were all either completely ignorant or extremely imprudent.

But another little incident also amused me on the third day after the duel. A Jesuit came to speak to me privately in the name of the Bishop of Poznan,[36] of which diocese Warsaw was a part. I send everyone out of the room, and I ask him what he wants.

"I come at the behest of Monseigneur" (he was a Czartoryski, and brother to the Palatine of Russia), "to absolve you from the ecclesiastical censures you have incurred by fighting a duel."

"I have no need of that, for I do not admit it. I was attacked, and I defended myself. Convey my thanks to Monseigneur; yet if you wish to absolve me of the sin without my confessing it, you are free to do so."

"If you do not confess the crime, I cannot absolve you of it. But do this: Ask me for absolution in case you fought a duel."

"With pleasure. If it is a duel, I ask you to absolve me, and I ask you for nothing if it is not one."

He gave me absolution with the same ambiguity. The Jesuits were admirable at finding subterfuges for everything.

Three days before I go out the Grand Marshal to the Crown withdrew the troops which were at the doors of the monastery. On going out (it was Easter Sunday) I went to mass, then to Court, where the King, giving me his hand to kiss, let me go down on one knee; he asked me (it was prearranged) why I had my arm in a sling, and I replied that it was because of an attack of rheumatism; he replied that I should beware of catching it again. After seeing the King, I told my coachman to take me to the door of the mansion in which Count Branicki was staying. I thought I owed him a visit. He had sent a lackey every day to inquire how I was doing; he had sent me back my sword, which I had left on the field of battle; he was to stay in bed for at least six more weeks because it had been necessary to enlarge the two wounds, in which the packing had become embedded, preventing his recovery. I owed him a visit. Then too, people were calling to congratulate him on the King's having appointed him Lowczy (which means Master of the Royal Hunt) on the previous day. The post ranked below that of Podstoli, but it was lucrative. It was jestingly said that the King had not given it to him until after seeing that he was an excellent shot; but that day I was a better shot than he.

I enter his anteroom; the officers, the lackeys, the chasseurs are surprised to see me. I ask the Adjutant to announce me to Monseigneur if he is receiving. He does not answer, he sighs, and he goes in. A minute later he comes out, he orders both leaves of the door opened, and he tells me to go in.

Wearing a dressing gown of some gold-glazed stuff, Branicki was lying in bed with his back supported by pillows with rose-colored ribbons. Pale as a corpse, he took off his nightcap.

"I have come, Monseigneur, to ask you to pardon me for not having been able to overlook a trifle to which, were I wiser, I should have paid no attention. I have come to tell you that you have honored me far more than you offended me, and I ask your protection in the future against your friends, who, not knowing your character, believe they must be my enemies."

"I admit," he replied, "that I insulted you, but you will likewise admit that I have certainly paid for it in my own person. As for my friends, I will declare myself the enemy of all those who will not respect you. Bisinski has been banished and stricken from the roster of the nobility, and it was rightly done. As for my protection, you do not need it, the King esteems you as I do and as do all those who know the laws of honor. Be seated, and in the future let us be good friends. A cup of chocolate for Monsieur. So you are cured?"

"Completely, except for the joint, the use of which I shall not recover for a year."

"You put up a good fight against the surgeons, and you were right to tell someone that the fools thought they would be pleasing me by leaving you with only one hand. They measure another's heart by their own. I congratulate you on having routed them and kept your hand; but I have never been able to understand how my ball could have gone into your hand after wounding you in the abdomen.''

Just then I was served chocolate, and the Grand Chamberlain came in, looking at me with a smile. In five or six minutes the room was filled with ladies and gentlemen who, having learned that I was with the Lowczy, and curious to hear what we would say to each other, had come to be present at our dialogue. I saw that they did not expect to find us on such good terms, and that they were delighted by it. Branicki took me back to the subject which had been interrupted.

''How could my ball have entered your hand?''

''You will permit me to assume the same position?''

''Whatever you like.''

So I rise, and displaying myself as I had been, he understands.

''You should,'' a lady[37] said to me, ''have held your hand behind your body.''

''I was more concerned, Madame, with keeping my body behind my hand.''

''You meant to kill my brother, for you aimed at his head.''

''God forbid, Madame; it was to my interest to leave him alive, so that he could defend me, as he did, against those who were with him.''

''But you told him you would aim at his head.''

''That is what one always says; but the wise man aims at the center of the target; the head is at the edge. Accordingly, when I raised the muzzle of my pistol I stopped it just before it would have gone beyond the middle line.''

''That is so,'' said Branicki; ''your tactics are better than mine, you taught me a lesson.''

''The lesson Your Excellency gave me in heroism and coolness is one far more worth learning and applying.''

''It is obvious,'' his sister Sapieha resumed, ''that you must have practiced a great deal with the pistol.''

''Never. It was my first unlucky shot; but I have al-

ways had a clear idea of the straight line, the accurate
eye, and the hand which does not shake.''

''That is all that is needed,'' said Branicki; ''I have
all that, and I am delighted that I did not shoot as well
as I usually do.''

''Your ball, Monseigneur, broke my first phalanx. Here
it is, flattened by my bone. Permit me to return it to
you.''

''I regret that I cannot give you back yours.''

''Your wound is getting better, I am told.''

''My wound is healing with great difficulty. If I had
done what you did that day, the duel would have cost
me my life. From what I hear, you dined very well.''

''The cause of it was my fear that the dinner would be
my last.''

''If I had dined, your ball would have pierced my intestines, whereas, they being empty, it only grazed them.''

What I learned for certain was that, as soon as he
knew he was to fight at three o'clock, Branicki went to
mass, confessed, and communicated. The confessor had
to absolve him when he told him that his honor obliged
him to fight. All this was still in accordance with the
ancient code of chivalry. As for me, perhaps more, perhaps less a Christian than Branicki, I addressed God in
only these few words: *''Lord, if my enemy kills me, I am
damned; so save me from death.''* After a number of
cheerful and interesting remarks, I took leave of the hero
to call on the nonagenarian Grand Marshal to the Crown,
Bielinski[38] (Countess Salmour[39] was his sister), who, by
virtue of his office, is the only administrator of justice in
Poland. I had never spoken to him, he had defended me
from Branicki's Uhlans, he had spared my life, it was
my duty to kiss his hand.

I send in my name, I enter, he asks me what I want of
him.

''I come to kiss the hand which signed my pardon,
Monseigneur, and to promise Your Excellency that I will
be wiser in future.''

"I advise you to be so. But as for your pardon, go thank the King, for if he had not asked me to grant it I should have had you beheaded."

"Despite the circumstances, Monseigneur?"

"What circumstances? Is it true or not true that you fought a duel?"

"It is not true; for I fought only because I was forced to defend myself. What I did could be called a duel if Count Branicki had taken me out of the Starosty, as my first challenge instructed him to do, and as we had agreed to do. So I believe that Your Excellency, properly informed, would not have had my head cut off."

"I do not know what I should have done. The King directed me to pardon you; it shows that he thought you deserve it, and I congratulate you. If you will come to dine with me tomorrow, I shall be pleased to see you."

"You shall be obeyed, Monseigneur."

The old man was renowned and very intelligent. He had been the great friend of the famous Poniatowski, the King's father. The next day at table he talked to me at length about him.

"What a comfort it would have been for Your Excellency's worthy friend if he had lived long enough to see the crown on his son's head!"

"He would not have wanted it."

The energy with which he made this reply showed me his soul. He was of the Saxon faction.[40] The same day I went to dine[41] with the Prince Palatine, who said that reasons of policy had prevented him from going to see me at the monastery; but that it should not make me doubt his friendship, for he had thought of me.

"I am having an apartment made ready for you here," he said. "My wife enjoys your company; but the apartment will not be ready for six weeks."

"Then I will use the time, Monseigneur, to pay a visit to the Palatine of Kiowia,[42] who did me the honor to send me an invitation."

"Through whom did he transmit the invitation?"

"The Starost Count Brühl,[43] who is in Dresden and whose wife is the Palatine's daughter."

"You will do well to make this little journey now, for your duel has made you many enemies, who will seize every occasion to get you into a quarrel, and Heaven preserve you from fighting again. Heed my warning. Be on your guard, and never go about on foot, especially at night."

I spent two weeks going to dinners and suppers to which I was invited, and at all of which I was summoned to tell the story of the duel in the greatest detail. The King was often present, always pretending not to listen to me; but once he could not refrain from asking me if, being in my native country Venice, and receiving an insult there, I would have challenged the insulter to a duel, supposing that he was a Venetian patrician.

"No, Sire, for I should have guessed that he would not come to fight."

"What would you have done then?"

"I should have champed the bit. But if the same Venetian patrician dared to insult me in a foreign country, he would account to me for it."

Having gone to call on Count Moczynski, I found La Binetti there; she vanished as soon as she saw me.

"What has she against me?" I asked Moczynski.

"She is the cause of the duel, and you are the cause of her losing her lover, for Branicki will have nothing more to do with her. She hoped he would treat you as he did Tomatis, and you nearly killed her bravo. She openly criticizes him for having accepted your challenge; but he will not see her again."

This Count Moczynski was as agreeable as possible, he was more than intelligent; but, generous to the point of prodigality, he was ruining himself at Court by making presents. His wounds were beginning to heal. The person who should have been the most attached to me was Tomatis; but, quite the contrary, he was no longer as pleased to see me as he had been before the duel. He saw in me a man who tacitly reproached him for cowardice and for preferring money to honor. He would perhaps have liked it better if Branicki had killed me, for then the author of his dishonor would have become the most odious person in all Poland, and people would perhaps have more easily forgiven him for the freedom with which he continued to show himself in the great houses with a stain on his honor which rendered him contemptible, despite the good society which made much of him and which he frequented; for it was obvious that all the favor he enjoyed came from the fanatical admiration which La Catai owed rather to her beauty and her sweet and modest manner than to her talent.

Determined to pay a visit to the malcontents who had recognized the new King only under compulsion, and several of whom had even refused to recognize him, I set out with Campioni, in order to have the companionship of a man who loved me and who had courage, and with one manservant. I had two hundred sequins in my purse, one hundred of which the Palatine of Russia had given me privately and in such an obliging way that I should have done very wrong to refuse them. I had won the other hundred backing Count Clary in a game of quinze which he played against a Starost Sniatinski,[44] who was light-heartedly ruining himself in Warsaw. Count Clary, who never lost when playing a two-handed game, that day won two thousand ducats from him, which the young man paid the next morning. Prince Charles of Kurland had left for Venice, where I had recommended him to my powerful friends, with whose treatment of him he had reason to be very well satisfied. The Anglican clergyman who had recommended me to Prince Adam had then arrived in Warsaw from Petersburg. I dined with him at the Prince's; the King, who knew him, was present by his own wish. There was also talk at that time of Madame Geoffrin,[45] an old friend of the King's, who was about to arrive in Warsaw at the invitation and the expense of the King himself, who, despite the difficulties which his enemies made for him, was always the soul of all the social occasions which he honored with his presence. He said to me one day when I chanced to find him sad and thoughtful that the crown of Poland was the crown of martyrdom. Yet this King, to whom I give all the praise which is his due, was weak enough to let calumny prevent him from making my fortune. I had the pleasure of convincing him that he was mistaken. I shall speak of it in the proper place, an hour or two hence.

I arrived at Leopol [46] six days after leaving Warsaw, because I stopped for two days at the young Count Zamojski's, the Ordynat of Zamosc, [47] who had an income of forty thousand ducats and was subject to epileptic fits. He told me that he was ready to give all that he possessed to the doctor who could cure him. I pitied his young wife. She loved him, and she did not dare to go to bed with him, for his affliction descended on him precisely when he tried to give her tokens of his fondness; she was in despair because she had to refuse his urgings and even to run away when he insisted. This magnate, who died not long afterward, lodged me in a very handsome apartment in which there was nothing. It is the Polish way; a gentleman is supposed to travel with everything he needs.

I put up at the inn in Leopol, which they call Lemberg; but I had to leave it to lodge in the house of the famous Castellane Kaminska, [48] a great enemy of Branicki, of the King, and of his whole faction. She was extremely rich, but the confederations ruined her. [49] She put me up for a week, but without pleasure on either side, for she spoke only Polish and German. From Leopol I went to a small city, whose name I have forgotten, in which lived the lesser General Joseph Rzewuski, [50] to whom I brought a letter from the Straznik Prince Lubomirski; he was a robust old man, who had a long beard which he wore to show his friends his sorrow at the novelties which were troubling his country. He was rich, learned, a superstitious Christian, extremely polished. He kept me for three days. He commanded, as might be expected, the small fortified place in which he lived and in which he kept a garrison of five hundred men. The first day on which he lodged me, I was in his room an hour before noon with three or four officers. Just as I was speaking with him about something interesting, an officer enters, goes to him, whispers something into his ear, and the same officer also whispers to me:

"Venice and St. Mark."

I reply aloud that St. Mark was the patron saint of Venice; everyone laughs, and I realize that it is the password for the day which His Excellency had given and of which I was informed as an honor. I begged pardon, and the word was immediately changed. The magnate talked politics to me at length; he had never gone to Court; but he had decided to go to the Diet to oppose the Russian laws in favor of the dissidents with all his might. He was one of the four whom Prince Repnin ordered seized and sent to Siberia.[51]

After taking leave of this great republican I went to Christianpol,[52] the place of residence of the famous Palatine of Kiowia, Potocki, who had been one of the lovers of the Russian Empress Anna Ivanovna. He had himself built the city in which he lived, and he had named it Christianpol after his own name. This nobleman, who was still handsome, kept a splendid Court; he honored Count Brühl's letter by keeping me with him for two weeks and sending me traveling every day with his physician, who was the celebrated Hyrneus, sworn enemy of the still more celebrated Van Swieten.[53] Hyrneus, though very learned, was something of a madman; he was an empiric, he followed the system of Asclepiades,[54] which has become untenable since the great Boerhaave; nevertheless he made astonishing cures. Back in Christianpol every evening, I paid my court to the Palatiness, who never came down to supper because the devotions she performed in her room did not permit it. I never saw her except with her three daughters and two Franciscan friars, who were her directors of conscience turn and turn about.[55]

I amused myself for a week in Leopol with a very beautiful girl who soon afterward made Count Potocki, Starost of Sniatyn, fall so much in love with her that he married her.[56] From Leopol I went to stay for a week in Pulawy,[57] a magnificent palace on the Vistula eighteen leagues from Warsaw, which belonged to the Prince Palatine of Russia. He had had it built. Campioni left me there, to go to Warsaw. A place can be as delightful as you please and yet be certain to bore a man who is condemned to live there alone, unless he has some work of literature in hand. At Pulawy a peasant girl who came into my room pleased me, and she ran away crying out one morning when I tried to do something with her; the caretaker came running, asking me coldly why I did not go about it in the straightforward way if the girl pleased me.

"What is the straightforward way?"

"Talk to her father, who is here, and ask him amicably if he will sell you her maidenhead."

"I do not speak Polish, make the bargain yourself."

"Gladly. Will you give him fifty florins?"

"You are jesting. If she is a maiden, and gentle as a lamb, I will give him a hundred."

The thing was done the same day after supper. Afterward she ran away like a thief. I learned that her father had had to beat her to make her obey him. The next day I was offered several girls without even being shown them.

"But where is the girl?" I asked the caretaker.

"What use is it to see her face when you are assured that she is a maiden?"

"Understand that what interests me is the face, and that the maidenhead of an ugly girl is taskwork for my odd taste."

After that I was shown them, and on the evening before I left I came to terms for another. In general the sex is ugly in that country. I left for Warsaw. It was in this fashion that I saw Podolia, Pokucie, and Volhynia,[58] which a few years later were renamed Galicia and Lodomeria,[59] for they could not become possessions of the House of Austria except by having their names changed. It is said, however, that these fertile provinces became happier after they ceased to be Polish. Today there is no Poland any more.[60]

At Warsaw I found Madame Geoffrin, who was being entertained everywhere and who was looked at with astonishment because of the simplicity of her dress. Not only did I find myself received very coldly by everyone, I was even badly received.

"We did not think," I was bluntly told, "that we should see you appear here again. What have you come here to do?"

"I have come to pay my debts."

I found it disgusting. Even the Palatine of Russia seemed to me a different man. I was received at the tables which I had frequented, but no one spoke to me. However, the Princess, Prince Adam's sister, pleasantly invited me to sup with her. I go there, and at a perfectly round table I find myself opposite to the King, who never spoke a word to me. He talked to no one but the Swiss Bertrand. It had never happened to me before that day.

The next day I go to dine at the house of Countess Oginska, daughter of Prince Czartoryski, Grand Chancellor of Lithuania, and a Countess Waldstein,[61] a greatly respected lady who lived to be ninety years old. At table this lady asks where the King had supped the evening before, nobody knew, and I remain silent. General Ronikier arrives as we are getting up from table. The Palatiness asks him where the King had supped, he replies that he had supped at the Princess Straznikowa's, and that I was there. So she asks me why I had said nothing at table when she had expressed her curiosity; I reply that it was because I was sorry to have been there, for the King had never said a word to me or looked at me.

"I am in disgrace, and I cannot guess the reason."

Leaving the house of the Palatine of Vilna, Oginski, I go to make my bow to the sagacious Prince Augustus Sulkowski, who, after receiving me very cordially, as he always did, told me that I had made a mistake in returning to Warsaw, for everyone had changed his mind about me.

"What have I done?"

"Nothing; but such is our character in general: inconstant, inconsistent, false. *Sarmatarum virtus veluti extra ipsos* ['The virtues of the Sarmatians are as it were outside them'].[62] Your fortune was made; you missed the moment, I advise you to leave."

"And I shall do so."

I go home, and at ten o'clock my servant gives me a letter which had been left at my door. I open it, I see no signature, and I find that a person who loves and esteems me, and who does not sign because he had learned the thing from the King himself, informs me that the King no longer wishes to see me at his Court because he had learned that I had been hanged in effigy in Paris for having left there taking with me a large sum which belonged to the funds of the Military School Lottery,[63] and that in addition I had practiced the base trade of actor in Italy, wandering from province to province with troupes of strolling players.

These are calumnies which it is very easy to put forth, and which it is very difficult to confute. Such are Courts, where hatred is ever at work, urged on by envy. I should have liked to be able to treat the thing with contempt and leave immediately; but I had debts, and not money enough to go to Portugal, where I was sure of a great resource.[64]

I stopped going anywhere, I saw only Campioni; I was writing to Venice and wherever I had friends, to try to replenish my purse, when the same Lieutenant-General who had been present at my duel comes with a gloomy countenance to tell me in the King's name to leave the Starosty of Warsaw within eight days. At this announcement I draw myself up, and I tell him to answer the King that I did not feel inclined to obey such an order.

"If I leave," I said, "I want everyone to know that I am leaving under compulsion."

"I will not convey such an answer. I will tell the King that I have carried out his order, and that is all. You shall do what you consider best."

In a towering rage, I write the King a long letter. I show him that my honor demanded that I disobey his order. "My creditors, Sire, will forgive me when they learn that I have left Poland without paying them only because Your Majesty compels me to leave it."

When I was thinking by whom I might send my strong letter to the monarch, I saw Count Moczynski in my room. I told him all that had just happened to me, and, after reading him my letter, I asked him by whom I could send it, and he replied, with great feeling, that he would deliver it himself. After that I went for a walk to get a breath of air, and I came upon Prince Sulkowski, who was not surprised when I told him that I had received an order to leave.

The Prince thereupon told me the whole story of what had happened to him in Vienna, where the Empress Maria Theresa had sent him an order to leave within the short space of twenty-four hours for no other reason than that he had conveyed compliments to the Archduchess Christine from Prince Louis of Württemberg.[65]

The next morning the Stolnik to the Crown, Count Moczynski, came, bringing me a thousand ducats. He said that the King did not know that I was in need of money, for I was in much greater need of saving my life, and that it was for this reason that His Majesty had sent me an order to leave, since, staying in Warsaw and going about by night, I was always exposed to obvious dangers. The dangers came from five or six people who had sent me challenges and whom I had not even answered. These people, to avenge themselves for my disregard, might attack me, and the King no longer wished to be uneasy on my account. In addition he told me that the order His Majesty had given me was in no way dishonorable to me in view of the person who had brought it to me, the circumstances, and the time I had been given so that I could easily make my arrangements to leave. The result of this harangue was that I not only gave Monsieur Moczynski my word that I would leave, but I begged him to thank His Majesty on my behalf for the favor he was doing me and the proof he gave me that he was concerned for my life.

The generous Moczynski embraced me and begged me to accept the small present he was going to make me of a carriage, since I had none, and he asked me to write to him. He told me that La Binetti's husband had left with his wife's chambermaid, with whom he had fallen in love, taking with him all that she possessed in the way of diamonds, watches, gold snuffboxes, and even thirty-six silver table services she had. He had left her to the dancer Pic, with whom she slept every night. La Binetti's protectors, the chief of whom was the King's brother, the Prince General, had united to console her and had given her enough so that she need not regret all that her scoundrel of a husband had taken from her. He said that the wife of the Grand General to the Crown, the King's sister,[66] had arrived from Bialystok[67] and that she was lodged at the Court, where the greatest honors were shown her. He said it was hoped that her husband would finally make up his mind to come to Warsaw. He was Count Branicki, who died declaring himself the last member of his family and consequently ordering that his arms, as was the custom, should be buried with him. The Branicki who had honored me with the duel was neither related to him nor bore his name except unrightfully. His name was Bragnecki.[68]

The next day I paid my debts, which came to two hundred ducats, and I prepared to leave on the next day but one for Breslau with Count Clary, he in his carriage and I in mine, which Count Moczynski at once sent me.

Count Clary was leaving without ever having been at Court, but he did not mind, he liked neither good company nor well-bred women; he wanted only gamesters and trollops. He had arrived in Warsaw with La Durant,[69] a dancer whom he had carried off from Stuttgart where she was in the service of the Duke,[70] which had deeply offended the sovereign, whose great virtue was not that of tolerance. At Warsaw Clary, tired of La Durant, had got rid of her by sending her to Strassburg; so he was leaving alone, as I was, with a manservant. He told me that he would part from me at Breslau because he wanted to go to Olmütz to see his brother, who was a canon.[71] He made me laugh when he told me his story without my asking him, for there was not a word of truth in anything he said to me. I knew three men of birth who had this ugly vice. Those who have it are to be pitied; they are in the unhappy situation of no longer being able to tell the truth to anyone, even when it is to their interest to make their listeners believe them. This Count Clary, who did not belong to the family of Clary of Teplitz, could go neither to his country nor to Vienna because he had deserted on the eve of a battle. He was lame, but no one knew it, for when he walked it did not show. It was the only truth he could hide without wronging anyone. He died in poverty in Venice; I will speak of him ten or twelve years hence. He was a handsome man, with a pleasant, attractive face.

We arrived in Breslau, traveling day and night, without anything untoward befalling us. Campioni traveled sixty leagues with me, he accompanied me as far as Wartenberg,[72] and he left me there to go back to Warsaw, where he had an affair of the heart. He came to join me in Vienna seven months later; I will speak of it in the proper place. Not having found Baron Treyden in Wartenberg, I stopped there only two hours. Count Clary having left Breslau the next day at dawn, I thought, as soon as I found myself alone, that I would give myself the pleasure of making the acquaintance of the Abate

Bastiani,[73] the celebrated Venetian whose fortune the King of Prussia had made. He was a canon of the cathedral.[74]

He received me as well as I could wish, cordially and unceremoniously; we were equally curious to know each other. He was blond, handsome, well built, and six feet tall; he had great intelligence, was very well read, had a persuasive eloquence, a natural gaiety, a good library, a good cook, and a good cellar. Very well lodged in an apartment on the ground floor, on the floor above he gave lodging to a lady of whose children he was very fond, perhaps because he was their father. Though a worshiper of the fair sex, he was not exclusive; from time to time he fell in love with some youth, and he sighed to conquer him in the Greek fashion when he encountered the obstacles which arise from education, prejudice, and what are called "manners." During the three days which I spent in Breslau, dining and supping at his house every day, his passion was evident. He sighed for the young Abate the Count of Cavalcabo.[75] He never stopped looking at him with eyes which burned with love; he swore to me that he had not yet come to a declaration, and that perhaps he would never come to one, in order not to risk compromising his dignity. He showed me all the fond notes he had received from the King of Prussia before he was made a canon; the monarch had been positively in love with Bastiani, he wanted to become his mistress, and he recompensed him royally by the gift of an ecclesiastical laurel. The Abate was the son of a Venetian tailor, had become a Franciscan friar, and had fled from the persecution of his tyrannical superiors. Having fled to The Hague, he found the Venetian Ambassador, Tron,[76] who lent him a hundred ducats, and he went to Berlin, where the great Frederick found him worthy of his affection. It is often by such roads that men come to fortune. *Sequere Deum* ("Follow the god").[77]

At eleven o'clock in the morning on the day before my departure I went to the house of a Baroness to give her

Russian Nobleman

Czarina Catherine II of Russia

a letter from her son, who was in the King's service in
Warsaw. I send in my name, and I am asked to wait for
half an hour to give the lady time to dress. I sit down
on a sofa beside a pretty, well-dressed girl with a cloak
and a workbag; she interests me; I ask her if she is there
to speak to the Baroness too.

"Yes, Monsieur; I have come to offer myself as French
governess to her three young daughters."

"A governess at your age?"

"Alas, age makes no difference when one is in need. I
have lost my father and my mother, my brother is a poor
lieutenant who can give me no help; what do you expect
me to do? I cannot live decently except by profiting
from the small share of good education which I received."

"And what will you earn by the year as a governess?"

"Alas! Fifty miserable crowns to buy my clothing."

"That is very little."

"It is all one gets."

"And where are you living now?"

"With a poor aunt, where I earn my living by sewing
shirts all day long."

"If instead of a children's governess you would like to
become governess to a man of honor, come to live with
me, and I will give you the fifty crowns, not per year but
per month."

"I your governess? To your family, of course."

"I have no family, I am alone, and I am traveling. I
leave for Dresden tomorrow at five o'clock in the morning, alone in my carriage, where there is a place for you
if you want it. I am staying in such-and-such an inn;
come with your trunk before I leave, and we will leave
together."

"It's a joke, and besides I do not know you."

"I am not joking, and as for knowing me, I ask you
which of the two of us has better reasons for knowing
the other. We shall know each other perfectly well in
twenty-four hours, it takes no longer."

My serious tone, my frank manner, convinced the girl

that I was not joking; but she was utterly astonished. On my side, I felt surprised to have given a serious turn to something which I had begun only for the sake of saying something amusing. Trying to persuade the girl, I had persuaded myself; what had happened seemed to me to be within all the wise rules of folly, I was pleased to see that she was thinking about it, turning her eyes to my face from time to time to see if I was making game of her. I thought I knew what thoughts were occupying her, and I interpreted everything in her favor. She was a girl whom I was going to bring into the light of day, whom I should educate in the ways of the great world. I had no doubt either of her decency or of her feelings, and I congratulated myself on being the fortunate man who would enlighten her by destroying the false ideas she entertained on the subject of virtue. Infatuated, I take two ducats from my pocket, and I give them to her as an advance on the first month. She takes them, shy and uncertain, and finally convinced that I was not imposing on her.

The Baroness receives me, she has already read the letter through twice, she asks me countless questions about her dear son, she invites me to dine with her the next day, and she is very sorry when I tell her that I am leaving at dawn. So I thank her, I take my leave, and I go to Bastiani's, not even noticing that when I came out of the Baroness's room the young woman was no longer where I had left her.

I dined with the Abate, and after spending the whole day playing ombre,[78] we sup well, then we embrace each other, and good-by. Early the next morning everything is ready, the horses are harnessed, I set off, and a hundred paces outside the city gate my postilion stops. The window at my right being down, I see a package come in, I look, and I see the young woman, whom to tell the truth I had forgotten; my manservant opens the door for her, she sits down beside me, I find the thing done to perfection, I praise her, swearing that I had not expected such shrewdness, and we are off. She told me that she instructed the postilion a quarter of an hour earlier to stop when he saw her, and had given him the order in my name.

"You took your measures very well, for God knows what they would have said at the inn. You might even have been prevented from leaving."

"No fear of that. It won't even be known in Breslau that I left with you, unless the postilion blabs. Yet I should not have made up my mind to come if I had not taken the two ducats. I did not want to give you reason to think me an adventuress."

CHAPTER IX

My arrival in Dresden with Maton. Her present to me. Leipzig. La Castel-Bajac. Schwerin. Return to Dresden and my departure. Prague. La Calori. My arrival in Vienna. Pocchini's ambuscade.

SEEING MYSELF with this girl who had dropped from the clouds, it seemed to me that I was the venerable agent of her destiny. It was her beneficent Genius who bestowed me on her, for I was sure that I was incapable of harming her. But was it my good or my evil Genius which bestowed her on me? I could not know. So thinking, I went on my way, not wanting to reflect that I was beginning to be young no longer, and that the power to please at first sight, which I had so long possessed in such measure, was beginning to fail me.

I was certain that, if the girl had any intelligence at all, she could not have decided to come with me unless she was ready to submit to my will with no reservations; but that did not satisfy me; my fancy was to be loved, and after Zaïre I had not again found myself in the arms of love, for the actress Valville had been only a passing inclination, and the adventuress Potocka[1] in Leopol had been only a bit of hawking, the due recompense for my money. No affairs of the heart in Warsaw. I was to remember that capital only because it was there that I had had the good fortune to convince all who knew me that I valued honor above life.

The girl I had with me was named Maton;[2] it was her family name, I did not trouble to find out her Christian name. Since she spoke French very well, I asked her if she wrote it as well, and she showed me a letter she had written which proved to me that she had had a good education. She told me that she had left Breslau not only without asking anyone's advice but without even telling her aunt and her cousin that they might not see her again.

"And your clothes?"

"My clothes weren't worth gathering together. In this package I have a shift, a pair of stockings, handkerchiefs, and some rags."

"What will your lover say? For it is impossible that you do not have one."

"Alas, I have no lover. I have had two; the first was a scoundrel who seduced me and abandoned me; the second, who was honest but a poor lieutenant, left a year ago because he was sent to join the regiment which is in garrison in Stettin."

Nothing was simpler than her story, and nothing had more the appearance of truth. I supposed that the girl had left with me only to seek a fortune, or at least a competence. At the age of twenty, having never left Breslau, she must be curious to see what the rest of the world was like, and she must be delighted to begin with Dresden. I saw very well that I had done a very foolish thing in taking on this burden, for Maton was bound to cost me a great deal of money, but I thought I could be excused, for when I proposed to her that she come with me, the odds were a hundred to one against her accepting my proposal. Despite these reflections, I congratulated myself on the pleasure I should take in being alone in the company of a pretty girl, all of whose merit I should discover in a few days; and in order for the discovery to be complete, I decide to attempt nothing with her on the journey; I wanted to see if her qualities would make me fall in love with her, for as yet I was only curious. So at nightfall I stopped at a post station where I saw that I should find a good supper and a good bed. Maton, who was dying of hunger, and who had not dared to tell me so, ate with ravenous appetite, and, not accustomed to wine, she would have fallen asleep at the table if I had not asked her to retire to her bed, which she did, repeatedly begging me to excuse her and assuring me that it should not happen again. She had not slept at all on the previous night, and she had eaten only bread for supper. Laughing at it all, I remained at the table, not even turning around to see if she got into bed dressed or undressed. I went to bed two or three minutes later, and I rose at five o'clock to order horses and coffee. Maton was dressed and asleep, sweating in great drops. It was the end of June. She woke slowly, finding it difficult to recover her senses.

"Get up, get up; you are very pretty, but another time undress, for you must be soaked to the skin."

She quickly put her feet in her slippers and hurried out of the room, coming back later much more at ease, dropping me a curtsy, wishing me good morning, and asking me if I would kiss her.

"Yes, and with great pleasure; sit down, we must eat breakfast quickly, for I want to be in Dresden this evening."

But something wrong with the carriage having made me lose five hours, we did not arrive there until the next day. Maton got into bed undressed, and I had the firmness not even to look at her.

Arrived in Dresden, I took the whole apartment on the second floor of the inn[3] on the square. I at once went to see my mother, who was in the country, and who was overjoyed to see me with my arm in a sling, which made a dramatic picture; then I saw my brother Giovanni and his Roman wife Teresa Roland,[4] whom I had known before he did and who made much of me; then I saw my sister, the wife of Peter August;[5] and after that I went with my brother to make my bow to the Starost Count Brühl, and his wife, the daughter of the Palatine of Kiowia, who was delighted to hear news of her family. Everyone made much of me, and I had to tell the story of my duel everywhere; I was glad to tell it, for I was proud of it.

The Estates[6] were assembled in Dresden at the time. The Elector who now reigns being then in his minority, Prince Xaver, the eldest of his uncles, was Regent.[7] He is the Count von der Lausitz who is still alive and who has children by a Spinucci[8] whom he married and whom he was courting at that time; she was a lady in waiting to the Dowager Electress.[9] Toward nightfall that evening I went to the Italian *opera buffa*, where there was a bank at faro,[10] and where I began playing, but with restraint, for my entire wealth consisted in eight hundred ducats. It was at the faro bank that I made the acquaintance of the unfortunate Agdollo,[11] who then did not look unfortunate. Young, with intelligence and courage, he was already a major, and the valor he had shown in war had won him general esteem. In addition, he was secretly the husband of the widowed Countess Rutowska.[12] This amiable man, who would be a Lieutenant-General today, had the misfortune to become involved in a very dangerous intrigue, together with the widowed Electress, mother of the Elector, whom she hated. Agdollo was imprisoned in Königstein,[13] where he still is after nearly thirty years, for the reigning Elector, so it is said, showed clemency in sparing him from the death penalty which was his due in punishment for his crime.

The evening of the first day I was in Dresden Maton greatly pleased me at supper. I asked her gently and fondly if she would sleep in my bed, and she replied that it was what she wanted, so the nuptials were celebrated, and we rose the next morning the best friends in the world. I spent the whole morning furnishing her with everything she needed: dress, shifts, stockings, petti-

coats, bonnets, shoes—everything, in short, for she had
nothing. I had many visitors; but I shut her up in her
room, replying to those who asked to see her that I would
do her that honor if she were my wife but, since she was
only my housekeeper, I did not want to introduce her
to society. For this reason she never let anyone who came
to see me enter my apartment when I was not there. I
had forbidden her to do so, and she made no objection
to it. She worked in her room on the linen I had had
made for her, with a young girl who helped her, and
whom I paid so that she should not be bored by being
left alone all day long. Sometimes, however, I took her
with me for a walk outside Dresden, and then she could
speak to any friends of mine who met me and joined us
in our walks.

This secretiveness on my part, which continued for all
of the two weeks the girl remained with me, began to
nettle all the young officers in Dresden, and especially
Count Bellegarde,[14] who was not accustomed to finding
a girl to his taste and being denied her when he took steps
to obtain her. Young, handsome, daring, generous, he
came into my room one day just as I was sitting down at
table with her and asked me for dinner, so I could neither
refuse him nor send Maton to her room. Throughout dinner he teased her good-naturedly with military jokes,
which I accompanied by others, but always keeping
within the bounds which it was his duty to observe. Maton
behaved very well, neither playing the prude nor departing from the respect which she owed to me and to herself.

It being my habit to take a siesta, I bluntly asked the
Count to leave half an hour after we rose from table.
He asked me with a laugh if Mademoiselle took one too,
and I answered that she did. At that, going for his sword,
he invited me to dinner the next day with Maton; I told
him that I did not take her to dinner anywhere, but that
he was free to come and take potluck with me at dinner
every day, where he would certainly find me with her. At

this refusal, to which he did not know what to answer, he took his leave, if not angrily at least very coldly. In this way I spent a week, very well pleased with Maton.

My mother having come back from the country, I went to see her the next day. She lived on the fourth floor of a house[15] from which, since it was not very far from my inn, I saw the *Erker*[16] (that is, the projecting bay) of the apartment I occupied. I chance to look there, and at one of the windows of the *Erker* I see Maton, standing sewing and at the same time talking to Monsieur de Bellegarde, who was at the window of a room near to the one with the *Erker,* which formed the corner and which did not belong to me though it belonged to the same inn. This discovery makes me laugh; I was sure I had not been seen, and I had decided, as on other occasions, that I would not let myself be cuckolded. My jealousy was more of the mind than of the heart.

Two hours later I go to dine in high spirits, Maton being equally gay. Turning the conversation to Bellegarde, I tell her that he is certainly in love with her; she replies that flirting was the habit of all officers and that she did not believe he was more in love with her than with any other girl.

"What? Did he not come here this morning to call on me?"

"Certainly not. And if he had come, the little girl would have gone to the door to tell him you were not at home."

"But when the guard was changed did you not see him walking about the square under our windows?"

"Certainly not."

It was all I needed. Maton was keeping her secret; I should be a cuckold in twenty-four hours if I did not at once do something to prevent it. I dissimulate perfectly, I do not change my humor. I give Maton some caresses after coffee, I leave, I go to the theater, I play with some success; I return to my inn at the second act; it was still light. At the door of the inn I find one of the inn servants,

I ask him if there are other rooms on the second floor besides the four I was occupying, and he replies that there are two more, with windows giving on the street.

"Excellent. Tell your master that I want those too."

"They have been taken since last evening."

"Who took them?"

"A Swiss officer who is in the service and who will sup there tonight with some other officers."

I say no more, to keep him from becoming suspicious; but it was a fact that nothing was easier than to pass from the window of the room in question to the bay by way of the window which was close to the other. In addition, there was a door in the room itself, in which I often had Maton sleep with the little girl when I did not want to have her sleep with me. The door was fastened with a bolt on our side; but she was there, and with keys it could be opened from the farther side.

I go up, I go to see Maton, who was sitting precisely in the bay, where a pleasantly cool breeze was blowing. After speaking of other things, I told her that I wanted to change rooms.

"You shall occupy mine, and I will come here, where in the morning I shall enjoy the delightful coolness."

She praises my idea, adding that it will not prevent her from coming to sew in the *Erker* in the afternoon.

From this reply I see that Maton is as clever as I am. I no longer loved her. I have her bed taken to the next room and mine put where hers had been, together with my table and all my papers. We sup gaily, and though I have not invited Maton to come to bed with me she has not the shadow of an idea of my change of humor. I go to sleep in my new room, I hear the voices of Bellegarde and of those who are drinking with him, I go to the window in the *Erker,* and I see the curtains in the windows of the other room drawn, which was supposed to show me that there was no plot afoot; but I learned afterward that Mercury had informed Jupiter that Amphitryon had changed his room.[17]

The next morning a bad headache, to which I was not usually subject, made me spend the day in the house; I had myself bled, and my kind mother came to keep me company and to dine with Maton. She was fond of her, she had several times asked me to send her to keep her company, and I would never do it. The day after the bleeding, my head being very heavy, I took a dose of medicine. That night when I went to bed I found myself attacked by a love token whose symptoms were very ugly. I knew enough about it not to be mistaken. Extremely chagrined, I am convinced that it can only be a present from Maton, for after the time at Leopol I had had to do with no other woman. I spend the night very angry with the trollop, I rise at daybreak, I go into her room, I draw the curtains, she wakes, I sit down on her bed, I throw off the sheet, and I pull from under her a towel folded double, the sight of which disgusts me. After that, she not daring to hinder me, I examine all that I had not taken the trouble to examine before, and I see a hideous pesthouse. She confesses with tears that she has had the malady for six months; but that she had believed she had not infected me with it because she had always taken great care to keep clean and to wash herself each time she foresaw that I would make love to her.

"Wash yourself, you wretch! Look at what you have done to me. You have robbed me of my one treasure, my health. But no one must know it, for it is my own fault and I am ashamed of it. Meanwhile get up, and you will see how kind I am."

She gets up; I have a trunk packed for her with all the things I had had made for her, and I send my servant to another inn to see if there is a small room to be rented for her. He goes, and he comes back to tell me that at the inn on the great square[18] there is a small room on the fifth floor at four groschen a day. I tell him to wait outside, and I tell Maton that she must go there at once, for she could no longer live with me. I let her weep, and I give her fifty crowns, telling her that she is free to spend

them where and as she wishes, for I want to hear no more
of her, and I make her give me a receipt truthfully setting forth the circumstances, humiliating as they were
for her. She had to submit when she saw that I was ready
to send her away without giving her a copper. She copied
everything I wanted her to sign.

"What am I to do here where I know nobody?"

"If you want to go to Breslau I will send you there
without its costing you a copper."

She made no answer. I sent her to her new room with
her possessions, turning my back on her when I saw her
go down on her knees, thinking it would move me. I
performed this act of justice without being troubled by
the slightest feeling of pity, for what she had done, and
what she was engaged in doing, showed me that she was
a little monster who would perhaps in one way or another
have cost me my life.

I left the inn on the next day but one, renting for six
months at thirty-five crowns the whole second floor of
the house in which my mother was living, putting into it
the furniture I needed to take the great cure, for the
glands in my groins were swollen and hard. Maton's
ablutions had the effect that she did not infect me with
gonorrhea but sent all the poison into my blood, which
finally had to show itself. If it had delayed another week
or two I should have been as ill as I had been at Augsburg
and at Wesel. The answer I made to all those who asked
me for news of my housekeeper was perfectly simple.
She was a servant whom I had dismissed and in whom
I took no more interest.

It was a week later that my brother Giovanni came to
tell me that Bellegarde and four or five other young men,
whom he named to me, were in the care of a physician,
reduced to a very bad state by my housekeeper.

"I am sorry for them; but it is their fault. Why did
they expose themselves to it?"

"She is a girl who came to Dresden with you."

"And whom I have dismissed. It is enough for me that they had nothing to do with her during the time she was living with me. Tell these young men that if they complain of me they are in the wrong; and that they are wrong to make their shame known. Let them learn to be wise, and let them go about being cured in silence. Otherwise, sensible people will laugh at them, and they will look like fools. Do you agree with me?"

"The thing does not do you honor."

"That I know; and so I do not boast of it, for I am not fool enough to make it public. They must be very stupid. If they had any intelligence they should have supposed that I could not but have had very good reasons for dismissing her so suddenly, and hence have suspected everything and kept away from the monster. They deserve the disease she has given them."

"They are all amazed that you are in good health."

"Go console them; tell them you have seen me in the state in which you see me, but that no one has heard a word of it, for I am not a fool."

Seeing that he was proved a fool himself, he left, and I submitted to remedies which, by the middle of August, made me as healthy as I had been when I left Warsaw. About this time the Princess Straznikowa,[19] Prince Adam Czartoryski's sister, came to Dresden; Count Brühl gave her lodging. I made my bow to her, and I learned from her own lips that her royal cousin had been weak enough to let himself be imposed on by calumny. I told her that I was of Ariosto's opinion, who wrote that the virtues were estimable only under the veil of constancy.

"Did you notice, Princess, that the last time I ate with the King at your table, His Majesty was pleased to pretend that he did not see me?"

"Certainly I noticed it."

"I feel sorry for the monarch who at that moment became unworthy of the esteem of a philosopher. You are going to Vienna now, and to Paris next year. You will see me there, Princess, and you shall write the King your cousin that you would not have seen me there if I had been hanged in effigy.''

The September fair[20] at Leipzig being a brilliant occasion, I wanted to be there in order to regain my weight by eating larks.[21] Playing with careful economy at Dresden, though always punting, I won three or four hundred ducats, so that I went to Leipzig with a letter of credit for three thousand crowns on the banker Hohmann,[22] who introduced me to an intelligent octogenarian who was High Commissioner[23] of the Saxon mines. It was from this worthy man that I learned something which is only a trifle but which is remarkable because no Russian knows it. The Empress Catherine II, whom all Russia and all those who saw her believed to be a brunette and even to have very black hair, was a blonde. The Commissioner, who had seen her at Stettin every day for three years from the year she was seven to the year she was ten, told me that at that time her hair began to be combed with lead combs, which have the property of coloring the hair black. This was done because from then on she was destined to be the wife of the Duke of Holstein, who was the unfortunate Peter III. It was the settled policy at the Russian Court to do everything possible to make the reigning family brunette rather than blonde, a color which is too common in Russia and therefore is not liked there. For this reason steps were taken to darken the hair of the august and immortal Catherine, who did so many fine things without caring that the cost of them impoverished her vast Empire. She would have had to live another ten years in peace in order to make up for her extravagance.

An adventure which I had in Leipzig, and which I still remember with pleasure, was that Princess Auersperg,[24] having arrived from Vienna and put up at the same hostelry in which I was staying,[25] took a notion to go to the fair incognito. Having a large suite with her, she made one of her chambermaids act the part of Princess, and she followed her, acting that of chambermaid. I suppose the reader knows that she was extremely pretty, that she had a very pleasant wit, and that she had been the favorite of the Emperor Francis I. Having been informed of this masquerade, I leave the inn at the same time she does, and when the false Princess stops at a shop to look at the fine jewels which were there I approach the real Princess, who did not know me, and speaking to her as unceremoniously as one speaks to a chambermaid, I ask her if it is true that that lady there is the celebrated Princess Auersperg.

"Certainly she is."

"I find it hard to believe, for she is not pretty, and besides she has not the look of a Princess."

"Apparently you do not know very much about Princesses."

"I know so much about them that I will tell you it is you who have the look of one, for the devil take me if I would not give you a hundred ducats to spend the night with you."

"A hundred ducats? It would serve you right if I took you at your word; but then you would break it."

"No. Try me. I am staying in the same inn as you are. Think of a way, and I will make you the present in advance, as soon as I am sure that I shall have you, for you might play me one of the tricks of your trade."

"Very well; say nothing, and try to speak to me at the inn before or after supper, and if you are brave enough to take some risks we will spend the night together."

"What is your name?"

"Carline."

Sure that nothing would come of it, but delighted to have amused the Princess and to have let her know that she pleased me, I think of going on with the role of dupe which I had begun so well. After eating a bite in the public room downstairs, I go up, and I hover about the Princess's apartment, stopping three or four times as I

pass the door of the room in which her real chambermaids were. One of them asks me if I want something.

"No, Mademoiselle; excuse me; I was looking to see if
I saw one of you with whom I talked at the fair, but I
imagine she is busy."

"It must be Carline. She is waiting on the Princess at
table. She will come out in half an hour."

I go up to my room; a half hour later I go down again,
and the same chambermaid tells me to hide in a closet
which she shows me, to which Carline will come in a
moment. I go there, the closet was dark, I wait, and
Carline arrives. I was sure that it was the real Carline;
but I continue to play my role. No sooner has she come
in than she takes me by my free hand [26] and says in a
very low voice that I have only to stay there and she will
come without fail as soon as her mistress has been put to
bed.

"Without a light?"

"No light. People going up and down in the house
would see that there was someone."

"Without a light I have no weapon, my charming
Carline. Then too, this is not a place to spend at least
five or six hours in. Do this. The first room at the top
of that staircase is mine. I will be alone, and I assure
you that no one will come in; go up there, and you will
make me happy. I have the hundred ducats here."

"It is impossible. I shouldn't dare go up for a million."

"Too bad. Nor will I stay here all night, where there
is nothing but a chair, for a million. Good-by, beautiful
Carline."

"Wait. Let me go out first."

She hurries out; but I take care to catch hold of her
dress; so when she tried to shut the door she could not.
I went out with her, she going to the left to her room
and I to the right to the stairs up to mine. Delighted
with the adventure, in which I had carried off the victory,
I went to bed the most contented of men. It is clear that
their intention was either to cheat me out of a hundred

ducats or to lock me in the closet and leave me there all night.

At noon on the next day but one, as I was bargaining for a pair of lace cuffs, Princess Auersperg entered the same shop, escorted by Count Zinzendorf,[27] whose acquaintance I had made in Paris at La Cavamacchie's[28] twelve years earlier. Just as I was withdrawing to make room for the Princess, the Count recognized me, spoke to me of those days in Paris, and asked me who was the Casanova who had fought a duel six months before in Warsaw.

"Alas, it is I. Here is my arm still in a sling."

"Aha! I congratulate you. The story of your duel must be interesting."

He then presents me to the Princess, asking her if she had heard of the duel.

"Oh, I have read of it in the gazettes. So this is the gentleman. I am delighted," she said to me, "to have made your acquaintance."

She showed no sign of recognizing me; and, as was only proper, I was as discreet as she. In the afternoon I paid a call on the Count, who asked me to go with him to the Princess, who would be delighted to hear the story of my strange adventure from my own lips, and I did so with great pleasure. The Princess, listening to my story most attentively, continued to play the role she had assumed, and even her chambermaids did not look at me. She left the next day.

At the end of the fair I saw in my room the beautiful Castel-Bajac.[29] I was about to sit down at table alone to revel in eating a dozen larks and then go to bed.

"You here, Madame?"

"Alas yes, unfortunately for me. I have been here three weeks; I have seen you a score of times, and we have always avoided you."

" 'We'?"

"Schwerin." [30]

"He is here?"

"Here, and in prison because of a forged bill of exchange which could not be falser and which he discounted, and I don't know what they will do to him. The poor wretch should at least have run away; but he would not. The man is absolutely determined to get himself hanged."

"And you have been with him ever since you left England? That was three years ago."

"Exactly. Stealing everywhere, cheating, deceiving, escaping, and I don't know what else. There is not an unhappier woman in the world than I. The forged bill of exchange is only for three hundred crowns. Forget everything, Casanova, do a noble act, save a man of illustrious birth from the gallows or the galleys, and my unhappy self from death, for I will kill myself in despair."

"Madame, I will let him be hanged, for he tried to get me hanged too with the forged bank notes; but I admit that you arouse my pity. In proof of which I invite you to come to Dresden with me day after tomorrow and I promise you three hundred crowns as soon as the scoundrel has been made to suffer what his destiny decrees for him. I do not understand how such a woman as you can have fallen in love with a man who has neither looks nor intelligence nor talent. His only asset consists in the name Schwerin."

"Then let me tell you that I have never been in love with him. Since that other scoundrel Castel-Bajac—who, by the way, was never my husband—introduced him to me, I never lived with him except under compulsion, and often touched by his tears and moved by his despair. I will tell you further that, despite my face and my character, which does not declare me vicious, I have never found a decent man who has seriously offered me a settled income to live with him. I assure you I would have accepted it, and that I would have left the wretch who will one day or another be the cause of my death."

"Where are you lodging?"

"Nowhere at the moment. Everything I had was taken, and I was put out into the street. Have pity on me."

So saying, she threw herself on her knees before me, and she broke into such a flood of tears that her grief went to my soul. The inn servant stood there in amazement, watching the scene and waiting for me to order him to serve me supper. My own manservant had gone to Dresden at my order. She was one of the prettiest women in all France, she was perhaps twenty-six years of age, she was the wife of an apothecary in Montpellier when Castel-Bajac had seduced her. She had made no impression on me in London because I was then too much in love with another;[31] but the woman had everything a woman could have to please me.

I force her to rise, I tell her she has touched me, I promise to help her; but I insist that she calm herself and even eat a bite with me. The waiter, admiring my noble action, goes to fetch another table service, and has a bed put in my own bedroom, which made me want to laugh.

The unfortunate woman, eating with wonderful appetite, though very melancholy, reminded me of the Matron of Ephesus.[32] It was after supper that I gave her her choice: either I would do nothing for her and leave her to her fate in Leipzig, or I would try to recover all her possessions, take her to Dresden with me, provide her with everything she needed, and pay her a hundred gold ducats when I was sure that she would not give them to the wretch who had reduced her to the state she was in. She did not think long before accepting the second choice; she gave me a sound and sensible reason, which was that if she stayed in Leipzig, she did not see how she could be of any use to the unfortunate man or how she herself could survive even for twenty-four hours, for she had not a copper or anything to sell. She was reduced to beggary or to turn prostitute. She made a still more sensible reflection. She said that if I gave her the hundred ducats then and there, and if she used them to get the poor prisoner released, she would still be in a wretched situation, not knowing how to leave, or, if she left, where to go. She said that all her possessions were in the hands of the proprietor of the inn in which she had stayed for three weeks, and that he might give them back if he were paid what was owed him, disregarding the order of sequestration which the banker who had discounted the bill of exchange had obtained upon all her effects. I promised that on the next day I would find a clever man who would try to do all that, and after embracing her I told her to go to bed. But here is what surprised me.

"I foresee," she said, "that either from inclination or from politeness you may approach me to demand a recompense which is certainly your due, and which I would grant you from both inclination and gratitude; but I must not wait for that moment to tell you something as repulsive for you as it is humiliating for me. Look at this shift, and divine what condition I am in."

Striking my head with my hand, I answered her only with:

"Go to bed, Madame, you deserve a better fate."

I still do not know to this day if I should have taken the risk of losing my health again, recently as I had been cured of the same disease, without first making investigations which would reassure me, but it is certain that it would have been in her power to deceive me, and that this fresh misfortune would have greatly degraded me in my own eyes and perhaps have disgusted me with life once and for all. This Frenchwoman had delicacy and an excellent heart, an unkind gift which nature had made her, which was the cause of all her misfortune.

The next morning I found an honest broker, who as soon as I explained the matter to him undertook to persuade the innkeeper to return everything which might belong to the lady upon payment of what was due him, leaving him all the sequestered articles which belonged to the imprisoned Count. He came back to the coffeehouse an hour later to tell me that the thing was done if I would give him sixty crowns. He assured me that he would see to it that he was given everything of hers, together with her trunk, which he would at once have carried to my inn. It was this broker whom I instructed to inform me in Dresden of all that happened to the Count. A half-hour after I returned to my inn the trunk arrived, in which the poor woman found all her clothes which she had never hoped to see again; she could not find words enough to express her gratitude to me, and she deplored her condition, which prevented her from showing me all that she felt for me.

This is natural: a woman of feeling thinks she cannot do anything more for a man who has done her a kindness than give herself to him body and soul. I believe that a man thinks differently; the reason is that man is made to give, woman to receive.

The next morning, an hour before we left, the broker came to tell us that the banker whom Schwerin had cheated had sent an express to Berlin to ask the Minister if the King would object to his proceeding according to all the rigor of the law against the Count, whose family had so many titles to respect.

"It is," said La Castel-Bajac, "the death blow which Schwerin has always feared. He is done for. The King will pay, but he will send him to end his days in Spandau.[33] Would that he had been imprisoned there four years ago!"

She left with me, very happy and full of gratitude when I told her I had a house, that she would live with me, and that I would at once put her in the care of a surgeon whose skill I knew from experience. She assured me that it was Schwerin himself who had made her the present only a month before at Frankfurt, and that he was even more ill than she, lying in prison as he was, where he must be worse off than in hell, since he had not a copper or a shirt to change into. Such was the state to which a man could find himself reduced. The reflection made me tremble.

At Dresden my appearance with the lady caused great surprise. She did not look like a girl of Maton's sort, she was presentable, she had distinction, her manner was modest and inspired respect; I gave her the name of Countess Blasin,[34] I introduced her to my mother and all my relatives, I gave her my room, removing to the one on the back, and I made the surgeon to whose care I confided her swear silence; he had to say that he was still coming for me, since I was not completely cured of my severe illness. I took her with me to the theater, I enjoyed making her play the part of a person of consideration. What consoled her was that she did not have to undergo the great cure. Two pints a day of a cooling infusion of herbs restored her to perfect health. Toward the end of November she found herself so well that she thought she could invite me to sleep with her. I could believe her, and I desired it. Our nuptials were a secret of which no one knew. At this time I received a letter from the broker giving us the news that the cheated banker had been paid by order of the King, and that the Count had been taken to Berlin under guard. Six weeks later[35] I learned in Vienna, when I was no longer with La Castel-Bajac, that the King had had him imprisoned in Spandau, where, if he has not died there, he must still be.

The time having come when I must pay a hundred ducats to the beauty, with whom I had fallen really in love, for she was as sensible and sweet as she was beautiful, I told her so. I told her too, sincerely and frankly, that both my heart and my mind commanded me to go to Portugal, and that I could not go there in the company of a beautiful woman except at the risk of my good fortune, besides which the very long and costly journey would be beyond my resources. La Castel-Bajac had so many proofs of my fondness that she could not believe I had tired of her or wanted to get rid of her in order to live with another woman. She told me that she owed me everything, and that I owed her nothing; but that if I wanted to do her one last kindness I should give her the means to return to Montpellier. She had relatives there, she was sure they would not abandon her, and she hoped to go back to her husband. I gave her my word of honor that I would send her back to her native city.

I left Dresden with her in the middle of December, having only four hundred ducats at my disposal, because luck had been against me at the faro bank and because my journey to Leipzig with all that followed on it had cost me three hundred ducats. I told my beauty nothing of these difficulties, I thought only of seeing that she wanted for nothing and of giving her continual proofs of my affection. We stopped for four days in Prague,[36] and we arrived in Vienna on Christmas Day. We went to lodge at the "Red Ox," [37] Mademoiselle Blasin, Modiste, in one room, I in another next to it, which, however, did not prevent me from going in to sleep with her. No later than eight o'clock the next morning two men enter La Blasin's room just as I was taking coffee with her.

"Who are you, Madame?"

"My name is Blasin."

"Who is this gentleman?"

"Ask him."

"What are you doing in Vienna?"

"I am taking coffee, as you see."

"If the gentleman is not your husband, you shall leave within twenty-four hours."

"The gentleman is only a friend of mine, and I will not leave until I see fit, unless I am driven out by force."

"Very well. We know, Monsieur, that you have another room, but it makes no difference."

One of the two police then enters my room, and I follow him.

"What do you want?"

"I am looking at your bed, which shows no sign of having been unmade; you slept with your friend."

"Damnation! I did not go to bed, either alone or with anyone. What is this accursed spying?"

He returns to La Blasin's room, and they both go, repeating the order to her to leave within twenty-four hours. I tell La Blasin to dress quickly and to go to tell the French Ambassador[38] the whole story, continuing to say that her name is Blasin, that she is unmarried, that she is a modiste, and that she is only waiting for the first opportunity to go on to Strassburg, from there to Lyons, and from Lyons to Montpellier. While waiting for her to get dressed, I engage a carriage and I hire a lackey. La Blasin goes to the Ambassador, tells him everything in accordance with my instructions, and comes back an hour later to tell me that his answer to her had been not to worry and not to think of leaving until she saw fit. I dress, I take her to mass, then I dine with her, and not wanting to go out, for the weather was bad, I spend the whole day by the fire with her, she having decided to take a place in the coach which left for Strassburg.

At eight o'clock the innkeeper comes up and tells her that he has been ordered to give her a room which does not adjoin mine, and that he must obey. She laughs, and she tells him that she is quite ready. I ask him if she had to sup alone too, and he replies that he has received no order as to that. I then tell him that I will go to her room to sup with her. The coach for Strassburg was to leave on the 30th, and the innkeeper himself undertook to reserve a place for her. But despite this infamous tyranny, I ate and slept with her on all the four nights she spent in Vienna. I wanted to force her to accept fifty louis, but she would take only thirty, convincing me that she would still arrive in Montpellier with some louis in her pocket. She wrote to me from Strassburg, and after that I had no news of her until I saw her again in Montpellier, as I shall relate in the proper place.

On the first day of the year 1767 I engaged an apartment in the house of Monsieur Schrötter,[39] and I took my letters to Madame de Salmour,[40] Mistress of the Household to the Archduchess Marianne,[41] and to Madame Starhemberg.[42] Then I went to see the elder Calzabigi,[43] who was working for the Ministry under the orders of Prince Kaunitz.[44] I often went to see Metastasio,[45] and to the theater every day when Vestris[46] danced; the young Emperor[47] had sent to Paris for him in order to see what his beautiful dancing was. On the 7th or 8th of January I saw the Empress, his mother, come to the theater dressed all in black. Everyone clapped. It was the first time she had appeared in public since the Emperor's death. In Vienna I found the Count de la Pérouse,[48] who was petitioning the Empress for the repayment of a half million florins which his father had lent to Charles VI. With the Count I made the acquaintance of the Spaniard Las Casas,[49] a nobleman of great intelligence, and, a rare thing, without prejudices. At the Count's I also found the Venetian Uccelli,[50] with whom I had attended the Seminary of San Cipriano in Murano, who was then in Vienna as Secretary of Embassy with the Ambassador Polo Renier,[51] who died the Doge. The Ambassador, a man of intelligence, esteemed me; but my situation with the State Inquisitors kept him from receiving me. During this time my good friend Campioni arrived from Warsaw by way of Cracow. I was very glad to put him up. He was to go to London to mount ballets; but he had time to spend a couple of months with me.

Prince Charles of Kurland, who had spent a month in Venice during the summer, and whom Signor Bragadin and the two other friends[52] to whom I had recommended him had treated with the greatest esteem and friendship, had spent two months in Vienna and had left it two weeks before my arrival to return to Venice, where the Duke of Württemberg,[53] who died two years ago, was making a great stir. He was there openly, and he was spending immense sums. Prince Charles wrote me letters in which he tried to make me feel all his gratitude. He assured me that in all Europe he had never known persons more estimable than the three friends of mine to whom I had sent him. It was as much as to tell me that he and all his possessions were at my disposal until the day of his death.

So I was living in Vienna perfectly at ease, amusing myself and in good health, and still planning to go to Portugal in the spring. I saw no company, either good or bad, I went to the theaters, and often to dinner at Calzabigi's, who made a show of his atheism and who was forever shamelessly belittling Metastasio, who despised him; but Calzabigi did not care. A great political calculator, he was Prince Kaunitz's familiar spirit.

One day after dinner when I was still at table amusing myself with my dear Campioni, a pretty girl [54] twelve or thirteen years of age steals into my apartment, bold and timid, dropping me a curtsy, and sure that she will not be ill received, for on her face was the fatal letter of recommendation which calms every man, even the most savage. I ask her what she wants, and she replies in Latin heroic verse. She asks me for charity, and she says that her mother is in my anteroom and will come in if I wish it. I reply in Latin prose that I do not care to see her mother, and I tell her the reason plainly; she replies by four verses which, being inappropriate, show me that she had committed everything she had said to me to memory, not even knowing what she was saying. She goes on to tell me in verse that her mother must come in, because she would be put in prison if the Commissioners of Chastity had reason to suspect that, being alone with her, I was f . . . ing her.

This broad term, uttered in good Latin, makes me burst out laughing and rouses in me a desire to explain to her in her mother tongue what she has said to me. She tells me that she is Venetian, which, making me even more curious, leads me to say in our beautiful dialect that the spies could not suspect her of having come to my room to do what she had said, for she was still too young. To this objection, after thinking a little, she recited ten or twelve lines from the *Priapeia*[55] to the effect that fruit slightly green excites the palate more than fruit which is ripe. It took no more to make me ardent; Campioni, seeing that he is in the way, goes to his room.

I ask her if her father is in Vienna, and she says that he is, and she does not take fright at what my hand is doing to her even as I ask her questions. I come to something which is everything, though not yet fully formed, and, all smiles, she recites some verses in honor of the instrument of propagation and the act of love. I find it admirable, I make an end, and I dismiss her with two ducats. There are more verses to thank me, and an address in German, which was that of her house, accompanied by four Latin verses in which she told me that if I came there to go to bed with her I should find her Hebe or Ganymede[56] as I chose.

I admire the ingenious contrivance of the Venetian who was the girl's father to make his living by her. She was very pretty; but there are so many pretty girls in Vienna that they are almost all of them poor. He had made his surprising by this hocus-pocus; but in Vienna it could not go on very long. Toward dusk the next day I take a notion to go on foot to see the girl, who perhaps did not know what she had promised in the address she had left me. At the age of forty-two years, despite all my experience, I am so rash as to walk alone along the boulevard to which the address told me to go. She sees me from the window, and, guessing that I am looking for her house, she calls to me, she shows me the door, I enter, I go upstairs, and I see the vile thief, the infamous Pocchini.[57] It was too late for me to retreat; turning round and leaving would have made me seem to be running away, and I never even thought of it. I saw there his supposed wife Catina,[58] two Slavonians[59] armed with sabers, and the decoy duck. All desire to amuse myself having gone, I choose the wise course of dissimulating, intending to leave five or six minutes later.

Pocchini, swearing and blaspheming, begins reproach-

ing me for the harshness with which I had treated him
in England, he says that the time for his revenge has
come, and that my life is in his hands. The horrible
Slavonian who seemed to be the master, for the other
looked like a servant, says to me that we must make
peace, hands me a chair, opens a bottle, and insists that
we drink. I decline; Pocchini, walking up and down the
room like a madman, says that I refuse to drink so that
I shall not have to pay for the bottle, I say he is mistaken, that I am ready to pay, and I put my right hand
in my pocket to take a ducat from my purse without
taking my purse from my pocket. The Slavonian says
that I can take out my purse without fear of being
robbed of it, for I am among honest people. At that I
take out my purse, and, since I have difficulty untying
it because I have my other hand in a sling, the Slavonian
takes it from me, Pocchini tears it from his hands and
says that it belongs to him to repay him in part for all
that I had made him lose. I laugh, I say that it is at his
disposal, and I rise to leave. The Slavonian wants me
to embrace him; I reply that there is no need of that,
and he draws his saber and the other does the same. I
thought my last moment had come. I embraced them all,
and I was astonished when they let me leave. I returned
to my lodging more dead than alive, not knowing what
to do. I went to bed.

CHAPTER X

I receive an order to leave Vienna. The Em-
press modifies it but does not revoke it. Za-
woiski in Munich. My stay in Augsburg. Piece
of bravado in Ludwigsburg. The gazetteer at
Cologne. My arrival in Aix-la-Chapelle.

THE GREATEST mistake one can make in punishing a scoundrel is to let him outlive the punishment, for
it is little short of certain that, once punished, he will
think of nothing but taking a scoundrel's revenge. If I
had had any kind of weapon I would have defended myself, but the cutthroats would have hacked me to pieces
and taken my watches, my snuffbox, and everything I
had, and the courts would have done nothing to them,
for they would have put my body out of the house. At
eight o'clock Campioni came to my bedside and was
greatly astonished at the story. Without indulging himself in blaming the victim, as all fools do when they hear
someone complain of some flagrant wrong to which he
has been subjected, he seconds me in thinking of ways
to obtain justice for me and to get back my purse; but
we foresee that they will all prove useless, for the scoundrels can take refuge in denying everything. There were
no witnesses except the cutthroats themselves, and the
woman and the girl could only have agreed with them.

Nevertheless, the next day I write the whole veracious story of the affair, beginning with the girl who recited Latin verses; then I make a fair copy of them, intending to present the whole to the Chief of Police or to the criminal magistrate, according to what an advocate to whom I should go would tell me.

I dine, and just as I was about to go out in my carriage, a policeman comes and orders me to go to speak with Count Schrattenbach,[1] who was called the Statthalter. I reply by telling him to inform my coachman of the place to which he is to take me, adding that I will go there immediately.

I enter a room in which I see a fat man standing, and a number of others, at some distance from him, who seem to be there only to carry out his orders. As soon as he sees me he holds a watch before my eyes and tells me to take note of the hour.

"I see it."

"Very well. If tomorrow at this same time you are here, I will have you shown out of Vienna by force."

"Why do you give me this order, than which nothing could be more unjust?"

"In the first place, I am not accountable to you; and I can tell you in the second place that you would not receive the order if you had not broken Her Majesty's laws which forbid gambling and which condemn sharpers to hard labor. Do you recognize this purse, do you recognize these cards?"

I had no idea what the cards were; but I recognize my purse, which must contain no more than a quarter of the gold which was in it when it was taken from me. Furious at the calumny, I reply only by handing him the statement I had written in four pages. The hangman reads it, then he laughs, saying that I had a reputation for being intelligent, that it was known who I was, why I had been expelled from Warsaw, and finally that the whole story I had given him to read was nothing but a pack of lies, which common sense rejected because they had no probability.

"In short, you shall leave," he repeats, "within the time I have prescribed, and I want to know now where you will go."

"I will not tell you until I have made up my mind to leave."

"What! You dare to tell me that you will not obey me?"

"It is yourself who have given me the choice by saying that if I do not leave willingly you will make me leave by force."

"Very well. I have already been told that you have a brain; but it will be of no use to you here. I advise you to avoid harsh treatment and to leave."

"Be so good as to give me back my written statement."

"I will give you back nothing. Go."

That, my dear reader, was one of the terrible moments which I have had in my life and which make me tremble every time I remember them. It was only a cowardly love of life which stopped me from quickly unsheathing my sword and running it through the body of that fat pig of a Statthalter of Vienna, who was disposing of me in this fashion.

Returning to my inn, I think of going to inform Prince Kaunitz[2] of the matter, though he did not know me. I proceed there, I go upstairs, and a footman tells me to wait where I am. He was to pass there on his way to dinner, followed by all his guests. It was five o'clock.

I see the Prince appear, and I notice following him Signor Polo Renier, Ambassador of my country. The Prince asks me what I want, and speaking in a loud voice *coram omnibus* ("in the presence of all") I tell him the whole story.

"I am ordered to leave, Monseigneur, but I shall not obey; I implore Your Highness's help so that my justified complaint can be laid at the foot of the throne."

"Write a petition; I will send it to the Empress; but I advise you only to beg her to suspend the order, for you would irritate her by telling her that you will not obey."

"But if the royal grace is delayed, violence will oppress me in the meanwhile."

"Take refuge with the Minister of your country."

"Alas, Prince, I no longer have a country. A legal though unconstitutional violence deprives me of the rights of a citizen and a man. I am a Venetian, and my name is Casanova."

The Prince thereupon looks in surprise at the Ambassador, who, smiling as he always did, spends ten minutes speaking to him in a low voice.

The Prince says to me that it is unfortunate for me that I cannot claim the protection of some Minister. At these words a nobleman six feet tall says to me that I can claim his, since my whole family is in the service of the King his master, and since I had served him myself.[3] And it was literally true.

"He is Count Vitzthum," [4] the Prince said to me; "so go at once and write to the Empress, and I will send her your petition immediately, and if the answer is delayed, take refuge with him. You will be safe from violence until you are ready to leave at your good pleasure."

After ordering writing materials brought to me, the Prince goes to dine.

Here is my petition, which I wrote and copied in ten minutes, and with a copy of which the Venetian Ambassador saw fit to favor the Senate of Venice.[5]

"Madame,

"I am sure that if, when Your Imperial and Royal Austrian Majesty is walking, an insect should say to you in a plaintive voice that you are about to crush it, you would turn your foot, if only a little, in order not to deprive the poor creature of life.

"I am the insect, Madame, who dares implore you to order Monsieur the Statthalter Schrattenbach to put off

King Stanislaus Poniatowski of Poland

IV   5

Vous etes homme de Parole
je Vous ai Comtel, puisse un
meilleur Sort Vous atendre
dans les Pais que vous aler
habiter et Souvenez vous que
Vous avez en moi un ami

                    A Moczynski

ayant reçu mille ducats du roi de Pologne lorsqu'il m'ordonna
de quitter l'Ussovie trois mois après mon duel, j'ai envoyé a
son ministre les quitances de tous mes créanciers.
Il m'écrivit cette lettre, et je suis parti le même jour
avec le comte Clari 9 juin 1766

379

Count Moczynski to Casanova

crushing me with Your Imperial and Royal Majesty's slipper for one week. It is possible that after that short time he will not crush me, but that you will remove from his hands the august slipper which you entrusted to him only to crush malefactors and not a man who remains a Venetian despite his flight from the Leads, and who is profoundly obedient to your Imperial and Royal Majesty's decrees.

"January 21, 1767.   Casanova."

After writing out this petition in a very round hand, I ask the footman who is there to deliver it to the Prince. Five or six minutes later he returns calmly, with my petition in his hands, telling me on the Prince's behalf that he will send it to the Empress at once but that he asks me to leave him a copy of it.

"Instantly."

I copy it, I hand both copies to the footman, and I leave. I was shaking like a paralytic, I feared that if I stayed there until the dinner was over I should be driven into doing a piece of work which would perhaps have cost me my life, for I was hot with anger from head to foot. I go home, and I sit down to write in the form of a manifesto the statement which I had put in the hands of the hangman Schrattenbach and which he had refused to return to me. About seven o'clock Count Vitzthum enters my room. He asks me to tell him the whole story of the girl whom I had gone to see, drawn by the four verses in which she promised that I should find her either Hebe or Ganymede. I give him the written address itself, he copies the verses, and he says it is enough to prove to an enlightened judge that I had been attacked and calumniated by scoundrels, but that even so he doubted if I would obtain justice.

"What! I shall have to leave tomorrow?"

"Oh, not that, for it is impossible that the Empress will not grant you the week for which you petitioned her."

"Why impossible?"

"Heavens! Have you forgotten what you wrote her? I have never seen a petition in that style. The Prince read it in his cold way, he smiled afterward, and he sent it to me; after me, he had it read by the Venetian Ambassador, who looked grave and asked him if he would send it to the Empress as it was. He replied that your petition was fit to be sent to God, if anyone knew the way there; and he immediately sent it to one of his secretaries with orders to put it in an envelope and send it to the Empress at once. After that we talked of you until the end of dinner, and what pleased me was that the Venetian Ambassador said that no one in Venice could guess what you could have done to deserve to be put under the Leads. Afterward there was talk of your duel, but no one could say any more about it than what had been read in the gazettes. Do me the favor to give me a copy of your petition to the Empress, for Schrattenbach holding her slipper delighted me."

I at once made him a copy from the original, which I have before me and which has only one correction, and I also gave him a copy of the manifesto. Before he left he repeated the order to go to lodge with him if I was not informed before the designated hour that the Empress had granted me the grace which I had asked of her.

At ten o'clock I saw in my apartment the Count de la Pérouse, the Marquis de Las Casas, and the Venetian Secretary of Embassy, Uccelli, who came to ask me for a copy of my petition on behalf of the Ambassador. I also sent him one of my manifestoes. The only thing which rather spoiled my manifesto, giving it a touch of the comic, was the four verses on the address, which in a way made it seem that I had gone to see Pocchini's daughter only in the hope of finding her Ganymede; it was not true; but the Empress, who knew Latin and knew the myth, might believe it, and that would have ruined me.

I went to bed two hours after midnight after making

six copies. The next day at noon Hasse,[6] son of the famous chapelmaster and the celebrated Faustina, and Secretary of Count Vitzthum's legation, came to tell me on his behalf that I had nothing to fear, either at home or if I went out in a carriage, but not on foot, and that he would come to see me at seven o'clock. On my asking him to write it all down for me he did me the favor, then he left.

So the order is suspended, the grace granted, it can only be at the Empress's behest! I have no time to lose; I shall have justice, the infamous cutthroats will be sentenced, I will get back my purse with two hundred ducats in it, and not as I saw it in the hands of the unworthy Statthalter, who would at least be dismissed from his office. Such were my castles in Spain, what I imagined was certain; *quod nimis miseri volunt hoc facile credunt* ("what those in misery ardently desire, they easily believe"),[7] says Seneca, in his knowledge of the human heart, somewhere in his tragedies. Before sending my manifesto to the Empress, to the Emperor, to Prince Kaunitz, to all the Ministers, I think of going to see Countess Salmour, who spoke to the Empress morning and evening. The reader knows that I had taken a letter to her.

The lady first receives me by saying that I ought to stop wearing my arm in a sling.

"It is an imposture, for after these ten months you cannot need it any longer."

I answer her with the voice and the expression of a man astonished that if I did not need the sling I would not wear it and that I was not an impostor.

"I have come, Madame, to trouble Your Excellency in regard to another matter."

"I am aware of that; but I will have nothing to do with it. You are all scapegraces like Tomatis."

I left instantly without making her a bow. I went home, unable to comprehend how I could be in such a pass. Assaulted, insulted by scoundrels and people of breeding alike, powerless to crush the latter or to exterminate the former, cast out by justice, where am I? What have I done? I am ridiculed for my sling? No one but Madame Salmour had said as much to me. If a man had said it to me I would have taken off my glove and given him a slap with my right hand. I could neither recover freedom of motion in it nor keep it from swelling as soon as I let it hang down for an hour. I was not completely cured until twenty months after I received the wound. But when I thought of the word "scapegrace" with which the Polish Countess had honored me I was sorry I had done all too little by merely turning my back on her. Old harridan unworthy of life, who yet lived ninety years.[8] Before that day I did not know the meaning of the word "scapegrace." Every time I hear someone utter it I remember that the honor of it was bestowed on me by a woman worthy of my utmost contempt.

Count Vitzthum came at seven o'clock to tell me that the Empress had said to Prince Kaunitz that Schratten-bach called the whole story I had written to exculpate myself pure romance. He was certain that I had kept a bank at faro with the sharpers' cards which were in his possession, that I had dealt with both hands, my sling being nothing but a deceit. One of the punters catching me in the act, they had rightly seized my bank and taken back the money I had won by cheating. The same punter, a police spy, had brought him my purse, containing forty ducats, which were duly confiscated. The Empress was obliged to believe everything Schrattenbach had told her about the matter, for even if I had been in the right she could make me reparation only by dismissing Schratten-bach, which would put her in a very difficult situation, for she could find no one willing to fill the onerous office which he filled, at a great cost in effort but always keeping Vienna clear of a verminous crew who dishonored the human race.

"That is the sum total of what Prince Kaunitz ordered

me to tell you. In any case, you have nothing more to fear. You shall leave when you please.''

''I shall have been robbed of two hundred ducats with impunity. But if the Empress, for reasons of policy, does not want me to bring a criminal suit, let her at least reimburse me. I beg you to ask Prince Kaunitz if I may prove to the sovereign in appropriate terms that she owes me that satisfaction as the least I can demand.''

''I will ask him.''

''Otherwise, I will leave, for what am I to do in a city where I cannot go about on foot, and where the government has cutthroats in its pay!''

''You are right. We are all persuaded that this Pocchini has slandered you. The girl who recites Latin verses is well known, but her address was not. I will tell you too that, as long as you remain in Vienna, you will do well not to publish this story, for it blackens Schrattenbach, whom the Empress unfortunately has to coddle.''

''I see all that, and I must champ the bit. I will leave as soon as the laundress brings me my linen. But I will print this story in all its atrocious details.''

''The Empress is prejudiced against you, I do not know by whom.''

''I know. It is by an old woman accursed in the eyes of God, by Madame Salmour, who told me to my face that I am a scapegrace.''

After hearing the whole of the incident, he left. The next morning he wrote me a note in which he told me that the Prince advised me to forget my two hundred ducats. He also told me that the little girl and her self-styled mother were apparently no longer in Vienna, for someone who had read the address and become curious about her had had her searched for in vain.

Thereupon, seeing that I should never obtain my rights in this accursed business, I decided to calm myself and to leave, nevertheless resolved to do two things, which I did not do. One was to print the story, the other was to

hang Pocchini with my own hands wherever I might find
him. At this same time a young lady of the Salis family,[9]
of Coire, arrived in Vienna by post coach, alone and with
no servant. The imperial hangman Schrattenbach sent
her an order to leave two days after her arrival, and she
sent him the answer that she intended to stay in Vienna
as long as she chose. The hangman had her shut up in
a convent. She was still there when I left. The Emperor,
who, though he despised his mother, never dared to question her orders, went to see the young lady in the convent, and his mother, having learned of it, asked him
what impression she had made on him; he replied that
she had impressed him as being far more intelligent than
Schrattenbach. It is a fact beyond question that a noble
soul will never believe that it cannot be free. Yet who is
free in this hell which we call the world? No one. Only
the philosopher can be so, but at the cost of sacrifices
which are perhaps not worth the phantom freedom.

I left Campioni my apartment, which was mine until
the end of the month, and my wood, of which I had laid
in a good supply, promising him that I would wait for
him in Augsburg, a city in which law alone reigned and
in which I had enjoyed life. I left all alone, without a
servant, in the carriage Count Moczynski had given me,
six days after receiving the order from the man who
cheated me in the end by dying[10] before I found a good
opportunity to kill him. I arrived in Linz on the next
day but one after my departure, stopping there all night
only to write him a letter, the most ferocious of all those
which I can have written in my life to people whose
despotism has crushed me, worse than the one I wrote in
1760 to the late Duke of Württemberg.[11] I went to the
post myself to get a receipt for it, so that he could not
say he had not received it. The letter was necessary to
my health. Anger kills if one does not succeed in purging
oneself of it in one way or another. From Linz I reached
Munich in three days, paying a visit there to Count

Gaetan Zawoiski, who died in Dresden seven years ago.[12] I had known him in Venice when he was in need, and I had been useful to him. As soon as I told him what had happened to me in Vienna he surmised that I might need money, and he gave me twenty-five louis. To tell the truth, it was perhaps less than he owed me if he intended it as repayment for all the money I had given him in Venice; but since I had never intended to lend it to him, I was grateful to him. He gave me a letter for Count Maximilian of Lamberg,[13] who was Marshal at the Court of the Prince-Bishop of Augsburg, who already knew me.

I went to lodge at Mayr's at the "Golden Grapes." [14] There were no plays or operas, but there were masked balls, where one found the nobility, the citizenry, and the girls of easy virtue; there were also small gatherings at which faro was played and at which one could amuse oneself at little expense. Sick and tired of all the pleasures, the misfortunes, the disappointments, the intrigues, the griefs which had been my lot in three capitals, I prepared to spend four months in a free city like Augsburg, where the foreigner enjoyed the same privileges as the canons. My purse had become very slender; but since my course of life cost me very little I had nothing to fear. Known, and not far from Venice, I was sure to have a hundred ducats at my disposal if I happened to need them. So I indulged in play for small stakes, making war on the sharpers, who, in my time, have become more numerous than the dupes, as doctors are more numerous than patients. I thought of ways to find a mistress, sorry that I had looked in vain for Gertrude.[15] The engraver had died, and no one could tell me what had become of his daughter.

Two or three days before the Carnival ended, having to attend a ball outside the city, I go to a stable to hire a carriage, and while waiting for the horse to be harnessed I go in to the stove; a girl asks me if I want wine, and I say no. She repeats the question, and I brusquely tell her no for the second time. I see her laugh, and, seeing that she is ugly, I tell her to be off.

"Yes, yes, I'm going. I know you cannot recognize me."

At these words I look at her more closely, and I see the pretty Annemirl,[16] the little maidservant of Gertrude's father the engraver, become ugly.

"You are," I said, "Annemirl."

"Alas, I once was. I know I am no longer fit to be loved, but you are the cause of it."

"I?"

"Yes, you. The four hundred florins you gave me led Count Fugger's[17] coachman to marry me. Not only did he spend everything I had and leave me, he gave me a disease which brought me to death's door; I recovered, but such as you see me."

"You distress me. Tell me what has become of Gertrude!"

"Don't you know that the ball you are going to is at her house?"

"At her house?"

"Yes. After her father's death she married a man of property and good conduct. His house is a short league from here; he provides lodging and meals, and you will be pleased."

"Is she still pretty?"

"She is as she was, except that she is six years older and has children."

"Does she indulge in gallantry?"

"I don't think so."

Annemirl had told me the truth. I went to the ball; Gertrude was glad to see me; she told her husband that I had lodged in her house; but when in the course of the night I spoke to her privately I found her behaving as her duty prescribed that she should.

Campioni arrived in Augsburg at the beginning of Lent with Binetti,[18] who was on the way to Paris to buy a post.[19] He had left his wife for ever, after taking everything she had. Campioni told me that no one in Vienna doubted the truth of my story in the terms in which I had made it public. He said that Pocchini and the Slavonian had disappeared a few days after I left, and that everyone called the Statthalter a plague.[20] Campioni left for London after spending a month with me.

As soon as I took my letter to Count Lamberg his reproaches flattered me, as did those of the Countess, who, though not a beauty, had everything to make anyone who approached her love her; she was a Countess Dachsberg,[21] who was his second wife, she was then six months pregnant. Three months later, not thinking that her time had come, she accepted an invitation from Count Fugger, Dean of the Chapter, to go with him in his carriage to eat at an inn at three-quarters of an hour's distance from Augsburg; I was one of the party. As she was eating an omelet the pains take her with such violence that she fears she will give birth instantly; she does not dare tell the Canon so; it is to me that she confides it. Quick, quick, out I go, I tell the coachman to bridle the horses quickly, I give her my arm, I put her in the carriage, the astonished Canon follows us, asking what is the matter, I reply that I will tell him all in the carriage, he gets in, he is uneasy, I ask him to tell the coachman to drive fast even if he kills the horses, and he does it all; but he insists on knowing the reason.

"Madame will give birth here if we do not go faster."

I saw her pains in her face. But I thought I should die laughing when I saw the Canon turn every color, terrified at the thought that she might really give birth in his carriage. He was in despair, for what would people say? The laughter such news would arouse horrified him. The Bishop was at Plombières,[22] he would be written to, the thing would appear in the newspapers.

"Quick, coachman! Quick, I say!"

We arrive at the castle, I fly to her room with her, she shuts herself in, a midwife is sent for; but it was too late; two minutes afterward Count Lamberg comes to tell us that Madame has given birth, and Monseigneur goes home to be bled.

I spent four months in Augsburg as pleasantly as possible, supping at Count Lamberg's two or three times a week, where I made the acquaintance of a man adorned to a rare degree with the qualities of the amiable gentleman; he is the Count of Thurn and Valsassina,[23] now Dean of the Chapter of Ratisbon, then page to the Prince-Bishop, a Prince of Darmstadt[24] who was a legless cripple. The page was always present at supper, as was Dr. Algardi,[25] physician to the Prince, who was charming too. He died fifteen or sixteen years later in the service of the Elector of the Palatinate, who now resides in Munich as the Elector of Bavaria.[26]

In Augsburg, most frequently at Count Lamberg's, I became well acquainted with a Baron Sellentin,[27] an officer in the Prussian service, who always lived in Augsburg to enlist recruits for his master. He was amiable, a wit in the Gascon manner, fond of gaming and well able to play his hand. He left the service ten or twelve years later and went to marry in Saxony near the Bohemian border. He wrote me from Dresden six years ago that, though he was now an old man, he greatly repented of having married.

During my stay in Augsburg several Poles who were leaving their country because of the troubles which were breaking out came to see me. Among others the Grand Notary to the Crown Rzewuski, whom I had known in Petersburg in love with the unfortunate Langlade, passed through Augsburg, and I at once went to see him at the "Three Moors,"[28] where he was staying. What a Diet![29] What intrigues! Fortunate were those who could keep away from it. He was going to Spa, where, he assured me, if I went there I should find the Princess, Prince Adam's sister, Tomatis, and La Catai, who had become his wife. It was he who decided me to go there too, and, being short of money, I took steps to go there with three or four hundred ducats in my purse. To that end I wrote to Prince Charles of Kurland, who was in Venice, to send me a hundred ducats. To persuade him to send them to me immediately, I sent him an infallible recipe for making the philosopher's stone. Since my letter, which contained so great a secret, was not in cipher, I advised him to burn it, assuring him that I had a copy of it with me; but he did not do so, he kept my letter, and it was taken from him in Paris with his other papers when he was sent to the Bastille.[30]

My letter in the archives of the Bastille would never have seen the light; but here is what happened to make my secret public. Twenty years later the populace of Paris, incited to riot by the Duke of Orléans, tore down the Bastille;[31] the archives were seized, my letter was found, and it was printed, together with several other curious documents which were later translated into German and English.[32] The ignoramuses who exist in the country in which I now live, and who, naturally, are all my enemies, for the donkey could never be the friend of the horse, triumphed when they read this chief article of accusation against me. They were stupid enough to reproach me with being the author of the letter, and they thought they could confound me by telling me that it had been translated into German to my eternal confusion. The Bohemian beasts who thus reproached me were astonished when I replied that my letter did me immortal honor and that, if they were not donkeys, they ought to admire it.

I do not know, my dear reader, if my letter was changed for the worse, but, since it has been published, permit me to record it in these memoirs to the honor of truth, the only God I adore. I copy it from my original, which I wrote at Augsburg in May of the year 1767; today is January 1, 1798.[33] Here is my letter:

"Monseigneur:
"Your Highness will burn this letter after reading it,

or will preserve it in your portfolio with all possible care, but it will be better to burn it, keeping a copy of it under the disguise of a cipher, so that, if it is stolen or lost, the reader will not understand a word of it. The attachment which you have inspired in me is not the only spring of my action; I confess to you that my interest has played an equal part in it. Permit me to tell you that it does not suffice me to be loved by you because of the qualities which you may have found in me, though that reason is infinitely flattering to me, for I must fear the inconstancy so natural to all princes; I wish you, Monseigneur, to have a much sounder reason for loving me; I want you to be obliged to me for an inestimable gift which I am about to make you. I give you the secret of augmenting the one material in the world of which Your Highness is in need. Gold. You would be rich if you had been born avaricious; having been born generous, you will always be poor without the secret which I shall communicate to you, and of which I am the sole possessor. Your Highness told me at Mitau that you wished me, before my departure, to give you the secret by which I transmuted iron into copper for you; I did not do so. I now give you the means to perform a much more important transmutation; but the place where you are is not the one suitable for the operation, though you can easily procure the materials. The operation requires my presence in respect to the construction of the furnace and to extreme care in the execution, for the slightest error would make it fail. The transmutation of Mars[34] is easy and mechanical, but the one which I give you is entirely philosophical. When your gold is assayed, which is very easy, it will be equal to that of which you see Venetian zecchini to be made. Consider, Monseigneur, that I may be putting you in a position to do without me, and, what is more, consider that I am putting my life in your hands as well as my freedom.

"The step I am taking must gain me your good will for ever, and must make you leave behind the prejudice which is entertained concerning the usual procedures and language of chemists. My self-esteem is wounded if Your Highness does not distinguish me from the crowd. The only favor I ask of you is to wait until we are together again to perform the operation. Since you cannot work alone, you cannot trust anyone; for even if the operation succeeded, the person who helped you would betray your secret. I will tell you that it was with these same ingredients, with the addition of niter and mercury, that I made the tree of projection[35] in the house of the Marquise de Pontcarré d'Urfé, the vegetation of which, calculated by the Princess of Anhalt-Zerbst,[36] gave an augmentation of fifty in the hundred. My fortune would now be at the highest pitch in regard to wealth if I had been able to trust a prince who controlled a mint. This good fortune has not fallen to me until today, and my utmost hopes are fulfilled, for your divine character frees me from all fear. Let us come to the point.

"One must take four ounces of good silver and dissolve it in aqua fortis, then precipitate it *secundum artem* with a sheet of copper; washing it afterward with warm water to separate all the acids from it; then it must be well dried and mixed with a half ounce of sal ammoniac, and so be put in a tortoise[37] of a kind which can be used as a recipient. After this preparation one must take a pound of alum feather and a pound of Hungarian crystal, four ounces of verdigris, four ounces of natural cinnabar, and two ounces of virgin sulfur. All these ingredients must be pulverized and mixed well together, and be put in a cucurbit of such a size that, when they are in it, they fill it only halfway. This cucurbit must be set on a furnace with four drafts, for the fire must be raised to the fourth degree. It is necessary to begin with a slow fire, which must only extract the phlegms, or hydropic parts, and when the spirits begin to appear the recipient in which is the Moon with the sal ammoniac must be subjected to it. All the joints will be sealed with the luting of Sapience, and, as the spirits pass, the fire must be regulated to the third degree. When the sublimation is seen to begin, the fourth draft must be boldly opened without any fear; but care must be taken to keep the sublimate from passing into the recipient, or tortoise, in which the Moon is. After this the whole must be allowed to cool. When the whole has been cooled, one must take the recipient in which the Moon is, close its spout with a bladder knotted three times, and put it in a circulating furnace with its spout directed upward; it must be given this slow circulating heat for twenty-four hours, and then the bladder must be removed, turning the tortoise toward the center so that it can distill. The fire must be increased to bring about the passage of the spirits which may be in the mass until complete desiccation. After this operation is performed three times, gold will be seen in the tortoise. The gold must then be taken out and melted with the addition of perfect body. Melting it with two ounces of gold and afterward putting it in water to work, one will find four ounces of gold which will meet every test, perfect in weight and malleable, but pale.

"There, Monseigneur, is the gold mine for your mint in Mitau, by means of which a director with four journeymen can give you a revenue of a thousand ducats a week, and twice that and four times that if Your Highness will multiply the workmen and the furnaces. I ask you for the directorship for myself, stipulating for my share only such material as it will please Your Highness to assign to me, having it struck with a die which I will describe to you. Remember, Monseigneur, that this must be the State's secret. You, a Prince, must understand the force of that expression. Give this letter to the flames, and if Your Highness wishes to give me a recompense in advance, I ask you only for a fond attachment to myself, who adores you. I am happy if I can flatter myself that my master will be my friend. My life, Monseigneur, which I put in your power with this letter, I shall be ready to give for your service, and I shall kill myself if it ever happens that I must repent of having confided in Your Highness, of whom I have the honor to be the inviolably attached servant, and to the end of my days.''

If this letter, in whatever language it is printed, speaks differently, it is not mine, and I give the lie to all the Mirabeaus[38] in France. I am called an exile from France, and it is untrue, for a man who leaves the kingdom by virtue of a *lettre de cachet* is neither exiled nor deported, he is obliged to obey an order from the monarch, who, by an act of his despotism, puts out of his house someone who inconveniences him, without thinking himself bound to tell him the reason. He regards his whole kingdom as his house. Every private citizen is entitled to act thus in his own domicile.

As soon as I saw my purse well filled I left Augsburg, all alone in my carriage, with a sufficient outfit. I left on June 14th. I was at Ulm when a courier from the Duke of Württemberg, who was in Venice, passed through it to go to Ludwigsburg to announce that His Most Serene Highness would arrive in five or six days. The courier had a letter for me, which had been given him by Prince Charles of Kurland, assuring him that he would find me at Augsburg lodged at the ''Grapes.'' Not having found me there, for I had left the day before, and knowing the road I had taken, he was sure to overtake me, and he overtook me at Ulm. Delivering the letter and drinking a glass, he asked me if I was the Casanova who had escaped from arrest at Stuttgart[39] because of a quarrel over gaming with three officers, and since I have never learned the art of denying any truth when someone asked me to testify to it, I replied that I was he. An officer of the Duke's who was present when I replied to the question said to me in a friendly manner that he was in Stuttgart at that time and that everyone blamed the three officers. Instead of answering him, I read the letter, which spoke only of our private business. After reading it, I took a whim to tell him a little lie, which could harm no one.

"In fact, Monsieur," I said, "after seven years I have succeeded in making the Duke your sovereign listen to reason, and here is a letter which informs me that His Most Serene Highness gives me a satisfaction which is very dear to me. I am engaged in his service as his secretary, at a salary of twelve hundred crowns; but in these seven years God knows what has become of the officers."

"They are all three of them at Ludwigsburg, Monsieur, and xxx is a Colonel. This is a piece of news which will surprise them, and which they will learn tomorrow, for I leave in an hour."

"If they are there," I replied, "my highest hopes are fulfilled. I am sorry that I cannot keep you company, for I mean to sleep here, and to sleep tomorrow wherever I stop; but we shall see each other day after tomorrow."

The courier left at once, and the officer in a post coach, after supping with me. Going to bed, I laugh at the effect this news will produce in Ludwigsburg, which was then the Duke's favorite residence.[40] I wake in the morning, and I adopt the charming idea which comes to me of going to Ludwigsburg in person, not to fight the officers but to flout them, to avenge myself for the old insult by scorning them. I also entertain the most agreeable idea of the demonstrations of pleasure with which I shall be greeted by all the acquaintances I must have in that city, where, besides La Toscani, the Duke's mistress, I should also find Balletti and Vestris, who had married a mistress of the Duke's[41] who later became a celebrated actress. Knowing the human heart, I had nothing to fear. The sovereign's return being imminent, no one could suppose the thing false. The Duke on his arrival would not find me, for I should make my escape as soon as the courier who preceded him came to announce his arrival. I would tell everyone that I was going to meet my new master.

Never did an idea strike me as so happy; proud of having conceived it, I should have found myself unworthy to have a mind if I had not adopted it: I was avenging myself to the full on the Duke, whose claws I must fear, for my reader may remember the excruciating letter[42] I had written him. I sleep badly the next night because of the impatience which gnawed at me, and I arrive at Ludwigsburg, giving my name without adding my pretended office, for the joke must not be carried too far. I go to lodge at the posthouse inn, I have my trunk taken upstairs, and just as I am asking where La Toscani lives, in she comes with her husband.[43] They both fall on my neck, they devour me with kisses and overwhelm me with congratulations on my arm, still in a sling, and on my second victory.

"What second victory?"

"Your appearance here, the circumstances of which have rejoiced the hearts of all your friends."

"I am in the Duke's service, but how can you know it?"

"It is all over the city. His Highness's courier, who brought you his letter, himself announced it, and so did the officer who was present and who arrived yesterday morning. But you cannot imagine the consternation of your enemies the three officers. Nevertheless, we are afraid that you will be obliged to come to a duel, for they still have the letter in which you challenged them at Fürstenberg." [44]

"Why didn't they come?"

"Two could not, and one arrived too late, and that is the truth."

"Very good. If the Duke permits it, they will do me honor by granting me a duel each in turn. With pistols, of course, for no one fences with one arm in a sling."

"We will discuss that. My daughter[45] wants to make peace between you before the Duke arrives, and you will be well advised to let her do so; for they are three, and it is safe to wager that you will not kill all three of them."

"Your daughter must have become a beauty."

"You shall sup with her tonight at my house, for she

is no longer the Duke's mistress. She is going to marry Messieri.'' [46]

"If your daughter makes it up between us I shall prefer peace to war, provided that my honor is not compromised."

"But why the sling after sixteen months?"

"I am in good health, but my hand swells as soon as I let it hang down for an hour. You shall see it after dinner, for you shall dine with me if you want me to sup with you."

In comes Vestris, whom I did not know, with Balletti, whom I loved dearly, a woman of their circle whom I did not know, and an officer who was in love with another of La Toscani's daughters. They all came to congratulate me on having entered the Duke's service so honorably. But Balletti was mad with joy. He had played the greatest part in my flight from Stuttgart; the reader knows that I was to marry his sister. The young man had a soul above that of a dancer, and great intelligence, besides the talent by which he distinguished himself; the Duke esteemed him. He had a small house adjoining the open countryside, in which there was an excellent room for me, he begs me to accept it, he admits that he is proud that the Duke should know that I am his best friend, and that I am staying with him until his arrival, for then of course I should be given a lodging at the Court. I yield to his insistence, and I accept. It was early, we all go to call on Toscani's daughter.

I had loved her in Paris,[47] when she was still not fully formed; and, displaying herself to me as she was then, she was not wrong to be ambitious. She showed me all of her fine house and her jewels, she told me the story of her liaison with the Duke, of her breaking with him because of his constant infidelities, and of her marriage to a man whom she scorned but whom her situation forced her to marry. At dinnertime we all went to the inn, and we came upon the Colonel who was the prime mover in trying to make me a soldier.[48] He put his hand to his hat first, and he left.

With this company of friends I ate dinner very gaily. After dinner I went to stay at Balletti's, putting my post chaise under cover, and toward nightfall we went to La Toscani's, where I found two beauties whose charms intoxicated me: her daughter, and Vestris's wife, whom the Duke had given to him after having two children by her, whom he recognized. La Vestris, though extremely pretty, enchanted me only by her turn of mind and by the graces which declared her born to be an actress. She had one fault: she slurred her *r*'s. Since La Toscani's daughter still maintained a reserved manner, at table I permitted myself to pay my particular court to La Vestris, of whom her husband was not jealous, because, in perfect accord with her, he did not love her. That day the parts of a short comedy had been given out, to be performed on the Duke's arrival; a young author[49] who was in Ludwigsburg had composed it, in the hope that it would convince the sovereign that he deserved to enter his service as a poet.

After supper, the conversation turning to this little comedy, in which La Vestris played the leading role, which was that of an affected young woman, she was asked to read it, and she did so with the greatest readiness.

"Your acting is from the soul," I say to her, "you express feeling in such a way that one would wager that all you say is yours and not someone else's. What a pity, Madame, that the point of your tongue cannot pronounce the canine letter." [50]

At that, the whole table boos me. I am told that it is not a fault but a charm, the expression became soft, more interesting, attracting more attention, an actress who did not speak thus was jealous of one who had the prerogative. I do not reply, but I look at La Vestris.

"Do you think," she asks me, "that I am the dupe of all that?"

"No, I do not think so, for I do you justice."

"A man who loves me, and who sincerely says 'What a pity!' pleases me far more than those who think they flatter me by telling me it is a beauty; but there is no remedy for it."

"What, Madame? No remedy for it? I have one in my infallible pharmacopoeia. Slap me in the face if by tomorrow I do not have you reading the role so that your fault does not appear; but if I have you reading it as your husband, for example, would read it, permit me to embrace you fondly."

"I accept. But what must I do?"

"Nothing except to let me cast a spell on your part book, and I am not joking. Give it to me. You don't need to read it tonight. Tomorrow I will bring it to you at nine o'clock in the morning to receive the slap or the kiss, if your husband has no objection."

"None at all, but we do not believe in spells."

"If my spell fails I shall get the slap."

She lets me have the part book. We talk of other things. I am pitied, for my hand is seen to be somewhat swollen; I tell the company the story of my duel, everyone loves me, I go back to the house in love with everyone, but especially with La Vestris and La Toscani. Balletti had a little daughter[51] three years old, who was miraculously beautiful.

"How do you happen to have that angel?"

"There is her mother, who, by the law of hospitality, will sleep with you."

It was his maid, of extreme beauty.

"I accept your offer, my dear friend, for tomorrow evening."

"Why not for tonight?"

"Because the spell will keep me busy all night."

"What? It is not a joke?"

"No. It is perfectly serious."

"Have you gone mad?"

"No. You'll see. Go to bed and just leave me a light and writing materials."

He goes to bed, and I spend six hours copying La Vestris's part, changing nothing in it except the phraseology, substituting words without *r*'s.[52] It was an arduous task, but I wanted to kiss La Vestris's beautiful lips in her husband's presence. "This man's procedures outrage me and make me desperate; I must think how to get rid of him." I change this sentence; I put: "This man has ways which offend me and desolate me. I must send him away." "He credits me with being crazy about him." I put: "He thinks that I love him." And so I go on to the end, then I sleep for three hours, I dress, and Balletti, who sees my work, predicts that the young writer will lay every imaginable curse on me, for La Vestris will certainly tell the Duke that he must command him to write for her without *r*'s. And that is what happened.

I go to La Vestris's, she was getting up. I give her her part, written out in my hand, she reads, she exclaims, she calls her husband; she swears she will never play another part in which there are *r*'s; I calm her, and I promise her I will copy all her parts as I had spent the whole night copying that one.

"All night? Come and take your payment. You are more than a wizard. It is charming. We shall laugh. We must have the author of the play come to dinner with us. Either he will undertake to write all my parts without *r*'s, or the Duke will not take him into his service. He will laugh, he will say I am right. It is a discovery. Oh, how well he has done to take you as his secretary! I should have thought it could not be done; but it must be very difficult."

"Not at all. If I were a pretty woman with that small fault, I would speak without ever using words which have *r*'s."

"Oh, that is too much."

"It is not too much. Let us wager again, a slap or a

kiss, that I will talk to you all day without an *r*. Come, let's begin.''

''If you like,'' said Vestris; ''but without a wager, for I think you are too greedy.''

The author came to dinner, and it was at table that La Vestris plagued him unmercifully, for she began by telling him that the authors of plays should be gallant to actresses and that the least gallantry an author could show one of them who slurred her *r*'s would be to write parts for her without them. The author laughed at the proposal, saying that the thing was impossible or that it could never be done except by impoverishing the language; and thereupon La Vestris handed him the part, commanding him to tell her if the language was impoverished. On the contrary, the poor man was forced to agree with La Vestris that it could not be done except by virtue of the richness of the language; and she was right.

This trifle made us very gay; but it was in perfect seriousness that La Vestris determined to insist that authors should submit to this law. At Paris, however, she met with opposition. All the authors there made common cause and swore they would make her lose her case. I heard her acting and slurring her *r*'s in Paris.[53] On that same day she asked me if I would undertake to transcribe the part of Zaïre[54] without *r*'s; but I begged her to excuse me, for, since it was a matter of writing verse, it became too difficult for me.

''How,'' the young author asked me, ''to pay court to her, would you go about telling her that she is 'charming,' a 'rare' woman, 'worthy of adoration'?''

''I should tell her that she 'enchants me,' that she is 'unique,' that she should be 'hailed like a goddess.' ''

She wrote me a letter without *r*'s, which I still keep; if I could have remained in Stuttgart the little game would have led to my conquering her; but after a week of festivities, triumphs, and complete satisfaction, the courier who preceded the Duke arrived at ten o'clock in the morning to announce the arrival of His Most Serene Highness at three or four o'clock in the afternoon. No sooner did I hear the news than I said to Balletti with perfect coolness that I wished to show my master the politeness of going to meet him and so enlarging his suite on his entrance into Ludwigsburg, and that, wanting to join him at least two stages away, I must leave at once. He praised my idea, and he sent his beautiful maid to engage horses at the post. But when he saw me hurriedly packing my trunk, and saw that I refused to listen to his perfectly sound objection that I had only to leave it in his house, he guessed everything, and he found it all most amusing. I confessed it to him. He became sad upon reflecting that he was losing me; but he prepared to laugh at the effect my piece of bravado would produce in the minds of the three officers and on the Duke. He promised to write me everything at Mannheim, where I had already decided I would spend a week to see my dear Algardi,[55] who had entered the service of the Elector of the Palatinate, and Monsieur de Sickingen,[56] to whom I had to give a letter from Count Lamberg, as well as another to Baron Beckers,[57] Minister to the Elector of the Palatinate.

When the horses were harnessed I kissed my dear friend, his little girl, and his maid, and I told the postilion to take the road to Mannheim.

Arrived in Mannheim, I found that the Court was at Schwetzingen,[58] and I went there to sleep. There I found all the people I wanted. Algardi had married; Monsieur de Sickingen was paying his court in order to go to Paris as the Elector's Minister, and Baron Beckers presented me to the Elector. On the fifth or sixth day I was there, Prince Frederick of Zweibrücken died;[59] but here is an anecdote which I heard on the eve of his death. Dr. Algardi was the physician who had attended him in his illness. On the eve of the day on which that handsome and brave Prince died, I was supping at Verazi's,[60] poet to the Elector, when Algardi arrived.

"How is the Prince?" I asked him.

"The poor Prince has at most twenty-four hours still to live."

"Does he know it?"

"No, for he hopes. He has just torn my heart. A moment ago he adjured me to tell him the undisguised truth, and he made me give him my word of honor that I would tell it to him. He asked me if he was in absolute danger of death."

"And you told him the truth."

"Certainly not. I was not such a fool. I replied that it was true that his disease was mortal, but that nature and art could perform what are vulgarly called miracles."

"So you deceived him? You lied."

"I did not deceive him, for his recovery is among possible things. I did not want to make him desperate. The duty of a wise physician is never to drive his patient to despair, for despair can only hasten his death."

"But admit that you lied, despite the word of honor by which he adjured you to tell him the truth."

"No, I did not lie, for I know that he may recover."

"Then you are lying now?"

"No again, for he will die tomorrow."

"By God, nothing is more Jesuitical than that."

"It is not Jesuitical. My first duty being to prolong the patient's life, I had to spare him news which could but shorten it, if only by a few hours, and that by a physical necessity; and I truthfully told him what after all is not among impossibilities. So I did not lie, and I am not lying now, for on the basis of my experience I prognosticate to you what I presume must happen. Thus I do not lie, for the fact is that I would wager a million to one that he will not recover, but I would not wager my life."

"You are right; but you nevertheless deceived the Prince, for his intention was to learn from you not what he knew himself but what you must know from experience. Nevertheless, I grant you that, being his physician, you could not shorten his life by telling him the dreadful news. I conclude by deciding that you practice a wicked profession.''

After two weeks I ended my delightful stay in Schwetzingen, leaving the poet Verazi a few of the things I had with me, which I promised him I would go to reclaim one day or another; but I never had time again. Verazi still has everything[61] I left with him thirty-one years ago. As a poet, he is the greatest oddity I have ever known. To distinguish himself from the others, he cultivated eccentricity. He tried to bring into fashion a style completely opposite to that of the great master Metastasio, making harsh verses and claiming that, so fashioned, they gave more scope to the science of the master who was to set them to music. Jommelli[62] had persuaded him to accept this extravagant notion.

I went to Mainz, where I hired a large boat on which I loaded my carriage. I arrived in Cologne about the end of July, looking forward with real pleasure to renewing my acquaintance with the Burgomaster's beautiful and charming wife, who detested General Kettler and who had made me happy during all the time I spent in that city seven years earlier; but it was not the only reason which obliged me to stop in the ugly, pretentious town. At Dresden I had read in a gazette published in Cologne: ''The Sieur de Casanova having reappeared in Warsaw after an absence of two months received an order to leave, the King having heard several stories which obliged him to defend his Court from that adventurer.'' [63] This article, which I could not stomach, had decided me to pay a call on Jacquet,[64] the writer of the gazette. The time had come.

I dine in haste, I go to pay a call on Burgomaster *xe*;[65] I find him at table with his family, sitting beside his beautiful Mimi. My story kept them occupied for two good hours. Some ladies arrived, Mimi *xe* had to go out, I was invited to dinner on the next day.

The woman seemed to me more beautiful than she had been seven years earlier; I imagine a renewal of our old pleasures, and, after spending a night made wakeful by illusions, I dress in Court attire and I go to the Burgomaster's early to seize the opportunity to speak to his wife. I find her there, she was alone, I begin by a transport, she wards me off gently, but her expression freezes me. She tells me in a few words that time, the excellent physician, has cured her heart of a malady which mingled too much bitterness with sweetness, and so she did not want to run the risk of succumbing to it again.

"What! The confessional——"

"The confessional must now serve us only to go to it to repent of our past sins."

"God preserve me from repentance and from the remorse whose source is only in prejudice. I will leave tomorrow."

"I do not tell you to leave."

"If I cannot hope, I must not stay. Can I hope?"

"No, absolutely not."

At table, however, she was charming; but I was so disheartened that I was found gloomy. Women always had the power to sharpen and to dull my wits. The next morning at seven o'clock I get into my chaise, and as soon as I am away from the posthouse[66] which sets me on the road to Aix-la-Chapelle I get out, telling the postilion to wait for me. I go to Jacquet's, armed with a pistol and my cane, with no other intention than to give him a caning.

I arrive there, the maidservant shows me the room in which the gazetteer Jacquet was working alone on his gazette, it was on the ground floor, and the door, the day being hot, was open. I enter, and he asks who is there, neither looking at me nor ceasing to write. I take my stand in front of him, and he asks me what my orders are, looking at me. He was a man with whom I could have dueled, I should therefore have no scruples about giving him a caning.

"I am, infamous gazetteer, the adventurer Casanova whose name you defamed in your gazette fourteen months ago."

So saying, I take out a pistol with the hand which I freed from the sling, and I raise my cane, but the wretch had instantly dropped to the floor at my left, and, down on his knees, was begging for mercy, offering to show me the original letter from Warsaw in which I could read the name of the person who wrote him the thing in the same terms.

"Where is the letter?"

"Instantly."

I move away to let him pass, and I bolt the door. He begins, shaking like a leaf, to look for the letter in question among the letters from Warsaw, which, instead of being in order by their dates, were every which way. I show him the date in his infamous gazette; but it is no use. At the end of an hour, shaking, blubbering, he falls to his knees again and tells me to do as I will with him. I give him a kick in the stomach, I put the pistol back in my pocket, and I tell him to come with me. He follows without protest and even without a hat, which I did not let him go to fetch, and he accompanies me to my post chaise, into which he sees me get, thanking God that he has escaped the storm.

I arrived that evening at Aix-la-Chapelle, where I found the Princess Lubomirska Straznikowa, the Grand Notary[67] Rzewuski, General Ronikier, Tomatis and his wife, and some Englishmen whom I knew.

CHAPTER XI

My stay in Spa. The blow. A sword thrust.
Crosin. Charlotte, her lying-in and her death.
A lettre de cachet *makes me leave Paris within*
twenty-four hours.

THEY ALL showed that they were charmed to see
me again, and I was no less delighted than they to see
that I was sure of moving in the best circles. They were
about to leave for Spa,[1] where there were a great many
people; the season at Aix being ended, everyone was
going to Spa, and those who were not going there were
remaining in Aix because there was simply no more room
for anyone in Spa. Everyone assured me of it; several
people had come back because they had found nowhere
to put up. I pay no attention to them, telling the Princess
that I will leave when she does, sure of finding a room
somewhere. We leave the next morning, we arrive in Spa
early; the Princess, the Grand Notary, Ronikier, and
Tomatis all had houses which they had taken beforehand,
I alone am left in my carriage not knowing where to go,
for the postilion had been everywhere. I decide to get out
and go to look for a room myself on foot; but before
running about Spa I enter a hatter's shop[2] to buy a hat,
having lost mine on the journey. I tell the shopwoman

my plight, she understands it, she looks at her husband; they talk together in Walloon, and she tells me that if it is for only a few days she will let me have her room, sleeping with her husband in the shop; but she says that she has absolutely no place for my manservant.

"I have no servant."

"So much the better, have your things unloaded."

"Where shall I put my carriage?"

"I will see that it is put in a safe place and under cover."

"How much shall I pay you?"

"Nothing; and nothing if you want to eat with us without expecting fine fare."

I accept everything in a manner which assures them that they have not been so polite to a scoundrel. I go up a short flight of stairs, I see a room and a closet, a good bed, a chest of drawers, a large table and two small ones; and I see that I am well off. The shopwoman takes down what she needed and what would inconvenience me, leaving me two drawers empty. I ask her why they would not rather sleep in the closet than in the shop, where they cannot but be very cramped, and they reply together that they would be in my way, whereas their niece would certainly not trouble me in the least.

At the word "niece" I am plunged in thought. The closet had no door, it was scarcely bigger than the bed it contained; it was an alcove without a window, and for this reason no door had been made for it, since it had to be lighted by the light from the room itself. I must inform my reader that the shopwoman, who was from Liège like her husband, was revoltingly ugly. "It is impossible," I said to myself, "that their niece can be uglier; but if they abandon her in this way to the first comer she must certainly be above temptation." However that may be, I agree to everything, I do not ask to see the niece, for the request might have been considered offensive, and I go out without even having opened my trunk. In a night bag I had the few things I needed. I

tell them that I shall not come in until after supper, and
I give them money to buy candles for me; I also tell them
that I must have a night lamp.

I go to see the Princess, at whose house I was to sup,
and all the others; they are all delighted with my good
luck in finding a lodging. I go to the concert, to the faro
bank simply to see of what sort it was, I enter the rooms
where the gaming is going on, and I see the Marquis
d'Aragon,[3] who was playing piquet with an old Count
of the Empire. I am at once told the story of a duel he
had fought with a Frenchman who had picked a quarrel
with him. It had happened three weeks earlier. The Marquis d'Aragon had given the Frenchman a wound in the
chest from which he was still suffering, and he was
waiting for him to be cured in order to give him the revenge for which he had asked him when he withdrew.
Such is the style of the French: as soon as they see their
own blood they are calmed; our style in Italy is entirely
different: we are not phlegmatic enough to amuse ourselves asking for a revenge at some indefinite time when
we are in the presence of the enemy who has already
opened our veins. But each nation has its particular
character. This custom in France makes dueling very
common.

The person whom I was delighted to see in Spa was
the Marchese Caraccioli,[4] whom I had left in London.[5]
He had obtained a leave of absence from his Court, and
he was amusing himself in Spa. He was a man of sound
intelligence, kind, humane, compassionate, a friend to
youth—male or female, he did not care—but not in
excess. He did not gamble, but he liked gamesters who
knew how to play, and he despised dupes. Being of this
happy character, he made the Marquis d'Aragon's fortune. He vouched for his name and his nobility to a fifty-
year-old English widow who was then in Spa and who fell
in love with him. On the word of the Ambassador Caraccioli, she married him and brought him sixty thousand
pounds sterling as her dowry. She can only have fallen

in love with his six feet of stature and with the proud
name of D'Aragon, for he had neither wit nor manners
and his legs were covered with venereal sores; but since
he always wore boots the Englishwoman cannot have
seen them until after their wedding. I saw him some time
afterward in Marseilles, and some years later he went
to Modena, where he bought two fiefs. His wife died and
left him rich. I believe he is still alive. The excellent
Caraccioli congratulated himself on having thus made
the fortune of the adventurer, whose name was Dragon.
By borrowing an *A*, he had made himself d'Aragon.

After supper I returned to my lodging, and I went
to bed without having seen the niece, who was already
asleep. I was waited on by her aunt, the very ugly shopwoman, who begged me not to take a servant as long as
I was in her house, for, according to her, they were all
thieves.

When I woke in the morning the niece had already
gone down to the shop; I dressed to go to the fountain,[6]
telling my kind hosts that I would come to eat dinner
with them that day. They could eat only in my room, and
I was amazed when they asked my permission to do so.
I did not see the niece, she had gone to take hats to a number of houses. I was beginning to feel no more curiosity
about her. At the morning promenade I fell in with
someone who informed me concerning all the feminine
beauties we saw there. The number of adventuresses who
frequent Spa during the watering season is incredible,
they all go there expecting to make their fortunes, and
they are all disappointed. The circulation of money there
is astonishing, but it is all among gamesters and merchants. The restaurant keepers, the innkeepers, the vint-
ners, and the moneylenders absorb a great part of it,
and the adventuresses find themselves reduced to momentary liaisons. The passion for play is stronger than
the passion for gallantry; the gamester at Spa has neither
time to stop to consider the merits of a woman nor the
courage to make sacrifices for her. As for gaming, the

money which comes from it is divided into three shares. One, which is the smallest, goes into the pocket of the Prince-Bishop of Liège, another share, somewhat larger, is divided among the small fry of cheats, who are very numerous and who do very poorly, for people avoid them and they have no established and authorized place to serve as their thieves' alley. So the largest share, which, take one year with another, is reckoned at half a million, goes to an association of twelve professional sharpers authorized by the sovereign. All this money comes from the pockets of the dupes who hasten from four hundred leagues around to ruin themselves in the hole called Spa. Going there to take the waters is usually only a pretext. People go there only for business, for intrigues, to gamble, to make love, and also to spy. A very small number of decent people go there to amuse themselves or to rest from the fatigues which their duties impose on them all year in the places in which they reside.

In such a place, where all one does is eat, drink, walk, gamble, dance, and look at courtesans, living is not expensive. At a table d'hôte where thirty made dishes are served, one pays only a French petit écu, and for the same amount one is well lodged. Those who live there the year round make in three months what they need to spend during the other nine months while they wait for the season to return.

I went back to my lodging at noon, after winning some twenty louis. I had four hundred sequins at my disposal, and I was determined to lead what is called a "virtuous life."

I enter the shop to go up to my room, and I see a girl nineteen or twenty years of age, tall, dark-haired, with big black eyes, very well built, serious-looking, measuring ribbon. She must be the niece who slept in the closet six paces from my bed. I am surprised, but do not show it. I sit down for a moment; but she scarcely greets me; she has not time enough. Her aunt comes down to tell me that dinner is about to be served, I go upstairs, I see

The Old Market Place in Dresden

Costumes for the Viennese Production of an Italian Opera

four places set, and a moment later the maid who brings in the soup asks me outright for money to buy wine with if I want any, for her master and mistress drink only beer. This pleases me, and I give her enough to buy two bottles of Burgundy.

The hatter comes up and shows me a repeating gold watch, with a gold chain, both from Paris, modern, and by a well-known maker. He asks me what it may be worth.

"Forty louis at least."

"A gentleman wants to sell it to me for twenty, but on condition that I will return it to him if he gives me twenty-two tomorrow."

"Do it."

"I haven't the money."

"I shall be glad to lend it to you."

I give him twenty louis, he hurries downstairs, he comes back and gives me the watch, which I put in my jewel case, and we sit down at table. A hole in the floor with a grill over it showed anyone who might enter the shop while we were dining. I had the wife at my right, the husband at my left, and, facing me, the niece, at whom I took care not to look and who did not speak twenty words during the whole dinner. I find the soup excellent, the boiled beef, the entrée, and the roast exquisite; the shopwoman tells me that the roast is at my expense, for they are not rich. I consider this sincerity admirable, and the procedure very polite. I ask her to drink some of my wine, and she accepts, saying that she would like to be a little better off only so that she could drink a measure of wine a day; her husband says the same.

"But it seems to me that your business——"

"The merchandise we have does not belong to us, we have debts in Liège, and our expenses are enormous. So far we have sold very little."

"I am most sorry for that. I hope things will go better. You have nothing but hats?"

"I beg your pardon—we have handkerchiefs from

China, stockings from Paris, and cuffs. People find everything too expensive, and they go away.''

''I will buy some of each, and I will bring my friends here. Leave it to me. I want to be of use to you.''

''Merci,[7] go get one or two packets of those handkerchiefs, and some socks in a large size, for Monsieur has a big leg.''

Merci goes for it all. I find the handkerchiefs superb, and the stockings very fine. I buy a dozen handkerchiefs and six pairs of stockings, and I promise her that I will see to it that she sells all the handkerchiefs and all the stockings in the shop in less than twenty-four hours. They thank me, and they beg me to continue my good offices. After the coffee, which was at my expense too, the aunt tells her niece to be very careful not to wake me in the morning when she gets up; she replies that she will always go to the shop to put on her shoes. I told her not to be concerned, for I slept soundly.

After dinner I go into a gunsmith's shop to buy pistols, which I wanted to present to my brother, for I had already decided to go to Paris immediately after Spa. Weapons from Liège are not expensive. They are handsome, but they are not as good. I ask him if he knows the merchant So-and-so, in whose house I am lodging.

''We are first cousins.''

''Is he rich?''

''In debt.''

''Why?''

''Because he is unlucky, like all honest people.''

''And his wife?''

''It is she who keeps him afloat by her careful economy.''

''Do you know her niece?''

''Certainly. She is a fool who is a bigot, and who because of her scruples drives customers from the shop.''

''What do you think she should do to attract the customers?''

"She should be more polite and stop playing the prude when some man wants to kiss her."

"Is she really like that?"

"Is she? Try, and you will see. It is not a week since she slapped an officer. My cousin scolded her, and she wanted to go back to Liège; but his wife soothed her. She is certainly pretty. Don't you think so?"

"Yes, but if she is what you say, the thing to do is to let her alone."

Armed with this information I decided to leave the house, for Merci had so pleased me at table that I foresaw that it could not be long before she saw me sitting on her bed, and I loathed Pamelas[8] and Charpillons. In the course of the afternoon I went into the shop with Rzewuski and Ronikier, who, to please me, bought more than fifty ducats' worth of merchandise, and the next day the Princess and La Tomatis bought all the handkerchiefs. Back at the house at ten o'clock, I found that Merci had gone to bed, as on the night before. The next morning the merchant came up to get the watch from me, giving me twenty-two louis, but I would take only my twenty. I told him that, if I was insured by a pledge, I would always open my purse to him, but that I absolutely refused to take any profit. He went downstairs overcome by gratitude, and his wife came up to express hers to me.

Being invited to dinner by Tomatis, I could not dine with them; but, curious about the beautiful bigot, I told them that I would sup there and that I would pay the extra outlay; and they gave me a good supper, at my expense as was only right, with good Burgundy, which Merci would never consent to taste. Toward the end of supper, she having gone out somewhere, I told her aunt that her niece was charming and that it was a pity she was so gloomy. She replied that her character would surely change, or she would not remain long in her shop.

"Is she like that with all men?"

"All."

"She has never loved ?"

"So she says, but I do not believe it."

"I am astonished that she sleeps peacefully, knowing that there is a man six paces away from her."

"She is not afraid."

She comes back, and she wishes us good night, I offer to kiss her, she declines, and, in order to undress freely, she puts a chair in front of the entrance to the closet, meaning to keep me from seeing her in her shift. They leave, I go to bed too, finding her procedure intolerable, and even not natural, for Merci knew and must know that she had the right to please. Nevertheless, I go calmly to bed, and when I wake in the morning I do not see her. I wanted to get her to talk with me privately, and afterward to decide on my course in accordance with what she said; but I did not know how to go about it. In the meanwhile the merchant availed himself of my offer by bringing me pledges and taking the interest himself. I procured this advantage for him at no risk to myself; I was delighted to do it; and both he and his wife said they were happy to have persuaded me to go on living in their house. So I decided to turn their self-interest to my profit.

On the fifth or sixth day I wake before Merci, I get up. I put on only my dressing gown, she instantly wakes, and, seeing me approaching her, she asks me what I want. Sitting down on her bed, I reply with a very gentle expression and the most humane manner that I want only to wish her good morning and to talk with her a little. She had wrapped herself in her sheet, for the weather was very hot; but, her bed being very narrow, that could not prevent me from putting my arms around her. Clasping her, I ask her to let me kiss her, and she curtly refuses. Her tone irritates me, I slip my hand under the sheet from the bottom, and I move rapidly from her legs to the most important place. Merci quickly pulls out one arm, and with her clenched fist she gives me a blow on the nose of a vigor to destroy all tenderness in me. I at once bleed very copiously, and, possessing myself to perfection, I withdraw and I wash with cold water until the blood is stanched, and meanwhile Merci dresses and goes downstairs.

After the bleeding stops I am left with a contusion which makes my face hideous. From the window I call the wigmaker who lives upstairs, he gives me a hasty combing, he puts my hair in a cadogan,[9] and he leaves. The shopwoman comes up to show me some trout, and she is astonished to see me disfigured. I tell her the reason, mildly and not only without complaining but putting the blame on myself. I pay for the trout and I go out, not listening to her useless excuses. Covering my bruise with a handkerchief, I enter a house across the street,[10] which I had the day before seen the Duchess of Richmond [11] leaving. Half of the apartment, the landlord told me, was let to an Italian Marchese who was to arrive from Liège; he offers me the other half, and I take it. I also engage a manservant, and I instantly go to have all my things conveyed from the house of the woman from Liège, paying no attention not only to her supplications but to her tears. Besides, what she said could have not the slightest power to persuade me, for by promising that Merci should not again appear before my eyes, she was satisfying Merci and punishing me, supposing, as she must, that I wanted a taste of her or, more reasonably, that I wanted to give the creature a whipping.

So I go to my new lodging, where I had two rooms and a closet. An Englishman promises that he will rid me of the swelling in an hour and of the bruise in twenty-four, and, I letting him do as he would, he kept his word. He rubbed me with spirits of wine. Feeling ashamed to show myself in such a state, I spend the day at home. The shopwoman comes at noon to bring me my trout, and, assuring me that Merci has repented with tears of having treated me so, she promises me that if I will return to her house the girl will make it up to me in any way I may wish.

"You must understand that, if I did that, what has

happened to me would become known, which would make me ridiculous, and also put a stain on the honor of your house, and on your niece herself, who could no longer pass as pious.''

I remind her of the incident of the slap,[12] the story of which she is astonished that I know, and I reproach her with the thoughtlessness of her conduct in exposing me to the wretched girl's fury. I end by saying that, without being very clever, I could suspect her of complicity. At these last words the woman shows that she is in despair and bursts into tears. Since they might spring from decent feeling, I soothe her, asking her to excuse me, and she goes. A half hour later her husband comes, bringing me twenty-five louis which I had lent on a gold snuffbox with diamonds, and he proposes that I give two hundred louis for a ring which was worth four hundred. It would belong to me, he said, if the owner of it did not give me two hundred and twenty louis in a week. Not being short of money, I look at the stone, which appeared to be of the six carats it was said to weigh, the water was excellent, I tell him that I will do it if the owner will give me a bill of sale.

''I will draw it up myself in the presence of witnesses.''

''Very good; in an hour I will give you the money, for I want to have the stone unset. It should make no difference to the owner, for I will have it reset as it is at my expense. If he redeems it, the twenty louis shall be for you.''

''I must ask him if he is willing to have it unset.''

''Very well, but tell him that if he does not consent I will not pursue the business.''

He goes, and he comes back with a jeweler who tells me that he is willing to guarantee me that the stone weighs at least two grains more.

''Have you weighed it?''

''No, but that makes no difference.''

''Then do the business yourself.''

''I haven't the money.''

"Why does the owner object to having it unset? It will cost him nothing."

"He refuses absolutely."

"That is his privilege, as it is mine not to give him a sou."

They went away; and I congratulate myself on having held out. It was obvious that, if the owner would not consent to its being unset, supposing he needed the money for which he asked, either the stone was false, which would have been shown by its weight, or it had an artificial base.

I spend the day writing, having sent away all visitors; I sup, I go to bed, and at daybreak I get up to see who is knocking at my door. I see Merci. I let her come in, and, getting back into bed, I ask her what she has come to me at that hour for. She sits down on my bed, and she begins pouring out vain excuses. Arguing to prove someone wrong being a passion with me, I ask her why, since her principle was to resist like a tigress the caresses of a man who was seduced by her charms, she could have put me in the position of having to do what I had done.

"Sleeping in the closet, I obeyed my aunt. Giving you the blow, which I greatly regret, I obeyed the involuntary impulse of my soul, which felt itself outraged; and it is not true that I am sure that every man who sees me is bound to lose his reason. I count on duty, and you will admit that your duty was to respect me, as mine was to defend myself."

"If that is the way you think, I confess that you were right, and indeed I conceded it; I did not protest when you drew my blood, and, since I left you, you are certain that I will respect you in future. Did you come here to hear this? You have done so. You can want nothing else. Only permit me to laugh at you for having asked me to excuse you, for what you have just said makes it laughable."

"What did I say?"

"That in breaking my nose you were doing your duty.

Do you think one must ask to be excused for having done what one ought to do?"

"I should have defended myself by gentleness. Alas, forget it all and forgive me. I will no longer defend myself in any way, I am yours, I love you, and I am ready to convince you of it."

She could not say more. As she utters the words, she falls on me, she weeps, and she rubs her face against mine. Ashamed of the victory which she is about to win, I do not repulse her, but I withdraw. I tell her to come back when my face has recovered its original shape. She left, very much mortified.

The Italian whom my landlord was expecting from Liège had arrived during the night, I had heard a great commotion; curious to know his name, I ask what it is, and I see the visiting card which had already been written to be distributed to all the self-styled sick people who were at Spa to recover their health. I am surprised to read: "The Marchese Don Antonio dalla Croce." Could it be Crosin? [13] It was perfectly possible. He was asleep. I am told that he has a wife, a secretary, also with a wife, a chambermaid, and two menservants. I cannot wait to see his face.

I did not have to wait long. As soon as he was up and informed that I was his neighbor, he presented himself. Two hours which we spent in telling each other our adventures since we had parted at Milan passed very quickly. He had learned how I had made the happiness of the girl he had left me;[14] in the last six months he had traveled over half of Europe, always at strife with Fortune; he had made much money in Paris, as he had done again in Brussels, where, having fallen in love with a young lady of birth whom her father had shut up in a convent, he had carried her off, and he had her with him, six months gone with child. He presented her as his wife, for he intended to make her so. He told me that he had fifty thousand francs, and as much again in jewels and other possessions, and that he intended to deal at his lodging, giving suppers, for he was sure to lose all that he had if he trusted himself to the run of the cards and did not tamper with luck. I encouraged him to adhere to his resolution. He expected to go to Warsaw, where he was sure that I would send him to all my acquaintances, but he was mistaken. I did not even let him hope that I would present him to the Poles who were in Spa. I told him that he could easily manage to make their acquaintance, and I assured him that I would do him no harm. I promised to dine with him that day. The man he passed off as his secretary was a Veronese named Conti,[15] a clever scoundrel whose wife played a leading part.

But about noon in comes the merchant from Liège again with the ring and its owner, who looked like a bravo. They were accompanied by the jeweler and another man. The owner repeats his request that I give him two hundred louis. If I had been more sensible and less talkative I would have asked him to excuse me, and it would have been all over. But not a bit of it, I wanted to convince him that his objection to allowing the stone to be unset was enough to prevent me from doing him the favor he asked of me. Once the stone was unset, I said to him, what it really was would appear.

"If, when it is unset," I said, "it weighs twenty-six grains, I will give you not two hundred but three hundred louis; set as it is, I will give you nothing."

"You are making a mistake to doubt what I tell you, for your obstinacy wounds my honor."

"My argument attacks no one's honor. My reason is free. I propose a wager to you. Let the stone be unset, and if it weighs twenty-six grains I lose two hundred louis, if it weighs much less you shall lose the ring."

"Your proposal is insulting, for it implies that I am lying."

At these words I go to the chest of drawers on which I had a pair of pistols and I ask the brawler to leave me in peace. Just then General Ronikier arrives, and the man with the ring tells him the story. Ronikier looks at the ring and says that if he were made a present of it he would not have the stone unset, but that if he had to buy it he would have it unset even if the seller were the greatest monarch on earth, and that he was astonished that he would not consent to it. The scoundrel then left, without bowing to anyone, and the ring remained in the hands of the merchant from Liège.

"Why," I asked him, "did you not give him back his ring?"

"Because I advanced him fifty louis yesterday; but if he does not give them to me tomorrow I will have the stone unset before the magistrate and put up at auction."

"I do not like the man. I ask you to not bring anyone to me henceforth."

The thing ended as follows: The impostor did not redeem the ring, and the merchant had it unset on the next day but one before witnesses. The stone was found to be flat and lying on the flat side of a crystal which made up two thirds of the entire bulk. However, the covering stone was worth the fifty louis, and the merchant from Liège obtained them from an Englishman whose curiosity the thing aroused. The knave vanished from sight. A week later, having found me walking alone to a fountain which is a quarter of a league from Spa,[16] he asked me to be so good as to follow him to a place where we should not be seen, for he had a word to say to me, sword in hand. Strangely enough, I had my sword with me. That same morning I had been to a meeting between two hot-heads who were also to duel and who had made it up. When one goes to see such a meeting at Spa one never goes unarmed.

I replied that I would not follow him, and that he need only speak to me where we were.

"We are seen."

"So much the better. Make haste and draw your sword first, I promise you I will not call for help."

"It is an advantage."

"So I know, and it is mine by right, and if you do not unsheathe I will publicly proclaim you the coward I know you to be."

At these words he quickly draws his sword; but, I jumping back, he finds me ready to receive him. He approaches me *à la Donadieu*,[17] and when he makes to cross swords I lunge straight at his chest, and I give him a pink which the surgeon found to be three inches deep. I should have finished him off if he had not lowered his sword, saying that he would find an opportunity to have his revenge. He leaves.

Twenty people who had seen us were already about me, no one troubling to overtake the other, for they were all witnesses that he had been the aggressor. I put the hilt of my sword on the ground to clean it, for I had my left hand in a sling, and we all go back to Spa. The affair had no consequences. When I left Spa he was still in the surgeon's care. He was an adventurer, with whom all the Frenchmen who were in Spa would have nothing to do. But let us come to Crosin and the dinner he gave me.

The Marquise, his pretended wife, was a girl sixteen or seventeen years of age, beautiful, blonde, very tall, and with all the manners and bearing of the nobility of the country in which she was born. The story of her elopement is known to her brothers and sisters; there is no need for me to tell the reader her name.[18] I have already said too much. When her husband, who had mentioned me to her beforehand, presented me to her she received me as one receives a well-tried friend. She showed neither the dejection which arises from repentance nor the embarrassment which follows a bold step contrary to the precepts which she must have received from her education and to the duties upon which the world makes honor depend. Six or seven months gone with child, she seemed already to have reached her term because of the extreme inward curvature of her back. She had all the appearance of the most perfect health, a candid physiognomy, prominent blue eyes, natural coloring, a mouth made for smiles, and two magnificent rows of teeth which were even whiter than her skin. Priding myself on being a physiognomist, I at once concluded that the young woman not only should be happy herself but should bring perfect happiness to the man she loved; I was soon forced to admit the vanity of that pretended science. She had beautiful earrings and two beautiful rings, which gave me an excuse to admire the beauty of her hands. Monsieur Conti's wife cut no figure at all. I had eyes only for Charlotte; such was her baptismal name. She surprised me so greatly that, in constant distraction, I almost never made appropriate answers to all the remarks she addressed to me at this dinner on the first day of her arrival.

I reflected on Crosin, with whom girls of superior merit fell in love, and for some reason which I could not comprehend. He had neither looks nor a cultivated mind nor the manners of good society nor a winning tongue nor the art of making a sufficient impression to reduce well-bred girls to forsaking their homes. Despite that, I had before me the second such,[19] whose merits were far superior to those of the first. I was far from foreseeing what nevertheless happened in five or six weeks.

After dinner I took Crosin aside and treated him to a wise and moving discourse. I pointed out his extreme need to behave with the utmost circumspection, for he would become the most execrable of villains if ever the excellent creature whom he had seduced should be brought to unhappiness on his account. He replied that he was determined no longer to trust in Fortune, whose capriciousness he had too often experienced. He intended to count only on his skill, and he was sure to live thenceforth a rich man.

"Does she know that your only income is the money of dupes?"

"She knows nothing, she knows that I am a gamester, and, loving me more than herself, she has no will but mine. I shall marry her in Warsaw before she bears her child. This one I shall not have to leave to your care. If you need money, avail yourself freely of my purse.''

I was not in need of money. Playing prudently, I was three or four hundred louis ahead. When luck was against me I had the strength to stop. Though the bruise from Merci's fist was still very visible, I took the Marquise to the gaming room alone, where she drew all eyes. She liked *piquet à écrire*,[20] and I kept her amused for a couple of hours. She had wanted to play for money, and, having lost twenty counters, she insisted on giving me twenty écus. Back at the house, we found Crosin and Conti, who had both won too—Conti a score of louis at faro, and Crosin a hundred-odd guineas at *passe-dix*[21] at an English club[22] to which I do not remember how he obtained an introduction. At supper I had more presence of mind than at dinner. Charlotte laughed a great deal at the amusing stories I told her.

After that I made only a few short calls on the Poles[23] and the Tomatises. At the end of a week they even stopped reproaching me. I was in love with the beautiful Italian,[24] and no one could find anything to say against it. But at the end of the same week Crosin, tired of seeing that he found no dupes and that those whom he brought home to supper did not punt when he put down a thousand louis and opened a pack of cards, began playing at the big bank in the gaming room and losing constantly. Accustomed to suffering losses, he was no less gay, he ate with no less appetite, he bestowed no fewer caresses on his excellent spouse, who knew nothing about it. I knew it, but I should have been worse than a fool to inform her of it. I loved her fondly, but I did not dare to tell her so; I thought I could aspire to no more than her friendship, and I feared that it would diminish if she came to know that I loved her and that I was even jealous of the happiness of the scoundrel who had seduced her. In short, I was afraid of losing the confidence she was beginning to have in me.

At the end of three weeks Conti, who, playing prudently, was ahead by two hundred louis, left Crosin and went to Verona with his wife and his manservant; and a few days later Charlotte sent her chambermaid, with whom she was not satisfied, back to her native Liège.

At the middle of September all the Poles and Tomatis left Spa to return to Paris, where I promised to rejoin them. I remained in Spa only perforce of the attachment Charlotte had inspired in me. I foresaw misfortunes, and I could not abandon the excellent creature. Crosin, losing every night and every day, emptied his purse of its last copper. He sold (for he never pawned) all his jewels, his watches, his rings. He asked his wife for her earrings, her rings, her watches, and everything she had, and he lost them all without her ever letting me see the slightest change in her angelic humor on account of it. Finally, on the last day, he took all her laces and her finest dresses, and adding them to all his coats, he sold the whole and went to assault Fortune for the last time with two hundred louis, which he lost in my presence in the most lamentable fashion, always trying to force the cards. He rises, he sees me, he beckons to me, I follow him, and we go outside of Spa.

"My dear friend," he says, "one of two things: I must either kill myself here and now, or leave as I am without going back to the house even for a moment. I shall go to Warsaw on foot, I know that you will take care of my wife, for you adore her and you do justice to her merits. It is for you to tell her the dreadful news that my destiny forces me to leave her. Assure her that if I live I will replenish my purse and will rejoin her. Take her to Paris, look after her, and I will write to you, addressing my letter in care of your brother. I know that you have money, but I would die before I would ask you for or accept a single louis. Here are three or four which I have in small coins, and I assure you that I am richer now than I was two months ago. Good-by. I commend Charlotte to your care; she would be happy if I had never known her."

After these words he embraces me, still shedding tears, and he goes off without another shirt in his pocket, in silk stockings, walking stick in hand; and he leaves me there motionless, petrified, and in despair that I must go to tell this terrible news to a young woman with child who adored the wretch who, despite everything, loved her. The only consolation which my soul found was that, knowing that I was in love with her, I was certain that she would not be left without support. I thank God and Fortune that I am rich enough to provide her with a comfortable life.

I go to her lodging, and to spare her I say that we can dine, for the Marquis was engaged in a game which would go on all evening. She sighs, she wishes him good luck, and we dine. I disguise my emotion so well that she cannot imagine that anything is wrong. After dinner I urge her to go to walk with me in the garden of the Capuchin monastery,[25] which was a hundred paces from our lodging, and she is glad to come. To prepare her to receive the news with equanimity, I ask her if she would praise her lover if, having had an affair of honor, he risked being murdered by his enemies in order to bid her good-by, rather than thinking of escaping.

"I should blame him," she said. "He should think of escaping, if only to preserve himself for me. Did my husband make that choice? Speak clearly. My soul is strong enough to bear such a blow, especially since I have such a friend as I believe you to be. Speak."

"Very well. I will tell you all. But be certain, as you hear me, that you must consider me a fond father who loves you, who will never let you want for anything, and who will remain so until death."

"Then I am not unfortunate. Speak."

I thereupon told her the whole brief story, and, word for word, the speech he made to me when he parted from me, which ended with the words: "I commend Charlotte to your care; she would be happy if I had never known her."

For half a quarter of an hour she remained motionless and thoughtful, with her beautiful eyes cast down, then she wiped away two tears, and, looking at me sadly and tenderly, she said that if she could count on me she was far from considering herself unfortunate.

"I swear to you," I said, "that I will never leave you except to restore you to your husband, unless I die before then."

"That is enough. I vow you eternal gratitude and all the obedience of a good daughter."

She then made some brief reflections on the unfortunate man's precipitate departure, and she saw despair in the alternative of killing himself. She commented on his conduct only to pity him. Attributing everything to a mad passion for play, she never condemned him. As he had several times told her the story of the girl from Marseilles whom he had left behind at an inn in Milan, leaving her nothing but the advice to entrust herself to me, she declared it a unique combination of circumstances which for the second time made me the guardian of a girl whom the unfortunate gamester abandoned when she was eight months with child.

"The difference is," I said, "that I made the fortune of the first by finding her a husband, whereas I should never have the courage to make the fortune of the second in the same way."

"As long as Croce[26] lives, I will never be any man's wife; and though I am very firm in that resolve, I am nevertheless very glad to be free."

Back at our lodging, I advised her to dismiss her manservant, paying for his journey as far as his native Besançon, where she had engaged him; this was to avoid the harmful things he might say. I made her sell all her poor lover's shirts and old coats, and his carriage too, since mine was better. She showed me everything she had left, which was only some linen and three or four plain dresses. We remained in Spa for four days after the poor wretch left, never going out. She saw that I loved her more than paternally, she told me so, and she was grateful to me for forbidding myself to act toward her as a lover. I held her in my arms for hours, kissing her beautiful eyes and demanding no other recompense for my affection; I enjoyed seeing that my restraint filled her with gratitude. When I felt tempted to believe that I was deceiving myself, I rejected the idea with indignation. Such is the man of feeling who has the misfortune to fall in love.

Since I needed a traveling hat, the inn servant went to look for one at the hatter's from Liège, and Merci brought several. She blushed when she saw me, and I said nothing; but my new friend laughed heartily when I told her, after Merci had gone, that it was from her that I had received the blow which had given me the bruise she had seen on my face when she arrived in Spa. She admired my courage in not having surrendered to her demonstrations of repentance. She thought the whole thing had been hatched up between the girl and her mistress.

We left Spa without a servant, and at Liège we took horses for Luxembourg, going by way of the Ardennes. It was necessary to do this to avoid Brussels, where she was afraid she might be set upon. At Luxembourg we engaged a manservant, who, by way of Metz and Verdun, waited on us until we came to Paris. On the journey my dear daughter always insisted on going to bed with her new father and putting him to sleep in her arms. My love grew calm, and this toying made her laugh. She said that, setting ourselves these limits, we did nothing with which we could reproach ourselves, and we assured ourselves that we would love each other most fondly all our lives. I foresaw that things would be different after her confinement, and I indulged myself in sweet imaginings of that time; but the event was to be otherwise. We went to stay at the Hôtel de Montmorency,[27] on the Rue de Montmorency.

Paris seemed to me a new world. Madame d'Urfé was

dead,[28] my old acquaintances had different houses and different fortunes, I found the rich become poor, the poor rich, brand-new courtesans, the ones I had known having gone to cut a figure in the provinces, where everything which comes from Paris is welcomed and acclaimed. I found not only new buildings which kept me from recognizing the streets, but whole new streets and so strange in their architecture that I lost my way in them. Paris seemed to me to have become a labyrinth. Being on foot, and wanting to walk from the Church of Saint-Eustache[29] to the Rue Saint-Honoré to go to the Louvre, and not finding the old site of the Hôtel de Soissons,[30] I got completely lost. Vast round buildings with unsymmetrical exits, and little streets wider than long—it was the height of French architectural folly, which, to the innovating genius of the nation, seemed a masterpiece. Taste in spectacles was governed by new principles: new rules, new actors, and new actresses; everything had become more expensive, the poor, to alleviate their sorrows, crowded to enjoy themselves on the new promenades which policy and avarice had built for them on the false ramparts[31] of the great city. The luxury of those who appeared there only in carriages seemed to be displayed only for the sake of contrast. The two extremes were, in turn and reciprocally, spectacle and spectators. No city except Paris needs only four or five years to present the observant eye with so great a change.

The first person whom I went to see was Madame du Rumain,[32] who saw me with the greatest joy. I at once returned to her the money which she had conveyed to me by the draft she had sent me at Wesel.[33] She was in good health, but a great many family concerns by which she was troubled made her think I had arrived in Paris most opportunely to rid her of them by my cabala. She found me ready to meet her at all the times she set; it was the least I could do for a woman of her character.

My brother had gone to live beyond the Pont-aux-

Choux[34] on the Rue des Amandiers in the Faubourg Saint-Antoine. Delighted to see me, as was his wife, who loved him alone and whom he made unhappy because of his inability to perform the act of love, he joined her in urging me to come to lodge with them; and I promised that I would do so after a lady who was with me had been confined. I saw no reason to tell them the story, and they did not urge me to tell it. On that same day I paid my only calls on Princess Lubomirska and on Tomatis, warning them that I should see them very seldom because of the lady they had seen at Spa, who was nearing her term and whom I must not leave alone.

After fulfilling these duties, I no longer left Charlotte, who, having a prodigiously big belly, expected to be confined from day to day.

It was on the 7th or 8th of October that I thought I would send Charlotte to stay in the house of the midwife Lamarre, who lived on the Rue du Faubourg Saint-Denis. Charlotte wanted to go there. We went together, she saw her room, she learned what attendance she would receive, how she would eat, and what I would pay for her board and her confinement, and we went there at nightfall of the same day in a hackney carriage into which I put a trunk containing all her possessions.

As we came out of the Rue de Montmorency our carriage had to wait for a quarter of an hour to let the funeral procession of some rich person pass. Charlotte held a handkerchief to her eyes, and, resting her beautiful head on my shoulder, said that it was stupid but that, even so, meeting the funeral procession in the state she was in seemed to her a very bad omen.

"Do not becloud your intelligence, my charming Charlotte, with the least apprehension; omens are nothing but vanities which can become real only with the help of superstition; a woman who is about to lie in is not ill, and no woman has ever died in childbirth except from some other disease. We will set out, my dear friend, for

Madrid as soon as you have recovered, leaving your child here at nurse, and I shall not be happy until I see you content.''

As soon as I saw that she was comfortably lodged and assured myself that she would want for nothing, I went home; and the next day I took all my things to my brother's; but as long as Charlotte lived I returned there only to sleep. I went to her room at nine o'clock in the morning and did not leave it until an hour after midnight. On October 13th Charlotte was attacked by a high fever which never left her. On the 17th in my presence she gave birth to a boy with no difficulty, and the next morning the midwife, at Charlotte's express order, took him to the church to be baptized,[35] she herself giving her the name she wanted him to bear written in her own hand: Jacques (which was my name) Charles (which was hers), son of Antonio La Croce and Charlotte xxx (she gave her real name). When they came back from the church she insisted that Madame Lamarre herself take him to the Foundling Hospital, with his baptismal certificate and the place where he was born and the address in his linen. I tried in vain to persuade her to leave the child in my care. She said that if he lived nothing would be easier than for his father to take him from the orphanage in which she was putting him. On the same day, October 18th, the midwife brought me the following certificate, which I have kept:

''We, J. Baptiste Dorival, Councilor to the King, Commissary of the Châtelet[36] in Paris, formerly superintendent of police in the quarter of La Cité,[37] certify that by our order there was taken to the Foundling Hospital a male child apparently one day old, brought from the Faubourg Saint-Denis by the midwife Lamarre, dressed in swaddling clothes in which was found a certificate stating that he was baptized on this same day at Saint-Laurent under the name of Jacques Charles, son of Antoine La Crosse and of Charlotte xxx. In testimony whereof we have delivered the present certificate at our residence on the Rue des Marmousets[38] in La Cité, this 18th October 1767 at seven o'clock in the evening. Dorival.''

If there is a reader who is curious to know the mother's name, I have enabled him to satisfy himself. After this matter was attended to, I did not leave Charlotte's bedside again day or night. The fever which remained with her despite the efforts of the physician Petit ended her life in my presence on the 26th of the same month at five o'clock in the morning. Before closing her beautiful eyes, an hour before she died, she gave me her last farewell, saying that it was the last, and before letting go of my hand she raised it to her lips in the presence of the priest who had confessed her at midnight. The tears which I now shed as I write this account will apparently be the last[39] with which I shall honor the memory of that charming creature, victim of love and of a man who still lives and who seems bound to make people unhappy only in obedience to his cruel destiny.

Breaking into tears again and again, I sat beside the bed on which lay what had been Charlotte, now a corpse, refusing to listen to the midwife, who tried to persuade me to come down to her quarters. At noon I saw my brother and his wife, who had not seen me for a week. Seeing the spectacle and my tears, they could not hold back theirs. They had to leave me there. I slept there, and I did not leave the room until after Charlotte had been carried away to be buried, and until I received the following certificate two hours later. Here is a copy of it:

''Extract from the registry of burials of the Church of Saint-Laurent, Paris, 27th October 1767. Charlotte XXX, spinster, aged seventeen years, deceased yesterday on the Rue du Faubourg Saint-Antoine in this parish, was buried in the cemetery of this church with the offices of three priests in the presence of Claude Louis Ambezar, who has signed. Collated with the original and delivered by me, the undersigned, priest. Besombet.''

On the evening before that fatal day my brother had

given me several letters which the post had brought to his house. Before leaving the ill-omened house of the good midwife, I open them to read them, and in the first, which came from Venice, written by Signor Dandolo,[40] I find the dreadful news of the death of Signor Braga-din.[41] The spring of my tears was dried up. It was the news of the death of a man who for twenty-two years had been as a father to me, living himself with the greatest economy and going into debt to support me. His estate being entailed, he could leave me nothing. His furniture, his library were to be sold to satisfy his creditors in part. His two friends, who were also mine, were poor. I could count only upon their hearts. This terrible news was accompanied by a bill of exchange for a thousand écus, which the deceased, foreseeing his imminent death, had sent me twenty-four hours before he rendered up his soul.

Overwhelmed as I was, I defied Fortune to give me a blow which I could feel. I spent three days without leaving my brother's house. On the fourth I began paying assiduous court to Princess Lubomirska, who had written the King, her cousin,[42] a letter which must have mortified him, for it showed the monarch that he had listened to calumny; but Kings are not mortified by such trifles; and the King of Poland had at that time received the most outrageous insult from Russia. The abduction of the three Senators[43] by the violence of Prince Repnin because they had spoken like free men in the Diet was a blow which must have pierced the heart of Stanislaus Augustus. Princess Lubomirska remained away from Warsaw more from hate than from love; and people were deceived. Since I had already decided to go to Madrid and to see and know that Court before going to Portugal, the Princess gave me a letter for the Count of Aranda,[44] who was then very powerful, and the Marchese Caraccioli, who was still in Paris, gave me three, one for Prince della Cattolica,[45] the Neapolitan Minister at that Court, another for the Duke of Losada,[46] Grand Steward to the

King[47] and his favorite, and the third for the Marquis of Mora Pignatelli.[48]

On the 4th of November I went to a concert opposite the Cul-de-sac de l'Orangerie[49] with a ticket which Princess Lubomirska had given me. Halfway through the concert I hear my name spoken behind me and a laugh; I turn, and I see that the person who was speaking scornfully of me was a tall young man[50] between two elderly people. I stare at him, and, turning his eyes from me, he continues his insolent remarks, and among other things I hear him say that I had cost him at least a million which I had stolen from his late aunt the Marquise d'Urfé.

"You can be nothing but an upstart," I said to him. "If you were out of this place I would teach you to talk by kicking you in the behind."

So saying, I rise and I go out, seeing the two sensible people holding back the blockhead. I get into my carriage, and I wait at the entrance to the Cul-de-sac for a quarter of an hour to see if he will come, and, not seeing him, I go to the play at the Théâtre de la Foire,[51] where I find myself in a box with the actress Valville.[52] She tells me that she is no longer on the stage and that she is being kept by the Marquis de Brumoy.[53] She urges me to sup with her. I excuse myself, assuring her that it was impossible for me to enjoy the pleasure, but that I would go to see her if she would be so good as to give me her address. So saying, I hand her a roll of fifty louis which I owed her.

"What is this?"

"The money you lent me in Königsberg."

"This is neither the time nor the place to return it to me. I will accept it only in my house, and do not insist."

I put the roll back in my pocket, she takes out her pencil, writes her address, and gives it to me. I was too sad to accept a supper alone with the charming and giddy Valville.

On the next day but one I was at table with my

brother, my sister-in-law, and some Russians who were boarding with him to learn to paint battle pictures, when I was told that a Chevalier of St. Louis[54] was in the anteroom wanting to speak to me. I go to hear what he has to say, and, without any preamble, he hands me a paper. I read it, I see that it is signed Louis. That monarch, in the letter he wrote me, ordered me to leave Paris within twenty-four hours and his kingdom within three weeks, and the reason he gave me was that such was his good pleasure.[55]

My departure from Paris. My journey to Madrid. The Count of Aranda. Prince della Cattolica. The Duke of Losada. Mengs. A ball. La Pichona. Doña Ignacia.

"VERY WELL, Chevalier" (he was Buhot),[1] "I have read, and I will try to gratify the monarch as soon as possible. However, if in twenty-four hours I have not been able to make ready to leave, His Majesty will enjoy the other gratification of doing as he will with me."

"Monsieur, the twenty-four hours are allotted you only by way of form; sign an acknowledgment of the order, give me a receipt for the *lettre de cachet,* and you shall leave at your convenience. I ask only for your word of honor that you will go neither to the theater nor to public promenades on foot."

"Very well, Monsieur, I give you my word for that, and I thank you for relying on it."

I take him into my room, and I write everything he tells me to write, and, he having said that he would be glad to see my brother, whom he already knew, I take him to the dining room, where he was still at table, and I tell him bluntly, but cheerfully and without recrimination, the purport of the visit. My brother laughs, telling the Chevalier Buhot that I do not need the order, for I was planning to leave within the week.

"So much the better. If the Minister[2] had known that, he would not have gone to the trouble of having the letter signed this morning."

"Is the reason for the letter known?"

"I heard something about a proposal to 'kick the behind' of someone who, though young, cannot be treated in that fashion."

"You no doubt understand," I said, "that those words are a formality, like the phrase 'within twenty-four hours,' for if he had come out he had a sword with which he could easily have defended his behind."

I told him the whole story, and Buhot admitted that I was entirely in the right, but he said that the police also had the right, so far as it was in their power, to prevent encounters of the sort. He advised me to present myself the next morning to Monsieur de Sartine, who knew me and who would be delighted to hear the whole story from my own lips; and I made no answer.[3]

It was November 6th. I did not leave until the 20th. I exchanged my carriage, which had four wheels, for one with two and room for only one person; and I informed all my acquaintances of the honor done me by the royal order, having absolutely refused the kind offices of Madame du Rumain, who wanted to go to Versailles expressly for the purpose, saying she was sure that she could get the letter withdrawn. My passport from the Duke of Choiseul authorizing me to order post horses is dated the 19th,[4] and I still keep it. I left on the 20th, all alone, without a servant, sad because of Charlotte's death, but calm, with a hundred louis in my purse and a bill of exchange for eight thousand francs on Bordeaux. I enjoyed perfect health, and I thought I was armed with new principles. I was going to a country in which I should need them, in respect both to my conduct and to the circumspection with which I must speak. Aside from that, I had lost all my resources, death had isolated me; I was beginning to see myself arrived at the "certain age" which Fortune commonly scorns, and for which women care little. I did not see La Valville until the day before I left. I found her splendidly lodged and well supplied with diamonds. When I wanted to return the fifty louis to her she asked me if I had at least a thousand, and when she learned that I had only five hundred she refused to take them. After that time I heard no more of her.

I embraced my brother and my sister-in-law at six o'clock by moonlight, and, determined to travel all night to dine at Orléans, where I wanted to see an old acquaintance, I found myself at Bourg-la-Reine in half an hour. I began to sleep, annoyed that I was constantly being waked to pay the post; I was in Orléans at seven o'clock in the morning. Oh, my dear France! where in those days everything went well, despite the *lettres de cachet*, the forced labor and the misery of the peasants, and the good pleasure of the King and the Ministers— what have you become today? Your king is the people. The most savage, the most insane, the most uncontrollable, the most rascally, the most fickle, the most ignorant of all peoples. But everything will perhaps return to its place before I finish writing these memoirs; in the meanwhile, may God keep me far from that country under his curse.

I had myself driven to the house of Bodin,[5] once a respectable dancer, who had married La Geoffroi, of Marseilles, whom I had loved twenty-two years before[6] and whom I had afterward seen at Turin, Vienna, and Paris; but I had still to see her at home. These renewed acquaintances, these surprises, these recognitions, which summoned up old memories, which recalled old joys, were my theater; I seemed to become again what I once was, and my soul rejoiced equally in narrating its vicissitudes and in hearing those of the object it saw before it. Such was my inclination, for cruel repentance did not gnaw my conscience; but often the object which interested me was in a frame of mind entirely different from mine.

Bodin's wife,[7] who had become even uglier than older, had turned pious to please the taste of her husband, who, living on a small property he had bought, attributed all the little misfortunes which befell his fields in the course of the year, and which damaged him to the extent of fifty écus, to the justice of an avenging God. I ate a fast-day dinner with them, for it was a Friday, and the rule was inviolable. I gave them a brief account of my vicissitudes, and at the end of my story I heard nothing but reflections on the irregularity of man's conduct when his guide in all that he does is not religion. They told me that there was a God, and that I had a soul, as if I had not known it, and that it was time that I thought, as they did, of renouncing all the vanities of this world. What La Bodin bitterly reproached me with was my having stayed with Charlotte until her last breath, and she was astonished at the priest who had allowed me to do so, for he must at least have known that I was not her father.

Despite all this stupidity, I was not sorry to have spent six hours with the two good creatures; I embraced them, and I traveled all night. I stopped at Chanteloup[8] to see the monument to the magnificence and the taste of the Duke of Choiseul. I spent twenty-four hours there; a man who had the air of a courtier and who seemed to have full powers, who did not know me and to whom I brought no letter, lodged me in a very fine room, gave me supper, and did not sit down at table with me until I had insisted on it; the next day at dinner he did the same, he took me everywhere, and, without ever asking me who I was, he showed me the honors due to a prince. He had the courtesy to see to it that not one servant should be present when I got into my chaise to leave. It was a deliberate arrangement to save the traveler from giving a louis. The beautiful castle, which cost the Duke immense sums, had not burdened him in the least, for he owed everything it cost,[9] but that made no difference to him. He was the declared enemy of "mine" and "thine"; he paid no one, and he pressed no one who owed him to pay him. He liked to give. A lover of the arts, a friend to people of talent and taste, he enjoyed the pleasure of being useful to them and of seeing them in his presence paying court to him from gratitude. He had, furthermore, a great deal of intelligence, though always from an embracing and summarizing point of view, disregarding every kind of detail, for he was lazy and a worshiper of pleasure. "There is time for everything," was his favorite saying. It was he who covered with ineffaceable ridicule those Ministers who shut their doors to everyone on post days; and so he succeeded in making them live the same life every day.

At Poitiers two young ladies protested when they saw me at seven o'clock determined to go on to sleep at Vivonne.[10]

"It is very cold; the road is not of the best. You are not a courier, sup here, you will find that we will give you an excellent bed, and you shall leave in the morning."

"I must leave, but if you will sup with me I will stay."

"Oh, that would cost you too much."

"There's no such thing. Quick, make up your minds."

"Very well, we will sup with you."

"Then have three places set. I will leave in an hour."

"In three, if you please, for our dear father cannot serve you for two hours."

"In that case I will not leave; but you shall keep me company all night."

"If Papa consents we are willing, and we will have your chaise brought in."

The two young mischiefs, having arranged things with their father, gave me a supper which could not have been more exquisite, with wines than which better were not to be had. They held me at table until midnight, keeping up with me in both eating and drinking, gay, playful, always ready with a charming remark, and in general such that I thought my moderation most extraordinary. I could attribute it only to a certain sadness which Charlotte's death had left in my soul, for I was gay, and I was thoroughly aware of all their charms; but I never felt that kindling sensibility to which I have all my life been so susceptible. I did not recognize myself.

Their father came into the room at midnight, smiling and asking me if I had been pleased with the supper.

"Very well pleased, but far more by the company. Your daughters are both enchanting."

"I am delighted to hear it. When you come this way again they will always eat with you; but at this hour everyone must go to bed."

I do not know if he would have left them with me, but I know that I did not propose it to him, for fear of being taken at my word. I had neither the inclination nor the ability to imagine a pleasure worthy of succeeding to the noble Charlotte. I wished them a good night's rest, and I believe I would not even have kissed them if their father had not urged me to do him that honor. My self-esteem inspired me to carry it off with ardor. They thought they left me a prey to desires, and I was glad to leave them deluded. When I was alone I saw that if I did not forget Charlotte I was lost. I slept until nine o'clock, and I told the maid who made my fire to order coffee for three and horses.

The pretty girls then came to breakfast with me, and I thanked them for having persuaded me to stay. I asked for the bill, and the elder said it came to a round sum. It was a louis a head for everything. I then gave three louis, saying that I had three heads. I left very well satisfied, not finding the entertainment too expensive. I wanted to pass that way again, but the opportunity never arose.

I made my journey two short leagues longer in order to go to Angoulême. I hoped to find Noël there, the King of Prussia's cook, with whom I had supped three or four times in Berlin at La Rufin's;[11] but I found only his father, who treated me very well and whose skill in pâtés I found to be immense. A man of persuasive tongue, he told me that he would undertake to send any pâtés I might order to any place in Europe, directly to the houses of the persons to whom I ordered him to send them.

"What? Even to Venice, to London, to Warsaw, to Petersburg?"

"Anywhere; you have only to write down the addresses, and, to assure yourself that I do not mean to cheat you, you shall not pay me until you hear that the pâtés are in the hands of the person to whom you want them sent."

I sent some, paying him for them, to Venice, Warsaw, and Turin, and I received thanks for them. The man had grown rich by this trade. He told me that he sent some to America. They were pâtés of partridge, of turkey, stuffed with truffles. They kept without spoiling until summer. On the next day but one I arrived in Bordeaux, where I spent a week. After Paris it is the first city of all France. I left after transferring my eight thousand francs to Madrid by a bill of exchange on a Genoese; and, by way of Les Landes,[12] I went to Saint-Jean-d'Angély,[13] where I sold my post chaise. I went to Pamplona after crossing the Pyrenees riding a mule and with another carrying my trunks. I thought those mountains much more imposing than the Alps.

At Pamplona the carter Andrea Capello took charge of me and my baggage, and we set out for Madrid. The first twenty leagues did not tire me, for the road was as good as in France. It was a monument which honored the memory of Monsieur de Gages,[14] who, after the Italian war, was made Governor of Navarre. He had, I was told, had the fine road built at his expense. This famous general, who twenty-four years earlier had had me arrested,[15] thus found the true way to gain immortality and to deserve it. As a great soldier he had won laurels only to declare himself a famous destroyer of the human race;

but this fine road declared him its benefactor. His fame was permanent and secure.

But after such a fine road I cannot say that I found a bad one, for I found none at all. Uneven stony climbs and descents, where one nowhere saw the least sign to indicate that carriages passed there. Such was the whole of Old Castile.[16] No one supposes that travelers who are fond of comfort think of going to Madrid by that route, so I was not surprised to find only wretched inns[17] fit to lodge muleteers who lodge with their mules. Señor Andrea was careful to choose the most habitable places for me, and after procuring everything his mules needed he would go through the village finding me something to eat. The master of the miserable establishment at which we stopped did not stir; he showed me a room and told me that I was at liberty to sleep in it, and a fireplace in which I was free to make a fire if I went to fetch the wood myself and to cook what I wanted to eat, not even troubling to tell me where I could go to buy it for my money. On leaving in the morning I paid him the small sum he asked for my lodging and a *peseta por el ruido,* "a small coin for the noise." [18] He smoked the *cigarro*[19] and his poverty stood him in the stead of riches, provided that the departing stranger could not say that he had bestirred himself in the slightest to wait on him. What causes this is an indolence mingled with pride; one is a Castilian, one must not lower oneself to wait on a *gabacho*;[20] this is the title which the whole Spanish nation confers on a foreigner. This word *gabacho* is much more insulting than the "dog" which the Turks apply to us and the "French dog" [21] which the English apply to all foreigners. It goes without saying that the nobility and people polished by travel or education do not think in this way. The foreigner who has good introductions and who behaves himself properly finds reasonable people in England as well as in Spain and in Turkey.

I slept the second night in Agreda. It is called a city. It is a prodigy of ugliness and gloom. It is a place where

Casanova's Passport
for His Journey to Spain

*Churchgoers in Front of the Church
of San Isidro*

a man whom some employment does not keep busy cannot but go mad, suffer from black bile, and become a
visionary. It is there that Sister María de Agreda went
mad to the point of writing the life of the Blessed Virgin
dictated by herself. I had been given her work to read
under the Leads, and my reader may remember that the
visionary's dreams very nearly made me lose my mind.[22]
We traveled twenty leagues a day. One morning I thought
I was preceded by ten or twelve Capuchins who were
moving more slowly than the mules harnessed to my
carriage. We pass them, I look at them, and I see that
they are not Capuchins but women of all ages.

"What is this?" I asked Señor Andrea. "Are these
women mad?"

"Not at all; they wear the Capuchin habit from devotion, and I am sure that not one of them has on a
shift."

It was the more likely because shifts in Spain are very
rare, but the notion of wearing the Capuchin habit to be
more pleasing to the Creator struck me as very strange
indeed.

Here is an adventure which amused me.

At the posthouse of a city not far from Madrid I am
asked for my passport, I hand it over, and I get out of
my carriage to amuse myself. I see the chief official angry
with a foreign priest who wants to go on to Madrid and
who has no passport for the capital. He showed one with
which he had been to Bilbao,[23] and the official was not
satisfied. The priest was a Sicilian, he was being badg-
ered; I take an interest in him, I ask him why he has
put himself in this predicament, and he replies that he
had not thought that he needed a passport to travel in
Spain once he was there.

"I want to go to Madrid," he said, "where I hope to
enter the household of a grandee[24] as his confessor. I have
a letter to him."

"Show the letter, and you will certainly be allowed to
pass."

"You are right."

From his portfolio he takes the letter, which was not sealed, he shows it to the official, who unfolds it, looks at the signature, and exclaims when he reads the name Squillace.[25]

"What, Abate! you are going to Madrid recommended by Squillace, and you dare to show his letter?"

The clerks, the police who were there, as soon as they understand that the Abate had no recommendation but one from the Minister who was the object of the entire nation's hatred, and who would have been stoned to death if the King had not arranged his escape, raise their sticks and begin to bestow a sound beating on the wretched Abate, who would never have expected such a lamentable effect from a letter of recommendation from a man upon whose favor he hoped to construct the edifice of his fortune.

This Squillace was sent by the King, who loved him, as Ambassador to Venice, where he died at a great age. He was a man to be hated by all the subjects of the monarch, whose Minister of Finance he would have liked to be, for to increase receipts he was pitiless in regard to taxes.

The door of the room which the innkeeper gave me had a bolt outside, and nothing inside which I could use to fasten my door when I went to bed; the door opened and shut only by means of the latch. I said nothing for the first night and the second; but on the third I told my carter that I would not put up with it. He replied that I should have to put up with it in Spain; since the Holy Inquisition[26] must always be able to send to see what foreigners might be doing at night in their rooms, foreigners must not have the means to lock themselves in.

"What can your accursed Holy Inquisition be curious to know?"

"Everything. To see if you eat meat on a fast day. To see if there are several people of both sexes in the room, if the women sleep alone or with men, and to learn if the women who sleep with men are their legitimate wives, and to be able to take them to prison if their marriage certificates do not speak in their favor. The Holy Inquisition, Señor Don Jaime,[27] is ever on the watch in our country for our eternal salvation.''

When we met a priest who was carrying the blessed sacrament to a dying person Señor Andrea stopped and imperatively told me to get out of the carriage and kneel, even in the mud if there was any; I had to obey. The great uproar in matters of religion at that time in the two Castiles[28] was over breeches without a codpiece. Those who wore them were taken to prison, and the tailors were punished; nevertheless both wearers and tailors persisted, and the priests and monks vainly wore out their throats in their pulpits inveighing against such indecency. A revolution was expected which would have set all Europe laughing; but fortunately the thing was settled without bloodshed. An edict was promulgated, and printed copies of it were displayed on every church door. It said that no one would be allowed to wear breeches so made except the executioner. The fashion then went out, for no one wanted either to be thought an executioner or to avail himself of such a privilege.

Thus learning, little by little, to know the country among whose people I was to live, I arrived at Guadalajara, Alcalá, and Madrid. Guadalajara and Alcalá! What are these words, these names, in which I hear only the vowel *a*? It is because the language of the Moors, whose country Spain had been for several centuries, had left a quantity of words there.[29] Everyone knows that the Arabic language abounds in *a*'s. The learned are even not unjustified in deducing thence that Arabic must be the oldest of all languages, since *a* is the easiest of all the vowels, because it is the most natural. Hence it is not just to regard as barbarisms the words in the beautiful Spanish language in which there are no other vowels: ala, achala, Aranda, Almada, Acara, bacala, Agapa, Agrada, Agracaramba, Álava, Alamata, Al-

badara, Alcántara, Alcaraz, Alcavala,[30] and a thousand more, which have the effect of making the
Castilian language richer than all languages, a richness which, as the reader easily understands, can
consist only in synonyms, since it is as easy to imagine
words as it is difficult to find new qualities and as it is
impossible to create things. However that may be, the
Spanish language is beyond contradiction one of the
most beautiful in the world, sonorous, energetic, majestic, to be pronounced *ore rotundo* ("with rounded
mouth"),[31] capable of the harmony of the most sublime
poetry, and which would be equal to Italian for music
if it had not the three guttural letters[32] which mar its
sweetness, despite all that is said by the Spaniards, who,
naturally, are of a different opinion. They must be allowed to go on saying so; *quisquis amat ranam ranam
putat esse Dianam* ("he who loves frogs thinks that
Diana is one").[33] Nevertheless, to unprejudiced ears its
tone makes it seem more imperative than any other
language.

As I entered by the Puerta de Alcalá,[34] I was searched,
and the greatest attention of the officials was directed to
books; they were disappointed when I was found to have
only the *Iliad* in Greek. It was taken from me, and it
was brought to me three days later in the Street of the
Cross,[35] at the coffeehouse where I went to lodge,[36] despite Señor Andrea, who wanted to take me elsewhere.
A reliable man had given me this address in Bordeaux.
A ceremony to which I was subjected at the Alcalá gate
annoyed me greatly. A clerk asked me for a pinch of
snuff. I give it to him; it was rappee.

"Señor, this snuff is accursed in Spain."

So saying, he throws all my snuff into the mud and
gives me back my snuffbox empty.

Nowhere is there such strictness in the matter of snuff
as there is in Spain, where, nevertheless, the contraband
trade flourishes more than elsewhere. The spies of the
tobacco monopoly, which is especially protected by the

King, are everywhere on the watch to discover people who have foreign snuff in their boxes, and when they find them they make them pay very dearly for their daring. This indulgence is forgiven only to foreign envoys; the King knew it and had to put up with it; but he did not allow them to use it in his presence. For his part, he put into his big nose only a big pinch of his Spanish snuff in the morning when he got out of bed, and he took no more of it all day. Spanish snuff is excellent when it is pure, but it is rare. On my arrival no good Spanish snuff was to be had. What had been found among the effects of the late Queen[37] had all been sold, and I had to go three or four weeks without taking snuff, except when I went to visit the fat Prince della Cattolica,[38] who, to give me an especial mark of his affection, received me, after the first time, seated on his commode, where he remained all morning and where he began the business of the day as soon as, left alone, he fell to writing his dispatches. In any case, Spaniards prefer rappee to their snuff, just as many of us prefer the Spanish. What pleases mankind is everywhere what is forbidden. A way of making men of a certain cast of mind do their duty would be to forbid them to do it; but lawmaking is nowhere philosophical.

Fairly well lodged, all I lacked was a fire; the cold was dry and more penetrating than in Paris, despite the forty degrees of latitude. The reason is that Madrid is the highest city[39] in all Europe. Those who go there from some city on the seacoast insensibly ascend, I believe, to an altitude of a thousand toises.[40] In addition, the city is surrounded by distant mountains and by hills close by, as a result of which when the wind blows it is bitterly cold. The air of Madrid is bad for all foreigners because it is pure and rarefied; it is good only for Spaniards, all of whom are thin, undersized, and susceptible to cold to the point that when there is the slightest wind even in August they do not expose themselves to it without being wrapped up to the eyes in great woolen cloaks. The minds

of the men in that country are limited by an infinity of
prejudices, those of the women are in general compara-
tively unprejudiced; and both men and women are subject to passions and desires as keen as the air they
breathe. All the men dislike foreigners, and they are
unable to allege one good reason for it, for their dislike
springs from nothing but an innate hatred; add to this
hatred a scorn which can certainly arise only from the
fact that the foreigner is not a Spaniard. The women,
who recognize the injustice of this hatred and scorn,
avenge us by loving us, but taking great precautions, for
the Spaniard, jealous by nature, is determined to have a
reason for his jealousy as well. He has bound his honor
to the slightest slip on the part of the woman who belongs to him; in this way he conceals the cowardice of
a timorous soul under the respectable veil which envelops
the sanctuary of honor and even of religion. Superstitious
to excess, he cannot be cured of it, for he does not know
that he is so. Gallantry in that country can only be a
mystery, for its goal is an enjoyment which is above
everything else and which is also forbidden. Hence secrecy, intrigue, and the trouble of a soul which hesitates
between the duties imposed by religion and the force of
the passion which struggles against them. The men of
that country are generally more ugly than handsome;
but the women are very pretty, burning with desires, and
all ready to lend a hand in schemes intended to deceive
all those who surround them to spy on their doings. The
lover who most boldly faces and defies dangers is the
one they prefer to all those who are timid, respectful,
guarded. Their coquetry makes them want to keep them,
but at bottom they despise them. In the public walks, in
churches, at the theaters, they speak with their eyes to
those to whom they wish to speak, possessing that seductive language to perfection; if the man, who must understand it, can seize the occasion and take advantage of
it, he is sure to be successful; he need not expect the

slightest resistance; if he neglects the opportunity or does not profit by it, it is not offered him again.

Needing to live in a comfortably warm room, since the brazier made me ill and there was no fireplace, I asked for a stove; and with great difficulty I found someone intelligent enough to make me one, following my instructions, of heavy tin with a long pipe which went out one of my windows to join another very long one which ascended to the gutter on the roof. The workman, proud of having succeeded, made me pay a great deal for his trial piece. During the first days until my stove was built I was told where I should go to warm myself an hour before noon and stay there until dinnertime; it was a place called the Gate of the Sun;[41] it was not a gate, but it was so named because it was there that the beneficent luminary, prodigal of his wealth, distributed the heat of his rays to all who went to walk there to warm themselves and thus enjoy their influence. I saw a large number of men of fashion walking about, either alone and rapidly, or slowly and talking to their friends; but I did not care for this sort of hearth. Needing a servant who spoke French, it was an endless task to find one; I did find him at last, but at a very high price, for he was what is called in Madrid a page; I could make him neither get up behind my carriage, nor carry packages anywhere for me, nor light me at night with a torch or a lantern. He was a man thirty years of age, with a face which could not be uglier. As a page, he was better fitted for the duties of his office being ugly than if he had been handsome, for he was not one to make the husbands of the ladies whom he went to serve jealous for fear they would fall in love with him. A woman of a certain station in Madrid does not dare to go out in a carriage unless she is accompanied by a so-called page, who sits up in front and who is with her only to spy on her. Such a rascal is more of a hindrance to a seduction than a duenna,[42] who is by nature a tyrant over the girls she guards. So, since I could find no one else, it was a fellow of this stamp whom I had to take into my service.

I delivered all my letters, beginning with the one by which Princess Lubomirska presented me to the Count of Aranda. The Count was then more powerful in Madrid than the King himself. It was he who in a single day had banished all the Jesuits in all Spain,[43] he had been able to proscribe hats with turned-down brims and cloaks coming down to the heel;[44] he was President of the Council of Castile,[45] he was all-powerful, he never went out except followed by one of the King's bodyguard, whom he always had eat at his table. As was to be expected, he was hated by the whole country, but he did not care. A man of profound intelligence, a great politician, bold, determined, reasoning correctly, a great epicurean, maintaining appearances, doing in his house everything that he forbade in other houses, and not caring if people said so. This rather ugly nobleman, who squinted to the point of deformity, received me rather coolly.

"What have you come to do in Spain?"

"To learn by observing the manners and customs of an estimable nation which I do not know, and at the same time to profit by my feeble talents if I can make myself useful to the government."

"To live here decently and quietly you do not need me, for if you behave in accordance with the laws which maintain order in the city no one will trouble you. As for your wish to use your talents to make your fortune, address yourself to the Ambassador of your Republic;[46] he will present you, and you can make yourself known."

"The Venetian Ambassador will do me no harm, but he will do me no good either, for I am in disfavor with the State Inquisitors. I am sure he will not receive me."

"In that case you can hope for nothing at Court, for the King will first ask the Ambassador about you. If the Ambassador will not present you, I advise you to think of nothing but amusing yourself."

I call on the Neapolitan Ambassador,[47] and he tells me

the same thing; the Marquis of Mora,[48] the most amiable of all Spaniards, is of the same opinion. The Duke of Losada, Grand Steward to His Catholic Majesty and his favorite, sorry that he could do nothing despite his good will, advises me to try to obtain admission to the residence of the Venetian Ambassador and to do what I could to gain his support, despite a disgrace of which he could pretend to be unaware since he did not know the reasons for it. I prepare to follow the wise old man's advice, so I write a strong letter to Signor Dandolo[49] in Venice, in which I asked him for a letter of recommendation to the Ambassador himself, which would oblige him to lend me his countenance at Court despite the State Inquisitors. My letter was so composed that it could be shown to the State Inquisitors themselves, and should have a good effect.

After writing this letter I go to the residence of the Venetian Ambassador, and I present myself to Signor Gasparo Soderini,[50] the Secretary of Embassy, a man of intelligence, prudent and honest, but who nevertheless took it upon himself to say that he was astonished that I had had the audacity to present myself at the Ambassador's residence.

"I present myself, Signore, in order not to have to reproach myself with the fault of not presenting myself, for I have done nothing which can make me suppose myself unworthy of it. I should think myself far more audacious if I stayed in Madrid without presenting myself here at least once than if I had never presented myself. In the meanwhile I am glad to have taken this step, which I regard as a duty, and I leave unhappy and disappointed to have learned that if the Ambassador thinks as you do he will consider temerity what is only an act of respect on my part. If, furthermore, the Ambassador is of the opinion that he may not do me the honor to receive me because of a private quarrel which exists between the State Inquisitors and myself, and the nature of which he cannot know, permit me to be surprised, for he is not here as Ambassador of the State Inquisitors but of the Republic, of which I am still a subject, for I defy him to tell me what crime I can have committed to make me unworthy of being so. I believe that if my duty is to respect in the Ambassador the image and the representative of my sovereign,[51] his duty is to extend his protection to me.''

Soderini had blushed at this discourse, which too clearly set forth palpable truths. He asked me why I did not write the Ambassador everything I had just said to him.

''I could not write him that before I knew if he would receive me or not; now that I have reason to believe that he thinks as you do, I will write to him.''

''I do not know if His Excellency thinks as I do, and despite what I have said to you it is possible that you still do not know what I think; but meanwhile write to him, and you may be given a hearing.''

Back at my lodging, I the same day wrote His Excellency everything that I had said to the Secretary of Embassy; and the next day Count Manuzzi[52] was announced to me. I see a handsome, rather well-built youth who makes a very good impression. He said that he lodged at the Ambassador's, who, having read my letter, had sent him to tell me that, having reasons for not receiving me publicly, he would nevertheless be delighted to talk with me in private, for he knew me and esteemed me. The young man told me that he was a Venetian, that he knew me by reputation from having heard his father and mother talk of me many times, lamenting my misfortune. I finally understand that the young Manuzzi whom I had before me was the son of the Giovanni Battista Manuzzi who had served the State Inquisitors as a spy in order to get me imprisoned under the Leads, the same man who had cleverly obtained from me the books of magic I had [53] and which were apparently the incriminating evidence which, without any other legal proceedings, had brought on me the terrible punishment to which I had been subjected. I tell him none of this, but I see that it is he; I knew his mother, who was the daughter of a valet in the service of the Loredan[54] family, and his father, who, as I said in my account of my imprisonment under the Leads, was a poor jeweler. I ask him if he is called Count in the Ambassador's household, and he says that he is, because he was in fact one by virtue of a patent he had received from the Elector of the Palatinate. He frankly tells me the truth about everything, and since he was aware that I knew of Ambassador Mocenigo's inclination, he does not hesitate to tell me with a laugh that he is his antinatural mistress. He assures me that he will do everything in his power for me; and it was all that I could ask, for such an Alexis was bound to obtain whatever he wanted from his Corydon.[55] We embrace, and he leaves, saying that he expects me after dinner at the palace in the Calle Ancha[56] to take coffee with him in his room, to which the Ambassador would certainly come as soon as he sent him word that I was there.

I went there, and the Ambassador gave me a very gracious reception, speaking with feeling of his regret that he dared not receive me publicly, for it was true that he could have done everything, and even taken me to Court without compromising himself, for he was under no obligation to know anything of the summary treatment I had received from the State Inquisitors, but he feared to make enemies. I replied that I hoped soon to receive a letter from someone which would tell him, on behalf of the Inquisitors themselves, that he could countenance me without fear, and he replied that in that case he would present me to all the Ministers.

The Ambassador was the Mocenigo who afterward got himself so much talked about in Paris because of his unfortunate inclination for pederasty, and who was later sentenced by the Council of Ten to spend seven years in the fortress of Brescia[57] for having tried to leave Venice for Vienna, where he had been appointed Ambassador, without first having been given permission to leave by

the Cabinet. The Empress Maria Theresa had intimated
that she did not want such a man in her capital, and in
Venice it had been proving difficult to make the appointee
understand the situation, when, by committing the error
of trying to leave without permission, he made it possible
for the Senate to appoint another Ambassador[58] to Vienna, who had the same taste as Mocenigo but who confined himself to women.

At Madrid he was liked, despite its being common
knowledge that he was of the wristband clique,[59] and
his often being seen driving through the streets of
Madrid with his paramour. I laughed when a Spanish
grandee told me at a ball that everyone knew that Manuzzi played the part of wife to His Excellency the
Ambassador; he did not know that the wife was the
Ambassador, to whom Manuzzi played husband. The
same inclination was shared by Frederick I, King of
Prussia, and by nearly all the men of Antiquity, who
were called "hermaphrodites" to designate their two
passions. However, Mocenigo kept Manuzzi at a distance
and did not have him dine with him when he gave formal
dinners.

I had already called two or three times on the painter
Mengs,[60] who for six years had been in the service of
His Catholic Majesty at an excellent salary, and he had
given me fine dinners with his friends. His wife was in
Rome with his whole family, he was alone with his servants, lodged in a house which belonged to the King, and
respected by everyone, for he talked with His Majesty
whenever he pleased. At his house I made the acquaintance of the architect Sabatini,[61] a very talented man,
whom the King had summoned from Naples to make
Madrid clean, whereas before he arrived it was the dirti-
est and most stinking city in the universe. Sabatini had
constructed drains and subterranean conduits, and had
had latrines built in fourteen thousand houses. He had
become rich. He had married by proxy the daughter of
Vanvitelli,[62] another architect, who was in Naples and

who had never seen him. She had arrived in Madrid at the same time that I did. She was a beauty eighteen years of age, who had no sooner seen her husband than she had said she would never consent to become his wife. He was neither young nor handsome. However, the charming girl decided to swallow the pill when he told her that she would have to choose between him and a convent. Afterward she had no cause to repent, for she found in him a rich husband, tender and considerate, who granted her all the decent freedom she could want. I went to their house a great deal. *Brûlant pour elle, et soupirant tout bas* ("Burning for her and sighing inaudibly"),[63] for aside from the fact that the wound Charlotte had made in my heart had not yet healed over, I was beginning to feel discouraged to see that women no longer welcomed me as they had done in the past.

I began going to the theater which was a hundred paces from the house in which I lived, and to the masked balls, which the Count of Aranda had established in Madrid in a hall built for the purpose called "Los Caños del Peral." [64] The Spanish theater was full of absurdities, but it did not displease me. I saw some *autos sacramentales*,[65] which soon afterward were forbidden in Madrid, and I observed the shamelessness of a base police administration in the way in which the *aposentos*, as they call the boxes, were constructed. Instead of having boards in front, which prevents people in the parterre from seeing the man's legs and the ladies' skirts, all the boxes were open, having, instead of boards, only two pillars which supported the rail. A precisian who was sitting next to me said devoutly that it was a very wise regulation and declared it surprising that the same policy was not in force in Italy.

"Why do you think it surprising?"

"It is surprising because a lady and gentleman, being sure that people in the parterre do not see their hands, might put them to evil use."

"What use?"

"*Valgame Dios* ['God help me']! The lady could do the *puñete*[66] to the gentleman."

After laughing heartily, and finding out what the *puñete* was, I told him that the Italians and the French did not dirty their minds with such suspicions. In a large box with a grating opposite the stage sat *los padres* of the Inquisition, to make sure that the audience and the actors indulged in nothing contrary to morality. All of a sudden I heard the voice of the sentinel who was at the entrance to the parterre shout: "Dios!" At the sound the whole audience, men and women, and the actors who were on the stage, broke off, fell to their knees, and remained there until a bell which was being rung in the street was no longer heard. The bell indicated that a priest was going past carrying the viaticum to a sick person. The people of Spain are edified by everything which proves that in all that they do they never lose sight of religion. There is not a courtesan who, being with her lover and yielding to amorous desire, decides to perform the act without first having put a handkerchief over the crucifix and turned the pictures of saints to face the wall. Anyone who laughed at it, a man who called the ceremony absurd and superstitious, would be considered an atheist, and the courtesan would perhaps denounce him to the authorities.

Any man in Madrid who goes to an inn with a woman and orders dinner in a private room is accommodated at once; but the headwaiter of the inn always remains present throughout the dinner so that he can swear afterward that the two people did nothing in the room but eat and drink. Despite these prohibitions, and even because of these prohibitions, profligacy runs riot in Madrid. Both men and women think of nothing but making all surveillance fruitless. All the women have a disease which they call "the whites," but men incautious enough to expose themselves to it find at the end of twenty-four hours that it is nothing less than white. This malady is general among the women, and I was assured that even

nuns are afflicted with it without ever having wronged
their divine spouse in any way.

The masked ball became my favorite pleasure. The
first time I went to it, alone and wearing a domino,
merely to see what it was, it cost me only a doubloon;
but all the other times it cost me four. This was in consequence of a discourse to which I was treated by a
masker in a domino, a man of perhaps sixty years, who
happened to sit beside me in the room in which one
supped. Seeing that I was a foreigner from the difficulty
I had in making myself understood by the waiter, he
asked me where my female masker was.

"I have no women with me, I came alone to see this
charming establishment, where a pleasure and an order-
liness reign which I had not expected to find in Madrid."

"Very well; but to enjoy this fine spectacle you must
come with a companion, for you seem to be a man to
enjoy dancing, and, alone, you cannot dance, for every
woman you see here has her *parejo* ['partner'] who will
not let her dance with anyone else."

"In that case I will come and never dance, since I do
not know a woman in this city whom I can invite to
come to the ball with me."

"As a foreigner you can obtain the company of a
woman or a girl much more easily than a Spaniard from
Madrid. Under the new regime of gaiety and freedom
introduced by the Count of Aranda, the ball which you
see has become the passion of all the women and girls in
Madrid. You see here some two hundred of them dancing,
for I do not count those who remain in the boxes, and it
is certain that four thousand girls who have no lover
who will or can bring them here are at home crying, for
as you know all women are forbidden to come here alone.
Now, I am certain that, if you give merely your name
and your address, there is not a mother or a father who
will have the heart to refuse you their daughter if you
present yourself to ask for the honor of offering her the

pleasure of the ball, sending her domino, mask, and gloves, and going to fetch her in a carriage, in which you will undertake, of course, to bring her back home."

"And if I am refused?"

"You bow and leave, and afterward the girl's father and mother are very sorry they have refused you, for she cries, falls ill, and goes to bed, cursing and swearing at their tyranny and calling God to witness that she has never seen you in her life and that nothing was more innocent than your request."

This novel discourse, which had the stamp of truth, and which already raised my spirits by the prospect that it would introduce me to some rare adventure, for which I still had an appetite, both interested me and authorized me to ask the masker who thus addressed me in very good Italian some questions. I thank him, and I promise him I will apply the fine lesson he has given me and will inform him of the outcome and of the acquaintance he will have led me to make, for I would consider the next morning to which of all the beauties in Madrid I would throw my handkerchief. He replies that he will be delighted to hear everything, and that I should find him every evening in a box to which he would take me to introduce me to the lady who was in it then and who would also be there on the following nights. More than obliged by such politeness, I tell him my name, I pay for my supper at the posted price, I follow him, and we enter a box in which are two women and an elderly man; he introduces me as a foreigner of his acquaintance; all goes smoothly, they speak French, they discuss the fine ball, I offer my comments, I make some remarks bright enough to please the company; one of the two ladies, who still showed signs of a great, faded beauty, asks me which *tertulias* ("receptions, circles") I frequent, and when she hears me say that I usually go nowhere she invites me to go to her house, saying that her name is Pichona[67] and that everyone knows where she lives. I promise her I will go there.

The great spectacle which enchanted me came toward the end of the ball, when to the music of the orchestra, after general applause, a dance for couples began than which I had never seen anything wilder or more interesting. It was the fandango,[68] of which I thought I had an accurate notion, but I was very much mistaken. I had seen it danced only in Italy and France on the stage, where the dancers did not perform one of the national gestures which make the dance truly seductive. I cannot describe it. Each couple danced face to face, never taking more than three steps, striking the castanets, which are held in the fingers, and accompanying the music with attitudes than which nothing more lascivious could possibly be seen. Those of the man visibly indicated love crowned with success, those of the woman consent, ravishment, the ecstasy of pleasure. It seemed to me that no woman could refuse anything to a man with whom she had danced the fandango. The pleasure I took in watching it made me exclaim aloud; the masker who had brought me there told me that to have a true idea of the dance one had to see it performed by *gitanas* ("gypsy girls") with a man who also danced it to perfection. I asked if the Inquisition had no objection to make to a dance which set the soul on fire, and I was told that it was absolutely forbidden, and that no one would have dared to dance it if the Count of Aranda had not given his permission for it. I was told that when he took it into his head not to give the permission everyone left the ball dissatisfied; but that on the other hand everyone left praising him when he permitted it.

The next morning I ordered my infamous page to find me a Spaniard whom I would pay to teach me to dance the fandango, and he brought me an actor, whom I engaged to give me lessons in the Spanish language; but in three days the young man taught me the motions of the dance so well that, by the testimony even of Spaniards, there was no one in Madrid who could boast that he danced it better than I.

Three days later there was a ball, and I wanted to do
justice to the lesson the masker had taught me. I wanted
neither a public courtesan nor a married woman. Nor
could I think of some rich or well-born lady, who would
have refused me and have found me ridiculous into the
bargain. It was St. Anthony's[69] day—the one who is
called "St. Anthony the Great" and who is depicted with
a pig; I pass by the Church of La Soledad,[70] and I enter
it to hear a mass, still thinking of finding a *pareja* for
the next day, which was a Wednesday. I see a tall girl
coming out of a confessional, beautiful, with an air of
contrition and keeping her eyes cast down. She kneels in
the middle of the church, directly on the floor, of course,
for that is the fashion in Spain. Imagining that she must
dance the fandango like an angel, I set my heart on having her as my partner at my début at Los Caños del
Peral. To find out where she lives, I think of following
her, she seemed neither rich, nor noble, nor a prostitute.
At the end of the mass the priest distributes the eucharist,
I see her rise, go to the altar, receive it devoutly, then
take a place apart to finish her prayers. I had the patience to wait until the end of the second mass. She goes
out with another girl, and I follow them at some distance;
at the end of a street the one on whom I had no designs
leaves her and goes upstairs to her home, mine retraces
her steps some twenty paces, enters another street, and
then a house which had only two stories. I cannot be
mistaken, I see the name of the street, del Desengaño,[71]
I walk for half an hour so that she shall not think I
followed her. Thoroughly prepared to be refused and to
leave with a bow afterward, as the masker had told me
to do, I go upstairs, I ring at the only door I see, I am
asked who is there, I reply "peaceable people," which
in Madrid is the password which the henchmen of the
Inquisition, who inspire terror, never use. The door is
opened, and I see a man, a woman, the girl in question,
and an ugly one.

Speaking Spanish very badly but well enough to be understood, with my hat in my hand, and a serious and respectful manner, I say to the father, without even looking at the devout beauty, that, being a foreigner and having no *pareja*, I had come to his house by chance to ask him for permission to take his daughter, if he had one, to the ball, assuring him that I was a man of honor and that I would bring her back to him as he had entrusted her to me at the end of the evening.

"Señor, there is my daughter, but I do not know you, and I do not know if she wants to go to the ball."

"If you will permit me to go, my Father and my Mother, I should think myself fortunate."

"Then you know this gentleman?"

"I have never seen him, and I think it almost impossible that he should have seen me anywhere."

"I swear to you that I have never seen you."

The man asks me my name and my address, and he promises to give me his answer at dinnertime, if I dine at home. I ask him to excuse the liberty I had taken, I leave begging him not to fail to give me his answer, for if he will not let me have his daughter I shall have to look for another *pareja* at random, knowing none but rich girls who were all engaged.

I go home, and exactly an hour later, just as I was about to dine, I see my man. I ask him to sit down, I send away my page, and as soon as he sees we are alone he says that his daughter will accept the honor I am so good as to offer her, but that her mother will come too and will sleep in the carriage and wait for her. I reply that she would be free to do so, and that I was only sorry that she would be cold in the carriage. He says that she will have a good cloak, and he tells me that he is a shoemaker by trade.

"Then please measure me for a pair of shoes at once."

"I do not dare, for I am a hidalgo.[72] Taking someone's measure would debase me, I am a *zapatero de viejo* (cobbler),[73] and so, not being obliged to touch anyone's feet, I neither derogate from my nobility nor wrong my birth.''

''Then will you mend these boots for me?''

''I will return them to you so that you will think them brand-new; but I see that they need much work, it will cost you a peso duro.'' [74]

It was a hundred French sous. I tell him that I am perfectly satisfied with the price, he takes the boots, and he leaves, absolutely refusing to dine with me.

Here was a cobbler who despised shoemakers who in their turn must have looked down on him. The lackeys in livery in France despise valets, because they are obliged to help their masters at moments when they must lower themselves to perform menial services.

The next day I sent a man with dominoes, masks, and gloves to my devout beauty, neither going there myself nor using my page, whom I could not bear, and at nightfall I got out at her door from a closed carriage which seated four. I found her all ready, her face prettily flushed with animation. We got into the carriage with her mother, who had on a great cloak, and we got out at the entrance to the ballroom, leaving her mother in the carriage. On the way the daughter told me that her name was Doña Ignacia.[75] The dancing had already begun, and there was a great crowd.

VOLUME 10 · NOTES

CHAPTER I

1. *Chapter I:* At the beginning of this chapter in C.'s ms. there is a marginal note, *Duobis omissis* ("two [pages] omitted"). Again, however, there is no break in the narrative.

2. *Baltimore:* See Vol. 9, Chap. XI, n. 14.

3. *Caraccioli:* Domenico Caraccioli, Marchese di Villa Marina (1715-1789), Envoy Extraordinary of the Kingdom of Naples in Paris (1752-1754), in Turin (1754-1763), and in London (1764-1774); in 1780 he was made Viceroy of Sicily, and in 1786 Prime Minister of the Kingdom of the Two Sicilies. His first audience at the Court of St. James's took place on Jan. 11, 1764.

4. *Pembroke:* See Vol. 9, Chap. VIII, n. 2.

5. *Richmond:* See Vol. 9, Chap. XII, n. 12.

6. *La Charpillon:* See Vol. 9, Chap. V, n. 6.

7. *Count So-and-so:* Probably Chamberlain von Schwicheldt; see Vol. 9, Chap. XIII, n. 44.

8. *Goudar:* See Vol. 9, Chap. VIII, n. 17.

9. *My vintner:* See Vol. 9, Chap. XII, n. 57.

10. *Pontacq:* Dry red or white wine from the vicinity of Pontacq, near Pau, in southern France.

11. *B . . . . . s . . . wh . . . s:* C. writes "b . . . . ." (for *bougresses*) and "p . . . . ." (for *putains*).

12. *Pawnbroker:* C. writes "pingbros."

13. *Jarba:* See Vol. 9, Chap. VII, n. 55.

14. *Sara:* See Vol. 9, Chap. XIII, n. 17.

15. *Necessity:* C. writes "une bisogne," an Italianism for French *besoin*.

16. *Victoire:* Probably Luise Charlotte Sophie von Schwicheldt (born 1749). C. may have chosen this name to conceal her identity because she represented his first "victory" among the five sisters. He makes her pun on it a few lines later on.

17. *Covent Garden:* See Vol. 9, Chap. VII, n. 46.

18. *Tenducci:* Giusto Fernando Tenducci, called "Il Senesino" from his birthplace, Siena (ca. 1736 - after 1790), Italian castrato, who appeared in Venice, Dresden, and London. He married Dorothy Mansell in 1766 or 1767; the marriage was annulled on the ground of nonconsummation in 1775. Court records show that in 1784 his marriage to the daughter of a Dublin advocate was dissolved for the same reason. But nothing is known of his being married when C. met him in London in 1764.

19. *Pettina:* Nothing is known of him except what C. relates.

20. *His King:* Ferdinand IV (Don Ferrante), also known as "Il re Lazzaroni" (1751-1825), King of Naples from 1759.

21. *Caraccioli . . . Turin:* The Marchese Caraccioli (cf. note 3 to this chapter) had been Envoy Extraordinary from the Kingdom of Naples to the Court of the Kingdom of Sardinia in Turin from 1754 to 1763.

22. *Éon:* See Vol. 9, Chap. VII, n. 45.

23. *Tanucci:* Bernardo, Marchese di Tanucci (1698-1783), began his career as Professor of Law at Pisa, from 1735 to 1767 he was the Neapolitan Secretary of State, from 1759 to 1767 Regent during the minority of Ferdinand IV, and from 1767 to 1776 Prime Minister; he was hostile to the Jesuits.

24. *A large . . . volume: Lettres, mémoires et négociations particulières du Chevalier d'Éon, ministre plénipotentiaire de France auprès du roi de la Grande-Bretagne* (London, 1764). It contains d'Éon's correspondence with the Comte de Guerchy (see Vol. 9, Chap. VII, n. 41), as well as confidential letters from the French Government; 1500 copies were sold in a few days. Its publication caused a scandal and it was attacked in a number of pamphlets, some of them written by Goudar.

25. *Twenty thousand pounds . . . wager:* According to contemporary English sources, wagers laid at the time in London on the sex of the Chevalier d'Éon amounted to 100,000 pounds sterling.

26. *Three years later:* D'Éon was a secret agent in the service of Louis XV. The King granted him a pension in 1766. But he did not return to Versailles until 1777, appearing there as a woman until 1785. He had been awarded the Cross of

St. Louis in 1763 for his courage in the Seven Years' War; he was granted permission to wear it on his woman's clothing.

27. *Cross of St. Louis:* The order of St. Louis was established by Louis XIV in 1693; it was abolished in 1830.

28. *Fleury:* André Hercule de Fleury (1654-1743), Bishop of Fréjus from 1698, Cardinal from 1726; from 1715 he was tutor to the young Louis XV. As Prime Minister, he directed French foreign policy from 1726.

29. *Augusta . . . third of the sisters:* The eldest of the Von Schwicheldt sisters was Bertha Augusta (born 1744); the third sister, Amalia Oelgarde, was not born until 1755 and hence was too young to be C.'s mistress in 1764.

30. *Nancy Stein:* An invented name. In C.'s ms. two words are blotted out and replaced by "Nenci Stein"; he may have first written her real name.

31. *The bit . . . :* C. writes "boug . . ." (for *bougresse*).

32. *Oeil-de-perdrix:* Term applied to certain wines, meaning "light claret-colored" (from the color of a pheasant's eye), and especially to a champagne from the Ville-Allerand district.

33. *The Vicaria:* The fortress of Castel Capuano, built in the 13th century in the northeastern quarter of Naples, was also known as La Vicaria from its having once been the viceregal residence. From the 15th century it served as the seat of the supreme court and as a prison.

34. *Hippolyte:* Hippolyte was one of the Christian names of Frau von Schwicheldt herself; C. apparently transfers it to the daughter. Cf. Vol. 9, Chap. XIII, n. 44.

35. *Pyrmont:* C. writes "Pirmont," doubtless for the then well-known watering place Bad Pyrmont, in Westphalia.

36. *Pagus:* See Vol. 9, Chap. XII, nn. 56 and 57.

37. *Gabrielle:* Another of C.'s fictitious names.

38. *Barnes:* Then a village on the Thames on the road to Richmond; now a part of Greater London.

39. *Pembroke . . . Saint Albans:* Lord Pembroke had a house in Saint Albans; but it seems improbable that he would have gone there by way of Barnes, which is on the south bank of the Thames whereas Saint Albans is northwest of London.

40. *Be my husband:* Frau von Schwicheldt's husband did not
    die until 1766, though he may have been seriously ill in
    1764. Cf. Vol. 9, Chap. XIII, n. 44.

CHAPTER II

1. *Chapter II:* At the beginning of this chapter in his ms. C.
   made the marginal notation: "Vigintiquinque paginis sublatis" ("twenty-five pages removed"). Again there is no
   break in the narrative, so the reference would seem to be to
   an earlier version.
2. *His Lordship:* I.e., Lord Pembroke.
3. *Would end by marrying her:* Pembroke was already
   married (cf. Vol. 9, Chap. VIII, n. 2).
4. *Mr. Frederick:* See Vol. 9, Chap. VIII, n. 18.
5. *Neuhoff:* See Vol. 9, Chap. VIII, n. 19.
6. *Du Clau:* Assumed name of the Jesuit Antoine de Lavalette
   (1707-1767); Superior of the order in Martinique from
   1753, he engaged in financial speculations which bankrupted
   him in 1759. The Society of Jesus was compelled to pay
   his debts (1760 and 1761). These events increased the already hostile attitude toward the Jesuits in France, and the
   order was forbidden there in 1764. Lavalette, expelled from
   the order, lived for some years in London, but later returned to France and died in Toulouse.
7. *Determined to go to Lisbon:* See Vol. 9, Chap. IX, n. 43.
8. *Portraits:* Snuffboxes and other small boxes were frequently
   ornamented with portraits, set either in the cover or in the
   bottom of the box.
9. *Mrs. Mercier:* A Susanna Mercier is documented as having
   lived on Greek Street, near Soho square, from 1762 to 1764.
   C. writes "Mistriss Mercier."
10. *Bragadin:* Matteo Giovanni Bragadin (1689-1767), Vene-
    tian patrician and Senator and faithful friend to C. (cf. Vol.
    9, Chap. II, n. 2).
11. *Zecchini:* The Venetian zecchino was a gold coin worth 22
    lire.
12. *The "Cannon" tavern:* See Vol. 9, Chap. XII, n. 23.
13. *Henau:* See Vol. 9, Chap. XIII, n. 42.
14. *Young Englishwoman . . . La Sartori:* See Vol. 9, Chap.
    XIII, and *ibid.*, n. 41.

15. *Maravedis:* See Vol. 9, Chap. IX, n. 42.

16. *Lisbonines:* See Vol. 9, Chap. IX, n. 20.

17. *Vanneck . . . Bosanquet . . . Lee:* London bankers. For Vanneck see Vol. 9, Chap. XIII, n. 28; for Bosanquet, see Vol. 9, Chap. VII, n. 49; Lee was a member of the banking firm of Brassey, Lee & Co., Lombard Street.

18. *Penny post:* See Vol. 9, Chap. XI, n. 23.

19. *Daturi:* Obviously an illegitimate son and a godson of C.'s; but there is no mention in C.'s memoirs of a love affair of which he could have been the offspring. He may be a certain Giacomo Tantini, known as Datur, who appeared in Venice from 1770 to 1779 with an Anna Tantini. Between 1756 and 1765 several members of the Datur family are documented as appearing as dancers in Venice (Angela, Anna, Enrico, Luigi, Maddalena). Daturi may have been appearing at the Little Theater in the Haymarket as an acrobat when C. was in London.

20. *Pagliaccio:* Italian, "clown."

21. *Three times:* By this year C.'s memoirs have already described him as suffering from venereal disease more than three times.

22. *Across the entire Atlantic Ocean:* See Vol. 9, Chap. IX, n. 14.

23. *Venus was born in that element:* In Greek and Roman mythology the goddess Venus (Aphrodite) was said to have been born from the foam of the sea.

24. *The great cure:* Treatment by mercury.

25. *Treves:* Gershon Treves, of Portuguese descent, banker in London in the second half of the 18th century.

26. *Algarotti:* Bonomo Algarotti (born before 1712) was ennobled with his brother, the celebrated writer Francesco Algarotti, by Frederick the Great in 1740; he was a banker in Venice.

27. *Salvador:* Joseph Jeshurun Rodriguez Salvador (died 1786), partner in the banking firm of Francis & Joseph Salvador in London.

28. *Dandolo:* Marco Dandolo (1704-1779), Venetian patrician, friend of Senator Bragadin and of C. (cf. Vol. 9, Chap. II, n. 2).

29. *Rochester:* See Vol. 9, Chap. VII, n. 6.

30. *Sittingbourne:* On the road from London to Dover, some 10 miles east of Rochester.

31. *The "Golden Arm":* See Vol. 9, Chap. VI, n. 45. C. had left his carriage there before crossing to England in June 1763. His precipitate flight from London must have taken place about the middle of March 1764.

32. *Celtic humors:* C. writes "glandes embibées d'humeurs celtiques." "Embibées" is no doubt for "imbibées"; "celtiques," as applied to "humeurs," has so far defined the efforts of the commentators.

33. *Gravelines:* On the English Channel, about halfway between Calais and Dunkirk.

34. *The "Conciergerie":* Still known in 1782 as the best inn in Dunkirk; it probably occupied a part of the municipal building known as "La Conciergerie." (Note 12 to Chap. IV of Vol. 5 should be corrected accordingly.)

35. *Teresa:* In his account of his liaison with her (Vol. 5, Chap. III), C. called her "Mademoiselle de la M-re." After her marriage he referred to her as "Madame P." (Vol. 5, Chap. IV).

36. *Tiretta:* Count Edoardo Tiretta (1734 - ca. 1809), of Treviso, friend of C.'s and adventurer (cf. especially Vol. 5, Chap. III).

37. *He would be of interest to me:* According to C.'s account Mademoiselle de la M-re was his mistress in Paris in May 1757. Her marriage to Monsieur P. (or S.) must have taken place immediately afterward, for C. saw her again in Dunkirk in Aug. or Sept. of the same year as Madame P. Since the meeting with her described in this chapter took place in March 1764, Madame P.'s 6-year-old son could well have been C.'s.

38. *The Dutch East India Company:* Founded in 1602 for trade with the former Dutch East Indies (now Indonesia). (Cf. Vol. 5, Chap. VII, n. 15.)

39. *Batavia:* Dutch name for the capital of Java (now Djakarta).

40. *Tournai:* Old Belgian city, some 20 miles east of Lille.

41. *Count of Saint-Germain:* Also Count Tzarogy, Prince Racoczy, General Soltikoff, Marquis of Montferrat, etc. (ca. 1696-1784), adventurer extraordinary, whose real origin is unknown. In his *Soliloque d'un penseur* (Prague, 1786), C.

maintains that he was an Italian violinist named Catalani. For C.'s previous encounters with him, see Vols. 5, 6, and 8, and Vol. 9, Chap. III.

42. *I . . . translate into French:* C. does not state in what language Saint-Germain wrote to him. Under the circumstances, one would expect it to have been in French. It has been suggested that C. may here be trying to support his contention that Saint-Germain was Italian (see the preceding note).

43. *Cobenzl:* Count Karl (Johann Karl Philipp) Cobenzl (1712-1770), was Minister Plenipotentiary in the Austrian Netherlands from 1753. Saint-Germain, who called himself Monsieur de Surmont at the time, had gained the Count's confidence and persuaded him to establish manufactories in Tournai. The manufactories having failed to show a profit, Saint-Germain lost Cobenzl's favor and left Tournai in Aug. 1763; hence C. cannot have seen him there in March or April 1764. Perhaps the meeting took place elsewhere.

44. *Madame d'Urfé . . . had poisoned herself:* Madame d'Urfé did not die until 1775 (cf. Vol. 9, Chap. IX, n. 39).

45. *Archeus:* According to occult doctrine, the vital principle which directs and maintains the growth and continuation of living beings.

46. *Atoeter:* C. writes "Atoétér"; the name has not been explained.

47. *Twelve-sou piece:* French silver coin, submultiple of an écu (60 sous). (Cf. Vol. 5, Chap. IV, n. 18.)

48. *Six or seven years ago:* Saint-Germain died on Feb. 29, 1784, in Eckernförde, near Kiel, in the then Duchy of Schleswig.

49. *Keith:* George Keith, Earl Marischal of Scotland (ca. 1693-1778); as a Jacobin, he was exiled in 1716; he settled in Berlin about 1745, and was Prussian Ambassador in Paris from 1751 to 1754 and in Madrid from 1758 to 1760; he was pardoned in 1759 and returned to England and Scotland, but in 1764 he went back to Potsdam and remained there as an intimate friend of Frederick the Great until his death.

50. *Dutch ducats:* The Dutch ducat was a gold coin minted in the United Provinces from 1586 to 1875. In C.'s day it was worth about 10 French francs.

51. *Madame Nettine:* Also de Nettine; the owner of well-known exchange banks in Brussels and Antwerp; she was widowed in 1752.

52. *The Hereditary Prince, who now reigns:* See Vol. 9, Chap. XII, n. 41.

53. *After twenty-one years:* This would put C.'s liaison with Daturi's mother in 1743, before he left Venice for Rome.

54. *Roermond:* Dutch town, then in the Austrian Netherlands, at the confluence of the Roer and Maas rivers.

55. *Madame Malignan:* She was the wife of the French or Flemish officer at whose house C. had renewed his acquaintance with La Charpillon (cf. Vol. 9, Chaps. X-XII). According to C. she had become a widow since he had seen her in London.

56. *Beckwith:* A Charles Frederick Beckwith commanded a regiment in Wesel from 1763 as an English officer in the Prussian service. Probably the reference is not to him but to the English Brigadier-General John Beckwith (died 1787), whose acquaintance C. had made in London (see Vol. 9, Chaps. X-XII).

57. *The school at Leiden:* The medical faculty of the University of Leiden had become celebrated in the 18th century through the teaching of Hermann Boerhaave (1668-1738), whose fame as a clinician brought him a great many pupils.

58. See Vol. 9, Chap. XII, n. 33.

59. *Peipers:* Heinrich Wilhelm Peipers (C. writes "Piper") was the son of the physician Adam Peipers (died 1758), who practiced in Wesel for 24 years. He studied medicine at Duisburg and Leiden, took his degree at Duisburg, and practiced there from about 1766.

CHAPTER III

1. *Madame de Pompadour was dead:* Madame de Pompadour died on April 15, 1764.

2. *Three teeth:* C. omits the word *dents* ("teeth"), but it is guaranteed by the later context.

3. *Salenmon:* Constantin Nathanael von Salenmon, also Salonmon (1710-1797), officer first in the French, then

in the Prussian service, was in 1764 Commandant of Wesel and Geldern as Prussian Lieutenant-General.

4. *As he might have been . . . all:* C. writes simply "d'être fait soldat quand même il les aurait eu toutes." The "as he might have been" of the translation seems necessary to make sense.

5. *Pyrotechnics:* By the 17th century, fireworks, first used in China, in classical antiquity, and in Europe, for military purposes, had increasingly become the crowning feature of elaborate celebrations. The 18th century was the period of the greatest popularity of fireworks, for which surprisingly high prices were paid. Italian pyrotechnists were the most celebrated of all, particularly the elder and younger Ruggieri, of Vicenza, who, in C.'s day, were even summoned abroad to practice their art.

6. *Madame du Rumain:* See Vol. 9, Chap. VI, n. 2.

7. *Balletti:* See Vol. 9, Chap. VI, n. 3.

8. *She died . . . fulfill the obligation:* Madame du Rumain did not die until 1791. In Chap. XI of this volume C. says that he did repay her loan.

9. *Gabrielle:* One of the Hanoverian sisters (see Chap. I of this volume).

10. *Stöcken:* See Vol. 9, Chap. XIII, n. 44.

11. *Redegonda:* Parmesan singer, whom C. had first met in Florence in 1761 (cf. Vol. 7, Chap. VIII).

12. *Livret:* In basset and faro, the 13 cards given to each punter.

13. *Notes . . . payment . . . in London:* See Vol. 9, Chap. XI.

14. *Brunswick:* Duke Karl I of Brunswick (1713-1780), acceded to the Duchy in 1735.

15. *Nicolini:* Filippo Nicolini (died after 1773), theatrical director for the city of Brunswick and for the ducal Court from 1749; fell into disfavor ca. 1769 for dismissing a mistress of the Hereditary Prince, perhaps Redegonda, went to Hamburg in 1771, and later retired to a monastery near Goslar, where he died.

16. *Reproaching me . . . Florence and Turin:* See Vol. 7, Chap. VIII, and Vol. 8, Chap. V.

17. *Her brother:* See Vol. 7, Chap. VIII.

18. *La Palesi:* See Vol. 9, Chap. X, n. 29.

19. *La Corticelli:* See Vol. 9, Chap. VI, n. 18.

20. *Waited at table on the ladies from Soleure:* See Vol. 6, Chap. IV.

21. *Miss Chudleigh . . . Kingston:* See Vol. 9, Chap. VII, n. 70.

22. *Salbottière:* This word is unknown to the French language; C. may have been trying to Gallicize the Italian *zabaglione.*

23. *Estate:* It was in Stöcken; see note 10 to this chapter.

24. *A good inn:* Perhaps the inn which James Boswell in his diaries calls "The Gulden Arm." C. gives the name "Le Bras d'Or" ("The Golden Arm") to an inn in Calais. See Vol. 9, Chap. VI, n. 45.

25. *Anna:* Anna van Oploo (died 1788), of The Hague, was Nicolini's adopted daughter.

26. *Crown Prince of Prussia:* Frederick William (1744-1797), Crown Prince from 1758, succeeded to the throne as Frederick William II in 1786.

27. *His future wife:* Elisabeth Christine Ulrike, Princess of Brunswick (1740-1840), married to the Crown Prince of Prussia in 1765.

28. *Turned out badly:* The marriage was dissolved in 1769, and in the same year the Crown Prince married Friederike Luise of Hesse-Darmstadt. His first wife lived alone in Stettin until her death.

29. *Hereditary Prince:* See Vol. 9, Chap. XII, n. 41.

30. *Made his acquaintance . . . freedom of the City of London:* See Vol. 9, Chap. XII.

31. *The third-finest library in Europe:* The Herzog-August-Bibliothek, in Wolfenbüttel, founded in 1568, still exists and is especially celebrated for its wealth of manuscripts and incunabula, of which it possesses some 5000.

32. *Pope:* Alexander Pope (1688-1744) published translations of the *Iliad* and the *Odyssey.*

33. *My translation of the* Iliad: C.'s partial translation of the *Iliad* (*Dell'Iliade de Omero tradotta in ottava rima, da G. Casanova Viniziano*) was published in Venice in 3 volumes from 1755 to 1788.

34. *Here:* At Dux in Bohemia. Cf. Vol. 9, Chap. XII, n. 4.

35. *A sister of the King of England:* See Vol. 9, Chap. XII, n. 41.

36. *The fortress:* Magdeburg, an old fortified town, was almost completely destroyed in 1631, during the Thirty Years' War. It was rebuilt, and the fortifications were enlarged, under Frederick I and Frederick William I of Prussia. In the 18th century Magdeburg was considered one of the most modern Prussian fortresses.

37. *"City of Paris":* In C.'s day the "Zur Stadt Paris" was probably the best inn in Berlin; it was located on Bruderstrasse. But in 1764, as appears from what follows, C. stayed at the "Three Lilies" ("Zu den drei Lilien") in Poststrasse, also known, from the name of its proprietor, as "Rufin's Inn" ("Rufin's Gasthaus"). It was there on Sept. 1, 1764, that James Boswell met C., to whom, however, he refers as "Ne[u]haus," the German translation of the name Casanova; C. does not mention the meeting.

38. *Treyden:* Baron von Trotha, known as von Treyden, was probably the brother of Benigna Gottliebe Biron, Duchess of Kurland (1703-1782).

39. *Biron:* Ernst Johann Biron (1690-1772), Duke of Kurland from 1737, married in 1723 to Benigna Gottliebe von Trotha, known as von Treyden.

40. *Greve:* See Vol. 9, Chap. XIII, n. 39.

41. *Noël:* Probably a native of Périgueux, he was, with Joyard of Lyons, head cook to Frederick the Great, who highly esteemed him and referred to him in an occasional poem as "Newton de la cuisine" ("the Newton of cooking"). Contemporary sources show that the two cooks had 12 assistants under them.

42. *Noël, Minister:* François Joseph Michel Noël (1755-1841), of Saint-Germain-en-Laye, near Paris, was not, as C. assumes, the son of Frederick the Great's cook. He was French Envoy to The Hague from 1792 to 1800.

43. *Directory:* French, *Directoire;* the supreme governing body of France in accordance with the Constitution of Sept. 23, 1795; it had 5 members. Napoleon replaced it by the Consulate on Nov. 11, 1799.

44. *La Mettrie:* Julien Offray de la Mettrie, also Lamettrie (1709-1751), French physician and philosopher, pupil of the celebrated physician Boerhaave in Leiden and contributor to the *Encyclopédie*. Because of his materialistic doctrines he was forced to leave France in 1746, and Leiden

later, and took refuge with Frederick the Great, who in 1748 appointed him his physician in ordinary; he was a member of the Prussian Academy of Sciences. It is a fact that he died in 1751 as the result of eating a truffled pâté which had been made with spoiled fat and which he had been served in the house of the Earl of Tyrconnel. In the same year Frederick the Great ordered the publication of his *Oeuvres philosophiques*, in 2 volumes, including his most celebrated work, *L'Homme machine*.

45. *Tyrconnel:* Richard Francis Talbot, Earl of Tyrconnel (1710-1752), entered the French service and became a Field Marshal in 1748; from 1748 to 1752 he was French Ambassador in Berlin.

46. *The Academy:* The Royal Prussian Academy of Sciences (Königliche Preussische Akademie der Wissenschaften) was founded in 1700 by Frederick I, neglected by Frederick William I, and reopened by Frederick the Great in 1744, with Maupertuis as President. The funeral oration, *Éloge de M. de la Mettrie*, was written by Frederick the Great but was read by Darget at the public session of the Academy on Jan. 19, 1752.

47. *Matter . . . mind:* Text: "la matière . . . l'esprit." The antithetical word play is impossible to reproduce in English, for *esprit* means not only "mind, spirit, intelligence," but also "wit."

48. *Calzabigi:* Giovanni Antonio Calzabigi, also de' Calzabigi (born after 1714, died in Italy in 1767); in 1750 he became Secretary to the Ambassador of the Two Sicilies in Paris, where in 1757, with his brother and C., he established the Military School Lottery (see especially Vol. 5, Chap. II); about 1760 he was summoned to the Prussian Court by Frederick the Great.

49. *Pâris-Duverney:* Joseph de Pâris-Duverney (1684-1770), of plebeian ancestry, became a purveyor to the army and was ennobled and made a Councilor of State in 1720; in 1751 he was appointed Intendant of the Military School. (Cf. Vol. 5, Chap. II.)

50. *La Générale Lamothe:* Simone, née Dorcet, widow of General Antoine Duru de Lamothe, married Giovanni Antonio Calzabigi in 1750.

51. *Cobenzl:* See note 43 to Chap. II of this volume.

52. *Lottery . . . directorship . . . Councilor of State:* Calzabigi was appointed "President of the Royal Prussian Lottery Directorate" by Frederick the Great, with the title of Privy Financial Councilor; he received a pension of 3000 thalers and was guaranteed 5 (not 10, as C. asserts) per cent of the profits. The first drawing of the lottery took place on Aug. 31, 1763, hence not two years before C.'s arrival in Berlin. On Aug. 1, 1764, Frederick turned the lottery over to Calzabigi against a payment of 50,000 thalers.

53. *Crowns:* Text, "écus." C.'s equivalents for the currencies of the German States being unclear, no attempt has been made to correct them.

54. *What the Italian opera cost him:* Frederick the Great ordered the building of the Royal Opera House on the Opernplatz, Berlin; it was inaugurated in 1742. During the Seven Years' War there was practically no theater in Berlin. After the peace was signed the King made every effort to revive theatrical life and to obtain good artists, which required considerable sums of money. He supported the opera, the ballet, and the Italian *opera buffa* from his private purse, so that the public (i.e., the nobility and the citizenry) could attend performances gratis.

55. *Mademoiselle Belanger:* C. mentions the Belangers, mother and daughter (he also writes "Beranger"), only in this passage of his memoirs.

56. *Brea:* Nothing is known of him.

57. *Castelletto:* See Vol. 5, Chap. II, n. 25.

58. *Ambo . . . terno . . . quaterna:* See Vol. 5, Chap. II, nn. 23, 27, 28, and 48.

59. *Biribissi:* See Vol. 9, Chap. I, n. 19.

CHAPTER IV

1. *Earl Marischal . . . Keith:* See note 49 to Chap. II of this volume. His brother, George Keith, died in 1758.

2. *Sans Souci:* Palace near Potsdam, built from 1745 to 1747 by order of Frederick the Great and from his own plans.

3. *"Fédéric":* Frederick always signed his personal letters thus.

4. *Picture gallery:* The gallery was a separate building, east of the palace, constructed from 1756 to 1763.

5. *Catt:* Henri Alexandre de Catt (1725-1795), of Morgues
   on the Lake of Geneva, was from 1756 reader and private
   secretary to Frederick the Great; he fell into disfavor in
   1780.

6. *Spent . . . in vain to bring water here for them:* The
   fountains and waterworks in the park in Sans Souci were
   a particular concern of Frederick's; the fountains especially
   failed to play because of lack of pressure. Not until 1842,
   when a steam engine was installed, did the waterworks
   finally function.

7. *Peristyle:* A peristyle, in the sense in which C. uses the
   word, is an open space enclosed by columns. Figuring in
   the Hellenistic period chiefly as the courtyard in a private
   house, in modern Europe it became an element in landscape gardening. After Frederick's death the peristyle at
   Sans Souci was demolished.

8. *Ephraim:* Veitel Heine Ephraim (died 1775), banker and
   jeweler in Berlin.

9. *Duchess of Brunswick:* Philippine Charlotte, Duchess of
   Brunswick, née Princess of Prussia (1716-1801), sister of
   Frederick the Great, married in 1733 to Karl I, Duke of
   Brunswick.

10. *Her daughter . . . next year:* See note 27 to the preced-
    ing chapter. The official betrothal took place on July 18,
    1764.

11. *The small theater in Charlottenburg:* The Italian comic
    opera *I portentosi effetti della natura* was performed in the
    Orangery Theater of Charlottenburg Palace on July 19,
    1764.

12. *The celebrated Denis:* Giovanna Denis, née Corrini (1728
    - after 1797), daughter of the actor Corrini who always
    played the role of Pantalone in *commedia dell'arte* per-
    formances; hence her nickname "la Pantaloncina." A cele-
    brated dancer, she was married in 1748 to Jean Baptiste
    Denis, ballet master and composer; they were in Berlin
    from 1749 to 1765.

13. *Gozzi:* Antonio Maria Gozzi (1709-1783), priest, Doctor
    of Civil and Canon Law; C. lived in his house and studied
    under him from the age of 10 until he entered the Univer-
    sity of Padua at 14. See especially Vol. 1, Chap. II.

14. *Pantalone:* One of the stock characters in the *commedia*

dell'arte, an elderly man of substance, usually a Venetian merchant.

15. *Pantaloncina:* Feminine diminutive of Pantalone.

16. *Giovannina . . . my mother's godchild:* C.'s mother's name was Giovanna Maria Casanova. Giovannina is the diminutive of Giovanna.

17. *Bettina:* Nickname of Elisabetta Maria Gozzi (1718-1777), younger sister of Antonio Maria Gozzi (cf. especially Vol. 1, Chaps. II-III).

18. *Banished him:* The documents show only that Jean Baptiste Denis ceased to be ballet master in 1765, being replaced by Franz Salomon. If, as seems likely, this was because of his age, it explains his wife's interest in C.'s bearing witness that she was 10 years younger than she really was. She was then probably living apart from her husband, perhaps at the insistence of her influential lover.

19. *Teplitz:* Now Teplice; well-known watering place in what was then Bohemia.

20. *Aubry:* Pierre Aubry, celebrated dancer; appeared in Venice in 1752 and 1758, in St. Petersburg from 1760 to 1764, in Berlin in 1764, and in Paris in 1765.

21. *La Santina:* Santina Zanuzzi (died after 1775), Italian dancer, born in Padua, documented as appearing in Vienna from 1756 and later in Parma, Venice, Milan, and St. Petersburg.

22. *Dall'Oglio:* Giuseppe B. dall'Oglio (died between 1791 and 1796), Italian musician from Padua or Venice; with his better-known brother Domenico, he was a violoncellist in the orchestra at the Imperial Court of St. Petersburg from 1735 to 1764.

23. *The service of the Empress of Russia:* Dall'Oglio came to St. Petersburg under the Empress Anna Ivanovna, remained there during the reigns of Elizabeth and Peter III, played an important part in the liaison between Catherine and Poniatowski, and did not leave the Court until two years after Catherine's accession.

24. *Madonis:* Luigi Madonis, also Madonnis (before 1700 - 1767), of Venice, celebrated violinist. His daughter was married to Giuseppe dall'Oglio.

25. *Your mother:* Giovanna Maria Casanova, née Farussi, called Zanetta, stage name La Buranella (1708-1776). She

played at the Dresden Theater from 1737 and remained in Dresden after she retired from the stage in 1756.

26. *The conspiracy:* Princess Sophie Augusta of Anhalt-Zerbst (1729-1796) was married in 1745 to the heir to the Russian throne, who succeeded in 1762 as Peter III and in the same year was murdered as the result of a conspiracy. She had herself proclaimed Czarina as Catherine II by the Guards on July 11, 1762. Her Court became one of the most brilliant cultural centers in Europe.

27. *Odart:* Probably Jean Dominique Joseph, Chevalier d'Odart, Piedmontese adventurer who, coming to the Russian Court in 1762, was soon made administrator of Catherine's estates and was given the title of Court Councilor; when Catherine ascended the throne he was forced to leave Russia with nothing but 1000 rubles for traveling money.

28. *A hundred thousand rubles:* Not 100,000, but only 1000 (see the preceding note). The ruble was a silver coin first minted in the 17th century. From 1756 there were also gold rubles, whose value was higher.

29. *A husband:* In 1742 Karl Peter Ulrich, Duke of Holstein-Gottorp (1728-1762), was summoned to Russia as the heir to the throne by the Czarina Elizabeth because he was a son of the daughter of Peter the Great. His marriage in 1745 to the later Catherine II (cf. note 26) was unhappy from the beginning.

30. *Her son:* Paul Petrovich, the future Paul I (reigned 1796-1801). Also see note 15 to the following chapter.

31. *The General:* Probably a certain General von Grumbkow.

32. The reference is to Suetonius's account ("Divus Julius," 2 and 49) of the homosexual relation between Julius Caesar and Nicomedes III Philopator, King of Bithynia, during Caesar's stay at his Court in 81 B.C., and more especially to a line from a mocking song of Caesar's soldiers which Suetonius quotes: *Caesar Gallias subegit, Nicomedes Caesarem* ("Caesar subjugated all the Gauls, Nicomedes subjugated Caesar"). It will be observed that C.'s "subjuguait" corresponds exactly to the "subegit" of the song; however, C. reverses subject and object.

33. *La Reggiana:* Santina Oliviera, called La Reggiana because she was a native of Reggio, Italian dancer, who had appeared in Berlin in 1752.

34. *La Barberina:* Barberina Campanini (1721-1799), Italian dancer, created a countess after her divorce from Charles Louis de Cocceji, son of the Grand Chancellor of Prussia, whom she married in 1749; she had not lived with him since 1759. She appeared in Berlin from 1744 to 1748. She was Frederick the Great's mistress until she fell into disgrace in 1748 upon his discovering that she was having an affair with De Cocceji. The portrait of her which C. mentions, painted by Pesne, hung in the King's bedroom at Potsdam, which visitors were allowed to see through a glass door.

35. *La Cochois:* Marianne Cochois (born ca. 1723), French dancer (Paris, 1741, Berlin, 1742), married to the ballet master Desplaces.

36. *D'Argens:* Jean Baptiste de Boyer, Marquis d'Argens (1704-1771), was from 1744 to 1769 Chamberlain to Frederick the Great and Director of the Prussian Academy of Sciences. He married Barbe Cochois (before 1722 - after 1771), French actress, elder sister of Marianne, in 1749.

37. *Half-burned notebooks:* There was a fire in the King's study on Oct. 1, 1763.

38. *It was published:* The *Histoire de la guerre de Sept Ans* did not appear until it was included in the *Oeuvres posthumes* of 1788.

39. *New corps of noble Pomeranian cadets:* C.'s description is not entirely accurate. The new Cadet School was to be an aristocratic academy, in which the fifteen most gifted cadets were to be instructed by renowned masters. Since the academy building was not to be ready until March 1, 1765, the pupils were provisionally accommodated on the upper floor of the Royal Stables. The German commentators are at pains to assert that in view of these facts, "there was nothing humiliating in the King's offer to Casanova." But it may be allowed that, after witnessing Frederick's treatment of one of the "renowned masters," C. was in a better position than they to judge whether the post was humiliating or not. The King's visit to this provisional installation took place on Aug. 19, 1764. After C. declined the post, it was conferred on a Swiss named De Meirolles.

40. *Q. Icilius:* Pseudonym of Carl Gottlieb Guichard, also Guischardt (1724-1775), of Magdeburg. He was the son of French Huguenots, he studied theology and oriental languages at Leiden; he entered the service of Frederick the Great in 1757 and became his adviser and friend.

41. *Cross . . . around my neck:* In Chap. II of this volume C. says that he sold his cross in London.

42. *Lambert:* According to contemporary documents, this servant of C.'s was named Franz Xaver Albert.

43. *Schaumburg:* C. writes "M. de Sauembourg," no doubt meaning the Baron von Schaumburg whom he had met in Sulzbach in 1762 (cf. Vol. 8, Chap. III).

44. *Bodissoni:* A Baron di Bodissoni is documented as an art dealer from 1738 in Venice; he was in Warsaw from 1768 to 1770 and in St. Petersburg in the latter year.

45. *Del Sarto:* Andrea del Sarto (1486-1531), celebrated painter of the Italian Renaissance.

46. *Keyserling:* Presumably Dietrich Karl, Baron von Keyserling, from 1759 Chancellor of the Duchy of Kurland, Count of the Empire from 1784. Originally a domain of the Teutonic Order, in C.'s time Kurland (later Latvia) belonged to the Kingdom of Poland.

47. *Lehwald:* Hans von Lehwald, also Lewald (1685-1768), from 1751 Prussian Field Marshal, from 1759 Governor of the Duchy of Prussia.

48. *Voeikov:* Fedor Matvoevich Voeikov, also Voiakov (1703-1776), Russian General and diplomat (in Mitau, 1744-1745; in Warsaw, 1759-1762).

49. *Bregonzi:* Catarina Bregonzi, or Brigonzi, Venetian singer, appeared in Venice in 1741 and in St. Petersburg ca. 1750.

50. *Mitau:* Lettish Jelgava, now a town in the Latvian S.S.R. southwest of Riga, was from 1562 the seat of the Dukes of Kurland.

51. *I went to lodge opposite the palace:* In 1738 Duke Ernst Johann von Biron had the 13th-century castle of the Teutonic Order demolished and a Baroque palace built in its place; the palace was destroyed in 1919, during the Russian Revolution, but was rebuilt in 1930. It is not known in what inn C. stayed.

52. *Friedrichsthaler:* The Friedrichsthaler (C. writes simply "Frédérics") was a Prussian gold coin minted from the reign of Frederick William I (1713-1740); it was worth 5 silver thaler, or about 38 Venetian lire.

53. *Papanelopulo:* Demetrio Papanelopulo was a banker in St. Petersburg ca. 1765.

54. *Biron:* Ernst Johann von Biron (1690-1772), Duke of Kurland from 1737. From 1561 to 1737 the Province of Kurland was under the rule of the ducal family of Kettler. The Czarina Anna Ivanovna made her favorite Biron Duke in 1737. However, he fell into disfavor in 1741 after the Czarina Elizabeth ascended the throne, and was banished to Siberia from 1741 to 1762. He was not reinstated in his dignities until 1763, under Catherine the Great. C. has mentioned him earlier (cf. the preceding chapter and Vol. 6, Chap. II).

55. *The "Amiable Conqueror":* Dance originated by the French dancing master Précourt at the Court of Louis XIV; it soon became popular.

56. *Regency:* The Regency (French "Régence") was the period from 1715 to 1723, during which, on the death of Louis XIV, the Duke of Orléans assumed the regency for King Louis XV until the latter reached his majority.

57. *Mademoiselle de Manteuffel:* Nothing is known of her.

58. *Ladies in waiting:* C. writes "frailes" (for German Fräulein).

59. *Zemgale:* The southeastern province of the Duchy of Kurland.

60. *Charles:* Karl Ernst von Biron, Prince of Kurland (1728-1801), Major-General in the Russian service from 1762.

61. *Albertsthaler:* Gold coin first minted in 1598 on the occasion of the marriage of the Grand Duke Albert of Austria (1559-1621) to the daughter of Philip II of Spain. It passed current in many European states, especially the Baltic countries (until 1810).

62. *Alexander Nevski:* The order of Alexander Nevski was the highest of Russian orders, with only one class; established by Peter the Great in 1722, it was first conferred by Catherine I in 1725. Prince Karl Ernst of Kurland received it in 1762. It survived until 1917.

CHAPTER V

1. *Chapter V:* At the top of the ms. page on which this chapter begins is the marginal note "octo rejectis" ("eight [pages] excised").
2. *Campioni:* Vicenzo Campioni, Italian dancer from Venice (cf. especially Vol. 2, Chap. VIII).
3. *Sainte-Hélène:* C. writes "Ste-Heleine." Probably the adventurer and professional gambler Sainte-Hélène, who assumed the title of Baron (died after 1768); he may have belonged to the family of Sainte-Hélène, Counts of Baschi.
4. *His mistress:* Perhaps Caterina Pulcinelli, of Rome, who in 1767 arrived with the Prince in Paris, where they were both arrested for presenting forged bills of exchange.
5. *Voeikov:* See note 48 to the preceding chapter.
6. *Lehwald:* See note 47 to the preceding chapter.
7. *Baroness Korff:* Baroness Konstanze Ursula von Korff, née von der Wahlen (1698-1790), wife of Johann Nikolaus, Baron von Korff (1710-1766), Chief of Police (with the title of General) to the Duke of Kurland.
8. *Madame Evtinov:* Nothing is known of her.
9. *Budberg:* Baron Woldemar Dietrich von Budberg (1740-1784), who after extensive travels lived from 1758 on his estate of Trastenhof, near Riga.
10. *The creator of Petersburg:* Peter the Great, who founded the city in 1703.
11. *Collins:* G. Collins (died after 1793), English merchant and Freemason, who had settled in Riga.
12. *Henau:* See Vol. 9, Chap. XIII, n. 42, and Chap. II of this volume.
13. *Tribunal of Commerce:* From the time of Peter the Great Russia had eight "Colleges," roughly corresponding to Ministries. The College of Justice comprised tribunals adjudicating matters pertaining to the Court and the Tribunal of Commerce. "The Russian" to whom C. refers is unknown.
14. *Elizabeth Petrovna:* Daughter of Peter the Great, and Czarina from 1741 (1709-1762).
15. *Peter . . . worshiped:* It is this and other acts of Germanophilism which have made C. declare Peter III the "enemy of the whole Russian nation." History tends to bear him out. See note 29 to the preceding chapter.

16. *At this same time:* Catherine the Great made the journey C. describes in June and July 1764. Since C. did not arrive in Riga until Oct. of that year, he cannot have seen her there.

17. *Poniatowski:* Stanislaus Augustus Poniatowski (1732-1798) was Polish Ambassador in St. Petersburg from 1758 to 1759; he was King of Poland as Stanislaus II Augustus from 1764 to 1795. See Vol. 8, Chap. VI, n. 38.

18. *Orlovs:* There were five Orlov brothers, of whom Grigori and Aleksei were most deeply involved in the conspiracy of 1762 against Peter III; it was probably Aleksei who strangled the Czar. Grigori succeeded Poniatowski as Catherine's favorite.

19. *Schlüsselburg:* The fortress of Schlüsselburg had existed from 1323 on an island in the Neva; under Peter the Great it was made a state prison and served as such until 1917.

20. *Ivan Ivanovich:* Ivan VI Antonovich (1740-1764) was proclaimed Czar in 1740, but was imprisoned by Elizabeth Petrovna first in a fortress on the White Sea and then in Schlüsselburg. It is possible that the person murdered on July 4, 1764, was not Ivan VI but a Swedish youth who had been substituted for him.

21. *The bold man:* Vasili Yakovlevich Mirovich (1739-1764), an officer in the Smolensk Regiment. His family's estates having been confiscated by the Crown, in order to avenge himself he attempted to free the pretender to the throne in 1764.

22. *Panin:* Nikita Ivanovich Panin (1718-1783), Count from 1767, President of the College of Foreign Affairs from 1762.

23. *Dragon . . . D'Aragon:* According to C. he was a Neapolitan. Two Russian officers of the Czarina's bodyguard, Grigori and Ilya Darragan, the first of whom made a journey to Germany, are documented; but the identity of C.'s Dragon-D'Aragon has not been discovered.

24. *Alexis:* Aleksei Orlov (1737-1808), Russian Major-General and Admiral.

25. *Ingria:* Also Ingermanland; region along the banks of the Neva River and the east shore of the Gulf of Finland, named after its original Finnish inhabitants, the Ingers. Peter the Great reconquered it from Sweden in 1702 and

founded St. Petersburg there in the following year. Its inhabitants spoke a dialect of Finnish.

26. *Holstein:* See note 29 to the preceding chapter.

27. *Sharpers:* C. writes "des grecs," slang of the period for cardsharpers; cf. Vol. 2, Chap. II, n. 12.

28. *Schlafwagen:* An especially commodious and comfortable traveling carriage, in which there was room to lie down and sleep. The word is German; C. spells it successively "Schlafsvagen," "Schlasfvagen" (*sic*), and "Schlaffswagen."

29. *Braun:* Count Yuri Yurievich Braun (1704-1792), son of an Irish emigrant named Brown; Russian General and Governor of Livonia.

30. *Verst:* Russian measure of distance, about two-thirds of a mile.

31. *Czernichev:* Count Zachar Grigorievich Chernichev (1722-1784), Russian General.

32. *Uchitel:* Russian "tutor," "major-domo"; in C.'s day such positions in Russia were usually held by Frenchmen.

33. *Narva:* City on the former border between Estonia and Russia, some 90 miles west of St. Petersburg.

34. *No Russian envoy in Venice:* Russia had a diplomatic representative in Venice only until 1724.

35. *Caporya:* The last post station on the road from Riga to St. Petersburg.

36. *A special language:* See note 25 to this chapter.

37. *Millionnaya:* Still a well-known street in Leningrad, leading from the Winter Palace.

38. *Channels:* C. writes "ruelles," whose meaning in this context is not clear.

39. *London:* C. first wrote "Paris," then crossed it out and substituted "Londres."

40. *The Imperial Palace:* The so-called Winter Palace, residence of the Czars, built from 1753 to 1762 by the Italian architect Rastrelli in Baroque style.

41. *Orlov:* Grigori Grigorievich Orlov (1734-1783), Count from 1762, Prince of the Empire from 1772; favorite of Catherine the Great from 1762 to 1777.

42. *Kopeck:* Russian coin of copper; 100 kopecks = 1 ruble.

43. *Bautta:* A sort of hood, used as part of a masking costume in Venice. (See Vol. 2, Chap. VIII, n. 27.)

44. *Bernardi:* A Venetian jeweler named Bernardi (died ca. 1760), lived in St. Petersburg from 1749.

45. *Volpati:* Nothing is known of him except what C. relates.

46. *I cannot tell you here:* C. traveled in Russia under the name of Comte de Farussi (from his mother's maiden name) and as Cazanov de Farussi. For the Venetian Count Volpati to recognize him, he had to give his real name, by which he was well known in Venice because of his escape from the Leads.

47. *Balls at the Opéra:* The Académie Royale de Musique (the Opéra) had the privilege of giving public balls (cf. Vol. 5, Chap. VIII, n. 48.)

48. *La Baret:* Madame Baret, née Gilbert, with whom C. had had a liaison in Paris. See Vol. 5, Chap. XI. The names Gilbert and Baret are both doubtless fictitious.

49. *Hôtel d'Elbeuf:* Parisian residence of the Duke of Elbeuf, by whom Baret was employed.

50. *Rue des Prouvaires:* Where Madame Baret lived after her marriage (cf. Vol. 8, Chap. I, n. 28.)

51. *Langlade:* Also L'Anglade, doubtless fictitious name for a Councilor of the Parlement of Rouen (cf. Vol. 8, Chap. I, nn. 28 and 29).

52. *Comic opera impresario:* The French comic opera in St. Petersburg was under the direction of a certain Renauld in 1764 and 1765; one of the actresses in the company was called "la belle Langlade."

53. *Rzewuski:* Count Franciszek Rzewuski (died after 1775), Grand Notary to the Polish Crown from 1752; Polish Envoy in St. Petersburg from June 1766. He may have been in St. Petersburg earlier.

54. *Recollect monks:* A branch of the Franciscan Order which adheres strictly to the Rule as laid down by the founder.

55. *Day . . . I really lost:* Taken by Laforgue to be an allusion to a remark attributed by Suetonius ("Titus," 8) to the Emperor Titus, who, after a day during which he had conferred no boon on anyone, is supposed to have said, "Friends, I have lost a day." The later commentators follow Laforgue; but he may rather be thought to have inquired too ingeniously, for there is really no reason to suppose that C. had Suetonius' anecdote in mind.

56. *Dall'Oglio:* See note 22 to Chap. IV of this volume.

57. *Poisoned . . . to tell:* The jeweler Bernardi had been one of the devoted adherents and confidants of Catherine when, still a Grand Duchess, she was preparing to seize the throne. In 1758, while Elizabeth still reigned, a certain General Apraksin fell into disgrace; papers confiscated on this occasion compromised the Grand Duchess and a number of her confidants, among them Bernardi. He was exiled to Kazan, where he died.

58. *Passport . . . . was about to leave:* This regulation remained in force in Russia until the end of the 19th century.

59. *La Fusi:* C. first wrote a name beginning with "S" and ending with "i," then crossed it out and substituted Fusi. She may have been a Giosetta Fusi, who appeared as a dancer in Venice in 1763.

60. *Melissino:* Pyotr Ivanovich Melissino (1726-1797 or 1803), a native of the island of Cephalonia. He was a General of Artillery in the Russian service.

61. *His elder brother:* Ivan Ivanovich Melissino (1718-1795), Russian Court Councilor, later Chancellor and Curator of the University of Moscow, and at the same time Procurator of the Holy Synod.

62. *The Synod:* The Holy Synod, instituted by Peter the Great in 1721 to replace the Patriarchate, was the supreme governing body of the Russian Church.

63. *The celebrated [Lefort]:* Jacques (= Franz Jakob) Lefort, also Le Fort, Leffort (1656-1699), of Geneva, confidant of Peter the Great. His only son died in 1703. The person to whom C. here refers is the son of Franz Jakob's nephew, Peter, Baron Lefort, who had been Master of Ceremonies to the Czarina Elizabeth.

64. *Matiushkin:* Dmitri Mikhailovich Matiushkin (1725-1800).

65. *Zinoviov:* Stepan Stepanovich Zinoviov, also Zinoviev (1740-1794), Russian officer and diplomat; he was appointed Russian Ambassador in Madrid in 1773.

66. *Macartney:* Sir George Macartney (1737-1806), English Envoy Extraordinary in St. Petersburg from 1764 to 1767.

67. *Mademoiselle Shitrov:* Anna Alekseevna Shitrov (died 1795), lady in waiting to Catherine the Great.

68. *Forgave:* According to contemporary sources she was forced to enter a convent.

69. *Brother . . . an officer:* The Shitrov family was very numerous; in C.'s time at least 4 Shitrovs were officers.

70. *Mademoiselle Sievers . . . now Princess N. N.:* Elizabeth Karlovna Sievers (1731-1808), daughter of Karl Sievers, a manservant and favorite of the Czarina Elizabeth, who made him a Count in 1760 and Court Marshal in 1762. Her second marriage was to Prince Nikolai Putyatin (1747-1830).

71. *Putini:* Bartolomeo Putini, also Puttini (born ca. 1730, died after 1766), Italian castrato, appeared in St. Petersburg from 1756.

72. *Galuppi:* Baldassare Galuppi (1706-1785), Italian composer, chapelmaster in St. Petersburg from 1745 to 1748 and from 1765 to 1768. He was called "Il Buranello" from his birthplace, the Island of Burano, Venice.

73. *Olsuviev:* Adam Vasilievich Olsuviev (1721-1784), Russian Councilor of State and Senator.

74. *Uppsala to study:* The Swedish University of Uppsala, founded in 1476, was one of the most celebrated institutions of higher learning in Europe in the 18th century.

75. *Locatelli:* Giovanni Battista Locatelli (between 1713 and '15 - 1785), of Milan, man of letters and theatrical impresario; he was in St. Petersburg in 1759-1762 and again later. C. had met him in Prague in 1753 (see Vol. 3, Chap. XI).

76. *Ekaterinhof:* A small palace near St. Petersburg, built by Peter the Great for his consort Catherine I.

77. *Teplov:* Grigori Nikolaevich Teplov (1711-1779), one of the leaders in the conspiracy against Peter III; after 1762 he became Secretary to Catherine the Great.

78. *Yelagin:* Ivan Porfirievich Yelagin (1725-1796), personal friend of Catherine the Great before her ascent to the throne; banished in 1758; appointed Secretary of State in 1762; so he could not have been in Siberia for more than 4 years.

79. *Mécour:* Giovanna Mécour, née Campi, Italian dancer from Ferrara, appeared in Petersburg from 1759.

80. *La Santina:* See note 21 to the preceding chapter.

81. *Luini:* Domenico Luini, called Il Bonetto, Italian castrato, appeared in St. Petersburg from 1765.

82. *La Colonna:* Perhaps Teresa Colonna, called La Venezianella (born 1734), Italian dancer, who appeared in Venice in 1746-1747 and later in Moscow. The singer Teresa Colonna

is documented in Venice in 1760-1761 and in St. Petersburg ca. 1763-1764. It is not known if they are the same person.

83. *Millico:* Giuseppe Millico (1739-1802), Neapolitan castrato, appeared in St. Petersburg ca. 1765.

84. *Naryshkin:* Semen Kirillovich Naryshkin (1701 or 1710 - 1775), Russian Envoy to London, 1742; Court Marshal and Master of the Hunt, 1757; Grand Chancellor, 1775.

85. *Maria Pavlovna:* Maria Pavlovna Naryshkin, wife of Semen Kirillovich Naryshkin, notorious for her love affairs.

86. *Kaloyer:* Russian, "monk."

87. *Platon:* Levshin Platon (1737-1812), Bishop of Tver, later of Moscow, from 1767 Archbishop of Novgorod.

88. *Princess Dashkov:* Ekaterina Romanovna Dashkov (1743-1810), wife of Prince Mikhail Dashkov (1736-1764). From 1782 to 1796 she was President of the Russian Academy of Sciences.

89. *Panin:* See note 22 to this chapter.

90. *A thing which I saw:* The same story is told in two contemporary sources, so it may be doubted if C. actually witnessed the incident.

91. *Bregonzi:* See note 49 to the preceding chapter.

92. *Signora Roccolino:* Vincenza Roccolino, née Montellato (died after 1775), known as "Signora Vincenza," had come to St. Petersburg with the French comic opera troupe (cf. note 52 to this chapter).

93. *Proté:* Nothing more is known of Proté and his wife.

94. *The Ridotto:* Name of the celebrated gambling casino in Venice; it was closed in 1774.

95. *Pun:* C.'s pun depends upon taking "Proté" as Latin *pro te* (= for thee) and turning it into Latin *pro me* (= for me).

96. *Bryus:* Yakov Aleksandrovich, Count Bryus (1729-1791), Russian General, from 1784 Governor of Moscow, from 1787 member of the Council of State; he was descended from a Scottish family named Bruce which had emigrated to Russia at the end of the 17th century.

97. *Zinoviov:* C. appears to have forgotten that he had already mentioned Zinoviov in this chapter (cf. note 65).

98. *St. Nicholas:* Patron saint of Russia; his feast celebrated on Dec. 6th.

99. *Zaïre:* Name of a Christian female slave of the Sultan of Jerusalem in Voltaire's tragedy *Zaïre.*

CHAPTER VI

1. *Görz:* Then in Austrian Friulia, now the Italian city of Gorizia, north of Trieste, on the Yugoslav border.
2. *Inconceivable:* The text has "inconvevable," which, not being annotated, may be presumed to be one of the numerous typographical errors which disfigure the Brockhaus-Plon edition.
3. *Russian baths:* A sweat bath, of the type of the Finnish sauna.
4. *The Villa Borghese:* See Vol. 7, Chap. XI, n. 45. In the contemporary guidebooks which list the sculptures in the Villa Borghese collection there is no mention of a Psyche. However, there was a Psyche in the Capitoline collection. C. may have confused the two places.
5. *Crèvecoeur:* Nothing is known of him.
6. *La Rivière:* Doubtless an adventuress. However, she can be neither the dancer Marguerite Rivière, also la Rivière, nor her sister Marie, whose acquaintance C. had made in Dec. 1756 (cf. Vol. 5, Chap. I), for he would certainly have recognized her.
7. *Baumbach:* He is not mentioned in C.'s account of his stay in England. C. writes "Bombac"; since he was a native of Hamburg the name must have been Baumbach.
8. *Krasni-Kabak:* Literally, "the Red Tavern," some three miles south of St. Petersburg on the road to Peterhof; it was well known, for it had been there that Catherine the Great spent some hours of the night of June 28-29, 1762, on which the uprising made her Czarina.
9. *Quinze:* A card game in which the player who ends with 15 points or the closest approximation to it is the winner.
10. *Wh . . . :* C. writes "p . . . . ." (for *putain*).
11. *The two Lunin brothers:* Aleksandr Mikhailovich Lunin (1745-1816), Russian Major-General, and his brother Pyotr (died 1822), a Lieutenant-General.
12. *Teplov:* See note 77 to the preceding chapter.
13. *B . . . . . . :* C. writes b . . . . . . (for *bougres*). And see note 10 to this chapter.
14. *Papanelopulo:* See note 53 to Chap. IV of this volume.
15. *Peterhof:* Villa built for Peter the Great by the French architect Leblond in 1720, some 25 miles from St. Petersburg

on the south shore of the Gulf of Finland. With its gardens, it somewhat resembled Versailles. C. spells it "Petrow."

16. *Muzhik:* Russian, "peasant." C. writes "mosik."

17. *Rastrelli:* Count Bartolomeo Rastrelli (1700-1771), celebrated architect and creator of the so-called "Russian rococo"; he retired in 1764, but then worked on the palace of the Dukes of Kurland in Mitau and probably died there.

18. *Rinaldi:* Antonio Rinaldi (ca. 1709-1794), Italian architect; he was summoned to the Russian Court in 1752 (not earlier, as C. asserts), remained there until 1785, and died in Rome.

19. *Impossible to hold the tournament:* It was in fact not held until June 16th of the following year, 1766.

20. *Izvozchik:* Russian, "coachman." C. writes "chevochik."

21. *Italian miles:* An Italian mile in the 18th century was 1.86 kilometers.

22. *To become French:* Here in C.'s ms. follows a sentence which he crossed out: "For I am sure that if the King of France were to give a caning to the National Assembly, the twelve hundred worthies would accept it, though they would not ask for more." Hence this chapter must have been written or copied between 1789 and 1792.

23. *Voeikov:* See note 48 to Chap. IV of this volume.

24. *Before the birth of Petersburg:* Voeikov was born in 1703; St. Petersburg was first built as a fortress in 1703 and then rebuilt in 1712 as the capital city of the Czars.

25. Slightly altered from Erasmus, *Adagia*, II, 2, 35.

26. After a fable of Aesop's, in which the fox mocks the lioness because, according to a belief current in Antiquity, she bears only one cub (ed. Halm, No. 240; ed. Perry, No. 257).

27. *Betskoi:* Count Ivan Betskoi (1702-1795), illegitimate son of Field Marshal Ivan Yurgievich Trubetskoi (in Russia in such cases the son often received his father's name abbreviated or slightly changed). Count Betskoi was a Lieutenant-General and at the same time Director of the Chancellery of Public Buildings and Curator of the Academy of Arts.

28. *Delamotte:* Vallen Jean Baptiste Delamotte (1729-1800), French architect, summoned to Russia in 1759.

29. *Where the staircases were:* Here in the ms. there follow two sentences which C. crossed out. "The Empire of Russia will finally become flourishing when another Catherine, or a male Catherine, ascends the throne and creates sumptuary laws.

The Russians need them, for luxury among them is a veritable frenzy."

30. *Built of stone . . . cross it:* Catherine the Great had 30 stone bridges built during her reign, all of the same design.

31. *Repnin:* Prince Nikolai Vasilievich Repnin (1734-1801), nephew of Count Panin, Russian Major-General and diplomat. He was Catherine the Great's favorite for a time.

32. *Torelli:* Stefano Torelli (1721-1784), of Bologna, Italian painter; he lived in Petersburg from 1762, became a professor at the Academy of Arts and, in 1771, its second Director.

33. *Protopapas, or bishop:* Text: "proto-papa évêque." C. is in error, the two designations being irreconcilable, for in the Eastern Church a protopapas (which incidentally is the Greek equivalent of the Russian *protopop*) ranks below a bishop.

34. *Olimpiade:* The *Olimpiade,* lyric drama by Metastasio, written in 1730, was set by more than 30 composers during the century. The reference here is probably to the setting by Manfredini or Galuppi, both of whose operas to this text were performed in Russia in 1762.

35. *Buranello:* I.e., Baldassare Galuppi (see note 72 to the preceding chapter).

36. *Is made up of four cities:* Moscow was in fact then made up of 4 cities: the Kremlin, Kitai-gorod, Beloi-gorod, and Semlijanoi-gorod; each was surrounded by walls and a moat.

37. *Demidov:* There were then two Demidovs, brothers, living in Moscow; C. very probably became acquainted with them both. The elder was Grigori Akinfevich (1710-1786), the younger Nikita Akinfevich (1724-1789). The latter was much interested in the arts and sciences and corresponded with Voltaire.

38. *The famous bell:* The "Anna Ivanovna," cast in 1735 by order of the Czarina Anna, was still the largest bell in the world in the 19th century, weighing more than two tons. As the result of a fire it fell in 1737 and was half buried in the ground. Napoleon tried in vain to have it conveyed to Paris. It was left at the foot of the bell tower as a curiosity.

39. *Gosti:* Russian, "guests."

40. *A delicious drink:* Perhaps kvass, or perhaps a favorite beverage in C.'s time made from raspberries flavored with various herbs.

41. *Sherbet:* Arabian drink, made from pomegranates.

42. *St. Nicholas:* See note 98 to the preceding chapter.

43. *Illyrian:* In antiquity Illyria was the name applied to the regions north of Greece bordering on the Adriatic and to its people, represented by the modern Albanians. C. probably uses it to mean "Slavic."

44. *Morskaya:* Street near the celebrated Millionnaya and the River Neva.

45. *Philosopher:* Text: "Ce philosophe," where it is not clear whether C. means "philosopher" in the general sense or in the sense of an adherent of the doctrines of the Enlightenment.

46. *Simolin:* Karl Matveevich, Edler von Simolin (1715-1777), from 1758 Russian Resident at the Court of the Duke of Kurland.

47. *Kamchatka:* Peninsula and province in Eastern Siberia. C. writes "Cams-Kacta."

48. *Bilioti:* The name Biliotis appears in a letter from the Duke of Kurland to C., written in 1765. Nothing more is known of him.

49. *Sinopaeus:* Damian Sinopaeus, clearly a Latinized name, entered the Russian service as a physician in 1730, became Municipal Physician in Moscow in 1736, then settled in St. Petersburg and became a State Councilor.

50. *The French Secretary of Embassy:* In 1765 the French Ambassador in St. Petersburg was replaced. Under Baron de Breteuil the Secretary was a Monsieur Bérenger; on April 29th the Marquis de Bausset arrived as the new Ambassador; his Secretary was the Abbé Guyot d'Ussières.

51. Horace, *Epistles,* I, 5, 19.

52. *Tartarian:* Cf. the proverb, "Scratch a Russian and you find a Tartar."

53. *Philosophy of History:* C. confuses two works by Voltaire, the *Essai sur l'histoire générale et sur les moeurs et l'esprit des nations,* which had been published in 1753 and included the "Philosophie de l'Histoire," and the *Dictionnaire philosophique portatif,* published in 1764 and dedicated to Catherine the Great.

54. *Stroganov:* Count Aleksandr Sergeevich Stroganov (1733 or '38 - 1811), Russian high official and diplomat, a great admirer of Voltaire and of France.

55. *Shuvalov:* Count Ivan Ivanovich Shuvalov (1727-1797 or

'98), favorite of Catherine the Great, Chief Gentleman of the Bedchamber; founded the University of Moscow in 1756.

56. *Dithyramb:* Originally designating a lyric or choric hymn in honor of the Greek god Dionysus, the term gradually came to mean a poem in irregular verse and characterized by enthusiasm.

57. C. quotes this saying several times in his memoirs, for example in Vol. 4, Chap. XIII, and in Vol. 8, Chap. VI, where he calls it a proverb.

58. *Beloselski:* Prince Aleksandr Mikhailovich Beloselski-Belozerski (1752-1809), Russian writer and diplomat; he was Ambassador in Dresden until 1790 and in Turin until 1792.

59. *Paul Petrovich:* Pavel Petrovich (1754-1801), son of Catherine II and Peter III; he was Czar as Paul I from 1796 to 1801.

60. *Francis I:* Francis Stephen (1708-1765), Duke of Lorraine, married Maria Theresa of Austria in 1736 and was Emperor from 1745. He died on Aug. 18, 1765.

61. *Krasnoe-Selo:* Town with an imperial palace, south of St. Petersburg.

62. *Lobkowitz:* Prince Joseph Maria Lobkowitz (1725-1802), Austrian Lieutenant-General and from 1763 to 1777 Ambassador in St. Petersburg.

63. *Esterházy:* Count Nikolaus Esterházy von Galantha (1711-1764), Austrian diplomat.

64. *Countess Bryus:* Countess Praskovia Aleksandrovna Bryus (1729-1786), wife of Count Yakov Aleksandrovich Bryus (see note 96 to the preceding chapter).

65. *A great infantry review:* The review, with splendid fireworks, was held near Krasnoe-Selo on June 28, 1765.

66. *Rousseau . . . a dialect of Greek:* C. refers to Rousseau's *Essai sur l'origine des langues.*

67. *Tott:* Brother of the better-known Baron François de Tott (1733?-1793), born in Paris but of Hungarian descent (cf. Vol. 5, Chap. VI).

68. *Difficulties . . . at the Battle of Minden:* Minden, one of the battles of the Seven Years' War, was fought on Aug. 1, 1759; in it the English troops won the day over the French. C. explained the "difficulties" in his ms. but then crossed the passage out: "Count Tott, with inconceivable stupidity, de-

camped on the eve of the battle on I know not what pretext, for it was not a desertion, but it was enough to dishonor him. Nevertheless he was brave."

69. *Madame Soltikov:* Matryona Pavlovna Soltikov (died before 1790), married in 1750 to Sergei Vasilievich Soltikov (1726 - after 1764), Catherine the Great's first lover, who was Russian Ambassador in Paris from 1762 to 1763.

70. *A handsome young man:* C. here added, then crossed out: "the only defect in his face being that his eyes were rheumy."

71. *The troubles in Poland:* Repnin, the Russian Ambassador in Warsaw, took advantage of the weakness of Stanislaus Poniatowski to rule Poland despotically. His measures aroused strong opposition, the leader of which was the Bishop of Cracow, in defense of the Roman Catholic faith against the pretensions of Russia. What amounted to a civil war broke out in 1768, during which the Russians conquered the opposing confederation (see note 49 to Chap. VIII of this volume) and pursued its members across the Turkish border. The result was a declaration of war by Turkey on Oct. 30, 1768. The Russo-Turkish War was not ended until 1774, by the Peace of Kuchuk Kainarji.

72. *Maruzzi:* There were three brothers of this name at the period: Constantino, Lambro, and Tano Maruzzi. The reference is probably to Lambro, who was first a banker in Corfu and then went to St. Petersburg, where he rose to be a Councilor of State.

73. *Tsarskoye-Selo . . . Kronstadt:* All 4 places were in the vicinity of St. Petersburg and all were the sites of imperial residences.

CHAPTER VII

1. *Summer Garden:* Garden with magnificent walks, extending from the left bank of the Neva to the Mikhailov Palace.

2. *Democritus . . . Avicenna:* Democritus (born ca. 460 B.C.), Heraclitus (576-480 B.C.), Greek philosophers; the statues reverse their usual attributes, the former having been known as the laughing, the latter as the weeping philosopher; Sappho (fl. 600 B.C.), Greek poetess; Avicenna (A.D. 980-1037), Arabian physician and philosopher.

3. *My worthy aunt:* The Czarina Elizabeth, aunt of Peter III, had no interest in art.

4. *Courtag:* From German *Cour-Tag* ("Court day"). The *courtag,* or simply *cour,* held regularly from the reign of the Czarina Anna, differed from the solemnity of great Court occasions by its informality.

5. *On those which were given there:* C. writes "sur qu'on y donnait" (omitting *ceux*).

6. *Gregorian calendar:* The Julian calendar, introduced by Julius Caesar in 46 B.C., in which the year was made to consist of 365 days, each bissextile year, or leap year, having 366 days, remained in use throughout the Middle Ages. Since the average length of the year thus obtained (365.25 days) differs slightly from that of the true solar year (365.2422 days), by the 16th century the accumulated difference amounted to 10 days. For this reason Pope Gregory XIII in 1582 ordered a reform of the calendar which, by a new distribution of the leap years, arrived at an average year of 365.2425 days. By the Gregorian calendar, the calendar year differs by a day from the solar year only after 3000 years. All the Roman Catholic countries adopted the reform immediately, whereas the Protestant countries did not introduce it until much later (England not until 1751). Countries of the Greek Orthodox religion did not introduce a new calendar similar to the Gregorian until 1923, when the difference had grown to be 13 days.

7. *Peter . . . ordered . . . first of January:* Peter the Great ordered this change made in 1700. In the pre-Julian calendar the year began on March 1st, as the names of our months from Sept. to Dec. testify.

8. *Year . . . Gregorian reform . . . not be bissextile:* The Gregorian reform prescribed that a year which began a new century should be a leap year (bissextile) only if it was exactly divisible by 400 (thus 1600 was a leap year, but not 1700, 1800, and 1900).

9. *The epact:* The number of days by which the last new moon has preceded the beginning of the year. It is one of the factors used in calculating the date of Easter.

10. *The tropical year:* The period in which the earth makes one complete revolution around the sun, reckoning from spring equinox to spring equinox.

11. *The law of the March moon:* According to the rules for calculating the date of Easter, it is always the first Sunday after the full moon that falls on or next after March 21st.

12. *Embolism:* Insertion of days, months, or years in an account of time, for regularity. To bring the lunar and solar years into agreement, the Jewish reckoning intercalated a lunar month in the third, fifth, and eighth years of an 18-year cycle.

13. *Council of Nicaea:* Held in A.D. 325; it promulgated the rules by which the date of Easter is still calculated.

14. *Catherine II died happy:* She died on Nov. 18, 1796, 37 hours after having an apoplectic stroke. She had long suffered from abnormal obesity. The text has "Catherine II mourut heureuse comme elle vécut," which could also be translated, "Catherine II was fortunate in her death as she had been in her life." The same double meaning of "heureux," for which there is no satisfactory rendering in English, recurs throughout the rest of the passage, and should be borne in mind by the reader of the translation.

15. *Only one each day:* This is not true, for the Roman Catholic Church also has more saint's days than there are days in the year.

16. *Begins the year on the first of March:* Venice had retained the old reckoning, according to which the year began on that date.

17. *M. V.:* Abbreviation for *More Veneto* ("according to the Venetian reckoning").

18. *Amusing figure . . . five Latin words . . . a grammatical error:* The emblem of Venice is a winged lion holding in its claws an open book with the words: *Pax Tibi Marce Evangelista Meus* ("Peace be unto thee, my Evangelist Mark"). According to the rules of Latin grammar, *meus,* which is in the nominative case, being in apposition to a vocative, should also be in the vocative (*mi*).

19. *Begin counting them at the beginning of the night:* In Italy until the end of the 18th century the hours of the day were counted from the ringing of the Angelus, that is, from a half hour after sunset. (Cf. Vol. 1, Chap. IV, n. 33.)

20. *Valville:* A Mademoiselle Valville is mentioned in a letter to C. by a certain Bilistein, dated Petersburg 1766. Nothing more is known of her.

21. *Les Folies amoureuses:* Comedy by Jean François Regnard (1655-1709), written in 1704. It was one of his most popular plays, and is still performed.

22. *Clairval:* Jean Baptiste Clairval (ca. 1735-1795), French singer and actor.

23. *Recruit a troupe of players:* Peter III, who had an aversion to everything French, had dismissed the French company which was playing in Petersburg; immediately after ascending the throne, Catherine the Great had a new French company brought to Russia.

24. *Seventy years of age:* Rinaldi, born in 1709, was then only 56 years old.

25. *Yelagin:* See note 78 to Chap. V of this volume.

26. *The Polish Resident:* Jakub Pisarski, first Polish Chargé-d'Affaires in St. Petersburg, then Resident from April 1765 to August 1766.

27. *Sulkowski:* Prince August Kazimierz Sulkowski (1729-1786), from 1764 Grand Notary to the Polish Crown. There were 5 Grand Notaries in all (cf. note 46 to this chapter).

28. *An Anglican clergyman:* Catherine the Great was a declared Anglophile and had several Englishmen among her trusted advisers. So it is understandable that an Anglican clergyman would have been in good standing with the pro-Russian faction in Warsaw.

29. *Czartoryski:* Prince Adam Kazimierz Czartoryski (1734-1823), Governor of the Province of Podolia.

30. *Caporya:* See note 35 to Chap. V of this volume.

31. *Countess Löwenwolde:* Nothing is known of her. (C. writes "Lowenvold.")

32. *Princess Dolgoruki:* Probably Princess Praskovia Vladimirovna Melissino, née Dolgorukaya, wife of the Court Councilor Ivan Ivanovich Melissino (1718-1795).

33. *Met in Riga the year before:* Cf. Chap. V of this volume.

34. *Villiers':* Villiers was the name of the proprietor of a then well-known inn in Warsaw.

35. *D'Aragon:* See note 23 to Chap. V of this volume.

36. *Tomatis:* Carlo Tomatis (born in Turin, died after 1787), created a Count in 1765 by King Stanislaus Augustus, whom he served as "directeur de plaisir"; he married the Italian dancer Caterina Catai.

37. *Catai:* Also Gattai and Gattei, Italian dancer, appeared in

Venice from 1760, in Warsaw from 1764; she was married to Count Carlo Tomatis in 1766.

38. *Giropoldi . . . Bachelier:* Nothing is known of either.

39. *Conservatorio dei Mendicanti:* One of 4 foundations in Venice devoted to the education of (chiefly orphan) girls. They were principally instructed in music.

40. *Saby:* Antoine Saby (ca. 1716 - after 1778), French adventurer and professional gambler (cf. Vol. 6, Chap. I).

41. *Sainte-Hélène:* See note 3 to Chap. V of this volume.

42. *Countess Fleming:* Princess Izabela Czartoryska, née Countess Fleming, also Flemming (1746-1835), married to Prince Adam Czartoryski in 1761.

43. *Saint-Pierre:* The Abbé Charles Irénée Castel de Saint-Pierre (1658-1743), French writer, propagandist for the Enlightenment, well known for his *Projet pour rendre la paix perpétuelle en Europe* ("Project for Maintaining Perpetual Peace in Europe").

44. *Repnin:* See note 31 to Chap. VI of this volume. Prince Repnin was Catherine the Great's favorite for a time; she sent him to Warsaw as Russian Ambassador to prepare the election of Stanislaus Poniatowski to the Polish throne.

45. *Krasicky:* Ignacy Krasicky (1735-1801), of the same family as the Counts of Krasicky, Prince of the Church and poet.

46. *Rzewuski:* Count Franciszek Rzewuski (died after 1775), from 1752 Grand Notary to the Crown, from 1766 to 1767 Envoy Extraordinary in St. Petersburg.

47. *Oginski:* Michal Kazimierz, Prince Oginski (ca. 1731-1800), from 1762 Voivod of Vilna. C. gives him the title "Palatine." There were some 34 Voivodships in Poland at the period.

48. *Ronikier:* Michal Ronikier (died ca. 1778), Polish General, decorated with the order of Alexander Nevski.

49. *Palatine of Russia:* Prince August Aleksander Czartoryski (1697-1782), Voivod (Palatine) of what was then called Red Russia (eastern Galicia, Volhynia, and Podolia).

50. *Augustus III:* From 1733 King of Poland and, as Friedrich August II, Elector of Saxony (1696-1763).

51. *The lady was a Dönhoff:* Maria Zofia von Granov-Siniavska, widow of Count Stanislaus Dönhoff, married in 1731 to Prince Czartoryski, who was consequently obliged to resign from the order of the Knights of Malta.

52. *Lubomirska:* Izabela Helena Anna, Princess Lubomirska, née Czartoryska (1736-1816), married in 1753 to Prince Stanislaus Lubomirski, Field Marshal from 1752; his military title in Polish was "Straznik wielki," hence his wife's title of "Straznikowa."

53. *His brother:* Prince Michal Fryderyk Czartoryski (1696-1775), from 1752 Grand Chancellor of Lithuania.

54. *Brühl:* Heinrich, Count Brühl (1700-1763), Prime Minister to King Augustus III of Poland.

55. *A young man . . . in the suite of an Ambassador:* Stanislaus Poniatowski had gone to St. Petersburg in 1755 in the suite of the English Ambassador, Sir Charles Hanbury Williams, and had become the lover of the future Catherine the Great. He left St. Petersburg for a time and returned there as Ambassador of King Augustus III of Poland, presenting his credentials on Jan. 11, 1757.

56. *This year 1797:* The year in which C. was writing. But Catherine the Great died, not in 1797, but in 1796.

57. *The famous Poniatowski:* Count Stanislaus Ciolek Poniatowski (ca. 1676-1762), married in 1720 to Princess Konstanzia Czartoryska; friend of Charles XII of Sweden and of Stanislaus Lesczinski, King of Poland and father-in-law of Louis XV.

58. *Charles XII:* 1682-1718, King of Sweden from 1697.

59. *Mount a throne:* C. writes "monter sur un" (omitting "trône").

60. The source of this quotation has not been determined.

61. *Diet:* The Polish Diet (*sejm*) met regularly every two years; its members were the higher clergy and the nobility. Extraordinary sessions of the Diet were held only for the election of a King.

62. *A Piast King:* Text: "un roi piaste," from Piast, the name of a 9th-century King of Poland elected from the peasantry. The line ended on the death of King Casimir III (1370). Later the word came to mean a native Polish candidate for the throne in contradistinction from foreign candidates. Inherited kingship was abolished in favor of electoral kingship by the constitution of 1572. The elections often led to conflict, for they gave foreign powers the opportunity to interfere in Polish internal affairs.

63. *The pretty Princess his sister:* See note 52 to this chapter.

64. *Starosts:* Government officials ranking immediately below the Voivods.

65. *Zaluski:* Jozef Andrzej Zaluski (1702-1774), Bishop of Kiowia from 1759. Kiowia was the name of the Polish part of the Ukraine, which had been divided between Russia and Poland in 1686. Zaluski's library was celebrated and was open to the public from 1746; he was known as a scholar and a great patron of scholars.

66. *Carried off . . . and sent to Siberia:* Zaluski was seized during the Diet of 1767 and taken to the prison of Zaluga, where he died in 1774.

67. *Tressetti:* Originally *tre sette,* Italian card game for two or four persons, in which the player who had three sevens won.

68. *Fifty sequins:* A few paragraphs earlier, C. had said that he received 50 *ducats* a month from Venice.

69. *Madame Schmidt:* Marie Schmidt (died after 1771), wife of the Swiss secretary and intendant to the Polish King, Schmidt (died 1769).

70. *Ghigiotti:* Gaetano Ghigiotti (died after 1790), private secretary to King Stanislaus Poniatowski, by whom he was ennobled in 1768.

71. Altered from Horace, *Epistles,* I, 18, 40.

72. *The first King of Sweden:* Gustavus Vasa (1496-1560), proclaimed King of Sweden in 1523.

73. Altered from Horace, *Epistles,* I, 17, 43-44.

74. Horace, *Satires,* I, 9, 58.

75. *"Wardrobe":* It was the last antechamber before the King's bedroom.

76. *Outliving his country:* The existence of Poland as an independent nation was ended by the third partition of Poland in Oct. 1795. Stanislaus Augustus died in 1798.

77. *Kosciuszko:* Tadeusz Kosciuszko (1746-1817), of a noble Lithuanian family, took part in the American War of Independence from 1778 to 1783 as an Adjutant to George Washington and in 1789 was appointed a General in Poland. He fought valiantly against the Russians before the second and third partitions of Poland, and after the defeat at Maciejowice (Oct. 10, 1794) was taken prisoner just as a Cossack was about to kill him. He was not released until

after Catherine's death, when he was allowed to go to America.

78. *Poninski:* Count Adam Antoni Poninski (1732-1798) became the Major-Domo to the Crown in 1762 and Royal Treasurer in 1772. In 1774 he obtained the title of Prince from the King and the Diet, in contravention of Polish law; in 1790 he was proscribed as a traitor.

79. *Pic:* Charles Pic, also Piq, Le Picq, and Lepicq (ca. 1743 - after 1783), celebrated French dancer; he won applause on many European stages and appeared in Warsaw in 1765 and 1766.

80. *The King's brother:* Andrzej Poniatowski (1734-1773), Prince from 1764; General in the Austrian army.

81. *Went to see her at Villiers' inn:* Earlier in this chapter C. says that he went to lodge at Villiers' inn when he arrived in Warsaw. It would seem that he moved elsewhere later, perhaps for reasons of economy.

82. *Moczynski:* August Nalecz, Count of Mosna-Moczynski (ca. 1735-1786), from 1752 Equerry (Stolnik) to the Crown; among his other offices, he was Director of the Royal Theater from 1755; he was the lover of the dancer Anna Binetti.

83. *Branicki:* Franciszek Ksawery Branicki (died 1819), from 1765 Count, from 1764 Chamberlain (Podstoli); in March and April 1765 he was in Berlin as Envoy of the King of Poland to treat with Frederick the Great.

84. *Lubomirski:* Prince Stanislaus Lubomirski (1722-1783), made Field Marshal (Straznik) in 1752; married to Princess Izabela Czartoryska in 1753 (cf. note 52 to this chapter).

85. *Xavier:* Branicki's given names (see note 83) are the Polish equivalent of Francis Xavier.

86. *The White Eagle:* Polish order founded by Augustus II in 1713.

87. *Vis-à-vis:* Light carriage for 2 persons on 2 facing seats.

CHAPTER VIII

1. *The two spectacles:* In the previous chapter C. has said that, on La Binetti's arrival in Warsaw, the dancer Pic arranged a ballet for which Tomatis spared no expense in supplying the costumes, scenery, and so on. The other

"spectacle" would seem to have been the ballet which Tomatis had already mounted for La Catai.

2. *He was . . . Russian:* Together with the Czartoryskis, Branicki was opposed to King Stanislaus Poniatowski, though the King heaped honors on him. His activities in the Russian interest brought him the rank of Grand Marshal to the Crown; in addition, he married Aleksandra Vasilievna, Baroness Engelhardt, a niece of the well-known favorite and Minister of Catherine the Great, Potemkin.

3. *The dissidents:* The Polish Diet of 1764 had made Roman Catholicism the only State religion; from then on Protestants and members of the Greek Orthodox Church were persecuted as "dissidents." Protecting them gave both Prussia and Russia the excuse to interfere in Polish internal affairs. It was not until the new constitution of 1791 that all faiths were granted equal rights.

4. *Under personal obligations to him . . . political reasons:* During the time Stanislaus Poniatowski was in St. Petersburg and was Catherine's lover, Branicki had helped to extricate him from a difficult situation. Politically, Poniatowski, King by the grace of Russia, was obliged to support the Russian faction.

5. *St. Casimir:* Born 1458, the patron saint of Poland and Lithuania. His feast was celebrated on March 4th: hence its eve was on March 3rd, not March 4th.

6. *The King's elder brother:* Kazimierz Poniatowski (1721-1780), Prince from 1764 and Grand Chamberlain.

7. *Casacci:* Teresa Casacci, also Casazzi and Casassi, Italian dancer from Turin, first appeared in Venice in 1762.

8. *Bisinski:* Perhaps an officer named Biszewski, who is mentioned in a contemporary Viennese document.

9. *Takes to his legs:* C. makes Branicki use the vulgar expression *fout le camp*.

10. *Sarmatians . . . Dacians:* The Sarmatians were a nomadic people who in Antiquity inhabited the southern Russian steppes and at the beginning of the Christian era advanced to the mouth of the Danube. The name was also extended to peoples north of that area. The Dacians inhabited the area north of the lower Danube and were brought under Roman rule by Trajan in 101-106; hence the name Dacia given to the new province, which, however, was evacuated

by the Romans in the 3rd century and roughly corresponds to the present Romania.

11. *Partner:* C. writes *"pertener,"* presumably for the English word.

12. *Pernigotti:* Carlo Pernigotti, of Italian descent, Chamberlain to the King of Poland and naturalized a Pole in 1767.

13. *Lubomirski:* Prince Kaspar Lubomirski (1734-1779), son of Prince Teodor Lubomirski, Voivod of Cracow.

14. *Starosty:* District governed by a Starost; originally a fief conferred on a nobleman by the King, later an administrative unit.

15. *Casanova:* Together with later passages this shows that C. did not travel in Poland as either Seingalt or Farussi.

16. *C. P.:* Abbreviation for *Coronae Poloniae* ("to the Crown of Poland").

17. *Thirty-two:* Substituted for twenty-seven, which had been substituted for the original twenty-six, which shows that C. returned to this chapter over a considerable period of years.

18. *Mniszek:* Doubtless the Counts Vandalin-Mniszek, whom Winckelmann mentions on their departure from Rome for Venice in 1767. However, there were two noble families of the name: the Counts Mniszek of Buzenin and the Counts Vandalin-Mniszek.

19. *Bertrand:* Élie (de) Bertrand (1713-1797), theologian and natural historian, from 1744 to 1765 pastor of the French church in Bern, from 1765 to 1768 in Poland, where he was ennobled. Cf. Vol. 6, Chap. VIII, n. 7.

20. *Berlin:* Large closed traveling carriage with 4 wheels.

21. *A beautiful garden:* Probably the duel, as C. himself says later, was fought in Wola in a garden belonging to Count Brühl. Wola, now a suburb of Warsaw, was then a village about half a mile from the capital and hence was still within the limits of the Starosty.

22. *Varsaw:* So C., to suggest the Polish pronunciation; elsewhere he Gallicizes the name to "Varsovie."

23. *Recollect:* See note 54 to Chap. V of this volume.

24. *Podlasie:* Polish province east of Warsaw; capital, Siedlce. The Voivod (C.'s "Palatine") from 1762 was Stanislaus Bernard Gozdzki.

25. *Kalisz:* Southwest of Warsaw, capital of a Voivodship; the Voivod from 1763 was Ignacy Twardowski.

26. *Jablonowski:* Jozef Aleksander Pruss Jablonowski (1712-
    1777), Prince from 1743, from 1755 Voivod of Nowogrodek;
    celebrated patron of the arts, scholar, and writer.

27. *Sanguszko:* Janusz Aleksander Sanguszko, son of the
    Prince and Grand Marshal Pawel Sanguszko.

28. *The Grand Marshal:* Count Franciszek Bielinski (1683-
    1766), from 1742 Polish Grand Marshal. His successor in
    1766 was Prince Stanislaus Lubomirski.

29. *The Grand Chamberlain:* Prince Kazimierz Poniatowski
    (cf. note 6 to this chapter).

30. Medical maxim of unknown source.

31. *Clary:* Johann Nepomuk Franz Borgia, Count Clary-
    Aldringen (1728 - ca. 1780), officer in the Imperial service.

32. *It was then that I:* In C.'s ms. there follows a canceled
    but still legible passage: "took the bit in my teeth and
    wrote a four-page letter to the King, all in a jesting tone,
    but cruel, in which I called all the surgeons in Warsaw
    ignoramuses and butchers and all the people who gave
    them the lie admirable, and all the others who claimed to
    know better than I did whether I had gangrene or not
    [*sic*]. I ended my rather impertinent letter by saying ——"

33. *Became visible:* There follows another canceled passage:
    "to my eyes, which had better sight than those of the
    ignorant surgeons who wanted me to trust them blindly."

34. *Gourel:* He remained in the service of Prince August
    Aleksander Czartoryski until 1772.

35. *I kept my hand:* There follows a canceled passage, a page
    in length, from which it appears that he asked Prince
    Sulkowski to bring him his French physician; it was not
    until this Frenchman had declared that gangrene had not
    set in that C. dismissed the 4 Polish surgeons. The French-
    man, having found C.'s wound not infected with gangrene,
    met the Polish surgeons the next morning and prevented
    the operation.

36. *Bishop of Poznan:* From 1738 to 1768 this office was held
    by Prince Teodor Kazimierz Czartoryski. Warsaw first be-
    came a bishopric in 1798 and an archdiocese in 1817.

37. *A lady:* As appears from what follows, she was Branicki's
    sister, Elzbieta Sapieha.

38. *Nonagenarian . . . Bielinski:* Bielinski was only 82 years
    old in 1765 (cf. note 28 to this chapter).

39. *Countess Salmour:* Countess Isabella Salmour, née Lubienska (not, as C. says, Bielinska), married in 1752 to Giuseppe Gabaleone, Count Salmour (1710-1759).

40. *The Saxon faction:* Poland was then divided into two great camps: the pro-Russian faction, led by the Czartoryskis, and the patriotic, pro-Saxon faction, which consisted largely of Roman Catholics.

41. *The same day I went to dine:* Either C. went to dinner twice in one day (first at the Grand Marshal's, then at the Prince Palatine's), or he is out in his reckoning by a day.

42. *The Palatine of Kiowia:* Count Franciszek Salezy Potocki (1700-1772), from 1753 Voivod of Kiowia; opponent of the Czartoryskis.

43. *Brühl:* Aloys Friedrich, Count Brühl (1739-1793), son of the celebrated Prime Minister to King Augustus III (see note 54 to the preceding chapter), was Starost of Warsaw.

44. *A Starost Sniatinski:* Text: "un Staroste Sniatinski." No Starost by this name is known. C. later mentions a Starost of Sniatyn, who may be the same person (see note 56 to this chapter).

45. *Madame Geoffrin:* Marie Thérèse Geoffrin, née Rodet (1699-1777), whose literary salon was one of the most celebrated in Paris. Stanislaus Poniatowski became a close friend of hers during his stay in Paris. She came to Warsaw at his invitation on June 6, 1766, and remained there until Sept. 13th of that year.

46. *Leopol:* Polish, Lwow. At the first partition of Poland (1772), it became Austrian and its name was changed to Lemberg.

47. *Zamojski . . . Zamosc:* Zamosc was a famous fortress between Warsaw and Leopol, founded in 1588 by Jan Zamojski. The fortress belonged to a so-called "ordynacja," a kind of fief of which there were only three in Poland at the period. In 1766 the Ordynat of Zamosc was Count Klemens Zamojski (died ca. 1767); he was married in 1763 to Countess Konstancja Zamojska, née Czartoryska (1742-1797).

48. *Kaminska:* Katarzyna Korsakowska, daughter of Franciszek Salezy, Count Potocki (cf. note 52 to this chapter); she was the Castellane Kaminska as the wife of the Castellan of Kamieniec, a fortress in Podolia.

49. *The confederations ruined her:* Noblemen who were op-
    posed to the decisions of the Diet had the right to unite
    in a confederation. The confederations were usually named
    from the towns in which they were formed; the best known
    of them was the general confederation of Bar (1768), of
    which Kaminska's husband was a leading member.

50. *Rzewuski:* C. has confused the Christian names. The
    reference is to Count Waclaw Rzewuski (1706-1779);
    "lesser" (C. writes "petit") because he had a superior officer
    whose title was "Grand General."

51. *One of the four . . . Siberia:* During the Diet of 1767
    Prince Repnin had 4 members of it abducted and banished
    to Siberia. They were the Bishop of Cracow, Kajetan
    Ignacy Soltyk, the Bishop of Kiowia (see note 65 to the
    preceding chapter), and Counts Waclaw and Seweryn
    Rzewuski.

52. *Christianpol:* Capital of the Voivodship of Kiowia, in
    southern Poland. The Voivod was Count Franciszek Salezy
    Potocki (see note 42 to this chapter). C.'s statement that
    he named the town after himself is not substantiated. The
    Count's given names are the Polish for François de Sales,
    but that is a far cry from "Christian."

53. *Van Swieten:* Gerhard van Swieten (1700-1772), physician
    in ordinary to the Empress Maria Theresa of Austria.
    Hyrneus (obviously a Latinized name) has not been iden-
    tified.

54. *Asclepiades:* Greek physician, born ca. 100 B.C., died at
    Rome ca. 30 B.C.

55. *Turn and turn about:* After this paragraph two unfinished
    and canceled paragraphs in C.'s ms. show that at Potocki's
    he encountered Baron Wiedau, his previous meeting with
    whom he has narrated in Vol. 6, Chap. I. The passage ends:
    "And from that time I never heard anything more of this
    Wiedau, upon whom I so fortunately took a sweet and just
    revenge."

56. *Potocki . . . married her:* Presumably a relative of Count
    Potocki (see note 52 to this chapter). Sniatyn was a place
    in Galicia, with a large castle. The "very beautiful girl"
    whom he married thus acquired the name Potocka, by
    which C. later refers to her.

57. *Pulawy:* A small town on the Vistula south of Warsaw;

it was the site of the principal palace of the Czartoryskis, in which there was a large library.

58. *Podolia, Pokucie, and Volhynia:* Names of southern provinces of Poland; the parts of them which became Austrian possessions by the partitions of Poland were renamed.

59. *Lodomeria:* This name survived until the third partition of Poland (1795); Austria took over the province as West Galicia.

60. *Today . . . Poland any more:* C. added this sentence between the lines after 1795.

61. *Countess Waldstein:* Eleonora Monika Czartoryska, née Countess Waldstein (1710-1792), married in 1726 to Prince Fryderyk Michal Czartoryski, who was Grand Chancellor of Lithuania from 1752. She was not 90 years of age (as C. writes) at the time of her death, but 82.

62. Altered from Tacitus, *Histories*, I, 79.

63. *Hanged in effigy . . . the Military School Lottery:* C.'s duel with Branicki aroused great interest and was reported in all the gazettes of the time. His consequent notoriety may have led to old rumors concerning his hasty departure from Paris in 1759 being revived (cf. Vol. 5, Chaps. X and XI).

64. *Portugal . . . resource:* Here again C. thinks of going to Portugal. What "resource" he expected to find there remains unexplained.

65. *Württemberg:* Prince Ludwig Eugen of Württemberg (1731-1795) was reputed to be a libertine and a freethinker; hence the pious Maria Theresa's refusal to consider him as a suitor for her daughter Christine.

66. *The King's sister:* Countess Izabela Branicka, née Poniatowska (born ca. 1730), married in 1748 to Jan Klemens, Count Branicki of Ruszcza, Grand General to the Polish Crown. He had received his appointment from King Augustus III in 1752; he was dismissed and banished in 1764, but returned in 1765 and supported the Confederation of Bar.

67. *Bialystok:* City in northeastern Poland, some 30 miles from the present boundary between Poland and the Soviet Union.

68. *Bragnecki:* He was probably a member of a family of the minor nobility named Branicki-Korczak.

69. *La Durant:* Perhaps the Durand who appeared as a dancer

in Stuttgart ca. 1764. A ballerina named Durand is documented with the Comédie Italienne in Paris in 1768.

70. *The Duke:* Duke Karl Eugen of Württemberg (1728-1793) reigned from 1737 (cf. especially Vol. 6, Chap. III).

71. *His brother . . . a Canon:* Count Clary had a brother who was a Canon, but in Brixen (Joseph, born 1731); the Canon in Olmütz was in all probability Waclaw Filip Benicjusz (born 1736), who belonged to another branch of the family.

72. *Wartenberg:* Wartenberg, in Schleswig, belonged to the domain of the Biron family; hence C. hoped to find the Duchess of Kurland's brother, Baron Treyden, there.

73. *Bastiani:* Niccolò Bastiani (died 1787), Venetian abate, installed as a Canon in Breslau by Frederick the Great.

74. *The cathedral:* The cathedral in Breslau was built in the Gothic style from 1244 to 1330.

75. *Cavalcabo:* Probably a Marchese Calvalcabo, whom Boswell met at the Court of Brunswick in 1764.

76. *Tron:* Andrea Tron (1712-1785), Venetian patrician and diplomat; he was Envoy in The Hague from 1743 to 1745.

77. See Vol. 9, Chap. XII, n. 33.

78. *Ombre:* A card game of Spanish origin, very popular in the 17th and 18th centuries.

CHAPTER IX

1. *Potocka:* See note 56 to the preceding chapter.

2. *Maton:* Probably a fictitious name; she has not been identified.

3. *The inn:* Probably the "Stadt Rom" ("City of Rome"), at the corner of the Neumarkt and the Moritzstrasse. The building had a projecting bay such as C. later describes.

4. *Roland:* Teresa Roland (1744-1779), daughter of a livery-stable keeper from Avignon who later had an inn in Rome. She had married Giovanni Casanova, the painter, in 1764, in which year he was appointed Director of the Academy of Fine Arts in Dresden.

5. *The wife of Peter August:* Maria Maddalena Antonia Stella Casanova (1732-1800) was married to the Saxon Court musician Peter August (died 1787). In 1787 her daughter

Marianna married Carlo Angioloni, and in 1821 their son
Carlo sold the manuscript of C.'s memoirs to the firm of
F. A. Brockhaus. (The "Angiolini" of Vol. 1, p. 10, of the
present translation rests on an error in the "Publisher's
Preface" to the Brockhaus-Plon edition [Vol. 1, p. 1] and
should be corrected to Angioloni.)

6. *The Estates:* The Assembly of the Estates was summoned
for the first time on May 12, 1766, by the Regent, Prince
Xaver. (Cf. the following note and Vol. 6, Chap. II, n. 39.)

7. *The Elector . . . in his minority . . . Regent:* The Elector
Friedrich Christian of Saxony died in 1763; his son Fried-
rich August III being then only 13 years of age, his uncle
Prince Xaver assumed the Regency.

8. *A Spinucci:* Chiara Rosa Maria, Countess Spinucci (1741–
1792), lady in waiting at the Electoral Court of Saxony,
married Prince Xaver of Saxony, Count von der Lausitz,
in 1765.

9. *The Dowager Electress:* Maria Antonia Walpurgis (1724–
1780), daughter of the Emperor Charles VII and widow of
the Elector Friedrich Christian, to whom she was married
in 1746 and who reigned for only a few weeks in 1763. (See
Vol. 8, Chap. I, n. 64.)

10. *A bank at faro:* Gambling was permitted in the Royal
Electoral Theater when Italian operas were given and at
performances by the Comédie Française (the resident company of French actors) until Dec. 17, 1766, when all games
of chance were prohibited.

11. *Agdollo:* Marchese Pietro Alvise Agdollo (died ca. 1800)
was arrested in 1766 for participating in a plot against the
reigning Elector and was imprisoned in the fortress of
Königstein.

12. *Countess Rutowska:* Princess Luise Amalie Lubomirska,
widow of Field Marshal Friedrich August, Count Rutowski.
She was married to Agdollo on Aug. 9, 1764.

13. *Königstein:* Saxon fortress south of Dresden on the Elbe,
partly built in the 12th century and used as a State prison
until recent times.

14. *Bellegarde:* There were several officers by this name in
the Saxon army at the time, so the one C. mentions cannot
be identified.

15. *A house:* Probably the house opposite to the "City of

Rome," the ground floor of which was occupied by another inn.

16. *Erker:* German, "projecting room or story, oriel."

17. *Mercury . . . Jupiter . . . Amphitryon:* Allusion to the legend of Amphitryon, King of Tiryns, whose wife Alcmena was deceived by Jupiter in the form of her husband; the offspring of their connection was Hercules. Mercury was the messenger of the gods.

18. *The inn on the great square:* Text: "l'auberge sur la grande place." C. having already said that the inn in which he was staying was on the square ("sur la place"), and the commentators referring both expressions to the same Neumarkt, and placing the inn over which C.'s mother lived there as well, they conjecture there was yet another inn on the square, of which nothing is known.

19. *The Princess Straznikowa:* See note 52 to Chap. VII of this volume.

20. *Fair:* There were then 3 annual fairs at Leipzig: at Easter, at Michaelmas (Sept. 29th), and at New Year's.

21. *Larks:* The cuisine of Leipzig was famous for its larks, which were snared in great quantities in the autumn. They were served roasted and were considered especially nourishing as late as the 19th century.

22. *Hohmann:* Probably Peter Hohmann, who settled in Leipzig in 1717 and was ennobled by Charles VI. Or C. may refer to his younger son, who was then director of the banking house of Hohmann.

23. *High Commissioner:* C. writes "président." The official referred to was either the "General-Berg-Commissarius" Friedrich Anton von Heinitz, or the "Ober-Berghauptmann" Friedrich Wilhelm von Oppeln auf Krebs.

24. *Princess Auersperg:* Marie Wilhelmine Josefa, née Countess Neipperg (1738-1775), Princess by her marriage in 1755 to Prince Johann Adam Auersperg (1721-1795), whose second wife she was.

25. *The . . . hostelry in which I was staying:* C. here writes "hôtel," but later refers to it as "auberge." Contemporary documents name no fewer than 120 inns in Leipzig at the time.

26. *My free hand:* As appears later, C. still had one arm in a sling.

27. *Zinzendorf:* Ludwig Friedrich Julius, Count Zinzendorf (1721-1780), nephew of the celebrated founder of the Herrnhuter Brotherhood, was converted to Roman Catholicism in 1739; he was in the diplomatic service first of Saxony, then of Austria, representing the latter from 1750 in St. Petersburg, Stockholm, and Copenhagen; Councilor of State from 1755, Minister from 1762. He was in Paris from 1750 to 1752; C. mentions him in passing in Vol. 3, Chap. IX.

28. *La Cavamacchie:* Giulia Ursula (Giulietta) Preato, called "La Cavamacchie" (1724 - ca. 1790). See especially Vol. 1, Chap. IV, and Vol. 3, Chap. I.

29. *The beautiful Castel-Bajac:* The wife of an apothecary in Montpellier, she called herself Castel-Bajac after the Marquis Louis de Castel-Bajac, an adventurer with whom she traveled; C. had already met them in Paris (cf. Vol. 5, Chap. X) and in London (cf. Vol. 9, Chap. X). She also used the name Madame Blazin (Blasin), perhaps after an earlier lover.

30. *Schwerin:* See Vol. 9, Chap. X, n. 17.

31. *No impression . . . in love with another:* In Vol. 9, Chap. X, C. compares Madame Castel-Bajac with Pauline, greatly to the disadvantage of the former.

32. *The Matron of Ephesus:* Heroine of the celebrated story "The Matron [or Widow] of Ephesus," perhaps of Near Eastern origin, the classic version of which occurs as an episode in Petronius' *Satyricon.* An Ephesian widow is so grief-stricken by her husband's death that she goes to live in the cave where he is buried. A soldier set to watch the body of a crucified convict nearby finds her there and becomes her lover. While they are engaged in intercourse the body of the convict is stolen from the cross. To save the soldier from punishment the widow lets him replace it by her husband's body.

33. *Spandau:* Then a small city some distance from Berlin, with a celebrated fortress which also served as a prison; now a suburb of Berlin.

34. *Countess Blasin:* See note 29 to this chapter.

35. *Six weeks later:* C. cannot have heard this news until May 1767, for Count Schwerin, who was then in Hamburg, was not arrested until that date. However, he was sent from there to Spandau.

36. *We stopped for four days in Prague:* In C.'s ms. there
follows a long canceled passage concerning his meeting with
La Calori, whose name he forgot to remove from the heading of this chapter when he canceled the passage concerning
her. It throws light on the identity of Bellino-Teresa, as
follows: "We stopped four days in Prague (where there
was Italian opera) and we went to it. When I entered the
box I had taken, the first person I see is the leading actress,
singing an air. It was La Calori, who, seeing me, lost her
composure. The same thing had happened to me in Florence
with Teresa. How delighted I was to see La Calori, and
sorry that I could not go to speak with her at once; I
wrote her a note the next morning, in which I asked her if I
might pay her a visit with my wife, and at what hour. She
replied that she would come to dine with me the next day,
for on that day she was engaged, and that she would be
most pleased to have me introduce her to my wife (. . .).

"The *virtuosa* gave us the greatest pleasure. We told each
other all our adventures from the time we had parted. We
spent six happy hours; La Castel-Bajac simply listened,
sighing from time to time when what we told each other
reminded her that she had spent three years in continual
misfortune. La Calori could not return our dinner because
she was in a boardinghouse. So we took leave of each other
after cordial embraces, and we left on the next day but
one with a passport from the government.

"My companion had taken the name of Mademoiselle
Blasin, lace-seller. I took this precaution as soon as I learned
of the (. . .) to which pretty women whose ill luck made
them pass through Vienna were subjected there."

37. *The "Red Ox":* There was no inn of this name in Vienna
at the period, though there was the well-patronized hostelry
the "Golden Ox" in the Seilergasse; however, in view of his
poor financial situation, it seems unlikely that C. could have
indulged himself in staying at the most expensive inn in
Vienna.

38. *The French Ambassador:* Émeric Joseph, Marquis de
Durfort-Civrac (died 1787), French diplomat, Ambassador
in Vienna from 1766 to 1770.

39. *Schrötter:* Franz Leopold Schrötter (ca. 1732-1794), of

Silesia, was Intendant to Count Neipperg and from 1771 the King of Prussia's agent in Vienna.

40. *Salmour:* See note 39 to Chap. VIII of this volume.

41. *The Archduchess Marianne:* Archduchess Maria Anna (Marianne) of Austria (1738-1789), eldest daughter of the Empress Maria Theresa; Abbess in Prague from 1766, in Klagenfurt from 1781.

42. *Madame Starhemberg:* Princess Maria Franziska Starhemberg, née Princess Salm (1721-1806), married in 1761 to Count Georg Adam Starhemberg, who was created a Prince in 1765.

43. *The elder Calzabigi:* Ranieri de' Calzabigi (1714-1795) organized the Military School Lottery in Paris with his brother and C. (cf. Vol. 5, Chap. II), and in 1761 was appointed Councilor of the Chamber of Accounts of the Austrian Netherlands in Vienna. He wrote some opera librettos for his friend Gluck.

44. *Kaunitz:* Count Wenzel Anton Kaunitz-Rietberg (1711-1794), Prince from 1764; Minister 1748, Chancellor 1753-1780.

45. *Metastasio:* Pietro Antonio Metastasio (1698-1782), Italian poet and man of letters, Austrian Court poet from 1730 and composer of many opera librettos (see especially Vol. 3, Chap. XII).

46. *Vestris:* Gaetano Apollino Baldassare Vestris (1729-1808), famous Italian dancer, so admired at the period that he was called "le dieu de la danse" ("the god of the dance").

47. *The young Emperor:* Joseph II (1741-1790) became Emperor upon the death of his father Francis I in 1765; son of Maria Theresa.

48. *De la Pérouse:* Gian Giacomo Marcello Gamba della Perosa (1738-1817), Count from 1758, called Comte de la Pérouse; son of Baron Gian Giacomo Gamba (1671-1751), purveyor to the Imperial army.

49. *Las Casas:* Simon de Las Casas (1742-1798), Spanish diplomat; he was Secretary of Embassy in Vienna from 1766 to 1772. Las Casas was a Freemason, an unusual thing in Spain at the time.

50. *Uccelli:* Francesco Antonio Uccelli (born 1728), first a notary in Venice, later Secretary of Embassy in Vienna. For the Seminary of San Cipriano, see Vol. 1, Chap. VI.

51. *Renier:* Polo (Paolo) Renier (1710-1789), Venetian patrician, from 1765 to 1768 Ambassador in Vienna, from 1779 Doge of Venice.

52. *Bragadin . . . two other friends:* For Bragadin, see note 10 to Chap. II of this volume. The two other friends were the patricians Marco Barbaro (1688-1771) and Marco Dandolo (1704-1779). See especially Vol. 2, Chap. VII.

53. *Württemberg:* Duke Karl Eugen of Württemberg died in 1793; he was in Venice from Dec. 1766 to June 1767.

54. *A pretty girl:* Presumably Adelaide Pocchini, illegitimate or pretended daughter of Antonio Pocchini (see note 57). She died of consumption on Aug. 31, 1767, in Leopoldstadt at the age of 9 years and 8 months.

55. *Priapeia:* Priapus was a Greek fertility god, also worshiped in Rome, whose representations were characterized by an enormous phallus. A collection of some 80 Latin poems, late literary imitations of inscriptions on his statues, many of them obscene, has been preserved under the title *Priapeia.*

56. *Hebe or Ganymede:* Allusion to the goddess Hebe, cupbearer of the gods, and the beautiful youth Ganymede who supplanted her in that position when Jupiter fell in love with him and translated him to Olympus.

57. *Pocchini:* See Vol. 9, Chap. XIII, n. 1. C.'s encounter with him in London is described in that chapter.

58. *Catina:* Pocchini was married to Lucia Fiorentin. Catina (died 1783) was a chambermaid from Serravalle, Italy, who was his companion on his travels for many years from 1757.

59. *Slavonians:* The militia of the Venetian Republic was made up partly of soldiers recruited in the Venetian territories in Dalmatia and Istria; they were called Slavonians (Venetian, Schiavoni).

CHAPTER X

1. *Schrattenbach:* Count Franz Ferdinand Schrattenbach (1707-1785), Statthalter of Lower Austria from 1759 to 1770; as such, he had extensive police powers. C. received the order to leave by Jan. 25 on Jan. 23, 1767. Through the intervention of Prince Kaunitz he was granted a prolongation of a few days.

2. *Kaunitz:* Wenzel Anton, Count Kaunitz, from 1764 Prince von Kaunitz-Rietberg (1711-1794), Austrian statesman; Minister, 1748; Ambassador in Paris, 1750-1752; Court and State Chancellor from 1765, and the Empress Maria Theresa's most trusted adviser. He was a patron of the arts.

3. *A nobleman . . . my whole family . . . served him myself:* The nobleman was the Saxon Ambassador at the Court of Vienna (see the following note). C.'s mother, his brother Giovanni, and his brother-in-law Peter August were all in the service of the Saxon Court in Dresden. C. himself during his first stay there had written two plays for the Court theater.

4. *Vitzthum:* Count Ludwig Siegfried Vitzthum von Eckstädt (1716-1777), Saxon diplomat; from 1765 to 1768 Ambassador in Vienna.

5. *Senate of Venice:* The Venetian Senate concerned itself only with the most important matters of state. C. was doubtless proud that a copy of his letter was transmitted to it.

6. *Hasse:* Franz Hasse, Secretary of Embassy to Count Vitzthum, son of the composer and chapelmaster Johann Adolf Hasse (1699-1783) and his wife (from 1730) Faustina, née Bordoni (1700-1781), famous singer known as "the tenth Muse"; she did not appear after 1753.

7. Seneca, *Hercules Furens*, 313 f.

8. *Ninety years:* It would follow from this that Countess Isabella Salmour, née Lubienska, died shortly before 1798, for C. first wrote, then crossed out, "who is still alive, a nonagenarian, in Dresden, where I saw her only two months ago." In the margin there is a note in C.'s hand: "I wrote this in the year 1798," where "1798" replaced "1794," which had replaced the original "1791."

9. *The Salis family:* A noble family whose seat was at Coire (German, Chur) in the Swiss Grisons. The "young lady" may have been a daughter of Ulysses von Salis (1728-1800), a prominent statesman.

10. *By dying:* Count Schrattenbach died in 1785, C. not until 1798.

11. *Worse than the one I wrote . . . to the late Duke of Württemberg:* In Chap. V of Vol. 6 C. says only that he

wrote the Duke a letter from Zurich "which must have left a bitter taste in his mouth."

12. *Seven years ago:* Count Gaetan Zawoiski died in 1788. For C.'s previous acquaintance with him, see Vol. 2, Chap. VII.

13. *Lamberg:* Count Maximilian Joseph von Lamberg (1729-1792), writer and great friend of C.'s during the latter's last years at Dux (cf. Vol. 8, Chap. I, n. 80). C. writes "Max. de Lamberg."

14. *The "Golden Grapes":* The "Zur goldenen Weintraube" inn (also "Goldene Traube") belonged from 1747 to 1790 to Johann Sigismund Mayr. It survived until 1896.

15. *Gertrude:* See Vol. 8, Chap. I.

16. *Annemirl:* See Vol. 8, Chap. I, n. 75.

17. *Fugger:* Among the many members of the Fugger family, it is impossible to identify this Count Fugger.

18. *Binetti:* Georges Binet (Binetti), French dancer and impresario, married in 1751 to Anna Binetti, née Ramon, one of the best-known Italian ballerinas of the period. She appeared until 1778 and then became a dancing teacher in Venice (cf. especially Vol. 6, Chap. III).

19. *To buy a post:* Until the French Revolution government positions could be bought in France.

20. *A plague:* Text: "que tout le monde disait *plagas* du Stathalter," where *plagas* is perhaps from Latin *plaga,* perhaps from Austrian "A Plag is" ("It's a nuisance").

21. *Countess Dachsberg:* Maria Josepha, Countess von Lamberg, née Baroness von Dachsberg (born 1746), became the second wife of Count von Lamberg in 1763.

22. *Plombières:* Watering place in the Vosges Mountains in eastern France.

23. *Thurn and Valsassina:* Perhaps Baron (not Count) Johann Benedikt von Thurn und Valsassina (1744-1825), from 1767 Canon ("Domicellarkanonikus") of the Cathedral of Ratisbon (Regensburg), from 1779 Dean ("Domdechant") of the Cathedral. (The identification is doubtful.)

24. *Darmstadt:* Joseph, Landgrave of Hesse-Darmstadt (1699-1768), from 1740 Prince-Bishop of Augsburg.

25. *Algardi:* Francesco Antonio Algardi (died 1789), Bolognese physician, from 1761 physician in ordinary to the

Prince-Bishop of Augsburg and later to the Electress of the Palatinate Elisabeth Auguste.

26. *Elector of Bavaria:* Karl Theodor von Wittelsbach (1724–1799), from 1742 Elector of the Palatinate, from 1777 Elector of Bavaria.

27. *Sellentin:* Baron von Sellentin (died after 1797), officer in the Prussian service. Cf. Vol. 8, Chap. I, n. 82.

28. *The "Three Moors":* See Vol. 8, Chap. I, n. 56.

29. *What a Diet!:* The reference is to the Polish Diet of 1766, at which Russia and Prussia demanded the political and civil emancipation of the dissidents (all those who were not Roman Catholics). The Catholic party was victorious, and the consequence was the formation of a large number of confederations (cf. notes 3 and 49 to Chap. VIII of this volume).

30. *When he was sent to the Bastille:* On Jan. 9, 1768.

31. *The populace of Paris . . . tore down the Bastille:* The States-General had been in session at Versailles from May 5, 1789; on June 17th the Third Estate withdrew and declared itself the National Assembly with power to draw up a constitution. Though this was in fact the first decisive step of the French Revolution, the storming of the Bastille on July 14, 1789, came to symbolize the raising of the revolutionary banner. The Duke of Orléans sided with the people.

32. *My letter . . . was printed . . . later translated into German and English:* The *Mémoires historiques et authentiques sur la Bastille* was published in 1789; C.'s letter appears on pp. 215-223 of it. The book was soon translated into several languages.

33. *January 1, 1798:* C. first wrote, then crossed out: "and today, on which I transcribe it, is April 6, 1792." The text of C.'s letter in his memoirs differs in some details from the one printed in the *Mémoires historiques* (see the preceding note).

34. *Of Mars:* Read "of iron," that being the metal ascribed to Mars by alchemical doctrine.

35. *Tree of projection:* In his description of Madame d'Urfé's laboratory (Vol. 5, Chap. V) C. calls it the "tree of Diana."

36. *The Princess of Anhalt-Zerbst:* Johanna Elisabeth, Prin-

cess of Anhalt-Zerbst (1712-1760), lived in Paris from 1758 under the name of Countess of Oldenburg and was an eager disciple of alchemy.

37. *Tortoise:* Text, "tortue," now the name of a kind of cooking pot, but used by C. to designate an alchemical implement.

38. *Mirabeau:* Honoré Gabriel de Riqueti, Count of Mirabeau (1749-1791), celebrated orator and greatly feared publicist, who virtually ruled the new National Assembly from 1789.

39. *Escaped from arrest at Stuttgart:* For this incident, which took place in April 1760, see Vol. 6, Chap. III.

40. *The Duke's favorite residence:* The castle in Ludwigsburg, north of Stuttgart, was built in 1711 and served Duke Karl Eugen of Württemberg as his second residence.

41. *A mistress of the Duke's:* Françoise Rose Gourgaud (1743-1804), French actress from Marseilles, married to the dancer Angiolo Vestris in 1767. She appeared in Paris at the Théâtre Français from 1768 to 1803.

42. *The excruciating letter:* See note 11 to this chapter. However, the reader cannot "remember" it, for C. nowhere gives the text of his letter to the Duke.

43. *Her husband:* Giovanni Battista Toscani, Italian actor, married to Isabella Toscani (on her, see especially Vol. 6, Chaps. II and III).

44. *The three officers . . . Fürstenberg:* See Vol. 6, Chap. III.

45. *My daughter:* Luisa Toscani, Italian dancer, appeared in Stuttgart from 1757.

46. *Messieri:* Gabriele Messieri, Italian singer, appeared in Dresden 1754-1756, in Stuttgart and Vienna 1766-1774; married Luisa Toscani in 1767.

47. *I had loved her in Paris:* C. first mentions her when he met her in Coblenz (see Vol. 6, Chap. II); however, he there refers to having met her earlier in Paris.

48. *Trying to make me a soldier:* The three officers had threatened C. that if he did not pay his gambling debts to them they would force him to enter the military service of Württemberg as a common soldier. See Vol. 6, Chap. III.

49. *A young author:* Perhaps a certain Joseph Uriot, who, however, had been an actor and author in Stuttgart from 1760.

50. *The canine letter:* Old name for the letter *r*, especially when trilled.

51. *A little daughter:* Nothing is known of her; she cannot have been Rosina Balletti, Balletti's daughter by his wife, for she was not born until 1767 or 1768.

52. *Words without r's:* Text: "des paroles sans erre" ("words without *erre*"), followed by: "or without *re*, for one no longer writes the letter *erre*, as my grandfather would have written it, one writes the letter *re*."

53. *Acting . . . in Paris:* C. added, then crossed out, "on my return from Spain." She appeared in Paris from 1768.

54. *Zaïre:* Heroine of Voltaire's tragedy *Zaïre* (1732).

55. *Algardi:* See note 25 to this chapter.

56. *Sickingen:* Karl Heinrich Joseph Sickingen (1737-1791), ennobled in 1773; diplomat in the service of the Elector Palatine.

57. *Beckers:* Heinrich Anton Beckers, Freiherr von Wester-stetten (1697 - after 1790), diplomat and Minister of State to the Elector Palatine.

58. *Schwetzingen:* Small town south of Mannheim, with a castle built in 1699. Mannheim had been the capital of the Palatinate from 1720.

59. *Prince Frederick . . . died:* Count Palatine Friedrich Michael von Zweibrücken-Birkenfeld, died on Aug. 15, 1767. An extant letter of C.'s to Count von Lamberg shows that C. was already in Spa (Belgium) on Aug. 11th. Probably the Count Palatine was already very ill when C. was in Schwetzingen.

60. *Verazi:* Mattia Verazi (died 1794), Roman poet, Court poet in Mannheim from 1756.

61. *Still has everything:* C. was misinformed. Verazi had died in 1794.

62. *Jommelli:* Niccolò Jommelli (1714-1774), Italian composer; from 1754 to 1769 he was in the service of Duke Karl Eugen of Württemberg. Verazi wrote several librettos for him.

63. *Defend his Court from that adventurer:* The item published in the *Gazette de Cologne* (No. 66, 1766) and dated Warsaw, July 30th, said only: "The Sieur de Casa-Nuova, well known in the newspapers, having wanted to reappear here recently, the Court ordered him to leave at once."

64. *Jacquet:* The editor of the *Gazette de Cologne* was Cas-

par Anton Jacquemotte de Roderique; he died in 1767 and was succeeded by the Abbé Jeaurinvilliers. C. left four versions of this incident; according to two of them the editor immediately undertook to publish a retraction dictated to him by C. However, no such retraction appeared.

65. *Burgomaster xe:* Franz Jakob Gabriel von Groote (1721-1792), Burgomaster of Cologne from 1756; married in 1749 to Maria Ursula Columba zum Putz, called Mimi. In Vol. 6, Chap. II, where C. relates his previous encounter with them, he writes Burgomaster *X* and Madame *X*.

66. *The posthouse:* The posthouses in Cologne were in the Glockengasse, as was the office of the *Gazette de Cologne*.

67. *The Grand Notary:* C. writes "le Picharge," for Polish *pisarz* ("Grand Notary"). See note 53 to Chap. V of this volume.

CHAPTER XI

1. *Spa:* Belgian watering place between Liège and Aix, with numerous mineral springs; also known for its games of chance.

2. *A hatter's shop:* The proprietor's name was Durieux, the shop (Au Cordon Rouge) was on the Rue de l'Assemblée.

3. *D'Aragon:* See note 23 to Chap. V of this volume.

4. *Caraccioli:* See note 3 to Chap. I of this volume.

5. *Had left in London:* In Chap. I of this volume C. says that he had met Caraccioli again in Turin after leaving him in London.

6. *Fountain:* Among the 16 mineral springs at Spa the best known is the "Pouhon."

7. *Merci:* Name (probably fictitious) of the niece; nothing is known of her except what C. relates.

8. *Pamelas:* Pamela is the name of the heroine of Richardson's novel *Pamela, or Virtue Rewarded,* published in 1740, and two years later in a French translation by the Abbé Prévost, author of *Manon Lescaut*. C. uses it generically to mean a girl of strait-laced virtue.

9. *Cadogan:* A knot or loop of ribbon in which the hair was tied back.

10. *A house across the street:* Its name was La Fontaine d'Or; it was not an inn, but a house which could be rented.

C. appears in the registry of visitors to Spa as "M. de Casanova, à la Fontaine d'Or."

11. *The Duchess of Richmond:* Mary Lennox, Duchess of Richmond (died 1796).

12. *The slap:* I.e., the slap Merci had given an officer, of which C. had learned from the gunsmith.

13. *Crosin:* See Vol. 9, Chap. I, n. 11. In the registry of visitors he appears as "Chevalier de la Croix d'Espagne."

14. *The girl he had left me:* The XXX or P.P. of Vol. 8, Chap. VIII, and Vol. 9, Chap. III.

15. *Conti:* He appears in the registry of visitors as "Monsieur Conty, capitaine au service du duc de Wurtemberg" ("captain in the service of the Duke of Württemberg").

16. *A fountain . . . a quarter of a league from Spa:* There were several mineral springs outside the city.

17. *À la Donadieu:* Other possible readings are "Doradieu" and "Doradien"; in any case, no such term has been found in manuals of fencing.

18. *Her name:* She was Charlotte de Lamotte (ca. 1749-1767), of Brussels.

19. *The second such:* See note 14 to this chapter.

20. *Piquet à écrire:* It differed from the usual game of piquet in its method of scoring.

21. *Passe-dix:* Game played with three dice; the winner must be ahead by more than 10 points.

22. *An English club:* There was a "Club des Anglais" in Spa in the 18th century.

23. *The Poles:* C. writes "le Polonais" (singular), probably a slip for the plural.

24. *The beautiful Italian:* Apparently an attempt by C. to conceal Charlotte's identity, though he later says that she was from Brussels.

25. *Capuchin monastery:* In the southern part of Spa; visitors to the city were invited to walk in the monastery garden and were expected to give alms in return.

26. *Croce:* As appears later, Crosin was known to Charlotte as Antonio La Croce.

27. *Hôtel de Montmorency:* See Vol. 9, Chap. V, n. 37.

28. *Madame d'Urfé was dead:* She did not die until 1775. Cf. Vol. 9, Chap. IX, n. 39.

29. *Saint-Eustache:* Celebrated old Parisian church, just north

of the former Halles Centrales (Central Market). On his way to the Rue Saint-Honoré, C. doubtless saw the Halle au Blé, built in 1765, which was in fact a round building (replaced in 1889 by another building with a similar ground plan, the Bourse de Commerce).

30. *Hôtel de Soissons:* It had been torn down in 1749; its site was occupied by the Halle au Blé (see the preceding note).

31. *The new promenades . . . on the false ramparts:* The ring of fortifications around Paris, some of them dating in part from the 14th century, began to be transformed into boulevards under Louis XIV, so they were not such a novelty as C. makes them out to be. However, some boulevards in the southern part of the city were not completed until 1761.

32. *Madame du Rumain:* See note 2 to Chap. VI of Vol. 9.

33. *The money . . . she had sent me at Wesel:* See Chap. III of this volume. There C. says that he was unable to return it to her before she died (cf. note 8 to that chapter).

34. *The Pont-aux-Choux:* Between the Porte Saint-Antoine and the Porte du Temple (now the Boulevard Beaumarchais) there was a bridge over the old moat of the fortifications which was called the Pont-aux-Choux ("Cabbage Bridge") because there were many vegetable gardens nearby, chiefly devoted to the cultivation of cabbages. The Rue des Amandiers starts where the present Avenue de la République crosses the Boulevard de Ménilmontant (20th Arrondissement).

35. *To the church to be baptized:* I.e., to Saint-Laurent, the parish church of the district, at the intersection of the Boulevard de Strasbourg and the Boulevard Magenta.

36. *The Châtelet:* The Grand Châtelet, a former fortress, was the seat of the justiciary of Paris until the French Revolution. The building, on the north bank of the Seine, was removed in 1802.

37. *La Cité:* The Île de la Cité, the island in the Seine which was the original site of Paris and from which the city gradually spread to both banks of the river.

38. *Rue des Marmousets:* This street no longer exists; it was near the Cathedral of Notre-Dame.

39. *Will apparently be the last:* C. would seem to have written this shortly before his own death.

40. *Dandolo:* See note 28 to Chap. II of this volume.

41. *Bragadin:* See note 10 to Chap. II of this volume.

42. *The King, her cousin:* See note 17 to Chap. V of this volume.

43. *The abduction of the three Senators:* See note 51 to Chap. VIII of this volume. Of the 4 notables who were carried off, all but Count Seweryn Rzewuski were Senators.

44. *Aranda:* Pedro Pablo Abarca de Bolea, Count of Aranda (1715-1798), President of the Council of Castille from 1766, Spanish Ambassador in Paris from 1772 to 1787; friend of Voltaire.

45. *Della Cattolica:* Giuseppe Agostino Bonanno Filingeri e del Bosco, Prince of Roccafiorita and della Cattolica (died 1779), Spanish grandee from 1748, and from 1761 to 1770 Envoy Extraordinary from the Kingdom of Naples to Madrid.

46. *Losada:* José Fernandez de Miranda, Duke of Losada, must already have been an old man in 1767.

47. *The King:* Carlos III (1716-1788), King of Naples, as Carlo Borbone, from 1735 to 1759, King of Spain, as Carlos III, from 1759.

48. *Pignatelli:* José María Pignatelli, Marqués de Mora (died 1774), friend of Mademoiselle de Lespinasse and of Voltaire.

49. *Cul-de-sac de l'Orangerie:* Now the Rue de Saint-Florentin, leading from the Place de la Concorde.

50. *A tall young man:* In his correspondence C. gives his name; he was the Marquis de Lisle.

51. *Théâtre de la Foire:* C. writes simply "à la foire." Originally nothing but a stage in the open air on which one or several buffoons performed, by the 18th century the Théâtre de la Foire, as an adjunct of the great seasonal fairs, had become almost a permanent institution, for which well-known authors (Lesage, for example) wrote comedies.

52. *Valville:* See note 20 to Chap. VII of this volume.

53. *Brumoy:* He has not been identified.

54. *Chevalier of St. Louis:* See note 27 to Chap. I of this volume.

55. *Such was his good pleasure:* "Car tel est notre bon plaisir" was a formula often used in royal orders.

CHAPTER XII

1. (*He was Buhot*): Added by C. between the lines. The reference is to Pierre Étienne Buhot (born ca. 1723), Royal Councilor and Inspector of the Saint-Germain-des-Prés quarter of Paris.

2. *The Minister:* César Gabriel, Count of Choiseul-Chevigny (1712-1785), from 1762 Duke of Praslin, had returned to the post of Minister of Foreign Affairs on April 8, 1766. It must have been he, therefore, who issued the *lettre de cachet* against C. Hence it is surprising that it was also he who, about the same time, gave C. a passport entitling him to demand special privileges in using the post from Paris to Bordeaux (see the reproduction in this volume).

3. *I made no answer:* Here C. added, then crossed out: "for I remembered too well what had happened to me nine years before, and I did not want to hear reproaches for long-past grievances." Cf. Vol. 5, Chaps. X and XI.

4. *Dated the 19th:* The passport was dated Nov. 15th and was valid for only two days.

5. *Bodin:* Pierre Bodin, French dancer, appeared in Naples in 1751 and after that in Vienna for some years until 1764; his wife was the dancer and actress Louise Geoffroi.

6. *Whom I had loved twenty-two years before:* C. mentions her in Vol. 3, Chaps. VII and XII, but he says nothing about a liaison between them.

7. *Bodin's wife:* C. begins this sentence with "Bodin et sa femme" ("Bodin and his wife"), but then goes on with a predicate the principal verb of which can refer only to the wife.

8. *Chanteloup:* Château near Amboise on the south bank of the Loire, which Choiseul bought in 1753 and enlarged in the style of Versailles. He spent the years of his exile from Court there (1770-1774). After the Revolution it fell into decay and was demolished in 1823. All that remains of it is a pagoda 120 feet high.

9. *He owed everything it cost:* Choiseul died (1775) leaving immense debts.

10. *Vivonne:* Then the first post station south of Poitiers.

11. *La Rufin:* See Chap. III of this volume.

12. *Les Landes:* District of France, consisting chiefly of a

great plain along the Bay of Biscay from Bordeaux nearly to the Pyrenees.

13. *Saint-Jean-d'Angély:* C. is in error. Saint-Jean-d'Angély is north of Bordeaux. He may mean Saint-Jean-de-Luz or, more probably, Saint-Jean Pied-de-Port, which is on the road to Pamplona.

14. *Gages:* Juan Bonaventura Thierry du Mont, Comte de Gages (1682-1753), in the Spanish service from 1703, was Captain General and Viceroy of Navarra from 1749.

15. *Had had me arrested:* See Vol. 2, Chap. II.

16. *Old Castile:* Province of Spain; when it was an independent kingdom its capital was Valladolid.

17. *Only wretched inns:* The highroad to Madrid ran and still runs through Burgos. From Pamplona C. must have traveled to Madrid by way of Tudela, Agreda, Soria, Medinaceli, Guadalajara, and Alcalá de Henares, part of which journey would have been by secondary roads.

18. *"A small coin for the noise":* So C. ironically translates the Spanish; but *ruido* in this context can also mean "disturbance."

19. *Cigarro:* This is C.'s only mention of the cigar, which about this time became fashionable in Spain, to which it was brought from South America. Cigar smoking was not taken up in the rest of Europe until the second half of the 18th century. The first cigar factory outside of Spain was established in Hamburg in 1778.

20. *Gabacho:* From *gave,* Pyrenean term for a mountain stream; literally, "uncouth person." The term was first applied to Pyrenean peasants and then extended to all Frenchmen.

21. *French dog:* C. writes "Frence-dogue."

22. *The visionary's dreams . . . lose my mind:* See Vol. 4, Chap. XII.

23. *Bilbao:* City in northern Spain near the Bay of Biscay, some 85 miles from the French border; today an important industrial center.

24. *Grandee:* In the kingdom of Castile "Grande" was the inheritable title of the highest nobility from the 13th century; under the Emperor Charles V (1520) it became the designation of a nobleman of the highest rank at Court.

25. *Squillace:* Leopoldo di Gregorio, Marchese di Squillace

(died 1785 in Venice) came from southern Italy, was Spanish Minister of Finance from 1759 and Minister of War from 1763. The heavy taxes he imposed and his numerous edicts directed against national customs led to an uprising in Madrid in 1766, which forced the King to dismiss him. Squillace retired to Naples and in 1772 was appointed Ambassador to Venice.

26. *The Holy Inquisition:* The Inquisition, though not confined to Spain, had more power there than in other European countries. It pronounced its last death sentence in Spain as late as 1781 and was not abolished there until 1834.

27. *Señor Don Jaime:* Jaime is the Spanish form of Jacques and Giacomo.

28. *The two Castiles:* For Old Castile, see note 16 to this chapter. New Castile as an independent kingdom had had Toledo as its capital.

29. *The language of the Moors . . . left a quantity of words there:* The Moors ruled the greater part of the Iberian Peninsula from 713 and developed a flourishing culture there, especially in the south. The Christian reconquest began as early as the 8th century from the mountainous northern provinces, but gained ground slowly; Toledo was not conquered until 1085, followed by Saragossa in 1118, Valencia in 1238, Seville in 1248. Gibraltar fell in 1462, and Granada not until 1492. Thus many Arabic elements entered the Spanish language, particularly its vocabulary. C. seems to have been struck by the large number of words containing the Arabic article *al*.

30. *Ala . . . Alcavala:* Since C. wrote words from foreign languages entirely by ear, it is impossible to identify all of his list of Spanish words, many of them proper names.

31. Horace, *Art of Poetry*, 323.

32. *Three guttural letters:* C. can only mean the Spanish pronunciation of *g* before *e* and *i*, and of *j* before all vowels, when those consonants have the sound of *ch* in Scottish "loch," though he may also be thinking of the Castilian lisped sound (th). He would have heard none of these in Italian.

33. Medieval hexameter (see *Proverbia Sententiaeque Latinitatis Medii Aevi*, ed. H. Walther, Vol. 4, No. 25, 531).

34. *Puerta de Alcalá:* The Puerta de Alcalá was one of the 15 old city gates of Madrid. The gate which bears the name today was not built until 1788, by the architect Sabatini.

35. *Street of the Cross:* The Calle de la Cruz is not far from the Puerta del Sol and still exists.

36. *The coffeehouse . . . lodge:* C. lodged in the "Hôtel garni du Café français."

37. *The late Queen:* Maria Amalia Walburga (1724-1760), daughter of King Augustus III of Poland, married in 1738 to King Carlo Borbone of Naples, who became King of Spain as Carlos III in 1759.

38. *Della Cattolica:* See note 45 to the preceding chapter.

39. *The highest city:* The altitude of Madrid is some 2130 feet, and so, with the exception of the pygmy states of Andorra and San Marino, it is the highest European capital.

40. *A thousand toises:* The Parisian toise was equal to just under six feet. This would make the altitude of Madrid 6000 feet! In his ms. C. first wrote, more reasonably, "three or four hundred toises," then substituted "a thousand."

41. *The Gate of the Sun:* The square La Puerta del Sol is still one of the most frequented places in the inner city. There was originally a gate there, whence the name.

42. *Duenna:* C writes "duegna" (for Spanish *dueña*).

43. *Banished all the Jesuits in . . . Spain:* The expulsion of the Jesuits from Spain took place on the night of March 31 to April 1, 1767. Portugal had expelled the Jesuits in 1759 and France in 1764.

44. *Proscribe hats . . . cloaks . . . heel:* They were used by questionable elements to avoid recognition. Squillace had issued his prohibition in March 1766; the result was the so-called *motín*, an uprising which forced the King to dismiss him (cf. note 25 to this chapter). His successor, the Count of Aranda, immediately rescinded the prohibition, but soon promulgated it again in a more acceptable form by a decree stating that the King would recognize true Spaniards by their cocked hats. Thereupon both slouch hats and long cloaks soon vanished.

45. *President of the Council of Castile:* The President of the Royal and Supreme Council of Castile was the most powerful person in Spain after the King. The Council was made

up of some 30 high-ranking magistrates, who not only drafted laws but made appointments to governmental positions and served as the highest court of appeal.

46. *The Ambassador of your Republic:* Alvise Sebastiano Mocenigo (1725-1780), Venetian Ambassador in Rome, and from 1762 to 1768 in Madrid; he was married and had two daughters.

47. *The Neapolitan Ambassador:* Prince della Cattolica (see note 45 to the preceding chapter).

48. *Mora:* See note 48 to the preceding chapter.

49. *Dandolo:* See note 28 to Chap. II of this volume.

50. *Soderini:* Gasparo Soderini, Venetian Secretary of Embassy in Madrid and Milan; appointed to the Venetian State Secretariat in 1775.

51. *My sovereign:* The Doge of Venice.

52. *Manuzzi:* Son of Giovanni Battista Manuzzi, who, as a spy for the Venetian State Inquisition, had contributed to C.'s being imprisoned under the Leads (cf. Vol. 4, Chap. XI). C. calls the son a Count. Nothing is known of him or of his title.

53. *The books of magic I had:* See Vol. 4, Chap. XI.

54. *Loredan:* The Loredans were an ancient Venetian patrician family.

55. *Alexis . . . Corydon:* In Vergil's second Eclogue the shepherd Corydon is in love with the beautiful youth Alexis.

56. *Calle Ancha:* The Calle Ancha de San Bernardo was in the northern part of the city. Ancha means "wide"; there was also a Calle Angosta ("narrow") de San Bernardo. The "palace" is the Venetian Ambassador's residence.

57. *Sentenced . . . Brescia:* Mocenigo was imprisoned in the fortress of Brescia in 1773; the city then belonged to the Republic of Venice.

58. *Another Ambassador:* Alvise Piero M. Contarini (1731-1786), Venetian patrician, appointed Venetian Ambassador in Vienna in 1773.

59. *Wristband clique:* Text: "de la manchette," slang for pederast.

60. *Mengs:* Anton Raphael Mengs (1728-1779), celebrated painter of the period, from Aussig (Bohemia); from 1754 Director of the Capitoline Academy in Rome, from 1761

to 1771 Court painter to King Carlos III of Spain. He was a close friend of C.'s (see especially Vol. 7, Chap. VIII).

61. *Sabatini:* Francesco Sabatini (Sabattino), Italian architect (1722-1797); he was summoned to Madrid by the King of Spain in 1760.

62. *Vanvitelli:* Luigi Vanvitelli, of Dutch descent (real name Lodewijk van Wittel), celebrated architect (1700-1773), worked on St. Peter's in Rome from 1726; his best-known work is the Palace of Caserta, near Naples.

63. C. indicates that this is a quotation. It is from a poem by an unknown author in reply to a poem of C.'s addressed to the Italian actress and dancer Giacoma Annetta Veronese, known as Camilla (see Vol. 3, Chap. XI, and Vol. 5, Chap. V). Both poems were published in the April 1757 issue of the *Mercure de France,* the reply under the title "Sur le portrait de Mlle Camille, fait en vers italiens."

64. *Theater . . . Los Caños del Peral:* In addition to the Buen Retiro, which had been closed in 1759, Madrid from the 17th century had had the Teatro de la Cruz (rebuilt in 1737) and the Teatro del Principe (rebuilt in 1745). To these in 1708 was added the theater called Los Caños del Peral, opened by the Italian actor and impresario Bartoli, and at first used for performances of Italian opera; from 1745 it was used for concerts and masked balls. (C. writes "los scannos.")

65. *Autos sacramentales:* Dramas, usually in one act, on sacred subjects, descendants of the medieval mystery plays but later composed by such famous writers as Tirso de Molina, Lope de Vega, and Calderón. From the 16th century they were performed on great feast days of the ecclesiastical calendar, the *autos sacramentales* on Corpus Christi Day and the *autos al nacimiento* on Christmas. Their performance had already been forbidden in 1765 at the instigation of the Archbishop of Toledo, Count Teba; so C. can hardly have seen one of them. Perhaps, however, the prohibition was not strictly enforced at first.

66. *Puñete:* C. writes "pugnetta." The word properly means "blow with the fist," but is here used in some obscene sense.

67. *Pichona:* Maria Teresa Palomino (1728-1795), called La

Pichona, famous Spanish actress from 1750, mistress of the Dukes of Medina Celi and of Medina Sidonia; celebrated for her beauty and, later, for her wealth.

68. *Fandango:* A lively dance in 3/8 or 6/8 time, brought to Spain from the West Indies.

69. *St. Anthony:* Ca. 250-350, the founder of Egyptian monasticism. His feast is celebrated on Jan. 17th. He is the patron saint of Spain, of tailors, and of swineherds.

70. *La Soledad:* There were two churches at the time named Nuestra Señora de la Soledad. The one to which Doña Ignacia went was probably the one in the Calle de Fuencarral, near the Puerta del Sol. It still exists.

71. *Del Desengaño:* The Calle del Desengaño still exists near the Puerta del Sol.

72. *Hidalgo:* Title denoting a Spanish nobleman of the lower class.

73. The parenthetical translation is C.'s. He writes "vieco."

74. *Peso duro:* Spanish silver coin minted from 1497 and worth 8 reales. It circulated, at least in the Spanish colonies, until 1868, when the peseta, which was worth half a peso, became the monetary unit.

75. *Doña Ignacia:* Nothing is known of her except what C. relates.